Data Communications & Computer Networks

A Business User's Approach

Ninth Edition

Jill West

Curt M. White

CENGAGE

Australia • Brazil • Canada • Mexico • Singapore • United Kingdom • United States

Data Communications & Computer Networks: A Business User's Approach, **Ninth Edition**

Jill West and Curt M. White

SVP, Higher Education Product Management: Erin Joyner

VP, Product Management, Learning Experiences: Thais Alencar

Product Director: Jason Fremder

Product Manager: Natalie Onderdonk

Product Assistant: Tom Benedetto

Content Manager: Arul Joseph Raj, Lumina Datamatics, Inc.

Digital Delivery Quality Partner: Jim Vaughey

VP, Product Marketing: Jason Sakos

IP Analyst: Ann Hoffman

IP Project Manager: Anjali Kambli, Lumina Datamatics, Inc.

Production Service: Lumina Datamatics, Inc.

Designer: Erin Griffin

Cover Image Source: Xuanyu Han/Getty Images

For product information and technology assistance, contact us at **Cengage Customer & Sales Support, 1-800-354-9706 or support.cengage.com.**

For permission to use material from this text or product, submit all requests online at **www.copyright.com**.

Library of Congress Control Number: 2021925306

ISBN: 978-0-357-50440-6

Cengage
200 Pier 4 Boulevard
Boston, MA 02210
USA

Cengage is a leading provider of customized learning solutions with employees residing in nearly 40 different countries and sales in more than 125 countries around the world. Find your local representative at **www.cengage.com.**

To learn more about Cengage platforms and services, register or access your online learning solution, or purchase materials for your course, visit **www.cengage.com.**

Notice to the Reader

Printed at CLDPC, USA, 04-24

Brief Contents

Contents

Chapter 3

Fundamentals of Data and Signals   74

Chapter 4

Frames and Errors   108

Chapter 5

Wired and Wireless Local Area Networks   141

Chapter 6

Network Systems and Software   175

Chapter 7

The Internet   215

Chapter 8

Chapter 9

Chapter 10

Connecting Networks and Resources   **336**

Chapter 11

Network Design and Management   372

Chapter 12

Business Principles in IT   414

Appendix A

CompTIA Cloud Essentials+ CLO-002 Certification Exam Objectives   **449**

Dedication

In memory of Curt M. White

Preface

Today's business world could not function without data communications and computer networks. Most people cannot make it through an average day without encountering or using some form of computer network. In the past, this field of study occupied the time of only engineers and technicians, but it now involves business managers, end users, programmers, and just about anyone who might use a phone or computer! Thus, *Data Communications & Computer Networks: A Business User's Approach*, Ninth Edition maintains a business user's perspective on this vast and increasingly significant subject.

In a generic sense, this book serves as an owner's manual for the individual computer user. In a world in which computer networks are involved in nearly every facet of business and personal life, it is paramount that each person understands the basic features, operations, and limitations of different types of computer networks. This understanding helps people become better managers, better employees, and simply better computer users. As a computer network *user*, you will probably not be the one who designs, installs, and maintains the network. Instead, you will have interactions—either direct or indirect—with the individuals who do. Taking this course should give you a strong foundation in computer network concepts, which will enable you to work effectively with network administrators, network installers, and network designers. Here are some of the many scenarios in which the knowledge contained in this book would be particularly useful:

> You work for a company and must deal directly with a network specialist. To better understand the specialist and be able to conduct a meaningful dialog with them, you need a basic understanding of the many aspects of computer networks.

> You are a manager within a company and depend on network specialists to provide you with recommendations for the company's network. To ensure that you can make intelligent decisions regarding network resources, you need to know the basic concepts of data communications and computer networks.

> You work in a small company, in which each employee wears many hats. Thus, you may need to perform some level of network assessment, administration, or support.

> You have your own business and need to fully understand the advantages of using computer networks to support your operations. To optimize those advantages, you should have a good grasp of the basic characteristics of a computer network.

> You have a computer at home or at work, and you simply wish to learn more about computer networks.

> You have realized that, to keep your job skills current and remain a key player in the information technology arena, you must understand how different computer networks work and become familiar with their advantages and shortcomings.

Audience

Data Communications & Computer Networks: A Business User's Approach, Ninth Edition is intended for a one-semester course in business data communications for students majoring in business, information systems, management information systems, and other applied fields of computer science. Computer science departments will also find the book valuable, particularly if the students read the Details sections accompanying most chapters. It is a readable resource for computer network users that draws on examples from business environments. In a university setting, this book can be used at practically any level above the first year.

Defining Characteristics of This Book

The major goal of this ninth edition is the same as that of the first edition: to go beyond simply providing readers with a handful of new definitions, and instead introduce them to the next level of details found within the fields of computer networks and data communications. This higher level of detail, framed within the context of real-world scenarios, includes the network technologies and standards necessary to support computer network systems and their applications. This book is more than just an introduction to advanced terminology. It involves introducing concepts that will help the reader achieve a more in-depth understanding of the often-complex topic of data communications. Hands-on projects provide memorable insights into the concepts, and pedagogical features help readers assess their own learning and progress. It is hoped that once readers attain this in-depth understanding, the topic of networks and data communications will become engaging in the pursuit of business objectives. To facilitate this understanding, the book strives to maintain high standards in three major areas: readability, a balance between the technical and the practical, and currency.

Readability

Great care has been taken to provide the technical material in as readable a fashion as possible. Each new edition has received a complete rewrite, in which every sentence has been reexamined to convey the concepts as clearly as possible. Given the nature of this book's subject matter, the use of terminology is unavoidable. However, every effort has been made to present terms in a clear fashion, with minimal use of acronyms and even less use of jargon.

Balance between the Technical and the Practical

As in the very successful first edition, a major objective in writing *Data Communications & Computer Networks*, Ninth Edition was to achieve a balance between the more technical aspects of data communications and its everyday practical aspects. Throughout each chapter, there are sections entitled "Details," which delve into the more specialized aspects of the topic at hand. Should readers not have time to explore this technical information, they can skip these Details sections without missing out on the basic concepts of covered topics.

Current Technology

Because of the fast pace of change in virtually all computer-related fields, every attempt has been made to present the most current trends in data

communications and computer networks. Some of these topics include:

> Integral coverage of cloud computing, especially from a business perspective

> An introduction to many new terms and concepts such as: IoT (Internet of Things), 5G (5th generation) cellular, SDN (software-defined networking), SD-WAN (software-defined wide area networking), data analytics, and AI (artificial intelligence)

> The most recent Wi-Fi standards of 802.11ac and 802.11ax

> Technologies to support remote workers

> Industry standards for cloud security

It is also important to remember the many older technologies still in prevalent use today. Discussions of these older technologies can be found, when appropriate, in each chapter of this book.

Organization

The organization of *Data Communications & Computer Networks*, Ninth Edition roughly follows that of the TCP/IP protocol suite, from the physical layer to the upper layers. In addition, the book has been carefully designed to consist of twelve, well-balanced chapters to fit into a typical 15- or 16-week semester (along with any required exams). The intent was to design a versatile introduction to the study of computer networks by creating a set of chapters that is cohesive but at the same time allows for flexibility in the week-to-week curriculum. Thus, instructors may choose to emphasize or de-emphasize certain topics, depending on the focus of their curriculums.

Coverage of CompTIA's Cloud Essentials+ exam objectives are deeply integrated into the material so that every objective is covered to or beyond the level required by the exam. Students who are taking this course and who engage in final exam preparation activities (such as review and practice testing) will be qualified to attempt the CompTIA Cloud Essentials+ certification exam. This exam sits at the crossroads of business and technology in cloud computing and encourages a common language for professionals from both areas of expertise.

Students who have taken other cloud computing courses, such as a course that covers CompTIA's more technical Cloud+ exam, can study Chapters 11 and 12 in preparation for the Cloud Essentials+ exam. These chapters focus on addressing the business-based language and concerns of cloud computing.

Features

To assist readers in better understanding the technical nature of data communications and computer networks, each chapter contains several significant features. These features are based on established, well-tested pedagogical techniques as well as some newer techniques.

Learning Objectives

The chapter opens with a list of learning objectives that should be accomplished by the end of the chapter. Each objective is tied to the main sections of the chapter. Readers can use the objectives to grasp the scope and intent of the chapter's content. The objectives also work in conjunction with the end-of-chapter summary and review questions, so that readers can assess whether they have adequately mastered the material.

Section Reviews

Each major section in each chapter concludes with a brief review of the main points students should remember from that section. This frequent review process helps students reflect on the material they've learned before moving on to the next section.

Self-Check Questions

Following the section review, self-check questions encourage students to practice recalling the information they've learned. This practice testing is proven in learning science research as one of the most effective methods to retain new information. Answers and explanations are provided for students at the end of each chapter so they can check themselves and identify gaps in their learning before moving forward.

Thought Experiments

Thought experiment boxes sprinkled throughout the reading invite students to consider a personal or business application of the concepts being discussed. These activities sometimes require outside research, and other times students draw upon their personal experiences and opinions.

Details

Most chapters contain one or more Details sections, which dig deeper into a particular topic. Readers who are interested in more technical details will find these sections valuable. Since the Details sections are physically separate from the main text, they can be skipped if the reader does not have time to explore this level of technical detail. Skipping these sections will not affect the reader's overall understanding of a chapter's material.

CompTIA Cloud Essentials+ Objectives Mapping

Where relevant, covered exam objectives are referenced within a section to support self-study efforts. All the exam objectives for the CompTIA Cloud Essentials+ certification are covered within this book at or beyond the level required by the exam.

End-of-Chapter Material

The end-of-chapter material is designed to help readers review the content of the chapter and assess whether they have adequately mastered the concepts. It includes:

> A bulleted summary that readers can use as a review of the key topics of the chapter and as a study guide.

> A list of the key terms used within the chapter.

> Review questions that readers can use to quickly check whether they understand the chapter's key concepts.

> A discussion starter designed to encourage readers to reflect on what they've learned in the chapter and how these topics might affect daily life, businesses and markets, and work processes in various industries.

> A Hands-On Project that gives students concrete experience with concepts from the chapter. These projects are carefully designed to work as effectively for a distance-learning student as for a student in the classroom. None of the projects require significant preparation beforehand for the instructor, hardware beyond a typical workstation or laptop, or paid subscriptions to any other service.

Glossary

At the end of the book, you will find a glossary that includes the key terms from each chapter.

New to This Edition

Just as networking technology continues to evolve, so does learning science and the insights available to course designers. In the interest of providing you with the most effective and durable learning experience, this latest edition is packed with improvements and enriched features.

> **Fully updated**—Content maps completely to CompTIA's Cloud Essentials+ CLO-002 exam for productive exam preparation.

> **"Remember this…" feature**—Section-specific learning objectives blend the Cloud Essentials+ exam objectives with the material covered in each section to help students focus on the most important points of that section.

> **Self-check questions**—Periodic multiple-choice questions placed throughout the readings help students mentally complete the "learning cycle" as they practice recalling the information to increase the durability of what they learn. With answers and thorough explanations at the end of each chapter, students can check their own learning and assess their progress toward mastering each chapter's objectives.

> **Flexible learning environment**—New skills-based projects encourage hands-on exploration of chapter concepts. These projects include thought-provoking questions that encourage critical thinking and in-depth evaluation of the material. The software tools used in the projects are included in Windows or freely available online, and hardware requirements are kept to a minimum, making these projects accessible to more students in a wide variety of learning environments.

> **Cloud, virtualization, and emulation technologies**—Projects at the end of each chapter challenge readers to explore concepts and apply skills with real-world tools. Some projects employ Cisco's network simulator, Packet Tracer, so learners can practice setting up a network from start to finish. Other projects guide students in accessing AWS so they can "get their hands dirty in the cloud" and discover why IT as an industry is becoming cloud-centric.

> **Certification preparation**—All exam objectives for the CompTIA Cloud Essentials+ certification are covered to or beyond the depth required by the exam. The CompTIA Cloud Essentials+ certification addresses the crossroads of business and technology in cloud computing. Training for the exam provides experts on both sides with a common language to encourage partnership and collaboration as companies increasingly migrate to the cloud.

Chapter Descriptions

To keep up with new technology in computer networks and data communications, this Ninth Edition has incorporated many updates and additions in every chapter, as well as some reorganization of sections within chapters. Here's a summary of the major concepts that can be found in each of the following chapters:

Chapter 1, Introduction to Data Communications and Computer Networks, introduces different types of computer networks, along with many of the major concepts that will be discussed in the following chapters, with an emphasis on the TCP/IP protocol suite followed by the OSI model. Cloud computing is introduced in this first chapter and is revisited in-depth in subsequent chapters.

Chapter 2, Conducted and Radiated Media, introduces the different types of wired and wireless media for transmitting data on personal and local area networks. Coverage of Wi-Fi, Bluetooth, and wireless IoT (Internet of Things) technologies reflects updated standards and evolution of wireless media.

Chapter 3, Fundamentals of Data and Signals, covers basic concepts describing how data is converted to signals for transmission on a network. Later chapters build on these concepts so students understand how to increase network performance and efficiency.

Chapter 4, Frames and Errors, discusses how a connection or interface is created between a computer and a peripheral device. The chapter explores types of noise and the errors they cause, how these errors are detected, and the actions that can take place in response to errors.

Chapter 5, Wired and Wireless Local Area Networks, explains the evolution of topology and Ethernet standards in wired local area networks, emphasizing the role a switch plays in modern networks. The chapter then describes standards used to handle collisions on wireless networks.

Chapter 6, Network Systems and Software, discusses various network services and the network operating systems that support them. New content discusses how to configure network devices and explains the concept and role of virtualization. The chapter concludes with new content explaining cloud computing services and pricing strategies.

Chapter 7, The Internet, is devoted to technologies that make the Internet work. The chapter covers IPv4 and IPv6 protocols and addressing as well as TCP, UDP, and a brief discussion of MPLS. It also discusses Internet services, such as DNS, SSH, and VoIP, and it presents new content on the IoT (Internet of Things) and data analytics.

Chapter 8, Risk, Security, and Compliance, addresses common network vulnerabilities and attack types, including updated information on ransomware and phishing emails. The chapter explains network security technologies, from physical security and anti-malware to firewalls and IDS/IPS. Encryption processes and uses are explained along with an updated discussion of authentication measures. The chapter concludes with a section devoted to wireless security.

Chapter 9, Wide Area Networks, introduces the basic terminology and concepts of campus area networks, metropolitan area networks, and wide area networks. Routing processes and common routing protocols are explored, followed by discussions on multiplexing and compression in wide area networks.

Chapter 10, Connecting Networks and Resources, delves into the details of how local networks connect to the Internet. The chapter includes DSL, cable modems, fiber, satellite, and cellular connections for consumer-level services and MPLS, Ethernet, VPN, and cloud connectivity for enterprise-grade connections. New content on SD-WAN, SD-Branch, and SASE helps prepare students for the CompTIA Cloud Essentials+ certification exam. And coverage of digital marketing, edge computing, and supporting remote workers prepares students for working in today's Internet-based businesses.

Chapter 11, Network Design and Management, introduces application lifecycle management, change management, and project management. In the context of creating or improving networks, the chapter explores network modeling, gap analysis, feasibility studies, capacity planning, and testing environments. A section on network monitoring covers monitoring tools and the importance of baseline studies. The chapter concludes with new content on cloud deployment and migration concepts, including migration strategies, automation/orchestration, and cloud monitoring.

Chapter 12, Business Principles in IT, offers new content addressing a network's human resources, including the need for administrative and training skills in addition to ongoing professional development. The next section focuses on relationships with vendors, important vendor documentation, and methods for evaluating proposed projects with vendors. New content covers financial aspects of the cloud, including a comparison of CapEx versus OpEx and a discussion of cloud cost optimization. The final section addresses business continuity and disaster recovery planning.

Instructor Resources

Additional instructor resources for this product are available online. Instructor assets include an Instructor's Manual, PowerPoint® slides, and a test bank powered by Cognero®. Sign up or sign in at www.cengage.com to search for and access this product and its online resources.

Acknowledgments

This book has been a long time coming. Through delays, multiple schedule rearrangements, the 2020 quarantines, and team members being promoted to other responsibilities, this edition has now come to fruition. I believe this is good timing—as the demand for cloud skills increases so does the perception of cloud as an integral part of IT.

Many people contributed to the production of this book, and many more helped move it along before the official drafting process began. I'd like to thank Emily Pope for her vision of blending this book's network instruction in a business context with CompTIA's business-centered cloud computing certification. I'm grateful for Staci Eckenroth's high standards in editing the drafts and ensuring inclusive language that shows the inherent value of people in all walks of life. And thank you to Jennifer Ziegler for picking up the reins of this project from others to see it through.

The work I do is only possible through the support and encouragement of my husband, Mike, and our four kids: Winn, Sarah, Daniel, and Zack. Thank you to each of you for the unique ways you each contribute. And finally, a special thanks to each of my students—your curiosity, struggles, dreams, and hard work fuel my passion for teaching and for writing. I'm grateful to play a part in your journey.

Chapter 1

Introduction to Data Communications and Computer Networks

Objectives

After reading this chapter, you should be able to:

- Use common networking terms
- Identify basic networking devices
- Describe common types of networks
- Describe the purpose of each layer of the TCP/IP protocol suite and the OSI model
- Explain the significance of cloud computing

Introduction

Making predications is a difficult task, and predicting the future of computing is no exception. History is filled with computer-related predictions so inaccurate that today they are amusing. For example, consider the following predictions:

> "I think there is a world market for maybe five computers."
> *Thomas Watson, chairman of IBM, 1943*

> "I have traveled the length and breadth of this country, and talked with the best people, and I can assure you that data processing is a fad that won't last out the year."
> *Editor in charge of business books for Prentice Hall, 1957*

> "There is no reason anyone would want a computer in their home."
> *Ken Olsen, president and founder of Digital Equipment Corporation, 1977*

Apparently, no matter how famous you are or how influential your position, it is very easy to make very bad predictions. Nevertheless, it's hard to imagine that anyone can make a prediction worse than any of those above. Buoyed by this false sense of optimism, consider these forecasts:

> Someday your home's heating and cooling system will automatically turn off when it detects you leaving home, turn on when it detects you're heading back, adjust its settings according to your daily activities and current energy prices, and shut down completely if it detects smoke in the house.

At some point, a hacker manages to steal your banking password and log into your online bank account, but the attack is detected and booted from your account before any damage is done because he didn't move his mouse the same way you do.

Someday your car battery will be capable of detecting when the power gets too weak to start the car, and it will call to inform you that you need a replacement or a charge.

One day you will use an app on your phone to request personal transportation. The app will show you the car's photo, provide a map of the car's current location, and you'll be notified when the car arrives at your location. However, when you enter the car, there will be no driver because the car drives itself.

Someday while driving in a big city, your car will navigate you to the nearest empty parking spot and allow you to pay the parking fee with your phone.

Do these predictions sound far-fetched and filled with mysterious technologies that only scientists and engineers can understand? They shouldn't because these scenarios are happening today with technologies that already exist. What's more, none of these advances would be possible today were it not for computer networks and data communications.

The world of computer networks and data communications is a surprisingly vast and increasingly significant field of study. Once considered primarily the domain of network engineers and technicians, computer networks now involve business managers, computer programmers, system designers, office managers, home computer users, and everyday citizens.

It is virtually impossible for the average person on the street to spend 24 hours without directly or indirectly using some form of computer network. Consider all the ways you might interact with computer networks when you're literally on the street: Most transportation systems use extensive communication networks to monitor the flow of vehicles and trains. Expressways and highways have computerized systems for controlling traffic signals and limiting access during peak traffic times. Some major cities are placing the appropriate hardware inside city buses and trains so that the precise location of each bus and train is known. This information enables transportation systems to keep buses evenly spaced and more punctual, and it allows riders to know when the next bus or train will arrive.

In addition, more people are using satellite-based GPS devices in their cars and on smartphones to provide driving directions and avoid traffic hotspots. Similar systems can unlock your car doors if you leave your keys in the ignition or can locate your car in a crowded parking lot by beeping the horn and flashing the headlights if you cannot remember where you parked.

Even if you didn't use public transportation today or a GPS device in your car to commute to work, school, or the store, there are many other ways to use a computer network. Businesses can order parts and inventory on demand and build products to customer-designed specifications electronically, without the need for paper. Online retail outlets can track every item you click on or purchase. Using this data, they can make recommendations of similar products and inform you in the future when a new product becomes available. ATMs can verify a user's identity by taking their thumbprint. Plus, many employees and students now work from home, relying heavily on data networks to access remote resources for work, school, and socializing.

To support current demands for network connectivity, cable television continues to expand, offering extensive programming, pay-per-view options, video recording, digital television and music, and (in some markets) gigabit connectivity to the Internet. The telephone system, the oldest and most extensive network of communication devices, continues to become more of a computer network every day. The most recent "telephone" networks can now deliver voice, Internet, and television over a single connection. Cellular telephone systems cover virtually the entire North American continent and include systems that allow users to upload and download data to and from the Internet, send and receive images, and upload or download streaming video such as television programs, movies, web conferences, and social media videos. Your smartphone can play music, make phone calls (even video calls), take pictures, browse the web, and let you play games while you wait for the next train, class, or appointment.

Welcome to the amazing world of computer networks! As you can see, it is nearly impossible to not have used some form of computer network and data communication. Because of this growing integration of computer networks and data communications into business and daily life, everyone—particularly those considering careers in information systems, business, or computer science—needs to understand the basic concepts. Armed with this knowledge, you not only will be better at communicating with network specialists and engineers, but also will become better students, managers, and employees.

Section 1-1: The Language of Computer Networking

Over the years, numerous terms and definitions relating to computer networks and data communications have emerged. To gain insight into the many subfields of study, and to become familiar with the emphasis of this textbook, take a moment to examine the more common terms and their definitions:

> A computer network is an interconnected group of computers and computing equipment using either wires or radio waves that can share data and computing resources.

> Wireless computer networks use different kinds of low energy radiation below the visible light spectrum and can involve broadcast radio, microwaves, or infrared transmissions.

> Networks spanning an area of a few centimeters to several meters around an individual are called PANs (personal area networks). PANs include devices such as laptop computers, smartphones, personal printers, and wireless peripheral devices (like a keyboard or speakers) that are typically used by one person at a time. A PAN can also include wearable devices, such as a smartwatch or smart glasses, although sometimes these devices are considered to be part of a BAN (body area network).

> Networks that are a little larger in geographic size—spanning a room, a floor within a building, or an entire building—are LANs (local area networks). Figure 1-1 shows the relative sizes of PANs, LANs, and other common network types described here.

> Collections of local area networks that cover a campus (such as a college campus or a business campus) are often called CANs (campus area networks).

> Networks that serve an area up to roughly 50 kilometers—approximately the area of a typical city—are called MANs (metropolitan area networks). Metropolitan area networks are high-speed networks that interconnect businesses with other businesses and the Internet.

> Large networks encompassing parts of states, multiple states, countries, and the world are WANs (wide area networks).

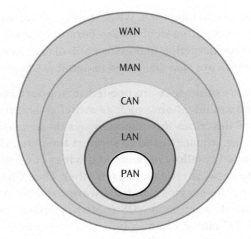

Figure 1-1   Relative sizes of common network types

There are many other terms you'll see repeatedly throughout this course. To put these terms in context, let's peruse the highlights of the coming chapters. It helps to think of the progression of these chapters in terms of how each chapter relates to a company's LAN, either internal to the LAN or external to it. For example, Chapters 2 through 6 concentrate on technologies used on LANs. Chapter 7 expands the discussion to see how networks function outside of the LAN environment, and Chapter 8 covers key security concepts when considering threats from outside the LAN. As you move away from the LAN, you find that several technologies can connect your network with other networks or with extensions to your own network. You'll learn about how WANs work in Chapter 9, and you'll discover many of the more common WAN connection types in Chapter 10. Let's take a more detailed look at what you can expect to learn during this course and some of the core vocabulary you'll be using.

The study of computer networks would be inadequate without the introduction of two important building blocks: data and signals. Data is information that has been translated into a form conducive to storage, transmission, and calculation. Data communications is the transfer of digital or analog data using digital or analog signals. Analog and digital signals are transmitted over conducted media or wireless (also called radiated) media, both of which are discussed in Chapter 2. These media are the foundational component of every network. Next, Chapter 3 evaluates how data is transformed into signals that can be transmitted on various network media.

Signals transmitted on a network must be formatted according to certain sets of rules, called protocols, a topic covered in Chapter 4. When the signals transmitted between computing devices are corrupted and errors result, error detection and error control are necessary. These topics are also discussed in detail in Chapter 4.

Many kinds of devices are needed to support network-based communications, such as switches and routers. Chapter 5 describes the different ways these *networking* devices (i.e., devices used to support the network) can be arranged to allow *networked* devices (i.e., devices using the network) to talk to each other. Then Chapter 6 evaluates the services and software used to manage the network, such as a NOS (network operating system), and Chapter 7 shows how you can connect your network to other networks using specialized networking protocols that enable communication across the Internet. As you open your network to the world, you need to keep it safe. Chapter 8 surveys common risks to your network and network security best practices that protect your network and your data when you're connected to the Internet.

Because sending only one signal over a medium at one time can be an inefficient way to use the transmission medium, many systems perform multiplexing. **Multiplexing** is the transmission of multiple signals on one medium, which is necessary with high-traffic connections like those that make up the Internet. For a medium to transmit multiple signals simultaneously, the signals must be altered so that they do not interfere with one another. **Compression** is another technique that can maximize the amount of data sent over a medium. Compression involves squeezing data into a smaller package, thus reducing the amount of time (as well as storage space) needed to transmit the data. Multiplexing and compression are covered in Chapter 9. Next, Chapter 10 shows how these techniques are used in different WAN technologies that connect your local network to the Internet and other remote networks.

Network management is the design, installation, and support of a network and its hardware and software. Chapter 11 discusses many of the basic concepts necessary to properly support the design and improvement of network hardware and software, as well as the more common management techniques used to optimize a network's performance.

A very common expression you may have heard is something like "back up your photos and documents to the cloud" or "the application is in the cloud." The key concept here is **cloud** and the way this term is currently used. Similar words or phrases that are commonly used today are **cloud computing** or *Anything* as a Service (XaaS), where the *X* can be replaced with other letters to refer to a particular service, such as SaaS (Software as a Service) or NaaS (Networking as a Service). Very often "the cloud" simply refers to the Internet or to some other remote network. When a company places data or applications on some website on the Internet and allows people to access them, you might say the application is cloud-based. One of the more visible examples of cloud computing is storing one's music and files at a remote location on the Internet rather than on a local device. Major corporations such as Amazon and Apple allow users to store personal data and recent media purchases on their clouds. Companies such as Microsoft and Google (as well as many others) offer cloud-based applications (called **web apps**) such as word processors and spreadsheets. The actual code that runs the web app does not exist on the user's computer but runs on the cloud provider's servers and is typically accessed across the Internet through the user's browser. This way, users don't have to download and install the application to an individual machine. You will examine cloud concepts in more detail throughout this course and specifically from a business perspective in Chapter 12.

Cloud Essentials+ Exam Tip

This course covers all the objectives for the CompTIA Cloud Essentials+ CLO-002 certification. Look for these Cloud Essentials+ Exam Tips to indicate which objectives are addressed in a section.

Remember this...

> Networks are often categorized according to their size and the types of devices connected to them.

> The study of data communications includes digital and analog signals that can be transmitted over conducted or wireless (radiated) media.

> Cloud computing often relies on the Internet in some way for access to resources at a remote location.

Self-check

1. You plug your new printer into a USB port on your computer. What kind of network supports this connection?
    a. CAN
    b. LAN
    c. WAN
    d. PAN

2. You connect your home network to your
   Internet provider using a single fiber cable.
   What technology allows you to download and
   upload data over this connection at the same
   time?
   a. Network management
   b. Multiplexing
   c. Compression
   d. Cloud computing

Check your answers at the end of this chapter.

Section 1-2: The Big Picture of Networks

If you could create one picture that tries to give an over-view of a typical computer network, what might this pic-ture include? Figure 1-2 shows one possibility. Note that this figure shows two wide area networks (WAN 1 and WAN 2), two local area networks (LAN 1 and LAN 2), and a personal area network. Although a full description of the different components constituting wide area and local area networks is not necessary quite yet, it is import-ant to note that most LANs often include the following hardware:

> Workstations—Personal computers (such as desktops, laptops, or tablets) or smartphones

> Servers—The computers that store network software and shared or private user files

> Switches—The collection points for the wires that interconnect the workstations on a LAN

> Routers—The connecting devices between LANs and WANs, such as the Internet

There are also many types of wide area networks. Although many different technologies are used to support WANs, all WANs include the following components:

> Nodes—Devices connected to the network, including endpoint devices (such as servers) and networking devices (such as routers) that make the decisions about where to route a piece of data

> Connecting media—Some type of wired or wireless high-speed transmission infrastructure (such as cables or radio signals) that connects one node to another

> A subnetwork—Collection of nodes and transmis-sion media working together in a cohesive unit

To see how LANs and WANs work together, consider User A (in the upper-left corner of Figure 1-2), who wishes to retrieve a web page from the web server shown in the lower-right corner. To do this, User A's computer must have both the necessary hardware and software required to communicate with the first WAN it encounters, WAN 1 (User A's Internet service provider).

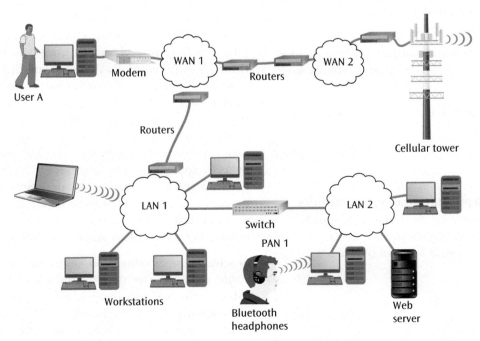

Figure 1-2 An overall view of the interconnection between different types of networks

Assuming that User A's computer is connected to this WAN through a DSL telephone line, User A needs some type of modem. Furthermore, if this WAN is part of the Internet, User A's computer requires software that speaks the language of the Internet: TCP/IP (Transmission Control Protocol/Internet Protocol).

Notice that no direct connection exists between WAN 1, where User A resides, and LAN 2, where the web server resides. To ensure that User A's web page request reaches its intended receiver (the web server), User A's software attaches the appropriate address information that WAN 1 needs to send User A's request to the router that connects WAN 1 to LAN 1. Once the request is on LAN 1, the node connecting LAN 1 and LAN 2 uses address information to pass the request to LAN 2. Additional address information then routes User A's web page request to the web server, whose software accepts the request.

Under normal traffic and conditions, this procedure might take only a fraction of a second. When you begin to understand all the steps involved and the great number of transformations that a simple web page request must undergo, the fact that it takes *only* a fraction of a second to deliver is amazing.

Remember this...

> LANs connect devices to each other using switches and connect to other networks using routers.

> WANs connect networks to each other using routing devices and are organized into groups of nodes called subnetworks.

> Specialized hardware and software are required for a workstation to communicate over a network such as the Internet.

> Addressing information is used to route information across a network.

Self-check

3. You plug your laptop into your local network's router and use your browser to visit a website. What type of device allows your router to communicate with your Internet provider's network?
   a. Switch
   b. Modem
   c. Server
   d. Subnetwork

4. You need to make some changes to a file stored on your office's network. On which device is the file located?
   a. Router
   b. Server
   c. Workstation
   d. Switch

Check your answers at the end of this chapter.

Section 1-3: Common Network Examples

The introduction of this chapter described a few applications of computer networks and data communications in everyday life. Think about the basic communications networks that you might encounter on any typical day while at school, at work, or living life in general. This will help you see how extensively you rely on data communications and computer networks. In Figure 1-3, Katrina is sitting at a desk at her college library. On the desk are two computers: a desktop PC (provided by the school) and her personal laptop. She is holding her smartphone. Try to identify each of the communications networks that Katrina might encounter in this scenario.

The Desktop Computer and the Internet

The desktop computer sitting on Katrina's desk is "connected" to the Internet via a cable at the back. ("Connected" was placed in quotations because, as this book will hopefully demonstrate, it is an intricate process to enable a device to communicate with other devices across the Internet and involves much more than simply plugging a cable into the computer's Internet port.) This is perhaps the most common network connection today and is found in virtually every business, every academic environment, and in many homes. The desktop computer—which is commonly known as the personal computer, PC, microcomputer, or workstation, and could also be a laptop or notebook—began to emerge in the late 1970s and early 1980s.

In a business or education environment, the Ethernet cable plugging the desktop into a wall jack travels through the walls to some collection point, such as a network switch. This network switch, as you will learn in Chapter 5, is part of a local area network. This LAN is possibly connected to other LANs, but eventually

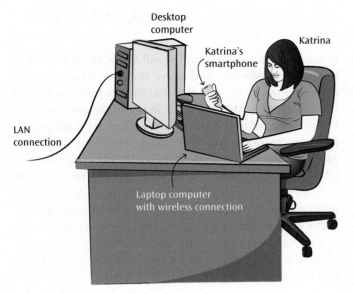

Figure 1-3 Katrina sitting at a desk at school, surrounded by networks and their connections

connects to a router. From the router, there is some form of high-speed connection to a site which specializes in high-speed connections to the Internet.

The LAN, as you'll see in Chapter 6, is an excellent tool for providing a connection to the Internet, as well as to other networks, software, and peripheral devices. In the business and education world, this network is called an **enterprise network** or a corporate network. The connection between workstations and the Internet in an enterprise network is handled by a client/server system. In a **client/server system**, a user at a computer, called the client machine, issues a request for some form of data or service. This could be a request for a database record from a database server,

a request for a web page from a web server, a request for a file from a file server, or a request to retrieve an email message from an email server. If the requested data is stored locally, the request travels across the local system to a local server. If the requested data is stored remotely, the request travels across the local system and then onto an external network, such as the Internet, to a remote server that contains a potentially large repository of data and/or applications. The remote server fills the request and returns the results to the client, displaying the results on the client's monitor. If users wish to print documents on a high-quality network printer, the LAN contains the network software necessary (a print server) to route their print requests to the appropriate printer. If users wish to access their email, the LAN provides a fast, stable connection between user workstations and the email server. If a user wishes to access the Internet, the LAN provides an effective gateway to the outside world. Figure 1-4 shows a diagram of this type of desktop-to-Internet connection.

Earlier, you met Katrina studying at her school library. What about connecting her personal computer to the Internet when she studies at home? Many years ago, most home users connected their computer to the Internet via a dial-up telephone line and a modem. Today, most home users either connect to the Internet using DSL (digital subscriber line) or a cable modem service, which is connected to a home router. DSL and cable modems can achieve much higher connection speeds (or data transfer rates) than dial-up connections, which are rarely used anymore. The home router functions as both a router and a switch, and it allows multiple devices to connect to the Internet at one time.

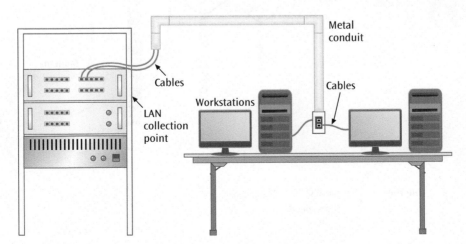

Figure 1-4 A desktop computer (or microcomputer) at a business or school connected from the user's desk to the company's local area network

To communicate with the Internet using a DSL or cable modem connection, a user's computer must connect to another device already communicating with the Internet. The easiest way to establish this connection is through the services of an ISP (Internet service provider). In this case, the user's computer needs to have the necessary software to communicate with the Internet. The Internet "talks" only in TCP/IP, so computers must have software that supports the TCP and IP protocols. Once the user's computer is talking TCP/IP, a connection to the Internet can be established. Figure 1-5 shows a typical home computer-to-Internet connection.

A Laptop Computer and a Wireless Connection

Back at the library, Katrina also has her laptop sitting on the desk. Many laptops do not connect to a network using a fixed wire but instead connect via a wireless connection. This type of network connection continues to grow in popularity. A user working with a laptop, tablet, or even a smartphone uses wireless communications (often called Wi-Fi) to send and receive data to and from a wireless access point (also called a wireless router). This access point is usually connected to a wired LAN and basically serves as the "bridge" between the wireless user device and the wired network. As you'll see in later chapters, there are different data communication protocols for wireless and wired LANs. While the flexibility of not having to physically cable your device to a wall jack is nice, you'll see there are also limitations as

to how far the wireless signals can travel and how fast they can carry data.

Because both wireless and wired LANs are standard in business, academic, and many home environments, it should come as no surprise that having just one LAN is not going to get the job done. Many organizations need the services of multiple LANs, and it may be necessary for these networks to communicate with each other. For example, the school that Katrina attends may want the LAN that supports its chemistry department to share an expensive color laser printer with its biology department's LAN. Fortunately, it is possible to connect two LANs so that they can share peripherals (such as the printer) as well as software and files. Depending on the situation, you might use a switch or a router to connect two or more LANs or segments of LANs.

In some cases, it may be more important to *prevent* data from flowing between LANs than to allow data to flow from one network to another. For instance, some businesses have political reasons for supporting multiple networks—each division may want its own network to run as it wishes. Additionally, there may be security reasons for limiting traffic flow between networks; or allowing data destined for one network to traverse other networks simply may generate too much network traffic. The switches that connect LANs can help manage these types of services as well. For example, the switch can filter out traffic not intended for the neighboring network, thus minimizing the overall amount of traffic flow. This process of separating network traffic is called segmentation. Figure 1-6 provides an example of two LANs connected by two switches.

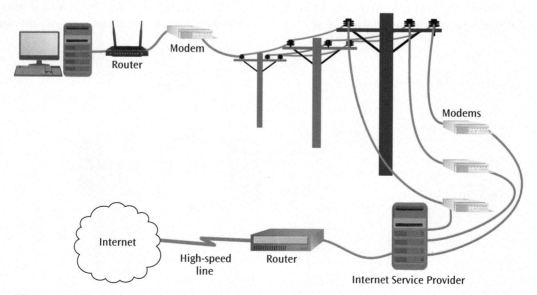

Figure 1-5   A computer sending data over a DSL line to an Internet service provider and onto the Internet

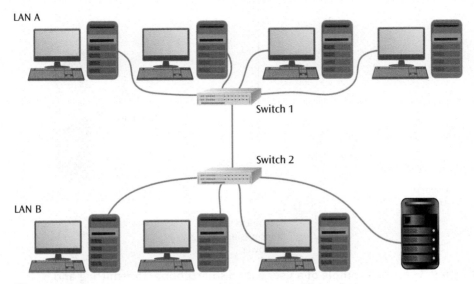

LAN A

Switch 1

Switch 2

LAN B

Figure 1-6 Two local area networks connected by switches

Cellular Network

While sitting in the library, Katrina can connect her smartphone to the Internet using Wi-Fi, but what if she needs to access her school email or assignments in a place where there is no Wi-Fi signal available? In this case, she can instead use a cell phone network, or cellular network.

One of the most explosive areas of growth in recent years has been cell phone systems. Originally, cell phones could only perform voice calls, but now your smartphone can send text messages, download pictures and videos from the Internet, stream music and video, and take high resolution photos and videos. The processing power built into modern smartphones rivals the mainframe computers of generations ago.

The network infrastructure that is needed to support modern smartphones has also increased in dramatic fashion. Large numbers of cell towers cover the face of North America and elsewhere throughout the globe. These cell towers are tied together into some form of network, allowing a user to send a text message all the way around the world. The data encoding technologies that support smartphones continue to increase in complexity so that users can access these networks at ever-increasing speeds.

For a more precise view, examine Figure 1-7. When a user talks into their smartphone, sends a text message or email, or interacts with a website, the data is transmitted across the cellular network to a telephone company building. The telephone company then transfers the smartphone's data over the public telephone network or through another high-speed connection onto the Internet.

All Things Considered

Thought Experiment

You've just taken a picture of your best friend with your smartphone. You decide to email it to a mutual friend across the country. List all the different networks possibly involved in this operation.

Other Common Network Systems

Cloud Essentials+ Exam Tip

This section discusses cloud deployment models, which is required by

• Part of Objective 1.1: Explain cloud principles.

The three sample networks you just viewed—a desktop computer connected to the Internet via a wired LAN, a laptop computer connected to the Internet via a wireless LAN, and a cellular network—are only a few of the many

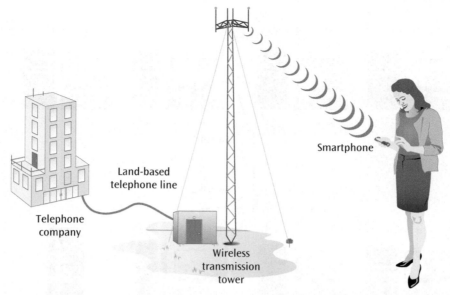

Figure 1-7 An example of a user with a smartphone transmitting and receiving data

examples of communication networks. Others that you will examine in more detail in later chapters include sensor networks, business mainframe networks, satellite networks, and cloud networks.

Sensor Networks

Sensor networks are often found in industrial and real-world settings. In this type of network, the action of a person or object triggers a sensor that is connected to a network. For example, in many left-turn lanes, a separate left-turn signal will appear if and only if one or more vehicles enter in the left-turn lane. A sensor embedded in the roadway detects the movement of a vehicle in the lane and triggers the left-turn mechanism

in the traffic signal control box at the side of the road. If this traffic signal control box is connected to a larger traffic control system, the sensor is connected to a LAN.

Another example of a sensor network is found within manufacturing environments. Assembly lines, robotic control devices, oven temperature controls, moisture detection or water level controls, and chemical analysis equipment, often use sensors connected to data-gathering computers that control movements and operations, sound alarms, and compute experimental or quality control results. These sensors are often interconnected via one or more LANs. Figure 1-8 shows a diagram of a typical sensor network in a manufacturing environment.

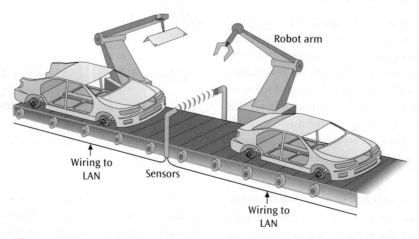

Figure 1-8 Automobiles move down an assembly line and trigger a sensor

Finally, don't forget all the sensor systems in people's homes and vehicles. Home appliances, such as washing machines, dryers, and dishwashers, include sensors to monitor water and air temperatures as well as water levels. Modern vehicles contain a myriad of sensors, monitoring fuel mixtures, oxygen levels, proximity detection, and wheel rotations (to trigger anti-lock brakes and anti-skid controls). Sensors and controllers have also been added to appliances such as refrigerators and thermostats so users can control these devices remotely through apps on their smartphones or through smart speakers. These speaker devices provide voice interaction with a digital assistant, such as Siri, Alexa, or Google. Smart appliances and other smart devices are part of the **IoT (Internet of Things)**. While there is some debate on exactly what is included in the IoT, this textbook will refer to IoT specifically as devices that would not normally be considered computing devices (like kitchen appliances or door locks) but are connected to the Internet to allow for remote and/or voice activated control.

Business Mainframe Network

Another fairly common network system is the business mainframe network. Many businesses still use mainframe computers to support their day-to-day operations. To "connect" to a mainframe, a user employs hardware and software that makes their computer act as a computer terminal. A **computer terminal**, or terminal, consists of essentially a keyboard and screen with no large hard drives, no gigabytes of memory, and little, if any, processing power. Computer terminals are used for entering data into a system, such as a mainframe computer, and then displaying

results from the mainframe. Because the terminal does not possess a lot of computing power, it's considered "dumb" and relies on the mainframe computer to control the sending and receiving of data to and from each terminal. This requires special types of protocols.

Business mainframe networks are still being used for inquiry/response applications, interactive applications, and data-entry applications. One example is the system that your bank might use to record ATM transactions from thousands of locations, as seen in Figure 1-9.

Satellite Networks

Satellite networks are continuously evolving technologies used in a variety of applications. If the distance between two networks is great and running a wire between them would be difficult, if not impossible, satellite transmission systems can be an effective way to connect the two networks or computer systems. Examples of these applications include digital satellite TV, meteorology, intelligence operations, mobile maritime telephony, GPS navigation systems, worldwide mobile telephone systems, and video conferencing. Figure 1-10 shows a diagram of a typical satellite system. You will examine these networks in more detail in Chapter 10.

Cloud Networks

Cloud networks connect resources that are said to reside "in the cloud." In reality, the cloud is essentially remote access to virtualized resources hosted in a software-defined environment. Let's break this down a little. **Virtualization** means that software is used

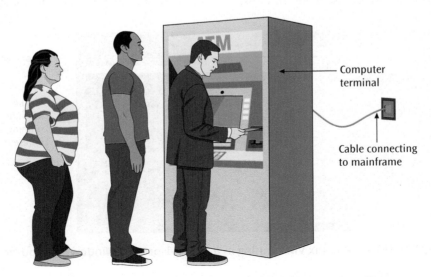

Computer terminal

Cable connecting to mainframe

Figure 1-9 Using an ATM terminal (or thin-client workstation) to perform a financial transaction

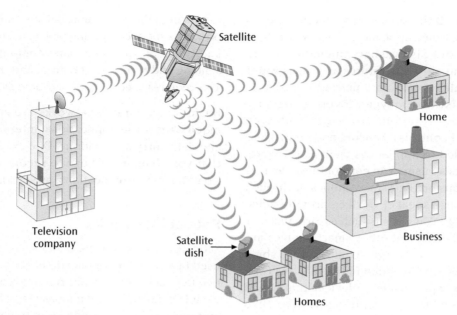

Figure 1-10 Example of a television company using a satellite system to broadcast television services into homes and businesses

to replicate the functions of hardware. For example, suppose you have a Windows computer like the one in Figure 1-11. You install virtualization software called a **hypervisor** on the Windows computer, and then you create a **virtual machine (VM)** in the hypervisor that functions as its own computer in a virtual environment. It needs its own OS (operating system), like Windows, or you can install a different OS, such as Linux. Figure 1-11 shows a Linux VM on the right where it's running on the Windows host computer. The hypervisor makes the Linux VM think it's the only computer running on the available hardware. The hypervisor allocates hardware resources to both the Linux VM and the Windows host.

A cloud network relies on a similar type of virtualization. A cloud hypervisor runs on top of a large collection of datacenter hardware, such as servers, routers, switches, and other devices. However, none of those physical devices are accessed directly by the cloud customer. The hypervisor abstracts the cloud network functions away from the physical devices so the customer only interacts with virtual resources, such as a virtual server. The cloud customer can create a new server VM, a process which is called "spinning up" a VM. From the customer's perspective, they're creating a new server that might run Linux or Windows or some other operating system. But the server is not an actual computer in

Figure 1-11 A Linux VM running in a hypervisor on a Windows computer

a rack—it's a virtual machine running in the hypervisor. The cloud network can run many other virtualized resources in the hypervisor, such as routing services or file storage services. You'll learn more about these service types later in this chapter.

Three primary types of cloud computing are as follows:

> Public cloud—These virtualized resources are hosted by a CSP (cloud service provider) at a remote location. While access control restrictions can protect these resources from unauthorized access, the hosting services can be used by anyone. For example, you might have files saved in a cloud storage service and only you can access them. However, thousands of other customers might use the same cloud storage service, and their files might be stored on the same physical server where your files are stored.

> Private cloud—These virtualized resources are hosted by the owner of the resources either in its own datacenter or at a remote location. The resources and the hosting services can only be accessed by the owner.

> Hybrid cloud—In a hybrid cloud, virtualized resources at a remote location and physical or virtual resources in the local datacenter are connected and interact at a functional level that is invisible to users. For example, you might sign into your computer at your desk, you open an application, and then you create and save a file. However, the application might be running on a server in your company's datacenter, and the file might be stored on a cloud-based server.

Cloud resources are collectively referred to as cloud computing, as you read earlier in this chapter. You'll learn more about cloud computing throughout this textbook.

Remember this...

> Many kinds of networks exist, depending on the connection technologies used, the types of communications the network supports, and the kinds of devices connected to the network.

> A client/server system provides client computers with a variety of services, such as a database, a web page, email, files, or printing.

> Protocols define the rules used by devices to communicate with each other over a network.

> Routers and switches can be used to connect devices across multiple LANs or segment traffic for security or traffic management purposes.

> Smartphones often rely on cellular networks to connect to the Internet and to provide calling and texting services.

> Other kinds of networks include sensor networks, wireless networks that use satellite technologies, and cloud networks that rely on virtualization.

Self-check

5. What kind of protocols support addressing and communication over the Internet?

   a. DSL

   b. TCP/IP

   c. LAN

   d. PC

6. You're setting up a small office network with a few desktop computers and a file server. You want to make sure only certain network users have access to the file server. What device will you need to configure to segment the network?

   a. Switch

   b. Cell phone tower

   c. Mainframe

   d. Router

7. Your school hosts its own cloud to provide students with virtual desktops. These desktops give students access to expensive software that most students couldn't afford to purchase on their own. Your school also stores student files in a cloud service that requires an Internet connection for students to access their files, even when they're on campus. What kind of cloud architecture is your school using?

   a. Public

   b. Enterprise

   c. Hybrid

   d. Private

Check your answers at the end of this chapter.

Section 1-4: Network Architectures

Now that you know the different types of networks, you need a framework to understand how all the various components of a network interoperate. When someone uses a computer network to perform a task, many pieces come together to assist in the operation. A network architecture, or communications model, places the appropriate network pieces in layers. The layers define a *model* for the functions or services that need to be performed. Each layer in the model defines what services either the hardware or software (or both) provides. The two most common architectures known today are the TCP/IP protocol suite and the OSI (Open Systems Interconnection) model. The TCP/IP protocol suite is a working model (currently used on the Internet), while the OSI model (originally designed to be a working model) has been relegated to a theoretical model. You will learn about these two architectures in more detail throughout the rest of this section. But first you should know a bit more about the components of a network and how a network architecture helps organize those components.

Consider that a typical computer network within a business contains the following components that must interact in various ways:

> Wires

> Printed circuit boards

> Wiring connectors and jacks

> Computers

> Centrally located wiring concentrators

> Storage drives

> Computer applications such as word processors, email programs, and software for accounting, marketing, and ecommerce

> Computer software that supports the transfer of data, checks for errors when the data is transferred, allows access to the network, and protects user transactions from unauthorized viewing

This large number of network components and their possible interactions inspires two questions. First, how do all these pieces work together harmoniously? You do not want two pieces performing the same function, or no pieces performing a necessary function. Like the elements of a well-oiled machine, all components of a computer network must work together to produce a product.

Second, does the choice of one piece depend on the choice of another piece? To make the pieces as modular as possible, you do not want the selection of one piece to constrain the options for another piece. For example, if you create a network and originally plan to use one type of wiring but later change your mind and use a different type of wiring, will that decision affect your choice of word processor? Such an interaction would seem highly unlikely. In contrast, can the choice of wiring affect the options for the protocol that checks for errors in the data sent over the wires? The answer to this question is not as obvious.

To keep the pieces of a computer network working together harmoniously, and to allow modularity between the pieces, national and international organizations developed network architectures, which are cohesive layers of protocols defining a set of communication services. Consider the following noncomputer example. Most organizations that produce some type of product or perform a service have a division of labor. Office assistants do the administrative work, accountants keep the books, laborers perform manual duties, scientists design products, engineers test the products, and managers control operations. Rarely is one person capable of performing all these duties. Large software applications operate the same way. Different procedures perform different tasks, and the whole system would not function without the proper operation of each of its parts. Computer network applications are no exception. As the size of the applications grows, the need for a division of labor becomes increasingly important. Computer network applications also have a similar delineation of job functions. This delineation is the network architecture. Now you're ready to examine the two network architectures or models in more detail: the TCP/IP protocol suite, followed by the OSI model.

The TCP/IP Protocol Suite

The TCP/IP protocol suite was created by a group of computer scientists to support a new type of network (the ARPANET) being installed across the United States in the 1960s and 1970s. The goal was to create an open architecture that would allow virtually all networks to inter-communicate. The design was based on several layers in which the user would connect at the uppermost layer and would be isolated from the details of the electrical signals found at the lowest layer.

The number of layers in the suite is not static. In fact, some books present the TCP/IP protocol suite as four layers, while others present it as five. Even then, different sources use different names for each of the layers. This textbook defines five layers, as shown in Figure 1-12: application, transport, network, data link, and physical.

Note that the layers do not specify precise protocols or exact services. In other words, the TCP/IP protocol suite does not tell you, for example, what kind of wire or what kind of connector to use to connect the devices of a network. That choice is left to the designer or implementer of the system. Instead, the suite simply says that if you specify a type of wire or a specific connector, you do that in a particular layer. In addition, each layer of the TCP/IP protocol suite provides a service for the next layer. For example, the transport layer makes sure the data received at the very end of a transmission is exactly the same as the data originally transmitted, but it relies upon the network layer to find the best path for the data to take from one point to the next within the network. With each layer performing its designated function, the layers work together to allow an application to send its data over a network of computers.

A common network application is email. An email communication that sends and accepts the message, "Blake, how about lunch? Najma," has many steps. Let's look at a simple analogy, as illustrated in Figure 1-13, to understand how the layers of the TCP/IP protocol suite work together to support this email message. Think of each layer of the TCP/IP suite as a worker. Each worker has its own job function, and Figure 1-13 shows how these workers cooperate to create a single package for transmission. Using the TCP/IP protocol suite, the steps might look like the following:

> The email "application worker" prompts the user to enter a message and specify an intended receiver. The application worker would create the appropriate data package with message contents and addresses, and send it to a "transport worker," who is responsible for providing overall transport integrity.

> The transport worker might establish a connection with the intended receiver, monitor the flow between sender and receiver, and perform the necessary operations to recover lost data in case some data disappears or becomes unreadable.

> The network worker would then take the data package from the transport worker and might add routing information so that the data package can find its way through the network.

> Next to get the data package would be the data link worker, who would insert error-checking information and prepare the data package for transmission.

> Finally, the physical worker would transmit the data package over some form of wire or through the air using radio waves.

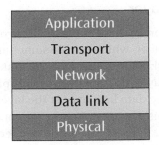

Figure 1-12   The five layers of the TCP/IP protocol suite

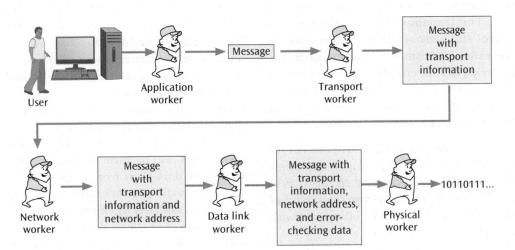

Figure 1-13   Several kinds of workers perform their job duties at each layer in the model

Application Layer

Now that you understand the big picture, let's examine each layer in more detail. The top layer of the TCP/IP protocol suite, the application layer, supports applications and might in some cases include additional services such as encryption or compression. Note that user applications, such as a browser or word processing application, don't reside in the application layer themselves. These applications rely directly on support provided by protocols that function within the application layer. The TCP/IP application layer includes several frequently used protocols:

> HTTP (Hypertext Transfer Protocol) allows web browsers and servers to send and receive web pages.

> SMTP (Simple Mail Transfer Protocol) allows users to send and receive email.

> FTP (File Transfer Protocol) transfers files from one computer system to another.

> SSH (Secure Shell) allows a remote user to securely log in to another computer system.

> SNMP (Simple Network Management Protocol) allows the numerous elements within a computer network to be managed from a single point.

Transport Layer

The TCP/IP transport layer commonly uses TCP (Transmission Control Protocol) to maintain an error-free end-to-end connection. To maintain this connection, TCP includes error control information in case one packet from a sequence of packets does not arrive at the final destination, and packet sequencing information so that all the packets can be sorted into the proper order as they're received. The transport layer performs *end-to-end* error control and *end-to-end* flow control, which ensures that the rate of transmitted packets does not overwhelm the device at the receiving end. This means the transport layer is not in use while the data packet is hopping from point to point within the network—it is used *only* at the two endpoints of the connection.

TCP is not the only possible protocol found at the TCP/IP transport layer. UDP (User Datagram Protocol) is an alternative also used, though less frequently, in the TCP/IP protocol suite. UDP does not provide the same kind of error control that TCP does and is most often used with streaming data, such as music or videos.

The two layers described so far are called end-to-end layers. They are responsible for the data transmitted

between the endpoints of a network connection. In other words, these layers perform their operations *only* at the beginning point and ending point of the network connection. The remaining three layers of the TCP/IP protocol suite—the network, data link, and physical layers—are not end-to-end layers. They perform their operations at each node (or device) along the network path, not just at the endpoints.

Network Layer

TCP/IP's network layer, sometimes called the Internet layer or IP layer, is used to transfer data within and between networks. IP (Internet Protocol) is the software that prepares a packet of data so that it can move from one network to another on the Internet or within a set of corporate networks. As this layer sends the packet from node to node, it generates the network addressing necessary for the system to recognize the next intended receiver. IPv4 (version 4) uses a 32-bit IP address, while IPv6 uses a 128-bit IP address. To choose a path through the network, the network layer determines routing information and applies it to each packet or group of packets.

Data Link Layer

The next lower layer of the TCP/IP protocol suite is the data link layer, which is also sometimes referred to as the network access layer or the link layer. Where the network layer deals with passing packets across the Internet, the data link layer is the layer that gets the data from the user workstation to the router connected to the Internet. In most cases, the connection that gets the data from the user workstation to the Internet is a LAN. Thus, the data link layer prepares a frame, or data packet, for transmission from the user workstation to a router sitting between the LAN and the Internet. This frame contains an identifier that signals the beginning and end of the frame, as well as spaces for control information and address information. In addition, the data link layer can incorporate some form of error detection software. If an error occurs during transmission, the data link layer is responsible for error control, which it does by informing the sender of the error. The data link layer might also perform flow control. In a large network where the data hops from node to node as it makes its way across the network, flow control ensures that one node does not overwhelm the next node with too much data. Note that these data link operations are quite similar to some of the transport layer operations. The primary difference is that the transport layer performs its operations only at the endpoints, while the data link layer performs its operations at every stop (node) along the path. This is also the last layer before the data is handed off for transmission across the medium.

All Things Considered

Thought Experiment

If the data link layer provides error checking and the transport layer provides error checking, isn't this redundant? Why or why not? Explain your answer.

Physical Layer

The bottom-most layer in the TCP/IP protocol suite (according to the layers as defined in this discussion) is the physical layer. The physical layer is where the actual transmission of data occurs. As noted earlier, this transmission can be over a physical wire, or it can be a radio signal transmitted through the air. To perform this transmission of bits, the physical layer handles voltage levels, plug and connector dimensions, pin configurations, and other electrical and mechanical issues. Furthermore, because the digital or analog data is encoded or modulated onto a digital or analog signal at this point in the process, the physical layer also determines the encoding or modulation technique to be used in the network. Note that some people combine the data link layer and physical layer into one layer.

Having distinctly defined layers enables you to "pull out" a technology used at one layer and insert an equivalent technology into that layer without affecting the other layers. For example, assume a network was designed for copper-based wire. Later, the system owners decide to replace the copper-based wire with fiber-optic cable. Even though a change is being made at the physical layer, it should not be necessary to make any changes at any other layers. In reality, however, a few relationships exist between the layers of a communication system that cannot be ignored. For example, if the physical organization of a LAN is changed (say from a wired network to a wireless network), it is likely that the frame description at the data link layer also will need to be changed. (You will examine this phenomenon in Chapter 4.) The TCP/IP protocol suite recognizes these relationships and merges many of the services of the physical and data link layers into one layer.

The OSI Model

Although the TCP/IP protocol suite is the model of choice for almost all installed networks, it is important to study both this architecture and the OSI model. Many books and articles, when describing a product or a protocol, often refer to the OSI model with a statement such as, "This product is compliant with OSI layer *x*." If you do not become familiar with the various layers of the OSI model and the TCP/IP protocol suite, you will struggle to understand more advanced concepts in the future.

The OSI model defines seven layers, as shown in Figure 1-14. Note further the relationship between the five layers of the TCP/IP protocol suite and the seven layers of the OSI model. As you examine descriptions of each of the OSI layers next, consider how their functions compare to the corresponding TCP/IP layer:

> The top layer in the OSI model is the application layer, which provides protocols to support applications using the network. Notice again that these protocols provide a support function—they are not the applications themselves, which do not reside on the network model. This OSI layer is similar to the application layer in the TCP/IP protocol suite.

> The next layer in the OSI model, the presentation layer, performs a series of miscellaneous functions necessary for presenting the data package properly to the sender or receiver. For example, the presentation layer might perform ASCII-to-non-ASCII character conversions, encryption and decryption of secure documents, and the compression of data into smaller units. There is no separate presentation layer in the TCP/IP protocol suite, as these functions are wrapped into the TCP/IP application layer.

> The session layer is another layer that does not exist separately in the TCP/IP protocol suite and is responsible for establishing sessions between users. It also can support token management, a service that controls which user's computer talks during the current session by passing a software

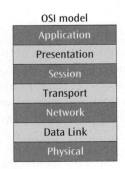
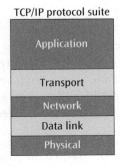

Figure 1-14   The seven layers of the OSI model compared to the five layers of the TCP/IP protocol suite

token back and forth. Additionally, the session layer establishes synchronization points, which are backup points used in case of errors or failures. For example, while transmitting a large document such as an ebook, the session layer might insert a synchronization point at the end of each chapter. If an error occurs during transmission, both sender and receiver can back up to the last synchronization point (to the beginning of a previously transmitted chapter) and start retransmission from there. Many network applications do not include a specific session layer and do not use tokens to manage a conversation. If they do, the "token" is inserted by the application layer, or possibly the transport layer, instead of the session layer. Likewise, if network applications use synchronization points, these points often are inserted by the application layer.

> The fourth layer in the OSI model, the transport layer, operates in the same way as the transport layer of the TCP/IP protocol suite. It ensures that the data packet arriving at the final destination is identical to the data packet that left the originating station.

> The network layer of the OSI model is similar to the network layer of the TCP/IP protocol suite and is responsible for getting the data packets from router to router through the network.

> The data link layer, similar to TCP/IP's data link layer, is responsible for taking data from the network layer and transforming it into a frame. It also handles addressing between devices within a LAN.

> The bottom layer in the OSI model—the physical layer—handles the transmission of bits over a communications channel. This layer is essentially identical to the physical layer of the TCP/IP protocol suite.

Logical and Physical Connections

An important concept to understand with regard to the layers of a communication model is the lines of communication between a sender and a receiver. Consider Figure 1-15, which shows the sender and receiver using a network application designed on the TCP/IP protocol suite.

Notice the dashed lines between the sender's and receiver's application layers, transport layers, network layers,

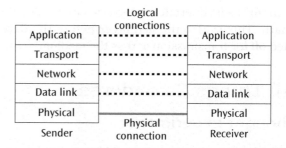

Figure 1-15 Sender and receiver communicating using the TCP/IP protocol suite

and data link layers. No data flows over these dashed lines. Each dashed line indicates a logical connection. A logical connection is a nonphysical connection between sender and receiver that allows an exchange of commands and responses. The sender's and receiver's transport layers, for example, share a set of commands used to perform transport-type functions, but the actual information or data must be passed through the lower layers of the sender and receiver, as there is no direct connection between the two transport layers. Without a logical connection, the sender and receiver would not be able to coordinate their functions. The physical connection is the only direct connection between sender and receiver, and is at the physical layer, where actual 1s and 0s—the digital content of the message—are transmitted over wires or airwaves.

For an example of logical and physical connections, consider what happens when you want to buy a house. Typically, you won't call homeowners directly. You'll first contact a real estate agent, who will show you several houses. Once you pick your favorite, you still won't communicate directly with the homeowner—your real estate agent will call the homeowner's agent. To negotiate the sales price, you and the homeowner will communicate through your respective agents as representatives of the best interests for each party. Figure 1-16 shows how this communication relies on layers of people and technology to send messages back and forth during the negotiation.

Note that the data did not flow directly between you and the homeowner; nor are the real estate agents likely to see each other face-to-face for the majority of these communications. Instead, the data had to flow down to the physical layer (in this case, the agents' smartphones) and then back up the other side. At each layer in the process, information that might be useful to the "peer" layer on the other side was added

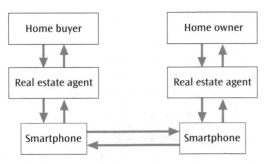

Figure 1-16 Flow of data through the layers of bureaucracy

(such as information about the house's address or information about the other agent's phone number). While this example illustrates the concept of layered communications, it is a bit overly simplified. Therefore, let's examine a more realistic example in which a person using a web browser requests a web page from somewhere on the Internet.

The TCP/IP Protocol Suite in Action

A more detailed and more challenging example of a request for a service moving through the layers of a communications model will help make the involved concepts clearer. Consider Figure 1-17, in which a user browsing the Internet on a personal computer requests a web page to be downloaded and then displayed on their screen.

Beginning in the upper-left corner of the figure, the process is initiated when the user clicks a link on the current web page. In response, the browser software (the application) creates a *Get web page* command that is given to the browser's transport layer, TCP. TCP adds a variety of header information to be used by the TCP software on the receiving end. Added to the front of the packet, this information will be used to control the transfer of data. This information assists

with end-to-end error control and end-to-end flow control, and it provides the transport-layer address of the receiving application on the web server (which likely is running several applications, and so each application has its own address called a port).

The enlarged packet is now sent to the network layer, where IP adds its header. The information contained within the IP header assists the IP software on the receiving end, and it assists the IP software at each intermediate node (router) during the data's progress through the Internet. This assistance includes providing the Internet address of the web server that contains the requested web page.

The packet is now given to the data link layer. Because the user's computer is connected to a LAN, the appropriate LAN headers are added. Note that sometimes, in addition to headers, control information is added to the end of the data packet as a trailer. One of the most important pieces of information included in the data link header is the address of the device (the router) that connects the LAN to the Internet.

Eventually, the binary 1s and 0s of the data packet are transmitted across the user's LAN via the physical layer, where they encounter a router. The router serves as the gateway to the Internet. The router removes the data link header and trailer. The information in the IP header is examined, and the router determines that the data packet must go out to the Internet. New data link header information, which is necessary for the data packet to traverse the Internet to the next router, is applied, and the binary 1s and 0s of the data packet are placed onto the WAN connection.

As the data packet moves across the Internet, it will eventually arrive at the router connected to the LAN that contains the desired web server. This remote router removes the WAN information, sees that the packet must be placed on its LAN, and inserts the LAN header and trailer information. The packet is placed onto the LAN; using the address information in the data link header, it travels to the computer holding the web server application. As the data packet moves up the layers of the web server's computer, the data link, IP, and TCP headers are removed. The web server application receives the *Get web page* command, retrieves the requested web page, and creates a new data packet with the requested information. This new data packet now moves down the layers and back through the routers to the user's network and workstation. Finally, the web page is displayed on the user's monitor.

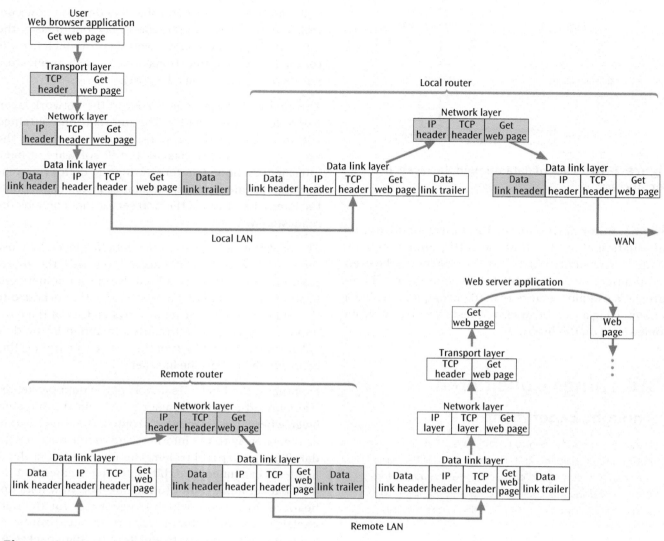

Figure 1-17   Path of a web page request as it flows from browser to Internet web server and back

It is interesting to note that, as a packet of data flows down through a model and passes through each layer of the system, the data packet grows in size. This growth is attributable to the fact that each layer adds more information to the original data. Some of this layer-added information is needed by the nodes in the data packet's path, and some is required by the data packet's final destination. This information aids in providing services such as error detection, error control, flow control, and network addressing. The addition of control information to a packet as it moves through the layers is called **encapsulation**. Note also that, as the packet moves up through the layers, the data packet shrinks in size as each layer removes the header it needs to perform its job. Once the job is complete, the header information is discarded and the smaller packet is handed to the next highest layer.

Details The Internet's Request for Comment (RFC)

Network models, like communications protocols, computer hardware, and application software, continue to evolve daily. The TCP/IP protocol suite is a good example of a large set of protocols and standards constantly being revised and improved. An Internet standard is a tested specification that is both useful and adhered to by users who work with the Internet. Consider the path a proposal must follow on the way to becoming an Internet standard.

All Internet standards start as an Internet draft, which is a preliminary work in progress. One or more internal Internet committees work on a draft, improving it until it is in an acceptable form. When Internet authorities feel the draft is ready for the public, it is published as an RFC (Request for Comment), a document open to all interested parties. The RFC is assigned a number, and it enters its first phase: proposed standard. A proposed standard is a proposal that is stable, of interest to the Internet community, and fairly well understood. The specification is tested and implemented by different groups, and the results are published. If the proposal passes at least two independent and interoperable implementations, the proposed standard is elevated to draft standard. If, after feedback from test implementations is considered, the draft standard experiences no further problems, the proposal is finally elevated to Internet standard.

If, however, the proposed standard is deemed inappropriate at any point along the way, it becomes an historic RFC and is kept for historical perspective. (Internet standards that are replaced or superseded also become historic.) An RFC also can be categorized as experimental or informational. In these cases, the RFC in question probably was not meant to be an Internet standard, but it was created either for experimental reasons or to provide information. Figure 1-18 shows the levels of progression for an RFC.

It is possible to obtain a printed listing of each RFC. See the IETF's (Internet Engineering Task Force) website at *ietf.org/ rfc/* for the best way to access RFCs.

The Internet is managed by the work of several committees, as described next:

> The topmost committee is the ISOC (Internet Society). ISOC is a nonprofit, international committee that provides support for the entire Internet standards-making process.

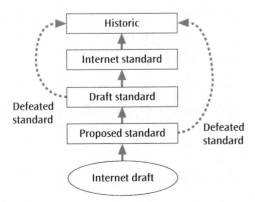

Figure 1-18 Levels of progression as an RFC moves toward becoming a standard

> Associated with ISOC is the IAB (Internet Architecture Board), which is the technical advisor to ISOC. Under the IAB are two major committees:

> > The IETF (Internet Engineering Task Force) manages the working groups that create and support functions such as Internet protocols, security, user services, operations, routing, and network management.

> > The IRTF (Internet Research Task Force) manages the working groups that focus on the long-range goals of the Internet, such as architecture, technology, applications, and protocols.

Internet committees are not the only groups that create protocols or approve standards for computer networks, data communications, and telecommunications. Another organization that creates and approves network standards is the **ISO (International Organization for Standardization)**, which is a multinational group composed of volunteers from the standards-making committees of various governments throughout the world. ISO is involved in developing standards in the field of information technology and created the OSI (Open Systems Interconnection) model for a network architecture.

Note

The shortened name for the International Organization for Standardization, *ISO*, is derived from a Greek word meaning *equal* and is not an acronym of the longer name.

Other standards-making organizations include the following:

> **ANSI (American National Standards Institute)**—A private, nonprofit organization not associated with the U.S. government, ANSI strives to support the U.S. economy and protect the interests of the public by encouraging the adoption of various standards.

> **ITU-T (International Telecommunication Union-Telecommunication Standardization Sector)**—Formerly the Consultative Committee on International Telegraphy and Telephony (CCITT), ITU-T is devoted to the research and creation of standards for telecommunications in general, and telephone and data systems in particular.

> IEEE (Institute of Electrical and Electronics Engineers)—The largest professional engineering society in the world, IEEE strives to promote the standardization of the fields of electrical engineering, electronics, and radio. Of particular interest is the work IEEE has performed on standardizing local area networks.

Remember this...

> Networks rely on a modular design based on various levels of functionality so that changes can be made at one layer without greatly affecting any other layer.

> The TCP/IP protocol suite defines four or five layers, the names of which can vary depending on the source. This text labels five layers: application, transport, network, data link, and physical.

> The OSI model defines seven layers: application, presentation, session, transport, network, data link, and physical.

> A logical connection identifies a conversation between the sender and receiver at each layer of communication, while a physical connection shows a direct connection between sender and receiver at the layer where actual 1s and 0s are transmitted over wires or airwaves.

> A message moves up and down the TCP/IP layers as it interacts with each protocol to carry information from one hop to the next across one or more networks.

Self-check

8. Which of these protocols do network admins use to help them identify problems on a network?
   a. HTTP
   b. SMTP
   c. FTP
   d. SNMP

9. Which OSI layer provides address information for a message to travel from a workstation to a router?
   a. Physical
   b. Data link
   c. Network
   d. Transport

10. A rat chews through a cable connecting two switches on your network. What layer of the OSI model has been compromised?
    a. Application
    b. Transport
    c. Network
    d. Physical

Check your answers at the end of this chapter.

Section 1-5: Cloud Computing

Throughout this course, you'll learn about cloud computing systems in the context of networking and data communications. While cloud computing is a relatively recent technological innovation, it's touching nearly every area of IT and, in many ways, revolutionizing the way datacenters and networks function. Why is this the case? Essentially, cloud computing provides a new way of running a company's IT resources. Cloud computing relies on the abstraction of compute, network, security, and storage functions away from the underlying physical hardware in ways that give network admins and other IT professionals almost unlimited resources at affordable prices. Let's start to break this concept down into bite-size pieces so you can see the significance of what cloud computing offers.

Cloud Computing Characteristics

Cloud Essentials+ Exam Tip

This section discusses cloud characteristics, which is required by

- Part of Objective 1.1: Explain cloud principles.
- Part of Objective 1.4: Summarize important aspects of cloud design.
- Part of Objective 2.4: Identify the benefits or solutions of utilizing cloud services.

To begin, you need a solid understanding of what characteristics define cloud computing and distinguish these technologies from more traditional options. NIST (National Institute of Standards and Technology) and similar organizations refer to the following characteristics to differentiate cloud computing from other types of IT resources:

> **Scalability** refers to the ability of resources to be adjusted over time in response to changing needs. Scalable resources can be increased or decreased either vertically or horizontally. For example, suppose a new doctor's office buys one server to hold their patient database. As their customer base grows, the database will continue to increase in size. Figure 1-19 illustrates two options for how to handle the growing demand. Vertical scaling would add more resources to the server, such as storage and memory, to increase its capacity, while horizontal scaling would add more servers to help host the database. With physical servers, this scaling up or scaling out is time-consuming and costly; cloud services are designed with scalability as a primary feature that can be performed quickly and even automatically, with little to no interruption in service.

> **Elasticity** means that resources can be increased or decreased quickly in response to changing needs, and in many cases, these shifts can be configured to occur automatically. Suppose you anticipate a huge increase in website traffic during a weekend

advertising campaign. With traditional computing, you would have to purchase additional servers many months ahead of time, and then spend hours installing and configuring the servers in preparation for a temporary traffic spike. After the campaign, the servers would no longer be needed, thereby wasting a lot of money. Elastic cloud resources can be temporarily increased only for the few days you need them, and then decreased as the traffic volume declines.

> **Pay-as-you-go** means the customer only pays for the resources they use. For example, when the customer no longer needs extra servers to handle increased traffic from the weekend advertising campaign, those extra servers are terminated and no longer accrue charges. The cloud customer does not have to pay for resources they're not using.

> **Self-service** resources can be increased, decreased, or otherwise altered by the customer without having to involve the cloud service provider. In many cases, the customer can configure these processes to happen automatically.

> **Broad network access** refers to a customer's ability to access and configure cloud resources from any Internet-connected computer. In other words, a technician or administrator does not have to be onsite at the cloud datacenter to make changes to their company's cloud resources. A company's IT team can access and control their cloud resources from home, from the company's own location, or from anywhere else where they have Internet access.

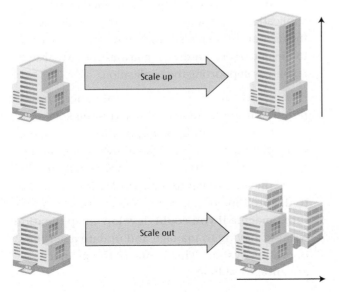

Figure 1-19 Resources can be scaled vertically by increasing an existing resource's capacity or horizontally by increasing the number of resources available

Note

Access to a customer's cloud console can be restricted to one or more specific locations based on IP address. However, this is a security measure, not a limitation of cloud capabilities.

> **Availability** refers to a cloud resource's ability to withstand losses or outages while minimizing disruption of service. **High availability (HA)** is the expectation that a service will be accessible for a certain percentage of time over the course of a year or a month and is usually listed by the number of 9s, such as 99.9% ("three nines") or 99.9999%

("six nines"). For example, if a service is down for less than 5.26 minutes per year, that service is said to have 99.999%, or five nines, availability. HA is achieved by providing **redundancy** within a system, which means that single points of failure (SPOFs), such as a network connection or a server, are duplicated. If one of these resources goes down, the other can take over and keep the system functioning.

Note

Various cloud services and ISPs offer three nines, four nines, five nines, or better availability, depending on what's defined in their **SLAs (Service-Level Agreements)**, which is a legally binding contract or part of a contract that defines certain aspects of a service. When shopping for cloud services, examine the SLA carefully so you'll know what parts of a service are guaranteed to be available.

However, be aware there's a difference between availability (the ability to access a resource) and **durability** (the resource's ongoing existence). For example, AWS lists its storage service, S3, at 99.999999999% durability (that's 11 nines!), but S3's *availability* is 99.99% for its Standard storage class. Why the discrepancy?

That 11 nines durability means you could store 10,000,000 objects in S3 and expect to lose one of those objects every 10,000 years on average (okay, not bad). This is because S3 stores each object on multiple devices in multiple, physical datacenters. The four nines availability means that, each year on average, there should only be 52.6 minutes when you can't get to your objects in S3—this is also pretty good, considering you can relax in knowing that your stored data isn't lost during that 52 minutes, even if you can't get to it for a bit.

Similar terms include **reliability**, which refers to how well a resource functions without errors, and **resiliency**, which refers to a resource's ability to recover from errors even if it becomes unavailable during the outage.

Cloud Service Models

Cloud Essentials+ Exam Tip

This section discusses cloud service models, which is required by

• Part of Objective 1.1: Explain cloud principles.

Now that you've read about the characteristics that are common to all cloud deployments, you're ready to learn about ways to differentiate various types of cloud services. You can think about each cloud service as a building block where you select the types of blocks that you need for your structure and connect them to work together. It helps to first think about these services in high-level categories, as described next:

> **SaaS (Software-as-a-Service)**, pronounced *sass*, is the type of cloud service most users are familiar with and provides access to an application that runs in the cloud environment. SaaS solutions tend to be highly scalable and require little to no understanding of the underlying architecture. SaaS applications also can be accessed from almost any kind of computer or mobile device. If you've used Google Docs or Dropbox, you've used SaaS. These cloud-based applications offer some level of configurability for the user or the administrator but provide no access to the underlying hardware, software, or virtualized resources supporting the application.

> **PaaS (Platform-as-a-Service)**, pronounced *pass*, requires more technical skill and often serves professional or hobbyist application developers or website developers. PaaS allows some underlying configurability, but developers can mostly focus on their development work without having to devote time to managing a network infrastructure. Imagine if you could develop an application without having to manage and update a server's operating system. This is one of the primary advantages of PaaS.

> laaS (Infrastructure-as-a-Service), pronounced *i-as*, requires the most technical skill for configuring cloud resources. While the customer cannot access the underlying hardware, IaaS allows the cloud customer to perform deep configurations to the cloud environment where they can most closely replicate a physical datacenter in the cloud, complete with virtual servers, firewalls, routers, and load balancers.

Notice that each of these categories varies on the type of person who would use a solution from that category. Figure 1-20 shows how each of these service models varies in the type of user the service is targeted to, and Figure 1-21 shows the different levels of technical skill required for each service model.

The progression of these categories reveals the fact that cloud customers and cloud providers each take part of the responsibility for managing and configuring cloud resources. As you can see in Figure 1-22, the placement of that dividing line determining who is responsible for what varies with the type of cloud service. In fact, this is one of the points that must be carefully studied and understood by cloud professionals for each service they use. It's important for cloud customers to know and consider what kinds of management tasks they must perform on their cloud services, what security precautions they must take, and what kinds of customization changes they can make. This reality is complicated by the fact that each cloud service provider handles the division of labor a little differently. For this reason, cloud professionals often specialize in one or a handful of cloud providers and service types.

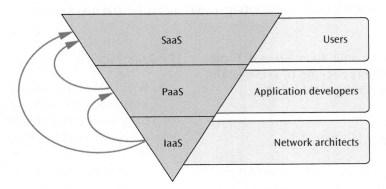

Figure 1-20 SaaS services are more immediately accessible to a wide market of users than other categories of cloud services

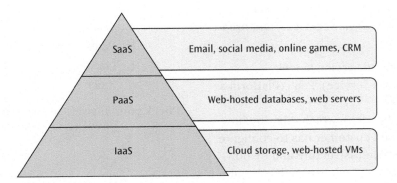

Figure 1-21 IaaS customers must understand more about configuring their cloud infrastructure—and they have more control—than do SaaS customers

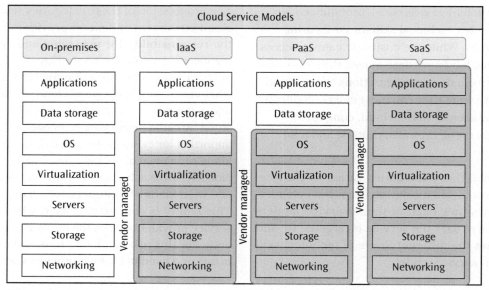

Figure 1-22   At each progressive level of these cloud service models, the vendor takes over more computing responsibility for the organization

In this chapter, you've laid a solid foundation of terminology and basic networking concepts to serve as the launching point for the remainder of this book.

Remember this...

> Cloud computing relies on the abstraction of compute, network, security, and storage functions away from the underlying physical hardware in ways that give network admins and other IT professionals almost unlimited resources at affordable prices.

> Characteristics that differentiate cloud computing from other types of IT resources include built-in scalability and availability, elastic resources, pay-as-you-go and self-service services, and broad network access.

> The three primary cloud service models are SaaS (Software-as-a-Service), PaaS (Platform-as-a-Service), and IaaS (Infrastructure-as-a-Service), which differ by how much access the cloud customer has to configure the underlying virtual infrastructure and by how much cloud management technical skill is required.

> It's important for cloud customers to know and consider what kinds of management tasks they must perform on their cloud services, what security precautions they must take, and what kinds of customization changes they can make.

Self-check

11. When schools suddenly closed and classes were held over the Internet instead, your company's video conferencing software suddenly needed to host five times more traffic than usual. What feature of your cloud-hosted web app allowed your service to automatically adapt to the changing demand?
    a. Accessibility
    b. Elasticity
    c. Self-service
    d. Broad network access

12. What kind of cloud service model is web-based email?
    a. SaaS
    b. PaaS
    c. IaaS
    d. XaaS

Check your answers at the end of this chapter.

Summary

Section 1-1: The Language of Computer Networking

> Networks are often categorized according to their size and the types of devices connected to them.

> The study of data communications includes digital and analog signals that can be transmitted over conducted or wireless (radiated) media.

> Cloud computing typically relies on the Internet in some way for access to resources at a remote location.

Section 1-2: The Big Picture of Networks

> LANs connect devices to each other using switches and connect to other networks using routers.

> WANs connect networks to each other using routing devices and are organized into groups of nodes called subnetworks.

> Specialized hardware and software are required for a workstation to communicate over a network such as the Internet.

> Addressing information is used to route information across a network.

Section 1-3: Common Network Examples

> Many kinds of networks exist, depending on the connection technologies used, the types of communications the network supports, and the kinds of devices connected to the network.

> A client/server system provides client computers with a variety of services, such as a database, a web page, email, files, or printing.

> Protocols define the rules used by devices to communicate with each other over a network.

> Routers and switches can be used to connect devices across multiple LANs or segment traffic for security or traffic management purposes.

> Smartphones often rely on cellular networks to connect to the Internet and to provide calling and texting services.

> Other kinds of networks include sensor networks, wireless networks that use satellite technologies, and cloud networks that rely on virtualization.

Section 1-4: Network Architectures

> Networks rely on a modular design based on various levels of functionality so that changes can be made at one layer without greatly affecting any other layer.

> The TCP/IP protocol suite defines four or five layers, the names of which can vary depending on the source. This text labels five layers: application, transport, network, data link, and physical.

> The OSI model defines seven layers: application, presentation, session, transport, network, data link, and physical.

> A logical connection identifies a conversation between the sender and receiver at each layer of communication, while a physical connection shows a direct connection between sender and receiver at the layer where actual 1s and 0s are transmitted over wires or airwaves.

> A message moves up and down the TCP/IP layers as it interacts with each protocol to carry information from one hop to the next across one or more networks.

Section 1-5: Cloud Computing

❭ Cloud computing relies on the abstraction of compute, network, security, and storage functions away from the underlying physical hardware in ways that give network admins and other IT professionals almost unlimited resources at affordable prices.

❭ Characteristics that differentiate cloud computing from other types of IT resources include built-in scalability and availability, elastic resources, pay-as-you-go and self-service services, and broad network access.

❭ The three primary cloud service models are SaaS (Software-as-a-Service), PaaS (Platform-as-a-Service), and IaaS (Infrastructure-as-a-Service), which differ by how much access the cloud customer has to configure the underlying virtual infrastructure and by how much cloud management technical skill is required.

❭ It's important for cloud customers to know and consider what kinds of management tasks they must perform on their cloud services, what security precautions they must take, and what kinds of customization changes they can make.

Key Terms

For definitions of key terms, see the Glossary near the end of the book.

application layer

availability

broad network access

CAN (campus area network)

client/server system

cloud

cloud computing

compression

computer network

computer terminal

data communication

data link layer

durability

elasticity

encapsulation

enterprise network

frame

FTP (File Transfer Protocol)

HA (high availability)

HTTP (Hypertext Transfer Protocol)

hybrid cloud

hypervisor

IaaS (Infrastructure-as-a-Service)

IEEE (Institute of Electrical and Electronics Engineers)

IoT (Internet of Things)

IP (Internet Protocol)

ISO (International Organization for Standardization)

LAN (local area network)

logical connection

MAN (metropolitan area network)

multiplexing

network architecture

network layer

network management

node

OSI (Open Systems Interconnection) model

PaaS (Platform-as-a-Service)

PAN (personal area network)

pay-as-you-go

physical connection

physical layer

presentation layer

private cloud

protocol

public cloud

redundancy

reliability

resiliency

router

SaaS (Software-as-a-Service)

scalability

segmentation

self-service

server

session layer

SLA (Service-Level Agreement)

SMTP (Simple Mail Transfer Protocol)

SNMP (Simple Network Management Protocol)

SSH (Secure Shell)

subnetwork

switch

TCP/IP protocol suite

transport layer

virtualization

VM (virtual machine)

WAN (wide area network)

web app

wireless

workstation

XaaS (Anything as a Service)

Review Questions

1. You are sitting at the local coffee shop, enjoying your favorite latte. You pull out your laptop and, using the wireless network available at the coffee shop, access your email. Which portion of the electromagnetic spectrum is your laptop most likely using?

   a. Ultraviolet waves
   b. Visible light waves
   c. Radio waves
   d. X-rays

2. Which of the following characteristics distinguishes a PAN from other types of networks?

   a. A printer is connected to the network.
   b. The network is intended to be used by one person at a time.
   c. The network supports wearable devices.
   d. The network is small in geographical coverage.

3. When you set up a network at your home with a home router, a few computers, a printer, multimedia devices, and your smartphone, which of the following statements is true?

   a. You can have several PANs, you have one LAN, and you probably have one WAN connection.
   b. You can have several LANs, you have one PAN, and you probably have one WAN connection.
   c. You can have several WANs, you have one MAN, and you probably have one LAN connection.
   d. You can have several PANs, you have one MAN, and you probably have one LAN connection.

4. Your company's network administrator mentions during a meeting that she has migrated your company's database to a DBaaS. What can you deduce about the database, given just this information?

   a. The database has been backed up.
   b. The database is now more secure than it was.
   c. The database is stored on a cloud provider's servers.
   d. The database has been archived.

5. When your work computer requests a web page, which device does the computer communicate with *first*?

   a. Web server
   b. Local server
   c. Router
   d. Switch

6. As you're setting up your home network, you connect one desktop and two laptops to your home router. You then connect your home router to your cable modem. When you test the connection with your desktop, the computer can access websites on the Internet. What functions is your home router providing for your home network?

   a. Web server and file server
   b. Web server and router
   c. Switch and web server
   d. Router and switch

7. What computer "language" is spoken over the Internet?

   a. WAN   c. TCP/IP
   b. NaaS   d. DSL

8. Using a laptop computer with a wireless connection to your company's LAN, you download a web page from the Internet. Which of the following statements can you know is true, given this information?

   a. Your web page request crossed at least two LANs.
   b. Your web page request crossed exactly one LAN.
   c. Your web page request was handled by exactly one router.
   d. Your web page request was handled by exactly one switch.

9. Your coworker, Raul, has stored a few documents on his workstation that you and several others in your office access regularly as you're writing emails to customers. What function is Raul's computer filling?

   a. Web server
   b. Switch
   c. Email server
   d. File server

10. Your family-owned business is growing and has just added a few new employees. The owners decide, for security purposes, that the network needs to be segmented so that only certain people can get to sensitive data. Which of these changes will accomplish this goal most effectively?

    a. Add a new WAN.
    b. Divide the network into two LANs.
    c. Divide the network into two WANs.
    d. Add a new PAN.

11. As you're riding the bus to work, you check your email on your smartphone. Your smartphone is using the cellular network to access the email server at your company's datacenter. What kind of network is this?

    a. Local area network
    b. Personal area network
    c. Body area network
    d. Wide area network

12. Which of the following is *not* an example of a sensor network?

    a. A doorbell sends an alert to the homeowner's smartphone when movement is detected.
    b. A security camera records some burglars robbing a gas station.
    c. A robot rejects a circuit board that does not meet manufacturing standards.
    d. An alarm sounds when water is detected on the datacenter floor.

13. Peggy owns a MacBook but needs to install and use an application that only works on the Windows operating system. How can she use the hardware she has to install and use the application?

    a. Wipe the macOS off her MacBook and install Windows instead.
    b. Spin up a macOS VM in the cloud and install the application on the VM.
    c. Create a VM on the MacBook and install Windows and the application on the VM.
    d. Change the hard drive on her MacBook and install Windows and the application on the new hard drive.

14. Which OSI layers does the TCP/IP architecture combine into one?

    a. Physical and network
    b. Network and application
    c. Application, transport, and physical
    d. Application, presentation, and session

15. Which of the following protocols functions at the transport layer?

    a. HTTP
    b. TCP
    c. IP
    d. SSH

16. Which of the following devices relies on IP addresses to send messages from network to network toward their destination?

    a. Routers
    b. Switches
    c. Servers
    d. Workstations

17. As you chat with a friend on social media, what type of connection maintains the immediacy of the conversation?

    a. Physical connection
    b. Logical connection
    c. Network connection
    d. Data link connection

18. In what part of a message on the Internet can a router find the destination IP address?

    a. Data link layer header
    b. Application layer header
    c. Transport layer header
    d. Network layer header

19. Mae sets up a database in the cloud for her new application, and she configures the database with automatic backups. The application runs on duplicate servers in her local area network. The local area network connects to the Internet through her router that was supplied by her Internet service provider. What is the single point of failure in Mae's architecture?

    a. The database
    b. The server
    c. The router
    d. The Internet

20. Kason creates a server in his private cloud where he will host his new website. Which cloud service model is Kason using for his VM?

    a. SaaS
    b. PaaS
    c. IaaS
    d. XaaS

Hands-On Project 1

Create a CloudWatch Alarm in AWS

Estimated time: 45 minutes

Resources:

> AWS account (instructions for free accounts and free credits are included below)

> Internet access

> **Context:**

Note

To Instructors: AWS Academy offers a plethora of helpful and free resources for schools, instructors, and students. At the time of this writing, students can only join AWS Academy when you post an invitation link in your LMS (learning management system) or when you send an email invite from the AWS Academy website, which provides students with free credits and tools for you to help them with their work in AWS. You can allocate free credits to your students for every class using a Learner Lab, and it does not count against their free credits in their own accounts. Creating an instructor's AWS Academy account is easy and free, and begins with a free AWS Academy application from your institution. Creating a Learner Lab in AWS Academy is even easier, and you can allocate free AWS credits for your students. For more information, visit **aws.amazon.com/training/awsacademy/**. If you have questions or need assistance, contact AWS Academy staff or email the author at *jillwestauthor@gmail.com*.

The Hands-on Projects in this course use the AWS (Amazon Web Services) public cloud platform. The steps below can help you create an AWS account if you don't have one already.

In this project, you'll create a CloudWatch alarm. Often, CloudWatch alarms are used to monitor availability and performance of cloud resources. In this case, you'll use CloudWatch to alert you if your cloud resources accumulate charges beyond a set maximum. While this shouldn't be necessary if you follow all project steps and properly delete all resources after you're finished with them, the alarm serves as a backup measure to help protect your liability. Note that these steps were accurate at the time of writing. You might need to do some research for updated information as things change. Search engines such as Google and documentation websites such as AWS and YouTube can be very helpful.

If you're using an AWS Academy account for this project, you'll be able to complete most of the steps and create the alarm; however, the alarm will not trigger because of a permissions limitation in AWS Academy. If you're using a standard AWS account, this alarm will help protect your liability for costs in AWS. Complete the following steps:

1. If you don't already have an AWS account, you'll need to create one. Choose one of the following options:

   a. Your instructor might have an AWS Academy course for you. In this case, your instructor should send you an invitation email to join the course, or your instructor might post a link in your LMS (learning management system). Follow the steps given in the email. No credit card is required.

   b. Alternatively, you can create a standard, free account with AWS directly. When you first create an AWS account, you get some Always Free services and 12 months Free Tier services that allow you to test-drive certain features within pre-defined limits. The AWS projects in this course can be completed within the limits of Free Tier services at the time of this writing, although that could change. Be sure to read and understand the terms and conditions of Free Tier services, which services are included, and what the defined limits are. To sign up, go to **aws.amazon.com/free/**. A credit card *is* required for this option.

2. After creating your AWS account, regardless of the approach you used, save your sign-in information in a safe place for future reference in later projects.

3. Sign into your AWS management console:

    a. If you're using an AWS Academy Learner Lab, you'll need to access your AWS management console through the AWS Academy website.

    b. If you're using a standard AWS account, sign in directly at **aws.amazon.com**.

Steps 4, 5, and 6 can only be completed using a standard AWS account. If you're using an account through AWS Academy, skip to Step 7. If you're using a standard AWS account, make sure you're signed in as the root user (this is the default) or as an IAM user with permission to view billing information, and then complete the following steps:

4. At the top of the console, make sure the **US East (N. Virginia)** region is selected.

5. At the top of the console, click the name of your account, and then click **My Billing Dashboard**.

6. In the navigation pane on the left, click **Billing preferences**. Select **Receive Billing Alerts**. Click **Save preferences**.

Regardless of the account type you're using, complete the following steps to create a billing alarm in CloudWatch:

7. At the top of the console, click **Services**. Services are grouped according to the kinds of resources they create. In the Management & Governance group, click **CloudWatch**.

8. In the navigation pane on the left, click **Alarms**. Click **Create alarm**. A CloudWatch alarm is a free resource in the CloudWatch service.

9. Click **Select metric**. On the Select metric page, you can drag up the two lines in the middle of the screen to resize the lower section, making it easier to see the available metrics. Under Metrics, click **Billing**. Click **Total Estimated Charge**. Check **USD**. Click **Select metric**.

10. By default, the Statistic field is set to Maximum, and the Period field is set to 6 hours. In the Conditions section, the Threshold type is set to **Static**, and the *Whenever Estimated Charge is…* field is set to **Greater**. Scroll to the bottom of the page to the *than…* field. Under *Define the threshold value*, type **5**. As shown in Figure 1-23, this metric will trigger the alarm if charges exceed $5 once within six hours. Click **Next**.

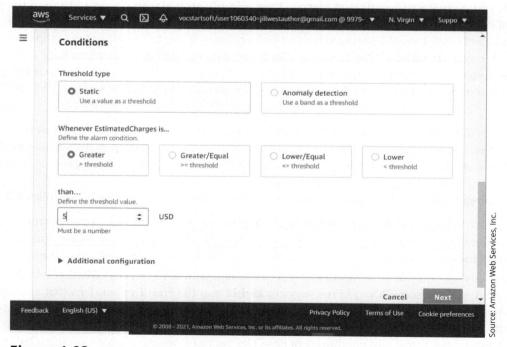

Figure 1-23 This will trigger if estimated charges exceed $5

In AWS, an alarm is an event that is triggered when certain conditions are met (similar to a smoke detector identifying smoke in the air). In contrast, an SNS (Simple Notification Service) topic handles any notifications that should be sent if the alarm is triggered (such as the noise a smoke detector emits when smoke is detected). Basically, an alarm identifies that something occurred, and the SNS topic is the communications channel in response to that alarm. In AWS, that response might be an email or text message sent to an admin, among other possibilities. Therefore, as you're setting up your alarm, you also need to set up a topic, as follows:

11. Under *Select an SNS topic*, select **Create new topic**. Give the topic an informative name. What name did you use?

12. In the Email endpoints field, enter your email address (an account you monitor regularly—this email does *not* have to be the same address you use to access your AWS console). Click **Create topic**. Scroll down and click **Next**.

13. Give the alarm an informative name and description. What name and description did you use? Click **Next**.

14. Study the information on the Preview and create page to make sure you understand the alarm you're creating. In your own words, give an example of what could trigger this alarm.

15. Click **Create alarm**.

Your email address was listed as a subscription, or communication endpoint, to the topic, meaning a message should be sent to your address if the alarm is triggered. However, to reduce spamming, you must first confirm your email subscription before you'll receive notices:

16. To confirm your email subscription to the topic you created, go to your email account, open the email from AWS Notifications, and click **Confirm subscription**.

17. Return to your AWS console and click the **Refresh** button (it shows a circle arrow icon) above the list of alarms. What is the initial state of the alarm?

18. If your alarm is not currently in the OK state, continue refreshing the data until your alarm reaches the OK state.

19. Click the alarm's name to see more information about it. **Take a screenshot** of the Details section of your alarm; submit this visual with your answers to this project's questions.

20. Currently, only your email address is subscribed to the alarm's topic. To see all current subscriptions in SNS (Simple Notification Service), click **Services**. In the Application Integration group, click **Simple Notification Service**. In the navigation pane, click **Topics**. Click the topic you created. What is the status of your email subscription? If there are any problems indicated for the email subscription, troubleshoot those now.

Reflection Discussion 1

As you read about in this chapter, you use many kinds of networks nearly every day, such as when you check your email, post on social media, use your smartphone, make a payment at a store, or even just drive down the road. Perhaps you've had some experience working with networks, either setting up a network or troubleshooting problems. Did you set up your own home network? Have you had to troubleshoot a problem with your employer's network?

Consider the following questions:

> What did you notice about how devices communicate with each other?

> What solutions did you find to problems you encountered?

> What questions do you have now that warrant further research?

Go to the discussion forum in your school's LMS (learning management system). Write a post of at least 100 words discussing your thoughts about the kinds of experiences you've had with networks, what you learned in those experiences, and what more you would like to learn. Then respond to two of your classmates' threads with posts of at least 50 words discussing their comments and ideas. Use complete sentences and check your grammar and spelling. Try to ask open-ended questions that encourage discussion, and remember to respond to people who post on your thread. Use the rubric in Table 1-1 to help you understand what is expected of your work for this assignment.

Table 1-1   Grading rubric for Reflection Discussion 1

Task	Novice	Competent	Proficient	Earned
Initial post	Generalized statements about experiences working with networks **30 points**	Some specific statements with examples about experiences working with networks and learning from those experiences **40 points**	Self-reflective discussion with specific and thoughtful statements about experiences working with networks, learning from those experiences, and questions for further research **50 points**	
Initial post: Mechanics	• Length < 100 words • Several grammar and spelling errors **5 points**	• Length = 100 words • Occasional grammar and spelling errors **7 points**	• Length > 100 words • Appropriate grammar and spelling **10 points**	
Response 1	Brief response showing little engagement or critical thinking **5 points**	Detailed response with specific contributions to the discussion **10 points**	Thoughtful response with specific examples or details and open-ended questions that invite deeper discussion of the topic **15 points**	
Response 2	Brief response showing little engagement or critical thinking **5 points**	Detailed response with specific contributions to the discussion **10 points**	Thoughtful response with specific examples or details and open-ended questions that invite deeper discussion of the topic **15 points**	
Both responses: Mechanics	• Length < 50 words each • Several grammar and spelling errors **5 points**	• Length = 50 words each • Occasional grammar and spelling errors **7 points**	• Length > 50 words each • Appropriate grammar and spelling **10 points**	
			Total	

Solutions to Self-Check Questions

Section 1-1: The Language of Computer Networking

1. You plug your new printer into a USB port on your computer. What kind of network supports this connection?

Answer: d. PAN

Explanation: A PAN (personal area network) includes devices connected within an area of a few meters, such as smartphones, music players, wireless keyboard or speakers, and a USB-connected printer.

2. You connect your home network to your Internet provider using a single fiber cable. What technology allows you to download and upload data over this connection at the same time?

Answer: b. Multiplexing

Explanation: Multiplexing is the transmission of multiple signals on one medium at the same time by altering each signal slightly to keep them from interfering with one another.

Section 1-2: The Big Picture of Networks

3. You plug your laptop into your local network's router and use your browser to visit a website. What type of device allows your router to communicate with your Internet provider's network?

Answer: b. Modem

Explanation: A modem allows communication over a DSL or cable connection between a local network and a wide area network.

4. You need to make some changes to a file stored on your office's network. On which device is the file located?

Answer: b. Server

Explanation: Servers store shared or private user files that can be accessed remotely.

Section 1-3: Common Network Examples

5. What kind of protocols support addressing and communication over the Internet?

Answer: b. TCP/IP

Explanation: The Internet "talks" in TCP/IP to provide an addressing scheme and establish communication connections, and users must use software that supports the TCP and IP protocols.

6. You're setting up a small office network with a few desktop computers and a file server. You want to make sure only certain network users have access to the file server. What device will you need to configure to segment the network?

Answer: a. Switch

Explanation: The switches that connect local area networks can help manage network segmentation as well, such as when separating some traffic from other network traffic.

7. Your school hosts its own cloud to provide students with virtual desktops. These desktops give students access to expensive software that most students couldn't afford to purchase on their own. Your school also stores student files in a cloud service that requires an Internet connection for students to access their files, even when they're on

campus. What kind of cloud architecture is your school using?

Answer: c. Hybrid

Explanation: In a hybrid cloud, virtualized resources at a remote location (such as the file storage accessed over the Internet) and physical or virtual resources in the local datacenter (such as servers hosting the virtual desktops) are connected and interact at a functional level that is invisible to users.

Section 1-4: Network Architectures

8. Which of these protocols do network admins use to help them identify problems on a network?

Answer: d. SNMP

Explanation: SNMP allows the numerous elements within a computer network to be managed from a single point, including receiving and processing error messages to identify problems.

9. Which OSI layer provides address information for a message to travel from a workstation to a router?

Answer: b. Data link

Explanation: The data link layer prepares a frame for transmission from the user workstation to a router sitting between the LAN and the Internet. The frame contains address information for this local transmission.

10. A rat chews through a cable connecting two switches on your network. What layer of the OSI model has been compromised?

Answer: d. Physical

Explanation: The physical layer is where the actual transmission of data occurs over a physical wire, such as a network cable, or by radio signal, such as with Wi-Fi. Problems at this layer usually involve physical equipment such as cables or access points.

Section 1-5: Cloud Computing

11. When schools suddenly closed and classes were held over the Internet instead, your company's video conferencing software suddenly needed to host five times more traffic than usual. What feature of your cloud-hosted web app allowed your service to adapt to the changing demand?

Answer: b. Elasticity

Explanation: Elasticity allows resources to scale up or down quickly in response to changing needs, and in many cases, these shifts can be configured to occur automatically.

12. What kind of cloud service model is web-based email?

Answer: a. SaaS

Explanation: SaaS (Software-as-a-Service) provides access to an application that runs in the cloud environment. Web-based email, such as Gmail or Yahoo, are good examples of SaaS.

Chapter 2

Conducted and Radiated Media

Objectives

After reading this chapter, you should be able to:

- Identify common cabling standards
- Compare types of network cables
- Compare wireless network technologies
- Evaluate the best media for network connections

Introduction

The world of computer networks would not exist if there were no medium by which to transfer data. Recall from Chapter 1 that network communications can be understood in terms of the TCP/IP protocol layers. The cables or wireless signals on which data travels is layer 1, the physical layer. In this book, you will begin your study of networking at this foundational layer.

All communications media can be divided into two categories: (1) conducted or wired media, such as copper cables and fiber-optic cables, and (2) radiated or wireless media, such as cell phones and Wi-Fi. This chapter will cover conducted media types such as USB that connect computers with peripheral devices and conducted media types found on a company's private LAN (local area network), including twisted pair cable, coaxial cable, and fiber-optic cable. In addition, this chapter examines the basic groups of wireless media used for data transfer on LANs: Wi-Fi, Bluetooth, Zigbee, and a few others. Chapters 9 and 10 will discuss wired and wireless technologies in the context of WANs (wide area networks).

As you read this, someone somewhere is undoubtedly designing new materials and building new equipment that is better than what currently exists. The transmission speeds and distances given in this chapter will continue to evolve. Please keep this in mind as you study the media. The chapter concludes with a comparison of the typical media types used most often on LANs, and yet, media preferences continue to shift as newer technologies become available and older technologies become cheaper.

Section 2-1: Cabling Standards

Connecting cables to network devices and workstations can be a challenging task. Various levels of hardware and software must agree completely before a device can "talk" to another device. Questions such as the following need to be resolved:

> Will the connector on the end of the cable coming from the network be compatible with the outlet on the device?

> Will the electrical properties of the two devices be compatible?

> Will these devices "speak the same language"?

Connecting devices to each other or to networks presents many pitfalls and obstacles. To better understand the interconnection between devices and the network, let's first discuss the concept of interfacing, which is the process of creating an interconnection between two devices, such as a computer and a network device. Considered primarily a physical layer activity, interfacing is a complex, relatively technical process that varies greatly depending upon the type of device and the connection desired between devices.

Many years ago, manufacturers of computers and other devices realized that, if one company made a computer and another company made a network device, the odds of the two being able to communicate with one another were slim. Thus, various organizations set about creating a standard interface between devices such as computers and modems. Because there were so many different transmission and interface environments, however, one standard alone did not suffice. As a result, hundreds of standards have been created. Despite their variations, all interface standards have two basic characteristics.

The first characteristic is that the standards have been created and approved by an acceptable standards-making organization. The primary organizations involved in making the standards used today are:

> International Telecommunication Union (ITU), formerly the International Telegraph and Telephone Consultative Committee (CCITT)

> Telecommunications Industry Association (TIA), which has taken over many of the now-defunct Electronic Industries Alliance (EIA) responsibilities

> Institute of Electrical and Electronics Engineers (IEEE)

> International Organization for Standardization (ISO)

> American National Standards Institute (ANSI)

Often, individual companies are in such a hurry to rush a product to market that they will create a new product that incorporates a nonstandard interface protocol. Although there is a definite marketing advantage to being the first to offer a new technology, there is also a considerable disadvantage to using an interface protocol that has not yet been approved by one of these standards-making organizations. For example, shortly after your company introduces its new product, one of the standards-making organizations might create a new protocol that performs the same function as your nonstandard protocol, and this might lead to your company's product becoming obsolete. In the quickly changing world of computer technology, creating a product that conforms to an approved interface standard is difficult but highly recommended.

Sometimes, when a company creates their own standard, they don't make it available for others to use. This is called a proprietary technology. Other times, a company will create a protocol and allow others to use it so that, although not an official standard, it becomes so popular that many other companies incorporate it into their own products. In this case, the protocol is considered a de facto standard. For example, Microsoft's operating system for personal computers is not an official standard. Nonetheless, more than 85 percent of all personal computers use the Microsoft operating system, thereby making the Windows desktop operating system a de facto standard. Systems running on a network must be compatible with the Windows OS.

The second basic characteristic of an interface standard is its composition. An interface standard can consist of four parts, or components, all of which reside at the physical layer: the electrical component, the mechanical component, the functional component, and the procedural component. All the standards currently in existence address one or more of these components, as follows:

> The electrical component deals with voltages, line capacitance, and other electrical issues. The electrical components of interface standards are primarily the responsibility of a technician.

> The mechanical component deals with items such as the connector or plug description. Questions typically addressed by the mechanical component include: What are the size and shape of a connector? How many pins are found on the connector? What is the pin arrangement?

> ## Note
>
> In comparing the various data transfer rates of services and devices over cables and other media, this book uses the convention in which lowercase k equals 1000, such as kb for 1000 bits. Also as part of the convention, lowercase b will refer to bits, while uppercase B refers to bytes, which is a collection of 8 bits. One Mb (megabit), then, equals 1000 kb. One Gb (gigabit) equals 1000 Mb. And One Tb (terabit) equals 1000 Gb.
>
> Most data transfer rates, or **throughput**, are measured per second, such as Mbps (megabits per second). Most of these data rates are theoretical maximums, meaning the medium theoretically could support that data rate just as a highway could theoretically support a certain number of cars driving bumper-to-bumper at the speed limit. However, data rates will rarely, if ever, approach these maximums because of the limitations of actual network communications and various environmental factors.

> The **functional component** describes the function of each pin (which is referred to as a circuit when you also consider the signal that travels through the pin and wire) used in an interface.

> The **procedural component** describes how the circuits are used to perform an operation. Although the functional component of an interface standard might, for example, describe two circuits, such as Request to Send and Clear to Send, the procedural component would describe how these two circuits are used so the device can transfer data over the connection.

Personal Area Network (PAN) Connection Standards

Although the bulk of this chapter focuses on cabling and interface standards used on LANs, there are a few standards for PAN (personal area network) connections you should be familiar with. This section covers a few of the most common wired PAN technologies. Wireless PAN technologies are covered in the wireless section later in this chapter because those technologies can also be used for LAN connections.

Universal Serial Bus (USB)

The USB interface is currently the most popular form of personal computer wired interface and will probably remain that way for some time. USB (Universal Serial Bus) is a modern standard for interconnecting many types of peripheral devices to computers. More precisely, USB is a digital interface that uses a standardized connector (plug) for all serial and parallel type devices. Because USB provides a digital interface, it is not necessary to convert the digital signals of the computer to analog signals for transfer over a connection. As you'll learn in Chapter 3, systems that undergo digital-to-analog or analog-to-digital conversions usually have more noise in their signals because of the conversion. USB avoids the introduction of such noise.

USB offers some other helpful features, as follows:

> USB is a relatively thin, hot-pluggable cable, meaning devices can be added and removed while the computer and peripheral are active. The idea behind **hot pluggable** capabilities is that the peripheral can simply be plugged in and turned on, and the computer should dynamically recognize the device and establish the interface. In other words, the casing of the computer does not have to be opened, nor do any software or hardware configurations have to be set.

> When using peripherals designed with a USB connector, it is possible to connect one USB peripheral to another without connecting back to the computer. This technique is known as **daisy-chaining**.

> USB offers the ability to provide the electrical power required to operate most peripherals. With this option, it is not necessary to find an electrical outlet for each peripheral.

> A USB 3.0 or better interface is a **full-duplex connection**, or connection in which both sender and receiver may transmit data at the same time. Older USB standards use a **half-duplex connection**, which allows only the sender or the receiver to transmit at one time.

As you just learned, interface standards consist of up to four components. Let's examine each of those components for the USB standard so you can see how much thought has gone into the design of cables and connectors.

Note

USB 3.0 refers to the specification that determines the protocols used over a USB cable. It's this generational version that identifies the data transfer rate of a USB cable and its capability for power delivery. Earlier USB versions include USB 1.0 (12 Mbps) and 2.0 (480 Mbps). The most recently released version at the time of this writing is USB 3.2 (recently renamed USB 3.2 Gen 2x2), which offers a greatly improved maximum throughput of 20 Gbps. Many USB connectors can be used with the USB 3.0 specification and above. You can often identify a USB 3.0 or better cable by its blue color, although this is not a completely reliable indicator.

With the USB standard, the electrical and functional components support the transfer of power and of the signal over a four-wire cable. Two of these four wires, VBUS (bus power) and GND (ground), carry a 5-volt signal that can be used to power the device. The other two wires, D+ and D–, carry the data and signaling information.

The mechanical component of USB strictly specifies the exact dimensions of the interface's connectors and cabling. While several types of USB connectors are specified, the most common today are Type-A, Type-B, Type-B Micro, and USB-C (see Figure 2-1). Connectors A and B each have four pins, one for each of the four wires in the electrical component, while the micro connector has five pins. The fifth pin is called the signal pin and is often simply connected to either the VBUS or GND pins. USB-C contains 24 pins to provide higher data transfer rates up to 10 Gbps, which is sufficient for video to extra monitors or a high-speed Internet connection. The connector can provide sufficient power transfer to charge a laptop and is

Figure 2-1 Four types of USB connectors (left to right): Type-A, Type-B, Type-B Micro, and USB-C

reversible, meaning the connector does not have a "top" or "bottom" and can be inserted either way.

The procedural component of USB is probably the most involved of the four components. To understand how it works, you first need to become familiar with the terms "bus" and "polling." A bus is simply a high-speed connection to which multiple devices can attach, and polling is a process in which a computer asks a peripheral if it has any data to transmit to the computer. The USB is a polled bus in which the host controller (the USB interface to the host computer) initiates all data transfers. The USB bus can recognize when a USB device has been attached to a USB port or to a USB hub (a device that is like an extension cord and can provide multiple USB ports). It can also recognize when that same device has been removed. In addition, the USB bus can support four basic types of data transfers, as follows:

> Control transfers are used to configure a peripheral device at the time of attachment.

> Bulk transfers are used to support large and bursty (i.e., produced in bursts) quantities of data.

> Interrupt transfers are used for timely but reliable delivery of data.

> Isochronous transfers are connections that require continuous and real-time transfers of data, such as audio and video streams.

In addition to USB, other interface standards have been created over the years to provide high-speed connections to various types of peripheral devices. Two of the most common are Thunderbolt and Lightning.

Thunderbolt

Thunderbolt is a proprietary standard developed by Intel. It was initially available only on Apple devices but has now been adopted by many other manufacturers. Thunderbolt uses the same USB-C connector you just learned about but provides a theoretical data rate of 40 Gbps. While the connector looks the same, you can usually identify a Thunderbolt capable port by the lightning bolt symbol, as shown in Figure 2-2. It was relatively easy to create this new, high-speed, daisy-chaining serial interface by combining two existing protocols. The first is PCI Express, which is a popular bus standard, and the second is DisplayPort, which is a video interface standard. Although Thunderbolt's design was originally conceived as a fiber-optic connector, it has become popular as a copper-wire connector, thus keeping down costs. Some predict that Thunderbolt will eventually hit 100-Gbps data rates in the future.

Jill West

Jill West

Figure 2-2   Thunderbolt cables use USB-C connectors

Lightning

The **Lightning** connector, as shown in Figure 2-3, is an Apple-proprietary standard. It has 8 pins designed to replace the older 30-pin connector and can be found as the primary connector on the newer versions of Apple's iPhone as well as many versions of the iPad and other devices. Lightning cables are most often used for charging devices, but data transfer speeds are similar to the USB 2.0 specification. While the Lightning connector is smaller than a USB-C connector and is also reversible, many questioned why Apple decided to go with a proprietary connector rather than an industry standard such as USB. In fact, European officials are pushing for Apple to abandon the Lightning connector entirely to increase standardization within the industry.

Remember this...

> All interface standards have two basic characteristics: they have been created and approved by an acceptable standards-making organization, and they can consist of one to four components, which include an

Jill West

Figure 2-3   Lightning cables only work on Apple devices

electrical component, a mechanical component, a functional component, and a procedural component.

> USB is a relatively thin, space-saving cable to which devices can be added and removed while the computer and peripheral are active. It is hot pluggable, supports daisy-chaining, offers the ability to provide electrical power, and is a full-duplex connection.

> Thunderbolt uses the USB-C connector but provides a theoretical data rate of 40 Gbps. Lightning is an Apple-proprietary standard that is smaller than a USB-C connector and is also reversible.

Self-check

1. In trying to identify an old cable, you check the connector on the end and count the number of pins. What component of the interface design are you using to help you identify this cable?

   a. Electrical

   b. Procedural

   c. Functional

   d. Mechanical

2. Which of these wired PAN standards does *not* use the USB-C connector form factor?

   a. USB 3.0

   b. Lightning

   c. Thunderbolt

   d. USB 2.0

3. Which of these wired PAN standards provides the fastest data throughput?

   a. USB 3.0

   b. Lightning

   c. Thunderbolt

   d. USB 2.0

Section 2-2: Conducted Media

Even though conducted media have been around since the telegraph, the progression of these technologies primarily focus on improved performance rather than developing new or unique cable types. Fiber-optic cable, the newest member of the conducted media family, became widely used by telephone companies in the 1980s and by computer network designers in the 1990s.

Altogether, there are three types of conducted media currently used on LANs. The oldest, simplest, and most common one is twisted pair cable.

Twisted Pair Cable

Twisted pair cable comes as two or more pairs of single-conductor copper wires that have been twisted around each other. The term "twisted pair" is almost a misnomer, as one rarely encounters a single pair of wires. As shown in Figure 2-4, each single-conductor wire is encased within plastic insulation and cabled within one outer jacket. Splicing segments of twisted pair cable is a relatively simple process that can be performed in the field with only a few simple tools. This makes installation and repairs simpler than some other types of cables. However, it also presents a security risk in that a hacker can break into the network without easily being detected.

Unless someone strips back the outer jacket, you might not see the twisting of the wires. The twists reduce the amount of interference one wire can inflict on the other, one pair of wires can inflict on another pair of wires, and an external electromagnetic source can inflict on any wire in a pair. You might recall two important laws from physics: (1) A current passing through a wire creates a magnetic field around that wire, and (2) a magnetic field passing over a wire induces a current in that wire. Therefore, a current or signal in one wire can produce an unwanted current or signal, called

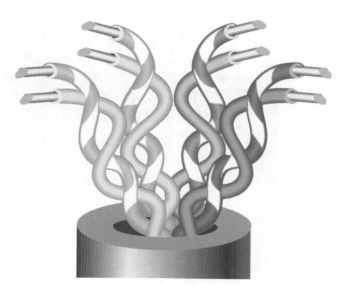

Figure 2-4 Example of four-pair twisted pair cable

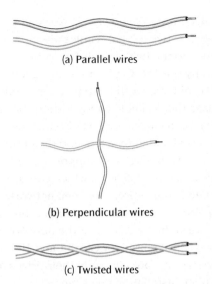

(a) Parallel wires

(b) Perpendicular wires

(c) Twisted wires

Figure 2-5 (a) Parallel wires—greater chance of crosstalk, (b) perpendicular wires—less chance of crosstalk, (c) twisted wires—crosstalk reduced because wires keep crossing each other at nearly perpendicular angles

crosstalk, in a second wire. If the two wires run parallel to each other, as shown in Figure 2-5 (a), the chance for crosstalk increases. If the two wires cross each other at perpendicular angles, as shown in Figure 2-5 (b), the chance for crosstalk decreases. Although not exactly producing perpendicular angles, the twisting of two wires around each other, as shown in Figure 2-5 (c), at least keeps the wires from running parallel and thus helps reduce crosstalk. More expensive twisted pair cables contain tighter twists for each pair, thereby reducing crosstalk further.

All Things Considered

Thought Experiment

List three different examples of crosstalk that do not involve wires and electric signals. (*Hint:* Look around you.)

Types of Twisted Pair Cable

As simple as twisted pair cable appears to be, it comes in many forms and varieties to support a wide range of applications. The following list provides a little more

detail about each category of twisted pair cables commonly found on networks today:

> **Cat 5 (Category 5)** twisted pair was designed to transmit data at 100 Mbps (called Fast Ethernet) for distances up to 100 meters (328 feet). Although the signal does not magically stop at 100 meters, it does weaken (attenuate), and the level of noise continues to grow such that the likelihood of the wire transmitting errors after 100 meters increases to an unacceptable level. The constraint of no more than 100 meters applies to the distance between the device that generates the signal (the source) and the device that accepts the signal (the destination). This accepting device can be either the final destination or a repeater. A **repeater** is a device that generates a new signal by creating an exact replica of the original signal. Thus, Cat 5 twisted pair and higher categories can run farther than 100 meters from its source to its destination as long as the signal is regenerated at least every 100 meters. Cat 5 twisted pair has a higher number of twists per inch than older categories of cables and, thus, introduces less noise. While Cat 5 is rarely used today, it's helpful to understand later standards by how they improved upon this one.

> Approved at the end of 1999, the specification for **Cat 5e (Enhanced Category 5)** twisted pair offers improved data rates for transmissions up to 1000 Mbps (1 Gbps, commonly called Gigabit Ethernet) for 100 meters. Many companies are producing Cat 5e cable at 125 MHz for 100 meters. Although the specifications for the earlier categories of cables described only the individual wires, the Cat 5e specification indicates exactly four pairs of wires (see Figure 2-6) and provides designations for the connectors on the ends of the wires, patch cords, and other possible components that connect directly with a cable. (You'll learn more about connector standards later in this section.) Thus, as a more detailed specification than Cat 5, Cat 5e can better support the higher speeds above 100 Mbps. (See the Details section "Gigabit Ethernet on Local Area Networks" to learn how Cat 5e can support 1000-Mbps LANs.) Cat 5e is commonly found on networks today, especially smaller networks, short connections within a network to a single workstation, or older networks where the cabling has not yet been upgraded.

Jill West

Figure 2-6   Four twisted pairs in Cat 5e cable

> Cat 6 (Category 6) twisted pair is designed to support data transmission with signals at or above 250 MHz for 100 meters. It has a plastic spacer running down the middle of the cable that separates the twisted pairs and further reduces electromagnetic noise. This makes Cat 6 cable a good choice for 100–meter runs in LANs with transmission speeds reaching 1000 Mbps. At shorter distances (37–55 meters, depending on crosstalk), Cat 6 can even support 10 Gbps data transmission rates. Also, Cat 6 twisted pair costs only pennies per foot more than Cat 5e twisted pair cables. Given a choice of Cat 5e or Cat 6 cables, you probably should install Cat 6, regardless of whether you will be taking immediate advantage of the higher transmission speeds.

> Cat 6a (Augmented Category 6) twisted pair cable offers some improvements over Cat 6 with a higher bandwidth of 500 MHz and reliably supports 10-Gbps speeds up to 100 meters. Cat 6a cable incorporates increased shielding to reduce crosstalk and support the higher data rates at greater distances.

> Cat 7 (Category 7) and Cat 7a (Augmented Category 7) twisted pair cables are more recent additions to the twisted pair family but were never ratified by the TIA. Cat 7 wire is designed to support 600 MHz of bandwidth for 100 meters while Cat 7a increases the available bandwidth to 1000 MHz (1 GHz). Both cables are heavily shielded—each pair of wires is shielded by a foil, and the entire cable has a shield as well. They can support up to 100 Gbps at a short 15 meters (49 feet), which can be useful for high-speed connections between networking devices sitting close to each other in a data center that interlace to form the backbone of the network. Cat 7 and Cat 7a are best suited for Gigabit and 10-Gigabit Ethernet networks, but currently their prices are relatively high, installation takes more space, and testing is trickier. Thus, using Cat 7 or Cat 7a wire may not provide the most cost-effective solution for many common Ethernet connections. Cat 7 and Cat 7a cables also require a special connector to reach their fullest potential speeds, which significantly increases the cost and complexity of installation.

> The Cat 8 (Category 8) standard was published in 2016, and Cat 8 products are now widely available for purchase. Cat 8 cables double the Cat 7a bandwidth, supporting up to 2 GHz, and relies on further improved and extensive shielding as shown in Figure 2-7. Cat 8 cables, also optimized for short-distance backbone connections within the datacenter, support up to 40 Gbps over 30 meters (98 feet), rivaling fiber-optic cables at these distances. Cat 8 cables are increasingly used to connect 25 Gb and 40 Gb networking devices within a datacenter, such as switches, modems, and routers. Additionally, Cat 8

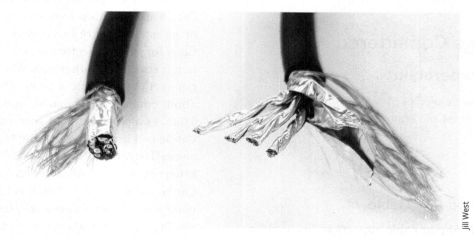

Jill West

Figure 2-7   Shielding around each twisted pair and additional shielding around all four pairs in a Cat 8 cable

Details | Gigabit Ethernet on LANs

If Cat 5e wire is designed to support 125-Mbps data transmission for 100 meters, how can it be used in 1000 Mbps (also known as Gigabit Ethernet) LANs? The first trick is to use all four twisted pairs for data transfer within the Cat 5e and later categories of cable for 1000-Mbps or faster LANs (as opposed to two pairs with 100-Mbps LANs). With four pairs, 250 Mbps is sent over each Cat 5e pair. Four pairs times 250 Mbps equals 1000 Mbps.

But that still does not answer how a pair of wires designed for 125-Mbps transmissions is able to send 250 Mbps. This answer involves a second trick:

Gigabit Ethernet networks use an encoding scheme called 4D-PAM5 (Pulse Amplitude Modulation). While the details of 4D-PAM5 are rather advanced and beyond the scope of this text, it can be simplified as a technique that employs four-dimensional (4D) data encoding coupled with a five-voltage level signal (PAM5). This combination enables Gigabit Ethernet to transmit 250 Mbps over each pair of wires in Cat 5e cables. With higher categories of cable that can transmit at increased bandwidths, data rates of 10 Gbps and better can be achieved over four twisted pairs.

Class I offers the advantage of using connectors that are backwards compatible with earlier standards (such as Cat 5e and Cat 6), which reduces the cost and complexity of installation. While more expensive than common Cat 6 cables, these Cat 8 Class 1 prices and installation needs are within reach for consumers who want to future-proof portions of their home networks. Cat 8 Class II cables, in the meantime, are backwards compatible with Cat 7 and Cat 7a specialty connectors.

Unshielded and Shielded Twisted Pair

Cat 5 through Cat 6a cables can be purchased as UTP (unshielded twisted pair) where none of the wires is wrapped with a metal foil or braid. In contrast, STP (shielded twisted pair), available in Cat 5 and up, is a form in which a shield is wrapped around each wire individually, around all the wires together, or both. This shielding provides an extra layer of isolation from unwanted electromagnetic interference (EMI), which

is a type of interference that can be caused by motors, power lines, televisions, copiers, fluorescent lights, or other sources of electrical activity. The shielding also makes it more difficult to detect the EMI generated along the cable itself, thereby reducing the chance the signal could be intercepted. Figure 2-8 shows an example of shielded twisted pair cable.

If a twisted pair cable needs to go through walls, rooms, metal conduits, or buildings where there is sufficient EMI to cause substantial noise problems, using shielded twisted pair can provide a higher level of isolation from that interference than unshielded twisted pair cable and, thus, a lower level of errors. EMI is often generated by large motors, such as those found in heating and cooling equipment or manufacturing equipment. Large sources of power can generate damaging amounts of EMI. Even fluorescent light fixtures generate a noticeable amount of EMI so it is best to avoid strapping twisted pair wiring to a power line that runs through a room or walls. Furthermore, even

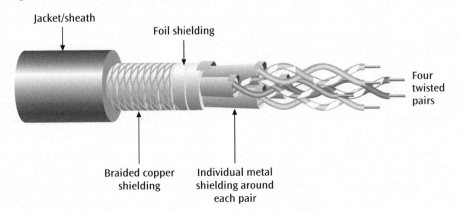

Figure 2-8   An example of shielded twisted pair cable

though shielded twisted pair cables have improved noise isolation, you cannot expect to push them past the 100-meter limit. Also, be prepared to pay a premium for shielded twisted pair. It is not uncommon to spend an additional $.50 or more per foot for high-quality shielded twisted pair. In contrast, Cat 5e, 6, and 6a unshielded twisted pair cables often cost between $.05 and $.20 per foot.

Table 2-1 summarizes the basic characteristics of UTP cables. Keep in mind that STP cables have basically the same data transfer rates and transmission ranges as UTP cables but perform better in noisy environments. Note also that the transmission distances and transfer rates appearing in Table 2-1 are not completely predictable. Noisy environments tend to shorten transmission distances and transfer rates.

Table 2-1 Characteristics of twisted pair cables

UTP Category	Typical Use	Maximum Data	Maximum Transmission Range	Advantages	Disadvantages
Cat 5	LANs	100 Mbps (100 MHz)	100 m (328 ft)	Inexpensive, easy to install and interface	Security, noise, obsolete
Cat 5e	LANs	250 Mbps per pair (125 MHz)	100 m (328 ft)	Inexpensive, easy to install and interface, supports Gigabit Ethernet	Security, noise
Cat 6	LANs	250 Mbps per pair (250 MHz)	100 m (328 ft)	Higher data rates than Cat 5e, less noise	Security, noise
Cat 6a	LANs	500 MHz	100 m (328 ft)	Support for 10 Gig Ethernet, increased shielding	Security, noise
Cat 7	Backbone connections	600 MHz	100 m (328 ft)	100 Gig Ethernet at very short distances (15 m)	Security, cost, requires special connectors
Cat 7a	Backbone connections	1000 MHz	100 m (328 ft)	Same as Cat 7, plus additional shielding	Security, cost, requires special connectors, thicker and more difficult to install
Cat 8 Class I and Class II	Backbone connections	2000 MHz	30 m (98 ft)	25 Gig and 40 Gig support at longer distances than Cat 7; Cat 8 Class I uses standard connectors	Security, cost

Details | More Characteristics of Twisted Pair Cable

When you are selecting a cable for a new network, you can choose from Cat 5e through Cat 8 and shielding options to make several distinctions between different types of twisted pair cable. In addition to knowing these distinctions, you need to consider where your cable will be placed and what kind of space the cable will run through. For example, when run between the rooms within a building, will the cable travel within a plenum or through a riser? A **plenum** is the space within a building's structure designed for the movement of breathable air—for example, the space above a suspended ceiling. A plenum can also be a hidden walkway between rooms that houses heating and cooling vents, telephone lines, and other cable services. Plenum cable is designed so that, in the event of a fire, it does not spread flame and

noxious fumes. To meet these standards, the cable's jacket is made of special materials; and this, of course, significantly increases the cable's cost. In fact, plenum cable can sometimes cost twice as much as standard twisted pair cable.

If, on the other hand, your cable is going to run through a riser—a hollow metal tube such as conduit that runs between walls, floors, and ceilings and encloses the individual cable—then flames and noxious fumes are not as serious of an issue. In this case, standard plastic jacketing can be used. This type of twisted pair cable is typically the cable advertised and discussed regarding new cable installations because a majority of these installations involve running cables through risers.

Coaxial Cable

Coaxial cable, in its simplest form, is a single wire, usually copper, wrapped in a foam insulation, surrounded by a braided metal shield or foil shielding, and then covered in a plastic jacket. The shielding is very good at blocking electromagnetic signals from entering the cable and producing noise. Some types of coaxial cable use multiple layers of shielding for increased resistance to EMI in noisy environments, such as a manufacturing floor or a conference center with busy wireless networks. Figure 2-9 shows a coaxial cable and its braided metal shield. Because of its shielding properties, coaxial cable is good at carrying analog signals with a wide range of frequencies. Thus, coaxial cable can transmit large numbers of video channels, such as those found on the cable television services that are delivered into homes and businesses. Coaxial cable has also been used for long-distance telephone transmission, under rare circumstances as the cabling within a LAN, and as a connector between a computer terminal and a mainframe computer.

Modern coaxial technology can typically support data transfer speeds up to 1 Gbps, although Internet providers are experimenting with more efficient encoding techniques to support even higher speeds. Compared to the data capacity of older twisted pair cable standards, coaxial cable is fairly robust. However, this bandwidth is no longer sufficient for long-distance transmission needs, which is better suited to fiber-optic cable. Cable companies now use coaxial cable mostly for cabling between multimedia devices within a customer's network, entry into a customer's location or, when needed, for last-mile connections.

Coaxial cable is available in a variety of thicknesses, rigidity, outer coating material, amount of shielding, and lengths of segments with various connectors on each end, depending on the purpose of the cable and the devices it will connect to, as shown in Figure 2-10. Some coaxial cable is jokingly referred to as frozen garden hose due to its thickness and rigidity. Coaxial cable prices vary depending on the quality and construction of the cable, but terminated cable lengths typically run $1.00 per foot or higher.

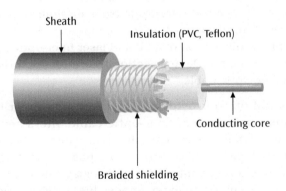

Figure 2-9 Example of coaxial cable showing braided shielding

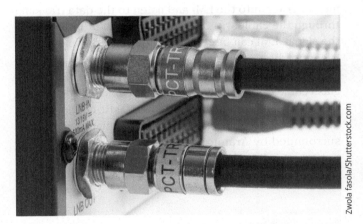

Figure 2-10 Coaxial cables connected to a satellite receiver

Zwola fasola/Shutterstock.com

Details | More Characteristics of Coaxial Cable

An important characteristic of coaxial cable is its ohm rating. Ohm is the measure of resistance within a medium. The higher the ohm rating, the more resistance in the cable. Although resistance is not a primary concern when choosing a particular cable, the ohm value is indirectly important because coaxial cables with certain ohm ratings work better with certain types of signals, and thus with certain kinds of applications. A coaxial cable's type is designated by RG (radio guide), a composite rating that accounts for many characteristics, including wire thickness, insulation thickness, and electrical properties. Table 2-2 summarizes three common types of coaxial cable, their ohm values, and applications.

Table 2-2 Common coaxial cables, ohm values, and applications

Type of Cable	Ohm Rating	Application
RG-6	75 Ohm	Cable television, satellite television, and cable modems
RG-59	75 Ohm	CCTV (closed-circuit TV); cable television (but RG-6 is better here) Note: You can also get "Siamese coaxial cable," which has a power cable bonded with the RG-59 or RG-6 cable to make CCTV installation faster.
RG-11	75 Ohm	Very thick cable built for long runs or where the cable must be buried

Fiber-Optic Cable

All the conducted media discussed so far have one great weakness: electromagnetic interference. As you've already learned, EMI is the electronic distortion that a signal passing through a metal wire experiences when a stray magnetic field passes over it. A related problem is that a signal passing through a metal wire also generates a magnetic field and thus itself produces EMI, which can interfere with nearby signals. Yet another related problem, and weakness of twisted pair cable and coaxial cable, is the possibility for someone to wiretap these media, or tap into the EMI and listen to the data traveling through the cable without being detected or interrupting the signal. EMI can be reduced with proper shielding, but it cannot be completely avoided unless you use fiber-optic cable. Fiber-optic cable (or optical fiber) is a thin glass cable or occasionally a plastic cable, a little thicker than a human hair, surrounded by a plastic coating. When fiber-optic cable is packaged into an insulated cable, it is surrounded by Aramid yarn and a strong plastic jacket to protect it from bending, heat, and stress. You can see some examples of fiber-optic cables in Figure 2-11.

Figure 2-11 Fiber-optic cables where each cable has a pair of connectors on each end

iStock.com/no_limit_pictures

How does a thin glass cable transmit data? A light source, such as a photo diode, is placed at the transmitting end and quickly switched on and off to produce light pulses. These light pulses travel down the glass cable at the speed of light and are detected by an optic sensor called a photo receptor on the receiving end. The light source can be either a simple and inexpensive LED (light-emitting diode) or a more complex and more powerful laser. The laser is much more expensive than the LED, and it can produce much higher data transmission rates. Fiber-optic cable is capable of transmitting data at more than 100 Gbps (i.e., 100 billion bits per second) over several kilometers. However, because many common LAN installations use an LED source, real-world fiber-optic transmissions are effectively limited to 10 Gbps for 300 meters. For a more technical discussion on LED and laser fiber-optic applications, see the Details section "More Characteristics of Fiber-Optic Cable."

In addition to providing high-speed, low-error data transmission rates, fiber-optic cable offers several other advantages over twisted pair cable and coaxial cable. Because fiber-optic cable passes electrically nonconducting photons through a glass medium, it is more difficult (though not impossible) to wiretap without interrupting the signal. While a skilled technician could redirect a small amount of light in the cable to a parallel fiber leading to a wiretapping detector, it's a delicate process that is often noticeable by the drop in the received signal's power levels. Also, because fiber-optic cable cannot generate nor be disrupted by EMI, no noise is generated from extraneous electromagnetic signals. Although fiber-optic cable still experiences noise as the light pulses bounce around inside the glass cable, this noise is significantly less than the noise generated in the metallic wire of twisted pair cables or coaxial cables. This lack of significant noise is one of the main reasons fiber-optic cable can transmit data for such long distances.

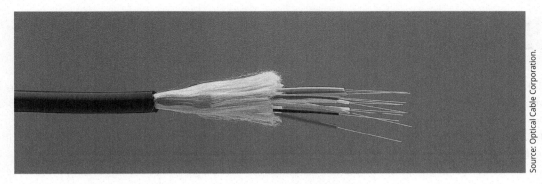

Source: Optical Cable Corporation.

Figure 2-12   A fiber-optic cable with multiple strands of fiber

Despite these overwhelming advantages, fiber-optic cable has two small but significant disadvantages:

> Due to the way the light source and photo receptor arrangement works, light pulses typically travel in one direction only. Thus, to support a two-way transmission of data, two fiber-optic cables are usually necessary. For this reason, most fiber-optic cable is sold with two cables melded together, as you might have noticed earlier in Figure 2-11, or with at least two (if not more) individual strands of fiber bundled into a single package, as shown in Figure 2-12. While bidirectional transmission is possible using different light wavelengths, it requires special equipment that offsets some of the cost savings.

> Fiber-optic cable costs more than twisted pair cable, but this disadvantage is slowly disappearing as materials become more affordable and widely available. For example, it is now possible to purchase bulk, general-purpose duplex (two-strand)

fiber-optic cable for $.10 to $.20 per foot (as opposed to paying a few dollars per foot many years ago), which is not much higher than the price of many types of twisted pair cable. When you consider its lower error rates and higher data transmission rates, fiber-optic cable is indeed a bargain. Interestingly, it is not so much the fiber-optic cable itself that is expensive. The technology's higher cost is due to the hardware that transmits and receives the light pulses at the ends of the fiber cable, however prices for transmitters and receivers continue to drop. It's common to use fiber-optic cable as the backbone of a network, and to use twisted pair cable from the backbone connection up to the workstation. An illustration of a fiber-optic backbone is shown in Figure 2-13. Today, fiber is increasingly used to connect individual servers or workstations to the network and to connect individual homes to an Internet service provider's network.

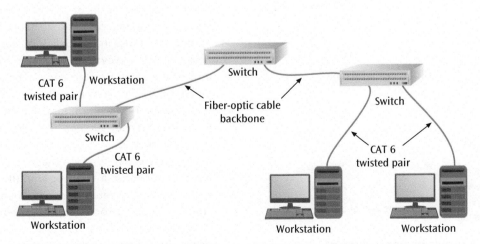

Figure 2-13   A fiber-optic backbone with CAT 6 twisted pair running to the workstations

Details | More Characteristics of Fiber-Optic Cable

When light from a source is sent through a fiber-optic cable, the light wave both bounces around inside the cable and passes through the cable to the outer protective jacket. When a light signal inside the cable bounces off the cable wall and back into the cable, this is called **reflection**. When a light signal passes from the core of the cable into the surrounding material, this is called **refraction**. Figure 2-14 demonstrates the difference between reflection and refraction.

Light can be transmitted through a fiber-optic cable using these two basic techniques:

> **Single-mode transmission** requires the use of a very thin fiber-optic core and a very focused light source, such as a laser. When a laser is fired down a narrow fiber, the light follows a tight beam so there is less tendency for the light wave to reflect or refract. This technique allows for a very fast signal with little signal degradation, and thus less noise, over long distances. Because lasers are used as the light source, single-mode transmission is a more expensive technique than the second fiber-optic cable signaling technique. Any application that involves a large amount of data transmitted at high speeds is a candidate for single-mode transmission.

> **Multimode transmission** uses a slightly thicker fiber core and an unfocused light source, such

as an LED. Because the light source is unfocused, the light wave experiences more refraction and reflection, or noise, as it propagates through the wire. This noise results in signals that cannot travel as far or as fast as the signals generated with the single-mode technique. Correspondingly, multimode transmission is less expensive than single-mode transmission. LANs that employ fiber-optic cables often use multimode transmissions.

Other characteristics that can differentiate the quality of the signal transmitted over a fiber-optic cable include the following:

> **Insertion loss** is a measure of **attenuation**, which is the continuous loss of a signal's strength as it travels through a medium. Insertion loss, then, measures the loss of signal strength between two points before and after an inserted connector or other passive network component or feature. Insertion loss can also be caused by low-quality cable, splices to join cable segments, and tight bends or coils in the cable. Insertion loss is measured by comparing input power to output power and is identified in decibels (dB), such as 0.3 dB or 0.5 dB. The lower this number, the better.

> When the signal reaches the other end of the fiber-optic cable, some of the light is reflected back into the cable to its source. This effect is called back reflection or **reflectance**, and it degrades the signal clarity. Reflectance identifies the amount of loss in decibels (dB), such as −55 dB or −14 dB; however, return loss is a measurement of the same performance benchmark but identifies the number as a positive, such as 55 dB return loss or 14 dB return loss. As you can see, higher reflectance, such as −14 dB, and lower return loss, such as 14 dB, both indicate the same lower quality signal, despite these numbers' different locations on a number line. (It might be helpful to think of return loss as a measure of a cable's resistance to reflectance; thus, higher return loss is good just as lower reflectance is good.) High reflectance (low return loss) could be caused by a dirty or poorly jointed connector or a

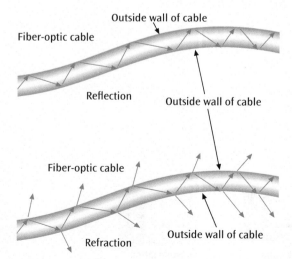

Figure 2-14 A simple demonstration of reflection and refraction in a fiber-optic cable

broken fiber. Reflectance is also a natural outcome of the tips of traditional UPC (Ultra Polished Contact) connectors and can be reduced by using an APC (Angled

Physical Contact) connector instead. APCs incorporate a slight angle at the tip of the fiber core to reduce light reflection at the joint (see Figure 2-15).

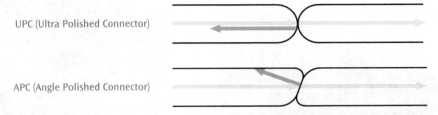

UPC (Ultra Polished Connector)

APC (Angle Polished Connector)

Figure 2-15 An APC connector uses a small angle to redirect and reduce back reflection

Cable Connectors

You've already learned about common connectors used to connect peripheral devices or charge computers, tablets, smartphones, and similar devices, such as USB and Thunderbolt. Network cables also require standardized connectors with a specific number and location of pins as well as different sizes and orientations. Let's explore the most common connectors used for each of the conducted media types you studied in this section.

Twisted Pair Cable Connectors

Most twisted pair cables use **RJ45 connectors** while a few twisted pair standards require a special connector. There's a bit more nuance to this statement that would be useful to dissect. The older standards, such as Cat 5e, can use an inexpensive, usually plastic or lightly shielded RJ45 connector, as shown on the left side of Figure 2-16. Technically, these are 8P8C (8 pins 8 conductors) connectors and are incorrectly but almost unanimously referred to as RJ45 throughout the industry. The additional cable shielding on later categories requires a thicker, more heavily shielded connector like the one shown on the right side of Figure 2-16. Or they might use a specialty connector that is better designed to maximize the cable's potential performance. These can be retrofitted to older equipment using specialty patch cables. Cat 8 Class 1 cables use shielded RJ45 connectors that can work with older devices, while Cat 8 Class 2 cables require a specialty connector that is compatible with Cat 7 connections. Although there is some flexibility for using connectors rated for one category on a different category cable, you might experience

Jill West

Figure 2-16 Two common types of twisted pair connectors: an unshielded RJ45 on a Cat 5e cable (left) and a shielded RJ45 on a Cat 8 cable (right)

decreased performance or increased crosstalk if the connector is not properly rated for the cable's category.

Coaxial Connectors

Both common coaxial cable types RG-6 and RG-59 can terminate with the following connector types:

> F-connectors, as shown in Figure 2-17 (a), attach to coaxial cable so that the pin in the center of the connector is the conducting core of the cable. Connectors are threaded and screwed together like a nut-and-bolt assembly. F-connectors are most often used with RG-6 cables.

Source: MCM Electronics, Inc.

Igor Smichkov/Shutterstock.com

Figure 2-17 Two types of coaxial cable connectors: (a) F-connector and (b) BNC connector

›A BNC connector, as shown in Figure 2-17 (b), is crimped, compressed, or twisted onto a coaxial cable. BNC stands for Bayonet Neill-Concelman, a term that refers to both an older style of connection and its two inventors. A BNC connector connects to another BNC connector via a turn-and-lock mechanism—this is the bayonet coupling referenced in its name. BNC connectors are used with RG-59 cables and, less commonly, with RG-6. Today, F-connectors are much more common.

Fiber Connectors

You read earlier about the UPC and APC options for fiber connectors that alter the type and amount of back reflection. Fiber cables can also be classified according to the type of cable they're used on (single mode vs. multimode) and according to the size of the ferrule. The ferrule is the extended tip of a connector that makes contact with the receptacle in the other connector, as shown in Figure 2-18.

Table 2-3 summarizes the most used fiber connectors.

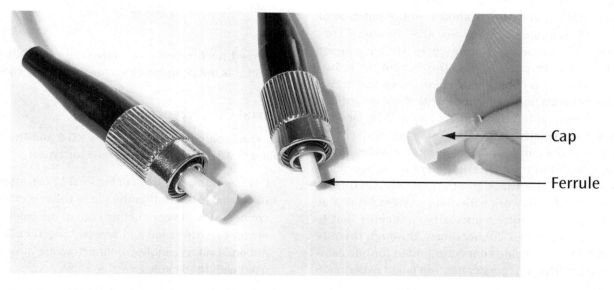

Cap

Ferrule

Figure 2-18 A cap protects the ferrule when the connector is not in use

Table 2-3 Common fiber connectors

Photo	Connector	Polish	Ferrule Size	Full-Duplex?
Source: Senko Advanced Components, Inc.	LC	UPC, APC	1.25 mm	Yes
Source: Senko Advanced Components, Inc.	ST	UPC	2.5 mm	No
Source: Senko Advanced Components, Inc.	SC	UPC, APC	2.5 mm	Can be
Source: Senko Advanced Components, Inc.	MTRJ	N/A	2 fibers	Yes

Summary of Wired LAN Technologies

Table 2-4 summarizes the conducted media discussed in this chapter. Category 5 through 8 wires have been grouped together because they are typically used for local area and data networks. In almost all cases, maximum data rate and maximum transmission range are typical values and can be less or more, depending on environmental factors.

Before leaving the topic of conducted media, there's one last important issue to address: the issue of right-of-way.

Table 2-4 A summary of the characteristics of conducted media

Type of Conducted Medium	Typical Use	Maximum Data Rate	Maximum Transmission Range	Advantages	Disadvantages
Twisted pair Cat 5, 5e, 6, 6a, 7, 7a, 8	LANs	100 Mbps–100 Gbps	100 m (328 feet)	Inexpensive, versatile	Noise, security
Coaxial cable	Cable TV, long-distance telephone, short-run computer system links	1 Gbps	5–6 kilometers (3–4 miles) (at lower data rates)	Low noise, multiple channels	Security
LED fiber optic	Data, video, audio, LANs	10 Gbps	300 meters (approx. 1000 feet)	Secure, high capacity, low noise	Expensive interface but decreasing in cost
Laser fiber optic	Data, video, audio, LANs, WANs, MANs	100s Gbps	100 kilometers (approx. 60 miles)	Secure, high capacity, very low noise	Expensive interface

Right-of-way is the legal capability of a business or a person to install a wire or cable across someone else's property. If a business wants to install a cable between two buildings, and the business does not own the property in between the buildings, the business must receive the right-of-way from the owner of the in-between property. This right might be a simple permission, but it might also involve payment. As you will see in the following sections, wireless transmissions generally do not have to deal with right-of-way issues. This often provides a strong advantage for wireless media over conducted media.

Remember this...

> Twisted pair cable in today's networks contains four twisted pairs, or eight wires total. Slower networks require only two pairs while faster networks use all four pairs.

> More twists in each twisted pair reduces crosstalk. Increasing categories of twisted pair cables use tighter twists, increased shielding, and other characteristics to offer increased data rates over 100-m segments.

> Cat 7 and Cat 7a cables must use specialty connectors to reach their maximum performance benchmarks. In contrast, Cat 8 cables can provide data rates rivaling fiber-optic cables at short distances (less than 30 m) and can use standard RJ45 connector types.

> Because of its good shielding properties, coaxial cable is good at carrying analog signals with a wide range of frequencies. Thus, coaxial cable can transmit large numbers of video channels, such as those found on the cable television services that are delivered into homes and businesses.

> The light source for a fiber-optic cable can be either a simple and inexpensive light-emitting diode (LED) or a more complex laser. The laser is much more expensive than the LED, and it can produce much higher data transmission rates, even exceeding 100 Gbps (i.e., 100 billion bits per second) over several kilometers.

> Although fiber-optic cable still experiences noise as the light pulses bounce around inside the glass cable, this noise is significantly less than the noise generated in the metallic wire of twisted pair cables or coaxial cables. This lack of significant noise is one of the main reasons fiber-optic cable can transmit data for such long distances.

> Single-mode transmission requires the use of a very thin fiber-optic cable and a very focused light source, such as a laser. Multimode transmission uses a slightly thicker fiber cable and an unfocused light source, such as an LED. Correspondingly, multimode transmission is less expensive than single-mode transmission. LANs that employ fiber-optic cables often use multimode transmissions.

Self-check

4. What is the lowest category of twisted pair cable that can support Gigabit Ethernet?
   a. Cat 5
   b. Cat 5e
   c. Cat 6
   d. Cat 6a

5. What is a primary weakness of all types of twisted pair cable?
   a. Cost
   b. Difficult to install
   c. Requires special connectors
   d. Security

6. How fast can signals travel along a fiber-optic cable?
   a. At the speed of sound
   b. At or near 100 Gbps
   c. At the speed of light
   d. At or near 10 Gbps

Check your answers at the end of this chapter.

Section 2-3: Radiated Media on LANs

The introduction of this chapter lists a few types of wireless media used on LANs. Even though each of these types might be used by a different application, and different sets of frequencies are often assigned to each, all wireless media share the same basic technology: the transmission of data using electromagnetic waves. Strictly speaking, in all these types of wireless technology, the actual *medium* through which the electromagnetic waves must travel is air or space. For the purposes of this discussion, however, the term "medium" includes the technology transmitting the signal.

This section will examine this growing technology and discuss each type of wireless media, along with their basic characteristics and application areas.

Wireless transmission became popular in the 1950s with AM radio, FM radio, and television. In 1962, transmissions were sent through the first orbiting satellite, Telstar. In the 70 or so years since wireless transmission emerged, this technology has spawned hundreds, if not thousands, of applications, some of which will be discussed in this chapter.

In wireless transmission, various types of electromagnetic waves are used to transmit signals. Radio transmissions, satellite transmissions, visible light, infrared light, X-rays, and gamma rays are all examples of electromagnetic waves or electromagnetic radiation. In general, electromagnetic radiation is energy propagated through space and, indirectly, through solid objects in the form of an advancing disturbance of electric and magnetic fields. In the case of, say, radio transmissions, this energy is emitted in the form of radio waves by the acceleration of free electrons, such as occurs when an electrical charge is passed through a radio antenna wire. The basic difference between various types of electromagnetic waves is their differing wavelengths, or frequencies, as shown in Figure 2-19.

Note that all types of transmission systems such as AM radio, FM radio, television, cell phones, terrestrial microwaves, and satellite systems are all confined to relatively narrow bands of frequencies. The FCC (Federal Communications Commission) keeps tight control over what frequencies are used by which application. The FCC will occasionally assign an unused range of frequencies to a new application. At other times, the FCC will auction off unused frequencies to the highest bidder. The winner of the auction is then allowed to use those frequencies for the introduction of a product or service. It is important to note, however, that only so many frequencies are available to be used for applications. Thus, it is crucial that each application use its assigned frequencies as well as possible. Wi-Fi, as you will see, provides a good example of how an application can use its assigned frequencies efficiently. Keep this conservative frequency allocation process in mind as you learn about six different areas of wireless communication systems, beginning with one of the most popular: Wi-Fi.

Wi-Fi

A LAN that is not based primarily on physical wiring, but instead uses wireless transmissions between workstations,

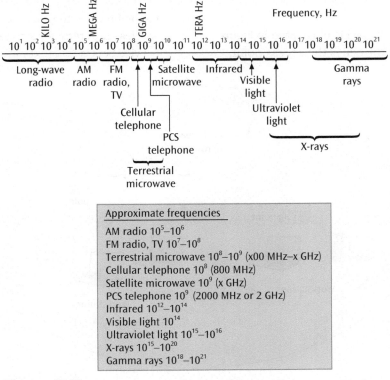

Figure 2-19 Electromagnetic wave frequencies

is a **wireless LAN**, often referred to by the trademarked term **Wi-Fi (wireless fidelity)**. By activating a transmitter/receiver on a computer or mobile device, and similar hardware on a device called an access point, it is possible to transmit data between a wireless client and network at speeds into the billions of bits per second. To create a wireless LAN, a few basic components are necessary:

> **Wireless clients (also called stations), such as a laptop, workstation, or smartphone**—A client has a special NIC that receives and transmits the wireless signals.

> **The wired LAN**—This is the conventional network component that supports standard workstations, servers, and medium access control protocols. A vast majority of wireless networks are connected to wired LANs.

> **The access point or a wireless router**—The **access point** is essentially the interface device between the wireless client and the wired LAN. The access point also acts as a switch/bridge and supports a medium access control protocol.

The workstation can be located anywhere within the acceptable transmission range. This acceptable range varies with the wireless technology used but typically falls somewhere between a few feet and several hundred feet. Wireless LANs are usually found in three basic configurations, as follows:

> The single-cell wireless LAN is illustrated in Figure 2-20. At the center of the cell is the access point,

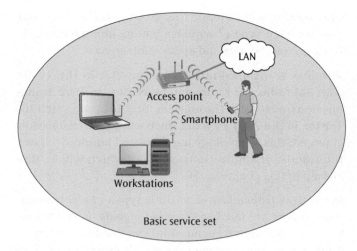

Figure 2-20 A single-cell wireless LAN configuration

which is connected to the wired LAN. All clients communicate with this one access point and compete for the same set of frequencies. Wireless LAN standards call this cell a **BSS (Basic Service Set)**.

> In the multiple-cell layout (see Figure 2-21), several cells are supported by multiple access points, as in a cellular telephone network. Clients communicate with the nearest access point and may move from one cell to another. Another way in which this configuration is like a mobile telephone cellular network is that each cell uses a different set of frequencies for communication between the client and the access point. The wireless LAN term for a collection of multiple Basic Service Sets is **ESS (Extended Service Set)**.

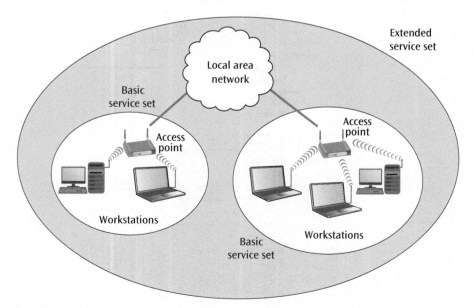

Figure 2-21 A multiple-cell wireless LAN configuration

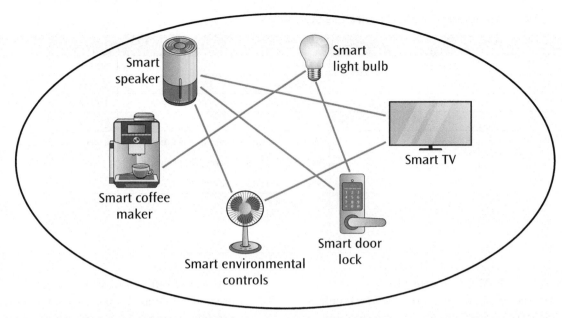

Figure 2-22 Many IoT devices can communicate with each other to expand their network coverage

❯ With the peer-to-peer, or ad hoc, layout (see Figure 2-22), there is no access point at the center of a cell. Each client communicates *directly* with the other clients. A configuration like this may be found in an IoT mesh network in which all clients are transmitting and sharing information directly with each other. Due to the intercommunications between all clients, ad hoc LANs work best with small numbers of devices.

Wireless LAN Standards

When wireless LANs first appeared, organizations were slow to accept them. The approval of the IEEE 802.11 wireless standard in June 1997 greatly helped with standardization of wireless networks and sped their growth and acceptance. The following list explores the progression of standards and 802.11 technology. Note that actual data transfer rates on wireless connections are roughly half or less of listed theoretical rates, due to noise interference. Consider the following standards:

❯ **802.11b**, which was ratified in 1999 and has been retroactively named Wi-Fi 1, can transmit data at a theoretical rate of 11 Mbps using 2.4-GHz signals. That same year, 1999, the Wi-Fi Alliance was formed to serve as a global non profit association of several companies with a common interest in the standardization of wireless LAN technologies.

❯ Also introduced in 1999, but not widely available commercially until a few years later, was **802.11a**, which is now called Wi-Fi 2. It supports a theoretical rate of 54-Mbps transmissions using the 5-GHz frequency range. This range is less crowded than the 2.4 GHz range and so results in less interference. However, signals at the 5-GHz frequency don't travel as far and so these networks require more access points.

Note

Why is 802.11a listed after 802.11b? While the 802.11a task group was launched first and named 802.11a, the 802.11b standard was completed first and was widely accepted in the market long before 802.11a devices became readily available.

❯ **802.11g**, introduced in 2002 and retroactively dubbed Wi-Fi 3, transmits data at a theoretical rate of 54 Mbps using the same 2.4-GHz frequencies used in 802.11b.

❯ The IEEE 802.11n standard in 2007 brought some new technologies to the wireless LAN market. Now called Wi-Fi 4, **802.11n** uses both the 2.4 GHz and 5 GHz frequency ranges and has a theoretical maximum data rate of 600 Mbps with actual data rates of

Table 2-5 Technical details for 802.11 wireless standards

Standard	Frequency Band	Maximum Theoretical Throughput	Geographic Range
802.11b (Wi-Fi 1)	2.4 GHz	11 Mbps	100 m
802.11a (Wi-Fi 2)	5 GHz	54 Mbps	50 m
802.11g (Wi-Fi 3)	2.4 GHz	54 Mbps	100 m
802.11n (Wi-Fi 4)	2.4 GHz or 5 GHz	600 Mbps	Indoor: 70 m Outdoor: 250 m
802.11ac (Wi-Fi 5)	5 GHz	Wave 1 (3 data streams): 1.3 Gbps Wave 2 (4 data streams): 3.47 Gbps Wave 3 (8 data streams): 6.93 Gbps	Indoor: 70 m Outdoor: 250 m
802.11ax (Wi-Fi 6 and Wi-Fi 6E)	2.4 GHz or 5 GHz or (Wi-Fi 6E only) 6 GHz	9.6 Gbps	Indoor: 70 m Outdoor: 250 m

roughly 100 to 145 Mbps. In order to support these higher speeds, this standard introduced a technology called MIMO. MIMO (multiple input multiple output) is a technique in which both the mobile device and the access point have multiple, smart antennae that help to reduce signal interference and reflections.

> Building on this success, 802.11ac (now called Wi-Fi 5) was published in December 2013 followed by an addendum for 802.11ac Wave 2 that was certified in 2016 and, later, an unofficial Wave 3 with additional improvements. This standard includes more advanced MIMO technology called MU-MIMO (multi-user MIMO), which supports MIMO transmissions to multiple wireless clients at one time. You'll learn more about how MIMO and MU-MIMO work in Chapter 9. Other 802.11ac advancements include wider channels in the 5-GHz bandwidth (but does not use the 2.4 GHz range) and more advanced modulation techniques. Data rates may reach the Gigabit threshold.

> The most current Wi-Fi standard with devices available on the market at the time of this writing is 802.11ax, commonly called Wi-Fi 6, which operates in both the 2.4 GHz and 5 GHz frequency ranges. Improvements include further development of modulation and MU-MIMO technologies to increase data speeds and transmission distances. A technique called BSS coloring also reduces interference from neighboring Wi-Fi networks. While theoretical maximum speeds for 802.11ax reach near 10 Gbps, actual speeds are expected to run about 30–60% faster than Wi-Fi 5. More significantly, however, Wi-Fi 6 can support higher speeds for more network

clients at the same time, which is particularly important for smart home environments with potentially dozens of IoT devices, or a stadium or conference center environment with hundreds or thousands of Wi-Fi clients.

> Building on the improvements of 802.11ax, Wi-Fi 6E will use the currently unlicensed 6 GHz frequency range. At a total of 1,200 MHz, this range is wider than either the 2.4 GHz (70 MHz wide) or 5 GHz (500 MHz wide) ranges, allowing for more available channels and much higher speed transmissions but at shorter distances.

Table 2-5 gives a brief summary of these Wi-Fi standards.

All Things Considered

Thought Experiment

Using a smartphone, install a free Wi-Fi detection app (such as Wifi Analyzer). Locate the wireless LANs on your campus or in your neighborhood, and then create a map of these networks.

Bluetooth

The Bluetooth protocol is named after the Viking crusader Harald Bluetooth, who unified several Danish tribes under a single government in the tenth century. Like its namesake, Bluetooth unites separate entities —such as mobile devices, computers, and accessories —under a single standard. It's a wireless technology that uses low-power, short-range radio frequencies to communicate between two or more devices, such as the Bluetooth speaker shown in Figure 2-23. More

Jill West

Figure 2-23 A Bluetooth speaker connected to a nearby smartphone

specifically, Bluetooth uses the 2.4-GHz ISM (Industrial, Scientific, and Medical) band.

The typical range for Bluetooth connections is determined by the class of the device, which is categorized according to the transmission power of the Bluetooth radio, as follows:

> Class 1 devices, such as laptops and desktops, boast a 100-mW (milliwatt) signal that can reach up to 100 meters (328 feet). However, at these longer distances, data throughput is greatly reduced.

> Class 2 devices, such as headsets and smartphones, are typically limited to distances of 10 meters (33 feet) with a 2.5-mW signal.

> Class 3 devices, such as a wireless keyboard, use a 1-mW signal and are intended to be used within a few meters of each other.

Bluetooth is not a line-of-sight technology and is capable of transmitting through nonmetallic objects such as walls. While a device that is transmitting Bluetooth signals can be carried in a pocket, bag, or briefcase and still maintain a connection, these obstacles will reduce the signal's range and throughput. The first Bluetooth standard was capable of data transfer rates up to roughly 700 Kbps. Later standards continued to increase

the data rates with the most recent version 5.2, released in early 2020, bursting to 2 Mbps at short distances. The available theoretical range of the latest Bluetooth long-range configuration also increased to 400 meters, which is a massive increase over Bluetooth 4.2's 100 meters. Other upgrades included in the latest versions reduce the power needed for IoT devices and add the capability of transmitting an audio signal to two headphones or two speakers at one time.

The most interesting aspect of Bluetooth is the list of applications that benefit from such a short-range transmission technology. Among many others, these applications include:

> Wireless transmission between a smartphone and earbuds

> Transmissions between a smartphone and computer

> Transmissions between peripheral devices (such as a keyboard and mouse) and a computer

> Wireless transmissions between a smartphone and an automobile, house, or workplace

To appreciate the potential power of Bluetooth technology, consider the following, more descriptive examples:

> You can automatically synchronize all email messages between your smartphone and your desktop/laptop computer.

> As you approach your car, your smartphone will tell the car to unlock its doors and change the radio to your favorite station.

> As you walk up to the front door of your house, your smartphone will instruct your house to unlock the front door, turn on the lights, and turn on an entertainment system.

> As you sit in a business meeting, your smartphone/laptop will wirelessly transmit your slide presentation to a projector and your notes to each participant's smartphone/laptop.

Zigbee

Zigbee is a relatively new wireless technology supported by the IEEE 802.15.4 standard. It's designed for data transmission between smaller, often embedded, devices that require low data transfer rates (20–250 Kbps) and corresponding low power consumption. While these speeds seem particularly low in comparison to Wi-Fi or wired connections, Zigbee works well for connections that communicate short signals to indicate status (such as a powered-on state), communicate a detected condition (such as water on the floor), or command a configuration change (such as unlocking a door). The Zigbee Alliance states that Zigbee is ideal for applications such as home and building automation (heating, cooling, security, lighting, and smoke and CO detectors), industrial control, automatic meter reading, and medical sensing and monitoring. It operates in the ISM radio band and requires very little software support and very little power. In fact, power consumption is so low that some suppliers claim their Zigbee-equipped devices will last multiple years on the original battery.

An interesting aspect of Zigbee is how devices are able to keep power consumption low. Zigbee employs two techniques in particular, as follows:

> Using mesh communications, not all the devices transmit directly to a single receiver. Instead, each device transmits its signal to the next closest Zigbee device, which in turn can pass this signal on to the next device. Each of these connections is called a hop, and each hop can typically jump 6–12 meters (20–40 feet) across potentially hundreds of hops. Eventually, the destination receiver will be reached, and an action will take place. Because transmission distances are typically shorter in a mesh configuration, less power is needed to transmit the signal. Interestingly, only devices plugged into a power source (not battery-powered) are used for repeating signals across the mesh network.

> Zigbee-enabled devices do not need to constantly communicate with other devices. When not transmitting a signal to a receiver, the device can put itself to sleep. When someone or something activates a device with Zigbee, the Zigbee circuit wakes up, transmits the signal, and then goes back to sleep.

Note

According to the Zigbee Alliance, the protocol's name comes from the zig zag dance bees use to communicate with each other on where to find food. The communication between devices that establishes and maintains the mesh network is based on this principle of intercommunication to establish relative distances and connections.

While many people confuse Zigbee with Bluetooth, it's interesting to notice that each technology targets a different application area: Bluetooth is best at replacing cables for short distances, while Zigbee is good at sending low-speed and low-power signals over short to medium distances.

Other Wireless Technologies in a LAN Environment

Three additional wireless technologies worth mentioning are infrared, ultra-wideband, and near-field communication transmissions. All three of these wireless technologies can be found in some smartphones for various purposes, and they also fill roles in other areas of a corporate, home, or personal network.

Infrared (IR)

IR (infrared) is a special form of radio transmission that uses a focused ray of light in the infrared frequency range (10^{12}–10^{14} MHz), which is just below the spectrum visible to the human eye. This focused ray of infrared information is sent from transmitter to receiver over a line-of-sight transmission. Usually these devices are no more than 10 meters (33 feet) apart, but infrared systems that can transmit up to 2–3 kilometers (1–2 miles) do exist.

IR is an old technology that has become new again. IR systems were often associated with media remote controls, laptop computers, handheld computers, peripheral devices such as printers and fax machines, digital cameras, and even children's handheld electronic games. Bluetooth has eclipsed IR in most of these use cases, although IR continues to play a key role in remote controls for multimedia devices. Just as IR was about to fade into history, modern networks gave new purpose to this technology in the context of IoT sensors. These IoT sensors can collect the following information:

> Presence or level of liquid, based on the quality of a reflection

> Variations in reflections from skin caused by variations in blood flow, which can be used to monitor heart rate

> Proximity to a device, which can trigger an action such as steering a vehicle away from an obstacle (see Figure 2-24)

> Commands from a control device, such as a game or TV remote control

In each of these examples, data is collected from the sensor but might be transmitted to a control device using

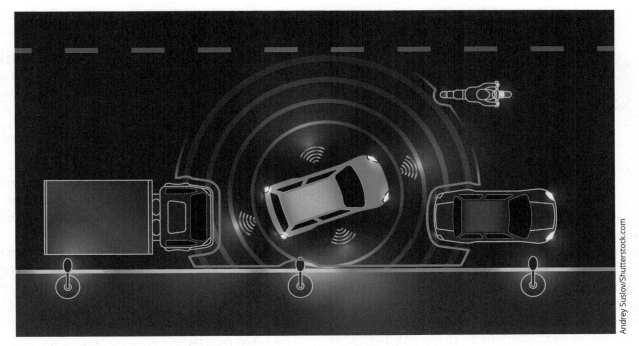

Andrey Suslov/Shutterstock.com

Figure 2-24 Designers of self-driving cars are experimenting with IR-based camera technologies to help the car detect objects and their movement even in low visibility conditions, such as fog or darkness, where regular cameras are insufficient

some other data transmission technology. When IR is used for data transmission, the transmitter and receiver are within the same room or a short distance apart, and there must be a line-of-sight connection between the two.

Ultra-Wideband (UWB)

Like IR, UWB (ultra-wideband) is an old technology finding new life in IoT, and like Zigbee, it's also based on the IEEE 802.15.4 standard. UWB transmits data over a wide range of frequencies rather than limiting transmissions to a narrow, fixed band of frequencies. The interesting aspect about transmitting over a wide range of frequencies is that some of those frequencies are used by other sources, such as cellular phone systems. So do UWB signals interfere with signals from these other sources? Proponents of UWB claim that, even though a wide range of frequencies is used, UWB transmits at power levels low enough that other sources should not be affected. Opponents of UWB argue that this is not correct—that UWB transmissions *do* affect other sources and, thus, should be carefully controlled. Despite this interference issue, UWB can support speeds up to 100 Mbps over local distances such as those found in wireless LANs.

So where are UWB signals used? You might find them in wireless systems that transfer data from a video camera to a computer or send pictures directly from a digital camera to a printer. Smartphone manufacturers, such as Apple, are beginning to add UWB to mobile devices for more precise location discovery. Perhaps one of the most interesting applications of UWB is systems that can see through walls. For example, these systems help firefighters detect humans within a burning building.

Near-Field Communication (NFC)

NFC (near-field communication) is a newcomer to the wireless market. It is used in very close proximity data transfers (usually less than 4 cm), often with the two devices touching each other. Rather than using radio transmission frequencies like Bluetooth, NFC uses magnetic induction as is commonly found with radio frequency ID (RFID) card readers, which are used in mass transit fare card systems. A common example of NFC is the transfer of data, such as photos or contact information, from one smartphone to another, or in contactless payment systems, such as Apple Pay and Google Pay digital wallets.

Passive NFC chips with no power source of their own can also be embedded in business cards, stickers, posters, or keychain tags (see Figure 2-25) to hold small amounts of information, such as a link to an app or a business's website. These tags can even be used to trigger tasks on your phone, such as disabling Wi-Fi when you get into your car

Figure 2-25 These programmable NFC tags have sticky backs for attaching to a flat surface like a wall, desk, or car dashboard

or muting the ringer when you walk through your front door. These passive tags collect power wirelessly from a nearby smartphone or other device by magnetic induction. When power is introduced to the NFC tag by the receiving device's proximity, the tag transmits its data, up to 32 KB depending on the tag's type.

Summary of Wireless LAN Technologies

Table 2-6 summarizes the wireless media discussed here, including the typical use, maximum data transfer rate, maximum transmission range, advantages, and disadvantages of each.

Now that you are familiar with the categories and types of wireless and conducted media available, you need to understand the criteria to consider when choosing media for a specific network application.

Remember this...

> Wireless media rely on various types of electromagnetic waves to transmit signals. In general, electromagnetic radiation is energy propagated through space and, indirectly, through solid objects in the form of an advancing disturbance of electric and magnetic fields. Electromagnetic waves can be identified by their wavelengths, or frequencies.

> A wireless LAN, often referred to by the trademarked term "Wi-Fi," consists of three primary components: wireless clients, a wired LAN, and an access point or wireless router.

> The most recent Wi-Fi standards offer several technologies to increase data throughput, such as MU-MIMO (MIMO transmissions for multiple wireless clients at one time), wider channels in the 5-GHz and 6-GHz bandwidths, more advanced modulation techniques, and BSS coloring to

Table 2-6 Summary of wireless media

Type of Wireless Medium	Typical Use	Maximum Data Transfer Rate	Typical transmission Range	Advantages	Disadvantages
Wi-Fi	Local area networks	10 Gbps	45–90 meters (150–300 feet)	Relative ease of use	Several standards
Bluetooth	Short-distance transfer	2 Mbps	A few feet to 100 meters (328 feet) depending on device class	Universal protocol	Limited distances
Zigbee	Short-to-medium distance, low-speed transfers	250 Kbps	Almost unlimited distance (mesh)	Low power	Low transfer speeds
IR	Short-distance data transfer	Varies by protocol used	10 meters (33 feet)	Fast, inexpensive, secure	Short distances, line of sight
UWB	Short-distance, high-speed transfers; location discovery	100 Mbps	100 meters (328 feet)	High speed, not restricted to fixed frequencies	May interfere with other sources
NFC	Very short distance data transfer	424 Kbps	About 4 cm	High-speed connections; allows for passive devices with no internal power supply	Very limited distance

reduce interference from neighboring Wi-Fi networks.

> Bluetooth uses the 2.4-GHz ISM (Industrial, Scientific, and Medical) band to reach ranges in three different device classes: Class 1 (up to 100 meters), Class 2 (up to 10 meters), and Class 3 (3–5 meters).

> Zigbee is designed for data transmission between smaller, often embedded, devices that require low data transfer rates (20–250 Kbps) and corresponding low power consumption.

> IR continues to be used in remote control devices and has found new life in IoT devices, which use IR (infrared) to collect data from sensors.

> Smartphone manufacturers, such as Apple, are beginning to add UWB (ultra-wideband) to mobile devices for more precise location discovery.

> NFC (near-field communication) is used in very close proximity data transfers (usually less than 4 cm), often with the two devices touching each other. Rather than using radio transmission frequencies like Bluetooth, NFC relies on magnetic induction.

Self-check

7. You're at school and trying to connect your smartphone to the school's wireless network, but your phone is not detecting a good signal. What device do you need to move closer to so you can get a stronger Wi-Fi signal?

    a. Access point

    b. Router

    c. Workstation

    d. Switch

8. Which of these 802.11 standards uses *only* the 5 GHz band?

    a. 802.11g

    b. 802.11n

    c. 802.11ac

    d. 802.11ax

9. Your new Bluetooth earbuds are listed as a Class 3 Bluetooth device. About how far away can you move from your smartphone sitting on your desk without losing a quality connection with your earbuds?

    a. 100 meters

    b. 30 meters

    c. 10 meters

    d. 3 meters

Check your answers at the end of this chapter.

Section 2-4: Media Selection Criteria

When designing or updating a computer network, selecting one type of medium over another is an important issue. Computer network projects have performed poorly and possibly even failed as a result of a poor decision about the appropriate type of medium. Furthermore, it is worth noting that the purchase price and installation costs for a particular medium are often the largest costs associated with computer networks. Once the time and money have been spent installing a particular medium, a business must use the chosen medium for a number of years to recover these initial costs. In short, the choice of medium should not be taken lightly. Assuming you have the option of choosing a medium, you should consider many media selection criteria before making that final decision. The principal factors you should consider in your decision include cost, speed, expandability and distance, environment, and security. The following discussion will consider these factors in relation to twisted pair cable, fiber-optic cable, Wi-Fi, and Bluetooth, which are the primary LAN media technologies.

Finally, keep in mind the issues of right-of-way and line-of-sight. Right-of-way involves the ability to place a physical cable over public property or someone else's private property. If you don't have the right-of-way, you cannot install any cabling. Line-of-sight deals with wireless signals. Some forms of wireless signals can only operate when the transmitter and receiver are within line-of-sight of each other.

Cost

Costs are associated with all types of media, and there are different types of costs. For example, purchasing twisted pair cable is generally less expensive than fiber-optic cable. To make a cost-effective selection decision, however, it is necessary to consider more than just the initial cost of the cable—you must also consider the cost of the supporting devices that originate and terminate the cables, the installation cost, and the price-to-performance ratio. For example, twisted pair cable is typically the least expensive medium to purchase. Each wire usually ends with a small modular jack that is mostly plastic and very inexpensive, costing only pennies each. Installation of twisted pair is typically straightforward, but it can still be costly depending upon the particular installation environment and who does the installation.

In comparison, fiber-optic cable, if purchased with two conductors and in bulk, is more expensive than twisted pair cable. The connectors that terminate fiber-optic cables are, as previously stated, more expensive than those of twisted pair. More importantly, if you need to connect a fiber-optic cable to a non-fiber-optic cable or device, the cost increase is even more dramatic because you must convert light pulses to electric signals and vice versa. Fiber-optic cable installation costs also tend to be higher than that of twisted pair cable. Consider, however, the price-to-performance ratio of fiber-optic cable compared to that of twisted pair cable. Although fiber is more expensive to purchase and install, it has the greatest transmission capabilities with the least amount of noise. Which is more important: saving money on the purchase of your cabling, or having cabling that is capable of very high transmission speeds?

In many cases, it is not possible to install your own cabling. For example, if you have two buildings that are separated by a public street, you might not have any way to connect a cable from one building to the other. Even if there were an overhead or underground passage through which a cable could be drawn, do you own the passage? In other words, you might not have the right-of-way to install the cables. If the passage is not yours, will the owner of the passage allow you to run cables through it? And if so, what will be the cost to you? If it is not possible or feasible to install your own cables, you might consider some form of wireless transmission. Or you might consider contacting a local telecommunications service provider (such as the local telephone company) to see what options are available (more on this in Chapter 10).

Each type of medium has the additional cost of maintenance. Will a certain type of wire last for x years when subjected to a particular environment? This is a difficult question to answer, but it should be asked of the company supplying the cable. Whereas it is easy to browse catalogs and learn the initial costs of a particular type of cable, it is more difficult to determine the maintenance costs two, five, or ten years down the road. Too often, overfocusing on initial cost inhibits decision makers from taking long-term maintenance cost into account and, therefore, considering better types of media.

Speed

To evaluate media properly, you need to consider expected speeds in the real world, not just theoretical maximums. Recall that data transmission speed is the number of bits per second that can be transmitted. The actual bits per second for a particular medium depends proportionally on the effective bandwidth of that medium, the distance the data must travel, and the environment through which the medium must pass (noise). If one of the requirements of the network you are designing is a minimally acceptable data transmission speed, then the medium you choose has to support that speed under realistic conditions.

This issue might sound trivial, but it is complicated by the difficulty of predicting network growth. Although a chosen medium might support a particular level of traffic at the moment, the medium might not be able to support a future addition of new users or new applications at the required speeds. Thus, careful planning for future growth is necessary for proper network support (you'll look at this issue in more detail in Chapter 11).

Expandability and Distance

Certain media lend themselves more easily to expansion. Twisted pair cable is easier to expand than fiber-optic cable. Fiber-optic connectors are elaborate, and joining two pieces of fiber-optic cable requires special training, practice, and the proper set of sophisticated tools.

Another expandability-related consideration is that most forms of twisted pair can operate for only 100 meters (328 feet) before the signal requires regeneration. Some forms of fiber-optic cable can extend for many miles before regeneration of the signal is necessary.

When considering expandability, do not forget the right-of-way issue. If you are trying to run a cable across land that does not belong to you, you must obtain permission from the landowner. Sometimes that permission might not be granted, and sometimes you might get the permission but have to pay a recurring fee to the landowner.

If you expect to create a system that might expand in the future, it is worthwhile to consider using a medium that can expand at a reasonable cost. Note, however, that the expansion of a system is, many times, determined more by the design of the system and the use of the supporting electronic equipment than by the selection of a type of medium.

Environment

Another factor that must be considered in the media selection process is the environment. Many types of environments are hazardous to certain media. Industrial environments with heavy machinery produce electromagnetic radiation that can interfere with improperly shielded cables. If your cabling might be traveling through an electromagnetically noisy environment, you should consider using shielded cable or fiber-optic cable.

Wireless transmission also can be disrupted by electromagnetic noise and interference from other transmissions. Wi-Fi standards must be selected carefully for their resistance to other signal types being used in the area as well as their ranges and the density of access points needed. Before selecting a medium, it is important to know the medium's intended environment and be aware of how this environment might influence or interfere with transmissions.

Security

If data must be secure during transmission, it is important that the medium not be easy to tap. Conducted media, even fiber-optic cable, can be wiretapped, meaning someone can "listen" to the signal traveling through the cable. Wireless communications also can be intercepted. Fortunately, there are means of improving the data security of both conducted and radiated media. Encryption and decryption software can be used with both types of media, making them virtually impervious to interception. Encryption techniques will be discussed in detail in Chapter 8.

This chapter surveyed common options for wired and wireless media on a LAN. As you read at the beginning of the chapter, WAN media will be covered later in Chapters 9 and 10. In the meantime, you're ready to learn the intricacies of how data is converted to signals and how signals are transmitted across these media. Chapter 3 will tackle these topics in detail.

Remember this...

> To make a cost-effective selection decision, it is necessary to consider more than just the initial cost of the cable—you must also consider the cost of the supporting devices that originate and terminate the cables, the installation cost, and the price-to-performance ratio.

> Data transmission speed is the number of bits per second that can be transmitted. The actual bits per second for a particular medium depends proportionally on the effective bandwidth of that medium, the distance the data must travel, and the environment through which the medium must pass (noise).

> An important expandability-related consideration is that most forms of twisted pair can operate for only 100 meters (328 feet) before the signal requires regeneration. Some forms of fiber-optic cable can extend for many miles before regeneration of the signal is necessary.

> If your cabling might be traveling through an electromagnetically noisy environment, you should consider using shielded cable or fiber-optic cable. Wi-Fi standards must also be selected carefully for their resistance to other signal types being used in the area as well as their ranges and the density of access points needed.

> If data must be secure during transmission, it is important that the medium not be easy to tap. Conducted media, even fiber-optic cable, can be wiretapped, and wireless communications also can be intercepted. Encryption and decryption software can be used with both types of media, making them virtually impervious to interception.

Self-check

1. Which of these network media is most resistant to EMI generated by a factory's manufacturing equipment?
   a. Bluetooth 5.2
   b. Cat 8 twisted pair cable
   c. 802.11 ax Wi-Fi
   d. Multimode fiber-optic cable

2. When installing a fiber-optic network, which factor will present the greatest concern relative to other media options?
   a. Security
   b. Cost
   c. Environment
   d. Speed

Check your answers at the end of this chapter.

Summary

Section 2-1: Cabling Standards

> All interface standards have two basic characteristics: They have been created and approved by an acceptable standards-making organization, and they can consist of one to four components, which include an electrical component, a mechanical component, a functional component, and a procedural component.

> USB is a relatively thin, space-saving cable to which devices can be added and removed while the computer and peripheral are active. It is hot pluggable, supports daisy-chaining, offers the ability to provide electrical power, and is a full-duplex connection.

> Thunderbolt uses the USB-C connector but provides a theoretical data rate of 40 Gbps. Lightning is an Apple-proprietary standard that is smaller than a USB-C connector and is also reversible.

Section 2-2: Conducted Media

> Twisted pair cable in today's networks contains four twisted pairs, or eight wires total. Slower networks require only two pairs while faster networks use all four pairs.

> More twists in each twisted pair reduces crosstalk. Increasing categories of twisted pair cables use tighter twists, increased shielding, and other characteristics to offer increased data rates over 100-m segments.

> Cat 7 and Cat 7a cables must use specialty connectors to reach their maximum performance benchmarks. In contrast, Cat 8 cables can provide data rates rivaling fiber-optic cables at short distances (less than 30 m) and can use standard RJ45 connector types.

> Because of its good shielding properties, coaxial cable is good at carrying analog signals with a wide range of frequencies. Thus, coaxial cable can transmit large numbers of video channels, such as those found on the cable television services that are delivered into homes and businesses.

> The light source for a fiber-optic cable can be either a simple and inexpensive light-emitting diode (LED)

or a more complex laser. The laser is much more expensive than the LED, and it can produce much higher data transmission rates, even exceeding 100 Gbps (i.e., 100 billion bits per second) over several kilometers.

> Although fiber-optic cable still experiences noise as the light pulses bounce around inside the glass cable, this noise is significantly less than the noise generated in the metallic wire of twisted pair cables or coaxial cables. This lack of significant noise is one of the main reasons fiber-optic cable can transmit data for such long distances.

> Single-mode transmission requires the use of a very thin fiber-optic cable and a very focused light source, such as a laser. Multimode transmission uses a slightly thicker fiber cable and an unfocused light source, such as an LED. Correspondingly, multimode transmission is less expensive than single-mode transmission. LANs that employ fiber-optic cables often use multimode transmissions.

Section 2-3: Radiated Media on LANs

> Wireless media rely on various types of electromagnetic waves to transmit signals. In general, electromagnetic radiation is energy propagated through space and, indirectly, through solid objects in the form of an advancing disturbance of electric and magnetic fields. Electromagnetic waves can be identified by their wavelengths, or frequencies.

> A wireless LAN, often referred to by the trademarked term "Wi-Fi," consists of three primary components:

wireless clients, a wired LAN, and an access point or wireless router.

> The most recent Wi-Fi standards offer several technologies to increase data throughput, such as MU-MIMO (MIMO transmissions for multiple wireless clients at one time), wider channels in the 5-GHz and 6-GHz bandwidths, more advanced modulation techniques, and BSS coloring to reduce interference from neighboring Wi-Fi networks.

> Bluetooth uses the 2.4-GHz ISM (Industrial, Scientific, and Medical) band to reach ranges in three different device classes: Class 1 (up to 100 meters), Class 2 (up to 10 meters), and Class 3 (3–5 meters).

> Zigbee is designed for data transmission between smaller, often embedded, devices that require low data transfer rates (20–250 Kbps) and corresponding low power consumption.

> IR continues to be used in remote control devices and has found new life in IoT devices, which use IR (infrared) to collect data from sensors.

> Smartphone manufacturers, such as Apple, are beginning to add UWB (ultra-wideband) to mobile devices for more precise location discovery.

> NFC (near-field communication) is used in very close proximity data transfers (usually less than 4 cm), often with the two devices touching each other. Rather than using radio transmission frequencies like Bluetooth, NFC uses magnetic induction.

Section 2-4: Media Selection Criteria

> To make a cost-effective selection decision, it is necessary to consider more than just the initial cost of the cable—you must also consider the cost of the supporting devices that originate and terminate the cables, the installation cost, and the price-to-performance ratio.

> Data transmission speed is the number of bits per second that can be transmitted. The actual bits per second for a particular medium depends proportionally on the effective bandwidth of that medium, the distance the data must travel, and the environment through which the medium must pass (noise).

> An important expandability-related consideration is that most forms of twisted pair can operate for only 100 meters (328 feet) before the signal requires regeneration. Some forms of fiber-optic cable can extend for many miles before regeneration of the signal is necessary.

> If your cabling might be traveling through an electromagnetically noisy environment, you should consider using shielded cable or fiber-optic cable. Wi-Fi standards must also be selected carefully for their resistance to other signal types being used in the area as well as their ranges and the density of access points needed.

> If data must be secure during transmission, it is important that the medium not be easy to tap. All conducted media, except fiber-optic cable, can be wiretapped easily, and wireless communications also can be intercepted. Encryption and decryption software can be used with both types of media, making them virtually impervious to interception.

 ## Key Terms

For definitions of key terms, see the Glossary near the end of the book.

802.11a	access point	Cat 5e (Enhanced Category 5)
802.11ac	attenuation	Cat 6 (Category 6)
802.11ax	backbone	Cat 6a (Augmented Category 6)
802.11b	Bluetooth	Cat 7 (Category 7)
802.11g	BSS (Basic Service Set)	Cat 7a (Augmented Category 7)
802.11n	Cat 5 (Category 5)	Cat 8 (Category 8)

coaxial cable	Lightning	RJ45 connector
crosstalk	mechanical component	single-mode transmission
daisy-chaining	MIMO (multiple input multiple output)	STP (shielded twisted pair)
de facto standard		throughput
electrical component	multimode transmission	Thunderbolt
EMI (electromagnetic interference)	MU-MIMO (multi-user MIMO)	twisted pair cable
ESS (Extended Service Set)	NFC (near-field communication)	USB (Universal Serial Bus)
fiber-optic cable	plenum	UTP (unshielded twisted pair)
full-duplex connection	procedural component	UWB (ultra-wideband)
functional component	proprietary	Wi-Fi (wireless fidelity)
half-duplex connection	reflectance	Wi-Fi 5
hot pluggable	reflection	Wi-Fi 6
insertion loss	refraction	Wi-Fi 6E
interfacing	repeater	wireless LAN
IR (infrared)	right-of-way	Zigbee

Review Questions

1. Just as you're about to connect your printer to your computer with a USB cable, your coworker walks in the room and says you must shut down your computer first. What USB feature is your coworker apparently not aware of?

   a. Daisy-chaining
   b. Hot pluggable
   c. Power delivery
   d. Full-duplex communication

2. What is one advantage USB-C offers over earlier standards?

   a. Reversible plug
   b. Power delivery
   c. Backwards compatibility
   d. Full-duplex connection

3. As you shop for a new Apple device, which of the following ports are you likely to find as options on most of these devices? **Choose two**.

   a. Lightning
   b. Coaxial
   c. MTRJ
   d. Thunderbolt

4. What characteristic of twisted pair cable reduces crosstalk within the cable?

   a. External shielding
   b. Connector type
   c. Distance limitations
   d. Twisted wires

5. Your small business has a network at each of two buildings that both use twisted pair cable. You've decided to connect these two networks, however, they're about 150 meters apart. How can you best get a stable signal between the two locations with at least Gigabit Ethernet speeds and without unnecessary expense?

   a. Upgrade all network cabling to Cat 8.
   b. Use coaxial cable for the link between networks.
   c. Use fiber-optic cable for the link between networks.
   d. Install a repeater between the two locations with Cat 5e cable.

6. Which category of twisted pair cable currently available for sale offers the fastest data

rates while using backwards compatible RJ45 connectors?

- **a.** Cat 6
- **b.** Cat 6a
- **c.** Cat 7a
- **d.** Cat 8

7. How many pairs of wires are required for Gigabit Ethernet?

- **a.** 1
- **b.** 2
- **c.** 4
- **d.** 8

8. As you're planning a cabling installation for a new office location, you notice the drop ceilings and realize this will help installation go faster than having to fish cable through the walls. What special cable rating must you be sure to budget for?

- **a.** Backbone
- **b.** EMI
- **c.** Gigabit Ethernet
- **d.** Plenum

9. What is the primary use for coaxial cable on today's networks?

- **a.** LAN networking
- **b.** Multimedia transmission
- **c.** WAN networking
- **d.** Digital data transmission

10. True or False: Transmissions on fiber-optic cable do not suffer from noise interference.

11. Which light source would provide the best performance for a fiber-optic connection?

- **a.** Infrared
- **b.** Laser
- **c.** LED
- **d.** Lightning

12. You just purchased a new home router. As you start setting it up, part of the setup requires you to assign a name to your 5-GHz wireless network. What wireless LAN characteristic does this name define?

- **a.** Frequency
- **b.** ESS
- **c.** Data rate
- **d.** BSS

13. Your company is setting up a Wi-Fi network for a school where multiple user devices need to be able to download files at the same time to reduce congestion. What is the minimum Wi-Fi standard that can accomplish this goal?

- **a.** 802.11n
- **b.** 802.11ac
- **c.** Wi-Fi 6
- **d.** Wi-Fi 6E

14. Which of the following is *not* a frequency range used by modern Wi-Fi?

- **a.** 1.2 GHz
- **b.** 2.4 GHz
- **c.** 5 GHz
- **d.** 6 GHz

15. Which of the following characteristics applies to NFC but *not* Bluetooth?

- **a.** Short-range transmission
- **b.** Low power demand
- **c.** Wireless power transfer
- **d.** Data transfer capability

16. Which wireless signal type would work best to control a garage door opener?

- **a.** IR
- **b.** Wi-Fi
- **c.** NFC
- **d.** Zigbee

17. Which of the following applications most likely uses infrared?

- **a.** Persistent connection between surround-sound speakers and controller hub
- **b.** Sending a print job from a smartphone to a nearby printer
- **c.** Auto-transmission of payment information at a self-checkout register
- **d.** Safety feature to stop an automatic garage door from closing

18. Which of the following transmission media offers the fastest potential data transfer rates?

- **a.** Bluetooth 5.2
- **b.** Wi-Fi 5
- **c.** Cat 5 cable
- **d.** USB 2.0

19. Which of the following transmission media provides the most security in transit?

- **a.** LED fiber optic
- **b.** Wi-Fi 6E
- **c.** Cat 8 cable
- **d.** USB 3.2

20. Which of the following wireless transmission media *cannot* transmit through solid objects?

- **a.** Zigbee
- **b.** Bluetooth
- **c.** IR
- **d.** UWB

Hands-On Project 2

Install and Use Cisco Packet Tracer

Estimated time: 1 hour

Resources:

> A computer and user account with application installation rights

> Internet access

> **Context:**

The Cisco Networking Academy website provides many useful tools for advancing your networking education. One of those tools is a network simulator called Packet Tracer. In this project, you download and install Packet Tracer and take a tour of the simulator interface. This version of Packet Tracer is free to the public, and your school does not have to be a member of Cisco's Networking Academy for you to download and use it.

In later projects, you'll return to Packet Tracer to build networks and even learn some basic Cisco IOS commands. Cisco IOS (Internetworking Operating Systems) is the operating system used on Cisco networking devices, such as routers and switches, with minor variations in the specific IOS for each different type of device. Many other manufacturers of networking devices use the same or similar commands, and those that use different commands typically use very similar functions, even if they call it something a little different.

To get the Packet Tracer download, you must first sign up for the free Introduction to Packet Tracer online course on the Cisco Networking Academy website. Complete the following steps to create your account:

1. Go to **netacad.com/courses/packet-tracer**. If the course is not listed on this page, do a search for *packet tracer site:netacad.com* and follow links to "Download Packet Tracer" or "Introduction to Packet Tracer" to find the current Packet Tracer introduction course. Enter your name, email, and text verification to enroll in the course.

2. Open the confirmation email and confirm your email address. Configure your account and save your account information in a safe place. You will need this information again.

3. Take the brief tour of the course.

Now you're ready to download and install Packet Tracer. If you need help with the download and installation process, use the Course Index to navigate to Page 1.1.2.1 for additional guidance. Complete the following steps:

4. Inside the course, under *Introductory Chapter*, click **Student Support and Resources**. Scroll down and click **Download and install the latest version of Packet Tracer**. Choose the correct version for your computer. After the download is complete, install Packet Tracer. When the installation is complete, run **Cisco Packet Tracer**. When Packet Tracer asks if you would like to run multi-user, click **No**.

5. When Packet Tracer opens, sign in with your Networking Academy account that you just created. If you see a Windows Security Alert, allow access through your firewall. Cisco Packet Tracer opens. The interface window is shown in Figure 2-26.

The Introduction to Packet Tracer course presents an excellent introduction to Packet Tracer and provides lab activities. Packet Tracer Activities are interactive labs in which you download a start file, make the changes instructed in the lab, and then grade the activity in Packet Tracer. Complete the following steps to access your course:

6. Return to your Introduction to Packet Tracer course. You've already downloaded Packet Tracer, so you can skip Chapter 1.

7. Complete Chapters 2, 3, and 4, including their videos and labs. (The later chapters provide excellent information on Packet Tracer but are not required for this project.) Answer the following questions along the way:

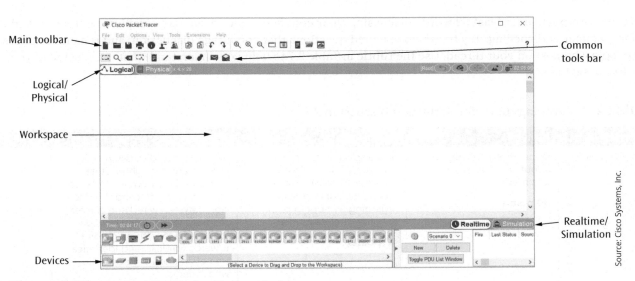

Figure 2-26   Explore the Packet Tracer window

a. What is the first step in deploying a Packet Tracer network?

b. When looking at a physical device's tabs in Packet Tracer, which tab is considered the learning tab?

c. What three questions can be answered using the Simulation Mode?

d. Which Packet Tracer feature do you think will be most helpful for you in learning how to manage a network? Why do you think this?

8. Back in your Packet Tracer window, deploy at least three physical devices into your workspace. You don't need to configure or connect them. **Take a screenshot** of your deployment; submit this visual with your answers to this project's questions.

9. When you're finished, you can close Packet Tracer. You do *not* need to save this network.

Reflection Discussion 2

Many factors must be considered when choosing a network medium: cost, speed, expandability and distance, environment, and security. Wireless media is increasingly evolving to offer sophisticated options that meet the demanding needs of businesses, while wired media, the traditional go-to technology, continues to decrease in cost. This progression offers many businesses the option to become an all-wireless workplace (AWW) for connections to workstations and other endpoints on the network, and even between many devices on the network backbone.

Consider the following questions:

> When choosing between wired and wireless media as the preferred standard for a network's endpoints, which factor do you believe is most relevant to making this decision?

> What improvements to wireless technology do you think will provide the "tipping point" so businesses start to think of wireless as the default solution?

> What is one characteristic of wired technology that you believe will ensure enterprise networks continue to use cables to endpoints to some degree?

Go to the discussion forum in your school's LMS (learning management system). Write a post of at least 100 words discussing your thoughts about wired and wireless media in the workplace. Then respond to two of your classmates' threads with posts of at least 50 words discussing their comments and ideas. Use complete sentences, and check your grammar and spelling. Try to ask open-ended questions that encourage discussion, and remember to respond to people who post on your thread. Use the rubric in Table 2-7 to help you understand what is expected of your work for this assignment.

Table 2-7 Grading rubric for Reflection Discussion 2

Task	Novice	Competent	Proficient	Earned
Initial post	Generalized statements about wired versus wireless media **30 points**	Some specific statements with supporting evidence about wired versus wireless media, including speculation regarding a "tipping point" towards wireless media **40 points**	Self-reflective discussion with specific and thoughtful statements and supporting evidence about factors affecting the decision between wired and wireless media, a well-formed opinion identifying the "tipping point" towards wireless, and identification of an enduring advantage of wired media **50 points**	
Initial post: Mechanics	• Length < 100 words • Several grammar and spelling errors **5 points**	• Length = 100 words • Occasional grammar and spelling errors **7 points**	• Length > 100 words • Appropriate grammar and spelling **10 points**	
Response 1	Brief response showing little engagement or critical thinking **5 points**	Detailed response with specific contributions to the discussion **10 points**	Thoughtful response with specific examples or details and open-ended questions that invite deeper discussion of the topic **15 points**	
Response 2	Brief response showing little engagement or critical thinking **5 points**	Detailed response with specific contributions to the discussion **10 points**	Thoughtful response with specific examples or details and open-ended questions that invite deeper discussion of the topic **15 points**	
Both responses: Mechanics	• Length < 50 words each • Several grammar and spelling errors **5 points**	• Length = 50 words each • Occasional grammar and spelling errors **7 points**	• Length > 50 words each • Appropriate grammar and spelling **10 points**	
			Total	

Solutions to Self-Check Questions

Section 2-1: Cabling Standards

1. In trying to identify an old cable, you check the connector on the end and count the number of pins. What component of the interface design are you using to help you identify this cable?

Answer: d. Mechanical

Explanation: The mechanical component determines the size and shape of the connection, the number of pins on the connector, and their arrangement.

2. Which of these wired PAN standards does *not* use the USB-C connector form factor?

Answer: b. Lightning

Explanation: Many USB specifications can use the USB-C connector, including USB 2.0 and USB 3.0. Thunderbolt also uses the USB-C connector but at a faster data rate. Lightning uses a proprietary connector that is smaller than a USB-C connector and is also reversible.

3. Which of these wired PAN standards provides the fastest data throughput?

Answer: c. Thunderbolt

Explanation: Thunderbolt uses the same USB-C connector as USB 2.0 and USB 3.0 but provides a theoretical data rate of 40 Gbps, which was twice the highest USB specification at the time of this writing in 2021.

Section 2-2: Conducted Media

4. What is the lowest category of twisted pair cable that can support Gigabit Ethernet?

Answer: b. Cat 5e

Explanation: The Cat 5e and higher specifications indicate exactly four pairs of wires with 250 Mbps sent over each pair. Four pairs times 250 Mbps equals 1000 Mbps.

5. What is a primary weakness of all types of twisted pair cable?

Answer: d. Security

Explanation: Splicing segments of twisted pair cable is a relatively simple process that can be performed by a malicious actor to tap into the network without easily being detected. Also, EMI generated along the cable can be intercepted, even when the cable is shielded.

6. How fast can signals travel along a fiber-optic cable?

Answer: c. At the speed of light

Explanation: Measurements such as 10 Gbps and 100 Gbps indicate the rate at which data can be communicated across a connection, which is affected by many factors other than the speed of the signal along the cable, such as back reflection, refraction, and insertion loss. The signal itself, however, travels at the speed of light.

Section 2-3: Radiated Media

7. You're at school and trying to connect your smartphone to the school's wireless network, but your phone is not detecting a good signal. What device do you need to move closer to so you can get a stronger Wi-Fi signal?

Answer: a. Access point

Explanation: The access point is the interface device between the wireless client and the wired LAN. While many products are advertised as wireless routers, the access point component of the wireless router is what connects to wireless clients.

8. Which of these 802.11 standards uses *only* the 5 GHz band?

Answer: c. 802.11ac

Explanation: 802.11ac includes wider channels in the 5-GHz bandwidth, but does not use the 2.4 GHz range.

9. Your new Bluetooth earbuds are listed as a Class 3 Bluetooth device. About how far away can you move from your smartphone sitting on your desk without losing a quality connection with your earbuds?

Answer: d. 3 meters

Explanation: Class 3 devices use a 1-mW signal and are intended to be used within a few meters of each other.

Section 2-4: Media Selection Criteria

10. Which of these network media is most resistant to EMI generated by a factory's manufacturing equipment?

Answer: d. Multimode fiber-optic cable

Explanation: Industrial environments with heavy machinery produce electromagnetic radiation that can interfere with improperly shielded cables. Wireless transmissions can be disrupted by electromagnetic noise. EMI can be reduced with proper shielding on copper cables, but it cannot be completely avoided unless you use fiber-optic cable.

11. When installing a fiber-optic network, which factor will present the greatest concern relative to other media options?

Answer: b. Cost

Explanation: Despite fiber-optic cable's many advantages, it's still more expensive than twisted pair cable, as are the various fiber-optic connectors and required converters. Fiber-optic cable installation costs also tend to be higher than that of twisted pair cable.

Chapter 3

Fundamentals of Data and Signals

Objectives

After reading this chapter, you should be able to:

- Evaluate the features of analog and digital data and signals

- Compare techniques for converting analog and digital data for transmission by analog and digital signals

- Compare character encoding schemes for storing and transmitting textual data as bits

Introduction

This chapter will deal primarily with two essential network elements that are difficult to physically see: data and signals. It is important to understand that the terms "data" and "signal" do not mean the same thing. For a computer network to transmit data across the cables and airwaves you learned about in Chapter 2, the data must first be converted into the appropriate signals. In all of this chapter's examples, data is converted to a signal by a computer or computer-related device, then transmitted over a communications medium to another computer or computer-related device, which converts the signal back into data. The originating device is the transmitter, and the destination device is the receiver.

A big question arises during the study of data and signals: Why should people interested in the business aspects of computer networks concern themselves with this level of detail? One answer to that question is that a firm understanding of the fundamentals of communication systems will provide a solid foundation for the further study of the more advanced topics of computer networks. Also, this chapter will introduce many terms that are used by network personnel. To be able to understand these professionals and to interact knowledgeably with them, you'll need to spend some time covering the basics of communication systems.

For example, imagine you are designing a new online inventory system and you want to allow various users within the company to access this system. The network technician tells you this cannot be done because downloading one inventory record in a reasonable amount of time (*X* seconds) will require a connection of at least *Y* billion bits per second—which is not possible, given the current network structure. How important is it that you understand the essence of the problem? What do you need to know so you can effectively evaluate the company's options for solving this problem?

The study of data and signals will also explain why almost all forms of communication, such as data, voice, music, and video, are slowly being converted from their original analog forms to the newer digital forms. What is so great about these digital forms of communication, and what do the signals that represent these forms of communication look like? This chapter will address all these questions and more.

Section 3-1: Data and Signals

Information stored within computer systems and transferred over a computer network can be divided into two categories: data and signals. **Data** conveys meaning within a computer system. Common examples of data include:

> A computer file of names and addresses stored on a hard disk drive

> The bits or individual elements of a movie stored on a DVD

> The binary 1s and 0s of music stored on a CD or streamed from a web server

> The pixels of a photograph that has been digitized by a digital camera and saved to a storage card

> The digits 0 through 9, which might represent sales figures for a business

In each of these examples, information has been electronically captured and stored on some type of storage device. If you want to transfer this data from one point to another, either via a physical wire or through radio waves, the data must be converted into a signal. **Signals** are the electric or electromagnetic impulses used to encode and transmit data. Common examples of signals include:

> A transmission of a video call between a smartphone and a cell tower

> A live news interview from Europe transmitted over a satellite system

> A term paper transmitted over the printer cable between a computer and a printer

> A web page transferred over cables between your Internet service provider and your home computer

In each of these examples, data, the static entity or tangible item, is transmitted over a wire or an airwave in the form of a signal, which is the dynamic entity or intangible item. Some type of hardware device is necessary to convert the static data into a dynamic signal ready for transmission and then convert the signal back to data at the receiving destination.

Before examining the conversion from data to signal, however, let's explore the most important characteristic that data and signals share.

Analog vs. Digital

Although data and signals are two different phenomena that have little in common, one characteristic they do share is that they can exist in either analog or digital form. This gives four possible data-to-signal conversion combinations:

> Analog data-to-analog signal, which involves amplitude and frequency modulation techniques

> Digital data-to-square-wave digital signal, which involves encoding techniques

> Digital data-to-(a discrete) analog signal, which involves modulation techniques

> Analog data-to-digital signal, which involves digitization techniques

Each of these four combinations occurs quite frequently in computer networks, and each has unique applications and properties, which are shown in Table 3-1 and further described next:

> Converting analog data to analog signals is fairly common. The conversion is performed by modulation techniques and is found in systems such as telephones, AM radio, and FM radio. Later in this chapter, you'll examine how AM radio signals are created.

> Converting digital data to square-wave digital signals is relatively straightforward and involves numerous digital encoding techniques. With this technique, binary 1s and 0s are converted to varying types of on and off voltage levels. They're called "square-wave" because the signal looks like a series of straight-line voltage changes, as you will see shortly. The local area network is one of the most common examples of a system that uses this type of conversion. In this chapter, you'll examine a few representative encoding techniques and discuss their basic advantages and disadvantages.

Table 3-1 Four combinations of data and signals

Data	Signal	Encoding or Conversion Technique	Common Devices	Common Systems
Analog	Analog	Amplitude modulation Frequency modulation	Radio tuner TV tuner	Telephone AM and FM radio Broadcast TV Cable TV
Digital	(Square-wave) digital	NRZ-L NRZI Manchester Differential Manchester Bipolar-AMI 4B/5B	Digital encoder	Local area networks Telephone systems
Digital	(Discrete) analog	Amplitude shift keying Frequency shift keying Phase shift keying	Modem	Dial-up Internet access DSL modem Cable modems Digital broadcast TV
Analog	Digital	Pulse code modulation Delta modulation	Codec	Telephone systems Music systems

> Converting digital data to (discrete) analog signals requires some form of a modem. This converts the binary 1s and 0s to another form, but unlike converting digital data to digital signals, the conversion of digital data to discrete analog signals involves more complex forms of analog signals that take on a discrete, or fixed, number of levels.

> Converting analog data to digital signals is generally called digitization. Telephone systems and music systems are two common examples of digitization. When your voice signal travels from your home and reaches a telephone company's switching center, it is digitized. Likewise, music and video are digitized before they can be recorded on a CD or DVD. In this chapter, two basic digitization techniques will be introduced and their advantages and disadvantages shown.

Let's examine the primary features of each type of data and signal.

Analog Data and Signals

Analog data and analog signals are represented as continuous waveforms that can exist at an infinite number of points between some given minimum and maximum. By convention, these minimum and maximum values are presented as voltages. Figure 3-1 shows that, between the minimum value A and maximum value B, the waveform at time t can exist at an infinite number of places.

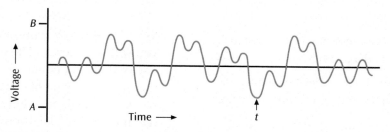

Figure 3-1 A simple example of an analog waveform

The most common example of analog data is the human voice. For example, when a person talks into a conventional telephone, the receiver in the mouthpiece converts the airwaves of speech into analog pulses of electrical voltage. Music and video, when they occur in their natural states, are also analog data. Although the human voice serves as an example of analog data, an example of an analog signal is the telephone system's electronic transmission of a voice conversation. Thus, you can see that analog data and signals are quite common, and many systems have incorporated them for many years.

One of the primary shortcomings of analog data and analog signals is how difficult it is to separate noise from the original waveform. Noise is unwanted electrical or electromagnetic energy that degrades the quality of signals and data. Because noise is found in every type of data and transmission system, and because its effects range from a slight hiss in the background to a complete loss of data or signal, it is especially important that noise be reduced as much as possible. Unfortunately, noise itself occurs as an analog waveform; and this makes it challenging, if not extremely difficult, to separate noise from an analog waveform that represents data.

Consider the waveform in Figure 3-2, which shows the first few notes of an imaginary symphonic overture. Noise is intermixed with the music—the data. Can you tell by looking at the figure what is the data and what is the noise? Although this example might border on the extreme, it demonstrates that noise and analog data can appear to be similar.

The performance of a record player provides another example of noise interfering with data. Many people have collections of vinyl albums that produce pops, hisses, and clicks when played; albums sometimes even skip. Is it possible to create a device that filters out the pops, hisses, and clicks from a record album without ruining the original data—the music? Various devices were created during the 1960s and 1970s to perform these kinds of filtering, but only the devices that removed hisses were (relatively speaking) successful. Filtering devices that removed the pops and clicks also tended to remove parts of the music. Filters now exist that can fairly effectively remove most forms of noise from analog recordings; but they are, interestingly, digital—not analog—devices. Even more interestingly, some people download software from the Internet that lets them insert noise sound effects into digital music to make it sound as though it were being played from a record album.

Digital Data and Signals

Digital data and digital signals are composed of a discrete or fixed number of values, rather than a continuous or infinite number of values. As you've already seen, digital data takes on the form of binary 1s and 0s. But digital signals are more complex. To keep the discussion as simple as possible, this discussion covers two forms of digital signal. The first type of digital signal is fairly straightforward and takes the shape of what is called a "square wave." These square waves are relatively simple patterns of high and low voltages. In the example shown in Figure 3-3, the digital square wave takes on only two discrete values: a high voltage (such as $+2$ volts) and a low voltage (such as -2 volts).

The second form of digital signal, which you'll learn about later in the chapter, involves more complex combinations of modulated analog signals. Even though the resulting signal is a composition of analog signals, you can treat the outcome as a digital signal because there are a discrete number of signal combinations and levels. Although this might be hard to visualize at this point, you'll see plenty of examples in this chapter to solidify your understanding.

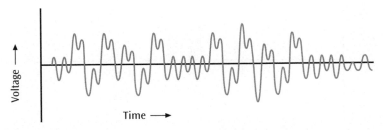

Figure 3-2   The waveform of a symphonic overture with noise

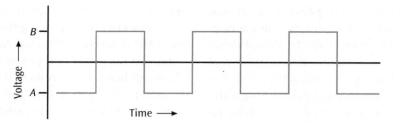

Figure 3-3 A simple example of a digital waveform

What happens when you introduce noise into digital signals? As stated earlier, noise has the properties of an analog waveform and, thus, can occupy an infinite range of values; digital waveforms occupy only a finite range of values. When you combine analog noise with a digital waveform, it is fairly easy to separate the original digital waveform from the noise. Figure 3-4 shows a digital signal (square wave) with some noise.

If the amount of noise remains small enough that the original digital waveform can still be interpreted, then the noise can be filtered out, thereby leaving the original waveform. In the simple example in Figure 3-4, as long as you can tell a high part of the waveform from a low part, you can still recognize the digital waveform. If, however, the noise becomes so great that it is no longer possible

to distinguish a high from a low, as shown in Figure 3-5, then the noise has taken over the signal and you can no longer understand this portion of the waveform.

The ability to separate noise from a digital waveform is one of the strengths of digital systems. When data is transmitted as a signal, the signal will *always* incur some level of noise. In the case of digital signals, however, it is relatively simple to pass the noisy digital signal through a filtering device that removes a significant amount of the noise and leaves the original digital signal intact.

Despite this strong advantage that digital has over analog, not all systems use digital signals to transmit data. One reason for this is that the electronic equipment used to transmit a signal through a wire, or over the airwaves,

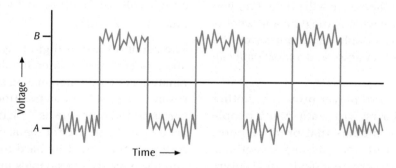

Figure 3-4 A digital signal with some noise introduced

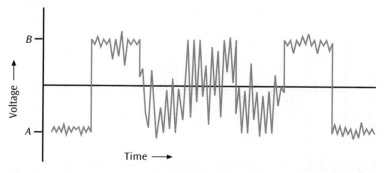

Figure 3-5 A digital waveform with noise so great that you can no longer recognize the original waveform

usually dictates the type of signals the wire can transmit. Certain electronic equipment is capable of supporting only analog signals, while other equipment can support only digital signals. Consider broadcast radio. It was originally and still is predominantly analog. In 2002, the FCC (Federal Communications Commission) approved standards to simultaneously broadcast digital with analog signals, and in 2020, they began allowing stations to broadcast only in digital if they choose. Still, most radio stations continue to broadcast in analog even if they've added a digital transmission. The digital transmission systems are expensive and also require users to switch to digital radio receivers. Because consumers have not yet made this transition en masse, the industry is still predominantly analog.

All Things Considered

Thought Experiment

You're working for a company that has a network application for accessing a database of corporate profiles. From your computer workstation, a request for a profile travels over the corporate LAN to a modem. The modem, using DSL, connects to the Internet and finally into the database service. The database service is essentially a modem and a mainframe computer. Create a table or draw a figure that shows every time data or signals are converted to a different form during this process. For each entry in the table or part of the figure, show where the conversion is taking place, the form of the incoming information, and the form of the outgoing information.

Now that you've learned data and signals share the primary characteristic of existing in either analog or digital form, along with the main feature that distinguishes them—analog exists as a continuous waveform while digital is discrete—you're ready to examine important characteristics of signals in closer detail.

Fundamentals of Signals

Three basic components of analog and digital signals are amplitude, frequency, and phase. A sine wave is used to represent an analog signal as shown in Figure 3-6. The amplitude of a signal is the height of the wave above or below a given reference point. This height often denotes the voltage level of the signal (measured in volts), but it also can denote the current level of the signal (measured

in amps) or the power level of the signal (measured in watts). That is, the amplitude of a signal can be expressed as volts, amps, or watts. Note that a signal can change amplitude as time progresses. In Figure 3-6, you see one signal with two different amplitudes.

The frequency of a signal is the number of times a signal makes a complete cycle within a given time frame. The length, or time interval, of one cycle is called its period. The period can be calculated by taking the reciprocal of the frequency (1/frequency). Figure 3-7 shows three different analog signals. If the time t is one second, the signal in Figure 3-7(a) completes one cycle in one second. The signal in Figure 3-7(b) completes two cycles in one second. The signal in Figure 3-7(c) completes three cycles in one second. Cycles per second, or frequency, are represented by Hz (hertz). Thus, the signal in Figure 3-7(c) has a frequency of 3 Hz.

Human voice, audio, and video signals—indeed most signals—are actually composed of multiple frequencies. These multiple frequencies are what allow you to distinguish between people's voices or different musical instruments. The frequency range of the average human voice usually goes no lower than 300 Hz and no higher than approximately 3400 Hz. Because a standard telephone is designed to transmit a human voice, the telephone system transmits signals in the range of 300 Hz to 3400 Hz. The piano has a wider range of frequencies than the human voice. The lowest note possible on the piano is 30 Hz, and the highest note possible is 4200 Hz.

The range of frequencies that a signal spans from minimum to maximum is called the spectrum. The spectrum of the telephone example is simply 300 Hz to 3400 Hz. The bandwidth of a signal is the absolute value of the difference between the lowest and highest frequencies. The bandwidth of a telephone system that transmits a single voice in the range of 300 Hz to 3400 Hz is 3100 Hz. Because extraneous noise degrades original signals, an electronic device usually has an effective bandwidth that is less than its theoretical bandwidth. When making communication decisions, many professionals rely more

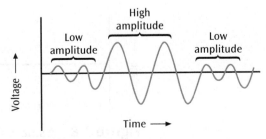

Figure 3-6 A signal with two different amplitudes

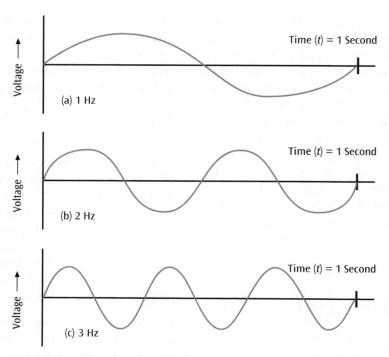

Figure 3-7 Three signals of (a) 1 Hz, (b) 2 Hz, and (c) 3 Hz

on the effective bandwidth than the theoretical bandwidth because most situations must deal with the real-world problems of noise and interference.

The **phase** of a signal is the position of the waveform relative to a given moment of time, or relative to time zero. In the drawing of the simple sine wave in Figure 3-8(a), the waveform oscillates up and down in a repeating fashion. Note that the wave never makes an abrupt change but is a continuous sine wave. A phase change (or phase shift) involves jumping forward or

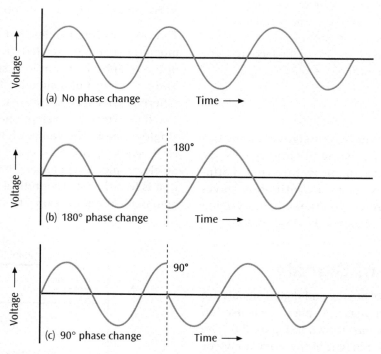

Figure 3-8 A sine wave showing (a) no phase change, (b) a 180-degree phase change, and (c) a 90-degree phase change

backward in the waveform at a given moment of time. Jumping forward one-half of the complete cycle of the signal produces a 180-degree phase change, as seen in Figure 3-8(b). Jumping forward one-quarter of the cycle produces a 90-degree phase change, as in Figure 3-8(c). As you will see in this chapter's "Transmitting digital data with discrete analog signals" section, some systems can generate signals that do a phase change of 45, 135, 225, and 315 degrees on demand.

When traveling through any type of medium, a signal always experiences some loss of its power due to friction. This loss of power, or loss of signal strength, is called attenuation, which you read about in Chapter 2. Attenuation in a medium such as copper wire is a logarithmic loss (in which a value decrease of 1 represents a tenfold decrease) and is a function of distance and the resistance within the wire. Knowing the amount of attenuation in a signal (how much power the signal lost) allows you to determine the signal strength. Decibel (dB) is a relative measure of signal loss or gain and is used to measure the logarithmic loss or gain of a signal. Amplification is the opposite of attenuation. When a signal is amplified by an amplifier, the signal gains in decibels.

Details | Composite Signals

Almost all of the example signals given in this chapter are simple, periodic sine waves. However, you will not always find simple, periodic sine waves. In fact, you are more likely to encounter combinations of various kinds of sines and cosines that, when combined, produce unique waveforms.

One of the best examples of this is how multiple sine waves can be combined to produce a square wave. Stated technically, multiple analog signals can be combined to produce a digital signal. A branch of mathematics called Fourier analysis shows that any complex, periodic waveform is a composite of simpler periodic waveforms. Consider, for example, the first two waveforms shown in Figure 3-9. The formula for the first waveform is $1 \sin(2\pi ft)$, and the formula for the second waveform is $1/3 \sin(2\pi 3ft)$. In each formula, the number at the front (the 1 and 1/3, respectively) is a value of amplitude, the term "sin" refers to the sine trigonometric function, and the terms "ft" and "3ft" refer to the frequency over a given period of time. Examining both the waveforms (also known as harmonics) and the formulas shows us that, whereas the amplitude of the second waveform is one-third as high as the amplitude of the first waveform, the frequency of the second waveform is three times as high as the frequency of the first waveform. The third waveform in Figure 3-9(c) is a composite, or addition, of the first two waveforms.

Note the relatively square shape of the composite waveform. Now suppose you continued to add more waveforms to this composite signal—in particular, waveforms with amplitude values of 1/5, 1/7, 1/9, and so on (odd-valued denominators) and frequency multiplier values of 5, 7, 9, and so on. The more waveforms you add, the more the composite signal would resemble the square waveform of a digital signal. Another way to interpret this transformation is to state that adding waveforms of higher and higher frequency—increasing bandwidth—will produce a composite that looks and behaves more like a digital signal. Interestingly, a digital waveform is, in fact, a combination of analog sine waves.

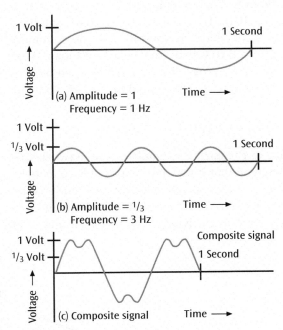

Figure 3-9 Two simple, periodic sine waves (a) and (b) and their composite (c)

All Things Considered

Thought Experiment

Locate a website that graphically shows the result of adding multiple sine waves to create composite waves such as square waves or sawtooth waves, or experiment with the following websites to create a variety of waveforms:

- geogebra.org/m/BOMfKCIK (Check the "Show/Hide $y_1 + y_2$" box to see the composite wave. Then adjust the y_1 and y_2 scrollbars to see how the composite wave is affected.)

- academo.org/demos/wave-interference-beat-frequency (Adjust the f_1 and f_2 scrollbars to see the effect on the composite wave. Be sure to check the "Sound on/off" checkbox to hear the changes as well.)

Because attenuation is a logarithmic loss and the decibel is a logarithmic value, calculating the overall loss or gain of a system involves adding all the individual decibel losses and gains. Figure 3-10 shows a communication line running from point A through point B, and ending at point C. The communication line from A to B experiences a 10-dB loss, point B has a 20-dB amplifier (i.e., a 20-dB gain occurs at point B), and the communication line from B to C experiences a 15-dB loss. What is the overall gain or loss of the signal between point A and point C? To answer this question, add all dB gains and losses:

$$-10 \text{ dB} + 20 \text{ dB} + (-15 \text{ dB}) = -5 \text{ dB}$$

Let's return to the earlier example of the network specialist telling you that it may not be possible to install a computer workstation as planned. You now understand that signals lose strength over distance. Although you do not know how much signal would be lost, nor at what

point the strength of the signal would be weaker than the noise, you understand this part of what the network specialist told you. But let's investigate a little further. If a signal loses 3 dB, for example, is this a significant loss or not?

The decibel is a relative measure of signal loss or gain and is expressed as

$$dB = 10 \times \log_{10} (P_2/P_1)$$

in which P_2 and P_1 are the ending and beginning power levels, respectively, of the signal expressed in watts. If a signal starts at a transmitter with 10 watts of power and arrives at a receiver with 5 watts of power, the signal loss in dB is calculated as follows:

$$dB = 10 \times \log_{10} (5/10)$$
$$= 10 \times \log_{10} (0.5)$$
$$= 10 \times (-0.3)$$
$$= -3$$

In other words, a 3-dB loss occurs between the transmitter and receiver. Because decibel is a relative measure of loss or gain, you cannot take a single power level at time t and compute the decibel value of that signal without having a reference or a beginning power level.

Rather than remembering this formula, you can use a shortcut. As you saw from the previous calculation, any time a signal loses half its power, a 3-dB loss occurs. If the signal drops from 10 watts to 5 watts, that is a 3-dB loss. If the signal drops from 1000 watts to 500 watts, this still is a 3-dB loss. Conversely, a signal whose strength is doubled experiences a 3-dB gain. It follows then that if a signal drops from 1000 watts to 250 watts, this is a 6-dB loss (1000 to 500 is a 3-dB loss, and 500 to 250 corresponds to another 3 dB). Now you have a little better understanding of the terminology. If the network specialist tells you a given section of wiring loses 6 dB, for example, then the signal traveling through that wire has lost three-quarters of its power.

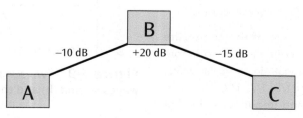

Figure 3-10 Example demonstrating decibel loss and gain

With a firmer understanding of the fundamentals of data and signals and the differences between them, you're ready to see how data is converted into signals for transmission.

Remember this…

> Data conveys meaning while signals are electric or electromagnetic impulses used to encode and transmit data. Both data and signals can exist in analog or digital forms.

> Analog data and analog signals are represented as continuous waveforms that can exist at an infinite number of points between some given minimum and maximum. Digital data and digital signals are composed of a discrete or fixed number of values, rather than a continuous or infinite number of values.

> Analog signals are represented by sine waves, which are defined by their amplitude, frequency, and phase.

> When traveling through any type of medium, a signal always experiences some loss of its power due to friction. This loss of power, or loss of signal strength, is called attenuation. Attenuation in a medium such as copper wire is a logarithmic loss in which a value decrease of 1 represents a tenfold decrease, and it's a function of distance and the resistance within the wire.

Self-check

1. Which of the following is most analogous to data transmitted across a network connection?
   a. The sound of a person's footsteps
   b. Lyrics of a song
   c. Light streaming through a window
   d. Ink on a sheet of paper
2. Which of the following is most analogous to digital data?
   a. The pitch of a lawn mower's engine
   b. A person's facial expression
   c. The growth progress of a tree
   d. Morse code sent by flashlight
3. Amplitude is to frequency as:
   a. The diameter of a bicycle wheel is to the speed of its rotation
   b. The speed a bicycle wheel's rotation is to its diameter

   c. The height of a mountain is to its width
   d. The width of a mountain is to its height

Check your answers at the end of this chapter.

Section 3-2: Converting Data into Signals

Analog signals often convey analog data, and digital signals convey digital data. However, you can use analog signals to convey digital data, and digital signals to convey analog data. The decision about whether to use analog or digital signals often depends on the transmission equipment and the environment in which the signals must travel. Recall that certain electronic equipment can support only analog signals, while other types of equipment support only digital signals. For example, the telephone system was created to transmit human voice, which is analog data. Thus, the telephone system was originally designed to transmit analog signals. Today, most of the telephone system uses digital signals. The only portion that remains analog is the local loop, or the connection from the home to the telephone company's central office.

Transmitting analog data with digital signals is also common. Originally, broadcast and cable television companies transmitted analog television channels using analog signals. More recently, the analog television channels are converted to digital signals in order to provide clearer images and higher-definition signals.

The four main combinations of data and signals are shown in the following examples:

> Analog data transmitted using analog signals

> Digital data transmitted using square-wave digital signals

> Digital data transmitted using discrete analog signals

> Analog data transmitted using digital signals

Transmitting Analog Data with Analog Signals

The analog data-to-analog signal conversion is probably the simplest of the four combinations of data and signals to comprehend. This is because the data is an analog waveform that is simply being transformed to another analog waveform, the signal, for transmission. The basic operation performed is modulation. **Modulation** is the process of sending data over a signal by varying its amplitude, frequency, or phase. Landline telephones (the local loop only), AM radio, FM radio, and broadcast television before June 2009 are the most common examples of analog data-to-analog signal conversion.

Consider Figure 3-11, which shows AM (amplitude modulation) radio as an example. The audio data generated by the radio station might appear like the first sine wave shown in the figure. To convey this analog data, the station uses a carrier wave signal, like that shown in Figure 3-11(b). In the modulation process, the original audio waveform and the carrier wave are essentially added together to produce the third waveform. Note how the dotted lines superimposed over the third waveform follow the same outline as the original audio waveform. Here, the original audio data has been modulated onto a particular carrier frequency (the frequency at which you set the dial to tune in a station) using amplitude modulation—hence, the name AM radio. Frequency modulation also can be used in similar ways to modulate analog data onto an analog signal, and it yields FM (frequency modulation) radio.

Transmitting Digital Data with Square-wave Digital Signals: Digital Encoding Schemes

To transmit digital data using square-wave digital signals, the 1s and 0s of the digital data must be converted to the proper physical form that can be transmitted over a wire or an airwave. Thus, to transmit a data value of 1, you transmit a positive voltage on the medium. If you wish to transmit a data value of 0, you could transmit a zero voltage. You could also use the opposite scheme: a data value of 0 is positive voltage and a data value of 1 is a zero voltage. Digital encoding schemes like this are used to convert the 0s and 1s of digital data into the appropriate transmission form. You will examine five digital encoding schemes that are representative of most digital encoding schemes: NRZ-L, NRZI, Manchester, differential Manchester, and 4B/5B.

Nonreturn to Zero Digital Encoding Schemes

The **NRZ-L (nonreturn to zero-level)** digital encoding scheme increases the charge for a value of 1 and decreases the charge for a value of 0. The reverse might be implemented as well: increase the charge for a value of 0 and decrease the charge for a value of 1. The point here is that the charge changes when the bit value changes. Figure 3-12(a) shows an example of the NRZ-L scheme. Notice that several 0s in a row or several 1s in a row would show a flatline voltage, which makes it difficult to maintain clock synchronization with the receiver. However, the NRZ-L encoding scheme is simple to generate and inexpensive to implement in hardware. Notice how the square-wave signal is very square-like in appearance.

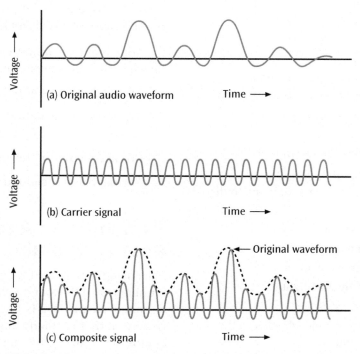

Figure 3-11   An audio waveform modulated onto a carrier frequency using amplitude modulation

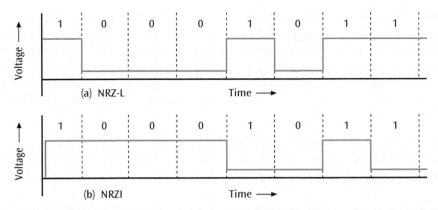

Figure 3-12 Comparison of NRZ-L and NRZI digital encoding schemes

The second digital encoding scheme, shown in Figure 3-12(b), is **NRZI (nonreturn to zero inverted)**. This encoding scheme has a voltage change at the beginning of a 1 and no voltage change at the beginning of a 0. A fundamental difference exists between NRZ-L and NRZI. With NRZ-L, the receiver must check the voltage *level* for each bit to determine whether the bit is a 0 or a 1. With NRZI, the receiver must check whether there is a *change at the beginning* of the bit to determine if it is a 0 or a 1. Look again at Figure 3-12 to understand this difference between the two NRZ schemes.

An inherent problem with both the NRZ-L and NRZI digital encoding schemes is that long sequences of 0s in the data produce a signal that never changes. Often the receiver looks for signal changes so that it can synchronize its reading of the data with the actual data pattern. If a long string of 0s is transmitted and the signal does not change, how can the receiver tell when one bit ends and the next bit begins? (Imagine how hard it would be to dance to a song if the volume is often muted for several seconds at a time.) One potential solution is to install in the receiver an internal clock that knows when to look for each successive bit. But what if the receiver has a different clock from the one the transmitter used to generate the signals? Who is to say that these two clocks keep the same time? A more accurate system would generate a signal that has a change for each and every bit. If the receiver could count on each bit having some form of signal change, then it could stay synchronized with the incoming data stream.

Manchester Code Digital Encoding Schemes

The Manchester class of digital encoding schemes ensures that each bit has some type of signal change, and thus solves the synchronization problem. Shown in Figure 3-13(a), the **Manchester code** encoding scheme has the following properties: To transmit a 1, the signal changes from low to high in the *middle* of the interval, and to transmit a 0, the signal changes from high to low in the *middle* of the interval. Note that there is always a

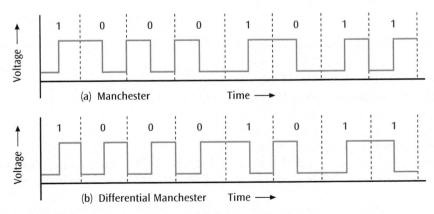

Figure 3-13 Comparison of Manchester digital encoding schemes

transition in the middle: a 1 is a low-to-high transition, and a 0 is a high-to-low transition. Thus, if the signal is currently low and the next bit to transmit is a 0, the signal must move from low to high at the *beginning* of the interval so that it can do the high-to-low transition in the middle.

The differential Manchester code was used in a now extinct form of local area network (token ring) but still exists in some unique applications. It is similar to the Manchester code in that there is always a transition in the middle of the interval. But unlike the Manchester code, the direction of this transition in the middle does not differentiate between a 0 or a 1. Instead, if there is a transition at the *beginning* of the interval, then a 0 is being transmitted. If there is no transition at the beginning of the interval, then a 1 is being transmitted. Because the receiver must watch the beginning of the interval to determine the value of the bit, the differential Manchester code is similar to the NRZI scheme in this one respect. Figure 3-13(b) shows an example of differential Manchester encoding.

The Manchester codes have an advantage over the NRZ schemes: In the Manchester codes, there is always a transition in the middle of a bit. Thus, the receiver can expect a signal change at regular intervals and can synchronize itself with the incoming bit stream. The Manchester codes are considered self-clocking because the occurrence of a regular transition is similar to seconds ticking on a clock. As you will learn in Chapter 4, it is very important for a receiver to stay synchronized with the incoming bit stream, and the Manchester codes allow a receiver to achieve this synchronization.

A major disadvantage of the Manchester codes is that roughly half the time there will be two transitions during each bit. For example, if the differential Manchester code is used to transmit a series of 0s, then the signal has to change at the beginning of each bit, as well as change in the middle of each bit. Thus, for each data value 0, the signal changes twice.

The number of times a signal changes value per second is called baud or the baud rate. In Figure 3-14, a series of binary 0s is transmitted using the differential Manchester code. Note that the signal changes twice for each bit. After one second, the signal has changed 10 times. Therefore, the baud rate is 10. During that same time period, only 5 bits were transmitted. The data rate, measured in bps (bits per second), is 5, which in this case is one-half the baud rate. Many individuals mistakenly

equate baud rate to bps (or data rate). Under some circumstances, the baud rate might equal the bps, such as in the NRZ-L or NRZI encoding schemes shown earlier in Figure 3-14. With these encoding schemes, there is at most one signal change for each bit transmitted. But with schemes such as the Manchester codes, the baud rate is not equal to the bps.

Why does it matter that some encoding schemes have a baud rate twice the bps? Because the Manchester codes have a baud rate that is twice the bps, and the NRZ-L and NRZI codes have a baud rate that is equal to the bps, hardware that generates a Manchester-encoded signal must work twice as fast as hardware that generates an NRZ-encoded signal. If 100 million 0s per second are transmitted using differential Manchester encoding, the signal must change 200 million times per second (as opposed to 100 million times per second with NRZ encoding). Therefore, the increased accuracy in clock synchronization with the Manchester codes requires significantly more bandwidth on the network to transmit the same amount of data. As with most things in life, you do not get something for nothing. Hardware or software that handles the Manchester codes is more elaborate and more costly than the hardware or software that handles the NRZ encoding schemes. More importantly, as you shall soon see, signals that change at a higher rate of speed are more susceptible to noise and errors.

4B/5B Digital Encoding Scheme

The Manchester codes solve the synchronization problem but are relatively inefficient because they have a baud rate that is twice the bps. The 4B/5B scheme tries to satisfy the synchronization problem and avoid the "baud equals two times the bps" problem. The 4B/5B encoding scheme converts 4 bits of data into a unique 5-bit sequence and encodes the 5 bits onto the medium using another scheme, such as NRZI. Because the data is broken into these 4-bit "nibbles" for translation, this encoding scheme is sometimes called block coding.

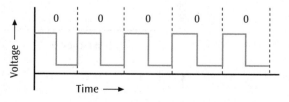

Figure 3-14 Transmitting five binary 0s using differential Manchester encoding scheme

The first step the hardware performs in generating the 4B/5B code is to convert 4-bit nibbles of the original data into new 5-bit patterns. Using 5 bits (or five 0s and 1s) to represent one value yields 32 potential combinations ($2^5 = 32$). Of these possibilities, only 16 combinations are used, so that no code has three or more consecutive 0s. This way, if the transmitting device transmits the 5-bit quantities using NRZI encoding for example, there will never be more than three 0s transmitted in a row even when adjacent 5-bit codes begin and end with a zero. If you never transmit more than three 0s in a row using NRZI encoding, then you will never have a long period in which there is no signal transition for clock synchronization. Figure 3-15 shows the 4B/5B code in detail.

How does the 4B/5B code work? Let's say, for example, that the next 4 bits in a data stream to be transmitted are 0000, which, you can see, has a string of consecutive zeros and therefore would create a signal that does not change. Looking at the first column in Figure 3-15, you see that 4B/5B encoding replaces 0000 with 11110. Note that 11110, like all the 5-bit codes in the second column of Figure 3-15, does not have more than two consecutive zeros. Having replaced 0000 with 11110, the hardware will now transmit 11110. Because this 5-bit code is transmitted using another method such as NRZI, the baud rate equals the bps and, thus, is more efficient. Unfortunately, converting a 4-bit code to a 5-bit code creates a 20 percent overhead (one extra bit). However, compare that to a Manchester code by itself, in which the baud rate can be twice the bps and thus yield a 100 percent overhead. Clearly, a 20 percent overhead is better than a 100 percent overhead.

Many of the newer digital encoding systems for high-speed LANs also use techniques that are quite similar to 4B/5B, such as 8B/10B paired with NRZ for fiber optic Gigabit Ethernet, or the more efficient 128B/132B used on USB 3.1. As networking technologies passed the Gigabit threshold, newer digital encoding schemes often combined techniques. For example, Gigabit Ethernet on twisted-pair cable uses 8B1Q4 and 4D-PAM5 encoding while Gigabit Ethernet on fiber optic cable uses 8B10B and NRZ. Let's dig into this a little.

Recall from Chapter 2 that Gigabit Ethernet on twisted pair cable uses all four pairs to send and receive data, not just two pairs. Data is divided into four lanes, so to speak, and each lane must support 250 Mbps. To achieve this goal, 8B1Q4 (8 bits to 1 set of four quinary symbols) encoding divides each byte into four 2-bit groups. A third bit is added to each group for error correction (you'll learn more about error correction in Chapter 4). Each of these 3-bit groups is then called a quinary symbol. Similar to 4B/5B, each of these symbols also avoids placing too many zeros in a row. A second layer of encoding, using 4D-PAM5 (4-dimensional Pulse Amplitude Modulation 5-levels), transmits each 3-bit group along a different twisted pair using a series of five

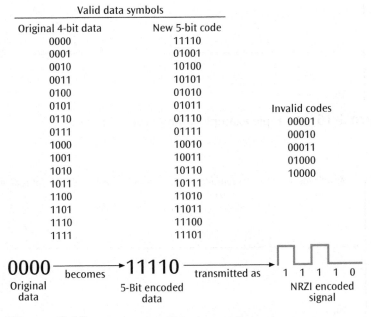

Valid data symbols	
Original 4-bit data	New 5-bit code
0000	11110
0001	01001
0010	10100
0011	10101
0100	01010
0101	01011
0110	01110
0111	01111
1000	10010
1001	10011
1010	10110
1011	10111
1100	11010
1101	11011
1110	11100
1111	11101

Invalid codes
00001
00010
00011
01000
10000

0000 ──becomes──▶ 11110 ──transmitted as──▶ 1 1 1 1 0

Original data / 5-Bit encoded data / NRZI encoded signal

Figure 3-15   The 4B/5B digital encoding scheme

different voltages. At 125 MHz per lane and 2 bits of data per quinary symbol, the overall throughput is 250 Mbps for each lane, totaling 1000 Mbps for the four lanes of traffic.

To reach even faster speeds of 10 Gbps, even newer encoding schemes are needed. Each new technology builds on these existing concepts of using a small amount of overhead to avoid long strings of any one bit value, and then using complex voltage patterns to maximize the efficiency of each clock cycle.

Transmitting Digital Data with Discrete Analog Signals

The technique of converting digital data to an analog signal is also an example of modulation. But in this type of modulation, the analog signal takes on a discrete number of signal levels. It could be as simple as two signal levels (such as amplitude shift keying described next) or something more complex, such as the 256 levels used with digital television signals. The receiver then looks specifically for these unique signal levels. Thus, even though they are fundamentally analog signals, they operate with a discrete number of levels, much like a digital signal from the previous section. So to avoid confusion, these are called discrete analog signals. Let's examine a number of these discrete modulation techniques, beginning with the simpler techniques and ending with more complex techniques used for systems such as digital television signals—quadrature amplitude modulation.

Amplitude Shift Keying

The simplest modulation technique is ASK (amplitude shift keying). As shown in Figure 3-16, a data value of 1 and a data value of 0 are represented by two different amplitudes of a signal. For example, the higher amplitude could represent a 0, while the lower amplitude (or zero amplitude) could represent a 1. Note that *during* each bit period, the amplitude of the signal is constant. Thus, there is only one change of baud for each bit. (The voltage oscillations within a bit do not count as baud changes.)

ASK is not restricted to two possible amplitude levels. For example, you could create an ASK technique that incorporates four different amplitude levels, as shown in Figure 3-17. Each of the four different amplitude levels would represent 2 bits. You might recall that, when counting in binary, 2 bits yield four possible combinations: 00, 01, 10, and 11. Thus, every time the signal changes (every time the amplitude changes), 2 bits are transmitted. As a result, the data rate (bps) is twice the baud rate. This is the opposite of a Manchester code in which the data rate is one-half the baud rate. A system that transmits 2 bits per signal change is more efficient than one that requires two signal changes for every bit.

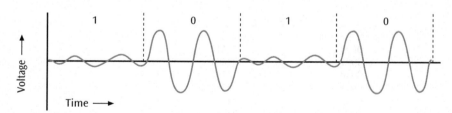

Figure 3-16   A simple example of amplitude shift keying

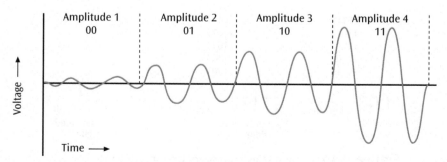

Figure 3-17   Amplitude shift keying using four different amplitude levels

Amplitude shift keying has a weakness: it is suscepti-ble to sudden noise impulses such as the static charges created by a lightning storm. When a signal is disrupted by a large static discharge, the signal experiences sig-nificant increases in amplitude. For this reason, and because it is difficult to accurately distinguish among more than just a few amplitude levels, amplitude shift keying is one of the least efficient encoding techniques and is not used on systems that require a high data transmission rate. When transmitting data over stan-dard telephone lines, ASK typically does not exceed 1200 bps.

Frequency Shift Keying

FSK (frequency shift keying) uses two different fre-quency ranges to represent data values of 0 and 1, as shown in Figure 3-18. For example, the lower frequency signal might represent a 1, while the higher-frequency signal might represent a 0. *During* each bit period, the frequency of the signal is constant.

Unlike amplitude shift keying, frequency shift keying does not have a problem with sudden noise spikes that can cause loss of data. Nonetheless, FSK is not perfect. It is subject to intermodulation distortion, a phenomenon that occurs when the frequencies of two or more signals mix and create new frequencies. Thus, like ASK, FSK is not used on systems that require a high data rate.

Phase Shift Keying

A third modulation technique is PSK (phase shift keying), which represents 0s and 1s by different changes in the phase of a waveform. For example, a 0 could indi-cate no phase change, while a 1 could indicate a phase change of 180 degrees, as shown in Figure 3-19.

This shift could also be represented on a grid showing the available values for each phase differential, as shown in Figure 3-20 (this grid will make more sense in a moment).

Phase changes are not affected by amplitude changes, nor are they affected by intermodulation distortions. Thus, phase shift keying is less susceptible to noise and can be used at higher frequencies. PSK is so accurate that the signal transmitter can increase efficiency by intro-ducing multiple phase-shift angles. For example, QPSK (quadrature phase shift keying) incorporates four differ-ent phase angles, as shown on the grid in Figure 3-21, each of which represents two bits:

> A 45-degree phase shift represents a data value of 11

> A 135-degree phase shift represents 10

> A 225-degree phase shift represents 01

> A 315-degree phase shift represents 00

Figure 3-22 shows a simplified drawing of these four dif-ferent phase shifts. Because each phase shift represents two bits, QPSK has double the efficiency of simple PSK. With this encoding technique, one signal change equals two bits of information; that is, 1 baud equals 2 bps.

But why not create a phase shift keying technique that incorporates eight different phase angles with 45-degree shifts? (See Figure 3-23.) This is called 8-PSK and allows transmission of three bits per phase change (3 bits per signal change, or 3 bits per baud).

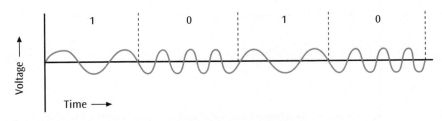

Figure 3-18   Simple example of frequency shift keying

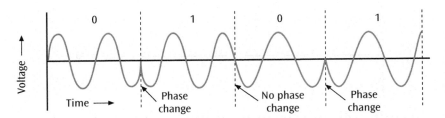

Figure 3-19   Simple example of phase shift keying

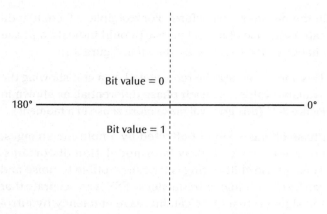

Figure 3-20 A phase change of 180 degrees is represented by a straight line on a grid

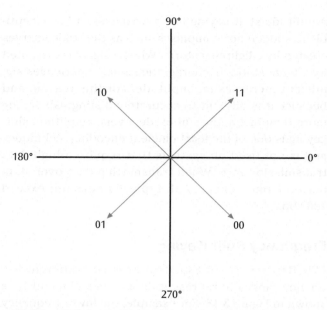

Figure 3-21   Phase changes at 90 degrees apart can represent four different data values

Sixteen phase changes (16-PSK) would yield 4 bits per baud; 32 phase changes (32-PSK) yield 5 bits per baud. Note that 2 raised to the power of the number of bits per baud equals the number of phase changes. Or inversely, the $\log_2$ of the number of phase changes equals the number of bits per baud. This concept is key to efficient communications systems: the higher the number of bits per baud, the faster the data rate of the system. You will revisit this concept.

What if you created a signaling method in which you combined 12 different phase-shift angles with two different amplitudes? Figure 3-24(a), known as a constellation diagram, shows 12 different phase-shift angles

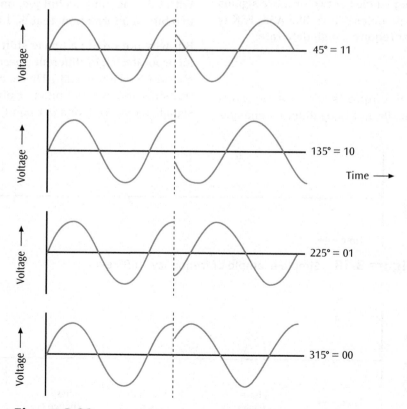

Figure 3-22   Four phase angles of 45, 135, 225, and 315 degrees, as seen in quadrature phase shift keying

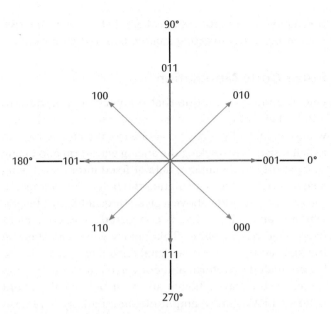

Figure 3-23 Phase changes at 45 degrees apart can represent eight different data values

have double amplitudes, resulting in 16 different combinations.

This encoding technique is an example from a family of encoding techniques termed **QAM (quadrature amplitude modulation)**, which is commonly employed in Wi-Fi and cell phones, and it uses each signal change to represent four bits (4 bits yield 16 combinations). Figure 3-25 shows an overlay of the grid from Figure 3-24 and the various values that can be determined by the 16 different states of the QAM signal.

The bps of the data transmitted using 16-QAM is four times the baud rate. For example, a system using a signal with a baud rate of 2400 achieves a data transfer rate of 9600 bps (4 × 2400). Interestingly, it is techniques like this that enable Internet access via DSL and digital television broadcasts on cable. In fact, newer Wi-Fi technologies (such as 802.11ax) employ 1024-QAM where the grid in Figure 3-25 would show 1,024 unique values rather than just 16. This dense constellation allows for significantly improved data throughput. Instead of just four bits per signal change, 1024-QAM communicates ten bits per signal change and so offers a bit rate ten times its baud rate. While there are additional factors that add complexity, it's clear that 1024-QAM plays a significant role in new Wi-Fi data rates.

with 12 arcs radiating from a central point. Two different amplitudes are applied on each of four angles (but only four angles). Figure 3-24(b) shows a phase shift with two different amplitudes. Thus, eight phase angles have a single amplitude, and four phase angles

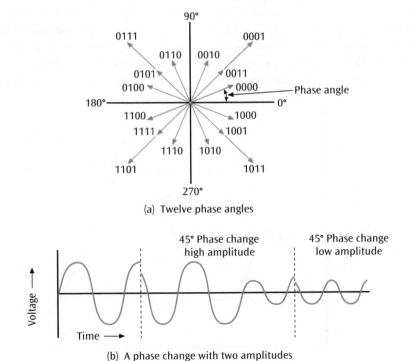

(a) Twelve phase angles

(b) A phase change with two amplitudes

Figure 3-24   Figure (a) shows 12 different phases, while Figure (b) shows a phase change with two different amplitudes

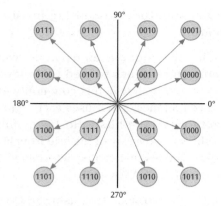

Figure 3-25 16-QAM yields 16 different 4-bit values

Transmitting Analog Data with Digital Signals

It is often necessary to transmit analog data over a digital medium. For example, many scientific laboratories have testing equipment that generates test results as analog data. This analog data is converted to digital signals so that the original data can be transmitted through a computer system and eventually stored in memory or on a storage disk. A music recording company that records songs for music albums also converts analog data to digital signals. An artist performs a song that produces music, which is analog data. A device then converts this analog data to digital data so that the binary 1s and 0s of the digitized music can be stored, edited, and eventually streamed over the Internet. When the song is played, the binary 1s and 0s are converted back to analog music

through your computer's speakers. Let's look at the two techniques for converting analog data to digital signals.

Pulse Code Modulation

One encoding technique that converts analog data to a digital signal is **PCM (pulse code modulation)**. Hardware—specifically, a **codec**—converts the analog data to a digital signal by tracking the analog waveform and taking "snapshots" of the analog data at fixed intervals. Taking a snapshot involves calculating the height, or voltage, of the analog waveform above a given threshold. This height, which is an analog value, is converted to an equivalent fixed-sized binary value. This binary value can then be transmitted by means of a digital encoding format. Tracking an analog waveform and converting it to pulses that represent the wave's height above or below a threshold is termed PAM (pulse amplitude modulation). The term "pulse code modulation" actually applies to the conversion of these individual pulses into binary values. For the sake of brevity, however, this text refers to the entire process simply as pulse code modulation.

Figure 3-26 shows an example of pulse code modulation. At time t (on the x-axis), a snapshot of the analog waveform is taken, resulting in the decimal value 14 (on the y-axis). The 14 is converted to a 5-bit binary value (such as 01110) by the codec and transmitted to a device for storage. In Figure 3-26, the y-axis is divided into 32 gradations, or quantization levels. (Note that the values on the y-axis run from 0 to 31, corresponding to 32 divisions.) Because there are 32 quantization levels, each snapshot generates a 5-bit value ($2^5 = 32$).

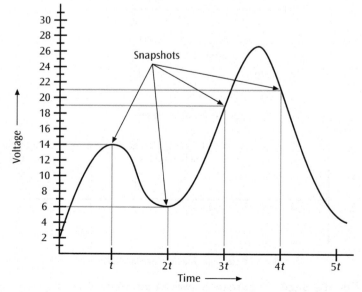

Figure 3-26 Example of taking "snapshots" of an analog waveform for conversion to a digital signal

What happens if the snapshot value falls between 13 and 14? If it is closer to 14, you would approximate and select 14. If closer to 13, you would approximate and select 13. Either way, your approximation would introduce an error into the encoding because you did not encode the exact value of the waveform. This type of error is called a quantization error, or quantization noise, and causes the regenerated analog data to differ from the original analog data.

To reduce this type of quantization error, you could tune the y-axis more finely by dividing it into 64 (i.e., double the number of) quantization levels. As always, you do not get something for nothing. This extra precision would require the hardware to be more precise, and it would generate a larger bit value for each sample (because having 64 quantization levels requires a 6-bit value, or $2^6 = 64$). Continuing with the encoding of the waveform in Figure 3-26, you see that at time $2t$, the codec takes a second snapshot. The voltage of the waveform here is found to have a decimal value of 6, and so this 6 is converted to a second 5-bit binary value and stored. The encoding process continues in this way—with the codec taking snapshots, converting the voltage values (also known as PAM values) to binary form, and storing them—for the length of the waveform.

To reconstruct the original analog waveform from the stored digital values, special hardware converts each n-bit binary value back to decimal and generates an electric pulse of appropriate magnitude (height). With a continuous incoming stream of converted values, a waveform close to the original can be reconstructed, as shown in Figure 3-27.

Sometimes this reconstructed waveform is not a good reproduction of the original. What can be done to increase the accuracy of the reproduced waveform? As you have already seen, you might be able to increase the number of quantization levels on the y-axis. Also, the closer the snapshots are taken to one another (the smaller the time intervals between snapshots, or the finer the resolution), the more accurate the reconstructed waveform will be. Figure 3-28 shows a reconstruction that is closer to the original analog waveform. Once again, however, you do not get something for nothing. To take the snapshots at shorter time intervals, the codec must be of high-enough quality to track the incoming signal quickly and perform the necessary conversions. And the more snapshots taken per second, the more binary data generated per second. The frequency at which the snapshots are taken is called the sampling rate. If the codec takes samples at an unnecessarily high sampling rate, it will expend much energy for little gain in the resolution of the waveform's reconstruction. Often, codec systems generate too few samples—use a low sampling rate—which reconstructs a wave form that is not an accurate reproduction of the original.

What is the optimal balance between too high a sampling rate and too low? According to a famous communications theorem created by Harry Nyquist, the sampling

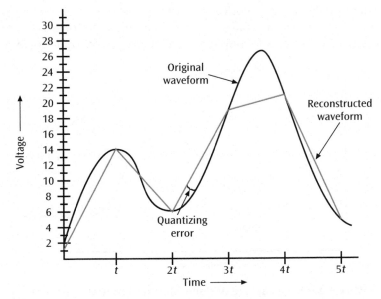

Figure 3-27   Reconstruction of the analog waveform from the digital "snapshots"

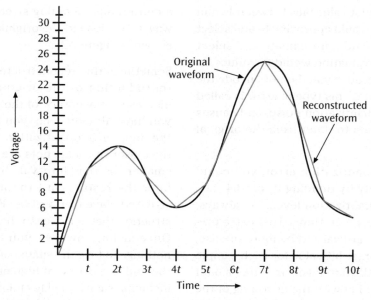

Figure 3-28 A more accurate reconstruction of the original waveform using a higher sampling rate

rate using pulse code modulation should be twice the highest frequency of the original analog waveform to ensure a reasonable reproduction. Using the telephone system as an example and assuming that the highest possible voice frequency is 3400 Hz, the sampling rate should be 6800 samples per second to ensure reasonable reproduction of the analog waveform. The telephone system actually allocates a 4000-Hz channel for a voice signal, and thus samples at 8000 times per second.

Delta Modulation

A second method of analog data-to-digital signal conversion is delta modulation. Figure 3-29 shows an example. With **delta modulation**, a codec tracks the incoming

analog data by assessing up or down "steps." During each time period, the codec determines whether the waveform has risen one delta step or dropped one delta step. If the waveform rises one delta step, a 1 is transmitted. If the waveform drops one delta step, a 0 is transmitted. With this encoding technique, only 1 bit per sample is generated. Thus, the conversion from analog to digital using delta modulation is quicker than with pulse code modulation, in which each analog value is first converted to a PAM value, and then the PAM value is converted to binary.

Two problems are inherent with delta modulation. If the analog waveform rises or drops too quickly, the codec may not be able to keep up with the change, and

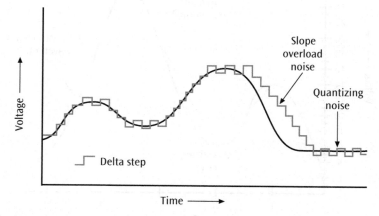

Figure 3-29 Example of delta modulation that is experiencing slope overload noise and quantizing noise

slope overload noise results. What if a device is trying to digitize a voice or music that maintains a constant frequency and amplitude, like one person singing one note at a steady volume? Analog waveforms that do not change at all present another problem for delta modulation. Because the codec outputs a 1 or a 0 only for a rise or a fall, respectively, a nonchanging waveform generates a pattern of 1010101010..., thus generating quantizing noise. Figure 3-29 demonstrates delta modulation and shows both slope overload noise and quantizing noise.

Details | The Relationship Between Frequency and Bits per Second

"Why is this network so slow? It's taking forever to download!" When a network application is slow, users often demand that someone, such as a network engineer, do *something* to make things go faster. What you now understand is that, in order to send data at a faster rate, one of two things must change: (1) the data must be transmitted with a higher-frequency signal, or (2) more bits per baud must be transmitted. Furthermore, neither of these solutions will work unless the medium that transmits the signal is capable of supporting the higher frequencies.

Note

It's important to understand the difference between the speed at which a signal travels along a cable or wireless connection versus the speed at which data is transmitted across that connection. Throughout this chapter, you've read about the delays caused by converting data to signals and back again, and the complications that arise when communicating data through a signal. At the same time, the signal itself experiences small delays. Although electrons travel rapidly, they still must travel, and a brief delay takes place between the instant when a signal leaves its source and when it arrives at its destination. These various delays collectively are referred to as **latency**. Other factors can also increase latency, such as cable limitations, number of transfers between devices, noise in the network, traffic congestion overwhelming network devices, processing delays, collisions with other messages, and conversion from one type of transmission to another.

To begin to understand all these interdependencies, it is helpful to both understand the relationship between bits per second and the frequency of a signal, and to

be able to use two simple measures—Nyquist's theorem and Shannon's theorem—to calculate the data transfer rate of a system.

An important relationship exists between the frequency of a signal and the number of bits a signal can convey per second: the greater the frequency of a signal, the higher the possible data transfer rate. The converse is also true: the higher the desired data transfer rate, the greater the needed signal frequency. You can see a direct relationship between the frequency of a signal and the transfer rate (in bits per second, or bps) of the data that a signal can carry. Consider the amplitude modulation encoding, shown twice in Figure 3-30, of the bit string 1010.... In the first part of Figure 3-30, the signal (amplitude) changes four times during a one-second period (baud rate equals 4). The frequency of this signal is 8 Hz (eight complete cycles in one second), and the data transfer rate is 4 bps. In the second part of the figure, the signal changes amplitude eight times (baud rate equals 8) during a one-second period. The frequency of the signal is 16 Hz, and the data transfer rate is 8 bps. As the frequency of the signal increases, the data transfer rate (in bps) increases.

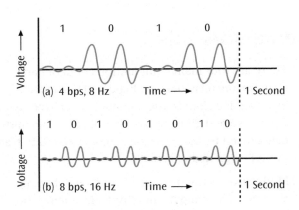

Figure 3-30 Comparison of signal frequency with bits per second

This example is simple because it contains only two signal levels (amplitudes), one for a binary 0 and one for a binary 1. What if you had an encoding technique with four signal levels, as shown in Figure 3-31? Because there are four signal levels, each signal level can represent two bits. More precisely, the first signal level can represent a binary 00, the second a binary 01, the third a binary 10, and the fourth signal level a binary 11. Now when the signal level changes, two bits of data will be transferred.

Two formulas express the direct relationship between the frequency of a signal and its data transfer rate: Nyquist's theorem and Shannon's theorem. **Nyquist's theorem** calculates the data transfer rate of a signal using its frequency and the number of signaling levels:

$$\text{Data rate} = 2 \times f \times \log_2 (L)$$

in which the data rate is in bits per second (the channel capacity), f is the frequency of the signal, and L is the number of signaling levels. For example, given

a 3100-Hz signal and two signaling levels (like a high amplitude and a low amplitude), the resulting channel capacity is 6200 bps, which results from $2 \times 3100 \times \log_2 (2) = 2 \times 3100 \times 1$. Be careful to use $\log_2$ and not $\log_{10}$. (If your calculator does not have a $\log_2$ key, as most do not, you can always approximate an answer by taking the $\log_{10}$ and then divide by 0.301.) A 3100-Hz signal with four signaling levels yields 12,400 bps. Note further that the Nyquist formula does not incorporate noise, which is always present. Thus, many use the Nyquist formula not to solve for the data rate, but instead, given the data rate and frequency, to solve for the number of signal levels L.

Shannon's theorem calculates the maximum data transfer rate of an analog signal (with any number of signal levels) and incorporates noise:

$$\text{Data rate} = f \times \log_2 (1 + S / N)$$

in which the data rate is in bits per second, f is the frequency of the signal, S is the power of the signal in watts, and N is the power of the noise in watts. Consider a 3100-Hz signal with a power level of 0.2 watts and a noise level of 0.0002 watts:

$$\text{Data rate} = 3100 \times \log_2 (1 + 0.2 / 0.0002)$$
$$= 3100 \times \log_2 (1001)$$
$$= 3100 \times 9.97$$
$$= 30{,}901 \ \text{bps}$$

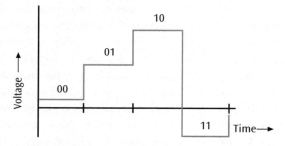

Figure 3-31   Hypothetical signaling technique with four signal levels

Remember this...

> There are four main combinations of data and signals transmissions: analog data transmitted using analog signals, digital data transmitted using square-wave digital signals, digital data transmitted using discrete analog signals, and analog data transmitted using digital signals.

> Modulation is the process of sending data over a signal by varying its amplitude, frequency, or phase. In the modulation process, the original audio waveform and the carrier wave are essentially added together to produce the third waveform.

> To transmit digital data using square-wave digital signals, the 1s and 0s of the digital data must be converted to the proper physical form that can be transmitted over a wire or an airwave. Digital encoding schemes convert the 0s and 1s of digital data into the appropriate transmission form. Five digital encoding schemes that are representative of most digital encoding schemes are NRZ-L, NRZI, Manchester code, differential Manchester code, and 4B/5B.

> The technique of converting digital data to an analog signal is also an example of modulation. But in this type of modulation, the analog signal takes on a discrete number of signal levels. Thus, even though

they are fundamentally analog signals, they operate with a discrete number of levels, much like a digital signal.

>Analog data often must be converted to digital signals so the original data can be transmitted through a computer system and eventually stored in memory or on a storage disk. PCM (pulse code modulation) converts the analog data to a digital signal by tracking the analog waveform and taking "snapshots" of the analog data at fixed intervals. With delta modulation, a codec tracks the incoming analog data by assessing up or down "steps."

Self-check

4. When a traffic light is green, it means you can go. When a traffic light is red, it means you must stop. Which digital encoding scheme does this analogy illustrate?

    a. NRZI

    b. Manchester code

    c. NRZ-L

    d. Differential Manchester code

5. What is one advantage Manchester codes offer over NRZ schemes?

    a. NRZ schemes offer a baud rate equal to the data rate.

    b. Manchester codes are better synchronized.

    c. Manchester codes are cheaper to implement in hardware.

    d. NRZ schemes are more resistant to noise and errors.

6. Which shift keying technique is most resistant to noise?

    a. FSK

    b. QSK

    c. ASK

    d. PSK

Check your answers at the end of this chapter.

Section 3-3: Characters and Codes

One of the most common forms of data transmitted between a transmitter and a receiver is textual data. For example, banking institutions that wish to transfer money often transmit textual information, such as account numbers, names of account owners, bank names, addresses, and the amount of money to be transferred. This textual information is transmitted as a sequence of characters. To distinguish one character from another, each character is represented by a unique binary pattern of 1s and 0s. The set of all textual characters or symbols and their corresponding binary patterns is called a **character set**. The most popular character set used to be ASCII; however, this standard presents some significant problems and has been augmented by the Unicode standard. Let's examine each of these to see how one builds on the other.

ASCII

ASCII (American Standard Code for Information Interchange), pronounced "askee," is a government standard in the United States and is one of the most widely used data codes in the world. The ASCII character set exists in a few different forms, including a 7-bit version that allows for 128 ($2^7 = 128$) possible combinations of textual symbols representing uppercase and lowercase letters, digits 0 to 9, special symbols, and control characters. Because the byte, which consists of 8 bits, is a common unit of data, the 7-bit version of ASCII characters usually includes an eighth bit. This eighth bit can be used to detect transmission errors (a topic that will be discussed in Chapter 4). Alternately, it can provide for 128 additional characters defined by the application using the ASCII code set, or it can simply be a binary 0. Figure 3-32 shows the ASCII character set and the corresponding 7-bit values.

To send the message "Transfer $1200.00" using 7-bit ASCII, the corresponding bits would be those shown in Figure 3-33.

Unicode

One of the major problems with ASCII is that it cannot represent symbols other than those found in the English language. It cannot even represent all the different types of symbols in the English language, such as many of the technical symbols used in engineering and mathematics. What if you need to represent characters from other languages around the world? In the interest of internationalization of web standards, you need a more robust character set—Unicode. **Unicode** is a more robust standard that provides a unique coding value, or code point, for every character in every language, no matter the platform. Currently, Unicode supports nearly 145,000 unique characters covering the world's languages,

Low-order bits (4, 3, 2, 1)	High-order bits (7, 6, 5)							
	000	001	010	011	100	101	110	111
0000	NUL	DLE	SPACE	0	@	P	`	p
0001	SOH	DC1	!	1	A	Q	a	q
0010	STX	DC2	"	2	B	R	b	r
0011	ETX	DC3	#	3	C	S	c	s
0100	EOT	DC4	$	4	D	T	d	t
0101	ENQ	NAK	%	5	E	U	e	u
0110	ACK	SYN	&	6	F	V	f	v
0111	BEL	ETB	'	7	G	W	g	w
1000	BS	CAN	(	8	H	X	h	x
1001	HT	EM	)	9	I	Y	i	y
1010	LF	SUB	*	:	J	Z	j	z
1011	VT	ESC	+	;	K	[	k	{
1100	FF	FS	'	<	L	\	l	|
1101	CR	GS	-	=	M	]	m	}
1110	SO	RS	.	>	N	^	n	~
1111	SI	US	/	?	O	—	o	DEL

Figure 3-32 The ASCII character set

101 0100	111 0010	110 0001	110 1110	111 0011	110 0110
T	r	a	n	s	f
110 0101	111 0010	010 0000	010 0100	011 0001	011 0010
e	r	[space]	$	1	2
011 0000	011 0000	010 1110	011 0000	011 0000	
0	0	.	0	0	

Figure 3-33   ASCII bits for the message "Transfer $1200.00"

symbols, and even emojis. For example, the Greek symbol β has the Unicode value of hexadecimal 03B2 (binary 0000 0011 1011 0010). ASCII is one of those supported code charts and so is now a subset of Unicode. Many of the large computer companies such as Apple, HP, IBM, Microsoft, Oracle, Sun, and Unisys have adopted Unicode as have a large majority of websites globally. Because the list of all Unicode characters is so large, it's not shown here. If you are interested, you can view the Unicode website at *unicode.org*.

Returning to the example of sending a text-based message, if you sent "Transfer $1200.00" using Unicode, the corresponding characters in binary would be those shown in Figure 3-34.

All Things Considered

Thought Experiment

Using the ASCII and Unicode character code sets, what are the binary encodings of the message "Hello, world"?

0000 0000 0101 0100	T
0000 0000 0111 0010	r
0000 0000 0110 0001	a
0000 0000 0110 1110	n
0000 0000 0111 0011	s
0000 0000 0110 0110	f
0000 0000 0110 0101	e
0000 0000 0111 0010	r
0000 0000 0010 0000	space
0000 0000 0010 0100	$
0000 0000 0011 0001	1
0000 0000 0011 0010	2
0000 0000 0011 0000	0
0000 0000 0011 0000	0
0000 0000 0010 1110	.
0000 0000 0011 0000	0
0000 0000 0011 0000	0

Figure 3-34   Unicode bits for the message "Transfer $1200.00"

Interestingly, Unicode is a global character set that matches each character to a code point (numerical value), but it does not define how each code point should be grouped into bits and bytes on a computer network or file like a web page. This step requires a character encoding scheme to determine number of bits or bytes per character and how to use bit spaces efficiently to avoid all those leading 0s you see in Figure 3-34. Two Unicode character encoding schemes still used today are UTF-8 and UTF-16, with UTF-8 being by far the more popular. UTF-8 dedicates one to four 8-bit bytes for each symbol in the Unicode character set. ASCII symbols can all be represented with a single UTF-8 byte, while other symbols require at least two bytes. UTF-16 takes a similar approach in using two or four bytes per symbol. UTF-16 is less efficient for ASCII characters, which are the primary characters used for most web pages written in English and other common languages, but it can be more efficient with the symbols of certain other languages.

The character encoding set is defined in a web page's header where **HTML (Hypertext Markup Language)**, which is the programming language used to build web pages, lists the charset attribute. This way, a web client knows how to map each bit combination in the page's content to Unicode code points. For example, the HTML code at the beginning of Google's home page, as shown in Figure 3-35, lists the charset attribute to specify the character encoding as UTF-8. This ensures that both web server and web client use the same key, so to speak, to match bit combinations to Unicode code points.

Remember this...

> The set of all textual characters or symbols and their corresponding binary patterns is called a character set. Two important character sets are ASCII and Unicode.

> The ASCII character set exists in a few different forms, including a 7-bit version that allows for

128 ($2^7 = 128$) possible combinations of textual symbols representing uppercase and lowercase letters, digits 0 to 9, special symbols, and control characters.

> One of the major problems with ASCII is that it cannot represent symbols other than those found in the English language or many of the technical symbols used in engineering and mathematics.

> Unicode is a more robust character set that provides a unique coding value for every character in every language, no matter the platform.

> Unicode does not define how each code point should be translated into bits on a computer network or file like a web page. This step requires a character encoding scheme. Two Unicode character encoding schemes still used today are UTF-8 and UTF-16, with UTF-8 being by far the more popular.

Self-check

7. Which character set contains the most symbols?
   a. Unicode
   b. UTF-8
   c. ASCII
   d. UTF-16

8. You're designing a website for your small business. Which character encoding scheme is most likely to be compatible with all the symbols you'll need while providing the most efficient use of hardware resources for your English-language website?
   a. ASCII
   b. UTF-8
   c. UTF-16
   d. Unicode

Check your answers at the end of this chapter.

```
<!DOCTYPE html>
<html itemscope itemtype="http://schema.org/WebPage" lang="en">
▼ <head>
    <meta charset="UTF-8">
    <meta content="origin" name="referrer">
    <meta content="At65Ued/
```

This web page uses the UTF-8 character encoding scheme

Source: Google LLC

Figure 3-35 The charset attribute in the HTML header specifies the character encoding scheme used for this web page

Summary

Section 3-1: Data and Signals

> Data conveys meaning while signals are electric or electromagnetic impulses used to encode and transmit data. Both data and signals can exist in analog or digital forms.

> Analog data and analog signals are represented as continuous waveforms that can be at an infinite number of points between some given minimum and maximum. Digital data and digital signals are composed of a discrete or fixed number of values, rather than a continuous or infinite number of values.

> Analog signals are represented by sine waves, which are defined by their amplitude, frequency, and phase.

> When traveling through any type of medium, a signal always experiences some loss of its power due to friction. This loss of power, or loss of signal strength, is called attenuation. Attenuation in a medium such as copper wire is a logarithmic loss in which a value decrease of 1 represents a tenfold decrease, and it's a function of distance and the resistance within the wire.

Section 3-2: Converting Data into Signals

> There are four main combinations of transmitting data and signals: analog data transmitted using analog signals, digital data transmitted using square-wave digital signals, digital data transmitted using discrete analog signals, and analog data transmitted using digital signals.

> Modulation is the process of sending data over a signal by varying its amplitude, frequency, or phase. In the modulation process, the original audio waveform and the carrier wave are essentially added together to produce the third waveform.

> To transmit digital data using square-wave digital signals, the 1s and 0s of the digital data must be converted to the proper physical form that can be transmitted over a wire or an airwave. Digital encoding schemes convert the 0s and 1s of digital data into the appropriate transmission form. Five digital encoding schemes that are representative of most digital

encoding schemes are NRZ-L, NRZI, Manchester code, differential Manchester code, and 4B/5B.

> The technique of converting digital data to an analog signal is also an example of modulation. But in this type of modulation, the analog signal takes on a discrete number of signal levels. Thus, even though they are fundamentally analog signals, they operate with a discrete number of levels, much like a digital signal.

> Analog data often must be converted to digital signals so the original data can be transmitted through a computer system and eventually stored in memory or on a storage disk. PCM (pulse code modulation) converts the analog data to a digital signal by tracking the analog waveform and taking "snapshots" of the analog data at fixed intervals. With delta modulation, a codec tracks the incoming analog data by assessing up or down "steps."

Section 3-3: Characters and Codes

> The set of all textual characters or symbols and their corresponding binary patterns is called a character set. Two important character sets are ASCII and Unicode.

> The ASCII character set exists in a few different forms, including a 7-bit version that allows for 128 ($2^7 = 128$)

possible combinations of textual symbols representing uppercase and lowercase letters, digits 0 to 9, special symbols, and control characters.

> One of the major problems with ASCII is that it cannot represent symbols other than those found in the

English language or many of the technical symbols used in engineering and mathematics.

› Unicode is a more robust character set that provides a unique coding value for every character in every language, no matter the platform.

› Unicode does not define how each code point should be translated into bits on a computer network or file like a web page. This step requires a character encoding scheme. Two Unicode character encoding schemes still used today are UTF-8 and UTF-16, with UTF-8 being by far the more popular.

Key Terms

For definitions of key terms, see the Glossary near the end of the book.

4B/5B

amplification

amplitude

analog data

analog signal

ASCII (American Standard Code for Information Interchange)

ASK (amplitude shift keying)

bandwidth

baud rate

bps (bits per second)

character set

codec

data

data rate

dB (decibel)

delta modulation

differential Manchester code

digital data

digital signal

digitization

effective bandwidth

frequency

FSK (frequency shift keying)

HTML (Hypertext Markup Language)

latency

Manchester code

modulation

noise

NRZI (nonreturn to zero inverted)

NRZ-L (nonreturn to zero-level)

Nyquist's theorem

PCM (pulse code modulation)

period

phase

PSK (phase shift keying)

QAM (quadrature amplitude modulation)

QPSK (quadrature phase shift keying)

self-clocking

Shannon's theorem

signal

spectrum

Unicode

Review Questions

1. Which of the following is an example of data?

    a. Cellular connection between your smartphone and the cell tower

    b. Bits saved on your hard drive

    c. Light pulses on a fiber-optic cable

    d. Wi-Fi signal transmitted through your house

2. What is the essential difference between continuous signals and discrete signals?

    a. Number of values within the signal

    b. Type of data the signal can carry

    c. Presence of noise

    d. Waveform shape

3. What is a primary advantage of digital signals over analog signals?

    a. Increased complexity

    b. Infinite number of values

    c. Can transmit analog data

    d. Decreased noise

4. Which of the following is *NOT* a basic component of all signals?

    a. Frequency

    b. Phase

    c. Bandwidth

    d. Amplitude

5. What is the frequency in Hz of a signal that repeats 75,000 times in one minute?

    a. 3100 Hz

    b. 1333 Hz

    c. 3400 Hz

    d. 1250 Hz

6. What is the period in seconds of a signal that repeats 75,000 times in one minute?

    a. .0008 second

    b. .006 second

    c. .00075 second

    d. 1 second

7. What is the spectrum of the human voice?

    a. 4200 Hz

    b. 300 Hz to 3400 Hz

    c. 30 Hz to 4200 Hz

    d. 3100 Hz

8. What is the bandwidth of a Wi-Fi channel whose lowest frequency is 2401 MHz (megahertz) and highest frequency is 2423 MHz?

    a. 24 MHz

    b. 2.4 GHz

    c. 22 MHz

    d. 5 GHz

9. A signal starts at point X. As it travels to point Y, it loses 8 dB. At point Y, the signal is boosted by 10 dB. As the signal travels to point Z, it loses 5 dB. What is the dB strength of the signal at point Z?

    a. −5 dB

    b. 13 dB

    c. −3 dB

    d. 7 dB

10. If a signal starts with a strength of 60 watts and experiences a 3-dB loss in transit to the receiver, what is the power level of the signal at the receiver?

    a. 30 watts

    b. 180 watts

    c. 57 watts

    d. 120 watts

11. Incorporating self-clocking in an encoding scheme resulted in a higher _____.

    a. bit rate

    b. data rate

    c. baud rate

    d. transmission rate

12. Which encoding scheme has the lowest baud rate?

    a. NRZ-L

    b. Manchester code

    c. 4B/5B

    d. 128B/132B

13. What is the equivalent 4B/5B code of the bit string 0001 1000?

    a. 11110 01001

    b. 01001 10010

    c. 01001 01111

    d. 01001 11011

14. Which type of shift keying can provide the highest data rates?

    a. 8-PSK

    b. ASK

    c. QPSK

    d. FSK

15. If 16-QAM is used to transmit a signal with a baud rate of 10,000, what is the corresponding data transfer rate?

    a. 2,000 bps

    b. 2,500 bps

    c. 32,000 bps

    d. 40,000 bps

16. Which of the following statements is true?

    a. AM radio uses ASK.

    b. FM radio uses FSK.

    c. Wi-Fi uses QAM.

    d. Cell towers use PAM.

```
geoz.js ></script>
▶ <style>…</style>
  <meta charset="utf-8">
  <meta name="viewport" content="width=device-width, initial-scale=1">
  <title>Digital Learning & Online Textbooks – Cengage</title>
  <script async src="https://www.googletagmanager.com/gtm.js?id=GTM-5ZZ9XQ9">
  </script>
▶ <script>…</script>
  <meta name="description" content="Cengage leads affordable learning:
  digital learning platforms, college textbooks, ebooks, and an unlimited
  subscription to over 22,000 digital products for one price.">
  <meta name="keywords" content="Cengage, digital learning, online textbooks,
  learning materials, online learning">
  <meta property="og:type" content="article">
  <meta property="og:title" content="Cengage Learning">
  <meta property="og:image" content="https://embed.widencdn.net/img/cengage/
```

Figure 3-36   HTML header for the Cengage home page

17. Using Shannon's theorem, calculate the data transfer rate to the nearest whole number given the following information:

    > Signal frequency = 10,000 Hz
    > Signal power = 2000 watts
    > Noise power = 180 watts

    a. 10,832 bps
    b. 45,076 bps
    c. 13,568 bps
    d. 35,986 bps

18. Which of these symbols is *NOT* part of the ASCII character set?

    a. Á
    b. @
    c. 9
    d. A

19. How many UTF-8 bytes are used for the Unicode symbol U+0041, which represents the English letter A?

    a. One
    b. Two
    c. Three
    d. Four

20. Based on the information shown in Figure 3-36, what character encoding scheme does the Cengage website use?

    a. ASCII
    b. Unicode
    c. UTF-8
    d. UTF-16

Hands-On Project 3

Latency around the World

Estimated time: 20 minutes

Resources:
> Internet access

❭ Context:

To communicate with devices on other networks—even around the world—your message must traverse a number of other devices, including several routers. The protocol IP (Internet Protocol) tracks the number of jumps or hops a message takes along the way to its destination. Each of these hops requires a tiny bit of time as the signal crosses each connection and is processed by each device to interpret the data within the signal. In this chapter, you learned that latency is the collective delay caused by the time it takes messages to travel between its source and its destination. This concept is easy to see in the real world, where it takes longer, for example, for you to travel across the country than it does to go down the street to the grocery store. Even though network messages travel much faster than a car or a jet plane, it still takes time for them to get from one place to another. And then the response must also travel across a similar number of hops, resulting in a longer RTT (round trip time).

In this project, you'll enter commands at a CLI (command line interface) to interact with your Windows computer and routers around the world. Typically you use a GUI (graphical user interface) to interact with your computer, such as the windows you click to browse to a website or open an email. A CLI can provide functionality you can't access through the GUI.

To see how distance affects a message's RTT, complete the following steps:

1. To open a CLI, right-click **Start** and click either **Windows PowerShell** or **Command Prompt**, depending on which of these tools is available by default in your Start menu.

2. The `tracert` command measures the latency from your location to each router along a path to a specific target. For example, if your message must cross three routers to reach a web server, `tracert` will tell you the latency to each of those routers and to the web server itself. To practice, type **tracert google.com** and press **Enter**. What results do you get? Do you recognize the location for any of the routers in the reported path? How can you tell where these routers are located?

3. Enter `tracert` on a website whose servers are located on a different continent from your location—across one ocean. For example, if you're located in the Midwest or Eastern United States, you can run the command **tracert london.edu** (London Business School). If you are on the West Coast, however, you might get more useful results for this step by targeting a server across the Pacific Ocean, such as **tracert www.tiu.ac.jp** (Tokyo International University). What command did you use?

4. Examine the output and find the point in the route when messages started jumping across the ocean. By what percentage does the RTT increase after the jump compared with before it? You can see an example in Figure 3-37.

   To calculate the percentage for this jump, select a time from just after the jump (129, for example) and divide it by a time from just before the jump (such as 27), then multiply by 100 percent: 129/27 × 100% = 478%. In this case, the sample data yields a 478 percent increase. It takes nearly five times as long for a message to go round-trip across the Atlantic from the United States to London, England (the location of this first European router) as

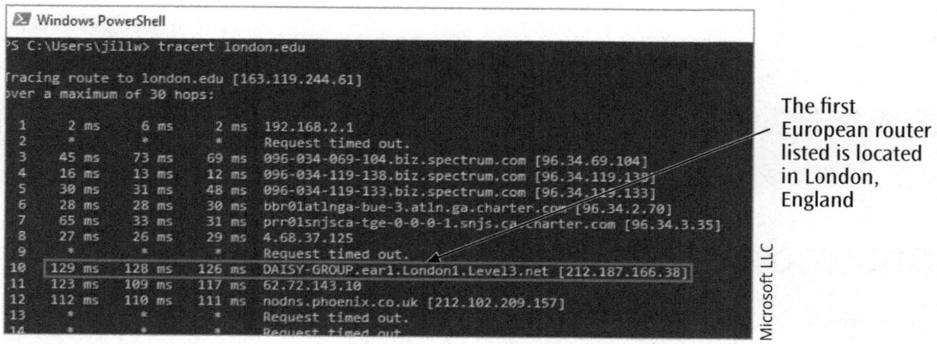

The first European router listed is located in London, England

Figure 3-37 The latency time increases significantly as messages start to cross the ocean

it does for a message to travel round trip between two servers that are both located on the U.S. East Coast (this local computer and the last U.S. router in the route).

5. Choose a website whose servers are on a continent even farther away from you. For example, if you are in the United States, you could trace the route to the University of Delhi in India at the address **du.ac.in**. What command did you use? How many hops did it take until the route crossed an ocean? What other anomalies do you notice about this global route?

6. Choose one more website as close to directly across the globe from you as possible. U.S. locations might want to use the University of Western Australia at **uwa.edu.au**. What command did you use? How many hops are in the route? Did the route go east or west around the world from your location? How can you tell?

7. Scott Base in Antarctica runs several webcams from various research locations. Run a trace to the Scott Base website at **antarcticanz.govt.nz**. What's the closest router to Scott Base's web server that your trace reached? If you can't tell from the command output where the last response came from, go to **iplocation.net** in your browser. Enter the final hop's IP address to determine that router's location.

8. Think about other locations around the world that might be reached through an interesting geographical route, such as traversing a place you would like to visit or tapping routers in an exotic location. Find a website hosted in that location and trace the route to it. Which website did you target? Where is it located? What are some router locations along the route of your trace? **Take a screenshot** of the output for your trace; submit this visual with your answers to this project's questions.

Reflection Discussion 3

Harry Nyquist and Claude Shannon developed their maximum data rate theorems in the mid-twentieth century, which was a busy time for data communications formulas and theorems. Noiseless and noisy data rates weren't the only issues being explored, defined, and theorized. Nyquist and Shannon are both famous for other theorems and conceptual work as well, including Nyquist's sampling theorem that sometimes is more aptly associated with Shannon and other researchers.

In this chapter, you learned about the importance of sampling rate in converting analog waveforms into digital data. Do some research online about the Nyquist-Shannon sampling theorem, then respond to the following questions:

› What does the Nyquist-Shannon theorem indicate?

› Who are the other researchers who contributed to the discovery of this principle?

› How is this principle useful in creating digital music recordings?

Go to the discussion forum in your school's LMS (learning management system). Write a post of at least 100 words discussing your thoughts about the Nyquist-Shannon theorem in response to the above questions. Then respond to two of your classmates' threads with posts of at least 50 words discussing their comments and ideas. Use complete sentences, and check your grammar and spelling. Try to ask open-ended questions that encourage discussion, and remember to respond to people who post on your thread. Use the rubric in Table 3-2 to help you understand what is expected of your work for this assignment.

Table 3-2 Grading rubric for Reflection Discussion 3

Task	Novice	Competent	Proficient	Earned
Initial post	Generalized statements about the Nyquist-Shannon theorem **30 points**	Some specific statements with supporting evidence about the Nyquist-Shannon theorem, the contributing researchers, and the effect on digital music **40 points**	Self-reflective discussion with specific and thoughtful statements and supporting evidence describing the Nyquist-Shannon sampling theorem, identification of at least four contributing researchers, and a clear and thorough statement explaining the effects of the sampling theorem on the parameters of recording music in digital format **50 points**	
Initial post: Mechanics	• Length < 100 words • Several grammar and spelling errors **5 points**	• Length = 100 words • Occasional grammar and spelling errors **7 points**	• Length > 100 words • Appropriate grammar and spelling **10 points**	
Response 1	Brief response showing little engagement or critical thinking **5 points**	Detailed response with specific contributions to the discussion **10 points**	Thoughtful response with specific examples or details and open-ended questions that invite deeper discussion of the topic **15 points**	
Response 2	Brief response showing little engagement or critical thinking **5 points**	Detailed response with specific contributions to the discussion **10 points**	Thoughtful response with specific examples or details and open-ended questions that invite deeper discussion of the topic **15 points**	
Both responses: Mechanics	• Length < 50 words each • Several grammar and spelling errors **5 points**	• Length = 50 words each • Occasional grammar and spelling errors **7 points**	• Length > 50 words each • Appropriate grammar and spelling **10 points**	
			Total	

Solutions to Self-Check Questions

Section 3-1: Data and Signals

1. Which of the following is most analogous to data transmitted across a network connection?

Answer: b. Lyrics of a song

Explanation: Of all these options, only lyrics of a song conveys the meaning of a message.

2. Which of the following is most analogous to digital data?

Answer: d. Morse code sent by flashlight

Explanation: Of all these options, only Morse code sent by flashlight relies on a discrete or fixed number of values rather than a continuous or infinite number of values.

3. Amplitude is to frequency as:

Answer: a. The diameter of a bicycle wheel is to the speed of its rotation

Explanation: Amplitude is the height of a signal wave. This is similar to the diameter of a bicycle wheel, which defines how high and low a point on the wheel will travel as the wheel turns. Frequency is the number of times a cycle is completed in a given time frame, which is similar to the speed at which a bicycle wheel rotates.

Section 3-2: Converting Data into Signals

4. When a traffic light is green, it means you can go. When a traffic light is red, it means you must stop. Which digital encoding scheme does this analogy illustrate?

Answer: c. NRZ-L

Explanation: The NRZ-L digital encoding scheme gives one charge for a value of 1 and a different charge for a value of 0. This is similar to how a traffic light works, which shows one color for "go" and a different color for "stop."

5. What is one advantage Manchester codes offer over NRZ schemes?

Answer: b. Manchester codes are better synchronized.

Explanation: In the Manchester codes, there is always a transition in the middle of a bit. Thus, the receiver can expect a signal change at regular intervals and can synchronize itself with the incoming bit stream.

6. Which shift keying technique is most resistant to noise?

Answer: d. PSK

Explanation: Phase changes are not affected by amplitude changes, nor are they affected by intermodulation distortions. Thus, phase shift keying (PSK) is less susceptible to noise and can be used at higher frequencies than other types of shift keying. In fact, PSK is so accurate that the signal transmitter can increase efficiency by introducing multiple phase-shift angles, such as QPSK (quadrature phase shift keying).

Section 3-3: Characters and Codes

7. Which character set contains the most symbols?

Answer: a. Unicode

Explanation: Unicode is a robust standard that provides a unique coding value (called a code point) for every character in every language. Currently, Unicode supports nearly 145,000 unique characters covering the world's languages, symbols, and even emojis. ASCII, however, is limited to a maximum of 256 possible values. UTF-8 and UTF-16 are character encoding schemes, not character sets.

8. You're designing a website for your small business. Which character encoding scheme is most likely to be compatible with all the symbols you'll need while providing the most efficient use of hardware resources for your English and Spanish-language website?

Answer: b. UTF-8

Explanation: ASCII symbols, which are the primary characters used for most web pages written in English and other common languages, can all be represented with a single UTF-8 byte. UTF-16 is less efficient for ASCII characters.

Chapter 4

Frames and Errors

Objectives

After reading this chapter, you should be able to:

- Explain the components of data link layer frames

- Identify types of network noise that cause transmission errors

- Describe the strengths and limitations of various error detection techniques

- Compare error control techniques and appropriate uses of each type

Introduction

In Chapter 3, you learned how the physical layer transmits bits across a physical or wireless medium. However, the physical layer has no awareness of the meaning of the data bits being transmitted. At this layer, there only exists streams of bits. Connecting a computer to a device requires more than just resolving connections at the physical layer. It is also necessary to define the packaging of the data as it gets transferred between a computer and other devices. In general, the basic configuration of this packaging is determined by data link layer standards. In this chapter, you'll learn about the packaging employed by the data link layer, the problems that can happen to a message in transit, and ways the data link layer handles those problems.

Section 4-1: Data Link Frames

As you read in Chapter 2, interface standards define the physical connection between a computer and a peripheral or another device on a network, and these standards reside at the physical layer of the TCP/IP protocol suite. But there is more to creating a connection than just defining the various physical components.

To transmit data successfully between two points on a network, such as between a workstation and a network server, you also need to define the data link connections. This refers to how data is packaged for transmission across a network connection. For example, think about what happens when you send a letter through the mail. You must package the letter inside an envelope, which acts as a carrier for the message itself. A data frame functions in much the same way. Bits at the beginning and end of the data signal serve as a package for the data as it traverses a network connection. This package is called a frame with special bits added to both the beginning and the end of the data bits, thereby "framing" the data. If you once again relate this to the TCP/IP protocol suite, you will note that the data link connection is performed at the data link layer.

Data Link Responsibilities

To appreciate the issues involved in defining a data link connection, first assume that the physical layer connections are already defined by the type of medium being used. These protocols define aspects such as modulation or encoding. Now, given that the sender and receiver are using the same physical layer protocol, the next questions that must be resolved are as follows:

> Which device is the message intended for?

> What is the basic form of the data frame that is passed between sender and receiver?

> When can data be sent along the medium to avoid overlapping signals interfering with each other?

> How are errors detected and handled?

Questions such as these define the type of communication that happens at the data link layer. While examining the data link connection, recall the duties of the data link layer from the TCP/IP protocol suite—two of which are to create a frame of data for transmission between sender and receiver, and to provide some way of checking for errors during transmission. Keep these duties in mind throughout this chapter. For now, let's look at what information the frame adds to each packet.

Frame Components

When a message is first created by an application to be transmitted across a network, the data contained within that message is called the payload. As the payload travels down the TCP/IP layers, some of these layers add extra bits at the beginning of the payload that contain information needed for the same layer on the receiving end. These extra bits for each layer are called a header. Figure 4-1 shows the various layers' headers added to the front of a payload. Recall from Chapter 1 that this process of adding layers of information to the front of a payload is called encapsulation. Each layer's protocols add their own pieces of information to their own headers and then pass the message on to the next layer, which then adds its header. The result is that each message traversing a network is preceded by a series of headers representing the layers of network communication.

At the end of the data, a much shorter trailer closes the frame around the data.

What information does each header contain? The fields of each header vary depending on the protocol that creates the header. You'll learn more about header fields in later chapters. One primary piece of information, however, is related to addressing. For example, the transport, network, and data link layers each need to add addressing information. Why are three layers of addresses required? Consider the following layers of addressing:

> The transport layer contains the port number that identifies which application on the receiving computer should process the message, such as a web browser (typically port 80 or port 443) or an email client (typically port 143 or port 993 to receive email).

> The network layer contains the IP address that identifies the destination computer uniquely across multiple networks. For example, a group of Google's servers resides at the IP address 8.8.8.8, and this IP address is unique on the Internet. Any message addressed to this IP address will be directed to Google's servers. Traffic crossing multiple networks is handled by routers, and so routers read the network layer's header to identify the destination computer's IP address. This information helps routers determine which route a message should take to reach the network of its destination.

> The data link layer contains the MAC (media access control) address that identifies each device's network port uniquely on its local network. Traffic on a local network is handled by a switch. The switch reads the data link layer's header to find the MAC address of the next device to receive the message.

A tool called a packet sniffer, such as Wireshark (wireshark.org), can capture packets as they traverse a network. By analyzing these packet captures, you can determine which protocol is adding header bits and where these headers are located in comparison to other headers. Figure 4-2 shows a capture of a packet that contains an Ethernet header at the data link layer,

Synchronization bits	Data link layer header(s)	Network layer header(s)	Transport layer header(s)	Original data (payload)	Data link layer trailer

Figure 4-1 Example of network packet with layers of header bits

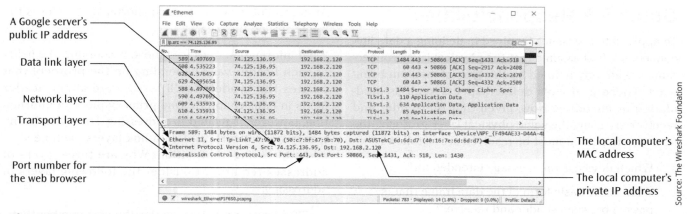

Figure 4-2 Wireshark capture of a network packet

Preamble	SFD (start frame delimiter)	Destination address	Source address	EtherType	Data (including important protocol information)	FCS (frame check sequence)
7 bytes of 10101010	10101011	6 bytes	6 bytes	2 bytes	46-1500 bytes	4 bytes

Physical layer spans Preamble and SFD. Data link layer spans Destination address through FCS.

Figure 4-3 Fields of an Ethernet header

an IP (Internet Protocol) header at the network layer, and a TCP (Transport Control Protocol) header at the transport layer. Also notice the transport layer's port number, the network layer's IP address, and the data link layer's MAC address.

The outermost header informs the receiver that an incoming data frame is arriving by starting with a preamble of alternating 1s and 0s, which allows the receiver to synchronize itself. Recall from Chapter 3 the importance of a receiver staying synchronized with the incoming data stream, especially if the data stream contains a long sequence of unchanging values. The fields in a header also contain flags that are each typically 8 or 16 bits in length (one or two bytes). Figure 4-3 shows the basic fields of an Ethernet header, which you'll learn more about in Chapter 5. Note that the "Data" portion inside the Ethernet frame also contains headers from higher-layer protocols.

Following the data and contained within the trailer is almost always some form of error detection and correction information, such as CRC (cyclic redundancy check). A message can sometimes encounter interference, which corrupts the integrity of the bits in the message. Other times, a message might collide with another message, which corrupts both messages. Each message, then, must contain information that the receiver can use to determine whether the message was corrupted

in transit. And in some cases, that information is sufficient for the receiver to correct the problem. You'll learn more about these technologies later in this chapter.

It might seem inefficient, but all these layers of headers and the trailer are added to every message before being transmitted onto the network media. Because each packet has its own sequencing, addressing, and error-checking information, a long message can be broken into smaller packets that can find their own route across a network, and then they're reassembled by the receiver. This kind of fragmentation—breaking longer messages into shorter messages for efficient travel—supports faster and more reliable network communication.

Remember this...

❯ Two functions of the data link layer are to create a frame of data for transmission between sender and receiver, and to provide some way of checking for errors during transmission.

❯ A data link layer frame consists of a header and a trailer surrounding the payload, which is the data contained within the message.

> The fields of each header vary depending on the protocol that creates the header. One primary piece of information is related to addressing. For example, the transport, network, and data link layers each need to add addressing information.

> Following the data and contained within the trailer is almost always some form of error detection and correction information. Each message must contain information that the receiver can use to determine whether the message was corrupted in transit. In some cases, that information is sufficient for the receiver to correct the problem.

Self-check

1. Which address identifies the receiving application?
    a. IP address
    b. Protocol
    c. MAC address
    d. Port

2. Which protocol adds a header at the network layer?
    a. IP
    b. Ethernet
    c. TCP
    d. Wi-Fi

3. In which part of a data link layer's frame can you find error checking information?
    a. Payload
    b. Outermost header
    c. Trailer
    d. Layer 2 header

Check your answers at the end of this chapter.

Section 4-2: Noise and Errors

The process of transmitting data over a medium often works according to Murphy's Law: if something can go wrong, it probably will. Even if all possible error-reducing measures are applied before and during data transmission, something will invariably alter the form of the original data. If this alteration is serious enough, the original data becomes corrupt, and the receiver does not receive the data that was originally transmitted. Even

with the highest-quality fiber-optic cable, noise eventually creeps in and begins to disrupt data transmission.

Noise is a problem for both analog and digital signals, and the transmission speed of the data can affect the significance of the noise. In fact, sometimes the influence of transmission speed is quite dramatic and can be easily demonstrated. Figure 4-4 shows a digital signal transmission at a relatively slow speed and at a relatively high speed. Notice in the figure that when the transmission speed is slower, you can still determine the value of a signal, but when the transmission speed increases, you can no longer determine whether the signal is a 0 or a 1.

Thus, despite one's best efforts to control noise, some noise is inevitable, and errors occur when the ratio of noise power to signal power becomes such that the noise overwhelms the signal. Given that noise is inevitable and errors happen, it is essential to detect error conditions. This chapter examines some of the more common error-detection methods and compares them in terms of efficiency and efficacy.

Before you begin to learn about error-detection techniques, it is vital that you understand the different forms of noise that commonly occur during data transmission. Having a better understanding of the different types of noise and what causes them to occur will enable you to apply noise-reduction techniques to communication systems and, thus, limit the amount of noise before it reaches the threshold at which errors occur.

As you might expect, several types of errors can occur during data transmission. From a simple blip to a massive outage, transmitted data—both analog and digital—is susceptible to many types of noise and errors. Copper-based media have traditionally been plagued by many types of interference and noise. Wireless transmissions of all kinds are also prone to interference and crosstalk. Even fiber-optic cables can introduce errors into a transmission system, although the probability of this happening is less than with other types of media. Let's examine several of the major types of noise that occur in transmission systems.

Gaussian Noise

Gaussian noise, which is also called thermal noise or white noise, is a relatively continuous type of noise and is much like the static you hear when a radio is being tuned between two stations. It is always present to some degree in transmission media and electronic devices, and it's dependent on the temperature of the

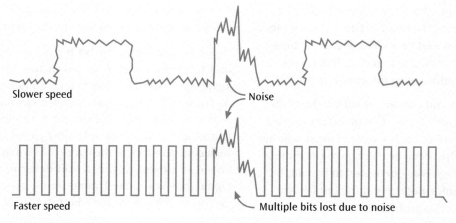

Figure 4-4   Transmission speed and its relationship to noise in a digital signal

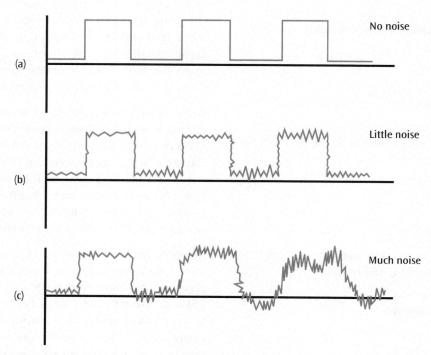

Figure 4-5   Gaussian noise as it interferes with a digital signal

medium. As the temperature increases, the level of noise increases due to the increased activity of the electrons in the medium. Because Gaussian noise is relatively continuous, it can be reduced significantly but never eliminated. Gaussian noise is the type of interference that makes an analog or digital signal become fuzzy (see Figure 4-5).

The process of reducing Gaussian noise from a digital signal is relatively straightforward if the signal is passed through a signal regenerator before the noise completely overwhelms the original signal. Reducing Gaussian noise from an analog signal is also possible to some

degree and involves passing the noisy analog signal through an appropriate set of filters, which (one hopes) leaves nothing but the original signal.

Impulse Noise

Impulse noise, or noise spike, is a noncontinuous noise and one of the most difficult errors to detect because it can occur randomly. The difficulty comes in separating the noise from the signal. Typically, the noise is an analog burst of energy. If the impulse spike interferes with an analog signal, removing it without affecting the original signal can be difficult. Recall the scratched record albums used as an example in Chapter 3. With albums, the impulse spikes correspond to the loud pops and clicks that are produced when an album is played and can interfere with some people's enjoyment of the music. For a second example of impulse noise, consider the plight of a small town in Wales where the residents consistently lost their Internet connection around 7:00 in the morning every day. After several months of investigations and replacing equipment and cabling, a team of engineers discovered in late 2020 that one resident's old television emitted a large burst of SHINE (single high-level impulse noise) when the owner turned it on every morning at 7. This caused line errors in the town's broadband connection and shut down the connection. As you can see, the intermittent nature of impulse noise can make it difficult and frustrating to track down the cause.

If impulse noise interferes with a digital signal, often the original digital signal can be recognized and recovered. When the noise completely obliterates the digital signal, the original signal cannot be recovered (see Figure 4-6).

Crosstalk

Crosstalk is an unwanted coupling between two different signal paths. This unwanted coupling can be electrical, as might occur between two sets of twisted pair wire (as in an Ethernet cable), or it can be electromagnetic (as when a microwave oven interferes with your home

Wi-Fi network). Telephone signal crosstalk was a more common problem when people used landlines more than cell phones, and before telephone companies used fiber-optic cables and other well-shielded wires. When crosstalk occurs during a phone conversation on a landline, you can hear another telephone conversation in the background, as shown in Figure 4-7. High humidity and wet weather can cause an increase in electrical crosstalk over an analog telephone system. Even though crosstalk is relatively continuous, it can be reduced with proper precautions and hardware.

Echo

Echo is the reflective feedback of a transmitted signal as the signal moves through a medium. Much like the way a voice will echo in an empty room, a signal can hit the end of a cable, bounce back through the wire, and interfere with the original signal. This error occurs most often at junctions where cables are connected, such as the back reflection on fiber-optic cables that you read about in Chapter 2. Figure 4-8 demonstrates a signal bouncing back from the end of a cable and creating an echo. To minimize the effect of echo, a device called an echo suppressor can be attached to a line. An echo suppressor is essentially a filter that allows the signal to pass in one direction only. For networks that use coaxial cable, a small filter is usually placed on the open end of each wire to absorb any incoming signals.

Time ————▶

Figure 4-6   The effect of impulse noise on a digital signal

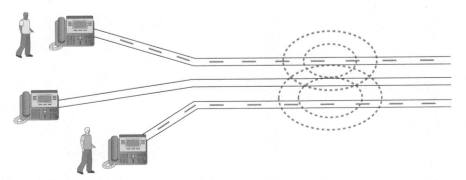

Figure 4-7   Three telephone circuits experiencing crosstalk

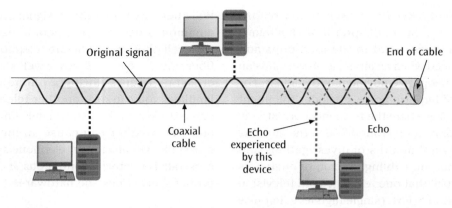

Figure 4-8 A signal bouncing back at the end of a coaxial cable and causing echo

Jitter

Jitter is the result of small timing irregularities that become magnified during the transmission of digital signals as the signals are passed from one device to another. To put it another way, when a digital signal is being transmitted, the rises and falls of the signal can start to shift, or become blurry, and thus produce jitter. If unchecked, jitter can cause video devices to flicker, audio transmissions to click and break up, and transmitted computer data to arrive with errors. If jitter becomes too great, correcting it can require the transmitting devices to slow down their transmission rates, which in turn limits overall system performance. Figure 4-9 shows a simplified example of a digital signal experiencing jitter.

Causes of jitter can include EMI (electromagnetic interference), crosstalk, passing the signal through too many repeaters, and the use of lower-quality equipment. Possible solutions to the jitter problem involve installing proper shielding, which can reduce or eliminate EMI and crosstalk, and limiting the number of times a signal is repeated.

Attenuation

Attenuation is the continuous loss of a signal's strength as it travels through a medium. It is not necessarily a form of error but can indirectly lead to an increase in errors affecting the transmitted signal. As you learned in Chapter 3, attenuation can be eliminated with the use of amplifiers for analog systems or repeaters for digital systems.

Error Prevention

Because there are so many forms of noise and errors, and because the presence of one form of noise or another in a system is virtually a given, every data transmission system must take precautions to reduce noise and the possibility of errors. An unfortunate side effect of noise during a transmission is that the transmitting station must slow down its transmission rate. For this reason, when a device first makes a connection with another device, the two devices participate in fallback negotiation. This means that, if the transmitting device sends data and the data arrives garbled, the receiving device may ask the

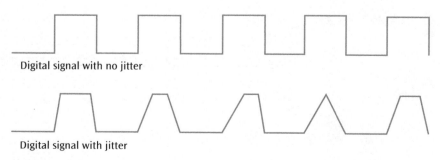

Figure 4-9 Original digital signal and a digital signal with jitter

transmitting device to fall back to a slower transmission speed. This slowdown creates a signal in which the bit duration of each 0 and 1 is longer—or in the case of QAM (quadrature amplitude modulation), a constellation diagram in which there are fewer discrete levels or targets—thus giving the receiver a better chance of distinguishing one value from the next, even in the presence of noise. If you can reduce the possibility of noise before it happens, however, the transmitting station may not have to slow down its transmission stream.

You can prevent the occurrence of many types of transmission errors by applying proper error-prevention techniques, including those listed here:

> Install wiring with the proper shielding to reduce EMI and crosstalk.

> Be aware that many types of wireless applications share the same wireless frequencies. Even some non-wireless devices generate signals that can interfere with wireless applications. For example, microwave ovens can interfere with some wireless LAN signals.

> Replace older equipment with more modern, digital equipment; although initially expensive, this technique is often the most cost-effective way to minimize transmission errors in the long run.

> Use the proper number of digital repeaters and analog amplifiers to increase signal strength, thus decreasing the probability of errors.

> Observe the stated capacities of a medium, and, to reduce the possibility of errors, avoid pushing transmission speeds beyond their recommended limits. For example, recall from Chapter 2 that twisted pair Category 5e/6 cable should not run longer than the recommended 100-meter (300-foot) distance when it is transmitting at 100 Mbps.

Reducing the number of devices, decreasing the length of cable runs, and reducing the transmission speed of the data can also be effective ways to reduce the possibility of errors. Although choices like these are not always desirable, sometimes they are the most reasonable alternatives available.

Table 4-1 lists the different types of errors that can arise and includes one or more possible error-prevention techniques for each.

Do not be fooled into believing that by simply applying various error-prevention techniques, errors will not happen. Appropriate error-detection methods still need to be implemented.

Remember this...

> Despite one's best efforts to control noise, some noise is inevitable. When the ratio of noise power to signal power becomes such that the noise overwhelms the signal, errors occur. It is at this point that error-detection techniques become valuable tools.

> Gaussian noise is a relatively continuous type of noise while impulse noise is a noncontinuous noise and one of the most difficult errors to detect because it can occur randomly. Noise is a problem for both analog and digital signals, and the transmission speed of the data can affect the significance of the noise.

> Crosstalk is an unwanted coupling between two different signal paths, while echo is the reflective feedback of a transmitted signal as the signal moves through a medium.

> Jitter is the result of small timing irregularities that become magnified during the transmission of digital signals as the signals are passed from one

Table 4-1 Summary of Errors and Error-Prevention Techniques

Type of Error	Error Prevention Technique
Gaussian noise	Install special filters for analog signals; implement digital signal regeneration for digital signals
Impulse noise	Install special filters for analog signals; implement digital signal processing for digital signals
Crosstalk	Install proper shielding on cables
Echo	Install proper termination on cables
Jitter	Use better-quality electronic circuitry; use fewer repeaters; slow the transmission speed
Attenuation*	Install device that amplifies analog signals; implement digital signal regeneration of digital signals

*Not a type of error, but indirectly affects error rates

device to another. Attenuation, which is not necessarily a form of error, is the continuous loss of a signal's strength as it travels through a medium.

Self-check

4. At which of these TCP/IP layers is error detection *not* typically performed?

   a. Transport

   b. Network

   c. Data link

   d. Physical

5. A forklift operating on the warehouse floor causes interference on the Wi-Fi network when it gets close to the data closet. What type of noise is this?

   a. Gaussian noise

   b. Echo

   c. Impulse noise

   d. Jitter

6. Which of the following techniques would *not* reduce noise on a network?

   a. Replace older equipment.

   b. Keep cable runs short.

   c. Choose highly shielded cables.

   d. Install cables close together.

Check your answers at the end of this chapter.

Section 4-3: Error Detection

Despite one's best attempts at prevention, errors will still occur. Because most data transferred over a communication line is important, it is usually necessary to apply an error-detection technique to the received data to ensure no errors were introduced into the data during transmission.

How do error detection and error-control fit into the TCP/IP suite introduced in Chapter 1? Most people associate error detection with the data link layer. When the data link layer creates a frame, it usually inserts an error-checking code after the data field. When the frame arrives at the next station, this error-checking code is extracted and the frame is checked for accuracy. Then, the data frame is reconstructed and sent to the next device in the transmission sequence. But the data link layer is not the only layer that performs some type of error detection. The transport layer also includes an

error-detection scheme. When the transport packet arrives at the final destination (and only the final destination), the receiver may extract an error-checking code from the transport header and perform error detection. Also, some network layer protocols, such as IP, include an error-detection code in the network layer header. In the case of IP, however, the error detection is performed on only the IP header and not the data field. Many applications also perform some type of error check such as detecting lost packets from a sequence of transmitted packets. For the moment, let's concentrate on the error-detection details covered in the data link and transport layers.

Regardless of where error detection is applied, all systems still recognize the importance of checking for transmission errors. The error-detection techniques themselves can be relatively simple or relatively elaborate. As you might expect, simple techniques do not provide the same degree of error checking as the more elaborate schemes. For example, the simplest error-detection technique is simple parity, which adds only a single parity bit to a character of data but catches the fewest number of errors. At the other end of the spectrum is the most elaborate and most effective technique available today: CRC (cyclic redundancy check). Not only is CRC more complex than simple parity, typically adding 8 to 32 check bits of error-detection code to a block of data, it is the most effective error-detection technique currently devised. This section will examine four error-detection techniques and evaluate their strengths and weaknesses.

Parity Checks

The most basic error-detection techniques are parity checks, which are more commonly used today with some types of data storage systems instead of for data transmission. Although there are various forms of single-character parity checking, one fact remains constant: Parity checks let too many errors slip through undetected. For this reason alone, parity checks are rarely, if ever, used on any kind of serious data transmissions. Despite this, two forms of parity checks—simple parity and longitudinal parity—do still exist and are worth examining.

Simple Parity

Simple parity, also known as vertical redundancy check, is the easiest error-detection method to incorporate into a transmission system. It comes in two basic forms:

even parity and odd parity. The basic concept of parity checking is that a bit is added to the end of a string of bits to create either even parity or odd parity. With even parity, the 0 or 1 added to the string produces an even number of binary 1s. With odd parity, the 0 or 1 added to the string produces an odd number of binary 1s. For example, if the 7-bit ASCII character set is used, a parity bit is added as the eighth bit. Suppose the character "k"—which is 1101011 in binary—is transmitted and even parity is being applied. In this case, a parity bit of 1 would be added to the end of the bit stream, as follows: 11010111. There is now an even number (six) of 1s. (If odd parity were used, a 0 would be added at the end, resulting in 11010110.)

Now, if a transmission error causes one of the bits to be flipped and a value is erroneously interpreted as a 0 instead of a 1, or vice versa, then the error can be detected if the receiver understands that it needs to check for even parity. Returning to the example of the character "k" sent with even parity, if you send 11010111 but 01010111 is received, the receiver will count the 1s, see that there is an odd number, and know there is an error.

What happens if 11010111 with even parity is sent and two bits are corrupted? For example, 00010111 is received. Will an error be detected? No, an error will not be detected because the number of 1s is still even. Simple parity can detect only an odd number of erroneous bits per character.

Note that, when the 7-bit ASCII character set is used, a parity bit is added for every 7 bits of data, resulting in a 1:7 ratio of parity bits to data bits. Thus, simple parity produces relatively high ratios of check bits to data bits, while achieving only mediocre (50 percent) error-detection results.

Longitudinal Parity

Longitudinal parity, also called longitudinal redundancy check, horizontal parity, or two-dimensional parity, tries to solve the main weakness of simple parity—that all even numbers of errors are not detected. To provide this extra level of protection, longitudinal parity needs to use additional parity check bits.

The first step of this parity scheme involves grouping individual characters together in a block, as shown in Figure 4-10.

	Data							Parity bit
Row 1	1	1	0	1	0	1	1	1
Row 2	1	1	1	1	1	1	1	1
Row 3	0	1	0	1	0	1	0	1
Row 4	0	0	1	1	0	0	1	1
Parity row	0	1	0	0	1	1	1	0

Figure 4-10   Simple example of longitudinal parity

Each character (also called a row) in the block has its own parity bit. In addition, after a certain number of characters are sent, a row of parity bits (also called a block character check) is also sent. Each parity bit in this last row is a parity check for all the bits in the column above it. If one bit is altered in Row 1, the parity bit at the end of Row 1 signals an error. In addition, the parity bit for the corresponding column also signals an error. If two bits in Row 1 are flipped, the Row 1 parity check will not signal an error, but two column parity checks will signal errors. This is how longitudinal parity is able to detect more errors than simple parity.

Note, however, that if two bits are flipped in Row 1 and two bits are flipped in Row 2, as shown in Figure 4-11, and the errors occur in the same column, no errors will be detected. This scenario is a limitation of longitudinal parity.

Although longitudinal parity provides an extra level of protection by using a double parity check, this method, like simple parity, also introduces a high number of check bits relative to data bits with only slightly better

	Data							Parity bit
Row 1	1	~~1~~0	~~0~~1	1	0	1	1	1
Row 2	1	~~1~~0	~~1~~0	1	1	1	1	1
Row 3	0	1	0	1	0	1	0	1
Row 4	0	0	1	1	0	0	1	1
Parity row	0	1	0	0	1	1	1	0

Figure 4-11   The second and third bits in Rows 1 and 2 have errors, but longitudinal parity does not detect the errors

than mediocre error-detection results. If n characters in a block are transmitted, the ratio of check bits to data bits is n+8:7n. For example, to transmit a 20-character block of data, a simple parity bit needs to be added to each of the 20 characters, plus a full 8-bit block character check is added at the end, producing a ratio of check bits to data bits that is 28:140, or 1:5.

Arithmetic Checksum

Many higher-level protocols on the Internet, such as TCP and IP, use a form of error detection in which the characters to be transmitted are "summed" together. This sum is then appended to the end of the message and the message is transmitted to the receiving end. The receiver accepts the transmitted message, performs the same summing operation, and essentially compares its sum with the sum that was generated by the transmitter. If the two sums agree, then no error occurred during the transmission. If the two sums do not agree, the receiver informs the transmitter that an error has occurred. Because the sum is generated by performing relatively simple arithmetic, this technique is often called **arithmetic checksum**.

More precisely, let's consider the following example. Suppose you want to transmit the message "This is cool." In ASCII, that message would appear in binary as: 1010100 1101000 1101001 1110011 0100000 1101001 1110011 0100000 1100011 1101111 1101111 1101100 0101110. (Do not forget the blanks between the words and the period at the end of the sentence.)

TCP and IP add these values in binary to create a binary sum. But binary addition of so many operands is a bit messy for humans to follow. Instead, you can convert the binary values to their decimal form to understand the basic concepts. You don't need to know binary to follow this example; the calculations are done for you as shown in Figure 4-12. (To see a complete calculation

Character	Binary value	Decimal value
T	1010100	84
h	1101000	104
i	1101001	105
s	1110011	115
<space>	0100000	32
i	1101001	105
s	1110011	115
<space>	0100000	32
c	1100011	99
o	1101111	111
o	1101111	111
l	1101100	108
	0101110	46
Total in decimal		1167

Figure 4-12 Binary values are converted to decimal and then added together

of the TCP/IP arithmetic checksum, read Details: Checksum Calculation Using Hexadecimal.)

The sum 1167 is then included in the outgoing message in binary form and sent to the receiver. The receiver will take the same characters, add their ASCII values, and if there were no errors during transmission, should get the same sum of 1167. Once again, the calculations in TCP and IP are performed in binary and the actual algorithm is more complex than what was shown here, but this provides a good foundation.

The arithmetic checksum is relatively easy to compute and does a fairly good job with error detection. Clearly, if noise messes up a bit or two during transmission, the receiver is more than likely not going to get the same sum. In an ideal scenario, it would be possible to "lower" the value of one character while "raising" the value of a second character so that the sum came out exactly the same. But the odds of that occurring are small.

Details | Checksum Calculation Using Hexadecimal

A more detailed example of how the arithmetic checksum is computed in TCP and IP might be helpful at this point. The binary calculations performed by TCP and IP are difficult for most humans to follow. So that you do not have to add all these binary values, first convert the binary values to their hexadecimal form. Hexadecimal converts easily with binary and, unlike decimal form,

maintains the separation of values within each byte. In other words, each hexadecimal digit represents exactly four binary digits, and two hexadecimal digits represent a single, 8-bit character. In a TCP checksum calculation, two characters or sixteen binary digits are grouped on each row for the calculations. For example, Figure 4-13 shows two columns of ASCII, binary, and hex values.

Character 1	Character 2	Binary 1	Binary 2	Hexadecimal 1	Hexadecimal 2
T	h	1010100	1101000	54	68
i	s	1101001	1110011	69	73
<space>	i	010000	1101001	20	69
s	<space>	1110011	0100000	73	20
c	o	1110011	1101111	63	6F
o	1	1101111	1101100	6F	6C
.	<empty>	0101110	0000000	2E	00

Figure 4-13 Place two characters on each row and convert to hexadecimal

If you add each column of hexadecimal digits starting from the right, you get the calculations shown in Figure 4-14. You can use a calculator app such as the one in Windows to perform these calculations. In the Windows calculator app, switch to the Programmer calculator and then choose HEX. Add each column of numbers separately, carrying a digit to the next column as needed.

Note how the left-most carry value of 2 is added back at the bottom to the right-most column. Some checksum operations will simply drop the left-most carry. Finally, the 1s complement of the result is computed in binary by switching each 1 for a 0 and each 0 for a 1, as shown in Figure 4-15.

This checksum is appended to the end of the transmission stream. The transmitted message will then look like the series of numbers in Figure 4-16 (again in hexadecimal).

The receiver will receive the original characters along with the checksum. The receiver then performs the same operations but includes the checksum value: add the four columns, bring down the left-most carry, and add to the sum. If there were no errors during transmission, the sum should equal all Fs in hexadecimal, which is all 1s in binary (see Figure 4-17). The 1s complement of all 1s is all 0s, which triggers the receiver to accept the data.

Carries	2	3	2	2	
		5	4	6	8
		6	9	7	3
		2	0	6	9
		7	3	2	0
		6	3	6	F
		6	F	6	C
		2	E	0	0
Partial sum:		5	2	3	F
Final carry:					2
Sum:		5	2	4	1

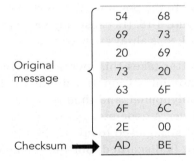

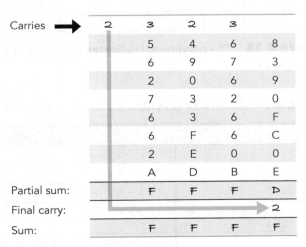

Figure 4-14 Note the handwriting font for calculated values; Add the hexadecimal numbers in each column and carry to the next column as needed

Sum from above:	5	2	4	1
Sum in binary:	0101	0010	0100	0001
1 s complement:	1010	1101	1011	1110
1 s complement in hexadecimal:	A	D	B	E

Figure 4-15 The 1s complement exchanges each 1 for a 0 and each 0 for a 1

Original message	54	68
	69	73
	20	69
	73	20
	63	6F
	6F	6C
	2E	00
Checksum →	AD	BE

Figure 4-16 The checksum is added to the end of the data

Carries	2	3	2	3	
		5	4	6	8
		6	9	7	3
		2	0	6	9
		7	3	2	0
		6	3	6	F
		6	F	6	C
		2	E	0	0
		A	D	B	E
Partial sum:		F	F	F	D
Final carry:					2
Sum:		F	F	F	F

Figure 4-17 The receiver includes the checksum in its calculations

Considering that arithmetic checksum can allow undetected errors, the question remains whether there is another error-detection method with almost no possibility that an error can escape detection. Indeed there is: the cyclic redundancy check.

Cyclic Redundancy Check

Unlike the simple parity and longitudinal parity techniques of error detection, which produce high ratios of check bits to data bits with only mediocre error-detection results, the CRC (cyclic redundancy check) method typically adds 8 to 32 check bits to potentially large data packets and yields an error-detection capability approaching 100 percent.

The CRC error-detection method treats the packet of data to be transmitted (the message) as a large polynomial. The far-right bit of the data becomes the x^0 term, the next data bit to the left is the x^1 term, and so on. When a bit in the message is 1, the corresponding polynomial term is included. Thus, the data 11001101 would be equivalent to the polynomial $x^7 + x^6 + x^3 + x^2 + 1$, as shown in Figure 4-18. (Because any value raised to the 0th power is 1, x^0 is always written as a 1.)

The transmitter takes this message polynomial and, using polynomial arithmetic, divides it by a given generator polynomial, and then produces a quotient and a remainder. A generator polynomial is an industry-approved bit string used to create the CRC remainder. The quotient is discarded, but the remainder (in bit form) is appended to the end of the original message polynomial, and this combined unit is transmitted over the medium. When the data and remainder arrive at the destination, the same generator polynomial is used to detect an error.

Table 4-2 shows some common generator polynomials. When a generator polynomial is referenced in code, it's often listed by its normal representation, which is a hexadecimal version of the polynomial coefficients.

All Things Considered

Thought Experiment

Why do all CRC generator polynomials end with a 1?

The receiver divides the incoming data (the original message polynomial plus the remainder) by the exact same generator polynomial used by the transmitter. If no errors were introduced during data transmission, the division should produce a remainder of zero. If an error was introduced during transmission, the arriving original message polynomial plus the remainder will not divide evenly by the generator polynomial and will produce a nonzero remainder, signaling an error condition.

The transmitter and receiver typically do not perform polynomial division with software. Instead, hardware designed into an integrated circuit can perform the calculation much more quickly. When software is used, the programming generally relies on lookup tables rather than repeated calculations.

The CRC method is almost foolproof. Table 4-3 summarizes the performance of the CRC technique. In cases where the size of the error burst is less than $r + 1$, where r is the degree of the generator polynomial, error detection is 100 percent. For example, suppose the CRC-CCITT is used, and so the degree, or highest power, of the polynomial is 16. In this case, if the error burst is less than $r + 1$ or 17 bits in length, CRC will detect it. Only in cases where the error burst is greater than or equal to

X^7	X^6			$+X^3$	$+X^2$		$+X^0$
1	1	0	0	1	1	0	1

Figure 4-18 The polynomial indicates the position of each 1 in the data byte

Table 4-2 Generator polynomials for common CRC methods

CRC Method	Generator Polynomial	Normal Representation	Common Use
CRC-8	$x^8 + x^7 + x^6 + x^4 + x^2 + 1$	0xD5	Digital satellite TV
CRC-12	$x^{12} + x^{11} + x^3 + x^2 + x + 1$	0x80F	Telecom
CRC-16	$x^{16} + x^{15} + x^2 + 1$	0x8005	USB
CRC-CCITT (also known as CRC-16-CCITT)	$x^{16} + x^{12} + x^5 + 1$	0x1021	Bluetooth
CRC-32	$x^{32} + x^{26} + x^{23} + x^{22} + x^{16} + x^{12} + x^{11} + x^{10} + x^8 + x^7 + x^5 + x^4 + x^2 + x + 1$	0x04C11DB7	Ethernet

Table 4-3 Error-detection performance of CRC

Type of Error	Error-Detection Performance
Single-bit errors	100 percent
Double-bit errors	100 percent if the generating polynomial has at least three 1s (they all do)
Odd number of bits in error	100 percent if the generating polynomial contains a factor x + 1 (they all do)
An error burst of length < r + 1	100 percent
An error burst of length = r + 1	Probability = $1 - (1/2)^{(r-1)}$ (very near 100%)
An error burst of length > r + 1	Probability = $1 - (1/2)^r$ (very near 100%)

r + 1 bits in length is there a chance that CRC might not detect the error. The chance or probability of an error burst of size r + 1 being detected is $1 - (\frac{1}{2})^{(r-1)}$. Assuming again that r = 16, $1 - (\frac{1}{2})^{(16-1)}$ equals 1 − 0.0000305, which equals 0.999969. Thus, the probability of a large error being detected is very close to 1.0 (100 percent). As you can see, increasing the power of the polynomial increases its accuracy. In contrast, the polynomial power can be reduced all the way to 1 (CRC-1), which is mathematically equivalent to a single parity bit.

Recall that parity checking, depending on whether it is simple parity or longitudinal parity, can only detect between 50 percent and approximately 80 percent of errors. You can perform manual parity calculations quickly, but hardware CRC methods are also fairly quick. As you learned earlier, parity schemes require a high number of check bits per data bits. In contrast, CRC requires that a remainder-sized number of check bits (either 8, 16, or 32—as you can see from the list of generator polynomials) be added to a message. The message itself can be hundreds to thousands of bits in length. Therefore, the number of check bits per data bits in cyclic redundancy can be relatively low.

CRC is a very powerful error-detection technique and should be seriously considered for all data transmission systems. Indeed, all local area networks use CRC techniques (CRC-32 is found in Ethernet LANs) and many wide area network protocols incorporate a CRC.

Now that you understand the basic error-detection techniques, let's look at what happens once an error is detected.

All Things Considered

Thought Experiment

Describe two situations in which error-free transmission is crucial to communications.

Remember this...

> When the data link layer creates a frame, it usually inserts an error-checking code after the data field. When the frame arrives at the next station, this error-checking code is extracted, and the frame is checked for accuracy.

> Simple parity is the easiest error-detection method to incorporate into a transmission system. It comes in two basic forms: even parity and odd parity. The basic concept of parity checking is that a bit is added to a string of bits to create either even parity or odd parity.

> Longitudinal parity tries to solve the main weakness of simple parity—that all even numbers of errors are not detected. To do this, characters are arranged in a matrix where each character has its own parity bit at the end of its row. In addition, after a certain number of characters are sent, a row of parity bits is also sent. Each parity bit in this last row is a parity check for all the bits in the column above it.

> Many higher-level protocols on the Internet use a form of error detection called arithmetic checksum where the characters to be transmitted are "summed" together. This sum is appended to the end of the message and then transmitted. The receiver performs the same summing operation, and essentially compares its sum with the sum that was generated by the transmitter. If the two sums agree, the message is accepted. If the two sums do not agree, the receiver informs the transmitter that an error has occurred.

> The CRC (cyclic redundancy check) method typically adds 8 to 32 check bits to potentially large data packets and yields an error-detection capability approaching 100 percent. It treats the message as a large polynomial. The transmitter takes this message

polynomial and, using polynomial arithmetic, divides it by a given generator polynomial, and then produces a quotient and a remainder. The quotient is discarded, but the remainder (in bit form) is appended to the end of the original message polynomial and transmitted over the medium. When the data and remainder arrive at the destination, the same generator polynomial is used to detect an error.

Self-check

7. Given the character 0110101, what bit will be added to support even parity?
    a. 0110101**0**
    b. 0110101**1**
    c. **0**0110101
    d. **1**0110101
8. Which error-detection method is designed to detect a corrupted IP address in a packet's IP header?
    a. Cyclic redundancy check
    b. Longitudinal parity check
    c. Simple parity check
    d. Arithmetic checksum
9. What is the largest size error burst the generator polynomial $x^{12} + x^{11} + x^3 + x^2 + x + 1$ can detect with 100% accuracy?
    a. 13 bits
    b. 12 bits
    c. 28 bits
    d. 29 bits

Check your answers at the end of this chapter.

Section 4-4: Error Control

Once an error in the received data transmission stream is detected, the receiver performs a process called error control, which essentially involves taking one of three actions:

› Toss the frame/packet (ignore the error). Although this seems like an irresponsible position, it has merit and is worth examining.

› Return an error message to the transmitter so the transmitter can resend the original data. This is the most common error-control action.

› Correct the error without help from the transmitter. This might sound like the ideal response, but

it is difficult to support and requires a significant amount of overhead.

Let's examine each of these options in more detail.

Toss the Frame or Packet

The first error-control option—tossing the frame or packet—hardly seems like a realistic option at all. Yet tossing the frame/packet for error control is a standard mode of operation for some network transmission techniques. For example, Ethernet supports the "toss the frame" approach to error control. If a data frame arrives at an Ethernet switch and an error is detected after the CRC is performed, the frame is simply discarded. Ethernet assumes that either the transport layer or the higher-layer application transmitting and receiving data will keep track of the frames and will notice that a frame has been discarded. It would then be the responsibility of the higher layer to request that the dropped frame be retransmitted.

Return the Message

The second option—sending a message back to the transmitter—is probably the most common form of error control. Returning a message was also one of the first error-control techniques developed, and it is closely associated with a particular flow control technique. Recall from Chapter 1 that flow control is a process that keeps a transmitter from sending too much data to a receiver, thus overflowing the receiver's buffer. Over the years, two basic versions of return-a-message error control have emerged: stop-and-wait and sliding window. Let's look at the stop-and-wait error control first.

Stop-and-wait Error Control

Stop-and-wait error control is a technique usually associated with the stop-and-wait flow control protocol where a sender waits for an acknowledgement on one message before sending the next message. This protocol and its error-control technique are the oldest, simplest, and thus most restrictive. A workstation (Station A) transmits one packet of data to another workstation (Station B), and then stops and waits for a reply from Station B. Four things can happen at this point:

› If the packet of data arrives without error, Station B responds with a positive acknowledgment, such as ACK. (ACK is one of the control codes in the ASCII character set and was introduced in the early days of stop-and-wait transmission systems.) When

Station A receives an ACK, it transmits the next data packet.

> If the data arrives with an error, Station B responds with a negative acknowledgment, such as NAK or REJ (for reject). If Station A receives a NAK, it resends the previous data packet. Figure 4-19 shows an example of these transactions.

> If a packet arrives at Station B uncorrupted, Station B transmits an ACK, but the ACK is lost or corrupted. Because Station A must wait for some form of acknowledgment, it will not be able to transmit any more packets. After a certain amount of time called a **timeout**, Station A resends the last packet. But now if this packet arrives uncorrupted at Station B, Station B will not know that it is the same packet as the last one received. To avoid this confusion, the packets are numbered 0, 1, 0, 1, and so on. If Station A sends packet 0, and the ACK for packet 0 is lost, Station A will resend packet 0. Station B will notice two packet 0s in a row (the original and a duplicate) and deduce that the ACK from the first packet 0 was lost.

> Suppose Station A sends a packet, but the packet is lost. Because the packet did not arrive at Station B, Station B will not return an ACK. Because Station A does not receive an ACK, it will resend the previous packet when the timeout is exceeded.

For example, Station A sends packet 1, the timeout limit is reached, times out, and Station A resends packet 1. If this packet 1 arrives at Station B, Station B responds with an ACK. How does Station A know whether the ACK is acknowledging the first packet or the second? To avoid confusion, the ACKs are numbered, just like the packets. In contrast to packets (which are numbered 0, 1, 0, 1, and so on), however, ACKs are numbered 1, 0, 1, 0, and so on. If Station B receives packet 0, it responds with ACK 1. The ACK 1 tells Station A that the *next* packet expected is packet 1. Because packet 0 just arrived, packet 1 is expected next.

One of the most serious drawbacks to the simple stop-and-wait error control is its high degree of inefficiency. Stop-and-wait error control is a half-duplex protocol, which means that only one station can transmit at one time. The time the transmitting station wastes waiting for an acknowledgment could be better spent transmitting additional packets. More efficient techniques than stop-and-wait are available.

All Things Considered

Thought Experiment

In a stop-and-wait error control system, Station A sends packet 0, and it is lost. What happens next?

Sliding Window Error Control

Sliding window error control is based on the **sliding window protocol**, which is a flow control scheme that allows a station to transmit a certain number of data packets at one time before receiving some form of acknowledgment. Sliding window protocols have been around since the 1970s, a time when computer networks had two important limitations. First, line speeds and processing power were much lower than they are today. For this reason, it was important that a station transmitting data did not send data too quickly and overwhelm the receiving station. Second, memory was more expensive, and so network devices had limited buffer space in which to store incoming and outgoing data packets.

Because of these limitations, standard sliding window protocols set their maximum window size to seven packets. A station that had a maximum window size of 7 (as some of the early systems did) could transmit only seven data packets at one time before it had to stop and

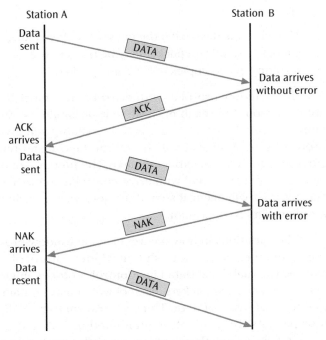

Figure 4-19   Sample dialog using stop-and-wait error control

wait for an acknowledgment. Because a window size of 7 was small, *extended* sliding window protocols were soon created that could support 127 packets. Today, the TCP protocol used on the Internet can dynamically adjust its window size into the thousands for optimum performance. For simplicity, the following examples will consider the standard protocol with a maximum window size of 7.

To follow the flow of data in a sliding window protocol with window size 7, packets are assigned numbers 0, 1, 2, 3, 4, 5, 6, or 7. Once packet number 7 is transmitted, the number sequencing starts back over at 0. Even though the packets are numbered 0 through 7, which corresponds to eight different packets, only seven data packets can be outstanding (unacknowledged) at one time. Because a maximum of seven data packets can be outstanding at one time, two data packets of the same number (both are numbered 4, for example) can never be transmitted at the same time. If a sender has a maximum window size of 7 and transmits four packets, it can still transmit three more packets before it must wait for an acknowledgment. If the receiver acknowledges all four packets before the sender transmits any more data, the sender's window size once again returns to 7.

Consider a scenario in which the sender transmits five packets and stops, such as the following:

> The receiver receives the five packets and acknowledges them.

> Before the acknowledgment is received, the sender can send two more packets because the window size is 7.

> On receipt of the acknowledgment, the sender can send an additional seven packets before it must stop again.

The acknowledgment that a receiver transmits to the sender is also numbered. In the sliding window protocol, acknowledgments always contain a value equal to the number of the *next expected* packet. For example, if the sender in Figure 4-20 transmits three packets numbered 0, 1, and 2, and the receiver wishes to acknowledge all of them, the receiver will return an acknowledgment (ACK) with the value 3 because packet 3 is the next packet the receiver expects.

What would happen if the protocol allowed eight packets to be sent at one time? Assume the sender sends packets numbered 0 through 7. The receiver receives all of them and acknowledges all by sending an acknowledgement numbered 0 (the next packet expected). But

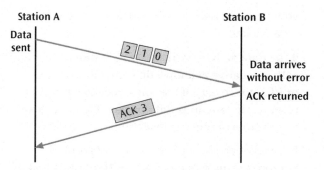

Figure 4-20 Example of a sliding window

what if none of the packets arrived at the receiver? The receiver would not respond with a positive acknowledgment, and the sender would hear nothing. If, after a timeout, the sender asked the receiver for the number of the next packet expected, the receiver would answer with 0. The sender would never know if that meant all the packets were received or none of the packets was received. This potential confusion could lead a sender to resend all the packets when it is not necessary, or to resend none of the packets when the receiver is trying to indicate an error.

Essentially four things can happen to a packet when it is transmitted:

> The packet arrives without error.

> The packet is lost; it never arrives.

> The packet is corrupted; it arrives but has a CRC error.

> The packet is delayed; if the packet is delayed long enough, a duplicate packet may be transmitted, resulting in two copies of the same packet.

A sliding window protocol with error control must be able to account for each of these four possibilities. An important distinction to note is that a sliding window protocol's function is simply to inform the transmitter what piece of data is expected next. The function of a sliding window protocol with error control is to further specify what will occur if something goes wrong during a sliding window operation.

Note the variations in how different sliding window protocols number data. Older sliding window protocols, such as the High-level Data Link Control protocol, number the transmitted packets, each of which may contain hundreds of bytes of data. Thus, if a transmitter sends four packets, they might be numbered 0, 1, 2, and 3, respectively. If something goes wrong with a packet, the receiver will request that packet *n* be transmitted again.

In contrast, newer sliding window protocols such as TCP number the individual bytes. In this case, if a transmitter sends a packet with 400 bytes of data, the bytes might, for example, be numbered 8001 to 8400. If something goes wrong with the packet, the receiver will indicate that it needs bytes 8001 to 8400 to be transmitted again.

Let's look at some examples that illustrate the four, basic error-control scenarios possible with sliding window protocols. For the first scenario, you will see a packet-numbering example, but in general, focus more on examples of the byte-numbering scheme of the TCP protocol, as it is the more popular of the protocols.

In Figure 4-21, the first scenario shows how one or more packets, numbered individually, are transmitted, and all arrive without error. More specifically, Station A transmits four packets numbered 2, 3, 4, and 5, and Station B receives them and sends an ACK 6 acknowledging all four. Notice that Station B is telling Station A what packet it expects next (packet 6). Station A responds by sending five more packets numbered 6, 7, 0, 1, and 2. Station B acknowledges all the packets by returning an ACK 3.

Figure 4-22 shows an example of the sliding window protocol numbering bytes instead of packets. Station A transmits one packet with bytes 0–400, followed by a second packet with bytes 401–800. Station B receives both packets and acknowledges all the bytes. Note once again that the ACK tells Station A the next byte that Station B expects (801).

An interesting question arises: Does a receiver have to acknowledge the data every time something is received? Or can a receiver wait a while to see if something more

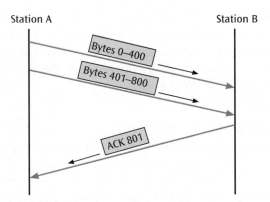

Figure 4-22   Normal transfer of data between two stations with numbering of the bytes

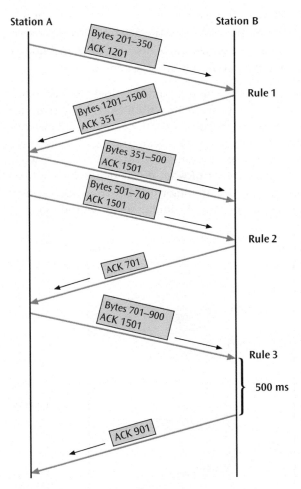

Figure 4-23   Three examples of returning an acknowledgment in TCP

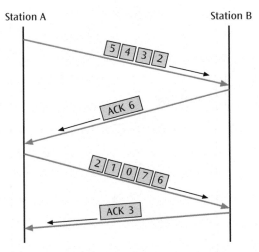

Figure 4-21   Normal transfer of data between two stations with numbering of the packets

is coming in before it sends an acknowledgment? In the world of TCP/IP, receiving stations follow a handful of rules for resolving this question. Figure 4-23 illustrates each of the following three rules:

> **Rule 1**—If a receiver just received some data and wishes to send data back to the sender, then the receiver should include an ACK with the data it is about to send. This is called **piggybacking**, and it saves the receiver from sending a separate ACK message.

> **Rule 2**—If the receiver does not have any data to return to the sender, and the receiver has just acknowledged the receipt of a previously sent packet of data, then the receiver must wait 500 milliseconds to see if another packet arrives. If a second packet arrives before the 500 milliseconds expire, however, then the receiver must immediately send an ACK.

> **Rule 3**—If the receiver is waiting for a second packet to arrive, and the 500 milliseconds expire, then the receiver does not wait for a second packet and instead issues an ACK immediately.

What happens when a packet is lost? Figure 4-24 illustrates the situation in which Station A transmits a sequence of packets and the second one is lost in the network. When the receiver, Station B, sees the third packet out of sequence, it returns an ACK with the sequence number of what it was expecting (byte 2401). Station A sees that something is wrong and retransmits the second packet. A similar result would occur if the

second packet arrived, but with a CRC error. In both cases, the packet is considered "lost."

What happens if a packet is delayed, or a duplicate packet arrives at the destination? If the packet is delayed enough that it comes in out of order, the receiver also treats this as a lost packet and sends an ACK with the appropriate value. When the delayed packet or a duplicate packet arrives, the destination will see a packet with a sequence number less than the previously acknowledged bytes and simply discard the duplicate.

Finally, what happens if an acknowledgment is lost? Two possible scenarios exist. If a lost acknowledgment command is followed shortly by another acknowledgment command that does not get lost, no problem should occur because the acknowledgments are cumulative (the second acknowledgment will have an equal or larger packet number). If an acknowledgment command is lost and is not followed by any subsequent acknowledgment commands, the transmitting station will eventually time out and treat the previous packet as a lost packet and retransmit it as shown in Figure 4-25.

Correct the Error

The last of the three actions a receiver can take if an error packet is deemed corrupted is to correct the error. This seems like a reasonable solution. The data packet has been received, and error-detection logic has determined that an error has occurred. Why not simply correct the error and continue processing?

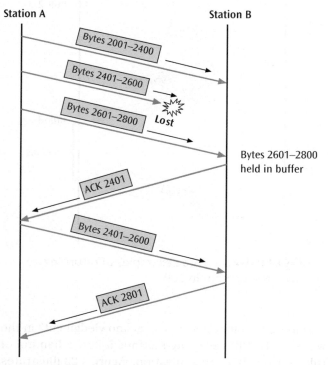

Figure 4-24 A lost packet and Station B's response

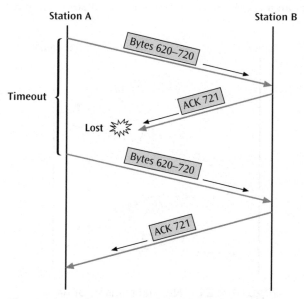

Figure 4-25 A lost acknowledgment and the retransmission of a packet

Unfortunately, correcting an error is not that simple. For a receiver to be able to fix an error—in a process called **FEC (forward error correction)**—redundant information must be present so that the receiver knows which bit or bits are in error and what their original values were. For example, if you were given the data 0110110 and informed that a parity check had detected an error, could you determine which bit or bits were corrupted? No, you would not have enough information.

To see the full extent of the problem, consider what would happen if you transmitted three identical copies of each bit.

For example, you transmitted 0110110 as 000 111 111 000 111 111 000.

Now, let's corrupt 1 bit: 000 111 111 001 111 111 000.

Can you determine which bit was corrupted? If you assume that only one bit has been corrupted, you can apply what is known as the majority rules principle and determine that the error bit is the final 1 in the fourth group, 001. Note that even in this simple example, FEC entailed transmitting *three times* the original amount of data, and it provided only a small level of error correction. This level of overhead limits the application of FEC.

A more useful type of FEC is a Hamming code. A **Hamming code** is a specially designed code in which special check bits have been added to data bits such that, if an error occurs during transmission, the receiver might be able to correct the error using the included check and data bits. For example, suppose you want to transmit an 8-bit character: the character 01010101 seen in Figure 4-26. Let's number the bits of this character from right to left as b3, b5, b6, b7, b9, b10, b11, and b12. (Leave spaces for the soon-to-be-added check bits.) Now add to these data bits the following check bits at positions represented by powers of 2, as follows:

> c8, which generates a simple even parity for bits b12, b11, b10, and b9

> c4, which generates a simple even parity for bits b12, b7, b6, and b5

> c2, which generates a simple even parity for bits b11, b10, b7, b6, and b3

> c1, which generates a simple even parity for bits b11, b9, b7, b5, and b3

Note that each check bit here is checking different sequences of data bits.

Let's take a closer look at how each of the Hamming code check bits in Figure 4-26 works:

> Check bit c8 "covers" bits b12, b11, b10, and b9, which are 0101. If you generate an even parity bit based on those four bits, you get 0 (there are an even number of 1s). Thus, c8 is set equal to 0.

> Check bit c4 covers b12, b7, b6, and b5, which are 0010, so c4 is set equal to 1.

> Check bit c2 covers b11, b10, b7, b6, and b3, which are 10011, so c2 is set equal to 1.

> Check bit c1 covers b11, b9, b7, b5, and b3, which are 11001, so c1 is set equal to 1.

Consequently, if you have the data 01010101, you generate the check bits 0111, as shown in Figure 4-26. This 12-bit character (data bits and check bits together) is now transmitted to the receiver. The receiver accepts the bits and performs the four parity checks on the check bits c8, c4, c2, and c1. If nothing happened to the 12-bit character during transmission, all four parity checks should result in no error.

But what would happen if one of the bits were corrupted and somehow ends up the opposite value? For example, what if bit b9 is corrupted? With the corrupted b9, you would now have the string 010000101111. The receiver would perform the four parity checks, but this time there would be parity errors, as follows:

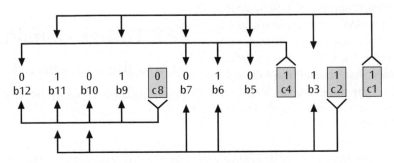

Figure 4-26   Hamming code check bits generated from the data 01010101

› Because c8 checks b12, b11, b10, b9, and c8 (01000), there would be a parity error. As you can see, there is an odd number of 1s in the data string, but the check bit is returning a 0.

› C4 checks b12, b7, b6, b5, and c4 (00101) and, thus, would produce no parity error.

› C2 checks b11, b10, b7, b6, b3, and c2 (100111), and would produce no parity error.

› C1 checks bits b11, b9, b7, b5, b3, and c1 (100011), which would result in a parity error.

If you examine just the check bits and denote a 1 if there is a parity error and a 0 if there is no parity error, you get 1001 (c8 error, c4 no error, c2 no error, c1 error). 1001 is binary for 9, telling you that the bit in error is in the ninth position. To learn more about the technical intricacies of a Hamming code, read the Forward Error Correction and Hamming Distance Details box.

Details | Forward Error Correction and Hamming Distance

For a data code such as ASCII to perform forward error correction, redundant bits must be added to the original data bits. These redundant bits allow a receiver to look at the received data and, if there is an error, recover the original data using a consensus of received bits. For a simple example, let's transmit three identical copies of a single bit (majority operation). Thus, to send a value of 1, three bits (111) will be transmitted. Next, consider what would happen if the three bits received have the values 101. In FEC, the receiver would assume that the 0 bit should be a 1 because the majority of bits are 1. To understand how redundant bits are created, you need to examine the Hamming distance of a code, which is the smallest number of bits by which character codes differ. The **Hamming distance** is a characteristic of a code. To create a self-correcting or forward error-correcting code, you must create a code that has the appropriate Hamming distance.

In the ASCII character set, the letter B in binary is 1000010, and the letter C is 1000011. The difference between B and C is 1 bit—the rightmost bit. If you compare all the ASCII characters, you will find that some pairs of characters differ by one bit, and some differ by two or more bits. Because the Hamming distance of a code is based on the *smallest* number of bits by which character codes differ, the ASCII character set has a Hamming distance of 1. Unfortunately, if a character set has a Hamming distance of 1, it is not possible to detect errors, nor to correct them. Ask yourself the following question: If a receiver accepts the character 1000010, how does it know for sure that this is the letter B and not the letter C with a 1-bit error?

When a parity bit is assigned to ASCII, the Hamming distance becomes 2. Because the rightmost bit is the parity bit, the character B, assuming even parity, becomes 10000100, and the character C becomes 10000111. Now, the last 2 bits of B must change from 00 to 11 for the character B to become the character C, and the difference between the two characters is two bits. Now that the Hamming distance is 2, it is possible to detect single-bit errors, but you still cannot *correct* errors. Also, if the character B is transmitted, but one bit is flipped by error, a parity check error occurs; however, you still cannot tell what the intended character was supposed to be. For example, the character B with even parity added is 10000100. If one bit is altered, such as the second bit, the binary value is now 11000100. This character would cause a parity check, but what was the original character? Any one of the bits could have changed, thus allowing for many possible original characters. You can correct single-bit errors and detect double-bit errors when the Hamming distance of the character set is at least 3. Achieving a Hamming distance of 3 requires an even higher level of redundancy and, consequently, cost.

All Things Considered

Thought Experiment

Devise a code set for the digits 0 to 9 that has a Hamming distance of 2.

Despite the additional costs of using forward error correction, are there applications that would benefit from the use of this technology? Two major groups of applications can in fact reap a benefit: digital storage systems and applications that send data over very long distances. Digital storage media, such as CDs, DVDs, and Blu-ray discs, use advanced forms of FEC called Reed-Solomon codes. Note that it is not possible to ask for retransmission of audio or video data if there is an error. It would be too late! The data needs to be delivered in real time, thus the need for FEC that corrects errors on the receiving end.

In the second example, if data must be sent over a long distance, it is costly to retransmit a packet that arrived in error. For example, the time required for NASA to send a message to a Martian probe is several minutes. If the data arrives garbled, it will be another several minutes before the negative acknowledgment is received, and another several minutes before the data can be retransmitted. If many data packets arrive garbled, transmitting data to Mars could be a very long, tedious process without error correction processes by the receiver.

Remember this...

> Error control involves taking one of three actions: toss the frame/packet, return a message to the transmitter asking it to resend the data packet that was in error, or correct the error without retransmission.

> Tossing the frame/packet for error control is a standard mode of operation for some network transmission techniques that assume a higher-layer protocol or application will notice that a frame has been discarded and request the dropped frame be retransmitted.

> Stop-and-wait error control is a technique usually associated with the stop-and-wait flow control protocol where a sender waits for an acknowledgement on one message before sending the next message. One of the most serious drawbacks to the simple stop-and-wait error control is its high degree of inefficiency. The time the transmitting station wastes

waiting for an acknowledgment could be better spent transmitting additional packets.

> The sliding window protocol is a flow control scheme that allows a station to transmit a certain number of data packets at one time before receiving some form of acknowledgment. Today, the TCP protocol used on the Internet can dynamically adjust its window size into the thousands for optimum performance. Newer sliding window protocols such as TCP number individual bytes and indicate in the ACK message which numbered byte is expected next. This allows the sender to adjust its transmission in response to lost packets.

> For a receiver to be able to fix an error—in a process called FEC (forward error correction)—redundant information must be present so that the receiver knows which bit or bits are in error and what their original values were. A Hamming code is a specially designed code in which special check bits have been added to data bits such that, if an error occurs during transmission, the receiver might be able to correct the error using the included check and data bits.

Self-check

10. Which of the following is *not* a legitimate option for how the receiver can handle a data transmission error?
    a. Correct the error
    b. Resend the packet
    c. Ask for retransmission
    d. Discard the message

11. Station A sends packets numbered 500-549. Station B replies with packets numbered 3000-3099 along with an ACK message. What packet number is included in the ACK message?
    a. 549
    b. 550
    c. 3099
    d. 3100

Check your answers at the end of this chapter.

Summary

Section 4-1: Data Link Frames

> Two functions of the data link layer are to create a frame of data for transmission between sender and receiver, and to provide some way of checking for errors during transmission.

> A data link layer frame consists of a header and a trailer surrounding the payload, which is the data contained within the message.

> The fields of each header vary depending on the protocol that creates the header. One primary piece of information is related to addressing. For example, the transport, network, and data link layers each need to add addressing information.

> Following the data and contained within the trailer is almost always some form of error detection and correction information. Each message must contain information that the receiver can use to determine whether the message was corrupted in transit. In some cases, that information is sufficient for the receiver to correct the problem.

Section 4-2: Noise and Errors

> Despite one's best efforts to control noise, some noise is inevitable. When the ratio of noise power to signal power becomes such that the noise overwhelms the signal, errors occur. It is at this point that error-detection techniques become valuable tools.

> Gaussian noise is a relatively continuous type of noise while impulse noise is a noncontinuous noise and one of the most difficult errors to detect because it can occur randomly. Noise is a problem for both analog and digital signals, and the transmission speed of the data can affect the significance of the noise.

> Crosstalk is an unwanted coupling between two different signal paths, while echo is the reflective feedback of a transmitted signal as the signal moves through a medium.

> Jitter is the result of small timing irregularities that become magnified during the transmission of digital signals as the signals are passed from one device to another. Attenuation, which is not necessarily a form of error, is the continuous loss of a signal's strength as it travels through a medium.

Section 4-3: Error Detection

> When the data link layer creates a frame, it usually inserts an error-checking code after the data field. When the frame arrives at the next station, this error-checking code is extracted, and the frame is checked for accuracy.

> Simple parity is the easiest error-detection method to incorporate into a transmission system. It comes in two basic forms: even parity and odd parity. The basic concept of parity checking is that a bit is added to a string of bits to create either even parity or odd parity.

> Longitudinal parity tries to solve the main weakness of simple parity—that all even numbers of errors are not detected. To do this, characters are arranged in a matrix where each character has its own parity bit at the end of its row. In addition, after a certain number of characters are sent, a row of parity bits is also sent. Each parity bit in this last row is a parity check for all the bits in the column above it.

> Many higher-level protocols on the Internet use a form of error detection called arithmetic checksum where the characters to be transmitted are "summed" together. This sum is appended to the end of the message and then transmitted. The receiver performs the same summing operation, and essentially compares its sum with the sum that was generated by

the transmitter. If the two sums agree, the message is accepted. If the two sums do not agree, the receiver informs the transmitter that an error has occurred.

> The CRC (cyclic redundancy check) method typically adds 8 to 32 check bits to potentially large data packets and yields an error-detection capability approaching 100 percent. It treats the message as a large polynomial. The transmitter takes this message polynomial and, using polynomial arithmetic, divides it by a given generator polynomial, and then produces a quotient and a remainder. The quotient is discarded, but the remainder (in bit form) is appended to the end of the original message polynomial and transmitted over the medium. When the data and remainder arrive at the destination, the same generator polynomial is used to detect an error.

Section 4-4: Error Control

> Error control involves taking one of three actions: toss the frame/packet, return a message to the transmitter asking it to resend the data packet that was in error, or correct the error without retransmission.

> Tossing the frame/packet for error control is a standard mode of operation for some network transmission techniques that assume a higher-layer protocol or application will notice that a frame has been discarded and request the dropped frame be retransmitted.

> Stop-and-wait error control is a technique usually associated with the stop-and-wait flow control protocol where a sender waits for an acknowledgement on one message before sending the next message. One of the most serious drawbacks to the simple stop-and-wait error control is its high degree of inefficiency. The time the transmitting station wastes waiting for an acknowledgment could be better spent transmitting additional packets.

> The sliding window protocol is a flow control scheme that allows a station to transmit a certain number of data packets at one time before receiving some form of acknowledgment. Today, the TCP protocol used on the Internet can dynamically adjust its window size into the thousands for optimum performance. Newer sliding window protocols such as TCP number individual bytes and indicate in the ACK message which numbered byte is expected next. This allows the sender to adjust its transmission in response to lost packets.

> For a receiver to be able to fix an error—in a process called FEC (forward error correction)—redundant information must be present so that the receiver knows which bit or bits are in error and what their original values were. A Hamming code is a specially designed code in which special check bits have been added to data bits such that, if an error occurs during transmission, the receiver might be able to correct the error using the included check and data bits.

 Key Terms

For definitions of key terms, see the Glossary near the end of the book.

arithmetic checksum	Hamming code	payload
CRC (cyclic redundancy check)	Hamming distance	piggybacking
echo	header	simple parity
error control	impulse noise	sliding window protocol
FEC (forward error correction)	jitter	stop-and-wait error control
Gaussian noise	longitudinal parity	timeout
generator polynomial	parity bit	trailer

Review Questions

1. Which of the following is *NOT* a function of the data link layer?

    a. Create a frame of data for transmission between sender and receiver

    b. Identify which application on the receiving device should process the message

    c. Provide a way to check for errors during transmission

    d. Address the receiving device's network port

2. Which network device is most concerned with MAC addresses?

    a. Router

    b. Packet sniffer

    c. Web server

    d. Switch

3. Which part of a message contains error detection and correction information for the entire message at every network device along the journey?

    a. Ethernet header

    b. IP header

    c. TCP header

    d. Ethernet trailer

4. Which of the following is most likely to cause Gaussian noise on a network?

    a. Loose cable connection

    b. Power spike

    c. Power outage

    d. Traffic on the highway

5. Which of the following is most likely to cause impulse noise on a network?

    a. Fluorescent lighting

    b. Infrared remote control

    c. Elevator motor

    d. Cables running alongside each other

6. Which of the following is the best example of crosstalk in a nontechnical context?

    a. Traffic lights directing traffic from multiple directions

    b. Security cameras monitoring several angles in a parking lot

    c. A teacher instructing a group of students

    d. A person participating in two conversations at one time

7. Which of the following is the best example of crosstalk on a network?

    a. A loose cable connection

    b. A power cord running alongside a network cable

    c. A laptop too far away from a Wi-Fi router

    d. An incompatible cable connector

8. When an echo interferes with a signal, what is the source of that interfering transmission?

    a. The device receiving the message

    b. The device sending the message

    c. The cable on which the message is sent

    d. A third device on the same connection

9. Which of the following transmissions is most susceptible to the degradation caused by jitter?

    a. File transfer

    b. Web page request

    c. Streaming video

    d. Email download

10. Which type of noise is continuous?

    a. Gaussian noise

    b. Impulse noise

    c. Echo

    d. Jitter

11. Which of the following factors will consistently decrease noise on a connection?

    a. Increased attenuation

    b. Increased parity

    c. Increased speeds

    d. Increased shielding

12. Which of these characters employs even parity?

    a. 11111001

    b. 11001000

    c. 11111110

    d. 00000001

13. Which of these error detection techniques potentially offers the most favorable ratio of data bits to parity bits while maximizing the chances of detecting an error?

    a. Simple parity

    b. Cyclic redundancy check

    c. Arithmetic checksum

    d. Longitudinal parity

14. With arithmetic checksum, what is being added?

    a. Binary values of transmitted characters

    b. A series of hexadecimal characters

    c. A series of TCP/IP characters

    d. Decimal values of transmitted numbers

15. Which of these errors could possibly escape a CRC-32 system?

    a. Odd number of bits in error

    b. Error burst of 32 bits

    c. Error burst of 34 bits

    d. Double-bit error

16. How many packets can be sent at one time using the stop-and-wait error control method?

    a. 1

    b. 7

    c. 127

    d. Thousands

17. In a sliding window error-control system, Station A sends three packets with bytes 0–99, 100–199, and 200–299, respectively. The second packet with bytes 100–199 is delayed somewhere along its path across the network long enough that the third packet arrives two seconds before the second one. What response will Station B send?

    a. ACK 0

    b. ACK 100

    c. ACK 200

    d. ACK 300

18. What condition must be met for error correction to be performed?

    a. The sender doesn't receive an ACK message

    b. The receiver sends a NAK message

    c. Redundant information is present

    d. The packet is not received

19. A system is going to transmit the byte 10010100. What are the four check bits c_8, c_4, c_2, and c_1 that will be added to this byte using even parity?

    a. **111**0**0**01**0**0100

    b. 100**1**00100**011**

    c. 1001**1**010**1**0**00**

    d. 1001**00**101**001**

20. The 12-bit string 010111110010 with embedded Hamming code bits (c_8, c_4, c_2, and c_1 using even parity) has just arrived. Is there an error? If so, which bit is in error?

    a. There is no error.

    b. The bit b_5 is in error.

    c. The bit b_9 is in error.

    d. The bit b_{12} is in error.

Hands-On Project 4

Install and Use Wireshark

Estimated time: 45 minutes

Resources:

❯ A computer and user account with application installation rights
❯ Access to a private network either owned by the student or which the student has explicit permission to scan
❯ Internet access

❯ **Context:**

Wireshark is a free, open-source network protocol analyzer that can help demystify network messages for you and help make the network layers easier to understand. For some students, using Wireshark for the first time can be an epiphany experience. It allows you to study the layers, all the information that is added to every message, and all the messages that have to go back and forth just to bring up a web page or simply to connect to the network. It becomes much more real when you see how many messages Wireshark collects during even a short capture.

During this project, you'll also encounter several network protocols that you will learn more about throughout this course. The point of this exercise is to show you how Wireshark works, so don't worry if the protocols are unfamiliar for now.

> # Note
>
> Take note that scanning a network you don't own or don't have permission to scan with Wireshark is illegal. Do not use Wireshark on public Wi-Fi networks at all. Also, don't use Wireshark on any network you don't own unless you have written permission from the owner to capture and analyze network communications using Wireshark.

Complete the following steps:

1. Open a browser and go to **wireshark.org**. Download and install the current stable release, using the appropriate version for your OS. Be sure to accept the Npcap option if it is offered. In the Wireshark setup window, you do *not* need USBPcap. If needed, reboot your computer to complete the Wireshark installation.

2. When installation is complete, open **Wireshark**.

3. In the Wireshark Network Analyzer window, select your network interface from the list. Then click the shark-fin icon to start the capture, as shown in Figure 4-27.

4. While the capture is running, open your browser and go to **cengage.com**. Then open a PowerShell or Command Prompt window and enter `ping 8.8.8.8`, which will send some messages to the Cengage server and prompt a response from the server. After the ping completes, click the red box on the command ribbon to stop the capture.

Look at some of the messages you've captured. You can adjust the pane sizes by grabbing a border between them and dragging. Expand the top pane so you can see more of the captured messages at one time. Let's start to decode this blur of numbers and letters.

5. Notice the column headers along the top of the capture, as shown in Figure 4-28. Of particular interest are the Source and Destination columns, the Protocol column, and the Info column. Find a UDP (User Datagram Protocol) message that has an IPv4 Source address—most likely starting with 192.168—and click on it. **Take a screenshot** of your capture with the UDP message selected; submit this visual with your answers to this project's questions.

Start capture

Stop capture

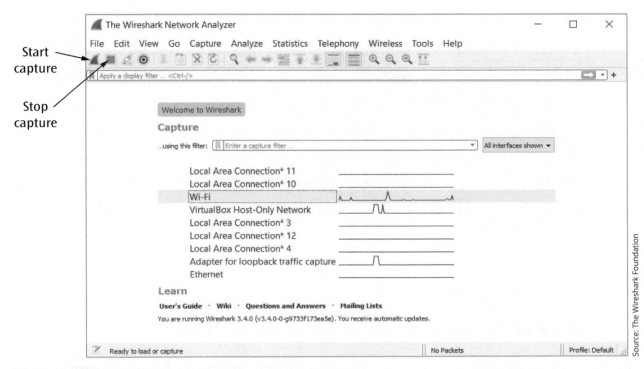

Figure 4-27   The Wireshark Network Analyzer window

Column headers

Filter box

Clear filter

UDP messages

OSI layers

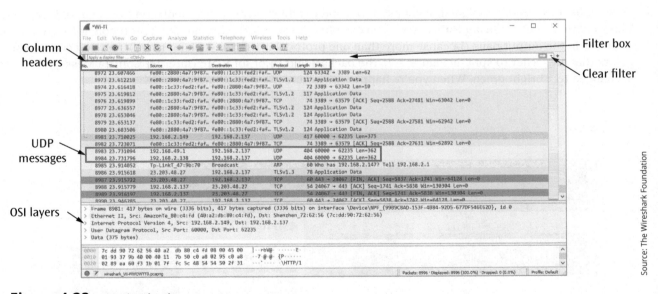

Figure 4-28   A Wireshark capture

6. In the middle pane, click on each line to expand that layer's information. What pieces of information stand out to you?

Color highlighting can make it easier to spot different protocols. Notice in Figure 4-29 that TCP (Transmission Control Protocol) messages are a light lavender or light green color (when it includes HTTP), and UDP and DNS (Domain Name Services) messages are a light bluish color. You can see the protocol names in the Protocol column. Note that if you have trouble distinguishing colors, you can choose colors or shades that work for you. For example, you might choose a very dark shade that stands out against lighter shades. If necessary, you could also use a phone app to help,

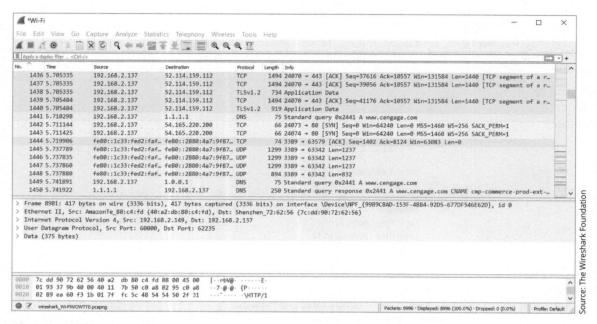

Figure 4-29 Different highlight colors correspond to different protocols

such as Be My Eyes (*bemyeyes.com*) that pairs users with a normally sighted volunteer to help identify colors, Color Blind Pal (*colorblindpal.com*) that provides descriptive information and offers a filter tool, or Pixolor that identifies colors of pixels in an image (website developers often use apps like this to define branding colors).

7. To see a list of currently assigned highlight colors and to adjust these assignments, on the main toolbar, click **View** and then click **Coloring Rules**. Here, you can change the priority for matching protocols within a message to colors in the output pane (because more than one protocol is used in each message), and you can assign colors that are easier to spot. In Figure 4-30, the background color for ICMP (Internet Control Message Protocol) is changed to a bright green. When you're happy with your color selections, click **OK**.

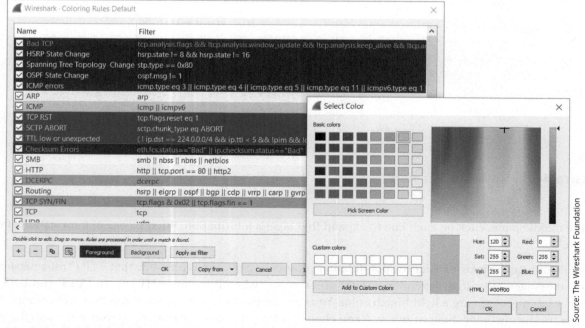

Figure 4-30 Choose colors that are easier to spot

8. To filter for a particular kind of message in your capture, type the name of the protocol in the Filter box (identified in Figure 4-28). Figure 4-31 shows a filter for ICMP messages, which are currently highlighted in bright green. These ICMP messages were generated when pinging another host on the network. Try filtering for other protocols you see listed in your capture, such as HTTP, and see how many different types you can find in your capture. Click the **X** to clear filters between searches. Which protocols did you find?

9. To compare which network layers are represented by each of these protocols, apply a slightly more complicated filter where you can see both HTTP messages and ICMP messages in the same search. Enter the following phrase into the Filter box: **http or icmp**.

10. Click on an ICMP message and count the layers of information available in the middle pane. In Figure 4-32, there are four layers of information, which correspond to layer 2 (Frame and Ethernet II) and layer 3 (Internet Protocol Version 4 and Internet Control Message Protocol).

11. Examine an HTTP message. Figure 4-33 shows five layers of information in the middle pane. This time, layer 7 (Hypertext Transfer Protocol) and layer 4 (Transmission Control Protocol) are represented, in addition to layer 3 (Internet Protocol Version 4) and layer 2 (Ethernet II and Frame).

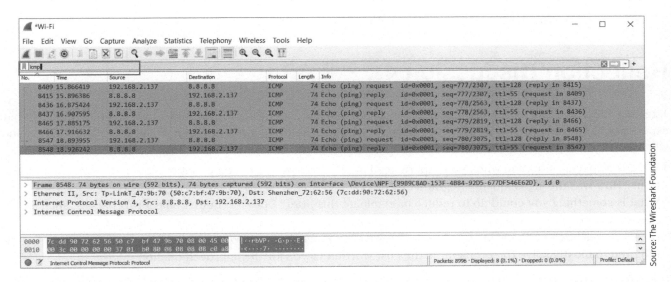

Figure 4-31   Use a filter to narrow your search

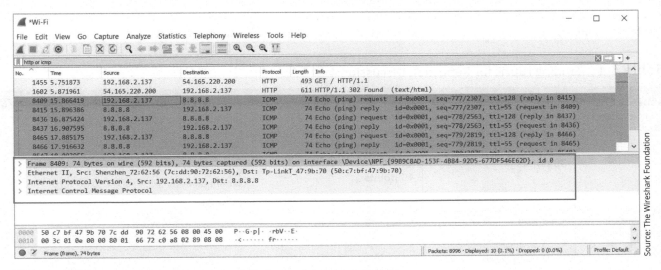

Figure 4-32   Use the middle pane to dig into each layer's headers

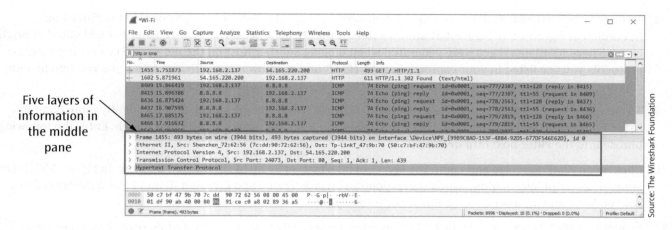

Five layers of information in the middle pane

Figure 4-33 This HTTP message uses TCP at the transport layer and IP at the network layer to contact a Cengage web server

12. You can close Wireshark and delete your capture. You do not need to save it for later.

Reflection Discussion 4

Jitter is a noise type that most computer and mobile device users experience fairly often to some degree. You might have experienced jitter when streaming a movie, talking on the phone, or playing a video game. Think about a specific situation when jitter caused problems in the quality of your network connection, and then answer the following questions:

> What is a specific situation when you experienced jitter? What were you doing that relied on network communications? How was the signal quality degraded by jitter?
> What is something you could do to reduce or eliminate this jitter? Does it require behavioral changes, such as moving your device, or does it require network changes, such as a hardware or software upgrade?
> Do a little research on the costs involved to improve your signal quality. What kind of investment would be required to mostly solve the problem? Is the cost worth it to you for the improved quality?

Go to the discussion forum in your school's LMS. Write a post of at least 100 words discussing your thoughts about your experiences with jitter. Then respond to two of your classmates' threads with posts of at least 50 words discussing their comments and ideas. Use complete sentences, and check your grammar and spelling. Try to ask open-ended questions that encourage discussion, and remember to respond to people who post on your thread. Use the rubric in Table 4-4 to help you understand what is expected of your work for this assignment.

Table 4-4 Grading rubric for Reflection Discussion 4

Task	Novice	Competent	Proficient	Earned
Initial post	Generalized statements about experiences with jitter **30 points**	Some specific statements with examples about experiences with jitter along with some possible, general solutions **40 points**	Self-reflective discussion with specific and thoughtful statements about experiences with jitter, well-defined proposals for solutions, and concrete cost-benefit analysis **50 points**	
Initial post: Mechanics	• Length < 100 words • Several grammar and spelling errors **5 points**	• Length = 100 words • Occasional grammar and spelling errors **7 points**	• Length > 100 words • Appropriate grammar and spelling **10 points**	

Response 1	Brief response showing little engagement or critical thinking **5 points**	Detailed response with specific contributions to the discussion **10 points**	Thoughtful response with specific examples or details and open-ended questions that invite deeper discussion of the topic **15 points**	
Response 2	Brief response showing little engagement or critical thinking **5 points**	Detailed response with specific contributions to the discussion **10 points**	Thoughtful response with specific examples or details and open-ended questions that invite deeper discussion of the topic **15 points**	
Both responses: Mechanics	• Length < 50 words each • Several grammar and spelling errors **5 points**	• Length = 50 words each • Occasional grammar and spelling errors **7 points**	• Length > 50 words each • Appropriate grammar and spelling **10 points**	
				Total

Solutions to Self-Check Questions

Section 4-1: Data Link Frames

1. Which address identifies the receiving application?

Answer: d. Port

Explanation: The transport layer contains the port number that identifies which application on the receiving computer should process the message, such as a web browser (typically port 80 or port 443).

2. Which protocol adds a header at the network layer?

Answer: a. IP

Explanation: The IP (Internet Protocol) header at the network layer contains the IP address that identifies the destination computer uniquely across multiple networks. Traffic crossing multiple networks is handled by routers, and so routers read the network layer's header to identify the destination computer's IP address. This information helps routers determine which route a message should take to reach the network of its destination.

3. In which part of a data link layer's frame can you find error checking information?

Answer: c. Trailer

Explanation: Following the data and contained within the trailer is almost always some form of error detection and correction information, such as CRC (cyclic redundancy check).

Section 4-2: Noise and Errors

4. At which of these TCP/IP layers is error detection *not* typically performed?

Answer: d. Physical

Explanation: When the data link layer creates a frame, it usually inserts an error-checking code after the data field. But the data link layer is not the only layer that performs some type of error detection. The transport layer also includes an error-detection scheme. Also, some network layer protocols, such as IP (Internet Protocol), include an error-detection code in the network layer header. In the case of IP, however, the error detection is performed on only the IP header, and not the data field. The physical layer involves other activities, such as modulation and encoding.

5. A forklift operating on the warehouse floor causes interference on the Wi-Fi network when it gets close to the data closet. What kind of noise is this?

Answer: c. Impulse noise

Explanation: Impulse noise, or noise spike, is a non-continuous noise and one of the most difficult errors to detect because it can occur randomly.

6. Which of the following techniques would *not* reduce noise on a network?

Answer: d. Install cables close together.

Explanation: Crosstalk is an unwanted coupling between two different signal paths and can occur when unshielded cables are installed closely together.

Section 4-3: Error Detection

7. Given the character 0110101, what bit will be added to support even parity?

Answer: d. Arithmetic checksum

Explanation: With parity checking, a bit is added to the end of a string of bits to create either even parity or odd parity. For even parity, the 0 or 1 added to the string produces an even number of binary 1s. In this case, the character already contains an even number of 1s, so a 0 parity bit is added to the end of the string: 0110101**0**.

8. Which error detection method is designed to detect a corrupted IP address in a packet's IP header?

Answer: d. Arithmetic checksum

Explanation: Many higher-level protocols on the Internet (such as TCP and IP) use a form of error detection called arithmetic checksum. IP's error-detection, however, is performed on only the IP header, and not the data field. Information such as the IP address is contained in the IP header.

9. What is the largest size error burst thegenerator polynomial $x^{12} + x^{11} + x^3 + x^2 + x + 1$ can detect with 100% accuracy?

Answer: b. 12 bits

Explanation: In cases where the size of the error burst is less than $r + 1$, where r is the degree of the generator polynomial, error detection is 100 percent. The degree of the polynomial listed is 12. In cases where the error burst is greater than or equal to $12 + 1$, or 13, there is a chance the CRC will not detect the error. Therefore, this CRC can only detect error bursts of 12 bits or less.

Section 4-4: Error Control

10. Which of the following is *not* a legitimate option for how the receiver can handle a data transmission error?

Answer: b. Resend the packet

Explanation: While the receiver might request that the sender resend the packet, the receiver would not be the one to resend a lost or corrupted packet. The receiver might also discard the message in some cases, or might be able to correct the error if error correction information is included.

11. Station A sends packets numbered 500-549. Station B replies with packets numbered 3000-3099 along with an ACK message. What packet number is included in Station B's ACK message?

Answer: b. 550

Explanation: The acknowledgment that a receiver transmits to the sender always contains a value equal to the number of the *next expected* packet from that sender. In this case, Station A sent packets 500-549. The next packet Station B would expect from Station A would be numbered 550.

Chapter 5

Wired and Wireless Local Area Networks

Objectives

After reading this chapter, you should be able to:

- Explain the purpose of LANs (local area networks) in a business or home

- Describe the evolution of LAN technologies

- Explain features offered by switches for network traffic management

- Compare Ethernet standards

- Explain the access control method used by wireless LANs

Introduction

So far in this course, you've learned about the networking layers of the TCP/IP suite and the OSI model. You've also learned about the activities of the physical layer of a network, whether a signal is transmitted on a wired connection or a wireless signal, and how data and signals are related. And then you read about frames that give structure to these messages, and how errors are handled. In this chapter, you'll continue your study of the data link layer, and you'll learn some of the specifics of how protocols at this layer function. Specifically, you'll read about Ethernet on both wired and wireless LANs.

A LAN (local area network) is a communications network that interconnects a variety of data communications devices within a small geographic area and transmits data at high data transfer rates. Several points in this definition merit a closer look. The phrase "data communications devices" covers computers such as personal computers, computer workstations, and mainframe computers, as well as peripheral devices such as disk drives, printers, and modems. Data communications devices could also include items such as motion, smoke, and heat sensors; fire alarms; ventilation systems; and motor speed controls. These latter devices are often found in businesses and manufacturing environments where assembly lines and robots are commonly used.

The next piece of the definition, "within a small geographic area," usually implies that a LAN can be as small as one room, or can extend across multiple rooms, over multiple floors within a building, and even through multiple buildings within a single campus. The most common geographic areas for a LAN, however, are a room or multiple rooms within a single building.

Lastly, the final phrase in the definition states that local area networks are capable of transmitting data at "high data transfer rates." While early LANs transmitted data at perhaps 10 million bits per second, the newest LANs can transmit data at 10 billion bits per second and higher.

Since the LAN first appeared in the 1970s, its use has become widespread in commercial and academic environments. It would be difficult to imagine a collection of computer workstations within a computing environment that did not employ some form of LAN. Many individual computer users now install LANs at home to interconnect two or more computers, printers, game systems, televisions, IoT (Internet of Things) systems, and other devices. Just as in office environments, one of the driving forces behind installing a LAN in a home is the capability of sharing peripherals such as high-quality printers and high-speed connections to the Internet. To better understand this phenomenon, it is necessary to examine several "layers" of LAN technology.

This chapter begins by discussing the primary function of a LAN as well as its advantages and disadvantages. Next, the basic physical layouts or hardware topologies of the most commonly found LANs are discussed, followed by a survey of the software (medium access control protocols) and network devices (switches) that allow a workstation to transmit data on the network. You'll then examine the most common LAN standards, such as the various Ethernet versions for both wired and wireless LANs.

Section 5-1: Using LANs

To better understand the capabilities of local area networks, let's examine their primary function and some typical activities and application areas. Most users need a LAN to provide access to hardware and software resources that will allow them to perform one or more of the following activities in an office, academic, or manufacturing environment: access to the Internet; access to files, databases, and applications; print services; email services; process control and monitoring; and distributed processing.

Perhaps the strongest advantage of a LAN is its ability to allow users to connect their computers to the Internet. In this way, you can use a web browser or other Internet software to access all the resources of the Internet. A LAN can interface with other LANs, with WANs (wide area networks) such as the Internet, and with mainframe computers, as well as with other network types. Thus, a LAN is the foundation that brings together many different types of computer systems and networks. A LAN's interfacing ability enables a company's employees to interact with people external to the company, such as customers and suppliers. For example, if employees wish to send purchase orders to vendors, they can enter transactions on their workstations. These transactions travel across the company's LAN, which connects to a WAN. The suppliers receive the orders through their own LAN that is also connected to a WAN.

Secondly, a LAN allows users to share hardware and software resources. For example, suppose the network version of a popular database program is purchased and installed on a LAN. The files that contain all the database information are stored in a central location such as a network server. When any user of the LAN wishes to access records from that database program, the records can be retrieved from the server and then transmitted over the LAN to the user's workstation for display. A LAN makes files available to network users by connecting a server or workstation with large storage disk drives that act as a central storage repository, aptly called a file server. Suppose two or more users wish to share a data set. In this case, the data set would be stored on the file server, while the network provides access to those users who have the appropriate permissions.

This file sharing capability also allows LANs to share access to applications. For example, when the LAN offers access to a high-level application such as commercial project management software, the network stores some or all of the application files on the file server and transfers a copy to the appropriate workstation on demand. By keeping all of the application on the server—or more likely, part of it on the server and part of it on the client workstation—the network can control access to the software and can reduce the amount of disk storage required on each user's workstation for this application.

A LAN can also provide access to one or more high-quality printers. LAN software called a print server provides workstations with the authorization to access a particular printer, accepts and queues print jobs, prints documents, and allows users access to the job queue for routine administrative functions.

Similarly, many companies support their own corporate email, although smaller companies and individuals often use a third-party service such as Gmail or Outlook instead. Companies with their own email services maintain email servers to store employee emails. The email servers are located somewhere on the corporate network as a database of email messages, both old and new. When users log in to access their email, their messages are retrieved from the email server.

Figure 5-1 shows typical interconnections between a LAN and other entities. It is common to interconnect

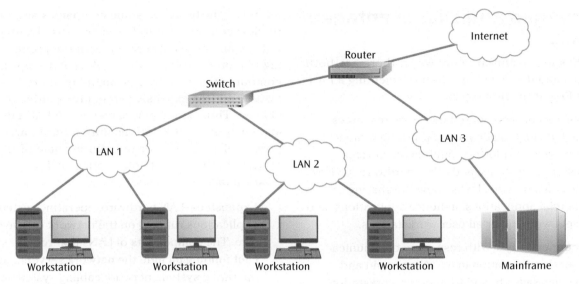

Figure 5-1   A LAN interconnecting another LAN, the Internet, and a mainframe computer

one LAN to another LAN using special configurations on a switch. Equally common is the interconnection of a LAN to a WAN or other LANs via a router. A LAN can also be connected to a mainframe computer to enable the two entities to share each other's resources.

In manufacturing and industrial environments, LANs are often used to monitor manufacturing events and report and control their occurrence. The LAN provides process control and monitoring. An automobile assembly line that uses sensors to monitor partially completed automobiles and control robots for assembly is an excellent example of a LAN performing process control functions.

Depending on the type of network and the choice of network operating system, a LAN may support distributed processing, in which a task is subdivided and sent to remote workstations on the network for execution. Oftentimes, these remote workstations are idle; thus, the distributed processing task amounts to "borrowing" CPU time from other machines (and is often called grid computing). The results of these remote executions are then returned to the originating workstation for dissemination or further processing. By delegating tasks to those computers that are most capable of handling specific chores, the distribution of tasks or parts of tasks can lead to an increase in execution speed and efficiency.

Putting LANs to Work

In addition to performing these common activities, a LAN can be an effective tool in many application areas:

> **Office environment**—A LAN in an office can support word processing, spreadsheet operations, database functions, email access, Internet access, electronic appointment scheduling, and graphic image creation capabilities over a wide variety of platforms and to many workstations. Completed documents can be routed to high-quality printers to produce letterheads, graphically designed newsletters, and formal documents.

> **Academic environment**—In a laboratory setting, a LAN can provide students with access to the tools necessary to complete homework assignments, send email, explore simulation activities, and utilize the Internet. In a classroom setting, a LAN can enable instructors to deliver tutorials and lessons with high-quality graphics and sound to students. Multiple workstations can be used to provide students with instruction at their own pace, while the instructor monitors each student's progress at every workstation.

> **Manufacturing environment**—Modern assembly lines operate under the control of LANs. As products move down the assembly line, sensors control position; robots perform mundane, exacting, or dangerous operations; and product subassemblies are inventoried and ordered. The modern automobile assembly line is a technological tour de force, incorporating numerous LANs and possibly mainframe computers.

Advantages and Disadvantages of LANs

While LANs are useful in many ways, there are both advantages and disadvantages to implementing a LAN. Let's look first at the primary advantages:

> **Shared resources**—Shared hardware resources can include high-quality and 3-D printers, tape-backup systems, plotters, multimedia devices, mass storage systems, and other hardware devices. On the software side, LANs allow the sharing of commercial applications, in-house applications, and data sets with one or all user workstations.

> **Interconnectivity**—With respect to communications, each workstation in a LAN can send and receive messages to and from other workstations and networks. This intercommunication allows users to send email, access websites, send print jobs, and retrieve database records.

> **Flexibility in system evolution**—In a LAN, component evolution can develop independently of system evolution, and vice versa. For example, if new workstations are desired, you can replace older workstations with newer ones, requiring few changes to the network itself. Likewise, if one or more network components become obsolete, you can upgrade the network component without replacing or radically altering individual workstations.

> **Mixed hardware**—Under some conditions, LANs allow equipment from different manufacturers to be mixed on the same network. For example, it is possible to create a LAN that incorporates Windows computers with macOS computers. You can also network mobile devices of various types and operating systems, printers from different manufacturers, and IoT devices that rely on various protocols.

> **High transfer rates and low error rates**—Today's LANs typically support data transfer rates between 100 megabits per second and 10 gigabits per second. Because of these rates, you can transfer documents across a LAN quickly and with confidence.

> **Privacy and autonomy**—Because LANs can be purchased outright, the entire network and all workstations and devices can be privately owned and maintained. Thus, a company can offer its desired services using the hardware and software it deems best for employees.

Interestingly, however, some companies are beginning to view equipment purchases as a disadvantage. Supporting an entire corporation with the proper computing resources is expensive. It does not help that, as a computer reaches its first birthday, there is a newer, faster, and less expensive computer waiting to be purchased. Thus, some companies lease LAN equipment and computer workstations, hire a third party to support their networks, or outsource some of their LAN services to the cloud. Implementing LANs incurs several disadvantages:

> **Expensive**—LAN hardware, operating systems, and applications running on the network can be expensive. The components of LANs that require significant funding include the network servers, network operating system, network cabling system including switches and routers, network-based applications, network security, and support and maintenance.

> **Compatibility challenges**—While a LAN can support many types of hardware and software, the different types of hardware and software may not be able to interoperate. For example, even if a LAN supports two different types of database systems, users may not be able to share data between the two databases.

> **User licenses**—Network admins must be careful to purchase the correct user license for LAN-based software. For example, it is almost always illegal to purchase a single-user copy of software and then install it on a LAN for multiple users to access. To avoid using software illegally, companies must be aware of the special licensing agreements associated with LANs.

> **Time commitment**—The management and control of the LAN require many hours of dedication and service. A manager, or network administrator, of a LAN should be properly trained and should not assume that the network can support itself with only a few hours of attention per week. Therefore, a LAN requires specialized staff and knowledge along with the right diagnostic hardware and software. Unfortunately, many hours of this support time are often spent fighting viruses and other network security issues (Chapter 8 is devoted entirely to a discussion of network security concerns).

> **Performance challenges**—A LAN is only as strong as its weakest link. For example, a network may suffer terribly if the file server cannot adequately

serve all the requests from network users. After upgrading a server, a company may discover that the cabling is no longer capable of supporting increased network traffic. After upgrading the cabling, it may become apparent that the network operating system is no longer capable of performing necessary functions. Upgrades to part of a network can cause ripple effects throughout the network, and the cycle of upgrades usually continues until it is once again time to upgrade the server.

Considering all the advantages and disadvantages associated with LANs, it should not be surprising that the decision to incorporate a LAN into an existing environment requires much planning, training, support, and money. Let's now look more closely at how the workstations in a LAN are interconnected to serve the activities and applications discussed so far.

Remember this...

> LANs provide access to hardware and software resources that support users' access to the Internet; access to files, databases, and applications; print services; email services; process control and monitoring; and distributed processing.

> It is common to interconnect one LAN to another LAN using special configurations on a switch. Equally common is the interconnection of a LAN to a WAN via a router.

> A LAN can be an effective tool in many environments, including offices, schools, and assembly lines.

> The primary advantages of a LAN include shared hardware and software resources, interconnectivity with networked devices and the Internet, flexibility in system evolution, compatibility between mixed hardware, high transfer rates and low error rates, and privacy and autonomy.

> Some companies lease LAN equipment and computer workstations, hire a third party to support their networks, or outsource some of their LAN services to the cloud.

> The challenges of maintaining a LAN include the expense of purchasing and maintaining equipment and software, compatibility challenges between network resources, management of user licenses, the time commitment for securing the LAN, and the

constant need to monitor the LAN for performance issues or plan for the ripple effects of changes to the LAN.

Self-check

1. Data stored on the network and accessed by multiple users is an example of _____.
   a. file services
   b. distributed processing
   c. email services
   d. print services
2. Which pair of devices would most likely *not* share the same LAN?
   a. Printer and laptop
   b. Switch and file server
   c. Web server and smartphone
   d. Smart TV and smart thermostat

Check your answers at the end of this chapter.

Section 5-2: Evolution of LAN Technologies

The way devices are connected on a LAN determine the types of rules, or protocols, they need to manage their communications with each other. For example, can a device send a message directly to another device, such as when you connect a small printer to your computer? Or can that transmission be detected by other devices on the network? If you connect all network devices along a single line, they all must share the same bandwidth, and all devices can eavesdrop on all other devices. Instead, is there a way to separate connections so every device has its own bandwidth and can send a private message to any other device? The way you organize these devices and their connections is called a network's **topology**.

Bus Topology

The **bus topology** was the first physical design when LANs became commercially available in the late 1970s. Since the 1970s, the use of a bus as a LAN configuration has diminished to the point of extinction; however, you can learn some important networking concepts from the technologies developed to overcome limitations of earlier technologies. A bus LAN essentially consisted of a cable, or bus, to which all devices were attached. As

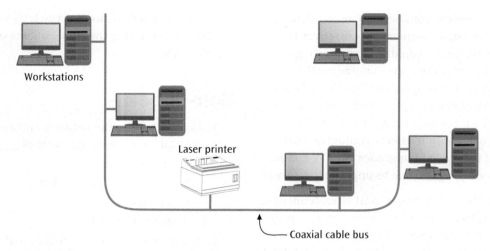

Figure 5-2 Simple diagram of a LAN bus topology

shown in Figure 5-2, the bus was simply a linear coaxial cable that connected multiple devices or workstations, similar to a bus line where you can board the bus at any point along its route. Any data transmitted on the bus was received by all devices connected to the bus, similar to how bus passengers can disembark at any point along the route.

Connecting to the cable required a simple device called a tap (see Figure 5-3). This tap was a passive device, as it did not alter the signal and did not require electricity to operate. In general, it was difficult to add a new workstation if no tap was available at the specified location. Because there was no tap, the cable had to be cut, and a tap had to be inserted. Cutting the cable and inserting a tap disrupted the traffic on the network and was a somewhat messy job. The best way to avoid this was to anticipate where workstations would be and have the installation team install all the necessary taps in advance. As you might expect, however, predicting the exact number and location of taps was virtually impossible.

On the workstation end of the cable was a network interface card, which is still used today. The **NIC (network interface card)** is an electronic device, sometimes in the form of a computer circuit board or part of a larger circuit board. It performs the necessary signal conversions and protocol operations that allow the workstation to send and receive data on the network.

When a device transmitted on the bus, all other attached devices received the transmission. Only one signal at a time could be transmitted on the cable. All workstations had to be aware that another workstation was transmitting, so they did not attempt to transmit and thereby inadvertently destroy the signal of the first transmitter. Allowing only one workstation access to the medium at one time was (and still is) the responsibility of the medium access control protocol, which will be discussed in detail a little later in this chapter.

As stated earlier, bus-based LANs have lost popularity to the point of near extinction. The next stage of LAN evolution was the star-wired bus topology, discussed next.

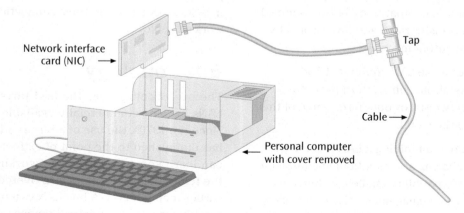

Figure 5-3 The NIC in a workstation connects to a LAN cable

Star-Wired Bus Topology

The star-wired bus topology, also now extinct, acted like a bus but looked like a star. To be more precise, the network logically acted as a bus with signals moving along a pre-defined path, but it physically looked like a star in the way all workstations connected to a single, central device.

The logical topology of a network determines how data moves around the network from workstation to workstation. The physical topology refers to the pattern formed by the locations of the physical elements of the network, as it would appear if drawn on a sheet of paper. Let's explore the details of this important distinction further, as the concepts here are still relevant today.

In star-wired bus networks, all workstations are connected to a central device called a hub, as seen in Figure 5-4. Hubs are no longer used on today's networks, but again, the progression of technology here laid the foundation for how today's networks function. The hub was a relatively nonintelligent device that simply and immediately retransmitted all data it received from any workstation out to all other devices connected to the hub. All workstations heard the transmitted data because there was only a single transmission channel, and all workstations used this one channel to send and receive data.

Sending data to all workstations and devices generated a lot of traffic but kept the operation very simple because there was no need to route traffic to any particular destination. Thus, regarding its logical design, the star-wired bus was acting as a bus—when a workstation

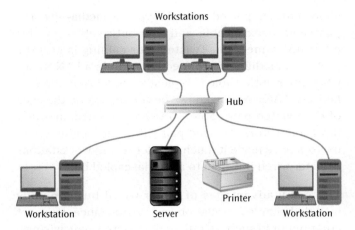

Figure 5-4 Simple example of a star-wired bus topology

transmitted, all connected devices immediately received the data. The network's physical design, however, was a star because all the devices were connected to a central hub and radiated outward in a star-like (as opposed to linear) pattern.

The hub at the center of a star-wired bus network came in a variety of designs. It could contain anywhere from two to hundreds of connections, or ports. For example, if you had a hub with 24 ports and more were desired, it was fairly simple to either interconnect two or more hubs, or purchase a larger hub. Figure 5-5 demonstrates that to interconnect two hubs, you simply ran a cable from a special connector on the front or rear of the first hub to a special connector on the front or rear of the second hub.

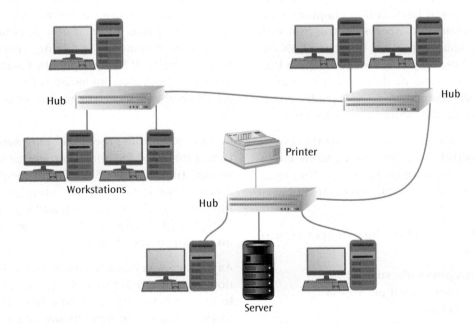

Figure 5-5 Interconnection of three hubs in a star-wired bus LAN

Many hubs supported multiple types of media—twisted pair cable, coaxial cable, and fiber-optic cable—for this interhub connection. Twisted pair cabling is still the preferred medium for connections within a LAN today, while fiber-optic cable is typically used as a connector between LANs. As you know, the connectors on the ends of the twisted pair cables are simple-to-use, modular RJ45 connectors. Twisted pair cable and modular connectors have made it much simpler to add workstations to a star-wired bus than to a coaxial-cabled bus.

The many advantages of a star-wired bus topology included simple installation and maintenance, low-cost components (such as hubs and twisted pair wiring), and a high volume of compatible products. The biggest disadvantage—and this is significant—was the amount of traffic its hub(s) had to handle. When two or more hubs were interconnected and a workstation transmitted data, all the workstations connected to all the hubs received the data. As has been noted, the hub was a relatively nonintelligent device. It did not filter out any data frames, and it did not perform any routing. This, as it turns out, became a major problem with hub-based LANs and has led to almost all hubs being replaced. But before you explore the hub's replacement, let's look at the software that operates over hub-based LANs because these concepts are still relevant today in other kinds of connections.

A medium access control protocol is the set of rules that allows a device to place data onto a hub-based LAN or onto other networks that require their workstations to compete for access to the same bandwidth (such as wireless LANs, discussed later in this chapter). Until several years ago, all medium access control protocols operated under the same restriction: Because a LAN was essentially a single bus, only one workstation at a time could be allowed to transmit its data onto the network. This imperative has changed with the introduction of full-duplex connections and switches to replace hubs.

For the moment, however, let's concentrate on one workstation transmitting at a time. Again, these limitations led the way for modern technologies that make the most sense when understood in the context of what they accomplished.

The two basic categories of medium access control protocols for LANs are:

> Contention-based protocols, such as CSMA/CD (carrier sense multiple access with collision detection)

> Round-robin protocols, such as token passing

Let's examine only the first protocol category, as it was the predominant form of medium access control for wired LANs.

Contention-Based Protocols

A contention-based protocol is a first-come, first-served protocol: the first station to recognize that no other station is transmitting data and then to place its data onto the medium is the first station to transmit. The most popular contention-based protocol for wired LANs was CSMA/CD (carrier sense multiple access with collision detection). The CSMA/CD medium access control protocol was found almost exclusively on bus and star-wired bus LANs, and for many years it was the most widely used medium access control protocol.

The name of this protocol is so long that it almost explains itself: it used collision detection to sense when access could be granted to one of multiple devices. Let's explain further. With the CSMA/CD protocol, only one workstation at a time could transmit, which is called a half-duplex connection as you might remember from Chapter 2. A workstation listened to the medium—that is, sensed for a signal on the medium—to learn whether any other workstation was transmitting. If another workstation was transmitting, the workstation wanting to transmit waited and then tried again to transmit. The amount of time the workstation waited depended on the CSMA/CD protocol used. If no other workstation was actively transmitting, the workstation transmitted its data onto the medium. The CSMA/CD access protocol was analogous to people carrying on a conversation at the dinner table. If no one is talking, someone can speak. If someone is talking, everyone else hears this and waits. If two people start talking at the same time, they both stop immediately (or at least polite people do) and wait a certain amount of time before trying again.

In most situations, the data being sent by a workstation is intended for one other workstation, but all the workstations on the CSMA/CD protocol-based network received the data. Only the intended workstation, as identified by the destination address, would do something with the data. All the other workstations would discard the frame of data.

As the data was being transmitted, the sending workstation continued to listen to the medium thereby listening to its own transmission. Under normal conditions, the workstation would hear its own data being transmitted. If the workstation heard a distorted, unstructured transmission, however, it assumed a collision had occurred. A collision was when two or more workstations transmitted their data across the same medium at the same time.

The two workstations did not actually need to *begin* transmission at exactly the same instant for a collision to occur. Consider a situation in which two workstations were at opposite ends of a bus LAN. A signal propagated from one end of the bus to the other end in time *n*. A workstation would not hear a collision until its data had, on average, traveled halfway down the bus, collided with the other workstation's signal, and then propagated back down the bus to the first station (see Figure 5-6). This interval, during which the signals propagated down the bus and back, was the collision window. During this collision window, a workstation might not hear a transmission, falsely assume that no one is transmitting, and then transmit its data.

As traffic on a CSMA/CD network increased, the rate of collisions increased, which further degraded the service of the network. If a workstation detected a collision, it would immediately stop its transmission, wait some random amount of time, and then try again. If another collision occurred, the workstation would wait once more. If the network was experiencing a small amount of traffic, the chances for collision were small. The chance for a collision increased dramatically when the network was under a heavy load and many workstations were trying to access it simultaneously. This is because all devices connected to a hub were part of the same collision domain. There was no traffic segmentation to reduce collisions or even to reduce the sheer volume of traffic traversing the networking media.

Because of these collisions, busy CSMA/CD networks rarely exceeded 40 percent throughput. In other words, these CSMA/CD networks wasted 60 percent of their time dealing with collisions and other overhead. Today's users find this rate unacceptable and so use more advanced networking devices called switches instead of hubs.

Before examining how switches function, let's answer the question: How do switches alter the network topology?

Star Topology

A modern-day star topology uses a more advanced central connection device called a switch, which you'll learn more about shortly. In a star LAN, both the physical and logical topologies are star shaped, as shown in Figure 5-7. Physically, each workstation connects directly to the central switch. And logically, each workstation communicates directly with the central switch, which then intelligently forwards messages to the port connecting the destination device rather than broadcasting messages out of every port.

Recall that all the devices connected to a hub receive every transmission and must choose what to ignore. In contrast, switches greatly reduce traffic by sending a message only to the intended destination. This is similar to how major shipping companies work. Consider

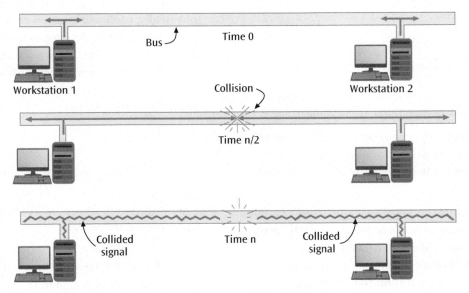

Figure 5-6 Two workstations at opposite ends of a bus experiencing a collision

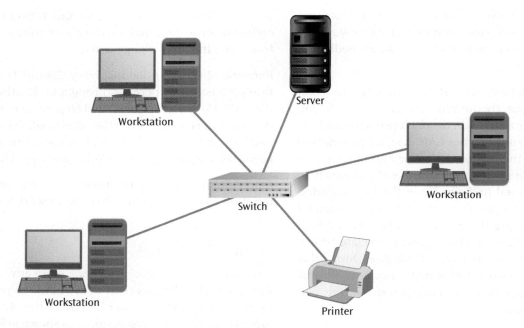

Figure 5-7 Simple example of a star LAN

what happens when you send a package by FedEx—your package does not travel along the same pre-defined route as all the other packages. Instead, it is routed to a central distribution facility, and then forwarded to its destination. The FedEx truck carries the package to the correct address, and the driver carries the package from the truck to the destination building. Similarly, the cabling connecting an end device and the switch is dedicated to those two devices and carries transmissions either going to or coming from the one workstation (with a few exceptions). In the next section, you'll see in more detail how a switch operates and the benefits it brings to today's LANs.

Remember this...

> A network's topology refers to the way networked devices and their connections are organized.

> A bus LAN essentially consisted of a cable, or bus, to which all devices were attached. Any data transmitted on the bus was received by all devices connected to the bus.

> The star-wired bus topology logically acted as a bus with signals moving along a pre-defined path, but it physically looked like a star. The logical design of a network determines how data moves around the network from workstation to workstation. The physical design refers to the pattern formed by the locations of the physical elements of the network, as it would appear if drawn on a sheet of paper.

> The most popular contention-based protocol for wired LANs was CSMA/CD (carrier sense multiple access with collision detection). It used collision detection to sense when access could be granted to one of multiple devices. All devices connected to a hub were part of the same collision domain.

> A modern-day star topology uses a more advanced central connection device called a switch, and both the physical and logical topologies are star shaped. Physically, each workstation connects directly to the central switch. And logically, each workstation communicates directly with the central switch, which then intelligently forwards messages to the port connecting the destination device rather than broadcasting messages out of every port.

Self-check

3. Four computers (Computers A, B, C, and D) are connected to a hub. Computer A sends a message to Computer D. Which device(s) will receive the message?

   a. Computer D

   b. Computers A and D

   c. Computers B, C, and D

   d. Computer A

4. An instructor lecturing to a classroom full of students is most analogous to which of the following?

    a. Bus topology

    b. Logical topology

    c. Physical topology

    d. Star topology

Check your answers at the end of this chapter.

Section 5-3: Switches

A hub is a simple device that requires virtually no overhead to operate. But it is also inefficient. When a network is experiencing a high volume of traffic, a hub compounds the problem by taking any incoming frame and retransmitting it out to all connections. In contrast, a switch uses addresses and processing power to direct a frame out of only a specific port, thus reducing the amount of traffic on the network. This functionality segments the collision domain so that only two devices exist on any collision domain, as illustrated in Figure 5-8. This nearly eliminates the possibility of collisions occurring unless there's an interface misconfiguration. Each device's connection with a switch is a dedicated segment, meaning the media making the connection is dedicated to that one workstation. This dedicated connection increases the available bandwidth for each workstation over time beyond what the bandwidth would be if the workstation were connected to a hub.

Additionally, the cabling on these dedicated segments can carry frames in both directions at the same time without causing a collision. This full-duplex connection allows for data to be simultaneously transmitted and received between a workstation and the switch. How can a cable support signals in both directions at the same time? By using two pairs of wire, each device transmits its send signal on one pair of wires, and it receives a signal on the other pair of wires. To enable a full-duplex connection, the cabling and the device on each end of the connection must be capable of supporting and configured to support full-duplex transmissions. If any of these configurations are not in place, the connection will suffer from a duplex mismatch. Most of the time, devices are configured by default to auto-negotiate the duplex configuration for a connection. This ensures full-duplex capability whenever possible.

Assuming the transmissions successfully arrive from one end of the connection to the other, how does a switch know where to send that transmission next? Let's look more closely at how switches use addressing to reduce and manage traffic on a network.

MAC (Medium Access Control) Addresses

A switch has one primary function: direct the data frame to only the addressed receiver. It does not send the frame out to all links, as a hub does, unless the data frame is a broadcast message. Instead, a switch greatly reduces the amount of traffic on a network by sending frames only to their intended destinations. Thus, a switch needs to know where all the devices are located on the network so it can send the data out the appropriate link. A switch does this by using address information stored within the switch.

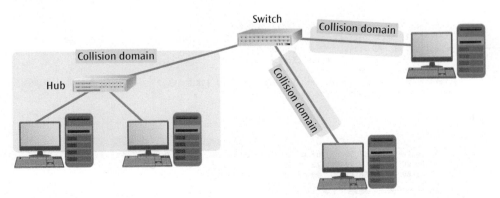

Figure 5-8 A modern switch segments the network into many isolated collision domains, thereby eliminating the problem of collisions

As a frame of data enters the switch, the switch examines the destination address stored within the frame, as shown in Figure 5-9. This frame address, called a **MAC (medium access control) address**, is a 48-bit address assigned to a NIC when the NIC is manufactured; all companies that produce NICs have agreed to use a formula that helps ensure every NIC in the world has a unique NIC address. The switch then determines if a data frame's destination address currently exists in its address table. If it does, the switch knows which port that device is connected to and forwards the frame only to that port. If it doesn't, the switch broadcasts the frame to all its ports except the port the frame came from. All these ports included in the broadcast are collectively called a **broadcast domain**.

> ## Note
>
> Switches are not the only devices that can transmit broadcast messages. End nodes such as workstations also send broadcast messages related to addressing and other network functions.

How does the switch know what addresses are on which ports? Did a technician sit down and type the address of every NIC on each connected port? Not likely. Most switches learn this information by themselves. Upon installation, the switch begins creating an internal port table by using a form of backward learning—that is, by observing the location each frame comes *from*. The switch identifies the source address from each frame as it enters one of the switch's ports, and it places that information into an internal table. After watching traffic for a while, the switch has a table of device addresses that shows which MAC address is connected to each of the switch's ports, which is called a **MAC address table**. If a frame arrives at the switch with a destination address that does not match any address in the table, only then will the switch send the frame to every one of its ports that has a device connected (except the port the frame came from).

For an example of how the switch learns, examine Figure 5-10 and the following scenario. The switch here has three active ports:

> Workstation A on port 10

> Workstation B on port 15

> Workstation C on port 20

When the switch is first activated, its MAC address table is empty except for some unrelated default entries. Figure 5-11(a) shows the table as initially empty. Now

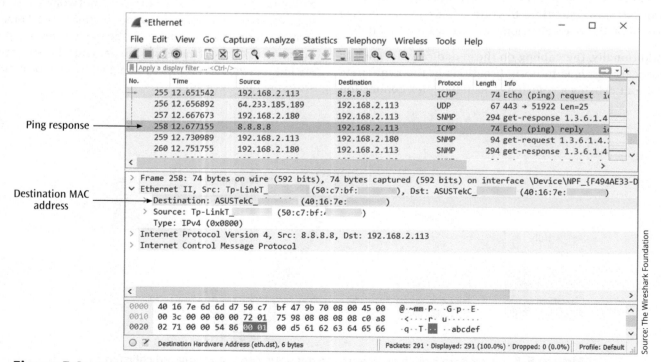

Figure 5-9 This frame, captured by Wireshark, shows the workstation's MAC address as the destination for this ping response from a Google server

Source: The Wireshark Foundation

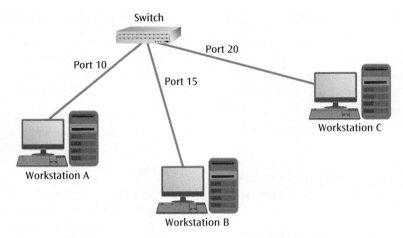

Figure 5-10   **A switch interconnecting three workstations**

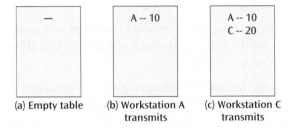

| (a) Empty table | (b) Workstation A transmits | (c) Workstation C transmits |

Figure 5-11   **A switch's MAC address table and its new entries**

suppose Workstation A transmits a frame intended for Workstation C. Before doing anything else with the frame, the switch adds Workstation A's MAC address to the switch's MAC address table and maps that address to Port 10. See Figure 5-11(b).

Because the switch does not yet know where Workstation C is located, the switch forwards the frame to all active ports except the port where it originated. Consequently, the frame successfully reaches Workstation C; however, the switch unnecessarily forwards the frame out of port 15 to Workstation B.

Now suppose Workstation C returns a frame to Workstation A. The switch extracts the address of Workstation C and places it in the MAC address table, as shown in Figure 5-11(c). The frame is destined for Workstation A, and the switch sees that there is an entry for Workstation A in the MAC address table. This time, the switch knows Workstation A is on port 10 and does not forward the frame to any other ports. In addition, if Workstation A sends another frame to Workstation C, the switch will see that Workstation C is on port 20 and will not forward the frame to any other ports.

If Workstation A sends a frame to Workstation B at this point, the switch will not recognize the address of Workstation B because there is no matching entry in the MAC address table. The switch will forward the frame to all active ports except the one where it originated. The switch will perform the same learning function for Workstation B only when that workstation transmits a frame. Thus, the switch learns where network devices are located as those devices transmit messages that include the device's own address information, and then the switch uses that information for future forwarding decisions. In the project at the end of this chapter, you'll experiment with a switch to see how and when it learns MAC addresses.

The above example showed a switch using only three active ports: one for each workstation. In reality, switches can have many active ports. A LAN can have fifty workstations, each one connected to a port on a switch. To support each of these ports efficiently, the main hardware of the switch—called the backplane—must be fast enough to support the aggregate or total bandwidth of all the ports. For example, if a switch has eight 1-Gbps ports, the backplane must support a total of 8 Gbps. This backplane is similar to a bus inside a computer, which allows you to plug in one or more NICs. Each NIC in a computer, switch, or other device supports one port, or connection, to the device. If the NICs are hot swappable, it is possible to insert and remove cards while the power to the unit is still on. This capability allows for quick and easy maintenance of a switch. As traffic enters each port, the MAC address table is updated to reflect the source address of the received frame. Later, when a frame is to be transmitted to another workstation, this table of forwarding addresses is consulted and the frame is sent out the optimal port.

Virtual LANs

One of the more interesting applications of a switch is to create a virtual LAN. Just as the switch segments a large collision domain into multiple smaller collision domains, switches can also segment a large broadcast domain into multiple smaller broadcast domains. As you just read, switches and workstations send broadcast messages to accomplish certain tasks on a network, such as addressing functions. However, high volumes of broadcast traffic can slow down a network, thus creating the need to break up a large and busy broadcast domain. This is one way that VLANs can be helpful.

A **VLAN (virtual LAN)** is a logical subgroup within a LAN created via switches and software rather than by manually moving wiring from one network device to another. For example, if a company wishes to create a workgroup of employees to collaborate on a new project, network support personnel can create a VLAN for that workgroup. Even though the employees and their actual computer workstations may be scattered throughout the building, LAN switches and VLAN software can be used to create a "network within a network" to enhance resource accessibility for that workgroup, regardless of where each employee's workstation is located in the building.

Alternatively, employees in different departments but sharing office space in close proximity can also be grouped according to VLAN. Two computers within inches of each other might be connected to the same switch but would not be able to communicate directly through their shared switch. In this case, VLANs are being used to enhance security by segmenting the network according to which computers should be able to communicate with each other, regardless of which switch each workstation is connected to.

Other reasons you might want to use VLANs include:

› Identify groups of devices whose data should be given priority handling, such as executive client devices or an ICS (industrial control system) that manages a refrigeration system or a gas pipeline.

› Isolate connections with heavy or unpredictable traffic patterns, such as when separating high-volume VoIP (Voice over IP) traffic from other network activities.

› Isolate groups of devices that rely on legacy protocols incompatible with most of the network's traffic, such as a legacy SCADA (supervisory control and data acquisition) system monitoring an oil refinery.

› Separate groups of users who need special or limited security or network functions, such as when setting up a guest network.

› Configure temporary networks, such as when making specific network resources available to a short-term project team.

› Reduce the cost of networking equipment, such as when upgrading a network design to include additional departments or new types of network traffic.

Consider Figure 5-12 in which two VLANs have been configured. VLAN 1 has Server 1, Workstation 1, and Workstation 2. VLAN 2 has Server 2, Workstation 3, and Workstation 4. The devices in VLAN 1 cannot access those in VLAN 2, and vice versa, because they are in different VLANs. Although this sounds restrictive, it increases available network bandwidth and security within and between VLANs. Traffic for one VLAN is not shared with devices on another VLAN. For example, network traffic for the HR Dept is not visible to workstations used by the Sales Dept.

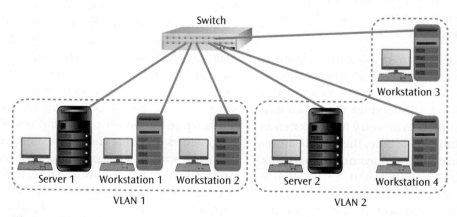

Figure 5-12 A switch with two VLANs configured

The IEEE 802.1Q standard (informally referred to as dot1q) was designed to allow multiple devices to work together to create a virtual LAN. Using this standard, it is also possible for a switch to be shared by multiple VLANs. To track this VLAN traffic, the 802.1Q standard defines a tag (a 4-byte field) that the switch inserts into each frame's header coming from a port assigned to a VLAN. That tag tells the switch which other ports the frame could be broadcast to. As the frame travels across multiple switches, other switches can also read the tag and limit traffic according to which ports have matching tags.

Only switches that support VLAN tagging can be used to configure VLANs on a network. Many switches, called managed switches, allow for this level of configuration. Unmanaged switches, however, are designed for plug-and-play simplicity and cannot be used to support VLANs. To aid with maintenance, most managed switches can have an IP address assigned to them, allowing a network administrator to effect a VLAN change over the network. All the 802.1Q operations on a managed switch can be performed remotely by a network administrator instead of sending a technician to a wiring closet to move a workstation cable from one switch to another. Thus, a workstation can be moved from one VLAN to another with a simple software change.

Link Aggregation

Sometimes one link does not provide enough bandwidth between a device and a switch for the traffic that crosses that link. Other times, a backup link might be required between a device and the switch. Link aggregation allows you to combine two or more data paths, or links, into one higher-speed link. Although a number of proprietary protocols have emerged over the years, the current link aggregation standard is IEEE 802.1AX. This IEEE standard can combine as many as eight identical links into one "fat" link called a LAG (Link Aggregation Group), thus allowing a much higher data transfer capacity between two devices. See Figure 5-13. In order to take advantage of the additional links, link aggregation attempts to balance the flow of data evenly across all shared links. However, if there is a flow of frames or packets belonging to a single conversation, it is more efficient to keep those packets in sequence over a single physical link rather than spreading them over multiple links. Thus, link aggregation can also recognize a sequence of packets and will not spread those packets over multiple links.

Link aggregation serves additional purposes beyond increasing a link's available bandwidth. It can also provide a backup link in the event of a primary link failure. If two or more links are aggregated and one of those links fails, the switches can recover from the link failure in less than a second. Finally, link aggregation can also be used to allow multiple parallel links to a server, as shown in Figure 5-14. This can be useful if a particular server has a high demand placed on it and is experiencing delays due to all requests traversing a single link. With link aggregation, the server requests can be spread across multiple links, thus doubling or tripling the server capacity (assuming that the server has the hardware and software necessary to support multiple simultaneous requests).

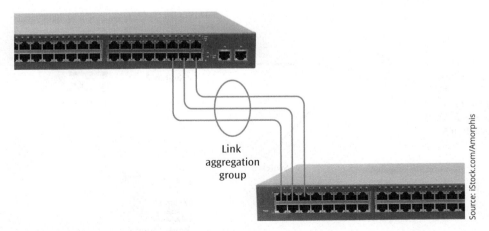

Source: iStock.com/Amorphis

Figure 5-13　Two switches treat these three physical links as one logical link

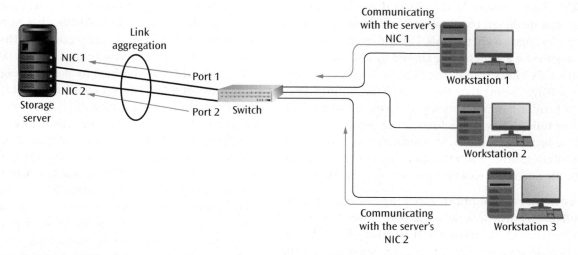

Figure 5-14 Link aggregation allows two workstations to communicate with a server at the same time

Spanning Tree Algorithm

Many businesses and schools use multiple switches and VLANs to support users spread over a large geographic area. It is often desirable to interconnect these networks such that campus-wide intercommunication can occur. As you've already seen, these VLANs are configured and interconnected with switches. Consider the interconnection of switches as shown in Figure 5-15 as an example.

Upon examining the network layout more closely, you might notice an interesting phenomenon: there is a circular connection from Switch 1 to Switch 2 to Switch 3 and back to Switch 1. Why was this done? Perhaps the network engineers were trying to create a system in which there were at least two possible ways to get to most nodes on the network, in case of a component failure. Or perhaps that's just the way the networks were

interconnected. Is this a problem? Actually, a number of things can go wrong.

Imagine Workstation A connected to Switch 1 sends a frame to Workstation C connected to Switch 3, but Switch 1 has not yet seen Workstation C's address and so the address is not listed in any lookup table. Because Switch 1 does not recognize the destination address, the frame is forwarded to all its ports except Workstation A's port. The frame then arrives at Switch 2. Once again, the switch does not recognize the destination address, so the frame is forwarded to all its ports except Switch 1's port, and the frame arrives at Switch 3. Not recognizing the destination address, the switch forwards the frame to all its other ports, which results in Switch 1 receiving the same frame again; and, not recognizing the destination address, Switch 1 will forward the frame to its other ports, and so on and so on.

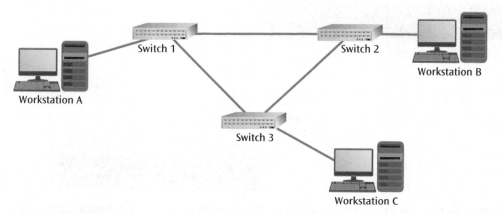

Figure 5-15 A circular interconnection of LANs and switches

At the same time, with the initial broadcast, the frame also traveled directly from Switch 1 to Switch 3, then from Switch 3 to Switch 2, and then back to Switch 1 from Switch 2, creating an endless loop with the frame traveling in both directions around the circle.

How can you stop this cycle of frame passing? It can be interrupted by simply breaking the circular interconnection of LANs and switches. You don't want to physically break the circular interconnection because there may be a reason for such an interconnection strategy. Instead, you can program the switches to locate circular interconnections and then prevent the looping transmissions by modifying the forwarding tables.

STP (Spanning Tree Protocol), originally defined by IEEE 802.1D, manages the traffic across redundant connections between switches. The protocol essentially consists of four steps:

Step 1—A root switch is designated (see Figure 5-16). Typically, the switch with the lowest-numbered MAC address becomes the root switch by default.

Step 2—Each switch must identify the port/connection that leads back to the root switch with the highest speed (such as 1 Gbps) in the fewest number of hops. To do this, the root switch begins a message trail from each of its ports that counts each hop from one switch to the next and also takes into consideration the speed of each connection. Each switch examines the message trail entering each of its ports and marks the best scoring port as the RP (root port).

Step 3—Each connection designated as an RP on one end is marked as a DP (designated port) on the other end of the connection so downstream messages from the root switch can be forwarded throughout the network to all connected switches.

Step 4—The ports that remain without either an RP designation or a DP designation are blocked. This means the internal forwarding tables are updated so data is not directly passed between, say, Switch 2 and Switch 3.

Although STP works well, there is one disadvantage: it can take between 30 and 50 seconds to recompute the spanning tree algorithm if a network failure or a topology change occurs. To fix this problem, the RSTP (Rapid Spanning Tree Protocol) was first issued in 2001 in IEEE's 802.1w standard, which can recompute the spanning tree algorithm in milliseconds. A similar protocol, SPB (Shortest Path Bridging), defined by IEEE's 802.1aq standard, increases network performance by keeping all potential paths active and managing traffic across those paths to prevent loops. Additionally, many vendors have developed their own, proprietary versions of STP.

Quality of Service

One final element that is supported by LAN switches is **QoS (quality of service)**. When LANs were created, all frames were essentially created equal. The protocol was often called a first-come, first-served protocol. It didn't matter if the network was delivering a low-priority email or was part of a high-priority video stream. Each device (and frame) competed with the other devices

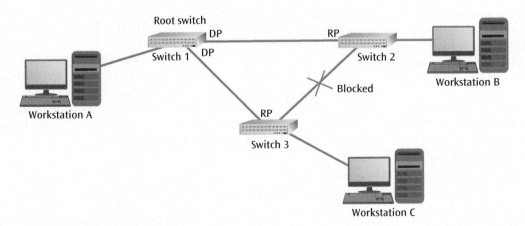

Figure 5-16 Network interconnection indicating root switch, root ports, designated ports, and removed connections

(and frames) for transmission over the medium. In the mid-1990s, IEEE created the 802.1p standard that adds a three-bit PCP (Priority Code Point) field to the header of an Ethernet frame by participating devices. This three-bit PCP field can specify eight different values, where each represents a different class of service or priority level. By default, all traffic is given a PCP value of 0 for "best effort." Level 1 is the lowest priority traffic above this default, and Level 7 is the highest priority traffic. How the system uses these PCP values is not defined by the standard and is left up to network personnel.

All Things Considered

Thought Experiment

Using the Internet or other external sources, collect literature on an Ethernet switch. What are the specifications (such as port speeds, number of ports, cable types supported, backplane speed, etc.) of the switch?

Remember this...

> A switch uses addresses and processing power to direct a frame out of only a specific port, thus reducing the amount of traffic on the network.

> As a frame of data enters the switch, the switch examines the destination address stored within the frame. This frame address, called a MAC (medium access control) address, is a 48-bit address assigned to a NIC when the NIC is manufactured.

> A VLAN (virtual LAN) is a logical subgroup within a LAN created via switches and software rather than by manually moving wiring from one network device to another. VLANs enhance security by segmenting the network according to which computers should be able to communicate with each other, regardless of which switch each workstation is connected to.

> Link aggregation combines two or more data paths, or links, into one higher-speed link. It can provide a backup link in the event of a primary link failure, or it can be used to allow multiple parallel links to a server, thereby increasing the server's performance.

> STP (Spanning Tree Protocol), originally defined by IEEE 802.1D, manages the traffic across redundant connections between switches.

> IEEE created the 802.1p standard that added a three-bit PCP (Priority Code Point) field to the header of an Ethernet frame specifying one of eight different values, where each represents a different class of service or priority level.

Self-check

5. Which device shrinks collision domains within a LAN?
   a. Switch
   b. Hub
   c. Router
   d. Workstation

6. What configuration on a switch could be used to prevent some connected devices from using a network printer?
   a. MAC address table
   b. RSTP
   c. Link aggregation
   d. VLAN

7. A message's header contains a 3 in the PCP field. How high of a priority is this message?
   a. Extremely high priority
   b. Moderately high priority
   c. Moderately low priority
   d. Best effort only

Check your answers at the end of this chapter.

Section 5-4: Wired LANs

Ethernet was the first commercially available LAN system and remains, without a doubt, the most popular wired LAN system today. Because Ethernet is so popular and has been around the longest, it has evolved into several forms. To avoid mass mayhem, IEEE created a set of individual standards specifically for Ethernet LANs, all under the category of 802.3. Let's examine some of the different 802.3 protocols in a little more detail. For your reference, the 802.3 standards to be discussed are summarized later in Table 5-1.

Ethernet Standards

Ethernet standards vary depending upon the underlying physical cabling being used. For example, fiber cable supports higher speeds at longer distances than copper twisted pair cabling. Some fiber cable is designed to maximize distance while other fiber cable is designed to maximize bandwidth. Similarly, cabling technologies have evolved over the years. For example, Cat (Category) 3 twisted pair cable is not nearly as capable of higher speeds and longer distances as is Cat 6 twisted pair cable.

Note

For a quick review of the various types and categories of fiber and copper cable, return to Chapter 2. Note that many of the Ethernet standards described below are supported by Cat 5e or better twisted pair cabling. Cat 5e is still a popular cable choice for residential and small office use because it is so inexpensive. However, newer categories of twisted pair (such as Cat 6) offer other benefits beyond the supported Ethernet standard. Very few new cabling installations for high-speed LANs, such as office buildings, would use Cat 5e or even Cat 6 cables today because the newer cable categories are much better.

Each of these cables can be used to support a variety of common Ethernet standards, each of which is a data link layer protocol to define the way signals are transmitted across a medium. Thinking back to the OSI model introduced in Chapter 1, the particular cable you're using is layer 1 (the physical layer) while the particular Ethernet standard you're using is layer 2 (the data link layer).

An early and extremely popular 802.3 standard was 10Base-T. A **10Base-T** system transmits 10-Mbps baseband (digital) signals over twisted pair cable for a maximum of 100 meters per segment length. (Note that these standards are based on the metric system.) Let's break down the significance of each piece of information indicated in the standard's name:

> The term "Base" is an abbreviation for baseband signals, which are digital signals.

> The "10" of 10Base-T represents a 10-Mbps transmission speed.

> The "T" refers to the twisted pair cabling.

When 10-Mbps Ethernet was first available, it was a fast protocol for many types of applications. Businesses, schools, and homes used 10Base-T for their LANs. As in most computer-based technologies, however, it was not fast enough for very long. In response to the demand for faster Ethernet systems, IEEE created the 100-Mbps

Ethernet 802.3u protocol. The 100-Mbps Ethernet standards are called **Fast Ethernet** to distinguish them from the 10-Mbps standards. The two most popular of these standards were as follows:

> **100Base-TX** was designed to support 100-Mbps baseband signals using two pairs of Category 5 unshielded twisted pair. Like its 10Base-T counterpart, 100Base-TX was designed for 100-meter segments.

> **100Base-FX** was created for fiber-optic systems. It can support 100-Mbps baseband signals using fiber-optic cable and for much greater distances: 1000 meters.

The next set of Ethernet standards to be developed was based on 1000-Mbps transmission speeds, or 1 gigabit (1 billion bits) per second, written as 1 Gbps. These standards (IEEE 802.3ab for copper cables and 802.3z for fiber) define **Gigabit Ethernet**, which is still a popular technology for high-speed LANs today. The most popular Gigabit Ethernet standards include the following:

> The first gigabit standard—**1000Base-SX**—supports the interconnection of relatively close clusters of workstations and other devices using multimode fiber-optic cables over short distances.

> **1000Base-LX** is designed for longer-distance cabling within a building and uses either single-mode fiber-optic cables or multimode fiber.

> A more recent and popular standard, termed simply **1000Base-T**, can use Cat 5 or better copper cable (although Cat 5e or better cable is preferred). More precisely, 1000Base-T incorporates advanced multilevel signaling to transmit data over four pairs of twisted-pair copper cable.

A slightly more recent Ethernet standard is 10-Gbps Ethernet. The initial **10-Gbps Ethernet** standard (transferring at a rate of 10 billion bits per second) was approved by IEEE in July 2002. This standard is also known as IEEE 802.3ae, 10G Ethernet, or 10-Gig Ethernet. The original 10-Gbps standard has already morphed into multiple secondary standards, such as 10GBase-SR for short-range cabling and 10GBase-LR for long-reach cabling. Most of these secondary standards involve fiber-optic cable as the medium for both short and medium distances. However, some copper-based standards have also emerged.

One such copper standard, **10GBase-T** (IEEE 802.3an), uses Cat 6a or better twisted pair cabling to allow transmission distances up to 100 meters (although lower category cables can be used for shorter distances). The development of this standard, while not relevant in many network environments, supports further development of 2.5GBase-T and 5GBase-T products (IEEE 802.3bz) using Cat 5e or better cabling. These technologies support high-speed demands from virtual reality, gaming, and teleconferencing applications.

Beyond the 10-gigabit threshold, standards for 25GBase-T, 40GBase-T, and even 100GBase-T also exist, although they're much less commonly implemented. These speeds are sometimes needed in data centers to span connections between backbone routers or switches, or to connect a SAN (storage area network) to the rest of the company's network. Cat 7 cabling can support these speeds at very short distances, and Cat 8 is preferred. For these short distance connections, you can see that newer copper cables rival fiber cable speeds.

Table 5-1 summarizes the various Ethernet standards just introduced. The table includes maximum transmission speed, cable type, and maximum segment length without a repeater. Note that special connectors are required to reach the higher speeds.

One additional improvement to Ethernet is PoE (Power over Ethernet), defined by IEEE standard 802.3af. Suppose you want to place a NIC in a device, but you do not want to or cannot connect the device to an electrical source. For example, you want to install a surveillance camera that transfers its signal first over Ethernet and then over the Internet. Normally, you would install the camera and then install both an Ethernet connection and an electrical connection. With PoE, you can send electrical power over the Ethernet cable, which can be used to power the camera. Although this sounds promising, one drawback is the capability to provide the Ethernet switch with enough power so that the power can then be distributed over Ethernet lines to various devices.

All Things Considered

Thought Experiment

Find the IEEE (or other) website and report on the latest advances in the 802 standards. Do any additional standards exist for >100-Gbps Ethernet or wireless LANs? Are there any new proposals for systems not mentioned in this chapter? Explain what you find.

Wired Ethernet Frame Format

When ISO created the OSI model in the 1970s, LANs were just beginning to appear. To better support the unique nature of LANs and to create a set of industry-wide standards, IEEE produced a series of protocols under the

Table 5-1 Summary of Ethernet Standards

Ethernet Standard	Maximum Transmission Speed	Cable Type	Maximum Segment Length
10Base-T	10 Mbps	Twisted pair	100 meters
100Base-TX	100 Mbps	2-pair Category 5 or higher unshielded twisted pair	100 meters
100Base-FX	100 Mbps	Fiber optic	1000 meters
1000Base-T	1000 Mbps	Twisted pair—four pairs	100 meters
1000Base-SX	1000 Mbps	Fiber optic	300 meters
1000Base-LX	1000 Mbps	Fiber optic	100 meters
2.5GBase-T	2.5 Gbps	Cat 5e or higher	100 meters
5GBase-T	5 Gbps	Cat 6 or higher	100 meters
10GBase-T	10 Gbps	Cat 6a or higher (Cat 7 is preferred)	55–100 meters
10GBase-R	10 Gbps	Fiber optic	Various lengths
25GBase-T	25 Gbps	Cat 7 or higher (Cat 8 is preferred)	30 meters
25GBase-R	25 Gbps	Fiber optic	Various lengths
40GBase-T	40 Gbps	Cat 7a or higher (Cat 8 is preferred)	30 meters
40GBase-R	40 Gbps	Fiber optic	Various lengths
100GBase-T	100 Gbps	Cat 7a or higher (Cat 8 is preferred)	15 meters
100GBase-R	100 Gbps	Fiber optic	Various lengths

number 802 (some of which you have already encountered in this text). One of the first things the IEEE 802 protocols did was to split the data link layer into two sublayers: the logical link control sublayer and the medium access control sublayer (see Figure 5-17).

The **LLC (logical link control) sublayer** is the upper portion of the data link layer (i.e., these fields are deeper into the packet, closer to the payload). Recall from Chapter 4 that protocols at various layers add headers with information relevant to that layer's protocols—this process is called encapsulation. It identifies the type of message included in the payload—this is the only LLC sublayer function in an Ethernet II frame—and handles multiplexing, flow and error control, and reliability (all of which requires other types of Ethernet frames).

The **MAC (medium access control) sublayer** is the lower portion of the data link layer (meaning the Ethernet fields related to the MAC sublayer are located closer to the outside of the frame). The MAC sublayer includes fields in the Ethernet header that identify the destination and source MAC addresses. It also provides the checksum in the frame's trailer.

The MAC sublayer defines the layout or format of the frame. There are several frame formats depending on the type of LAN. TCP/IP networks (such as the Internet)

use the Ethernet II standard, which defines the frame format shown in Figure 5-18.

The following list describes each field in Figure 5-18:

> The preamble and SFD (start frame delimiter) fields combine to form an 8-byte flag that the receiver locks onto for proper synchronization.

> The destination address and source address are the 6-byte MAC addresses of the receiving device's NIC and the sending device's NIC, respectively.

> The EtherType field identifies the protocol used at the next layer up, such as IPv4 or IPv6.

> The data field contains the frame's payload and must be between 46 bytes and 1,500 bytes long. The minimum size frame that any station can transmit is 64 bytes long. Frames shorter than 64 bytes are considered **runts**, or frame fragments, that resulted from a collision (in the earlier non-switched LANs) or some other error, and these are automatically discarded. Thus, if a workstation attempts to transmit a frame in which the data field is very short, padding is added to ensure that the overall frame length equals at least 64 bytes.

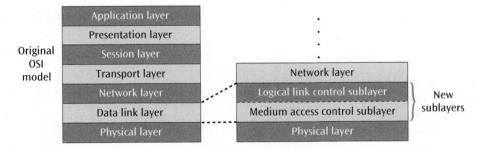

Figure 5-17   Modification of OSI model to split data link layer into two sublayers

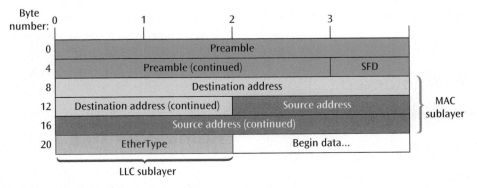

Figure 5-18   Ethernet II frame format

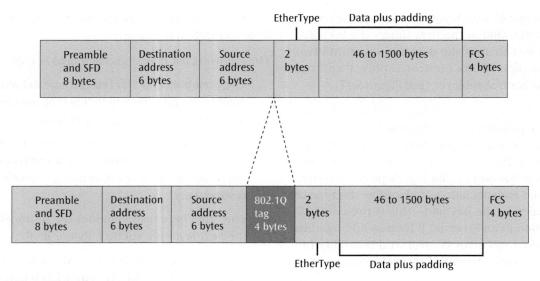

Figure 5-19 The 802.1Q VLAN tag is inserted after the Source field

> A checksum field in the trailer, which is not shown in the figure, is a 4-byte FCS (frame check sequence) calculated based on the CRC (cyclic redundancy check) algorithm.

In total, an Ethernet II frame (not counting the Preamble and SFD) is at least 64 bytes and no more than 1,518 bytes. Furthermore, additional fields can be added to this header as needed. For example, Figure 5-19 shows where the VLAN tag is inserted between the Source address field and EtherType field to track 802.1Q information as a message traverses a network.

This discussion of LAN technology first covered an historical progression of network topologies: bus, star-wired bus, and star. Then you learned about switches and the improvements these devices offer a LAN over older technologies. And now you've read about Ethernet standards that determine the way messages are transmitted at the data link layer over wired connections. Let's conclude this chapter with an examination of how these networking principles must adapt to wireless networking environments.

All Things Considered

Thought Experiment

You are working for a company that is composed of three departments: general support, marketing, and sales. General support occupies the first floor, while marketing and sales are on the second floor. General support has 28 workstations, marketing has 10 workstations, and sales has 30 workstations. Some applications require that data be transferred between departments, but generally each department has its own applications. Everyone needs access to the Internet, the company internal Internet (intranet), and email.

Design a LAN solution for this company. Show the locations of all workstations and interconnecting devices, such as switches and routers, if any are used.

Also show the connection that provides Internet access. What type of LAN wiring would you recommend? What type of LAN topology and protocols would you recommend? Draw a floor plan for each floor. If possible, show both floor plans on one page.

Use the following assumptions:

a. Available switches have a maximum of 24 ports.
b. Some software applications and large data sets reside on departmental servers.
c. To support email, a server is needed.
d. To support the company intranet, a server is needed.
e. The company does not have an unlimited budget but is willing to invest in quality technology.

Remember this...

> Ethernet standards vary depending upon the underlying physical cabling being used. For example, fiber cable supports higher speeds at longer

distances than does copper twisted pair cabling. And yet, some fiber cable is designed to maximize distance while other fiber cable is designed to maximize bandwidth.

> The most popular Gigabit Ethernet standards include 1000Base-T, 1000Base-SX, and 1000Base-LX.

> The LLC (logical link control) sublayer identifies the type of message included in the payload (this is the only LLC sublayer function in an Ethernet II frame) and handles multiplexing, flow and error control, and reliability (all of which requires other types of Ethernet frames). The MAC (medium access control) sublayer includes fields in the Ethernet header that identify the destination and source MAC addresses. It also provides the checksum in the frame's trailer.

Self-check

8. What is the minimum *preferred* category of twisted pair cable required for Gigabit Ethernet up to 100 meters?

   a. Cat 5e

   b. Cat 6

   c. Cat 6a

   d. Cat 5

9. Which OSI sublayer provides the destination device's physical address?

   a. LLC

   b. Physical

   c. MAC

   d. Data link

Check your answers at the end of this chapter.

Section 5-5: Wireless LANs

Now that you've read about the various Ethernet standards for wired networks, you're ready to turn your attention to the underlying medium access control technique that allows a wireless device to communicate with a wireless access point. You could argue that a wireless LAN is essentially a star topology because the wireless workstations typically radiate around and transmit data to the access point. Note that most wireless LANs are actually a combination of wireless and wired technologies. The wireless portion connects laptops, desktop computers, wireless printers and game stations, IoT

devices, handheld devices such as smartphones and tablets, and access points. On the other end of these access points (whose details will be examined shortly) is the wired LAN. The wired portion contains the usual Cat 5e or better wiring along with various combinations of switches, routers, and servers.

Clearly, one of the strongest advantages of a wireless LAN is that no cabling is necessary for the user's device to communicate with the network. This makes a wireless LAN a perfect solution for many applications. Consider an environment in which it is simply not possible to run cabling, such as in the middle of a warehouse or on the floor of a stock exchange. Wireless LANs also work well in historic buildings, or buildings with thick concrete or marble walls, where drilling holes through walls, ceilings, or floors is undesirable or difficult.

Many business offices have incorporated wireless LANs for other reasons as well. Suppose an employee is sitting in their cubicle working on their laptop over a wireless connection. Suddenly, the employee is called into a meeting. They pick up the laptop, walk into the meeting room, and continue work over the wireless connection. Likewise, most college and high-school campuses have wireless LANs so students can access network operations while sitting in class, working in the library, or enjoying a beautiful day on the quad. The most relevant question in this discussion, however, is: How do wireless devices decide which device gets to transmit next?

Wireless CSMA/CA

The contention-based medium access control protocol that supports wireless LANs has two interesting differences from the older CSMA/CD protocol found on older wired LANs. First, there is no collision detection. In other words, the transmitter does not listen during its transmission to hear if there was a collision with another signal somewhere on the network. Three reasons for this are:

> The cost of producing a wireless transmitter that can transmit and listen at the same time.

> The fact that there is no wire on which to listen to an increase in voltage (the collision of two signals).

> The fact that, if two workstations are so far apart that they cannot hear each other's transmission signal, then they will not hear a collision (this is called the hidden node problem or hidden station problem).

Instead, the algorithm of the protocol supporting wireless LANs limits when a workstation can transmit in an attempt to reduce the number of collisions. The algorithm that tries to avoid collisions is called **CSMA/CA (carrier sense multiple access with collision avoidance)**, and unlike CSMA/CD, it is still used on today's LANs.

How does the algorithm limit when a workstation can transmit? Part of that answer is tied to the second interesting difference: priority levels. To provide a certain level of priority to the order of transmission, the CSMA/CA algorithm functions according to the following rule: If a client wishes to transmit and the medium is idle, the device is not allowed to transmit immediately. Instead, the device is made to wait for a small period of time called the **IFS (interframe space)**. If the medium is still idle after this time, the device is then allowed to transmit. How does the IFS provide priority ranking? There are different IFS times that can be used. Check the flowchart in Figure 5-20 to follow along with this discussion.

Step 1—A device wants to transmit to an access point and if a device cannot transmit, it has to back off and wait. There is a limit to how many times a device will back off. To determine if this limit has been met, the device will use a back-off counter. Thus, to start, the device sets its back-off counter to 0 and then listens to the medium to see if anyone else is transmitting.

Step 2—If the medium is initially busy, the device simply continues to listen to the medium. Some software will have the device try again later after a random amount of time. When the medium becomes idle, the client doesn't transmit immediately but delays for the DIFS (differential interframe space). This procedure helps prevent clients from transmitting at the same instant the medium becomes idle, which would cause a collision.

Step 3—If the medium is still idle after the DIFS, the client sends an RTS (Request to Send) to the access point and sets a timer. Hopefully, a CTS (Clear to Send) will be received from the access point before the timer times out.

Step 4—If a CTS is received in time, the device once again waits an IFS, but this time it is a shorter IFS such as an SIFS (Short Interframe Space) or an RIFS (Reduced Interframe Space).

Step 5—After the SIFS or RIFS, the device finally transmits the frame.

Step 6—As shown in the flowchart in Figure 5-20, the device waits for an ACK (acknowledgment) that the frame was received properly.

Step 7—If anything goes wrong, the device increments its back-off counter by 1, checks to make sure it hasn't backed off too many times, and if not, tries the whole procedure over again.

There is one additional technique used to avoid collisions during this entire procedure. If some device wishes to transmit a frame, but it has just heard a CTS come from the access point, then it knows another device has beat it to the punch. When the device sees this CTS, it simply backs off and waits the approximate time necessary for the device that beat it to complete its transmission. This once again reduces the chance of two or more devices trying to transmit at the same time.

CSMA/CA Frame Format

To examine a final piece of information regarding wireless LANs, let's look at the format of the frame that is sent between devices within the wireless portion of the network. There are some interesting things going on here that are worth closer examination. The basic format for a CSMA/CA frame is shown in Figure 5-21 and described next:

› The Frame Control field holds information for controlling transmission.

› The Duration field indicates the anticipated duration of the transmission. Other devices use this information to determine how long to wait before attempting their own transmission.

› Notice that there are four address fields (recall standard Ethernet has only two). Why would wireless Ethernet need four? Besides the usual source and destination addresses, there are also two possible access point addresses. For example, if a device (the source address) sends its message to an access point (the second address) and then from there to a second access point (the third address) and finally to a destination device (the fourth address), then four addresses are necessary. This would be an example of a network with multiple Basic Service Sets (BSSs). If only one BSS is involved, then only three addresses of the four are used: destination, source, and access point.

› Sequence Control defines the sequence number of the current frame.

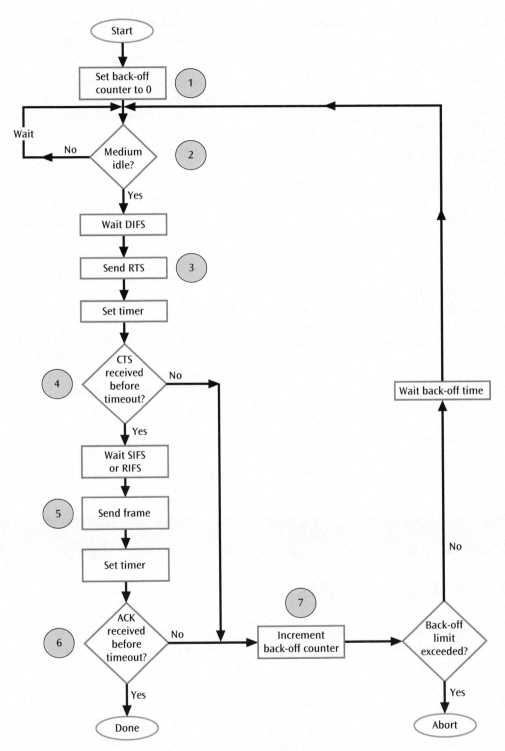

Figure 5-20   Flowchart showing the algorithm for CSMA/CA

Frame control	Duration	Addr 1	Addr 2	Addr 3	Sequence control	Addr 4	Payload	Frame check sequence
16 Bits	16 Bits	48	48	48	16	48	0–18496 Bits (0–2312 Bytes)	32 Bits

Figure 5-21   The various fields of the CSMA/CA frame

> The payload can be between 0 and 2312 bytes in length.

> The Frame Check Sequence is a 32-bit cyclic redundancy checksum.

All Things Considered

Thought Experiment

Create a map of your company or school's LAN. Are there any switches? If so, where are the switches located? Are there any routers? Show where these are located. What about access points? Identify these as well.

In this chapter, you explored the way messages are formatted to be transmitted across a LAN's wired and wireless connections. In the next chapter, you'll learn about the systems, services, and software that support LANs.

Remember this...

> Unlike CSMA/CD, the contention-based medium access control protocol that supports wireless LANs does not listen during its transmission to hear if there was a collision with another signal

somewhere on the network. Instead, the protocol limits when a workstation can transmit in an attempt to reduce the number of collisions.

> Interesting fields in the CSMA/CA frame include the Duration field, which indicates the anticipated duration of the transmission, and the four address fields, which allow for two possible access point addresses.

Self-check

10. Which of the following would a wireless client send on a wireless network?
    a. DIFS
    b. RTS
    c. CTS
    d. SIFS
11. Which field in the wireless Ethernet frame is of most interest to other wireless clients on the network?
    a. Sequence Control
    b. Frame Control
    c. Source Address
    d. Duration

Check your answers at the end of this chapter.

Summary

Section 5-1: Using LANs

> LANs provide access to hardware and software resources that will support users' access to the Internet; access to files, databases, and applications; print services; email services; process control and monitoring; and distributed processing.

> It is common to interconnect one LAN to another LAN using special configurations on a switch. Equally common is the interconnection of a LAN to a WAN via a router.

> A LAN can be an effective tool in many environments, including offices, schools, and assembly lines.

> The primary advantages of a LAN include shared hardware and software resources, interconnectivity with networked devices and the Internet, flexibility

in system evolution, compatibility between mixed hardware, high transfer rates and low error rates, and privacy and autonomy.

> Some companies lease LAN equipment and computer workstations, hire a third party to support their networks, or outsource some of their LAN services to the cloud.

> The challenges of maintaining a LAN include the expense of purchasing and maintaining equipment and software, compatibility challenges between network resources, management of user licenses, the time commitment for securing the LAN, and the constant need to monitor the LAN for performance issues or plan for the ripple effects of changes to the LAN.

Section 5-2: Evolution of LAN Technologies

> A network's topology refers to the way networked devices and their connections are organized.

> A bus LAN essentially consisted of a cable, or bus, to which all devices were attached. Any data transmitted on the bus was received by all devices connected to the bus.

> The star-wired bus topology logically acted as a bus with signals moving along a pre-defined path, but it physically looked like a star. The logical design of a network determines how data moves around the network from workstation to workstation. The physical design refers to the pattern formed by the locations of the physical elements of the network, as it would appear if drawn on a sheet of paper.

> The most popular contention-based protocol for wired LANs was CSMA/CD (carrier sense multiple access with collision detection). It used collision detection to sense when access could be granted to one of multiple devices. All devices connected to a hub were part of the same collision domain.

> A modern-day star topology uses a more advanced central connection device called a switch, and both the physical and logical topologies are star shaped. Physically, each workstation connects directly to the central switch. And logically, each workstation communicates directly with the central switch, which then intelligently forwards messages to the port connecting the destination device rather than broadcasting messages out of every port.

Section 5-3: Switches

> A switch uses addresses and processing power to direct a frame out of only a specific port, thus reducing the amount of traffic on the network.

> As a frame of data enters the switch, the switch examines the destination address stored within the frame. This frame address, called a MAC (medium access control) address, is a 48-bit address assigned to a NIC when the NIC is manufactured.

> A VLAN (virtual LAN) is a logical subgroup within a LAN created via switches and software rather than by manually moving wiring from one network device to another. VLANs enhance security by segmenting the network according to which computers should be able to communicate with each other, regardless of which switch each workstation is connected to.

> Link aggregation combines two or more data paths, or links, into one higher-speed link. It can provide a backup link in the event of a primary link failure, or it can be used to allow multiple parallel links to a server, thereby increasing the server's performance.

> STP (Spanning Tree Protocol), originally defined by IEEE 802.1D, manages the traffic across redundant connections between switches.

> IEEE created the 802.1p standard that added a three-bit PCP (Priority Code Point) field to the header of an Ethernet frame specifying one of eight different values, where each represents a different class of service or priority level.

Section 5-4: Wired LANs

> Ethernet standards vary depending upon the underlying physical cabling being used. For example, fiber cable supports higher speeds at longer distances than does copper twisted pair cabling. And yet, some fiber cable is designed to maximize distance while other fiber cable is designed to maximize bandwidth.

> The most popular Gigabit Ethernet standards include 1000Base-T, 1000Base-SX, and 1000Base-LX.

> The LLC (logical link control) sublayer identifies the type of message included in the payload (this is the only LLC sublayer function in an Ethernet II frame) and handles multiplexing, flow and error control, and reliability (all of which requires other types of Ethernet frames). The MAC (medium access control) sublayer includes fields in the Ethernet header that identify the destination and source MAC addresses. It also provides the checksum in the frame's trailer.

Section 5-5: Wireless LANs

❭ Unlike CSMA/CD, the contention-based medium access control protocol that supports wireless LANs does not listen during its transmission to hear if there was a collision with another signal somewhere on the network. Instead, the protocol limits when a

workstation can transmit in an attempt to reduce the number of collisions.

❭ Interesting fields in the CSMA/CA frame include the Duration field, which indicates the anticipated duration of the transmission, and the four address fields, which allow for two possible access point addresses.

Key Terms

For definitions of key terms, see the Glossary near the end of the book.

1000Base-LX

1000Base-SX

1000Base-T

100Base-FX

100Base-TX

10Base-T

10GBase-T

10-Gbps Ethernet

802.1Q

backplane

broadcast domain

bus topology

collision

collision domain

contention-based protocol

CSMA/CA (carrier sense multiple access with collision avoidance)

CSMA/CD (carrier sense multiple access with collision detection)

Ethernet

Fast Ethernet

Gigabit Ethernet

hot swappable

hub

IFS (interframe space)

link aggregation

LLC (logical link control) sublayer

logical topology

MAC (medium access control) address

MAC (medium access control) sublayer

MAC address table

managed switch

medium access control protocol

NIC (network interface card)

physical topology

PoE (Power over Ethernet)

QoS (quality of service)

runt

star topology

star-wired bus topology

STP (Spanning Tree Protocol)

topology

unmanaged switch

VLAN (virtual LAN

Review Questions

1. Your new laptop just arrived, and you need to connect it to the manufacturer's website for some updates. What kind of network will you *directly* connect to your laptop so you can access this information?

   a. PAN

   b. MAN

   c. WAN

   d. LAN

2. Which of the following is both an advantage and a disadvantage for a company deploying its own LAN?

   a. Equipment is owned and maintained by the company that uses the LAN.

   b. The network configuration is adaptable over time as needs change.

   c. Licenses must account for the number of users on the LAN.

   d. LANs support data transfer rates up to 10 Gbps or more.

3. Which of the following is the most common topology for today's LANs?

    a. Mesh

    b. Star

    c. Bus

    d. Star-wired bus

4. Which contention-based protocol attempts to avoid collisions?

    a. VLAN

    b. STP

    c. CSMA/CD

    d. CSMA/CA

5. Which of these Ethernet standards functions on fiber-optic cable?

    a. 100Base-TX

    b. 1000Base-SX

    c. 10GBase-T

    d. 100GBase-T

6. You're installing a wireless access point in an old building on a wall with no nearby power outlet. What Ethernet technology can you use to make this installation work anyway?

    a. PoE

    b. QoS

    c. STP

    d. VLAN

7. Suppose Workstation A wants to send the message "HELLO" to Workstation B. Both workstations are on an IEEE 802.3 LAN. For this example, suppose Workstation A has the binary address 1000, and Workstation B has the binary address 0111. Which of the following is the resulting MAC sublayer frame (in binary) that is transmitted?

    a. 0000 1111

    b. 0111 1000

    c. 1111 0000

    d. 1000 0111

8. Your wireless LAN device has just sent a request to send (RTS). What happens next?

    a. The device waits during the DIFS.

    b. The device sends a frame.

    c. The device increments the back-off counter.

    d. The device sets a timer.

9. You need to provide a secure segment of your network for executives at your company. Which standard will allow you to meet this goal?

    a. 802.1D

    b. 802.1Q

    c. 802.1AX

    d. 802.1p

10. What is accomplished by upgrading a network from hubs to switches?

    a. Combines data paths into one higher-speed link

    b. Segments broadcast domains

    c. Interconnects devices

    d. Segments collision domains

11. Which LAN topology uses a logical topology that is different than the physical topology?

    a. Star-wired bus topology

    b. Mesh topology

    c. Star topology

    d. Bus topology

12. You're connecting a web server to your network that will need to handle high volumes of traffic. Which standard is best to help you increase the bandwidth available to the server?

    a. 802.3af

    b. 802.1Q

    c. 802.1AX

    d. 802.3u

13. You're installing an email server that should be accessible by all employees on the internal network. Which network device is the best option to connect your email server to?

    a. Router

    b. Another server

    c. Workstation

    d. Switch

14. Which field identifies the protocol encapsulated in the data link header's payload?

    a. Preamble

    b. EtherType

    c. Checksum

    d. SFD

15. Which spanning tree protocol keeps all potential paths active?

    a. STP

    b. RSTP

    c. SPB

    d. PCP

16. Which of the following is *not* a type of protocol that determines which device can transmit on a connection at any given time?

    a. Medium access control protocol

    b. Round-robin protocol

    c. Link aggregation protocol

    d. Contention-based protocol

17. What is the minimum *preferred* category of twisted pair cable required for 10-Gig Ethernet up to 100 meters?

    a. Cat 5e

    b. Cat 6a

    c. Cat 7

    d. Cat 6

18. Which CSMA/CA transmission comes first?

    a. RTS

    b. ACK

    c. CTS

    d. Frame

19. Which of these devices encapsulates a message requesting a web page?

    a. Router

    b. Workstation

    c. Server

    d. Switch

20. Given the network in Figure 5-22, which labeled port would STP most likely block to eliminate a cyclic path?

    a. Port A

    b. Port B

    c. Port C

    d. Port D

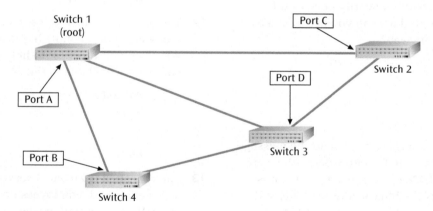

Figure 5-22 A hypothetical network with cyclic paths

Hands-On Project 5

Build a MAC Address Table in Packet Tracer

Estimated time: 45 minutes

Resources:

> Computer with Cisco Packet Tracer installed

> Internet access

> **Context:**

In Project 2, you installed Packet Tracer and practiced interacting with the user interface. Earlier in this chapter, you learned about MAC address tables that switches use to track which device is connected to each of a switch's ports.

In this project, you build a small network in Packet Tracer and observe changes to a switch's MAC address table. Complete the following steps:

1. Open Packet Tracer and, if necessary, sign in with your Networking Academy account.

2. In the Devices pane, click **Network Devices** category and then click **Switches**. Add a **PT-Switch** to your workspace. Give the switch a moment to boot.

3. Click **Switch0** to open its configuration window. Click the **CLI** tab. This takes you to the CLI (command-line interface) for this switch where you can enter commands to interact with the switch. While Packet Tracer offers some options for configuring devices through their GUIs (graphical user interfaces), the tasks in this project can only be completed from the CLI.

4. Click at the bottom of the IOS Command Line Interface pane in the empty space below "Press RETURN to get started!" Press **Enter** to activate the CLI. By default, you begin in user EXEC command mode, which has the lowest level of privileges in a Cisco device. You can see what mode you're in by looking at the prompt—user EXEC mode shows the prompt *Switch>*. To enter privileged EXEC mode, enter `enable`. The prompt changes to *Switch#*.

5. Now that you're in privileged EXEC mode, you can check the switch's current MAC address table. Enter `show mac address-table`. What entries are listed?

6. From the **End Devices** group in the Devices pane, add two **PCs** to your workspace.

7. Click **PC0**. In PC0's configuration window, click the **Desktop** tab and then click **IP Configuration**. In this project and most Packet Tracer projects in this course, you'll set static IP addresses. Enter the following information and then close the configuration window (the information saves automatically):

   IP address: **192.168.0.2**
   Subnet mask: **255.255.255.0**

8. Repeat Step 7 for PC1 and enter the following information for PC1:
   IP address: **192.168.0.3**
   Subnet mask: **255.255.255.0**

9. It's important to get in the habit of keeping good documentation as you work. In the toolbar above your workspace, click the **Place Note (N)** tool. Click under each PC and document that device's IP address and subnet mask, as shown in Figure 5-23.

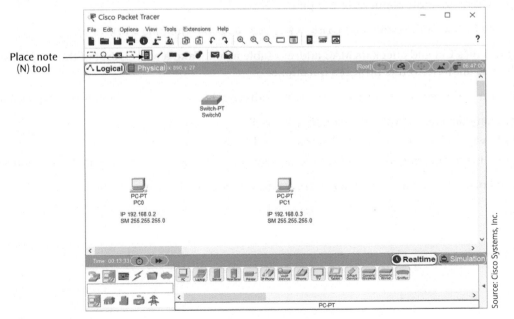

Figure 5-23   Use notes to document your network configurations

10. Now you're ready to connect your PCs to your switch. In the Devices pane, click **Connections** and then click the **Copper Straight-Through** cable, which is a thick, black line. Click **PC0** and select its **FastEthernet0** interface. Then click **Switch0** and select its **FastEthernet0/1** interface. Repeat this process for PC1, connecting PC1's **FastEthernet0** interface to Switch0's **FastEthernet1/1** interface. Wait for all indicator lights to turn to green triangles.

11. Access Switch0's CLI again. Click at the bottom of the CLI pane and press **Enter**. Check Switch0's MAC address table. What entries are listed?

Recall that the switch must see traffic crossing its interfaces to collect MAC addresses for connected devices. To generate traffic, run a ping from PC0 to PC1. Complete the following steps:

12. Click **PC0** and click the **Desktop** tab. Click **Command Prompt**. At the C:\> prompt, enter `ping 192.168.0.3` and wait for the ping to complete.

13. Return to Switch0's CLI and check its MAC address table again. **Take a screenshot** of the output; submit this visual with your answers to this project's questions.

A switch can only see network traffic that crosses its interfaces. It's possible for traffic from multiple devices to enter a switch at a single switch port. In this case, the switch will record multiple MAC addresses for a single interface. Complete the following steps:

14. Add a second **PT-Switch** and a third **PC**.

15. Configure PC2 with the following information and create a note to document this configuration:

    IP address: **192.168.0.4**

    Subnet mask: **255.255.255.0**

16. In the **Connections** group, click the **Fiber** cable, which is the solid orange line. Click **Switch0** and select its **FastEthernet4/1** interface. Then click **Switch1** and select its **FastEthernet4/1** interface.

17. Use a **Copper Straight-Through** cable to connect PC2's **FastEthernet0** interface to Switch1's **FastEthernet0/1** interface. Wait for all indicator lights to turn to green triangles.

18. Check Switch0's MAC address table again. What entries are listed? Given this information, which connected device is Switch0 currently aware of?

19. Sending a ping between PC2 and PC0 will inform Switch0 of three devices' MAC addresses. Which devices do you expect Switch0 to know about after the ping?

20. From PC2, ping PC0 with the command `ping 192.168.0.2`. Did the ping work?

21. Return to Switch0's CLI and check its MAC address table again. **Take a screenshot** of the output; submit this visual with your answers to this project's questions.

22. Examine the three devices listed in Switch0's MAC address table and answer the following questions:

    a. How many devices is Switch0 currently aware of?
    b. Which two devices communicated across Switch0's Fa4/1 interface?

23. Currently, PC1 is not showing in Switch0's MAC address table. What can you do to make Switch0 aware of PC1?

24. When you're finished, you can close Packet Tracer. You do *not* need to save this network.

Reflection Discussion 5

In this chapter, you read about the hidden node problem, also called the hidden station problem. Do some research online to understand this dilemma in more detail. And then answer the following questions:

> In your own words, how would you describe the hidden node problem to a layperson?

> What problematic symptoms would indicate your network is experiencing a hidden node problem?

> How can you fix this problem?

Go to the discussion forum in your school's LMS (learning management system). Write a post of at least 100 words discussing your responses to the listed questions. Then respond to two of your classmates' threads with posts of at least 50 words discussing their comments and ideas. Use complete sentences, and check your grammar and spelling. Try to ask open-ended questions that encourage discussion, and remember to respond to people who post on your thread. Use the rubric in Table 5-2 to help you understand what is expected of your work for this assignment.

Table 5-2   Grading rubric for Reflection Discussion 5

Task	Novice	Competent	Proficient	Earned
Initial post	Generalized statements about the hidden node problem **30 points**	Some specific statements with supporting evidence about the hidden node problem, including sufficient preventative measures **40 points**	Self-reflective discussion with specific and thoughtful statements and supporting evidence about the hidden node problem, a well-formed definition, clear symptoms, and identification of reasonable preventative measures **50 points**	
Initial post: Mechanics	• Length < 100 words • Several grammar and spelling errors **5 points**	• Length = 100 words • Occasional grammar and spelling errors **7 points**	• Length > 100 words • Appropriate grammar and spelling **10 points**	
Response 1	Brief response showing little engagement or critical thinking **5 points**	Detailed response with specific contributions to the discussion **10 points**	Thoughtful response with specific examples or details and open-ended questions that invite deeper discussion of the topic **15 points**	
Response 2	Brief response showing little engagement or critical thinking **5 points**	Detailed response with specific contributions to the discussion **10 points**	Thoughtful response with specific examples or details and open-ended questions that invite deeper discussion of the topic **15 points**	
Both responses: Mechanics	• Length < 50 words each • Several grammar and spelling errors **5 points**	• Length = 50 words each • Occasional grammar and spelling errors **7 points**	• Length > 50 words each • Appropriate grammar and spelling **10 points**	
			Total	

Solutions to Self-Check Questions

Section 5-1: Using Local Area Networks

1. Data stored on the network and accessed by multiple users is an example of _____.

Answer: a. files services

Explanation: A LAN performs file serving when it is connected to a workstation with large storage disk drives that act as a central storage repository, or file server. Data can be stored on the file server, and the network provides access to those users who have the appropriate permissions.

2. Which pair of devices would most likely *not* share the same LAN?

Answer: c. Web server and smartphone

Explanation: Most commonly, a web server is accessed by connecting with the Internet. A smartphone's LAN provides the interface to the Internet where the web server is located on a different LAN.

Section 5-2: Evolution of LAN Technologies

3. Four computers (Computers A, B, C, and D) are connected to a hub. Computer A sends a message to Computer D. Which devices will receive the message?

Answer: c. Computers A, B, C, and D

Explanation: A hub is a nonintelligent device that simply and immediately retransmits all data it receives from any device out to all other devices connected to the hub.

4. An instructor lecturing to a classroom full of students is most analogous to which of the following?

Answer: d. Star topology

Explanation: In a star topology, all devices are centrally connected to a hub or switch. In the given analogy, all the students are listening directly to the instructor.

Section 5-3: Switches

5. Which device shrinks collision domains within a LAN?

Answer: a. Switch

Explanation: A switch segments each collision domain within a LAN so that only two devices exist on any collision domain, thus nearly eliminating the possibility of collisions occurring unless there's an interface misconfiguration.

6. What configuration on a switch could be used to prevent some connected devices from using a network printer?

Answer: d. VLAN

Explanation: VLANs can be used to enhance security by segmenting the network according to which devices should be able to communicate with each other, regardless of which switch each device is connected to.

7. A message's header contains a 3 in the PCP field. How high of a priority is this message?

Answer: c. Moderately low priority

Explanation: By default, all traffic is given a PCP value of 0 for "best effort." Level 1 is the lowest priority traffic above this default, and Level 7 is the highest priority traffic. A PCP value of 3 places the message towards the low end of the priority scale.

Section 5-4: Wired LANs

8. What is the minimum *preferred* category of twisted pair cable required for Gigabit Ethernet?

Answer: a. Cat 5e

Explanation: 1000Base-T, the most popular Gigabit Ethernet standard for twisted pair cable, can use Cat 5 or better copper cable, but Cat 5e or better cable is preferred.

9. Which OSI sublayer provides the destination device's physical address?

Answer: c. MAC

Explanation: The MAC (medium access control) sublayer includes fields in the Ethernet header that identify the destination and source MAC addresses.

Section 5-5: Wireless LANs

10. Which of the following would a wireless client send on a wireless network?

Answer: b. RTS

Explanation: A wireless client sends an RTS to request that the access point reserve the channel for the client to send its data.

11. Which field in the wireless Ethernet frame is of most interest to other wireless clients on the network?

Answer: d. Duration

Explanation: The Duration field indicates the anticipated duration of the transmission. Other devices use this information to determine how long to wait before attempting their own transmission.

Chapter 6

Network Systems and Software

Objectives

After reading this chapter, you should be able to:

- Identify common network servers, software, and licensing models

- Compare server operating systems

- Explain how network devices are configured

- Identify common uses of virtualization on networks

- Explain the role of cloud computing in modern networks

Introduction

Although there are many types of network software—such as diagnostic and maintenance tools, utilities, and programming development environments—network operating systems and network support software are two of the most important. A network operating system (NOS) is essential if the network is going to allow multiple users to share resources. The NOS provides users with password protection on their accounts, and it networks administrators with services that help them control access to network resources as well as use and administer the network. Other NOSs allow network administrators to configure network devices, such as routers, switches, and firewalls, to manage and segment network traffic for increased performance and security. This chapter will outline these operating systems' basic features and capabilities, and it will compare their advantages and disadvantages.

The technologies that support network configuration have continued to evolve in ways that were unpredictable in earlier decades. Where network admins twenty years ago configured physical devices throughout the network, today's network admins work primarily with virtual devices. This chapter will explore the modern network's reliance on virtualization technologies and the emergence of cloud computing that is revolutionizing the way today's networks function.

Section 6-1: Network Servers and Software

To understand the significance of servers on a network, you first need to understand the role an operating system plays for any device, including smartphones, laptops, workstations, servers, and even routers and switches. An **OS (operating system)** is the software loaded into computer memory when a device is turned on; it manages all the other applications and resources (such as disk drives, memory, and peripheral devices) in a computer. Even once an application is running, the application relies on the OS when it makes service requests through a defined API. **APIs (application programming interfaces)** provide a means for different applications to communicate with each other, similar to how a GUI (graphical user interface) or a CLI (command line interface) allows humans to interact with software.

Because users are likely to run multiple applications at the same time, the OS must be capable of allocating the limited amount of main memory and other resources (such as processing time) in a way that provides each application with a sufficient amount of these resources to operate. A modern OS must also provide various levels of OS security, including directory and file security, memory security, and resource security. As applications and their users become more sophisticated, the capability of an OS to provide protection from unscrupulous users is becoming more crucial.

Finally, a function equally as important as memory, storage management, or security is communicating about the status of operations. An OS sends messages to applications, a user, or a system operator about the status of the current operation. It also sends messages about any errors that may have occurred.

Several OSs are available for different types of computer systems. Popular OSs for workstations include macOS, Linux, and Windows. The most popular smartphone and tablet OSs include Android and Apple's iOS. Popular OSs for larger computers (mainframes) include IBM's z/OS and z/TPF (Transaction Processing Facility), VSI's OpenVMS (Open Virtual Memory System), and again, Linux.

Like individual devices, networks also rely on operating systems. A **NOS (network operating system)** is a large, complex program that can manage resources commonly found on most LANs. A NOS needs a host machine from which to operate. Although a part of the NOS resides in each client computer, the bulk of the NOS operates in a network server. More precisely, a server is the computer that stores software resources such as the NOS, computer applications, programs, data sets, and databases, and performs one or more network-type services for connected clients.

There are many types of servers. As just mentioned, network servers support the NOS. There are also file servers for storing files, email servers, print servers for temporary storage of print jobs, database servers, web servers for storing web pages; FTP servers for supporting FTP (File Transfer Protocol) sites; and DNS servers for converting website addresses to IP addresses. The list goes on.

Let's examine the different forms of servers, along with some of the typical hardware and software features that they employ.

Servers range in size from small desktop computers to massive mainframe computers. Typically, the server is a powerful computer running an OS such as Linux or Unix, and they are typically equipped with redundant components: redundant disk drives, redundant power supplies, and even redundant cooling fans.

RAID Configurations

To protect the server from catastrophic disk failure, the storage drives on most servers are configured with a redundancy storage technique. **RAID (Redundant Array of Independent Disks)** is a collection of storage drives (called an array) interfaced in a way to ensure one or more layers of redundant copies of data across the drive array. There are many forms of RAID. Except for the first RAID technique explained below, which is called RAID 0, RAID offers the ability to recover lost data if one or more drives in the array is lost. Figure 6-1 illustrates some of the more common RAID techniques, as follows:

> **RAID 0**—Data is broken into pieces, and each consecutive piece is stored on a different drive. This technique is known as **striping**. There is no redundancy of data in this technique; if one drive fails, data is lost. The advantage of this technique, however, is the speed at which data can be read or written across multiple drives at the same time.

> **RAID 1**—Data is stored on at least two drives, in duplicate, to provide a level of redundancy (or fault tolerance) should one drive become corrupted. This technique is also known as **disk mirroring**. RAID 1, however, does not provide protection against certain risks to data such as ransomware or a virus, as those kinds of attacks would affect data on both drives. Therefore, RAID 1 is not considered a reliable data backup method.

> **RAID 3**—Data is stored across multiple drives (striping), and error-checking information concerning the stored data is kept on a separate drive.

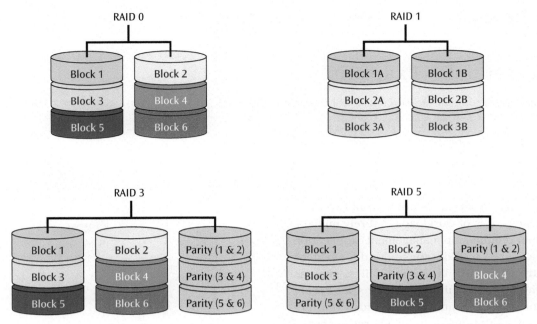

Figure 6-1 Each RAID technique uses a different approach to increase performance, redundancy, or both

This error-checking information, called parity, can be used to detect errors and possibly reconstruct the data should some of it become corrupted. RAID 3 is rarely used in modern RAID arrays and has been replaced by RAID 5.

> **RAID 5**—Data is broken into pieces (stripes) and stored across three or more drives. Parity information (error-checking code) is interleaved with the striped data, not separated onto a separate drive. This configuration maximizes performance while minimizing cost, and still provides reliable data recovery if a drive is lost. RAID 5 is the most popular of these RAID techniques in corporate environments. Keep in mind, however, that RAID 5 by itself is not a complete backup strategy.

Several more RAID techniques exist. They are essentially variations on and combinations of the above techniques, providing increased speed and increased redundancy while also requiring more disks.

Along with redundancy such as RAID, most servers also feature a powerful set of management software. This software allows a network administrator to monitor the status of the server, remotely deploy network applications, update the necessary drivers, install and fine-tune the NOS, and configure the RAID storage system.

Note

A reliable backup strategy will include at least three complete copies of data stored on at least two different types of media with at least one copy stored offsite and, for greater protection, at least one copy kept offline from the remainder of the network. This is called the 3-2-1-1 Rule, as illustrated in Figure 6-2.

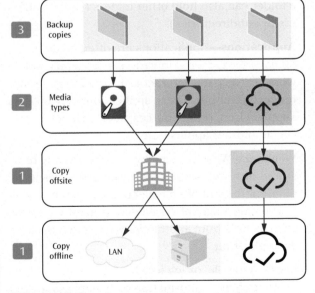

Figure 6-2 The 3-2-1-1 Rule for backups

Storage Types

Storing data directly on servers is not your only option. Consider the many kinds of workloads that rely on data. A CRM (customer relationship management) application draws on data stored in a database. Media services access what are often very large media files, such as videos or high-resolution images. Office staff create documents, spreadsheets, and presentations that are stored on their workstations or in file shares accessed across their company's network. All these examples of data might be stored on-premises (called on-prem for short) or in the cloud. Examples of data types stored on networks include the following:

> **Office and media files**—Probably the most recognizable type of data, office files include file types such as documents, spreadsheets, and presentations. Media files include file types such as photos or videos. Files are then typically stored in a hierarchical file system, as shown in Figure 6-3. Files are grouped within folders (also called directories), and a folder can also hold other folders (called subfolders or subdirectories).

> **Applications**—Applications are often made up of many parts stored in various places on a network. These parts interact as needed to generate requested output. These applications rely on data supplied from other sources, such as a database, an OS, or another application.

> **Websites**—Websites usually consist of many files stored on a web server. Each web page lives in a different file and often collects data from many files. A web page might also pull data from other sources, such as APIs from another website, a database, or an application.

> **Logs**—A log file, or log for short, is a special kind of file that collects information on events associated with a system or application. For example, a log might show information about traffic crossing a network interface. The information could include

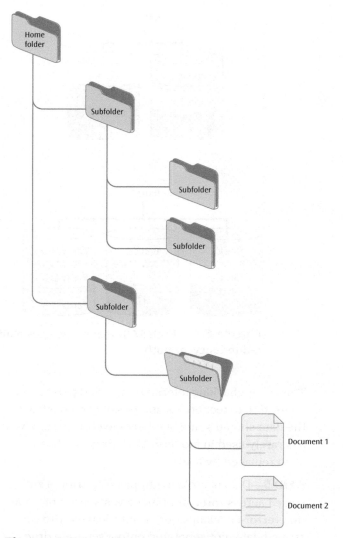

Figure 6-3 A file system consists of folders within folders

data about the time a particular network message was received, where it came from, where it was going, and whether it was allowed to pass. Keeping logs generates a tremendous amount of data in a short period of time and can take up a lot of storage space. But logs are important for troubleshooting problems or investigating security issues.

With all this data as the lifeblood of a business, the systems used to store the data are critical to a business's success. The following list explores storage types you might find in an on-prem network environment:

> **DAS (direct attached storage)** is the storage type most familiar to typical users and refers to a storage device attached directly to a computer (whether that's a smartphone, laptop, workstation, or server). If you have a hard drive in your

computer, you're using DAS. The file system hierarchy of these storage devices may be familiar, where files are organized inside folders inside folders.

> As previously mentioned, RAID is a way to increase data redundancy and requires multiple disk drives. If each server in a datacenter has its own RAID system with multiple hard drives, you're going to require a lot of space with limited ability to expand.

> **NAS (network attached storage)** is a device that provides a large amount of storage to users on a network. The device contains several hard drives, and the storage space on those drives are made available to multiple network devices. Like DAS, a NAS device stores files in a file system. A stripped-down OS running on the NAS is designed for the sole purpose of retrieving data for users. Typically, a NAS device does not have a keyboard or monitor. Access to its control operations is usually obtained through an assigned web address.

> Suppose you gathered all the hard drives for all your datacenter's servers into one place and made the entire pool available to all your servers. This is called a **SAN (storage area network)** and requires specialized, high-speed connections among the SAN drives and between the SAN and the servers. Data in a SAN array of drives is stored in blocks rather than in a file system hierarchy and is called **block storage**. Each block is a specified size, much like storage lockers in a U-Haul (*uhaul.com*) storage facility, and it contains data that is referenced by the block's LUN (logical unit number). A server sees each block as a separate volume and can treat that volume as an attached drive, even installing a file system on it if the block size is large enough. The server then adds data to the block over time.

This distinction between file system storage and block storage is a significant one. File system storage lends itself well to organizing a person's or small department's files, but it does not scale well for large amounts of different kinds of data used by many people. One of the advantages of file system storage is the metadata stored with each file. Metadata is data about the file, such as creation date, author, and permissions. This can be helpful when you're searching for a particular file or need to sort files by creation date, last edited date, or file size.

In contrast, block storage organizes data in a flat namespace so it scales up (increases in size) more easily to accommodate massive amounts of data. Every block in the storage network is addressed by a unique number called a LUN (logical unit number). This avoids the complexity from multiple layers of nested folders and allows for low-latency access to databases, virtual machines, and boot drives. Block storage provides no metadata, however, and requires specialized protocols, such as Fibre Channel (FC), that are expensive and complicated to manage.

In comparing file storage and block storage, think of it as the difference between a street address versus an account on Facebook or a similar social media site. Your home address is identified by a *number* on a *street* in a *zip code* that's in a *city* within a *state*. The street name represents a group of dwellings; that group is part of a larger group represented by a zip code; and that zip code is part of a larger group of zip codes in a city, which is joined by many cities in your state. These are groups within groups within groups. On Facebook, however, your account is identified only by an account name. Every other account on Facebook also has a unique name, and they're not grouped within groups in a hierarchical structure. Therefore, the namespace is said to be flat. Block storage works much the same way as Facebook's namespace. You'll revisit this distinction between file systems and block storage in the cloud discussion later in this chapter.

Utilities

Two other kinds of LAN software that work with and support the NOS are utilities and Internet software. Let's examine both in turn. **Utilities** are software programs that operate in the background and support one or more functions to keep the network running at optimal performance. To support a LAN and its OS, a wide variety of utility programs are available. Sometimes these utility programs come bundled with an OS, but many times they are separate and must be purchased individually. It's important when purchasing utility software (as well as any software product) to pay attention to the licensing agreements. Many utility programs are licensed for a single machine. If 200 workstations are on your LAN, you may have to purchase 200 licenses before your usage is within the letter of the law.

Some of the more common groups of network utility software are:

> **Anti-malware**—This utility is designed to detect and remove viruses and other malware that have infected a computer's memory, disks, or OS. Because new malware appears all the time, it is important to continuously update anti-malware

with the latest version. Many times, owners of purchased anti-malware can download these updates from the software company's website for no additional charge. The only time it is necessary to purchase a new version of the anti-malware is when the software has undergone a major revision. Some anti-malware manufacturers offer corporate deals in which a flat annual fee is paid, and the company can disperse and update as many copies of the software as desired.

> **Anti-spam software**—Spam, or unsolicited commercial bulk email, has become a major nuisance to corporate users as well as individuals. Some professionals estimate that tens of billions of spam messages are sent each day. This large volume of spam wastes the time of workers who must delete these messages, consumes billions of bytes of storage in email servers, and congests the networks that transfer this data. Anti-spam software is used to block unwanted emails and is available that can block spam for an individual computer or for the entire corporate network.

> **Anti-spyware software**—Business and home computer users have been victims of another type of intrusion from unscrupulous outsiders: spyware. Spyware is software that a user unknowingly downloads from the Internet, and when this software is executed on the user's machine, it begins spying on the user. Spyware may take the form of a remote-control program operated by a hacker, or it may be a program launched by a retailer hoping to gather information about your shopping habits for its own purposes or to share with other retailers. In the latter case, the program may simply be a harmless type of market research tool. Even so, most users feel that spyware is intrusive and should be blocked or eliminated. Anti-spyware software can locate and clean the spyware found in a computer's memory and hard disk drive. Home computer users, as well as network administrators, should install anti-spyware and either run it on a regular basis or program the OS to run it on a timed schedule. You should be careful, however, when searching the Internet for free anti-spyware programs as many of them (but not all) are spyware programs themselves.

> **Network monitoring software**—This software incorporates a fairly large number of network support tools. For example, there is software that can monitor servers and report on CPU utilization, network activities, and server requests. Devices called sniffers can be used on both wired and wireless networks. Sniffers can listen to traffic on a network and determine if invalid messages are being transmitted, report network problems such as malfunctioning NICs, and detect traffic congestion problems. Wireless sniffers can perform similar operations and can also detect how far wireless signals reach. Thus, if you are having wireless communication problems, a wireless sniffer can tell you if the signal is too weak at a particular location. Conversely, wireless sniffers can also tell you if your wireless signals go too far, such as outside your building or down the street, where they might be exploited by unauthorized users.

> **Remote access software**—This solution allows a user to access all the possible functions of a workstation from a mobile or remote location. The two most common users of remote access software are nomadic users, who must access software and data on their work computers while traveling or working at home, and support personnel, who need to enter a user's computer system to troubleshoot problems and suggest or make repairs. Many types of remote access software also create a VPN (virtual private network) between the remote user and the work computer. You will learn more about remote access in Chapter 7.

Software Licensing Models

Cloud Essentials+ Exam Tip

This section discusses the subscription licensing model, which is required by

- Part of Objective 2.2: Summarize the financial aspects of engaging a cloud provider.

The licensing agreement that accompanies a software product is a legal contract and describes a number of conditions that must be upheld for proper use of the software package. Most licensing agreements specify conditions in the following areas: software installation and use, network installation, backup copies, decompilation restrictions, rental restrictions, upgrades, copyright, and maintenance.

One of the most important issues that affects most users is software installation and use. When a software package is sold, it is usually intended for a particular type of installation, referred to as the user license. Software companies establish user licenses so that an individual in a company does not purchase one copy of a program and install it on, for example, 200 machines, thus avoiding purchase fees or royalties.

The terms of a license are usually built around one or more licensing models that define where the software can be installed, who can use it, and when payments are made.

Several licensing models exist:

> Under the terms of one of the most common user licenses, a single-user-single-station license, the software package may be installed on a single machine, and then only a single user at one time may use the software on that machine. Some software packages can track how many times the software has been installed and will allow only a single installation. To move the software to another machine requires that you first run the software's uninstall utility.

> A single-user-multiple-station license is designed for the user who might have a desktop machine at work and a laptop machine for remote sites, or another desktop machine at home. The user agrees to allow only one copy of the software to be in use at one time. For example, if the user is at work and operating a particular word-processing program with the single-user-multiple-station license, no one should be running the same program on the user's laptop at the same time.

> An interactive user license, floating license, and controlled number of concurrent users license, all refer to essentially the same scenario. When a software package is installed on a multiuser system, such as a server on a LAN, multiple users can execute multiple copies of the single program. Many multiuser software packages maintain a counter for every person currently executing the program. When the maximum number of concurrent users is reached, no further users may access the program. When a software counter is not used, the network administrator must estimate how many concurrent users of this software package are possible at any one moment and take the necessary steps to purchase the appropriate number of concurrent user licenses.

> A server license, also called a system-based license or cluster-wide license, is similar to an interactive user license. However, with a server license, there is rarely a software counter controlling the current number of users. A server license might actually be priced according to the number of CPU cores or sockets the server has.

> A site license allows a software package to be installed on any or all workstations and servers at a given site. No software installation counter is used. The network administrator must guarantee, however, that a copy of the software will not leave the site.

> A corporate license allows a software package to be installed anywhere within a corporation, even if installation involves multiple sites. Once again, the network administrator must ensure that a copy of the software does not leave a corporate installation and, for example, go home with a user.

> A subscription license relies on a monthly or annual payment schedule to continue using the application. In contrast to the traditional perpetual license, which is a pay-once-own-forever arrangement, a subscription license uses a pay-as-you-go model where the customer makes payments to continue using the service. This arrangement can be beneficial in many scenarios. Subscription licenses cost less upfront, and these expenses are categorized as OpEx (operational expenses) instead of as CapEx (capital expenses), which can provide certain tax benefits.

> The GPL (General Public License) is associated with software that is free to share and change. The license clearly stipulates that "free" implies the freedom to share and change the source code, but the creator of the software may still charge a fee. Users interested in either creating or using GPL software are encouraged to visit the GNU General Public License website (*gnu.org/copyleft/gpl.html*) for further details. GNU stands for "GNU's Not Unix" and is pronounced *G-new* with a hard g sound.

Every software company may create its own brand of user licenses and may name them something unique. It is the responsibility of the person installing the software—either the user, system administrator, or network administrator—to be aware of the details of the user license and follow them carefully.

All Things Considered

Thought Experiment

Consider the following software licensing scenario: Office Suite 1 costs $229 per single-user-single-station license, while Office Suite 2 costs $299 per interactive user license. You have 200 users on your network, and you estimate that at any one time only 60 percent of your users will be using the suite application. Determine the best license solution. At what level of interactive use will the cost of the interactive user licenses break even with that of the single-user-single-station licenses?

What happens if someone does not behave in accordance with the user license and installs a software package in an environment for which it was not intended? In these situations, some packages simply will not work. Other packages will not work correctly if the installation does not follow the license agreement. For example, some software packages maintain a counter and will not allow more copies than were agreed upon during the purchase. Some software packages, such as database systems, may be installable on multiple machines or may give the appearance of allowing multiple users access, but if they were not designed for multiple-user access, they may not work correctly. It is, in fact, important during multiuser database access that the database system lock out any other users while one user is currently accessing data records. If the system is intentionally not designed for concurrent multiuser access, violations of the licensing agreement may lead to unknown and problematic results.

Installing the software on more machines than have been agreed to in the user license is illegal. If you install more copies than the number for which you have licenses and the software manufacturer discovers this fact, you and your company may face legal consequences. This is a risk, therefore, that is definitely not worth taking. Be sure you have the proper user license in place before you install any software.

Remember this...

> A NOS (network operating system) is a large, complex program that can manage resources commonly found on most LANs. Although a part of the NOS resides in each client computer, the bulk of the NOS operates in a network server, or simply, a server.

> RAID (Redundant Array of Independent Disks) is a collection of storage drives (called an array)

interfaced in a way to ensure one or more layers of redundant copies of data are available across the drive array. The most basic RAID techniques are RAID 0 (called striping), RAID 1 (called disk mirroring), RAID 3 (which includes parity), and RAID 5 (which spreads parity information across multiple disks).

> Storage types you might find in an on-prem network include DAS (direct attached storage), NAS (network attached storage), and a SAN (storage area network). DAS and NAS devices store files in a file system. Data in a SAN array of drives is stored in blocks rather than in a file system hierarchy and is called block storage.

> To support a LAN and its OS, a wide variety of utility programs are available. Utilities are software programs that operate in the background and support one or more functions to keep the network running at optimal performance.

> The licensing agreement that accompanies a software product is a legal contract and describes a number of conditions that must be upheld for proper use of the software package. Licensing models define where the software can be installed, who can use it, and when payments are made.

Self-check

1. Which RAID technique spreads data across disks without the ability to recover lost data?
   a. RAID 5
   b. RAID 0
   c. RAID 3
   d. RAID 1

2. Which storage type identifies data locations with a LUN?
   a. NAS
   b. DAS
   c. RAID
   d. SAN

3. For which of these licensing models do you need to know the number of cores a computer has before you can install the licensed software?
   a. Server license
   b. Site license
   c. Interactive user license
   d. Corporate license

Check your answers at the end of this chapter.

Section 6-2: Server Operating Systems

The NOS that runs on a server is sometimes more specifically called a **server OS**. A server OS is a large, complex program that can manage the common resources on most LANs, in addition to performing the standard OS services mentioned previously. This NOS will make more sense as you read about its purposes. What functions do these operating systems perform? How is a server OS different from a workstation's OS?

The resources that a server OS must manage typically include one or more network services, multiple network printers, one or more physical networks, and a potentially large number of users who are directly or remotely connected to the network. A server OS also performs a wide variety of network support functions, including the coordination of all resources and services on the network and the processing of requests from client workstations, whether they're connected locally or remotely. It supports user interaction by prompting a user for network login, validating user accounts, restricting users from accessing resources for which they have not been granted access, and performing user accounting functions.

Interestingly, many current desktop OSs now incorporate many of the features described previously, thereby enabling individual users to create server OSs for their homes and small businesses. Thus, the line between a desktop OS (such as Windows 10) and a server OS (like Windows Server) has blurred in recent years. Even so, there are still, as you will see shortly, significant differences between the two types of systems. Let's look at some of the more popular server OSs on the market and see how each supports network functions.

Unix

Unix was a popular OS for mainframes and servers and can still be found on single-user workstations. It most often works via a text-based interface, although GUIs are available. Unix was initially designed at Bell Labs and was first implemented on a PDP-7 minicomputer in 1970. It is a relatively streamlined system, which explains why it operates quickly. Shortly after its introduction, the Unix software was rewritten in the popular C programming language. Owing to characteristics of the C programming language and Unix's design, the internal code of Unix is relatively easy to modify. For this reason, and because early versions of the OS were given away for free, Unix became extremely popular in academic institutions. One of the more popular variants of the Unix system is the BSD version originally released from University of California, Berkeley, and its modern, open-source distributions such as NetBSD, OpenBSD, and FreeBSD. An application is **open source** if its code is made available to the public for review and modification. These Unix versions are still in use today while commercial distributions are rarely marketed or sold anymore.

Because Unix is one of the older OSs and has grown in processing power over many years, it is quite stable. It handles network operations well, and a broad range of applications have been written to run in Unix. Various distributions of Unix are still customized for niche scenarios due to its stability and backwards compatibility with older applications. Today, however, many experts consider Unix to be outdated.

Linux

Since its early days, Unix has evolved into many versions and executes on several computer platforms. One version that generated a lot of interest in the 1990s was Linux. Linux, while based on the Unix concept, is a complete rewrite of the Unix kernel and borrows additional functions from the well-established Free Software Foundation's toolset called GNU and from the even larger free software community. Interestingly, some of the largest and fastest computer systems in the world run on Linux. Linux shares many of the same advantages and disadvantages of Unix, and it performs similarly to Unix as a server OS.

Several features, however, set Linux apart from Unix as well as from all other server OSs:

> **Cost**—Many Linux distributions, called distros for short, are completely free to download and use. Some distros require payment because of other components included in the package or to maintain vendor support, but the Linux code itself is still open source. One of the most popular Linux distros for desktops is Ubuntu, shown in Figure 6-4. These days, many companies are choosing to purchase a Linux server distro from a vendor that specializes in providing proprietary code in their distributions along with all the supporting applications and utilities, such as web page support tools, a GUI, and the latest versions of peripheral drivers. This package often includes professional-grade support from the vendor to maintain reliable uptime. An example of

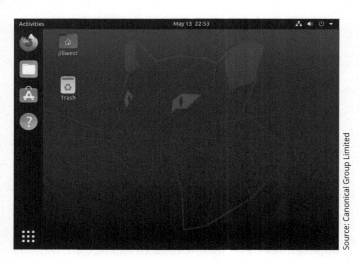

Source: Canonical Group Limited

Figure 6-4   Ubuntu Linux desktop

this type of package is RHEL (Red Hat Enterprise Linux). Even when Linux is purchased from a vendor, the cost of it is insignificant compared to the cost of purchasing either Unix or Windows Server. Whereas Unix and Windows Server can cost thousands to tens of thousands of dollars, depending upon the number of user workstations, commercial versions of Linux can cost as little as a few hundred dollars.

> **Open-source code**—When you purchase or download Linux, you can receive the original source code along with the compiled code for free. Having the original source code gives organizations a great amount of control over the software. In the hands of an experienced programmer, the Linux source code can be modified in almost limitless ways to provide a customized OS. The ability to customize the software, however, is a double-edged sword. In inexperienced hands, customized source code can be a source of constant trouble. At any rate, Linux is part of a growing family of open-source software that is rather highly regarded within the business and educational industries.

> **Size**—Since its debut, Linux has been able to operate on a system as small as an Intel 386 processor with only 4 MB of main memory. Although Linux will certainly run on larger systems, many administrators might even install a Linux system on an old personal computer to support simple network functions. These systems can run unattended with little or no support. Linux even runs on devices as small as the credit-card sized Raspberry Pi circuit board.

Linux shares many other advantages with Unix, such as fast execution (due to its relatively small size and efficient code), network support functions, and the option with some distros for a GUI.

These days, a clear majority of companies are running Linux on at least one server to support a particular application, and many companies rely extensively on Linux systems. In fact, some research is showing that Linux as a server OS is now more widespread than any other OS. Currently, Linux software is commonly used to support email servers, web servers, FTP servers, file/print servers, firewalls, proxy servers, and DNS servers. Outside the datacenter, Linux powers smartphones and smartwatches, gaming consoles, media streaming devices (such as Roku), televisions, cloud services, security or digital payment devices, robots, smart home devices (such as refrigerators and washing machines), and even cars. In or out of the datacenter, Linux is definitely a major player in the server OS arena and should not be overlooked. In the project at the end of this chapter, you'll experiment with a virtual Linux computer.

Microsoft Windows Server

In contrast to the familiar Windows desktop OS, Windows Server was designed to offer the necessary administrative tools to support multiple users, multiple servers, and a wide range of network peripheral devices. In addition, Windows Server supports many of the applications that allow users to create, access, and display web pages, as well as the software that allows a server to act as a web server. The Windows OS also works seamlessly with the hugely popular Microsoft application tools.

One of the most significant components of Windows Server is the directory service AD. **AD (Active Directory)** stores information about all the objects and resources in a network and makes this information available to users, network administrators, and applications. Microsoft created a directory service based on existing standards rather than designing its directory service from scratch. Thus, you may hear network specialists talk about how AD is built around the Internet's DNS (Domain Name System), which is discussed in Chapter 7, and a second standard, LDAP (Lightweight Directory Access Protocol).

AD creates a hierarchical structure of resources similar to a tree design:

> **Leaves**—Objects, such as users, groups of users, computers, applications, and network devices, are the leaf items within the tree.

› **OUs (organizational units)**—Leaf items are grouped in OUs (organizational units).

› **Domain**—One or more OUs can be grouped together into a domain, which is the main object in Windows Server.

› **Trees and forest**—Where these domains are hierarchically organized as a tree, a collection of trees is then a forest.

For example, two of the departments within an organization may be Marketing and Engineering (Figure 6-5). Both departments are OUs. Within each department are users and network servers. Grouping objects within the directory tree allows administrators to manage objects and resources on a macro level rather than on a one-by-one basis. With a few clicks of a mouse, a network administrator can allow all the users within Engineering to access a new engineering-related software application.

The basic idea underlying Microsoft's AD is that the network administrator must create a hierarchical tree that represents the layout of the organization. This hierarchical structure resembles an inverted tree, with the root at the top and the users and network resources—the leaves—at the bottom. This tree could correspond to the physical layout of the organization. For example, workstations 1 through 20 will be on the third floor of an office building, workstations 21 through 40 on the second floor, and workstations 41 through 60 on the first floor.

A more powerful and flexible hierarchical tree can be created based on a logical layout. A logical layout could describe the organization in terms of its departmental structure: the Engineering department (which could be scattered over floors 1 through 3), the Sales department (which could be situated on floors 2, 6, and 7), and the Marketing department (which might be physically located in two different buildings).

Throughout the entire tree-creation process, it is important to review your draft design for accuracy, flexibility, and completeness. Because an AD tree is going to be used by every server on the network and is probably going to be in place for many years, the creation of a well-designed tree is extremely important. A tree that is designed improperly will lead to difficulties in the future when you try to add new users, user groups, and resources to the network. A poorly designed tree may also create a sluggish system with poor response times.

Figure 6-6 shows an example of an appropriate tree design. Note that the design of a tree should ideally be like a pyramid. Fewer container objects should be at the top of the tree than at the bottom. Wide, flat trees are usually not a good design, as this layout causes too many inner-container communications, and users may have trouble finding the appropriate resources. Likewise, trees that are too narrow and tall may also be poorly designed because they incorporate too few containers, which can lead to future problems when a network administrator wants to add new users or resources.

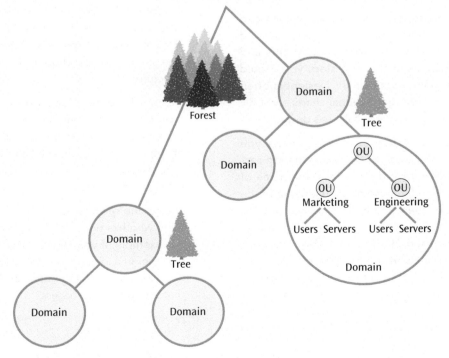

Figure 6-5 Example of a tree design in Windows Active Directory

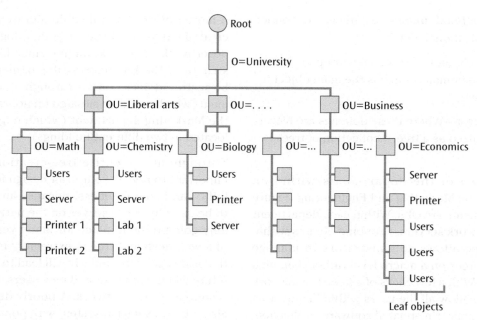

Figure 6-6 Possible design for a server OS tree

Details | Suggestions for Designing a Network Tree

Creating a good and appropriate tree design is not a trivial task; the following four basic steps will give the network administrator a good start:

1. Gather the appropriate corporate documents so that you know about the available hardware and software, and the employee departments and divisions. As part of this first step, you should obtain an organizational chart. Designers often consult corporate organizational charts and LAN maps to guide the hierarchical tree's design.

2. Design the top section of the tree before you design any lower sections. To design the top section of the tree, give the top level the name of the organization (in most cases, the name of the company) and then create the first layer of OUs, or container objects. An OU is an object that is further composed of additional objects (examples of which include servers, printers, users, or groups of users). For example, a division in a company that is composed of multiple departments

would be considered an OU. A department is also an OU because it, too, is further composed of objects, such as employees. If your network is very small, there may not be a need for any OUs. When designing a tree directory structure, some network designers feel that the top of the tree should be based upon the corporate WAN structure.

3. Design the bottom section of the tree, which includes the remaining hierarchy of OUs and leaf objects. Leaf objects are not composed of any objects and are usually entities such as the users, peripherals, servers, printers, queues, and other network resources.

4. Design the security access rights—that is, determine who has rights to the appropriate objects. For example, if you create a new user and place that user in a location on the tree, what rights will that user have? What printers and directories will that user be able to access?

All Things Considered

Thought Experiment

You are working for a company that has three divisions: Marketing, Research, and Sales. Each division has many employees, each with their own workstation. Each division also has its own network server and a number of high-quality printers. Draw a Windows Active Directory diagram to support this company's network structure.

Remember this...

› Unix was a popular OS for mainframes and servers and can still be found on single-user workstations. Various distributions of Unix are still customized for niche scenarios due to its stability and backwards compatibility with older applications.

› Many companies purchase a Linux distro from a vendor that specializes in providing proprietary code in their distributions along with all the supporting applications and utilities, such as web page support tools, a GUI, and the latest versions of peripheral drivers. Even when Linux is purchased from a vendor, the cost of it is insignificant compared to the cost of purchasing either Unix or Windows Server.

› One of the most significant components of Windows Server is the directory service AD (Active Directory), which stores information about all the objects and resources in a network and makes this information available to users, network administrators, and applications. AD creates a hierarchical structure of resources similar to a tree design. Objects, such as users, groups of users, computers, applications, and network devices, are the leaf items within the tree. Leaf items are grouped in OUs (organizational units). One or more OUs can be grouped together into a domain, which is the main object in Windows Server.

Self-check

4. Which of the following characteristics of Linux is both a positive and a negative factor in choosing a Linux distro?
   a. Price
   b. Stability
   c. Customizability
   d. Backwards compatibility

5. At what level would a printer fit in an AD tree design?
   a. OU
   b. Forest
   c. Domain
   d. Leaf

Check your answers at the end of this chapter.

Section 6-3: Network Devices

Servers and workstations are not the only devices on a network with installed OSs. Many routers and switches also run OSs that allow network admins to enable elaborate configurations on these devices. These configurations increase network performance and help ensure network security.

Unlike server OSs, NOSs on these network devices typically offer only a CLI (command-line interface). Network admins must learn the commands and best practices for managing these devices through a CLI. Additionally, the OS on these devices tends to be proprietary to the specific manufacturer. One of the most widely deployed network device brands is Cisco Systems, Inc. Cisco's routers and switches use various versions and flavors of the Cisco IOS (Internet OS). This software allows for internetwork configurations across multiple LANs and network segments. While there are variations in the OS for different devices, most of the commands work universally across all Cisco devices. Learning these commands is a critical skill for network admins, who are likely to work with Cisco devices at some point in their careers.

Command Modes

Like many OSs, Cisco's IOS relies on various command modes that determine what commands can be executed. These command modes are accessed from the CLI and, along the way, the prompt indicates which command mode is active. Table 6-1 shows the most common command modes and what the prompt for each mode looks like. Figure 6-7 shows how to enter each of these modes by entering an escalation command for each successive mode. Notice how the prompt changes each time the mode is escalated.

Table 6-1 Common modes on a Cisco router

Mode	Prompt on Device Named "Router"	Purpose
User EXEC	`Router>`	• Default mode for basic commands, such as viewing statistics • Can be password protected
Privileged EXEC	`Router#`	• Privileged mode for managing device configuration files but not for changing the device's configuration • Can be password protected
Global configuration	`Router(config)#`	• High-level mode for making device configuration changes • Organized into groups of device-specific configuration modes
Interface configuration	`Router(config-if)#`	• One of the global configuration mode's many sub-groupings and used to configure a specific interface on the device

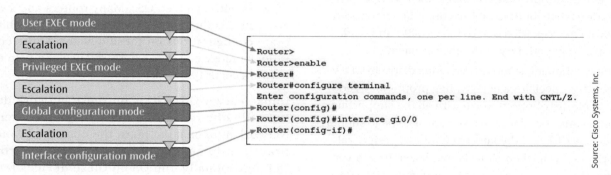

Source: Cisco Systems, Inc.

Figure 6-7 Some of the router's command modes

Configuring with Commands

A wide variety of commands are available within these command modes to configure each router, switch, and other network devices. For example, suppose you want to configure two VLANs on a switch, as illustrated in Figure 6-8. Beginning in the switch's global configuration mode, you would enter the commands shown in Table 6-2 to create and name the two VLANs and enable one of the interfaces for each VLAN. You could then continue adding more interfaces as needed using the same commands repeatedly. Notice how each series of commands must be performed in a particular command mode.

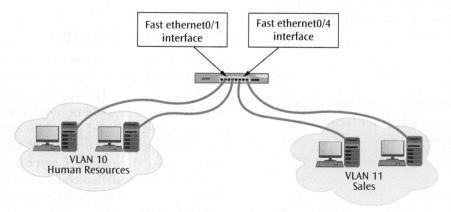

Figure 6-8 Create two VLANs, and assign each interface to a VLAN

Table 6-2 Configure two VLANs on a Cisco switch

Command	Purpose
`vlan 10`	Creates VLAN 10 and enters VLAN configuration mode for that VLAN
`name HR`	Assigns VLAN 10 the name HR
`vlan 11`	Creates VLAN 11 and enters VLAN configuration mode for that VLAN
`name Sales`	Assigns VLAN 11 the name Sales
`exit`	Returns to global configuration mode
`interface fastethernet0/1`	Enters interface configuration mode for the FastEthernet0/1 interface
`switchport mode access`	Sets access mode for this interface, which is required for endpoint devices in the VLAN
`switchport access vlan 10`	Assigns this interface to VLAN 10
`exit`	Returns to global configuration mode
`interface fastethernet0/4`	Enters interface configuration mode for the FastEthernet0/4 interface
`switchport mode access`	Sets access mode for this interface, which is required for endpoint devices in the VLAN
`switchport access vlan 11`	Assigns this interface to VLAN 11
`exit`	Returns to global configuration mode
`do show vlan`	Shows configured VLANs and associated interfaces
`exit` and press **Enter**	Returns to privileged EXEC mode
`copy run start` and press **Enter**	Saves the current settings

Other common configurations a network admin might apply to a switch or router are to set access passwords, define subnets and IP address pools, and add traffic security restrictions.

All Things Considered

Thought Experiment

As you can see, interface configuration mode is used to assign a switch's interface, or port, to a particular VLAN. Do some research online to find out what other configuration modes are available under global configuration mode.

While Cisco leads the market for routers, switches, and other network devices, you're just as likely to encounter devices from other manufacturers. In no particular order, popular competitors include Aruba, Dell, D-Link, MikroTik, Juniper, NETGEAR, Extreme, Huawei, Arista, and many others. It's common for network professionals in training to learn network administration on Cisco devices, and then they transfer those skills to other networking environments after they enter the workforce.

Remember this...

> Like many OSs, Cisco's IOS relies on various command modes that determine what commands can be executed. These command modes are accessed from the CLI and, along the way, the prompt indicates which command mode is active.

> A wide variety of commands are available within each of Cisco's command modes to configure a router, switch, and other network devices. Each series of commands must be performed in a particular command mode. Other manufacturers offer similar commands to configure their devices.

Self-check

6. Which Cisco command mode is most likely used to change the password for accessing the device?

    a. Global configuration

    b. User EXEC

    c. Interface configuration

    d. Privileged EXEC

7. Why might an admin use the show command on a Cisco switch?

    a. To save the device's configuration changes

    b. To change the device's password

    c. To change the device's command mode

    d. To confirm the device's configurations are correct

Check your answers at the end of this chapter.

Section 6-4: Virtualization

So far, you've learned about physical devices on a network—computers, routers, and switches that you can touch, that you must plug into a power source, and that take up space on a datacenter rack, shelf, or desktop—but not all devices on a network are physical. Especially these days, many devices are virtual and exist as software on another device.

For example, suppose you have a desktop computer that runs Windows 10, but you need a Linux computer for a website you're developing. You could buy a new computer and install a Linux OS on that computer, and then you'd have two computers cluttering your desk. Or you could create a virtual computer, called a VM (virtual machine), on your physical computer and then install an OS on that virtual system. Meaning, this VM is a software-based guest computer that runs on the hardware-based host computer. Figure 6-9 shows a physical host computer with two guest VMs sharing the host system's connection to the network.

Hypervisors

To make this work, software called a hypervisor runs on the host computer. The hypervisor allocates availability of hardware resources to the host computer and to each guest computer. The hypervisor also creates a kind of pocket within the host computer's OS where the guest system runs independently of the host system and any other guest systems. Each guest system can run any OS supported by the hypervisor and underlying hardware. For example, some hypervisors allow you to run an Android VM that functions just like your smartphone. Other hypervisors allow you to install a router's or switch's OS so you could practice configuring these network devices.

Figure 6-10 shows two types of hypervisors, aptly named type 1 and type 2 hypervisors:

> **Type 1 hypervisor**—Runs directly on the host system's hardware and does not require an underlying OS, such as Windows 10. A type 1 hypervisor is itself a minimal OS, many of which are built on the Linux kernel. The hypervisor controls all the physical resources and is therefore a very efficient method for a server to host many VMs at one time. Common examples include Citrix Hypervisor, ESXi by VMware, and Hyper-V by Microsoft.

> **Type 2 hypervisor**—Runs on top of an existing OS. In other words, the host must have an OS installed first, and then a hypervisor application can run inside that OS. For example, you could install Oracle VirtualBox, a free type 2 hypervisor application, on

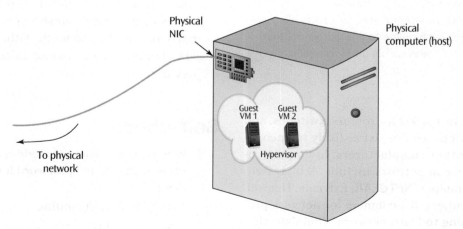

Figure 6-9 Elements of virtualization

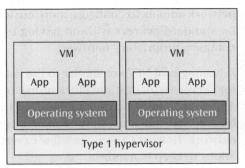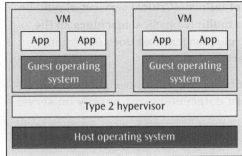

Figure 6-10   Type 1 and type 2 hypervisors

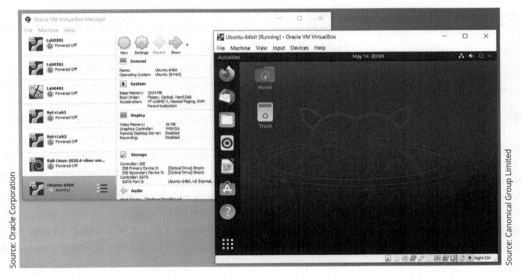

Source: Oracle Corporation

Source: Canonical Group Limited

Figure 6-11   Ubuntu Desktop is installed on a VM in Oracle VirtualBox

your Windows 10 computer. Then use VirtualBox to create a VM and install a Linux OS on that VM. To run the Linux VM, you would need to first open the VirtualBox application, and then start the VM. You could then install an application on the Linux VM.

Figure 6-11 shows the VirtualBox hypervisor installed on a Windows 10 computer. A VM is running, and its OS is Ubuntu Linux.

Advantages and Disadvantages of Virtualization

Virtualization offers several advantages:

> **Efficient use of resources**—Many servers can run on a single physical machine.

> **Cost and energy savings**—Fewer physical machines require less electricity to power and cool.

> **Fault and threat isolation**—Services running on one VM are isolated from those on other VMs, even when those VMs are hosted on the same physical device.

> **Simple backups, recovery, and replication**—An entire VM can be stored in a file called an image, which can be backed up, copied, or recovered.

At the same time, network admins must be aware of significant possible disadvantages:

> **Compromised performance**—If one VM on a host system is demanding a high level of hardware resources, other VMs on the same host can experience reduced performance and capacity.

> **Increased licensing costs**—Every instance of commercial software requires its own license, whether the software is running on a physical server or a virtual server.

> **Single point of failure**—Critical services should be spread across multiple physical machines so the failure of a single physical host does not compromise these services.

Overall, the advantages typically outweigh the disadvantages, and modern datacenters rely heavily on server virtualization.

Virtualizing Network Devices

Servers and workstations are not the only devices on a network that can be virtualized. Routers and switches can also run on a hypervisor designed for this purpose. This technology is called **NFV (network functions virtualization)**, and it can also be used to virtualize firewalls, load balancers, and other network devices. A **firewall**, as illustrated in Figure 6-12, is a security device or system that supports an access control policy between two networks. A **load balancer**, also shown in Figure 6-12, is a device that distributes traffic intelligently among multiple computers or connections, such as when handling traffic to a high-volume website that is hosted by a cluster of web servers. Any of these devices can run on a hypervisor, such as OpenStack, which allows network admins to configure more customized networks on standard servers without having to purchase more complex, proprietary hardware.

Advantages of NFV are similar to the list you read earlier for server virtualization: efficient use of resources, cost and energy savings, quick migration in case of device failure, and high scalability to meet changing needs of a network. However, there are a few caveats and considerations to keep in mind:

> You'll need licenses for each of the virtualized devices as well as for the type 1 hypervisor that will host them. Fortunately, the cost of these licenses amounts to a fraction of the cost of similarly featured hardware devices.

> The interaction between physical and virtual devices introduces a small degree of latency as data passes through the hypervisor and its connections. Usually, this delay is negligible. On the flip side, NFV also allows for migrating many network functions closer to their point of use, which can more than compensate for the delay in traversing the hypervisor.

> Many network admins, even those most committed to the advantages of virtualization, are uncomfortable using a virtual firewall to protect the entire network. The server hosting a virtual firewall occasionally needs to be restarted in the course of regular maintenance or failure, and in that event, the hosted firewall goes down with the server. Instead, many network admins believe that virtual firewalls are only appropriate for securing virtual-only portions of the network or serving as a backup to physical firewall devices.

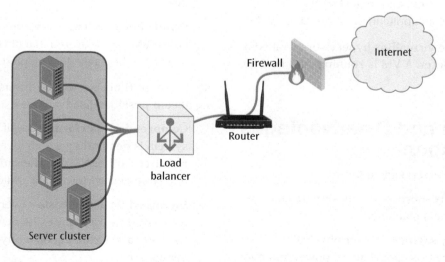

Figure 6-12 Common network devices

Software-Defined Networking (SDN)

Virtualization of network functions offers some significant technological advances in other ways. For example, SD-branch (software-defined branch) and SD-WAN (software-defined wide area network) technologies allow companies to extend their corporate networks to branch and other remote locations while keeping hardware deployment relatively simple, allowing for remote management of these network extensions and even incorporating programmable automation of services. Much of this functionality relies on **SDN (software-defined networking)** where decision-making processes are made at the software level by a network controller instead of being handled by individual hardware devices.

To understand this concept a little better, consider this very simple example with a switch configured to support three VLANs. When a packet enters a port on the switch where the packet does not match an existing set of instructions, the switch must decide which other ports to send the packet back out of and what VLAN-related modifications to make to the packet's header. This decision-making process is called the **control plane**, as shown in Figure 6-13. SDN allows a network controller

to make these decisions for the switch and then tell the switch what to do with the packet or, in some cases, the controller might handle the packet itself without sending the packet back to the switch. Note that the actual movement of the packet from device to device is called the **data plane**. So, the SDN controller handles the control plane while the switch only needs to handle the data plane.

While it might seem inefficient to move this decision-making function to a different device on the network, consider the benefits when managing dozens or even hundreds of switches, routers, load balancers, and firewalls. Traditionally, these devices would have to coordinate decision-making with each other, which increases traffic on the network and decreases efficiency. By shifting this responsibility to a central controller, cheaper and "dumber" network devices can support complex network configurations that can even adapt to constantly changing network conditions. Additionally, SDN provides central management of the network so technicians don't have to physically access every network device to make configuration changes, such as adding a new VLAN. For these reasons, SDN has become commonplace on modern networks.

Note

SDS (software-defined storage) is similar in concept to SDN in that SDS abstracts the control of storage management away from the physical or virtual disks storing the data. SDS allows users to store any kind of data on nearly any kind of storage device under a single management interface. Data might be stored on-prem or in the cloud. SDS is not limited by the hardware (physical or virtual) where the bits of data are saved. And the SDS system can be scaled almost indefinitely while maintaining high performance standards.

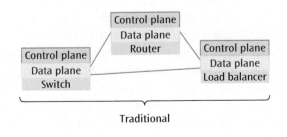

Traditional

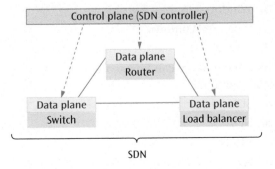

SDN

Figure 6-13 Distributed control planes in a traditional network versus a centralized control plane in an SDN network

Remember this...

> A type 1 hypervisor runs directly on the host system's hardware and does not require an underlying OS. A type 1 hypervisor is itself a minimal OS, many of which are built on the Linux kernel. A type 2 hypervisor runs on top of an existing OS. In other words, the host must have an OS installed first, and then a hypervisor application can run inside that OS.

> Virtualization offers the advantages of efficient use of resources; cost and energy savings; fault and threat isolation; and simple backups, recovery, and replication. Possible disadvantages include compromised performance, increased licensing costs, and single point of failure.

> NFV (network functions virtualization) can be used to virtualize routers, switches, firewalls, load balancers, and other network devices. This allows network admins to configure more customized networks on standard servers without having to purchase more complex, proprietary hardware.

> With SDN (software-defined networking), decision-making processes are made at the software level by a network controller instead of being handled by individual hardware devices. This decision-making process is called the control plane. The actual movement of the packet from device to device is called the data plane.

Self-check

8. If you install a hypervisor on a Linux host machine, which of the following OSs can you install in a VM on that server?

    a. Linux

    b. Windows

    c. Linux or Windows

    d. Any OS

9. Which technology can be used to create a virtual switch?

    a. SDN

    b. NFV

    c. VLAN

    d. SDS

Check your answers at the end of this chapter.

Section 6-5: Cloud Computing

Cloud computing is another trend toward increased virtualization. Where server and network function virtualization run virtualized devices in the company's own datacenter, cloud computing expands the flexibility and functionality of virtualization technologies to hardware owned and managed by dedicated cloud service providers (CSPs). Cloud computing also further abstracts the control plane from the data plane to the point where cloud customers don't need to access the underlying hardware hosting their cloud services when configuring cloud-based networks.

For example, suppose a company is running a cluster of five virtual web servers on their own hypervisor, and they're concerned that a power loss in their area would result in expensive downtime for their website. This company can migrate their web servers to a cloud platform, such as AWS or Azure, to ensure a power failure does not interrupt website service to their customers. The company can even configure redundant server clusters in different regions of the world to increase website performance to global customers and ensure increased availability of their website.

A logical question to ask at this point is: Who are these CSPs, and what are the differences between their platforms? Let's explore some of the more popular options on both fronts.

Popular Cloud Platforms

Several public CSPs have emerged over the past decade with AWS currently leading the market for IaaS and PaaS resources. (Refer back to Chapter 1 for a refresher on the various cloud service models.) The following list discusses the most notorious CSPs in these markets:

> AWS (Amazon Web Services) was founded in 2006 and essentially created public cloud computing, setting these technologies on a path to revolutionize the IT industry. With this early lead, no other provider has yet caught up. AWS is an especially popular choice for hosting IaaS resources, and they continue to innovate in all areas of cloud computing. Figure 6-14 shows AWS's management console.

> Currently the second largest provider of public cloud services, Microsoft Azure relies on its popularity with AD and Windows Server to expand its

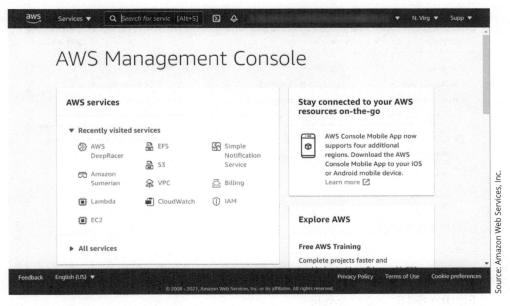

Figure 6-14 AWS management console

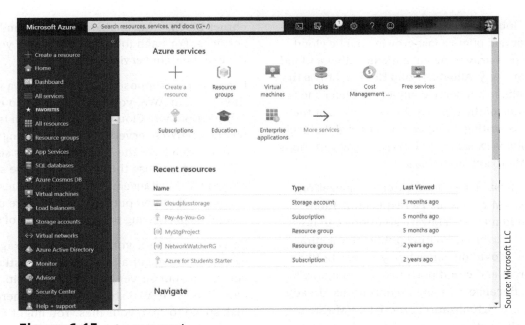

Figure 6-15 Azure portal

foothold from the on-prem datacenter to the cloud. Microsoft has recently reorganized their entire certification structure to center around Azure and its related technologies. Azure's portal is shown in Figure 6-15.

› In a distant third place, GCP (Google Cloud Platform) is hosted on the same infrastructure as other Google products and claims high popularity for PaaS resources, especially for application and

website developers. Interestingly, GCP has been growing faster in recent years than AWS or Azure. You can see GCP's console in Figure 6-16.

› IBM Cloud is a rebranding of earlier services from SoftLayer, which IBM acquired in 2013, and IBM's own Bluemix products. Depending on the statistics used, IBM Cloud arguably exceeds GCP in market share. With IBM's purchase of Red Hat in 2018, significant shifts in the cloud market are expected to emerge.

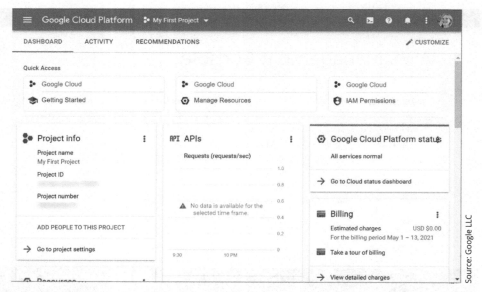

Figure 6-16 GCP console

> Alibaba Cloud, based in China, is a relative newcomer and offers a fast-growing public cloud platform primarily to Asian markets. Alibaba Cloud's parent company, Alibaba Group Holding Ltd, is the largest online commerce company in China and is listed as one of the top five global retailers at the time of this writing. Compared to other global tech firms, Alibaba ranks in the top ten, along with Apple, Google, Microsoft, and Amazon.

> A leading provider of datacenter virtualization solutions, VMware is also a respectable force in the cloud market. VMware solutions can now be installed over an existing public cloud infrastructure, providing consistency across both the on-prem and cloud portions of a company's network. Because so many organizations already use VMware virtualization products, VMware's partnerships with major cloud providers such as AWS provide a natural extension to a customer's existing VMware infrastructure to create a seamless hybrid cloud.

Service Categories

There are a vast number of services available in each cloud platform. At first, this can feel overwhelming. Imagine each of these different services as a building block. When you're building a structure from blocks, you might need a large block for one scenario, and next time you might need a very small block, or a

corner block, or an angled block. It's similar with cloud services. For each job you need done, you are able to choose the right service to do that job.

For example, suppose you want to run a web server in the cloud. In AWS, you might choose to create an EC2 (Elastic Compute Cloud) instance, which is a VM hosted on one of AWS's servers. If you're working in Azure, you would instead use the Virtual Machines service. And in GCP, you would use the Compute Engine service to create your VM instance in the cloud. All these options are categorized as compute services. You're paying for the computer processing power to do work of some kind.

To run a website, you also need storage space. For example, you might attach an EBS (Elastic Block Store) volume to your server instance to hold its OS and other files. This is an AWS storage service where you pay for disk space to save your files. You might also use an S3 (Simple Storage Service) bucket to hold other files that need to be available to your customers, or you might store a database in RDS (Relational Database Service), which is categorized as a database service and provides both storage space and compute processing when you sort and filter records. If you're instead using Azure or GCP, you would use similar storage and database services that accomplish the same tasks.

As you can see, cloud services are easier to learn and understand when you categorize the services according to their primary function, as shown in Figure 6-17. While there are dozens of categories, the main ones include compute, storage, databases, networking, security, and

Source: Amazon Web Services, Inc.

Figure 6-17 Service categories in AWS

billing. One of the first tasks when starting to learn a new cloud platform is to familiarize yourself with the most popular services in each of these categories. Knowing they exist is simply the beginning. Cloud professionals must learn what each service can do, what makes it different from similar services, and ways to optimize that service for best performance and price.

Pricing Strategies

Cloud Essentials+ Exam Tip

This section discusses the BYOL (bring your own license) licensing model and subscription services, which are required by

- Part of Objective 2.2: Summarize the financial aspects of engaging a cloud provider.

- Part of Objective 2.4: Identify the benefits or solutions of utilizing cloud services.

Understanding pricing strategies is another significant part of learning how to work with the cloud. While cloud customers already benefit from economies of scale when using cloud services, most cloud services offer a variety of pricing options to further customize your pricing structure. For example, part of the expense of an EC2 instance is the OS that you run on it. In AWS, you choose the OS when you choose the AMI (Amazon Machine Image). Some OSs are free, such as Amazon's Linux 2 AMI

shown in Figure 6-18. This is a Linux distribution that is optimized for deep monitoring in AWS, and it incurs no additional fees for use of this OS. Many other OSs, however, add expense to your EC2 instance to cover the cost of the OS license, such as macOS Big Sur or most of the Windows Server 2019 AMIs. Suppose you already have a batch of Windows Server licenses that you would like to use on your cloud VM instances. In AWS and most other cloud platforms, you can take advantage of their **BYOL (bring your own license)** policy so you can install Windows Server under the umbrella of your existing licenses.

Another decision you make as you build an AWS EC2 instance is whether you plan to keep this instance for a while or if you'll need it for only a short time. Suppose you're creating a web server that you'll keep running for at least a year. You might choose to reserve the instance for a lower price than the **on-demand pricing model**. This **subscription service** allows you to commit to paying for this instance for a full year at a lower rate. Then you can pay part of the fee up front, or you can pay all of it for an even more reduced rate, as shown in Figure 6-19. While these reserved instances are nonrefundable, you can modify or exchange reserved instances and even sell them on the Reserved Instance Marketplace.

These kinds of subscription-based pricing options are available for other services in AWS and for many services in other cloud platforms. However, reserving resources is not the only option for saving money in the cloud. Another popular strategy is storage tiering. To understand how this works, let's first discuss some basic principles of how storage services work in the cloud.

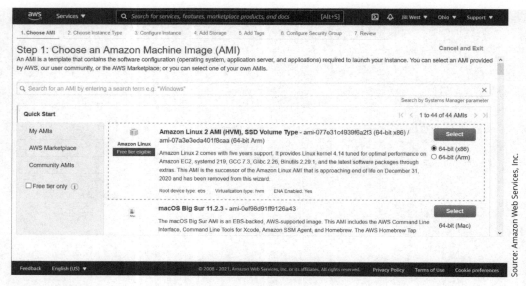

Figure 6-18 Some AMIs are free tier eligible

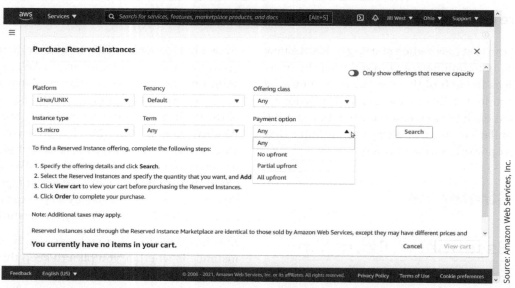

Figure 6-19 Reserved instances are cheaper than on-demand instances

Cloud Storage

As you can probably predict at this point, cloud providers offer a wide variety of cloud-based storage solutions. Knowing the key role data plays in business highlights the need for good data storage methodologies. Compromised data can destroy an organization. Therefore, as companies move their datacenters to the cloud, it's the responsibility of IT professionals to ensure that data is kept both safe and accessible.

Cloud-Native Storage

Recall from earlier in this chapter when you read about file systems and block storage. In contrast, **object storage** is a more cloud-native storage infrastructure—it takes some of the best characteristics of file and block storage, and it reimagines storage in a way that capitalizes on the cloud's auto-scaling functionality. Recall from Chapter 1 that scalability is a core feature of cloud technology. Automatic scaling, or auto-scaling, allows a cloud resource to adjust its capacity quickly according to the customer's need, avoiding unnecessary charges.

Object storage also offers increased performance inherent in its design. An object packages stored data with metadata about the object. This metadata can give extensive information about the stored data, and it's optimized for quick search and retrieval functions. Where file systems keep basic metadata on a file, such as creation date and author, object metadata can contain extensive and customized information about the data itself. This is especially useful when the data can't be easily searched, such as photos, videos, or complex CAD (computer-aided design) 3-D images.

Object storage also relies on a flat namespace; however, this space is not organized into consistently sized blocks. Objects are held in a single repository, or pool of storage. This space can be expanded indefinitely, even across geographies. However, the expansiveness and flexibility of the space also results in higher latency. Object storage lends itself well to unstructured data storage (such as massive collections of images or video), archival storage, or big data storage (such as IoT raw data stored in a data lake).

Object storage offers one more benefit specific to the cloud environment: simpler protocols. Where block storage relies on complex protocols such as FC, object storage uses APIs and HTTP.

Storage Optimization

Available storage options can be compared with each other based on several factors, as you've already seen. The organization of data, expandability of the storage space, and durability of the data all factor into storage decisions. Storage performance can be evaluated based on several measurable factors, three of which are described here:

> **Transfer rate or read/write throughput**—This measurement specifies the speed at which data is moved through the storage infrastructure and is measured in MB/s (megabytes per second).

> **IOPS (input/output operations per second)**—This number details how many read and write operations can be completed per second, as shown in Figure 6-20. It's typically given as an integer, such as 500 for an HDD in the cloud or as high as 16,000 for a cloud-hosted SSD.

> **Latency**—Latency results from bottlenecks in technology, geographical distances, or subpar optimization of data. It can be measured by TTFB (time to first byte), RTT (round-trip time), or similar metrics. You can decrease the latency of a storage solution by turning on data caching and by choosing carefully where data is located geographically.

One way to maximize storage performance is to optimize the data itself. Some cloud storage services—especially if they target specific kinds of storage, such as databases or websites—offer data compression. For

Figure 6-20   Virtual SSD burstable to 3000 IOPS

example, AWS Redshift, which is designed to warehouse massive databases, and AWS CloudFront, a high-speed CDN (content delivery network) service, both offer data compression options. Compression reduces the number of bits needed to store data by recoding the data in a more efficient manner.

Note

A **CDN (content delivery network)** is a distributed storage structure that allows customers to store files in locations closer to where their users are located. For example, suppose you run a video repository website. If your users in India try to stream a video that is stored on a server located in a datacenter in Virginia, those users will experience significant latency. A CDN such as AWS CloudFront allows you to store your video on a server that is physically located in India. This is called **caching**, which is the process of storing copies of data in locations closer to where the data is used. The proximity to your users will decrease latency and increase user satisfaction.

You might have used compression when you zipped large files into a smaller attachment to send by email. Many compression technologies exist, such as zip compressors like 7-Zip (*7-zip.org*), xz (*tukaani.org/xz/*), and gzip (*gnu.org/software/gzip/*), or RAR (Roshal Archive Compressed) compressors like WinRAR in Windows or the aforementioned 7-Zip. Figure 6-21 shows a folder being compressed in Windows.

Another option for reducing the sheer volume of stored data is data **deduplication**, which eliminates multiple copies of the same data. For example, suppose you email a video file to several members of a project team, and everyone saves their own copy of the file to the company network. Data deduplication stores only one copy of the video and tracks metadata references for all other copies back to that one file instance.

Regardless of the optimization of your data, you need to make sure you allow for sufficient storage space to host that data. In the traditional, on-prem datacenter, an IT admin must anticipate the organization's increasing needs well ahead of when those needs are realized. It can take months to get approval for new file servers, order the equipment, install the new infrastructure hardware, and provision higher-capacity storage spaces. This process incurs significant bulk expenses and work time, and results in frequent mismatches between used space and available space.

When using cloud storage services, however, most public cloud platforms charge you only for the storage space you use. Costs increase or decrease immediately and granularly, eliminating the budget cushion required for an on-prem storage solution. This capacity on demand is another way you can minimize cloud storage costs.

Cloud storage services also allow for storage tiers where you pay for storage services according to the kind of access you need to your data. For example, data that is accessed frequently can be stored using a service that charges more for the space used and less for the number of times you access it, as shown in Figure 6-22. This allows for frequent access while paying a more consistent premium for the storage space itself and is sometimes referred to as hot storage. In contrast, data that doesn't require regular access, such as archived data or backups, can be kept in cold storage where storage space is cheaper but each request for data costs more (and takes longer). This system replicates the on-prem process of transferring old data from active systems, such as fast flash storage, to cheaper but slower and less accessible storage media, such as tapes.

Cloud-Native Computing

Cloud Essentials+ Exam Tip

This section discusses microservices and containerization, which are required by

- Part of Objective 2.4: Identify the benefits or solutions of utilizing cloud services.

When considering a migration to the cloud, most people initially expect to take a "lift-and-shift" approach to the migration. Essentially, the expectation is that server VMs running in the on-prem datacenter can be shifted to the cloud and run as usual. While this approach is appropriate for some older applications not designed to function in the cloud, it does not take full advantage of what the cloud has to offer. Newer applications are developed with a "cloud-native" mindset that requires abandoning the monolithic systems hosted on traditional (physical or virtual) servers and creating instead a web of specialized and interconnected microservices. Let's explore what this means.

Traditionally, applications have been developed to function in a complete OS environment. To run the application, you must run the entire OS on a server (either physical or virtual), and you then run the application on top of the OS, as illustrated in Figure 6-23. The

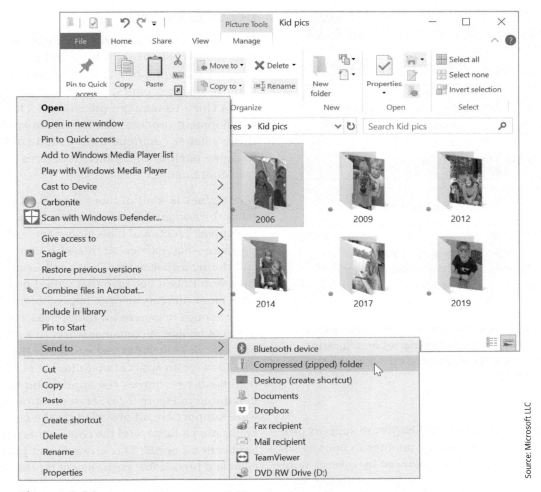

Source: Microsoft LLC

Figure 6-21   Compress a group of files to take up less storage space

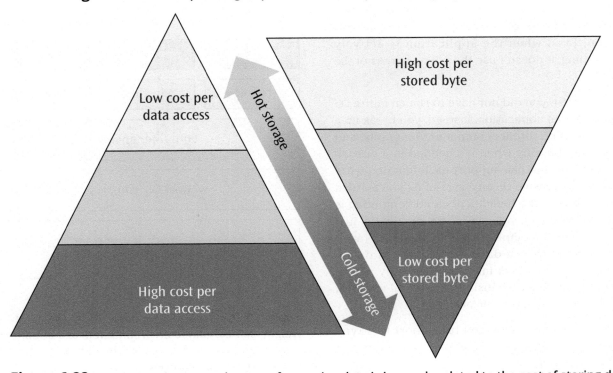

Figure 6-22   With tiered storage, the cost of accessing data is inversely related to the cost of storing data

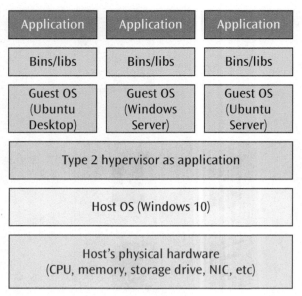

Virtual machines

Figure 6-23 VM-hosted software requires an entire OS, along with all its binaries and libraries, even if those components aren't used by the running application

app relies on services, files, and hardware support provided by the OS. It takes several minutes to boot an OS and then start an application, followed by several more minutes to shut everything down. Due to this lag time, servers are left running all the time so they're readily available. But either way, there's a lot of wasted processor runtime that is not directly supporting the needed application. Even when the application is actively doing something, it doesn't use the full resources of the server or its OS.

Suppose, however, you did not have to run an entire OS environment for an application. Instead, you break up a massive application into its component functions, and you run a function only when it's needed in a virtualized environment that can support each function without running an extensive OS on a server. As you learned in Chapter 1, one of the benefits of cloud computing is scalability. In the cloud, you can create, or spin up, just enough resources to complete an individual task (such as retrieving data from a database), and then delete those resources. This task might require only microseconds of processing time instead of several minutes, which is cheaper and more efficient.

Two technologies have emerged to support this type of microservice design for applications: containers and serverless computing.

Containerization

Many applications or services can be subdivided into smaller **microservices**. An online shopping website, for example, might include one component to manage user accounts, one for the product catalog, and a third to manage purchases. The application development process that breaks an application into these smaller components is called **containerization** because each of these microservices can run in its own container.

A container is kind of like a spacesuit. An astronaut takes the essential environmental components needed to support functional life—air, power, and appropriate pressure—and carries all this with them in the spacesuit during a spacewalk. They don't bring components they won't need because that would make the spacewalk more difficult or even impossible. And they only carry enough resources for themselves, not for an entire group of people. A container works in a similar fashion. The **container** includes just enough of the resources an OS offers for an application to function, but it does not include any resources the application won't need, as illustrated in Figure 6-24. Services, libraries, and hardware support are all provided by the container to the application it hosts, and the container is matched to the application's needs. This arrangement provides an efficient and predictable environment for the application to run in.

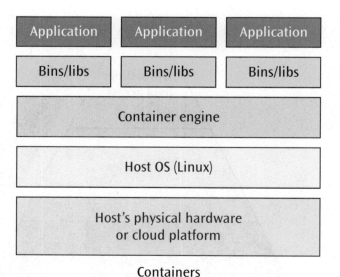

Containers

Figure 6-24 A container engine creates a lightweight, self-contained environment (like a bubble or a spacesuit) that provides only the files and services needed to run an application

This lightweight package offers flexibility and efficiency. Containers can be created and deleted quickly, running only when needed. Another advantage is that multiple containers can run on distributed hardware resources to achieve high availability and effective load balancing. For example, a cluster of physical servers can support a high number of containers where the application within each container might pull on the physical resources (such as CPU, memory, or storage) from any server in the cluster.

Serverless Computing

While this chapter has been heavily focused on servers, the discussion would be incomplete without mention of a cloud-native alternative for hosting cloud-based applications: serverless computing (serverless for short). Despite the name, servers are still involved with serverless computing. However, the cloud customer doesn't have to configure or manage the server—the CSP does this part.

When running a serverless application, the CSP provides short-term access to server processing only when the application needs to run, and then the server access is terminated as soon as the tasks are finished. In many cases, this access requires only microseconds to complete the task. This arrangement reduces overall costs to the consumer and transfers responsibility for managing the server (such as provisioning, patching, and maintenance) to the CSP.

Examples of serverless services include:

> **AWS**—Lambda for running code, S3 (Simple Storage Service) for object storage, and DynamoDB for NoSQL databases

> **Azure**—Cosmos DB for databases, Bot Service for intelligent serverless bots, and Event Hubs for consolidating mass data input from devices and sensors

> **GCP**—Cloud Functions for running code, App Engine for hosting web and mobile apps, and Cloud Dataflow for stream and batch data processing

Serverless computing is often ideal for handling databases, backing up or transferring data, and running apps for short spurts, such as for IoT. Serverless is also often used for backend tasks behind the scenes of complex websites or applications.

All Things Considered

Thought Experiment

When you talk to an Alexa device, your instructions are processed by Lambda, an AWS serverless compute service that processes code in milliseconds. Research online to find out which Google service processes your interactions with Google Assistant.

Remember this...

> The most popular CSPs (cloud service providers) for IaaS and PaaS services include AWS (Amazon Web Services), Microsoft Azure, GCP (Google Cloud Platform), IBM Cloud, Alibaba Cloud, and VMware.

> While there are dozens of cloud service categories, the main ones include compute, storage, databases, networking, security, and billing. One of the first tasks when starting to learn a new cloud platform is to become familiar with the most popular services in each of these categories.

> Cloud customers already benefit from economies of scale when using cloud services. Additionally, most cloud services offer a variety of pricing options to further customize a customer's pricing structure. For example, a BYOL (bring your own license) policy allows customers to install Windows Server under the umbrella of their existing licenses. Similarly, a subscription service allows the customer to commit to paying for an instance over an extended period of time at a lower rate than what's available in the on-demand pricing model.

> Object storage is a more cloud-native storage infrastructure—it takes some of the best characteristics of file and block storage, and it reimagines storage in a way that capitalizes on the cloud's auto-scaling functionality.

> Cloud-native applications rely on a web of specialized and interconnected microservices. Two technologies in particular support this approach. A container includes just enough of the resources an OS offers for an application to function, but it does not include any resources the application won't need. When running a serverless application, the

CSP provides short-term access to server processing only when the application needs to run, and then the server access is terminated as soon as the tasks are finished.

Self-check

10. What cloud service category would you most likely use to manage IP address assignment for your VM instances in the cloud?

    a. Compute

    b. Networking

    c. Security

    d. Storage

11. Which cloud service would allow you to run application code in the cloud without needing to manage a server?

    a. Lambda

    b. Cosmos DB

    c. S3

    d. DynamoDB

12. Which storage type is optimized for the cloud environment?

    a. File system storage

    b. Direct attached storage

    c. Object storage

    d. Block storage

Check your answers at the end of this chapter.

Summary

Section 6-1: Network Software and Servers

> A NOS (network operating system) is a large, complex program that can manage resources commonly found on most LANs. Although a part of the NOS resides in each client computer, the bulk of the NOS operates in a network server, or simply, a server.

> RAID (Redundant Array of Independent Disks) is a collection of storage drives (called an array) interfaced in a way to ensure one or more layers of redundant copies of data across the drive array. The most basic RAID techniques are RAID 0 (called striping), RAID 1 (called disk mirroring), RAID 3 (which includes parity), and RAID 5 (which spreads parity information across multiple disks).

> Storage types you might find in an on-prem network include DAS (direct attached storage), NAS (network attached storage), and a SAN (storage area network). DAS and NAS devices store files in a file system. Data in a SAN array of drives is stored in blocks rather than in a file system hierarchy and is called block storage.

> To support a LAN and its OS, a wide variety of utility programs are available. Utilities are software programs that operate in the background and support one or more functions to keep the network running at optimal performance.

> The licensing agreement that accompanies a software product is a legal contract and describes a number of conditions that must be upheld for proper use of the software package. Licensing models define where the software can be installed, who can use it, and when payments are made.

Section 6-2: Server Operating Systems

> Unix was a popular OS for mainframes and servers and can still be found on single-user workstations. Various distributions of Unix are still customized for niche scenarios due to its stability and backwards compatibility with older applications.

> Many companies purchase a Linux distro from a vendor that specializes in providing proprietary code in their distributions along with all the supporting applications and utilities, such as web page support tools, a GUI, and the latest versions of peripheral drivers. Even when Linux is purchased from a vendor,

the cost of it is insignificant compared to the cost of purchasing either Unix or Windows Server.

> One of the most significant components of Windows Server is the directory service AD (Active Directory), which stores information about all the objects and resources in a network and makes this information available to users, network administrators, and

applications. AD creates a hierarchical structure of resources similar to a tree design. Objects, such as users, groups of users, computers, applications, and network devices, are the leaf items within the tree. Leaf items are grouped in OUs (organizational units). One or more OUs can be grouped together into a domain, which is the main object in Windows Server.

Section 6-3: Network Devices

> Like many OSs, Cisco's IOS relies on various command modes that determine what commands can be executed. These command modes are accessed from the CLI and, along the way, the prompt indicates which command mode is active.

> A wide variety of commands are available within each of Cisco's command modes to configure a router, switch, and other network devices. Each series of commands must be performed in a particular command mode. Other manufacturers offer similar commands to configure their devices.

Section 6-4: Virtualization

> A type 1 hypervisor runs directly on the host system's hardware and does not require an underlying OS. In reality, a type 1 hypervisor is itself a minimal OS, many of which are built on the Linux kernel. A type 2 hypervisor runs on top of an existing OS. In other words, the host must have an OS installed first, and then a hypervisor application can run inside that OS.

> Virtualization offers the advantages of efficient use of resources; cost and energy savings; fault and threat isolation; and simple backups, recovery, and replication. Possible disadvantages include compromised performance, increased licensing costs, and single point of failure.

> NFV (network functions virtualization) can be used to virtualize routers, switches, firewalls, load balancers, and other network devices. This allows network admins to configure more customized networks on standard servers without having to purchase more complex, proprietary hardware.

> With SDN (software-defined networking), decision-making processes are made at the software level by a network controller instead of being handled by individual hardware devices. This decision-making process is called the control plane. The actual movement of the packet from device to device is called the data plane.

Section 6-5: Cloud Computing

> The most popular CSPs (cloud service providers) for IaaS and PaaS services include AWS (Amazon Web Services), Microsoft Azure, GCP (Google Cloud Platform), IBM Cloud, Alibaba Cloud, and VMware.

> While there are dozens of cloud service categories, the main ones include compute, storage, databases, networking, security, and billing. One of the first tasks when starting to learn a new cloud platform is to become familiar with the most popular services in each of these categories.

> Cloud customers already benefit from economies of scale when using cloud services. Additionally, most cloud services offer a variety of pricing options to further customize a customer's pricing structure. For example, a BYOL (bring your own license) policy allows customers to install Windows Server under the umbrella of their existing licenses. Similarly, a subscription service allows the customer to commit to paying for an instance over an extended period of time at a lower rate than what's available in the on-demand pricing model.

> Object storage is a more cloud-native storage infra-structure—it takes some of the best characteristics of file and block storage, and it reimagines storage in a way that capitalizes on the cloud's auto-scaling functionality.

> Cloud-native applications rely on a web of specialized and interconnected microservices. Two technologies

in particular support this approach. A container includes just enough of the resources an OS offers for an application to function, but it does not include any resources the application won't need. When running a serverless application, the CSP provides short-term access to server processing only when the application needs to run, and then the server access is terminated as soon as the tasks are finished.

Key Terms

For definitions of key terms, see the Glossary near the end of the book.
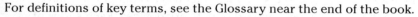

AD (Active Directory)

API (application programming interface)

auto-scaling

block storage

BYOL (bring your own license)

caching

CDN (content delivery network)

container

containerization

control plane

corporate license

CSP (cloud service provider)

DAS (direct attached storage)

data plane

deduplication

disk mirroring

file system

firewall

GPL (General Public License)

interactive user license

licensing agreement

licensing model

load balancer

microservice

NAS (network attached storage)

NFV (network functions virtualization)

NOS (network operating system)

object storage

on-demand pricing model

open source

OS (operating system)

pay-as-you-go model

perpetual license

RAID (Redundant Array of Independent Disks)

SAN (storage area network)

SDN (software-defined networking)

SDS (software-defined storage)

server license

server OS

serverless computing

single-user-multiple-station license

single-user-single-station license

site license

sniffer

spyware

striping

subscription license

subscription service

type 1 hypervisor

type 2 hypervisor

utility

Review Questions

1. Which of the following functions is specific to a server OS?

   a. Manage applications

   b. Prompt user for network login

   c. Allocate hardware resources

   d. Secure files and other resources

2. Which software interface is an application most likely to use to communicate with an OS?

   a. CLI

   b. SDK

   c. GUI

   d. API

3. Which type of RAID stores duplicate copies of data?

    a. RAID 0

    b. RAID 3

    c. RAID 5

    d. RAID 1

4. For a medium-sized company with five offices in three cities, which AD layer would most likely correspond to the company's name?

    a. Leaf

    b. Domain

    c. Forest

    d. Organizational unit

5. Which standards served as the template for AD's design? *Choose two.*

    a. RAID

    b. LDAP

    c. Unix

    d. DNS

6. Which of the following OSs is NOT open-source software?

    a. Windows Server

    b. NetBSD

    c. RHEL

    d. Ubuntu

7. Which of the following is NOT an advantage offered by Linux?

    a. Fast

    b. Free

    c. Easy

    d. Stable

8. Which OS would most likely be found on a router?

    a. Windows Server

    b. RHEL

    c. Ubuntu

    d. IOS

9. Which storage type requires specialized protocols to access stored data?

    a. SAN

    b. CDN

    c. NAS

    d. DAS

10. Why is Linux such a stable OS?

    a. Linux is open source.

    b. Linux is lightweight.

    c. Linux is adaptable.

    d. Linux is customizable.

11. As you plug a new workstation into a port on your Cisco switch, you realize you need to make sure the new workstation is assigned to the correct VLAN. Which command mode do you need to use to assign the connection to the VLAN?

    a. Interface configuration

    b. User EXEC

    c. Privileged EXEC

    d. Global configuration

12. Which of these hypervisors would be easiest for students to use on their home computers?

    a. ESXi

    b. Oracle VirtualBox

    c. Citrix Hypervisor

    d. Android

13. Which of the following is a potential disadvantage of using virtual resources in a corporate datacenter?

    a. Requirements for physical hardware

    b. VM isolation

    c. Licensing requirements

    d. Demand on energy resources

14. When you enter a Cisco router's CLI, which command mode do you start in?

    a. Privileged EXEC

    b. Global configuration

    c. Interface configuration

    d. User EXEC

15. Which cloud platform is natively compatible with AD?

    a. AWS

    b. IBM Cloud

    c. Azure

    d. GCP

16. Which of the following is a cloud-native technology?

    a. Serverless

    b. NFV

    c. VLAN

    d. Hypervisor

17. Which of these technologies is NOT used to minimize costs of cloud storage?

    a. Auto-scaling

    b. Anti-malware

    c. Compression

    d. Deduplication

18. To increase redundancy, you've created two copies of your database in the cloud. What virtual device can ensure you spread traffic evenly across both copies of the database to increase performance?

    a. Router

    b. Hypervisor

    c. Firewall

    d. Load balancer

19. Your client, a medical office, needs to store old patient records for at least seven years since the last date of service. What kind of cloud storage will provide the best price?

    a. Hot

    b. RAID

    c. Cold

    d. CDN

20. Which of the following is an AWS compute service?

    a. RDS

    b. EC2

    c. EBS

    d. S3

Hands-On Project 6

Create a Linux VM in VirtualBox

Estimated time: 45 minutes

Resources:

> Any edition of Windows 10 installed on a computer that supports UEFI. Note that instructions for projects using VirtualBox are written for Windows 10 hosts. However, Oracle VirtualBox can also be installed on a Windows 7/8/8.1, Linux, macOS, or Solaris host.

> Internet access

> If desired, instructor can provide Ubuntu Desktop image file

> **Context:**

In this project, you download and install Oracle VirtualBox, which is a free hypervisor, to create VMs (virtual machines) and a virtual network on a single workstation. You'll also install Ubuntu Desktop, a Linux distro, in the VM. Complete the following steps to install VirtualBox:

1. If you are using a 64-bit host computer and want to install a 64-bit OS in the VM, HAV (hardware-assisted virtualization) must be enabled in UEFI setup. If you are not sure it is enabled, click **Start** and **Power**. Hold down the **Shift** key and click **Restart**. When the computer reboots, click **Troubleshoot**, **Advanced options**, and **UEFI Firmware settings**. The computer reboots again, this time into UEFI setup.

2. Make sure hardware-assisted virtualization (HAV) is enabled. For the system shown in Figure 6-25, that's done on the CPU Configuration screen. Also make sure that any subcategory items under HAV are enabled. Save your changes, exit UEFI setup, and allow the system to restart to Windows.

3. Go to **virtualbox.org/wiki/Downloads** and download the most current **VirtualBox platform package** for Windows hosts to your desktop or other folder on your hard drive. Install the software, accepting default settings during the installation. The Oracle VM VirtualBox Manager window opens as shown in Figure 6-26.

Note

Some motherboards might not show "UEFI Firmware settings" as an option on the Advanced options screen. If this is the case for you, you'll need to do a little experimenting and troubleshooting.

First, determine your motherboard manufacturer and model. To do this, continue the boot to Windows, press **Win+R**, and enter **msinfo32**, which will list the motherboard manufacturer and model on the System Summary page.

Find the motherboard's documentation online to ensure it supports UEFI. If it does, you can try entering the UEFI settings during boot by pressing the required key, such as Esc, Del, F2, F4, F8, or F12. (If you're not sure which key to try, check your motherboard documentation or watch for a message during boot.) For this to work, you might first need to disable fast startup in the Windows Control Panel's Power Options menu.

If you have trouble with any of this, be sure to do a search online for the problem you're having and look for information to help you figure it out. Learning how to research a problem online is an important skill for anyone working with computers and networks.

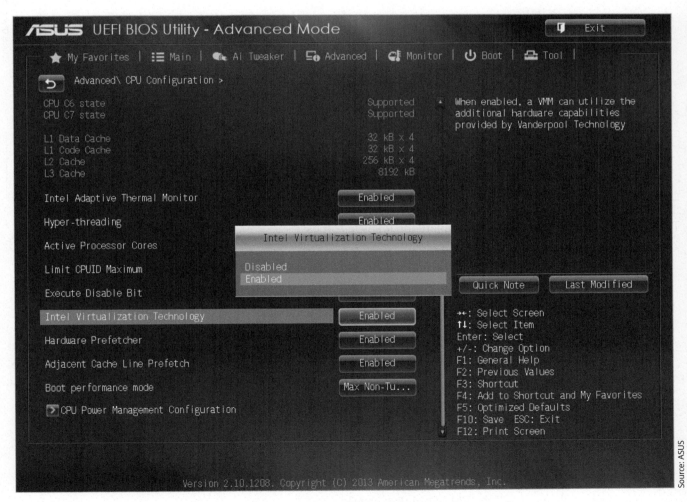

Figure 6-25   Virtualization must be enabled in UEFI setup for VirtualBox to work

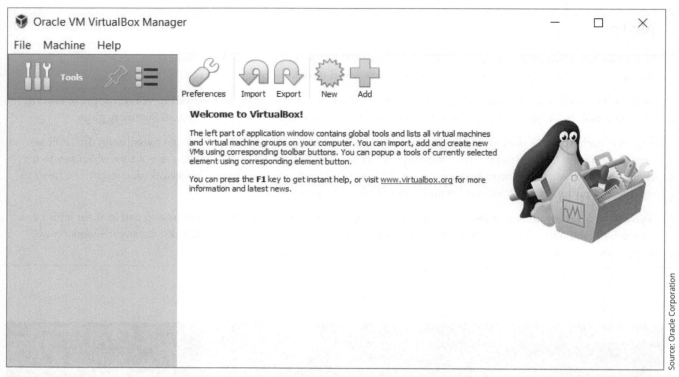

Figure 6-26 Use the VirtualBox Manager to create and manage virtual machines

Source: Oracle Corporation

Note

Your instructor might have special instructions for the following steps. Check with your instructor before proceeding.

To create a Linux VM in VirtualBox, complete the following steps:

4. Go to **ubuntu.com** and download the Ubuntu Desktop OS to your hard drive. While this project uses Ubuntu 21.04, you can use the most recent version. The download is free, so you can decline to make any donations. The file that downloads is an ISO file. Wait for the download to complete before continuing to the next step.

5. Back in VirtualBox, click **New** in the toolbar and follow the wizard to create a VM. Give your VM a name. When naming resources like VMs, be sure to think through what information the resource's name should provide and think about how this name will compare to other resource names when appearing in a list together. For example, you might want to include the VM's OS in the name, such as "Ubuntu-64bit," or you might want to reference the project in which you created the VM, such as "Proj6." What did you name your VM?

6. Choose the **Linux** type and the **Ubuntu (64-bit)** version. You can accept all other default settings for the VM unless directed otherwise by your instructor. As you go, notice the resources allocated to the VM and answer the following questions:

    a. How much memory will the VM have?
    b. What kind of file will hold the VM's virtual hard disk?
    c. How much space will the VM's hard disk have?

To install the Ubuntu OS, you'll first need to mount the ISO file that contains the Ubuntu Desktop image to a virtual DVD in your VM. Complete the following steps:

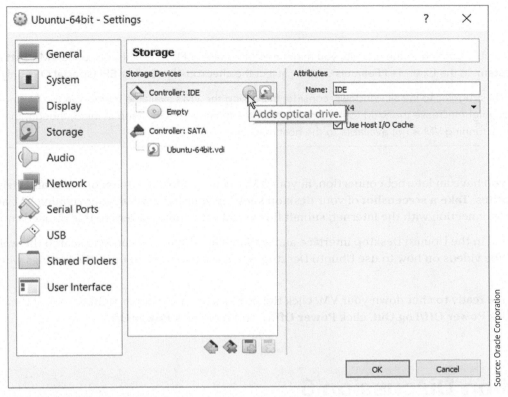

Figure 6-27   Storage Tree options allow you to mount an ISO image as a virtual CD in the VM

7. With the VM selected, click **Settings** in the VirtualBox Manager window. In the VM's Settings window, click **Storage** in the left pane.

8. In the Storage Tree area, in the Storage Devices pane, click the **Adds optical drive** icon, which looks like a CD with a plus (+) symbol, as shown in Figure 6-27.

9. The Optical Disk Selector window appears. Click **Add**. Browse to the location of the ISO file. Select the ISO file, click **Open**, click **Choose**, and click **OK**. You will now return to the VirtualBox Manager window.

Note

An ISO file (which has the .iso file extension) is a disc image file. It contains all the files and folders of a virtual CD or DVD merged into a single file. The file can be burned to a physical disc, or it can be mounted to a virtual device, such as a VM.

---

10. With your new VM selected in the left pane, click **Start** on the toolbar. Your VM starts up and begins the process of installing the operating system. Follow the prompts on the screen to install Ubuntu Desktop. Be sure to click **Install Ubuntu**; do not click Try Ubuntu. Accept all default settings except, when given the option, don't install any extra software bundled with the OS. Give permission to download updates while installing. Confirm that you want to erase the disk and install Ubuntu—it will only erase the virtual disk assigned to your VM, not your physical disk. Record your user credentials for your Ubuntu VM in a safe place. You'll need to restart the VM when the installation is finished.

> ## Note
>
> If you have trouble booting to the ISO file, you might need to enable EFI. To do this, go to the VM's **Settings** window and click **System**. In the Extended Features section, select the checkbox for **Enable EFI (special OSs only)**.
>
> Also, if the VM struggles to install Windows, consider increasing the VM's available memory in the Settings menu. For example, you might increase the RAM to 4 GB rather than the minimum 1 GB. Keep in mind, though, that any RAM dedicated to a running VM is not available to the host machine.

11. To verify you have an Internet connection, in your VM, open the Mozilla Firefox browser and visit two or three websites. **Take a screenshot** of your desktop showing your hypervisor, your running VM, and the VM's successful connection with the Internet; submit this visual with your answers to this project's questions.

12. Poke around in the Ubuntu Desktop interface and get familiar with it. You can also search the web for tutorials and YouTube videos on how to use Ubuntu Desktop. What are two ways to open the Settings window in Ubuntu Desktop?

13. When you're ready to shut down your VM, click the power icon in the upper-right corner of the Ubuntu Desktop screen, click **Power Off/Log Out**, click **Power Off...**, and then click **Power Off**.

Reflection Discussion 6

This chapter covered popular technologies that support virtualization and cloud computing. As you learned, cloud computing relies on virtualization to function, but they're not quite the same thing. Virtualization is often used in the on-prem datacenter, and public cloud is the most popular form of cloud computing. To help you better differentiate between the two types of technologies, answer the following questions:

> What are two business-related advantages of virtualization over cloud computing?
> What are two business-related advantages of cloud computing over virtualization?
> Which do you think is the most beneficial and why?
> What is your biggest concern when using cloud computing in a business environment?

Go to the discussion forum in your school's LMS. Write a post of at least 100 words discussing your thoughts comparing virtualization and cloud computing technologies. Then respond to two of your classmates' threads with posts of at least 50 words discussing their comments and ideas. Use complete sentences, and check your grammar and spelling. Try to ask open-ended questions that encourage discussion, and remember to respond to people who post on your thread. Use the rubric in Table 6-3 to help you understand what is expected of your work for this assignment.

Table 6-3 Grading rubric for Reflection Discussion 6

Task	Novice	Competent	Proficient	Earned
Initial post	Generalized statements addressing the benefits of virtualization and cloud computing **30 points**	Some specific statements with supporting evidence about advantages of virtualization and cloud computing, a clearly stated opinion regarding which is the most beneficial, and a statement identifying a concern related to cloud computing **40 points**	Self-reflective discussion with specific and thoughtful statements and supporting evidence about advantages of virtualization and cloud computing, a well-supported opinion regarding which is the most beneficial, and a thorough description of a concern related to cloud computing **50 points**	

Initial post: Mechanics	• Length < 100 words • Several grammar and spelling errors **5 points**	• Length = 100 words • Occasional grammar and spelling errors **7 points**	• Length > 100 words • Appropriate grammar and spelling **10 points**	
Response 1	Brief response showing little engagement or critical thinking **5 points**	Detailed response with specific contributions to the discussion **10 points**	Thoughtful response with specific examples or details and open-ended questions that invite deeper discussion of the topic **15 points**	
Response 2	Brief response showing little engagement or critical thinking **5 points**	Detailed response with specific contributions to the discussion **10 points**	Thoughtful response with specific examples or details and open-ended questions that invite deeper discussion of the topic **15 points**	
Both responses: Mechanics	• Length < 50 words each • Several grammar and spelling errors **5 points**	• Length = 50 words each • Occasional grammar and spelling errors **7 points**	• Length > 50 words each • Appropriate grammar and spelling **10 points**	
			Total	

Solutions to Self-Check Questions

Section 6-1: Network Software and Servers

1. Which RAID technique spreads data across disks without the ability to recover lost data?

Answer: b. RAID 0

Explanation: With RAID 0, data is broken into pieces, and each consecutive piece is stored on a different drive. This technique is known as striping. There is no redundancy of data in this technique; if one drive fails, data is lost.

2. Which storage type identifies data locations with a LUN?

Answer: d. SAN

Explanation: Data in a SAN (storage area network) array of drives is stored in blocks rather than in a file system hierarchy and is called block storage. Each block is a specified size and contains data that is referenced by the block's LUN (logical unit number).

3. For which of these licensing models do you need to know the number of cores a computer has before you can install the licensed software?

Answer: a. Server license

Explanation: With a server license, there is rarely a software counter controlling the current number of users. A server license might instead be priced according to the number of CPU cores or sockets the server has.

Section 6-2: Server Operating Systems

4. Which of the following characteristics of Linux is both a positive and a negative factor in choosing a Linux distro?

Answer: c. Customizability

Explanation: The ability to customize Linux is a double-edged sword. In the hands of an experienced programmer, the Linux source code can be modified in almost limitless ways to provide a customized OS. However, in inexperienced hands, customized source code can be a source of constant trouble.

5. At what level would a printer fit in an AD tree design?

Answer: d. Leaf

Explanation: In the hierarchical structure of AD, objects such as users, groups of users, computers, applications, printers, and network devices are the leaf items within the tree.

Section 6-3: Network Devices

6. Which Cisco command mode is most likely used to change the password for accessing the device?

Answer: a. Global configuration

Explanation: Global configuration mode is a high-level mode for making device configuration changes, such as the username and password to access the device. Other modes might be used to configure passwords for specific capabilities on the device.

7. Why might an admin use the show command on a Cisco switch?

Answer: d. To confirm the device's configurations are correct

Explanation: After making configuration changes on a device, the admin should use the show command, such as do show vlan, to view configurations and confirm all changes are implemented as intended.

Section 6-4: Virtualization

8. If you install a hypervisor on a Linux host machine, which of the following OSs can you install in a VM on that server?

Answer: d. Any OS

Explanation: The hypervisor allocates availability of hardware resources to the host computer and to each guest computer. The hypervisor also creates a kind of pocket within the host computer's OS where the guest system runs independently of the host system and any other guest systems. Each guest system can run any OS supported by the hypervisor and underlying hardware.

9. Which technology can be used to create a virtual switch?

Answer: b. NFV

Explanation: NFV (network functions virtualization) can be used to virtualize routers, switches, firewalls, load balancers, and other network devices.

Section 6-5: Cloud Computing

10. What cloud service category would you most likely use to manage IP address assignment for your VM instances in the cloud?

Answer: b. Networking

Explanation: While there are dozens of categories, the main ones include compute, storage, databases, networking, security, and billing. IP address assignment is a networking task and would be handled by a networking cloud service. For example, in AWS, you can define IP address spaces using the VPC (Virtual Private Cloud) service in the Networking category of services.

11. Which cloud service would allow you to run application code in the cloud without needing to manage a server?

Answer: a. Lambda

Explanation: With serverless computing, the cloud customer doesn't have to configure or manage the server—the CSP (cloud service provider) does this part. AWS's Lambda service is an example of serverless computing for running short-term code in the cloud.

12. Which storage type is optimized for the cloud environment?

Answer: c. Object storage

Explanation: Object storage is a cloud-native storage infrastructure—it takes some of the best characteristics of file and block storage, and it reimagines storage in a way that capitalizes on the cloud's auto-scaling functionality.

Chapter 7

The Internet

Objectives

After reading this chapter, you should be able to:

- Explain the ways IP supports communication across networks

- Explain the protocols and processes used to locate Internet resources

- Describe how common protocols work with IP to support network communications

- Describe popular Internet-based services

Introduction

During the late 1960s, a branch of the U.S. government called ARPA (Advanced Research Projects Agency) created one of the country's first wide area data networks, the ARPANET. Select research universities, military bases, and government labs were allowed access to the ARPANET for services such as electronic mail, file transfers, and remote logins.

In 1983, the Department of Defense divided the ARPANET into two similar networks: the original ARPANET and MILNET, which was for military use only. Although the MILNET remained essentially the same over time, the ARPANET was eventually phased out and replaced with newer technology. During this period, the National Science Foundation funded the creation of a new cross-country network backbone called the NSFNET. The NSFNET was the main telecommunications line through the network, connecting the major router sites across the country. It was to this backbone that smaller regional or mid-level (statewide) networks connected. A set of access or "campus" networks then connected to these mid-level networks (Figure 7-1). Eventually, this collection of networks became known as the Internet.

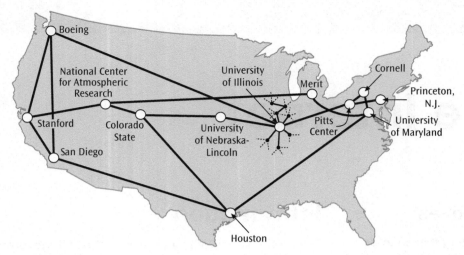

Figure 7-1 Old NSFNET backbone and connecting mid-level and campus networks

During the mid-1990s, the government essentially withdrew all direct support for the Internet and turned it over to private industries and universities. Thus, there is no longer a single backbone but multiple backbones supported by different businesses and organizations.

Current estimates suggest that there are over 1.5 billion active and inactive websites connected to the Internet, and billions of people around the world access the Internet daily. One fact is very clear: use of the Internet has grown at a phenomenal rate. Its early creators did not—could not—envision today's Internet.

In this chapter, you'll learn about how the Internet works, and you'll explore many of the services made available over the Internet—services that have deeply impacted and transformed businesses of all kinds. To support the many different types of Internet services and to support the layers of the TCP/IP protocol suite, numerous protocols have emerged. This chapter covers several of the more important Internet protocols, starting with IP (Internet Protocol).

an application (such as email) requires the use of the application layer, which in turn requires the use of the transport layer, which requires the use of the network layer, which requires the use of the data link layer, which places the signal on the physical layer for transmission. The layers build on one another in this hierarchy, and the user is not exposed to the details of those lower layers that the user does not have direct contact with.

Different protocols function at each layer. The most-used protocol at the network layer in the TCP/IP protocol suite—and arguably the most important protocol on the Internet—is called IP (Internet Protocol), which you first read about in Chapter 1. Its primary function is to perform the routing necessary to move data packets across the networks that collectively form the Internet.

To this end, IP provides the IP addressing scheme used by routing protocols. IP addresses in each packet identify the packet's source and destination. Routers read this information to determine the next hop that

Section 7-1: Internet Protocol (IP)

From simple email to the complexities of the web, many services are available on the Internet. What enables these varied services to work? How does the Internet itself work? Recall the layers of the TCP/IP protocol suite that were introduced in Chapter 1 (Figure 7-2). The layers are designed so that an Internet user who needs to use

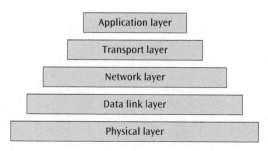

Figure 7-2 Hierarchy of layers as created by the Department of Defense

will move each packet towards its destination. Routing protocols, which you'll learn more about in Chapter 9, help determine these pathways quickly and efficiently. IP is the glue that holds this system together by providing the addressing scheme used to identify each network location across WANs like the Internet, and by organizing this addressing information in each packet's IP header. To understand IP, you'll need to understand IP headers and IP addresses.

IP Packets

Recall from earlier chapters that Ethernet frames at the data link layer encapsulate headers and data from higher layer protocols. One of the most common protocols encapsulated inside an Ethernet frame is IP. Similar to an Ethernet frame at the data link layer, IP's header at

the network layer contains standard fields that encapsulate headers and data from higher layers. An IP packet is the combination of the IP header and its payload. This packet is, in turn, encapsulated by the lower, data link layer's header(s) and trailer. The data link layer header provides information needed to traverse a LAN while the IP header provides information needed to traverse multiple networks, such as the Internet.

Consider once again the example of a workstation performing a network operation such as sending an email message to a distant workstation, a process that is depicted in Figure 7-3. Suppose both workstations are on LANs, and the two LANs are connected via a WAN. As the local workstation sends the email packet down through the layers for transmission on the first LAN, the IP header is added in front of the transport layer message, creating the IP packet. Next, the appropriate

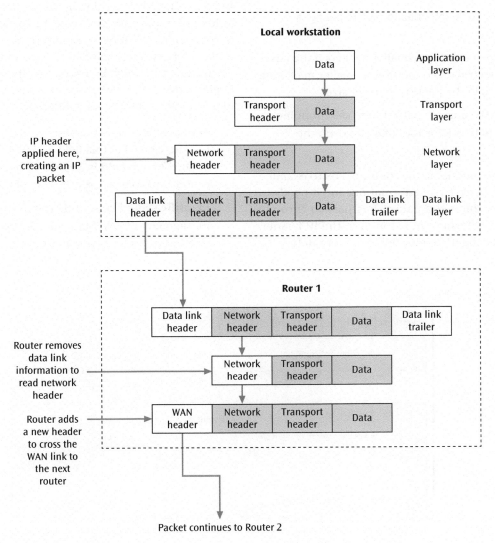

Figure 7-3   Progression of a packet from one network to another

MAC layer headers encapsulate the IP packet creating a frame, and this frame is sent through LAN 1 to the first router. Because the router interfaces LAN 1 to a WAN, the MAC layer information is removed, leaving the IP packet. At this time, the router may use some or all of the IP information to perform the necessary internetworking functions. The necessary WAN level information is applied, and the packet is sent over the WAN to Router 2. When the packet arrives at the second router, the WAN information is removed, once again leaving the IP packet. The appropriate MAC layer information is then applied for transfer of the frame over LAN 2, and the frame is transmitted to its destination. Upon arrival at the remote workstation, all header information is discarded, leaving the original data.

When a router receives an IP packet, it may make several decisions affecting the packet's future. In particular, the router might perform the following functions:

> Make routing decisions based on the packet's address portion

> Fragment the packet into smaller packets if the next network to be traversed requires a smaller maximum packet size than the packet's current size

> Decide that the current packet has been hopping around the network for too long and drop the packet

To perform these functions, the router needs to examine the address and packet size information, and it needs to know how many times the packet has passed through a router. All this information is found in the IP header. Before looking at the IP header fields in more detail, it's

important to note that there are currently two versions of IP: IPv4 (IP version 4) and IPv6 (IP version 6). IPv4 has been in existence since the early 1980s and is still the more common version. To support growing demands, IPv6 was introduced in 1998. Despite many advancements, IPv6 has been slow to take off. But that won't always be the case. Let's look at version 4 first.

Internet Protocol Version 4 (IPv4)

Figure 7-3 showed that the network layer adds an IP header to the transport layer message—thereby creating an IP packet—before passing the packet on to the data link layer. The information included in this IP header and the way the header is packaged allow networks to share data and create internetwork connections.

Exactly what is in this IP header that allows internetworking to happen? Figure 7-4 shows the individual fields of the IPv4 header in more detail. While all 14 fields are important, you need to know about the field that specifies the IP version and those that affect three of the primary functions of IP: fragmentation, packet discard, and addressing. By examining these fields, you will begin to discover how IPv4 works and why it is capable of interconnecting so many different types of networks:

> **Version**—Indicates the version of IP being used. IPv4 has the value 4 in this field and IPv6 has the value 6. The Version field is important because it tells the router how to interpret the rest of the IP packet.

> **Identification, Flags, and Fragment offset**—Used to fragment a packet into smaller parts. IP allows a router to break a large packet into smaller

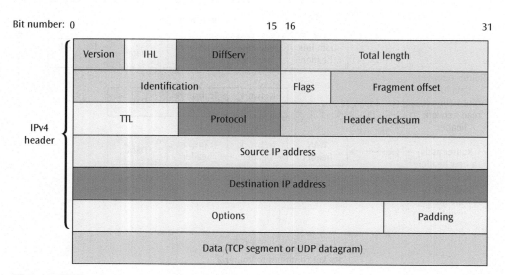

Figure 7-4   Format of the IPv4 packet

fragments so it will fit onto the next network if that network requires smaller packets. While this feature generally isn't required for today's networks, it can still be used as an attack vector for various fragmentation attacks. As you will learn shortly, IPv6 doesn't even have a field in the header to perform fragmentation, thus making IPv6 safer in this regard.

> **TTL (Time to live)**—Allows the router to discard a packet that has been traveling across networks for too long. This field indicates how long a packet is allowed to live—that is, how many bounces from router to router a packet can make within the system. You'll see the importance of the TTL field in Chapter 9 when you learn about hop count and hop limits for routing protocols on WANs.

> **Header checksum**—Performs an arithmetic checksum on only the header portion of the packet.

> **Source IP address and Destination IP address**— Contain the 32-bit IP source and destination addresses, respectively, of the packet. A 32-bit address uniquely defines a connection to the Internet—usually a workstation or other device, although a single device can also support multiple Internet connections. As an IP packet moves through the Internet, the Destination IP address field is examined by a router. The router, using a routing algorithm, forwards the packet onto the next appropriate communications link.

All Things Considered

Thought Experiment

What is the IP address of your workstation, laptop, or smartphone? How did you find this information? Is the address statically assigned or dynamically assigned? Did your IP address come from an ISP or from somewhere else? Explain your reasoning.

IPv4 Addresses

To make IPv4 addresses a little easier for humans to understand, these 32-bit binary addresses (see the top of Figure 7-5 for an example) are represented by dotted decimal notation. This dotted decimal notation is created by converting each 8-bit string in the 32-bit IP address into its decimal equivalent. Thus, the binary IP address in the top row becomes 128.156.14.7, as shown in the bottom part of Figure 7-5.

10000000	10011100	00001110	00000111
128	156	14	7

Figure 7-5   Four octets make up an IPv4 address

Keep in mind, however, that computers still see IP addresses at the bit-by-bit level. This is important when determining which network an IP address belongs to. Some of the bits in an IP address refer to the local network and are called the network ID, and some of the bits in the IP address refer to a specific host on the network and are called the host ID, as shown in the top part of Figure 7-6. In this IP address, 128.156.14 is the network ID, and .7 is the host ID. The value of the fourth octet could be anything from 0 to 255, and that IP address would still be on the same 125.156.14 network as this one.

To allow for flexibility, the number of bits for each part can vary depending on the network settings. When more bits are used for the network ID, the IP address range can support more networks but fewer hosts on each network. When more bits are used for the host ID, the IP address range can support more hosts on each network but fewer networks. For example, a network using 24 bits for the network ID and 8 bits for the host ID can have 2^8, or 256, host addresses. However, a network using 16 bits for the network ID and 16 bits for the host ID can have 2^{16} (which is 65,536) host addresses.

How do computers know how many bits to count towards the network ID and how many bits are used for the host ID? IPv4 addressing relies on a subnet mask for this task. The subnet mask contains a 1 for each bit that should be counted as part of the network ID and a 0 for each bit that should be counted as part of the host ID. The bottom part of Figure 7-6 shows how these bits line up with corresponding bits in the IPv4 address.

The subnet mask can also be written using decimal numbers, but it makes more sense to think about the subnet mask at a bit-by-bit level to understand why the numbers apply as they do. For example, instead of 24 bits for the network ID, suppose you decided to use only 23 bits. This allows for fewer network IDs while allowing for more host IDs on each network. In Figure 7-7, the subnet mask at a bit-by-bit level shows 23 1s, and when converted to decimal, each octet reflects the correct value.

Using 23 bits for the network ID allows for twice as many possible host IDs. There's the original range of IP addresses: 128.156.14.0-255. And there's now a second

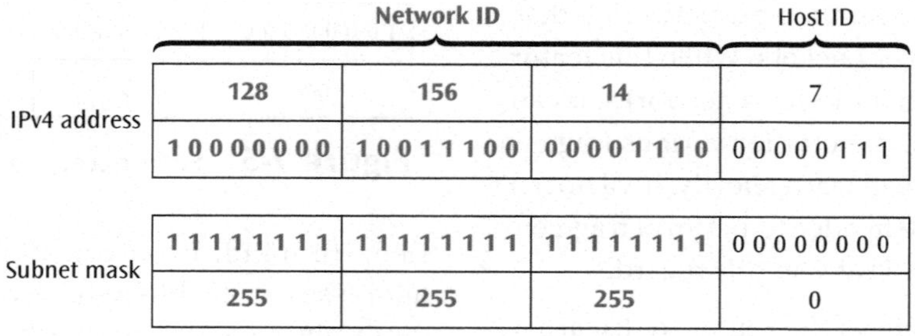

Figure 7-6 The bold red bits show the network ID as indicated by the 1s in the subnet mask

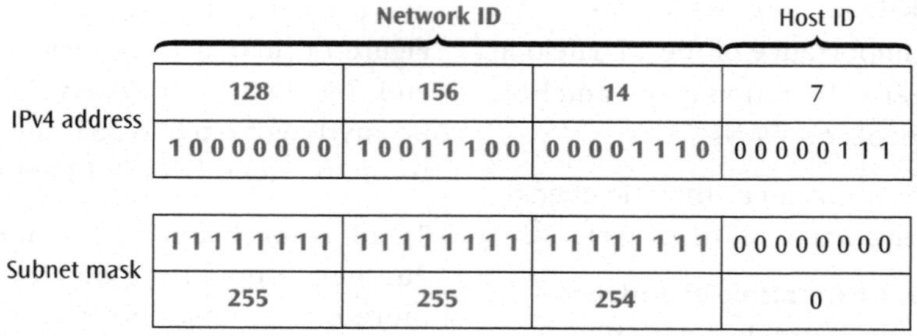

Figure 7-7 More bits for the host ID allow for more hosts on each network

available range of IP addresses within the same subnet: 128.156.15.0-255. In this example, all IP addresses from 128.156.14.0 through 128.156.15.255 are contained in the same network. Using this technique, an ISP (Internet service provider) and a company can take many host IDs and break them into subnets. Each subnet can then support a smaller number of hosts. This process of dividing larger networks into smaller subnets is called subnetting.

Here you've seen how the number of 1s in a subnet mask indicates how many bits in the IPv4 address are used to indicate the network and each host on that network. A network is, therefore, identified by its network ID and its subnet mask. A shorthand version of this information can be written 128.156.14.0/23. This format is called CIDR (Classless Interdomain Routing and pronounced "cider") notation or just slash notation. The address 128.156.14.0 is the beginning address of the block of addresses. The /23 indicates how many of the 32 bits in the address are allocated to the network ID portion. Thus, the first 23 bits are allocated to the network ID, leaving 9 bits for the host ID. If you have a 9-bit host ID, then you have 2^9, or 512, host IDs.

This form of addressing is called classless addressing. The term makes more sense in contrast to what it replaced: classful addressing. When IP and IP addresses

were created in the 1960s, subnet masks only varied by an entire octet at a time. Instead of adjusting the number of bits by one digit left or right, each class of subnet mask could only be adjusted by the number of octets used to identify the network and hosts. Therefore, the three main classes of IP addresses were A, B, and C, as shown in Table 7-1. Each class was also restricted by the bit values in the first few digits, which limited the IP address ranges used in each class. Figure 7-8 shows the relationship of assigned bit values, distribution of octets, and range of IDs for each of these three classes. Note that the first octet value of 127 is reserved and cannot be included in a network's usable IP address range. Two other classes, D and E, are also reserved for other purposes.

The last row in Table 7-1 indicates the private address range for each class of addresses. Only certain IP addresses can be used on the Internet. When a company or person applies for and receives an IP address for use on the Internet, that IP address will fall within a particular range of IP address values called public IP addresses. Routers will forward messages on to the Internet only if the message is addressed to a public IP address. In contrast, a defined range of IP addresses can be used by anyone on their private networks. These are called private IP addresses. Messages sent to a private IP address will not be forwarded by

Table 7-1 The three main classes of classful addressing

	Class A	Class B	Class C
Valid network range	1.0.0.0–126.0.0.0	128.0.0.0–191.255.0.0	192.0.0.0–223.255.255.0
Total networks	$2^7 = 128$	$2^{14} = 16,384$	$2^{21} = 2,097,152$
Host addresses per network	$2^{24} = 16,777,216$	$2^{16} = 65,536$	$2^8 = 256$
Network bits	8 (1 octet)	16 (2 octets)	24 (3 octets)
Host bits	24 (3 octets)	16 (2 octets)	8 (1 octet)
Subnet mask	255.0.0.0	255.255.0.0	255.255.255.0
Private address range	10.0.0.0–10.255.255.255	172.16.0.0–172.31.255.255	192.168.0.0–192.168.255.255

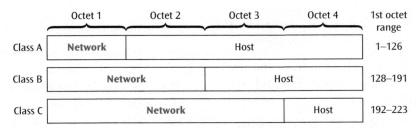

Figure 7-8 Each class uses a certain number of full octets for the network ID

a router. You can check your computer's IP address with the command `ipconfig` in Command Prompt or PowerShell on a Windows computer. On a Mac computer using a wired connection, open Terminal and enter the command `ipconfig getifaddr en1`. For a wireless connection, instead enter the command `ipconfig getifaddr en0`. Your computer should have a private IP address.

Note

Some of the calculated host addresses in a particular network are reserved and can't be used by host devices on the network. For example, the initial address, such as 128.156.14.0, refers to the network itself. The address at the back end of the address range, such as 128.156.14.255, is reserved for sending messages to all hosts on the network and is called the broadcast address. Depending on network settings, other addresses might also be reserved. For example, it's common for the first available host address, such as 128.156.14.1, to be assigned to the local network's router. This information must be accounted for when designing a network's IP address range to ensure there are enough IP addresses available for the anticipated size of the network.

Internet Protocol Version 6 (IPv6)

IPv6 (Internet Protocol version 6) was conceived to fix problems and limitations of IPv4. When IP was created in the 1960s, the computing climate was very different from today. There was nowhere near the number of people or devices currently using the Internet, and the telecommunications lines used to support high-speed networks were not as fast or error-free as they are today. Also, applications operating over the Internet involved smaller data packets with little need to transmit them in real time. As these demands on the Internet began to grow, the designers decided it was time to create a more modern IP that took advantage of current technology.

Several notable differences exist between IPv6 and the older IPv4. The first concerns addressing. With the explosive growth of the Internet, the system ran out of IP addresses, and the last blocks of IPv4 addresses were allocated to regional Internet registries in 2011. IPv6 calls for addresses to be 128 bits long, as opposed to the 32-bit addresses on IPv4, and a 128-bit address supports virtually unlimited addresses. With 128-bit addresses, one million IP addresses can be assigned every picosecond (10^{-12} seconds) for the known age of the universe! With IPv6, address space limitations will not be a problem.

Significant changes were also made to the IP header between IPv4 and IPv6. As you may recall from Figure 7-4, the IP header in IPv4 contains fourteen fields whereas in IPv6, the IP header contains eight fields, plus the payload (data) and optional extension headers, as shown in Figure 7-9. The most notable additions to the IPv6 header are the Priority field and the Flow Label field. Priority assigns a value from 0 to 7 for transmissions that can tolerate delays and from 8 to 15 to indicate real-time data that should receive priority processing. It helps ensure that a data stream with a higher priority will be serviced more quickly than a lower priority packet. The Flow Label field allows certain applications and connection types to establish a pseudo-connection with particular properties and requirements that support faster routing through the Internet. As you can see, speed and efficiency were high priorities in the IPv6 header design.

What fields do you notice are missing from the IPv6 header that were included in the IPv4 header in Figure 7-4? Consider the following points:

> IPv6 does not have a header length field. Because the header in the new version is a fixed length, a length field is unnecessary.

> IPv6 doesn't contain a field that allows fragmentation. The creators of IPv6 felt that almost all of the networks in current operation could handle packets of very large sizes, and that it would no longer be necessary to break a packet into smaller pieces. Even though IPv6 can perform fragmentation, this function is only available as an option in an extension header.

> Another difference is the absence of the Checksum field from IPv6. As network quality improves and higher-level protocols and applications can assume the role of error detector, modern networks are trending towards removing Checksum fields.

Although modifications to the IP header represent profound changes in the protocol, there are even more, significant differences between IPv4 and IPv6. Namely, IPv6 has:

> Better support for options using the extension headers

> Better security, with two extension headers devoted entirely to security

> More options in type of service

This last improvement to IP relates to QoS (quality of service), which is an important part of modern networks. This useful tool allows a network admin to specify a level of service for certain types of traffic such as VoIP (Voice over IP), which ensures the network will prioritize time-sensitive telephony traffic. IPv6 can deliver much better QoS management than IPv4.

Despite these improvements, IPv6 has still not completely replaced IPv4. Many organizations, if they support IPv6 at all, rely on a dual stack network that uses both IP versions simultaneously. Although the U.S. Office of Management and Budget announced in 2005 that it intended to require support for the protocol across government agencies by 2014, that date was unrealistic. The latest push will require 80 percent of

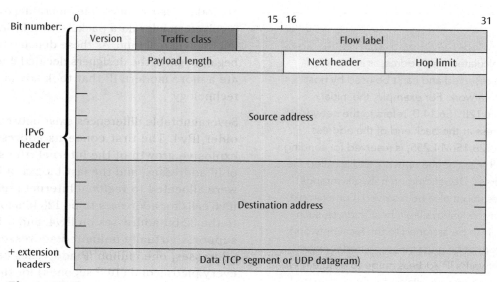

Figure 7-9   Format of the IPv6 packet

IP-enabled assets on federal networks to use only IPv6 by 2025 with several interim checkpoints along the way to that goal.

Mobile networks and cloud providers have offered evolved technologies to natively support IPv6 and ease the transition for everyone. The migration to cloud services, especially, makes IPv6 implementation as simple as using the default settings or choosing a simple configuration option.

IPv6 Addresses

The size of IPv6 addresses makes it challenging to reference them. Additionally, they're usually written in hexadecimal form where each four-bit quantity is replaced by a hexadecimal digit from 0 to F. Here is one example of an IPv6 address:

6A3E:BA91:7221:0000:01FC:922C:877B:FFEF

If there are four hex 0s in a row between two colons, as above, you can save a little space and incorporate a small abbreviation:

6A3E:BA91:7221:0:01FC:922C:877B:FFEF

Longer strings of 0s can be abbreviated further. For example,

6A3E:BA91:0:0:0:0:877B:FFEF

can be abbreviated as

6A3E:BA91::877B:FFEF

Notice that the abbreviation of two colons replacing a series of 0s can only occur once in an IP address to avoid confusion. To maximize efficiency, the two colons should replace the larger group of 0s if there is more than one group of 0s.

IPv6 addresses are also classless and use the slash notation. Thus, an address such as

6A3E:BA91::877B:FFEF/104

tells you that the first 104 bits are part of the network ID, and the remaining 24 bits are part of the host ID.

Remember this...

> IP (Internet Protocol) is a connectionless protocol that routes data packets across the networks collectively forming the Internet. IP provides the addressing scheme used to identify each network

location across WANs like the Internet, and organizes this addressing information in each packet's IP header.

> An IP packet is the combination of the IP header and its payload. This packet encapsulates headers and payload from higher layers, and is in turn encapsulated by the lower data link layer's header(s) and trailer.

> IPv4 (Internet Protocol version 4) addresses are 4 bytes, or 32 bits, in length whereas IPv6 (Internet Protocol version 6) uses 128-bit addresses to support virtually unlimited addresses, solving one of the core limitations of IPv4. IPv6 also offers better support for various options using extension headers.

Self-check

1. At what TCP/IP layer does IPv6 function?
   a. Network
   b. Application
   c. Data link
   d. Transport

2. Which of the following is NOT a valid IPv4 address?
   a. 192.168.0.1
   b. 10.0.0.2
   c. 172.13.155.2
   d. 168.256.127.1

3. Which of the following is NOT an advantage offered by IPv6 over IPv4?
   a. Better security
   b. Smaller header
   c. More efficient
   d. Faster transmission

Check your answers at the end of this chapter.

Section 7-2: Locating a Resource on the Internet

When a user is running a browser and clicks on a link, the browser attempts to locate the object of the link and bring it across the Internet to the user's device. This object can be a document, web page, image, FTP file, or any of several other types of data objects.

How is each object located on the Internet? Stated simply, every object on the Internet has a text-based address called a **URL (Uniform Resource Locator)**, which uniquely identifies each file, web page, image, or any other type of electronic resource that resides on the Internet. Routers on the Internet, however, do not recognize URLs directly. For a browser to find a resource, part of the resource's URL must be translated into the IP address that identifies the web server where the resource is stored. This translation from URL to IP address is performed by DNS (Domain Name System).

Uniform Resource Locator (URL)

Suppose you are using a web browser to access your school's website hosted at your school's datacenter. You click a link on the website to access your LMS (learning management system), which is hosted by the LMS provider at their datacenter. This click sends a command out to the Internet to fetch the web page from the LMS provider's server that is identified by the web page's URL. Your click on the URL starts a chain reaction of processes between your browser, various servers, and multiple routers. For this reason, every URL must be unique.

All URLs consist of four parts, as shown in Figure 7-10 and described next:

1. The first part of the URL, indicated by a 1 in the figure, is called the scheme and identifies the protocol that is used to transport the requested resource.

   › If you request a web page with http://, then HTTP (Hypertext Transfer Protocol) is used to retrieve the web page from the web server.

   › https:// is used more often to request a web page over a secure connection, which encrypts HTTP with TLS (Transport Layer Security).

› You might also request a file on an FTP (File Transfer Protocol) server with ftp://.

› Other schemes include telnet:// to perform an insecure remote login to a server or ssh:// for encrypted remote access, and mailto:// to send an email message.

2. The second part of the URL, indicated by a 2 in Figure 7-10, is the **domain name**. This portion of the URL specifies a host, which is one or more servers that contain the requested resource. Within the domain name are various parts:

   › Starting on the right, *com* is the top-level domain and indicates that the website is a commercial site. Some other top-level domains are edu (educational), gov (government), mil (military), org (nonprofit organization), net (network-based), biz, name, info, pro, museum, aero, and coop. Each country also has its own top-level domain name—Canada is ca and the United Kingdom is uk. For a high price tag, you can have a custom top-level domain.

   › The mid-level domain name is usually the name of the organization or host, often a company or school.

   › Any other lower-level domains to the left (such as *www* for a web server or *email* for an email server) are further subdivisions of the host and are usually created by the domain owner.

3. The third part of a URL, labeled 3 in Figure 7-10, is the detailed path to a specific resource. In Figure 7-10(b), the URL *https://p.widencdn.net/fzrlay* specifies that the requested PDF file is in the directory *fzrlay*.

4. The final part of the URL, specified by the number 4 in Figure 7-10, is the filename of the requested object. In Figure 7-10(b), it is a PDF

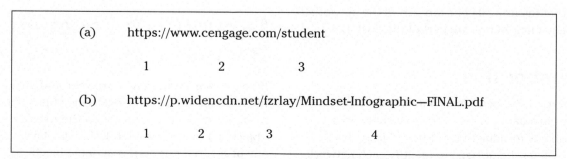

(a)   https://www.cengage.com/student

        1   2   3

(b)   https://p.widencdn.net/fzrlay/Mindset-Infographic—FINAL.pdf

        1   2   3   4

Figure 7-10   The parts of a URL for (a) a website home page and (b) a PDF file provided through a content delivery network

document titled *Mindset-Infographic—FINAL.pdf*. Not all URLs contain this information as not all resources are a single file. A static web page might consist of a single file named something like *index.htm*; however, most modern web pages are made up of many files. It's up to the web server to determine which files should be transmitted when a resource is requested.

Domain Name System (DNS)

Recall that all connections to the Internet are defined by either 32-bit binary addresses (IPv4) or 128-bit binary addresses (IPv6). Asking a user to enter a 32-bit address into a web browser would be cruel and unusual punishment. Or, can you imagine trying to enter a 128-bit address just to check your email?! Even the dotted decimal notation for IPv4 addresses and the hexadecimal form for IPv6 addresses are not convenient for most humans to use or remember. When referencing an Internet site, it's easier to refer to its domain name. Computers, however, use binary addresses.

The Internet converts the binary IP addresses into character-based domain names, and vice versa. To do this, it uses **DNS (Domain Name System)**, which is a large, distributed database of Internet addresses and domain names. This distributed database consists of a network of local DNS servers, mid-level DNS servers, and higher-level DNS servers. To keep the system manageable, the DNS database is distributed according to the top-level domains: .edu, .gov, .com, .mil, and so on.

Converting a domain name into a binary IP address can vary in complexity depending on whether the domain name is already cached somewhat locally. For example, when you leave a webpage and a domain name is resolved, that information is temporarily cached in your browser, your computer's operating system, the LAN's router, and your ISP's DNS cache. Your network might also have a dedicated DNS server.

The browser will first check with each of those resources to determine if the domain's IP address is already known, such as when you are navigating to a website you visit often. If none of these caches contains the information, your computer's designated DNS server will call upon a higher authority. The local DNS server will send a DNS message to the next higher DNS server until the address is found or it is determined that the address does not exist. If the address does not exist, an appropriate message is returned.

To understand this better, consider the scenario in Figure 7-11 where a user at *cs.waynestate.edu* in Wayne State University wants to retrieve a web page from *www.trinity.edu* at Trinity University.

Step 1—The message originates from *cs.waynestate.edu* and goes to the *waynestate.edu* name server.

Step 2—The *waynestate.edu* name server does not recognize *www.trinity.edu* because the domain name *www.trinity.edu* is not in a list of recently referenced websites. Therefore, the *waynestate.edu* name server sends a DNS request to *edu-server.net*.

Step 3—Although *edu-server.net* does not recognize *www.trinity.edu*, it does recognize *trinity.edu*, so it sends a query to *trinity.edu*.

Step 4—The *trinity.edu* name server recognizes its own *www.trinity.edu* and returns the result to *edu-server.net*, which returns the result to the *waynestate.edu* name server, which returns the result to the user's computer, which then inserts the result—that is, the appropriate 32-bit or 128-bit binary IP address—into the browser request. While this seems like a lengthy process, on average, it only takes milliseconds to complete.

Dynamic Host Configuration Protocol (DHCP)

When a company installs several computer workstations and intends to give them access to network resources, it must assign each workstation an IP address. This IP address, as you'll recall, allows a workstation to send and receive information over the Internet or other network.

Two basic methods are used to assign an IP address to a workstation: static assignment and dynamic assignment. With a static assignment, a person sits down at each machine and, using the network operating system, configures an IP address on the device. The person configuring the address must then record that IP address somewhere so it's not accidentally assigned to another device.

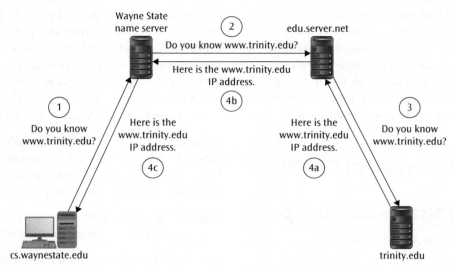

Figure 7-11 DNS resolution

If a workstation with an IP address that was statically assigned is then removed from service, someone must make sure the IP address assigned to that machine is made available for use in another machine. If the same IP address is mistakenly assigned to two machines, there would be an IP address conflict and a network administrator would have to locate the two machines with the same IP address to rectify the situation.

Another issue to consider is that a static assignment of IP addresses can lead to a waste of resources, including a high demand on the network admin's time. If a company has 1000 workstations and each workstation has access to the Internet, then it seems the company must acquire (typically lease) 1000 IP addresses. This is not cost-effective, particularly if only one-half of the users are on the Internet (using their IP address) at a time. Dynamic assignment of IP addresses contributes to solving these problems.

The most popular protocol that handles dynamic IP address assignment is DHCP (Dynamic Host Configuration Protocol). When a workstation running DHCP client software needs to connect to the network, the protocol issues an IP request, which prompts the DHCP server to look in its table of IP addresses. If this workstation has an entry, then that IP address is assigned to that workstation. If there is no entry in the table, the DHCP server selects an IP address from an available pool of addresses, as shown in Figure 7-12, and assigns it to the workstation.

The IP address assignment is temporary with the default time limit typically being one hour. DHCP clients may

negotiate for a renewal of the assignment if the workstation is still accessing the network when the temporary assignment is nearing expiration.

Thus, with DHCP, most of the problems introduced with static assignment are solved. No one has to assign IP addresses to workstations; two workstations never get assigned the same IP address; and if only 200 workstations out of 1000 are ever using the network at the same time, the company can get by with acquiring fewer IP addresses.

ISPs (Internet service providers) use this same process to manage available public IP addresses for residential customers. When your home network is actively connected with the Internet, the ISP's DHCP server assigns an IP address during the session creation period. Your router uses this temporary IP address as long as your connection is active. Once your connection is no longer active, the address is placed back into the pool to be ready for use by the next customer.

Network Address Translation (NAT)

NAT (Network Address Translation) is another protocol used to assign IP addresses. More precisely, NAT lets a router represent an entire LAN to the Internet as a single IP address, as illustrated in Figure 7-13.

When a user workstation on a company LAN sends a packet out to the Internet, NAT replaces the workstation's private IP address with a corporate public IP address. In fact, all packets that leave the corporate

Figure 7-12   DHCP address pool on a home router

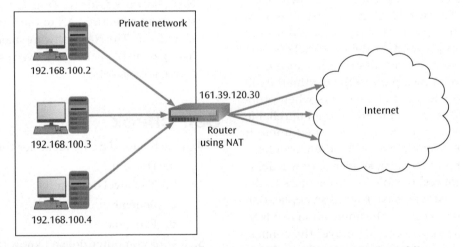

Figure 7-13   NAT translates private IP addresses into a single public IP address

network contain this public IP address. Thus, the only IP address that anyone sees outside of the corporate network is the one public IP address.

If all packets from all workstations leave the corporate network with the same IP address, the responses that come back from the Internet must get directed to the proper machine. The NAT software maintains a cache listing of all IP packets that were sent out and which device sent each packet. When a response comes back, NAT checks the cache to find out which device originally sent the request. When NAT finds the match, it removes

the public IP address, reinserts the user workstation's IP address, and places the packet on the corporate network.

If a packet arrives at the corporate NAT software and there is no cache entry with a matching outgoing request, the packet is discarded because someone has sent a packet to the corporate network that was not requested by a corporate workstation. The exception to this rule is if the company is supporting a server, such as a web server, then a packet may originate from a user on the Internet. In this case, when the web page request packet arrives at the NAT software, the IP address where the packet originated will not match any IP addresses in the local cache. Before the NAT software discards the packet, it examines the message's destination port. If the packet is a request for a web page from the corporate web server, the NAT software lets the packet in.

An interesting feature of using NAT is that, because external devices never see any of the private IP addresses used within the corporate network, a level of security has been added. Additionally, the company does not need to lease a public IP address for every device on the corporate network. To support this feature, the network admin ensures that only private IP addresses within a designated range are assigned to internal devices. These addresses can only be used within a LAN environment and cannot cross a router to the Internet. When a workstation with a private IP address issues an Internet request, the NAT software replaces the private IP address with the corporate public IP address. The use of NAT and private IP addresses is another way to save money on leasing IP addresses.

At this point, you've learned a lot about IP and that it works by sending each packet along its own route (which is called packet switching). It's important to note that IP is a connectionless protocol in that it does not keep track of lost, duplicated, or delayed packets, and packets might be delivered out of order because each packet has followed its own path to the destination. IP also does not inform senders or receivers when problems occur. Thus, IP is also referred to as an unreliable service. This doesn't mean IP can't be relied upon. It means that IP is not responsible for handling problems between the sender and receiver, similar to how a delivery truck driver is not responsible for problems with the items included in a customer's package. If an application requires a reliable service, then the application needs to include a reliable transport service "above" the connectionless, unreliable packet delivery service. The reliable transport service is provided by TCP (Transmission Control Protocol), which turns an unreliable network into a reliable network, free from lost and duplicate packets. This combined service is known as TCP/IP. In the next section, you'll learn about TCP and other protocols of the TCP/IP protocol suite that collaborate to make the Internet work.

Remember this...

> Every object on the Internet has a unique, text-based address called a URL. Routers on the Internet do not directly recognize URLs. For a browser to find a resource, part of the resource's URL must

be translated into the IP address that identifies the web server where the resource is stored.

> All URLs consist of four parts: the scheme, which indicates the protocol that is used to transport the requested resource; the domain name, which specifies one or more servers that contain the requested resource; the path information to the specific resource; and (sometimes) the filename of the requested object.

> DNS is a large, distributed database of Internet addresses and domain names and is used to convert binary IP addresses into character-based domain names, and vice versa.

> Two basic methods used to assign an IP address to a workstation are static assignment and dynamic assignment. With a static assignment, a person sits down at each machine and, using the network operating system, configures an IP address on the device. DHCP (Dynamic Host Configuration Protocol) handles dynamic IP address assignment on a network.

> NAT (Network Address Translation) lets a router represent an entire LAN to the Internet as a single IP address. The NAT software maintains a cache listing of all IP packets that were sent out and who sent each packet.

Self-check

4. Which part of a URL identifies the protocol used?
   a. Domain
   b. Top-level domain
   c. Scheme
   d. Filename

5. If your computer doesn't know the IP address for a new website you want to visit, which device does it ask first for this information?
   a. Web server
   b. Top-level DNS server
   c. The website's DNS server
   d. Local DNS server

6. Which technology can ensure no two devices on the same network have the same IP address?
   a. DHCP
   b. DNS
   c. URL
   d. NAT

Check your answers at the end of this chapter.

Section 7-3: Protocols of the Internet

IP is one of the most important communications protocols, but it's not the only one. Many other protocols work together to make communication on the Internet and other networks possible. This section covers several of the most common protocols on the Internet.

Transmission Control Protocol (TCP)

To create error-free, end-to-end connections across networks without lost or duplicate packets, IP relies on TCP (Transmission Control Protocol), whose primary function is to turn an unreliable network into a reliable network. Thus, TCP essentially manages the functions ignored by IP. In order for this transport layer protocol to make an unreliable network reliable, TCP performs the following six functions:

> **Create a connection**—The TCP header includes a port number that indicates an application. Together the port number and the IP address identify a specific application on a specific machine. When TCP creates a connection between a sender and a receiver, the two ends of the connection use a port number to identify the application's connection. This port number is found within the TCP segment and is passed back and forth between sender and receiver.

> **Release a connection**—The TCP software can also dissolve a connection after all the data has been sent and received.

> **Implement flow control**—To make sure the sending station does not overwhelm the receiving station with too much data, the TCP header includes a field called the sliding-window size that allows the receiver to tell the sender to slow down. This sliding-window size is similar in operation to the sliding window used at the data link layer. The difference between the two window operations is that the data link layer's sliding window operates between two adjacent nodes along the message's path, while the TCP window operates between the two endpoints (sender and receiver) of a network connection.

> **Perform error recovery**—TCP numbers each byte for transmission with a sequence number. As the packets of bytes arrive at the destination site, the receiving TCP software checks these sequence numbers for continuity. If there is a loss of continuity, the receiving TCP software uses an acknowledgment number to inform the sending TCP software of a possible error condition.

> **Establish traffic priority**—If the sender needs to transmit data of a higher priority, such as an error condition, TCP can set a value in the Urgent Pointer field that indicates all or a portion of the enclosed data is urgent.

> **Establish multiplexing**—Because the TCP header includes a port number instead of an IP address, it is possible to multiplex multiple TCP-layer connections over a single IP connection. Multiplexing is the transmission of multiple signals on one medium at essentially the same time.

An example of TCP multiplexing would be when your browser uses one port to download a web page and a second port to download an image on that web page at the same time. Recall that IP uses IP addresses to track devices connected to networks. Similarly, TCP uses ports to track applications on each device. Working together, the two create what is called a socket —a precise identification of an application on a device. What if your company has one server that handles both email and FTP connections? The server would have one IP address but two ports: one for the email application and one for the FTP application. Now consider the fact that this server is connected to a LAN, and thus has a NIC (network interface card) with a unique 48-bit MAC address. That makes three addresses:

> The MAC address, at the data link layer, is used only on the LAN to find the device.

> The IP address, at the network layer, is used to move the data packet across multiple networks, such as the Internet.

> The port number, at the transport layer, is used to identify an application on the device.

All three addresses at each layer of the TCP/IP suite work together to identify the device and the relevant application both locally and across multiple networks. The Ethernet header contains MAC addresses, the IP header contains IP addresses, and the TCP header contains port numbers.

TCP Segment Format

To perform the six functions listed earlier, TCP places a header at the front of every data packet that travels from one end of the connection to the other between

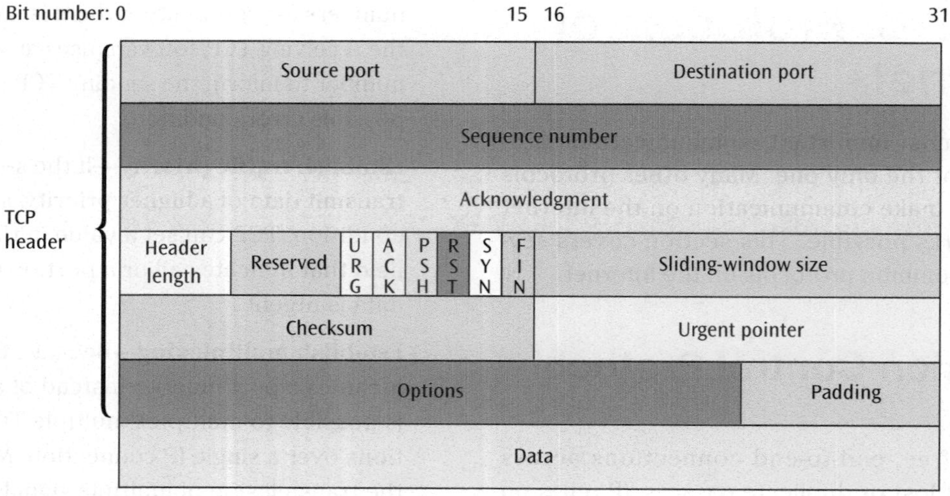

Figure 7-14 Format of a TCP segment

sender and receiver. This header encapsulates data from higher layer protocols and is in turn encapsulated by IP's header.

The TCP header contains the fields shown in Figure 7-14. Let's examine those fields that assist TCP in performing the six functions listed earlier:

> **Source port and Destination port**—Contain the addresses of the applications at the two ends of the transport connection. These port addresses are used in creating and terminating connections. The port can also be used to multiplex multiple transport connections over a single IP connection.

> **Sequence number**—Contains a 32-bit value that counts bytes and indicates a packet's data position within the connection. For example, if you are in the middle of a long connection in which thousands of bytes are being transferred, the sequence number tells you the exact position of this packet within that sequence. Packets crossing the open Internet don't necessarily take the same path to reach their destination. Therefore, it's common for packets to arrive out of order. This field can be used to reassemble the pieces at the receiving workstation and determine if any packets of data are missing.

> **Sliding-window size**—Contains a sliding window value that provides flow control between the two endpoints. This allows the receiver to request the sender slow the rate of transmission as needed. If the receiver wants the sender to fully stop sending data, the Sliding-window field can be set to 0.

> **Checksum**—Provides for an arithmetic checksum of the header *and* the data field that follows the header.

> **Urgent pointer**—Used to inform the receiving workstation that this packet contains urgent data.

TCP is the protocol used by most networks and network applications to create an error-free, end-to-end network connection. TCP is connection-oriented in that a connection via a port must be established before any data can be transferred between sender and receiver. What if you do not want to establish a connection with the receiver but simply want to send a packet of data without additional overhead? In this case, UDP is the protocol to use.

User Datagram Protocol (UDP)

UDP (User Datagram Protocol) is a no-frills transport protocol that does not establish connections, does not attempt to keep its datagrams in sequence, and does not watch for datagrams that have existed for too long. As illustrated in Figure 7-15, its header contains only four fields—Source port, Destination port, Length, and Checksum—and it is used by network services such as DNS that do not need to establish a connection before sending data.

A common use of UDP is for streaming audio or video where datagrams either make it to their destination or they don't—there's no time to replace a missing or corrupt datagram because the stream must continue in real time.

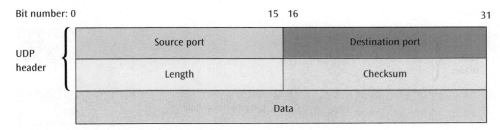

Figure 7-15   A UDP datagram

Address Resolution Protocol (ARP)

ARP is a small but important protocol supporting TCP/IP networks. ARP (Address Resolution Protocol) takes an IP address in an IP packet and translates it into the appropriate MAC layer address for delivery on a LAN. After an IP packet enters a LAN through a router, the router will check its ARP table to see if it already knows the destination's MAC address. If it does not, ARP broadcasts a message on the LAN asking which device belongs to this IP address. The workstation that recognizes its IP address sends an ARP reply essentially saying, "Yes, that is my IP address, and here is my 48-bit MAC address." The router sends the message to its destination according to the MAC address, which the router inserts in the data link layer header. The router then stores this 48-bit MAC address in its ARP table in case it will be needed again in the near future.

IPv6 does not use ARP. Instead, IPv6 relies on ICMPv6 (Internet Control Message Protocol for use with IPv6) to perform the functions that ICMPv4 and ARP perform

in IPv4 networks. This includes detecting and reporting data transmission errors and discovering other nodes on a network. To better understand this distinction, let's look at the role ICMP plays in a TCP/IP network.

Internet Control Message Protocol (ICMP)

Several things can go wrong as an IP packet moves through a network. As the packet nears its intended destination, a router might determine that the destination host is unreachable (e.g., the IP address is wrong or the host does not exist), the destination port is unknown (e.g., there is no application that matches the TCP port), or the destination network is unknown (again, the IP address might be wrong). If a packet has been on the network too long and its TTL (Time to Live) value expires, the packet will be discarded. Also, there could be something wrong with the entire IP header of the packet. In each of these cases, it would be nice if a router or some other device would send an error message back to the source device, informing the user or the application of a problem. IP was not designed to return error messages, so a different protocol must perform these operations.

ICMP (Internet Control Message Protocol), which is used by routers and other nodes, performs this error reporting for IP. As shown in Figure 7-16, all ICMP messages contain at least the following three fields:

> **Type**—A number from 0 to n that uniquely identifies the kind of ICMP message, such as invalid port number or invalid IP address.

> **Code**—A value that provides further information about the message type.

> **Payload**—The first eight bytes of the IP packet that caused the ICMP message to be generated.

Note

What's the difference between an ARP table, as just described, and a MAC address table, which you learned about in Chapter 5?

> The ARP table stores a mapping of IP addresses to MAC addresses. This information is used to update the Ethernet header as a message moves from device to device inside of a LAN.

> The MAC address table stores a mapping of MAC addresses to physical interfaces on a device. This information is used to tell a router or switch which interface (such as Ethernet0/0) a device is connected to.

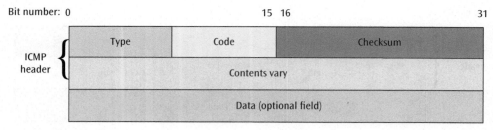

Figure 7-16   An ICMP packet

If you used tracert to communicate with servers around the world in Chapter 5, then you've seen ICMP in action. The tracert utility employs ICMP and a trial-and-error approach to discover the nodes at each hop from the source to the destination. To do this, tracert sends multiple ICMP echo requests to the destination node and listens for an ICMP echo reply from that node. However, tracert limits the TTL of each repeated trial message, thereby triggering routers along the route to return specific information about the route being traversed.

Details | Multiprotocol Label Switching (MPLS)

Encapsulation has been a key concept throughout this course so far. Recall that encapsulation is the layering of one layer's header over the existing data packet, and in the TCP/IP protocol suite, the TCP header is layered on top of (placed in front of) the packet that comes from the application layer. The information in the TCP header is used to perform transport layer connection functions at the endpoints of the connection. The IP header is then layered on top of the TCP packet, and the information in the IP header is used to perform network routing and TTL operations. Normally the next step would be to place the data link layer information on top of the IP packet, but WANs do not use data link layer information to route data packets. Thus, routers must "dig into" a data packet, extract the IP information, and use it for routing. This takes time, plus the time it takes to "dissect" the IP address and determine its next best path, and is typically not a fast process, at least not when compared to the forwarding operation that LAN switches can perform. If WANs could perform switching operations quickly, the Internet (as well as other WANs) would operate much more efficiently.

To provide this level of switching at the network level, network designers created MPLS. **MPLS (Multiprotocol Label Switching)** is a technique that enables a router to switch data from one path onto another path. To make this possible, one or more labels (headers with MPLS information) are encapsulated onto the front of an IP packet, as illustrated in Figure 7-17. Each label contains four fields:

> **Label**—A 20-bit Label value field tells the MPLS-enabled router which connection this packet belongs to and thus how to forward the packet.

> **Exp**—A 3-bit Experimental field is reserved for future use.

> **S=0**—A 1-bit Bottom of stack flag field indicates if there are multiple labels on this packet (0 if this is the last label and 1 if otherwise).

> **TTL**—An 8-bit Time to live field works similarly to the TTL field in the IP header.

When a packet enters the network, an MPLS-enabled router determines the connection the packet should

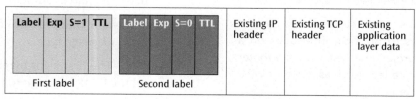

Figure 7-17   Two MPLS headers and their four fields

be in and inserts one or more labels in the newly created MPLS header. The packet is now called a *labeled packet*. Subsequent MPLS-enabled routers look at the information in the MPLS header and forward the labeled packet in the appropriate direction. For each labeled packet that enters, MPLS-enabled routers can have built-in routing tables that tell the router what kind of operation to perform based upon the packet's topmost MPLS label. This operation is performed quickly, often in hardware. When the labeled packet arrives at the destination router, the MPLS-enabled router removes the MPLS header, leaving the original IP packet.

MPLS is popular for large networks and across WANs, and it's an IETF (Internet Engineering Task Force) standard.

Remember this...

> The primary function of TCP (Transmission Control Protocol) is to turn an unreliable network into a reliable network that is free from lost and duplicate packets.

> TCP performs the following six functions: create a connection, release a connection, implement flow control, establish multiplexing, perform error recovery, and establish traffic priority.

> UDP (User Datagram Protocol) is a no-frills transport protocol commonly used for streaming audio or video where datagrams either make it to their destination or they don't.

> ARP (Address Resolution Protocol) takes an IP address in an IP packet and translates it into the appropriate MAC layer address for delivery on a LAN.

> ICMP (Internet Control Message Protocol), which is used by routers and other nodes, performs error reporting for IP.

Self-check

7. What is the best transport layer protocol to support Netflix traffic on a network?
   a. UDP
   b. IP
   c. ARP
   d. TCP

8. What information in the TCP header allows multiple, simultaneous conversations over a single connection?
   a. IP address
   b. MAC address
   c. Port number
   d. Traffic priority value

9. What header field enables tracert's trial-and-error process?
   a. ICMP's Type field
   b. IP's TTL field
   c. ICMP's Code field
   d. TCP's Sliding-window size field

Check your answers at the end of this chapter.

Section 7-4: Internet Services

When the Internet came into existence as the ARPANET, most people used it for email, file transfers, and remote logins. In addition to studying those services, let's examine several of the more popular services that the Internet provides today.

Email

Email is so integrated into modern business and life in general that, if it vanished tomorrow, some serious social and economic repercussions would be felt throughout the world. Many free or commercial email programs are available. Regardless of the program used, each transmitted email consists of two basic components: an envelope, which contains information describing the email message, and the message, which is the contents of the envelope. Most messages consist of plain text and are written in simple ASCII characters.

What if you want to send (or attach) a non-text-based item, such as a spreadsheet, database, or image? Or what if you need to communicate in a language that uses non-ASCII characters?

MIME (Multipurpose Internet Mail Extensions) converts data into a format that can be sent over existing email protocols, and then converts the data back into its original form on the receiver's end.

At a basic level, most email systems primarily consist of two parts:

> **MUA (mail user agent)**, also called the mail client —the portion of the email program that allows a user to create, edit, store, and forward email messages.

> **MTA (mail transfer agent)**, also called the mail server or SMTP (Simple Mail Transfer Protocol) relay server—the portion of the email program that prepares and transfers the email message.

SMTP is a key application-layer protocol that can transfer email to and between email servers. Once the email and optional attachment have been created, the email client uses SMTP or one of its variants to send the email to an email server. To do this, the source computer establishes a TCP connection typically to port 587 on the email server.

The email server has an email daemon—a utility that is always running in the background and waiting to perform its function—that supports the SMTP protocol. The email daemon monitors the SMTP port, accepts incoming connections, and copies messages to the appropriate mailbox if that account is also hosted on the same server. If not, the email server uses DNS to locate the appropriate email server and—still using SMTP but now, typically, on port 25—sends the email along to that server.

When you turn your computer or smartphone on and open your email client, a message informs you that you have a certain number of new email messages waiting. There are two options of software used most often to perform this operation:

> POP3 (Post Office Protocol version 3) allows the user to save email messages in a server mailbox and download them when desired from the server. POP3 is useful if you do not have a permanent connection to a network and must connect using a temporary Internet connection (which is unusual these days). POP3 will hold your email messages until the next time you connect and access your mailbox. Configuring your email client to use POP3 typically works well only if you use a single device to access your email. POP3 uses TCP port 110 (insecure) or port 995 (secure).

> IMAP4 (Internet Message Access Protocol version 4) receives and holds email messages on the email server. You can view just the heading of the email or view the sender of the message and then decide if you want to download the message. You can also

create and manipulate folders or mailboxes on the server, delete old email messages, or search for certain parts of an email message. The server maintains a copy of your email for access from multiple devices, and the organization of messages is synced across all your email client installations. IMAP4 uses TCP port 143 (insecure) or port 993 (secure).

Many email packages allow a user to encrypt an email message for secure transfer over an internal LAN or over the Internet using S/MIME (Secure/MIME), PGP (Pretty Good Privacy), or similar technologies. Figure 7-18 shows the option to turn on encryption in Microsoft Outlook with additional options to prevent the recipient from forwarding the message.

When an email message is encrypted, it is virtually impossible to intercept and decode the message without the proper encryption algorithm and key. For added security, a user can apply a digital signature to an important email message so that, in the future, the owner of the message can prove the email belongs to only them. Encryption techniques will be discussed in more detail in Chapter 8.

Another challenge related to email safety, besides privacy, is the management of spam email. Have you ever received a suspicious email asking for personal or financial information? Perhaps there were grammatical errors, misspelled words, or something else felt "off" about the email. If you checked the sender's address, you probably noticed that the sender was not from the domain of the company it claimed to come from—while the link might have been worded similarly to a legitimate domain, there were noticeable differences.

SPF (Sender Policy Framework) works to ensure that no one can send email from a domain without the domain owner's authorization. So hackers can't, for example, create an email address that appears to come from the cengage.com domain. For an additional layer of protection, DKIM (DomainKeys Identified Mail) adds a digital signature to the message's header which can be verified with information found in the domain owner's public DNS record. These techniques rely on cryptography, of which encryption is a part.

File Transfer Protocol (FTP)

FTP (File Transfer Protocol), which you first read about in Chapter 1, was one of the first services offered on the Internet. Its primary function is to allow a user to transfer files between a local computer and a remote site. These files can contain data, such as numbers, text,

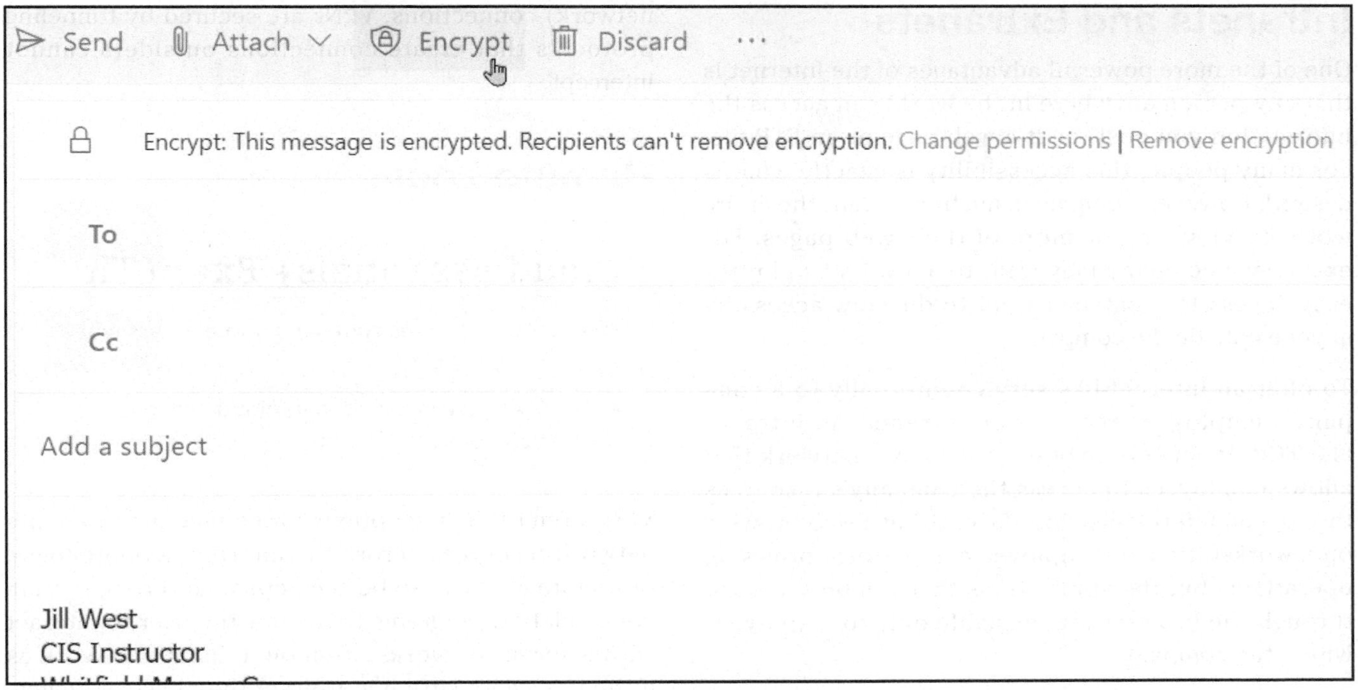

▷ Send   📎 Attach ∨   🛡 Encrypt   🗑 Discard   ...

🔒   Encrypt: This message is encrypted. Recipients can't remove encryption. Change permissions | Remove encryption

To

Cc

Add a subject

Jill West
CIS Instructor

Source: Jill West

Figure 7-18   Encryption can help maintain confidentiality of information included in an email

or images, or executable applications. Although HTTP-based websites (such as Dropbox) have become the major vehicle for sharing text- and image-based documents, many organizations still find it useful to create an FTP repository of data and application files, especially when these files are very large. For example, businesses in the AEC (Architecture, Engineering, and Construction) industry still use FTP sites to share large files containing architectural diagrams.

News agencies might receive live weather camera streams to FTP sites, and web developers might use FTP to transfer large website files from development computers to web servers. Using a web browser or specialized FTP software, you can easily access an FTP site or even host your own. If you desire privacy and wish to restrict access to an FTP site, the site can be designed to require a user ID and password for entry.

To access an FTP site via a web browser and download a file, you must know the address of the FTP site, the name of the directory or subdirectory in which to look for the file, and the name of the file that you want to download. Thus, downloading FTP files is not a "browsing" activity. You must have a good idea of what you are looking for and where it is located. Clicking the filename and specifying the receiving location of the downloaded material starts the download process. Two connections are created: the first connection on port 21 transfers the control

information, which sets up the file transfer, and the second connection on port 20 transfers the actual data.

When FTP was first developed, security was not a significant concern. FTP was not designed with security as a high priority. Today, FTP is considered too insecure to use extensively, especially in sensitive business communications or when handling regulated data such as medical or financial information. Usernames and passwords are transmitted in cleartext, meaning that anyone who intercepts these transmissions could easily read your username and password. Also, an FTP file itself is not encrypted so anyone intercepting the message could read all the contents of the file as well.

In response to these issues, a variety of techniques were developed to increase security for file transfer. Two commonly used protocols are the following:

> FTPS (FTP Secure) is an extension of FTP that uses TLS (Transport Layer Security) to encrypt both the control and data channels.

> SFTP (Secure FTP) is the file-transfer version of SSH (Secure Shell) that includes encryption and authentication. SFTP needs only a single connection, usually over port 22.

Note that SFTP and FTPS are incompatible with each other. SFTP is an extension of the SSH protocol, not of FTP.

Intranets and Extranets

One of the more powerful advantages of the Internet is that any person anywhere in the world can access the information you post, be it a web page or an FTP file. For many people, this accessibility is exactly what is desired. However, companies might not want the entire world to view one or more of their web pages. For example, a company may want to allow its employees easy access to a database, but to disallow access by anyone outside the company.

To offer an Internet-like service internally to a company's employees requires an intranet. An **intranet** is a TCP/IP network inside a company's network that allows employees to access the company's resources through an Internet-like interface. Using a web browser on a workstation, an employee can perform browsing operations, but the applications that can be accessed through the browser are available only to employees within the company.

Intranets use essentially the same hardware and software that is used by other network applications, which simplifies installation, maintenance, and hardware and software costs. If a company desires, it can allow an intranet and its resources to be accessed from outside the corporate walls. In these circumstances, a user ID and password are often required to gain access.

Employees might use their company's intranet to do the following tasks:

 > Establish access to internal databases such as human resource information, payroll data, and personnel records.

 > Interface with corporate applications.

 > Perform full-text searches on company documents.

 > Access and download training materials and manuals and perform daily business operations, such as filling out travel expense reports. There's a good chance you registered for classes using your college's intranet.

When an intranet is extended outside the corporate walls to include suppliers, customers, or other external agents, it becomes an **extranet**. Because an extranet allows external agents to have access to corporate computing resources, a much higher level of security is usually established. Essentially, an extranet is an interconnection of corporate intranets. The interconnection is usually performed over the Internet, using VPN (virtual private

network) connections. VPNs are secured by tunneling protocols that create connections outsiders cannot intercept.

Remote Login

Cloud Essentials+ Exam Tip

This section discusses common remote access types, which are required by

- Part of Objective 1.2: Identify cloud networking concepts.

VPNs aren't the only options for connecting to remote network resources across the Internet. Remote login, or remote access, can be accomplished through terminal emulation programs that allow the user to interact with a server or workstation on a distant network as if the user were sitting in front of the physical device. Similarly, most of the methods discussed in this section are also commonly used to remotely connect to cloud resources, such as a cloud-based server.

Telnet

Telnet is a terminal emulation program for TCP/IP networks, such as the Internet. It allows users to log in to a remote computer. The Telnet program runs on your computer and connects your computer to a remote device. Once you are connected to the remote server or host, you can enter commands at a CLI (command line interface) through the Telnet program, and those commands will be executed as if you were entering them directly at the terminal of the remote computer.

There are several reasons for using remote login software such as Telnet:

 > Allows a user to log in to a personal account and execute applications on a device in a different geographical location. For example, you might have a computer account at two different companies or two different schools. Although you may be physically located at one site, you can use Telnet to log in to the other computer site. Through this login, you can check your email, access files, or run an application.

 > Allows a user to access a public service on a remote computer.

> Enables a network administrator to control a network server and communicate with other servers on the network. This control can be performed from a remote distance, such as another city or the network administrator's home.

Secure Remote Login Protocols

Like FTP, Telnet is insecure and is rarely used on modern networks. Some popular options that provide improved security through encryption include the following:

> SSH (Secure Shell), first described in Chapter 1, is a collection of protocols that allows a user to log on to a host, execute commands on the host, and copy files to or from the host using a CLI. Figure 7-19 shows a SSH connection in Google Chrome to an Ubuntu instance in GCP (Google Cloud Platform). SSH encrypts data exchanged throughout the session. SSH also allows for password authentication or key-based authentication, which you'll learn more about in Chapter 8. In the project at the end of this chapter, you'll use SSH to remotely access a VM in the AWS cloud.

> RDP (Remote Desktop Protocol) is a Microsoft proprietary protocol used by Windows Remote Desktop and Remote Assistance utilities to connect to and control a remote computer. RDP supports the familiar Windows GUI (graphical user interface) that looks almost exactly as if you're sitting in front of the remote computer itself. Figure 7-20 shows an RDP connection where the remote computer's desktop appears in a window on the local computer's screen.

> VNC (Virtual Network Computing) is an open-source, cross-platform alternative to RDP. VNC is slower than Remote Desktop and requires more network bandwidth. However, because VNC is open source, many companies have developed their own software using VNC.

> HTTPS (Hypertext Transfer Protocol Secure) is an encrypted form of HTTP. Some resources—such as cloud-hosted servers and virtual desktops—can be accessed using a standard browser and HTTPS. Figure 7-21 shows a remote connection in the Google Chrome browser to a virtual desktop on a school network. This service is made available to students who need access to a Windows computer and its applications from their Macbooks or Chromebooks.

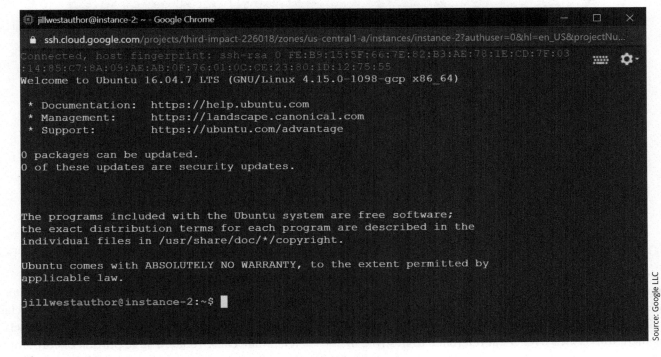

Figure 7-19   SSH connection to a cloud-based Linux instance

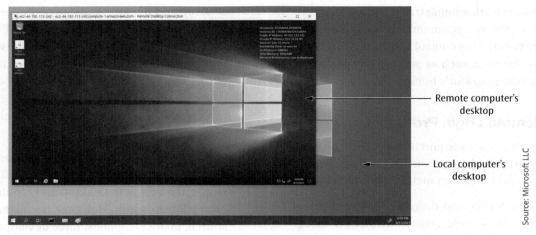

Remote computer's desktop

Local computer's desktop

Source: Microsoft LLC

Figure 7-20 RDP connection to a cloud-based Windows Server instance

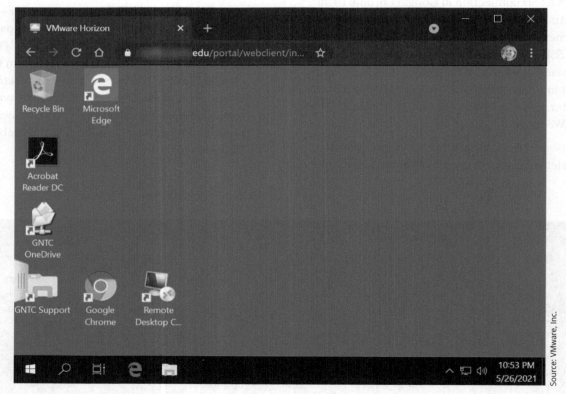

Source: VMware, Inc.

Figure 7-21 HTTPS connection to a virtual desktop

Voice over IP (VoIP)

A popular service that has attracted the interest of companies and home users alike is the sending of voice signals over an IP-based network such as the Internet. This practice of making telephone calls over the Internet is called VoIP (Voice over IP) in reference to IP's role in controlling the transfer of data over the Internet.

There are currently three ways to deliver VoIP to users:

> Many companies offer VoIP systems that operate over a corporate LAN. These systems involve a fair amount of equipment, such as VoIP servers, special IP-enabled telephones, and routers that can direct telephone calls. Today, a large portion of corporate sites have converted their older internal telephone

systems to VoIP systems that operate over their own networks, thus converging two systems into one.

> For home customers using existing telephones, a special converter is added between the telephone and a high-speed Internet connection (DSL or cable modem). The converter digitizes the voice signal and creates a stream of packets that are then sent over an IP connection.

> Modern cell phone technologies are all packet-based, thus requiring a telephone call to be converted to digital packets and sending those packets over IP networks.

One of the earlier advantages of VoIP was simply related to the fact that long-distance calls, especially overseas calls, are expensive, while sending data—or voice—over the Internet is essentially free. Many companies are finding other, more important advantages in being able to treat voice data like other forms of data. For one, if both voice and data can travel over the same network, companies can realize savings in equipment and infrastructure. This contributes to yet another significant advantage, eliminating the need for a separate telephone system. Thus, a company's management can be simplified.

VoIP has some disadvantages as well. The statement that sending data over the Internet is essentially free is misleading. Nothing, of course, is free. All Internet users must pay an Internet service provider for access, the interconnecting phone or cable line, and any necessary hardware and software. Also, additional hardware and software are necessary to handle the transmission of high volumes of voice packets over a corporate data network. Nonetheless, if you already have high-speed Internet access, adding VoIP may be a reasonable way to obtain both local and long-distance telephone service.

A second, and more important, disadvantage is that transmitting voice over a corporate network can be demanding on the network's resources. If the current corporate network system is straining to deliver data, adding voice to this system can cause severe service problems. These service problems can be compounded because voice systems require networks to pass voice data quickly and in real time. A network that delays voice data by more than 20 milliseconds from end to end will introduce a noticeable echo into the transmission. If the delay becomes longer than 250 milliseconds (that is only a quarter of a second), the system is basically unusable.

Further compounding this delay problem is the fact that each data packet on the Internet is routed individually, which, as you read earlier, is called packet switching. This individual routing can introduce a routing delay for each packet. In contrast, a public telephone network first establishes a route (a circuit) and then transmits all following packets down that established route, which is called circuit switching. Because the route is fixed, packets do not experience routing delays. To maintain a telephone conversation over the Internet, the voice packets must arrive at their destination in a continuous stream. If they do not, the voice conversation breaks up and is of poor quality. Currently, VoIP usually works well but sometimes does not.

Other issues that have been challenging for VoIP include the following:

> Security can be an issue because voice packets traverse the same Internet as other packets, which are always susceptible to interception.

> Emergency service has posed an interesting problem. Traditional telephone lines are associated with a fixed telephone number. When someone calls 911 from a traditional telephone line, the emergency operator immediately knows the location of the call source. This may not be the case with VoIP. Fortunately, enhanced 911 service has provided a reasonable solution to this problem.

> VoIP systems are susceptible to power failures because the telephone calls traverse LANs, which require constant power. Traditional telephone systems supply their own power and often survive power failures (except for cordless telephones).

For companies considering VoIP, one important and interesting fact to keep in mind is that the technology does not need to involve using the Internet. A company can use IP for transmission of data *within* its own network but use traditional telephone lines outside the company network. Many people call such systems **private VoIP**. Because these systems do not use the Internet but instead remain internal, packet delays are minimal, and this makes VoIP attractive. Today's systems can support both telephone operations and computer data operations over the same set of wires. This area of study—computer telephony integration—is a marriage of computer systems and telephone systems.

In order to gain a little better understanding of VoIP, consider the various steps necessary to create a VoIP packet from someone's voice:

Step 1—Convert voice signal to IP packets by performing an analog-to-digital conversion using a codec.

Step 2—Compress the data into a much smaller package and then convert into packet format.

Step 3—Encapsulate each voice packet with the appropriate UDP and IP headers and send over the IP network.

A common device that performs the conversion from an analog telephone call (voice *and* signals) into the packetized IP data is the VoIP gateway. The **VoIP gateway** can perform the digitization, compression, and encapsulation required, and it controls the setup of VoIP calls between the calling device and the called device. Currently, two basic sets of protocols support all these steps. The first set of standards, H.323, is from ITU-T and was first issued in 1996. **H.323** is a set of protocols named packet-based multimedia protocols, and it was designed for a wide range of applications (audio and video).

A simpler and increasingly popular option is **SIP (Session Initiation Protocol)**, which was introduced in 1998 by the IETF specifically for supporting the transfer of voice over the Internet. SIP is an application layer protocol that can create, modify, and terminate voice sessions between two or more parties. These voice sessions are not limited to simple telephone calls and can also include conference calls and multimedia transmissions.

Media Streaming

Streaming media, whether audio or video, involves the continuous download of a sequence of packets from a compressed audio or video file, which can then be heard or viewed on the user's device. Typical examples of streaming audio are listening to music apps, live radio broadcasts, and podcasts. Typical examples of streaming video include watching shows or movies on streaming apps, watching lectures through your school's website, and watching live news or sports broadcasts. Businesses can use streaming media to provide training videos, product samples, and video conferencing, to name a few examples.

To transmit and receive streaming media, the network server requires the space necessary to store the data and the software to deliver the stream. The user needs either a browser, an app for the service such as Spotify or Pandora, or a media streaming device such as a Roku or Amazon's Fire TV Stick. All media files must be compressed because an uncompressed data stream would occupy too much bandwidth and would not travel in real time (you'll learn about compression techniques in Chapter 9). Packets are delivered over a stream so the client device can play each packet while downloading and decompressing the next packet in the series.

RTP (Real-Time Protocol) and **RTSP (Real-Time Streaming Protocol)** are two common network protocols servers use to deliver streaming media to a user's browser or streaming device. Both RTP and RTSP are public-domain protocols and are available in several software products that support streaming data.

The Internet of Things (IoT)

Cloud Essentials+ Exam Tip

This section discusses IoT, which is required by

- Part of Objective 2.4: Identify the benefits or solutions of utilizing cloud services.

The IoT (Internet of Things), first mentioned in Chapter 1, is the collection of everyday objects and processes connected to or accessible through the Internet. For example, if you like jogging, perhaps you will purchase a smartwatch that tracks and then transfers all the data about your morning jog directly to the Internet during or after your run. To converse with the Internet, your smartwatch will of course need an IP address. What about all your home appliances, heating and cooling systems, garage door opener, and alarm systems? The IoT (Internet of Things) is made up of any device that can be connected to the Internet—that is, any sensor, computer, or wearable device that talks to other devices over a network.

One of the fastest-growing areas of IoT is personal monitoring devices, such as health monitors, exercise equipment, GPS locators, and smartwatches. Another exploding IoT market interconnects smart home devices. You might already be familiar with Amazon Echo, Apple HomePod, or Google Home. These voice-controlled **smart speakers** and their embedded personal assistant apps (such as Alexa, Siri, and Google Assistant) can interlink a plethora of devices, from locks and lights to security cameras and coffee pots. You can control these devices through voice commands while interacting with a smart speaker, or you can control IoT devices through an app on your smartphone (see Figure 7-22). All these connected devices within a home create a type of LAN called a HAN (home area network).

Let's briefly look at what some of these smart home devices might offer to better understand how your network should be designed to support them:

> **Smart thermostat**—More sophisticated than programmable thermostats, a smart thermostat allows users to adjust temperature settings based on daily schedules, shifting activity levels inside the home, current weather conditions outside, and in response to voice commands. You can control your home's temperature remotely from a smartphone, such as when the outdoor temperature drops unexpectedly while you're away from home. Further, the thermostat itself will monitor activity levels to automatically adjust its schedule for optimized energy savings and offer tips to save even more on utility bills. Some smart thermostats can be linked with other environmental control devices, such as smart humidifiers and air purifiers.

> **Smart doorbell**—This device monitors an entryway for movement. To minimize false alarms from animals, you can set it up to filter out everything except movement caused by humans. It allows users to communicate with visitors remotely by video, even while away from home. Some smart doorbells can play a pre-recorded message, and a few offer facial recognition to identify familiar faces. The video feed can be stored locally on the device's onboard storage drive (such as a microSD card), on a hub device inside the house, or to the cloud. Many smart doorbells now come with rechargeable batteries, so no wiring is required for installation.

> **Security camera**—These devices come with rechargeable batteries, wireless capability, and significant weather proofing to maximize installation options. Some cameras can also be connected to a solar panel so they don't need to be taken down to recharge. Many of these cameras can be installed almost anywhere, even on a tree trunk, for optimal perspective on a monitored area (see Figure 7-23). The camera sends alerts and video feeds through Wi-Fi to a smartphone app where the user can remotely monitor covered areas, such as entryways and parking areas. Most of today's cameras include some type of night vision capability, and many include two-way audio similar to a smart doorbell.

So that you may control them from a smartphone at a remote location, each of these devices will need their own IP address. This growth of Internet-connected devices all requiring IP addresses is part of the reason for IPv4's insufficiency. Now with a virtually unlimited supply of IPv6 addresses, imagine what creative opportunity you might invent using the IoT.

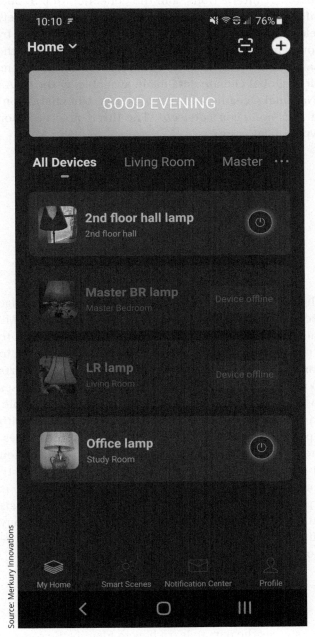

Figure 7-22   App-controlled IoT devices

Figure 7-23 This wireless security camera distinguishes between humans and animals to send more useful alerts and reduce false positives

All Things Considered

Thought Experiment

Thinking about the Internet of Things, what everyday actions would you like to see connected to the Internet? How would an Internet connection make these actions more meaningful? Are there any everyday actions done in your home or personal life that you think should not be connected to the Internet?

Data Analytics

Cloud Essentials+ Exam Tip

This section discusses data analytics, machine learning, and artificial intelligence, which are required by

- Part of Objective 2.4: Identify the benefits or solutions of utilizing cloud services.

One of the most impactful modern influences of the Internet and cloud-based technologies on businesses is in the area of data analytics. An industry in its own right, data analytics is the study of raw data to detect patterns, anomalies, and insights that can inform research, business processes, regulatory measures, and many other efforts. Cloud computing uniquely enables data analytics due to the simple fact that the cloud makes available nearly unlimited processing power, storage space, and network bandwidth. For example, extremely large data sets are made available through cloud platforms that inform the analysis work of many businesses and industries. Businesses themselves collect large volumes of data in the course of daily business activities, including transactions, research, customer interactions, and the collection of personal information. These massive data sets are collectively referred to as big data. This data might be collected by companies, governments, or entire industries, and the data might be structured or unstructured. One example is global climate data made available by the NOAA (National Oceanic and Atmospheric Administration) at *ncdc.noaa.gov/cdo-web/*. The three most common types of data are:

> Social data, such as that collected from social media platforms

> Machine data collected from sensors (such as traffic cams or medical devices), logs, and other automated sources

> Transactional data, such as purchases, payments, and invoices

The cloud and big data make possible other cutting-edge technologies such as AI (artificial intelligence) and ML (machine learning). AI (artificial intelligence) refers to a computer's ability to adapt its behavior according to ongoing input. This kind of computer processing starts to resemble human thought processes where responses to input aren't necessarily predictable. For example, have you attempted to carry on a conversation with a personal assistant such as Alexa or Siri? Sometimes, these assistants' responses can be surprising, even in humorous ways. Further, AI enables a computer to continue to learn and adapt. ML (machine learning) is a process where computers learn from data analysis rather than from explicit programming. There are many different approaches to the logic of ML. Three of the most common are:

> **Supervised learning**—The computer is given labeled data, such as videos of vehicles that are each identified by make and model. The computer studies the data to learn how to identify the same items later in unlabeled videos.

> **Unsupervised learning**—The computer is given unlabeled data and expected to identify patterns that might not be known to the human programmers. For example, a computer might be given medical data and asked to determine what factors might indicate the likelihood of someone developing heart disease or cancer.

> **Reinforcement learning**—The computer engages in trial-and-error learning where right responses are rewarded and poor responses are not. For example, AWS's DeepRacer service uses reinforcement learning to teach a virtual vehicle how to drive along a simulated road course. Turns that keep the vehicle on the road are preferred while turns that lead the vehicle off the road force-stop the simulation. In DeepRacer competitions, students develop algorithms to try to train their AI models faster and with fewer errors.

As these technologies continue to improve and expand, the Internet's relevance to business and to daily life will only increase. Additionally, new technologies will continue to emerge.

Remember this...

> SMTP (Simple Mail Transfer Protocol) is a key application-layer protocol that can transfer email to and between email servers. POP3 (Post Office Protocol version 3) allows the user to save email messages in a server mailbox and download them when desired from the server. IMAP4 (Internet Message Access Protocol version 4) receives and holds email messages on the email server.

> FTP (File Transfer Protocol) allows a user to transfer files between a local computer and a remote site. Although HTTP-based websites (such as Dropbox) have become the major vehicle for sharing text- and image-based documents, many organizations still find it useful to create an FTP repository of data and application files, especially when these files are very large.

> An intranet is a TCP/IP network inside a company's network that allows employees to access the company's resources through an Internet-like interface. An extranet allows external agents to have access to corporate computing resources.

> Telnet allows users to log in to a remote computer. However, Telnet is insecure and is rarely used on modern networks. Some popular options that provide improved security through encryption include SSH (Secure Shell), RDP (Remote Desktop Protocol), VNC (Virtual Network Computing), and HTTPS (Hypertext Transfer Protocol Secure).

> The practice of making telephone calls over the Internet is called VoIP (Voice over IP) in reference to IP's role in controlling the transfer of data over the Internet.

> Streaming media, whether audio or video, involves the continuous download of a sequence of packets from a compressed audio or video file, which can then be heard or viewed on the user's device.

> The IoT (Internet of Things) is made up of any device that can be connected to the Internet. Each of these devices requires an IP address.

> Data analytics is the study of raw data to detect patterns, anomalies, and insights that can inform research, business processes, regulatory measures, and many other efforts. Cloud computing uniquely enables data analytics due to the simple fact cloud makes available nearly unlimited processing power, storage space, and network bandwidth.

Self-check

10. Which protocol allows non-ASCII characters in email?
    a. MUA
    b. SMTP
    c. IMAP
    d. MIME

11. Which remote login protocol should you NOT use?
    a. RDP
    b. SSH
    c. Telnet
    d. HTTPS

12. Which technology requires computers to uncover hidden patterns?
    a. Supervised learning
    b. Artificial learning
    c. Unsupervised learning
    d. Reinforcement learning

Check your answers at the end of this chapter.

Summary

Section 7-1: Internet Protocol (IP)

> IP (Internet Protocol) is a connectionless protocol that routes data packets across the networks collectively forming the Internet. IP provides the addressing scheme used to identify each network location across WANs like the Internet, and organizes this addressing information in each packet's IP header.

> An IP packet is the combination of the IP header and its payload. This packet encapsulates headers and payload from higher layers, and is in turn encapsulated by the lower, data link layer's header(s) and trailer.

> IPv4 (Internet Protocol version 4) addresses are 4 bytes, or 32 bits, in length whereas IPv6 (Internet Protocol version 6) uses 128-bit addresses to support virtually unlimited addresses, solving one of the core limitations of IPv4. IPv6 also offers better support for various options using extension headers.

Section 7-2: Locating a Resource on the Internet

> Every object on the Internet has a unique, text-based address called a URL. Routers on the Internet do not directly recognize URLs. For a browser to find a resource, part of the resource's URL must be translated into the IP address that identifies the web server where the resource is stored.

> All URLs consist of four parts: the scheme, which indicates the protocol that is used to transport the requested resource; the domain name, which specifies one or more servers that contain the requested resource; the path information to the specific resource; and (sometimes) the filename of the requested object.

> DNS is a large, distributed database of Internet addresses and domain names and is used to convert binary IP addresses into character-based domain names, and vice versa.

> Two basic methods used to assign an IP address to a workstation are static assignment and dynamic assignment. With a static assignment, a person sits down at each machine and, using the network operating system, configures an IP address on the device. DHCP (Dynamic Host Configuration Protocol) handles dynamic IP address assignment on a network.

> NAT (Network Address Translation) lets a router represent an entire LAN to the Internet as a single IP address. The NAT software maintains a cache listing of all IP packets that were sent out and who sent each packet.

Section 7-3: Protocols of the Internet

> The primary function of TCP (Transmission Control Protocol) is to turn an unreliable network into a reliable network that is free from lost and duplicate packets.

> TCP performs the following six functions: create a connection, release a connection, implement flow control, establish multiplexing, perform error recovery, and establish traffic priority.

> UDP (User Datagram Protocol) is a no-frills transport protocol commonly used for streaming audio or video where datagrams either make it to their destination or they don't.

> ARP (Address Resolution Protocol) takes an IP address in an IP packet and translates it into the appropriate MAC layer address for delivery on a LAN.

> ICMP (Internet Control Message Protocol), which is used by routers and other nodes, performs error reporting for IP.

Section 7-4: Internet Services

> SMTP (Simple Mail Transfer Protocol) is a key application-layer protocol that can transfer email to and between email servers. POP3 (Post Office Protocol version 3) allows the user to save email messages in a server mailbox and download them when desired from the server. IMAP4 (Internet Message Access Protocol version 4) receives and holds email messages on the email server.

> FTP (File Transfer Protocol) allows a user to transfer files between a local computer and a remote site. Although HTTP-based websites (such as Dropbox) have become the major vehicle for sharing text- and image-based documents, many organizations still find it useful to create an FTP repository of data and application files, especially when these files are very large.

> An intranet is a TCP/IP network inside a company's network that allows employees to access the company's resources through an Internet-like interface. An extranet allows external agents to have access to corporate computing resources.

> Telnet allows users to log in to a remote computer. However, Telnet is insecure and is rarely used on modern networks. Some popular options that provide improved security through encryption include SSH (Secure Shell), RDP (Remote Desktop Protocol), VNC (Virtual Network Computing), and HTTPS (Hypertext Transfer Protocol Secure).

> This practice of making telephone calls over the Internet is called VoIP (Voice over IP) in reference to IP's role in controlling the transfer of data over the Internet.

> Streaming media, whether audio or video, involves the continuous download of a sequence of packets from a compressed audio or video file, which can then be heard or viewed on the user's device.

> The IoT (Internet of Things) is made up of any device that can be connected to the Internet. Each of these devices requires an IP address.

> Data analytics is the study of raw data to detect patterns, anomalies, and insights that can inform research, business processes, regulatory measures, and many other efforts. Cloud computing uniquely enables data analytics due to the simple fact cloud makes available nearly unlimited processing power, storage space, and network bandwidth.

Key Terms

For definitions of key terms, see the Glossary near the end of the book.

AI (artificial intelligence)

ARP (Address Resolution Protocol)

big data

CIDR (Classless Interdomain Routing) notation

data analytics

DHCP (Dynamic Host Configuration Protocol)

DNS (Domain Name System)

domain name

extranet

H.323

host ID

HTTPS (Hypertext Transfer Protocol Secure)

ICMP (Internet Control Message Protocol)

IMAP4 (Internet Message Access Protocol version 4)

intranet

IPv6 (Internet Protocol version 6)

MIME (Multipurpose Internet Mail Extensions)

ML (machine learning)

MPLS (Multiprotocol Label Switching)

NAT (Network Address Translation)

network ID

packet

POP3 (Post Office Protocol version 3)

port

private IP address

private VoIP

public IP address

RDP (Remote Desktop Protocol)

RTP (Real-Time Protocol)

RTSP (Real-Time Streaming
Protocol)

SIP (Session Initiation Protocol)

smart speaker

socket

subnetting

TCP (Transmission Control Protocol)

Telnet

UDP (User Datagram Protocol)

URL (Uniform Resource Locator)

VNC (Virtual Network Computing)

VoIP (Voice over IP)

VoIP gateway

Review Questions

1. Which is the best abbreviation of the IPv6 address
   FE80:0000:0000:0007:5C62:0000:6F91?

   a. FE80:0:0:0007:5C62:0:6F91

   b. FE80:0:0:0007:5C62::6F91

   c. FE80:0:0:07:5C62:0:6F91

   d. FE80::0007:5C62:0:6F91

2. Which protocol's information can NOT be encapsulated by an IP header?

   a. TCP

   b. Ethernet

   c. DNS

   d. UDP

3. Google's DNS server is located at 8.8.8.8, which is
   a(n) _____.

   a. URL

   b. IPv6 address

   c. IPv4 address

   d. MAC address

4. Which of the following is a responsibility of IP?

   a. Create a connection.

   b. Implement flow control.

   c. Establish multiplexing.

   d. Route data across networks.

5. Which of the following components together form
   a socket?

   a. MAC address and IP address

   b. IP address and packet number

   c. IP address and port number

   d. MAC address and port number

6. What service does ICMP provide to IP?

   a. Multiplexing

   b. Error reporting

   c. Error correction

   d. Connection management

7. Which technology conceals a server's IP address
   from Internet-based attackers?

   a. DHCP

   b. URL

   c. DNS

   d. NAT

8. When you click a link to go to a new web page on
   the Internet, what information will a DNS server
   return to your computer?

   a. A URL

   b. A private IP address

   c. A public IP address

   d. A MAC address

9. What is the network ID of the IPv4 address
   172.16.54.198/24?

   a. 172

   b. 172.16

   c. 172.16.54

   d. 172.16.54.198

10. Which protocol would best help you access and
    download detailed schematics for a machine your
    company's contractor is building?

    a. FTP

    b. IoT

    c. Telnet

    d. SSH

11. The Hop Limit field in IPv6 is 8 bits long (the same size as the equivalent Time to Live field in IPv4). Given that this hop count is reduced each time an IP packet enters a router, what are the implications of having such a small field size?

    a. The size of the packet's payload is limited.
    b. The number of possible hops is limited.
    c. The packet's latency to its destination is limited.
    d. The size of the packet is limited.

12. A company currently has a telephone system and a separate system of LANs. It is thinking about converting its telephone system to VoIP and running both voice and data over the same LANs. Which of the following protocols will the company need to begin supporting on its LANs to accomplish this goal?

    a. HTTP
    b. SIP
    c. FTP
    d. NAT

13. When you send an email to your friend, which protocol handles the transfer of the data between your email server and your friend's email server?

    a. POP3
    b. MIME
    c. IMAP4
    d. SMTP

14. Which device do you need to purchase to talk to Amazon's Alexa?

    a. Smart thermostat
    b. Security camera
    c. Smart speaker
    d. Smart doorbell

15. Considering the following hypothetical URL, which part is the scheme?

    https://www.cengage.com/student/pages/web.htm

    a. https://
    b. www.cengage.com
    c. /student/pages
    d. web.htm

16. Suppose there is a small commercial retail building in your town that has essentially one room. On one side of the room is a real estate agency, and on the other side of the room is a guy who sells tea. This situation is an analogy for which technology?

    a. Error checking
    b. Encapsulation
    c. Streaming
    d. Multiplexing

17. As you arrive home one evening after work, you realize you forgot to download some presentation files to your laptop, and you leave for a business trip early in the morning. What tool can you use to access your desktop this evening from home so you can transfer the files to your laptop without having to go back to your office?

    a. VoIP
    b. RDP
    c. SIP
    d. IoT

18. Your company recently launched a new web app to allow employees to apply for jobs posted internally. To maintain security and privacy, where should this web app's access portal be posted?

    a. Extranet
    b. Internet
    c. Telnet
    d. Intranet

19. Which of the following is an advantage of static IP address assignment?

    a. Decreased potential for mistakes
    b. Increased time investment
    c. Increased control
    d. Decreased cost efficiency

20. Which type of ML requires a labeled data set?

    a. Reinforcement learning
    b. Unsupervised learning
    c. Supervised learning
    d. Artificial learning

Hands-On Project 7

Create and Remote into an EC2 Instance in AWS

Estimated time: 1 hour

Resources:

> Windows computer with administrative privileges or with PuTTY already installed

> AWS account (created in Chapter 1)

> Internet access

> **Context:**

In Chapter 1, you created an AWS account and configured a CloudWatch alarm. In this project, you create your own VM in the AWS cloud. You'll then use SSH to remote into your cloud VM.

> ## Note
>
> Depending on the status of your account and the selections you make during this project, an EC2 instance and its supporting resources (such as storage) can deplete your credits or accrue charges. Make sure to follow these steps carefully and delete all created resources at the end of this project.

Complete the following steps to create your EC2 instance:

1. Sign into your AWS management console. If you're using an AWS Academy classroom, you'll need to access your AWS management console through the AWS Academy website. If you're using a standard AWS account, sign in directly at **aws.amazon.com**.

2. Most AWS resources reside in a specific geographical region in the world. Regular AWS accounts have access to nearly all these regions. However, AWS Academy accounts are limited. The region is listed in the top right corner of your console. Click the dropdown arrow to see all the available regions. What region is currently selected in your account?

3. At the top of the console, click **Services**. In the Compute group, click **EC2**. EC2 (Elastic Compute Cloud) is one of the oldest and most used AWS Academy. The EC2 dashboard shows you how many of each EC2 resource type you have in your account, which should currently be 0 across the board except for one security group. Scroll down and click the orange **Launch instance** button and then click **Launch instance** from the list.

4. Step 1 of creating an EC2 instance is to choose an AMI (Amazon Machine Image). This image determines the OS your instance will run. Notice that many of the AMIs are labeled as Free tier eligible. List three different OSs included in Free tier eligible AMIs.

5. Amazon has optimized a Linux AMI for use in the AWS environment. Next to the Amazon Linux AMI, click **Select**.

6. Step 2 is to choose an instance type. The instance type determines the virtualized hardware resources available to the instance. For example, the t2.micro type has 1 vCPU, 1 GiB (gibibyte) of memory, and low to moderate network performance. In contrast, a more robust instance type, c5.large, has 2 vCPUs, 4 GiB of memory, and up to 10 Gigabit network performance. Select **t2.micro** and click **Next: Configure Instance Details**.

Note

A gibibyte is similar to a gigabyte, but mathematically they are not the same. A gigabyte (GB) is typically calculated as a power of 10 (10^9 or 1,000,000,000 bytes). A gibibyte (GiB) is calculated as a power of 2 (2^{30} or 1,073,741,824 bytes). Many cloud platforms use GiB for certain metrics.

7. Step 3 gives you the opportunity to set several specific configurations for your instance. What options here stand out to you and why?

8. Keep all default settings for Step 3 and click **Next: Add Storage**.

9. By default, the instance is assigned one root volume, which is where the OS will be installed. Click **Next: Add Tags**.

10. Tags give you the option to define your own key-value pairs to further identify your instance and other resources. For example, you might want a key called "Name" so you can name all your instances. Or you might want a key called "Department" so you can track billing for each department at your company. Click **Add Tag**. Under Key, type **Name**. Under Value, give your instance an informative name. What did you name your instance? Click **Next: Configure Security Group**.

11. By default, your instance will be placed in a new security group with port 22 open for SSH (Secure Shell) access. The Source (0.0.0.0/0) is a wildcard IP address that indicates the SSH connection could come from any IP address. Normally, this would not be a secure option. Because you're just practicing for now, you can leave all these default settings as is. Click **Review and Launch**.

12. Review your instance configuration and click **Launch**. You'll need a key pair to remote into this instance—you'll learn about key pairs in Chapter 8. In the first field, select **Create a new key pair**. In the second field, give the key pair an informative name. What did you name your key pair? Click **Download Key Pair**, and save the file in a place where you can find it easily later. Then click **Launch Instances**.

Note

Students sometimes get an error at this point, possibly related to the restrictions placed on using AWS through the classroom account. If you do get an error, retry the process of launching an instance. Sometimes it takes a couple attempts.

13. Scroll down and click **View Instances**. At first, the instance is listed as Running and Initializing. Select the instance and scroll down to see additional details about the instance. What is your instance's private IPv4 address?

14. Your instance was automatically assigned a Public IP address. If you had a web server running on the instance, this is the IP address you would assign to your URL. You'll use the DNS information for this IP address to remote into your instance. **Take a screenshot** of the Instance summary information section that shows the Public IPv4 address; submit this visual with your answers to this project's questions.

If you don't already have PuTTY installed on your computer, you'll need to install it:

15. Go to **putty.org**. Download and install PuTTY. Be sure to choose the correct installer for your computer.

Now you need to convert the key pair to a file type that PuTTY can use:

16. Click **Start**, type **puttygen**, and press **Enter**.

17. With **RSA** selected under Parameters, click **Load**. Change the file type to **All Files (*.*)**.

18. Navigate to and select the key pair you downloaded in Step 12, and click **Open**. Click **OK**.

19. Click **Save private key** and then click **Yes**. Give the file an informative name. What did you name your private key file? Make sure the **.ppk** file type is selected and click **Save**. Close the PuTTY Key Generator window.

Now you're ready to collect some information about your EC2 instance:

20. In your AWS management console, refresh your list of running instances to ensure your instance is active. Select the instance and click **Connect**. Click **SSH client** for detailed information about your instance.

21. Under Example, select and copy the portion of the text from the username (ec2-user) through the URL (amazonaws.com), as shown in Figure 7-24. What is the information you copied?

You now have the information you need to remote into your EC2 instance using PuTTY:

22. On your local computer, open **PuTTY**. Paste the information you copied from your AWS console into the Host Name field. Make sure the Port field lists **22**, and make sure **SSH** is selected for the Connection type, as shown in Figure 7-25.

23. In the left pane, click **SSH** and then click **Auth**. On the right side, click **Browse** and find the private key file you created earlier in Step 19. Click **Open**, and then click **Open** again. In the security alert dialog box, click **Yes** to add your private key to PuTTY's cache.

24. When the SSH connection is established, interact with your Linux instance by entering the command `ifconfig`. Your VM's private IP address is listed under eth0. What is your VM's inet address?

You're now ready to power down the machine and delete it:

25. In your AWS console, click **Instances** so you can see your instance's state listed. Position your management console window and your PuTTY window so you can see both windows on your screen at the same time.

26. At the VM's shell prompt, enter the command `sudo poweroff`. The connection is severed. Click **OK** and close your PuTTY window. Refresh the data in your console. What state is your instance in now?

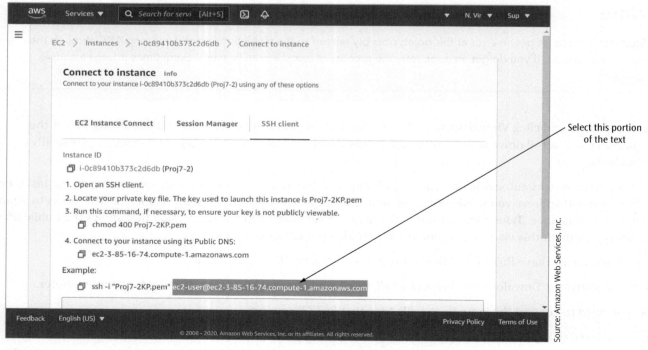

Figure 7-24   Select the sign-in information from the username through the URL

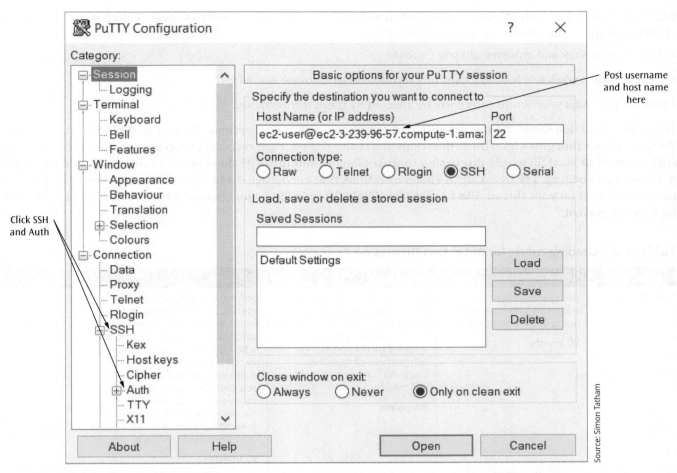

Figure 7-25   Paste the username and host name information from AWS in the Host Name field

27. Turning the instance off does not delete any resources in your AWS cloud. In some cases, you continue to be charged for resources even if they're turned off. To delete your instance, select the instance, click **Instance state**, and click **Terminate instance**. Click **Terminate**. Refresh your list of instances. What is the instance state now?

> **Note**
>
> Depending on the status of your account and the selections you made during the AWS projects, your EC2 instance and its supporting resources (such as storage) can deplete your credits or accrue charges. Double-check to make sure you've terminated all resources you created in the AWS projects.

Reflection Discussion 7

This chapter covered many technologies that make the Internet possible and many other, cutting-edge technologies made possible by the Internet. Many of these technologies have already deeply impacted a wide variety of industries and continue to revolutionize the work of these businesses. For example, data analytics processes are used in agriculture to determine which environmental factors most benefit crops, machine learning is used to support medical research, and artificial intelligence informs educational professionals as they assist students to optimize their learning.

Think about an industry that you're interested in and consider how one or more of these technologies affect your chosen industry. Then answer the following questions:

> Which technology and industry did you choose?

> What are some ways this industry uses this technology to innovate and adapt?

> How do you think your future career will be affected by these technologies?

Go to the discussion forum in your school's LMS (learning management system). Write a post of at least 100 words discussing your thoughts about these questions and technologies. Then respond to two of your classmates' threads with posts of at least 50 words discussing their comments and ideas. Use complete sentences, and check your grammar and spelling. Try to ask open-ended questions that encourage discussion, and remember to respond to people who post on your thread. Use the rubric in Table 7-2 to help you understand what is expected of your work for this assignment.

Table 7-2 Grading rubric for Reflection Discussion 7

Task	Novice	Competent	Proficient	Earned
Initial post	Generalized statements addressing Internet technologies in an industry **30 points**	Some specific statements with supporting evidence about ways a specific industry is affected by cutting-edge Internet technologies, and suggestions of how the student's future career will be affected **40 points**	Self-reflective discussion with specific and thoughtful statements and supporting evidence about ways a specific industry is being changed and improved by cutting-edge Internet technologies in ways that wouldn't be possible without the Internet, and creative insights into how the student's future career will need to adapt to and can benefit from these technologies **50 points**	
Initial post: Mechanics	• Length < 100 words • Several grammar and spelling errors **5 points**	• Length = 100 words • Occasional grammar and spelling errors **7 points**	• Length > 100 words • Appropriate grammar and spelling **10 points**	
Response 1	Brief response showing little engagement or critical thinking **5 points**	Detailed response with specific contributions to the discussion **10 points**	Thoughtful response with specific examples or details and open-ended questions that invite deeper discussion of the topic **15 points**	
Response 2	Brief response showing little engagement or critical thinking **5 points**	Detailed response with specific contributions to the discussion **10 points**	Thoughtful response with specific examples or details and open-ended questions that invite deeper discussion of the topic **15 points**	
Both responses: Mechanics	• Length < 50 words each • Several grammar and spelling errors **5 points**	• Length = 50 words each • Occasional grammar and spelling errors **7 points**	• Length > 50 words each • Appropriate grammar and spelling **10 points**	
			Total	

Solutions to Self-Check Questions

Section 7-1: Internet Protocol (IP)

1. At what TCP/IP layer does IPv6 function?

Answer: a. Network

Explanation: The most-used protocol at the network layer in the TCP/IP protocol suite is IP (Internet Protocol), including IPv6.

2. Which of the following is NOT a valid IPv4 address?

Answer: d. 168.256.127.1

Explanation: Each octet can range in value from 0 to 255. The number 168.256.127.1 contains an octet with a value over 255, which is not valid in IPv4.

3. Which of the following is NOT an advantage offered by IPv6 over IPv4?

Answer: b. Smaller header

Explanation: While the IPv6 header has fewer fields, IPv6 addresses are much longer, thus requiring more bits for the IPv6 header than IPv4's header.

Section 7-2: Locating a Resource on the Internet

4. Which part of a URL identifies the protocol used?

Answer: c. Scheme

Explanation: The first part of a URL (Uniform Resource Locator) identifies the protocol that is used to transport the requested resource and is called the scheme.

5. If your computer doesn't know the IP address for a new website you want to visit, which device does it ask first for this information?

Answer: d. Local DNS server

Explanation: If the IP address is not cached on the computer itself or on the network, the computer will then refer the request to a local DNS server. The local DNS server will send a DNS message to the next higher DNS server until the address is found or it is determined that the address does not exist.

6. Which technology can ensure no two devices on the same network have the same IP address?

Answer: a. DHCP

Explanation: When a device needs a dynamically assigned IP address, the DHCP (Dynamic Host Configuration Protocol) server selects an IP address from an available pool of unused IP addresses and assigns it to the device. This ensures no two devices are assigned the same IP address.

Section 7-3: Protocols of the Internet

7. What is the best transport layer protocol to support Netflix traffic on a network?

Answer: a. UDP

Explanation: UDP (User Datagram Protocol) is a no-frills transport protocol that does not establish connections, does not attempt to keep its datagrams in sequence, and does not watch for datagrams that have existed for too long. A common use of UDP is for streaming audio or video, such as streaming movies from Netflix, where datagrams either make it to their destination or they don't—there's no time to replace a missing or corrupt datagram because the stream must continue in real time.

8. What information in the TCP header allows multiple, simultaneous conversations over a single connection?

Answer: c. Port number

Explanation: Because the TCP header includes a port number instead of an IP address, it is possible to multiplex multiple TCP-layer connections over a single IP connection. Multiplexing is the transmission of multiple signals on one medium at essentially the same time.

9. What header field enables tracert's trial-and-error process?

Answer: b. IP's TTL field

Explanation: The tracert utility limits the TTL in the IP header of each repeated trial message, thereby triggering routers along the route to return specific information about the route being traversed.

Section 7-4: Internet Services

10. Which protocol allows non-ASCII characters in email?

Answer: d. MIME

Explanation: MIME (Multipurpose Internet Mail Extensions) converts data into a format that can be sent over existing email protocols, and then converts the data back into its original form on the receiver's end.

11. Which remote login protocol should you NOT use?

Answer: c. Telnet

Explanation: Telnet is insecure and is rarely used on modern networks.

12. Which technology requires computers to uncover hidden patterns?

Answer: c. Unsupervised learning

Explanation: With unsupervised learning, the computer is given unlabeled data and expected to identify patterns that might not be known to the human programmers.

Chapter 8

Risk, Security, and Compliance

Objectives

After reading this chapter, you should be able to:

- Compare common network security risks, response options, and policies

- Explain network security technologies

- Explain common methods to secure data

- Analyze elements of IAM (identity and access management)

- Describe methods to secure wireless connections

Introduction

Computer network security has reached a point at which it can best be characterized by two seemingly conflicting statements: never has network security been better than it is today, and never have computer networks been more vulnerable than they are today. How both these statements can be true is an interesting paradox. Today, anyone connected to the Internet can access or attempt to access any Internet-connected computer system or device anywhere in the world. This interconnectivity between devices and networks is both a benefit and a liability. It allows users to access corporate resources while working from home and order ride-share services, grocery deliveries, and vacation rentals from their smartphones. But this interconnectivity also exposes all Internet-attached systems to invasion. And the reality is that there are people who attempt to access forbidden systems through a variety of methods and intend to steal, destroy, or ransom sensitive documents and information.

Internet-connected systems are not the only systems subject to security problems. Studies show that many business thefts are committed by the employees working at the company. In today's environment, managing computer network security is a continuous, all-encompassing task.

This chapter's discussion of network security begins by examining common system attacks that are launched against computer users and their networks. You will then examine four basic areas of network security: preventing unauthorized access to physical or digital resources, securing data, managing legitimate network access, and securing wireless communications.

Section 8-1: Network Security Risks

You might remember the highly publicized Equifax data breach in 2017 when the personal information of nearly 150 million U.S. consumers was compromised. That's almost half of all U.S. residents. Or you might have read about the 2018 ransomware attack on the city of Atlanta that shut down most city functions for days, or the 2021 Colonial Pipeline ransomware attack that threatened fuel supplies throughout the U.S. East Coast. These attacks might seem distant and irrelevant to most people's daily lives, but they can touch supply chains and organizations that affect large portions of any population.

As a result of the large number of attacks on computers and networks in recent years, experts monitor attack vectors, called threats, being used to take advantage of loopholes and vulnerabilities in networks and other systems. While you will learn about many of these threats, two of the most popular attack methods for the last several years have been (1) socially engineered attacks and (2) exploiting known vulnerabilities in operating systems and applications (i.e., misconfigured or unpatched software).

Common Vulnerabilities and Attack Types

> ## Cloud Essentials+ Exam Tip
>
> This section discusses threats and vulnerabilities, which are required by
>
> - Part of Objective 4.4: Explain security concerns, measures, or concepts of cloud operations.

Typically, an attacker's goal is to somehow gain access to a system and then steal or damage data. To accomplish this goal, the attacker might install malware in the system, which is malicious software that can be used to monitor a system or otherwise damage data and other software. Attackers might use one or more of many available attack vectors, depending on what component in the system is compromised.

Compromise Users

A social engineering attack is a common attack type that tries to trick someone into giving up confidential information or otherwise allowing the attacker unauthorized access to a computer or network. Social engineering attacks often occur in the form of a link in a web page or email. If the user clicks the link, this often results in malware being downloaded to the user's computer. This malware can go on to erase sensitive data, erase the entire hard disk, or even hold the computer hostage unless the user pays a ransom to remove the malware, which is then called ransomware.

Compromise Software

Many attacks attempt to take advantage of bugs, loopholes, backdoors, or other software weaknesses called vulnerabilities. Hackers are dedicated to finding these openings in popular operating systems and applications. Once a vulnerability is found, the hacker will launch an attack that compromises the host computer or network server. Often, the company that created and supports the compromised software will issue a patch, a corrective piece of software designed to close the vulnerability. Unfortunately, not all computer owners and operators install the patch, or, even worse, the patch itself may have additional vulnerabilities. Many hackers watch for when a company announces the release of a patch. The released information and patch can direct the hacker to the vulnerability rather than searching for it themselves. Once the vulnerability is known, the hacker creates code to take advantage of that vulnerability, knowing that many companies and users will be slow to install the patch, if they install it at all.

Some system attacks do not need a user to open an email or web page. All a user does to become infected is connect to the Internet. While connected, a user's computer is constantly vulnerable to malware on the Internet scanning for unprotected computers (such as open TCP ports or unpatched software) and trying to exploit known operating system and application vulnerabilities. Unless the user maintains updated malware protection installed on the computer, the computer is likely to be compromised.

Compromise Availability

A common category of system attacks is the denial-of-service attack. DoS (denial-of-service) attacks and DDOS (distributed denial-of-service) attacks bombard a computer site or service with so many messages that the server is incapable of performing its normal duties. To understand how a DoS attack works, consider the following example illustrated in Figure 8-1. A hacker instructs a network of compromised web servers (called

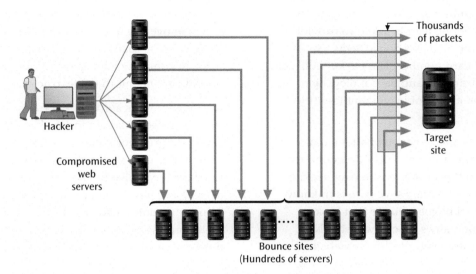

Figure 8-1   An example of a DDoS attack intended to cripple a web server

zombies) to send messages to a second set of servers. These messages contain the destination address of the target website. The second set of servers, called bounce sites, receives multiple spoofed requests and responds by sending multiple messages to the target website at the same time. The target site is then overwhelmed and essentially debilitated by the incoming flood of illegitimate messages, which leaves no room for legitimate messages.

Compromise Accounts

Another popular attack method is to abuse or take advantage of valid user accounts and the permissions associated with those accounts. For example, a user at a company or college who has a valid account will try to access forbidden documents, upload unauthorized files and datasets, use the company network as a site for illegal web and email attacks, or simply try to circum-navigate the system security features in an attempt to access forbidden services.

One of the most successful account attack strategies involves simply asking a user for their password. With some clever acting and strategic manipulation, an attacker can convince users that the attacker has a legitimate need for the user's password. Sometimes the attacker will pose as a company executive or as an IT admin. They might use psychological techniques, such as mixing truth with lies, creating a sense of urgency or scarcity, implying authority, playing on emotions,

intimidation, generalizing to cover for unknown details, feigning familiarity, appealing to empathy, or offering favors to create a sense of owing a favor in return.

Another common attack method is to try to guess or intercept valid IDs and passwords from authorized users. Hackers will try to steal passwords by guessing simple combinations or eavesdropping on transmissions in which a password is being transmitted. Some hackers will even go so far as to create an application that appears to be legitimate and prompts users for an ID and password, such as an app asking for credentials to a social media platform to provide added features and surreptitiously capturing those credentials from the user. Once an individual enters their ID and password, the software displays a message that gives the appearance of a system failure, or it might even act as a go-between with the real social media site and redirect the user's credentials for a successful login. The user moves on, not knowing that their ID and password have just been passed to a bogus program.

Other Attack Strategies

Additional attack types include the following:

> **Phishing**—This attack involves a form of communication, such as an email, text, or phone call, that appears to be sent from a legitimate source and requests access or authentication information. Hackers often create emails that seem to be a

legitimate request coming from a well-known company. The email even includes official-looking corporate logos, emblems, and signatures. In the email, the unsuspecting user is asked to provide private information such as a Social Security number or credit card number. The hacker collects this personal information and uses it illegally to purchase items or, even worse, commit identity theft.

> **Pharming**—This is another type of attack that involves tricking the user into supplying confidential information. In this attack, a web user seeking to visit a particular company's website is unknowingly redirected to a bogus website that looks exactly like the company's official website. Not knowing that they are visiting a bogus website, the user might enter confidential information to register for a service or make a purchase, which can then be stolen.

> **Rootkit**—This software is installed (usually unknowingly) in a user's operating system. It is installed so deep within the OS that normal protection software does not notice the rootkit, thus making it a highly effective form of attack. With a rootkit in place, a user's computer can essentially be taken over by a remote user. Although some rootkits are actually useful and can help with problems on company managed computers, most rootkits are meant to be destructive.

> **Keylogger**—This software captures and records all the keystrokes made at the keyboard. This can be a useful program for someone who wants to monitor a computer user's progress on a certain task. Unfortunately, it can also be used to capture someone's user ID and password or other private information. Some companies also use keyloggers to monitor their employees' productivity or habits. This purpose can be either good or bad depending upon your frame of reference.

Professionals who support computer networks, as well as individual computer users who have a computer at home or work, need to be aware of these common attacks so they can decide how best to protect their systems.

Details | Analyzing a Phishing Email

Figure 8-2 shows a phishing email that appears to come from Chase, a credit card company. If the intended victim has a Chase card, they might decide they at least should read the email to find out if it's real. The email creates a sense of urgency by saying the receiver's credit card might have been compromised. The

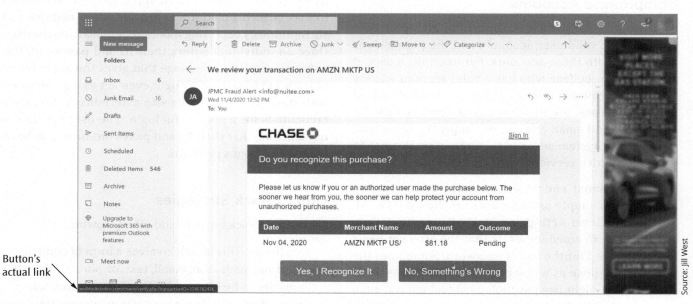

Button's actual link

Figure 8-2 Phishing emails often include legitimate-looking logos, buttons, instructions, and fine print

logo and formatting give the email a sense of formality, which implies authority. The seeming detail in the alleged charge gives a sense of credibility that builds trust. However, further investigation reveals this email to be a scam.

Notice the cursor in the figure is floating over the red "No" button at the bottom right of the figure, revealing the button's target address in the lower-left corner of the image. If you clicked the button, this is the address

the link would go to. Even though the link lists a transaction ID, which might be convincing, the link itself does not go to the Chase website. Scrolling to the bottom of the email, the fine print shown in Figure 8-3 is even more revealing—the email claims to come from Chase, but the company listed in the fine print is Capital One, a completely different company. Once you know what you're looking for, it can be fun to pick apart a phishing email to discover its flaws.

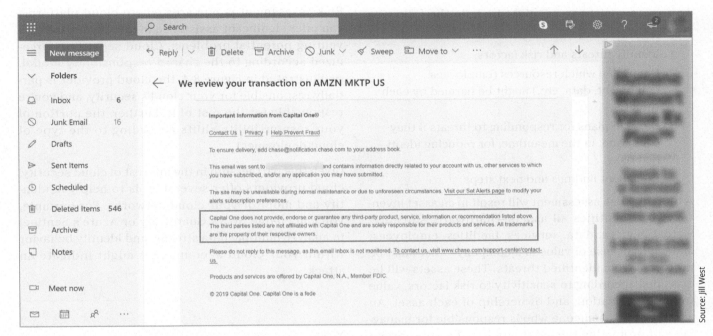

Figure 8-3 Careful investigation reveals clues the email is fake

Risk and Security Assessments

To evaluate the risks your network faces, you'll need to conduct several types of assessments. These assessments are designed to help you identify the resources

within your domain—including hardware, software, data, and cloud-based resources—and identify risks to those resources. Effective risk management happens at two layers:

> A security risk assessment evaluates threats to and vulnerabilities of the network.

> A business risk assessment evaluates the impact of potential threats on business processes.

To determine these risks to the business, you must first have a good understanding of the various processes the business relies on. An operations business process, for example, would be the series of steps involved in receiving an order from a customer, delivering a product or service, and billing the customer. Business and IT professionals use techniques to identify, define, evaluate, and analyze these various business processes and the potential impact of security threats on those processes.

A threat's consequences range from severe to mild —from a costly network outage or the dispersal of classified or sensitive information to lack of access for one user or the dispersal of relatively insignificant corporate data. The more devastating a threat's effects and the more likely it is to happen, the more rigorously your security measures should address it.

An assessment process might include the following steps:

1. Identify threats and risk factors.

2. Determine which resources (employees, equipment, data, etc.) might be harmed by each threat.

3. Develop plans for responding to threats if they occur and, in the meantime, for reducing identified risks.

4. Document findings and next steps.

A thorough risk assessment will result in an asset inventory that identifies all assets—hardware, software, virtual devices, data, services, facilities, employees, and anything else of value in a company—that must be protected from identified threats. These assets will be classified according to sensitivity to risk factors, value to the organization, and ownership of each asset. An asset owner is someone who is responsible for managing and protecting the asset and has the appropriate authority to do so.

Additional security assessments include the following techniques:

> **Application scanning**—These tools are used to analyze your network's applications for missing patches, identified vulnerabilities, and insecure configurations.

> **Vulnerability scanning**—IT staff search for vulnerabilities in their corporate network device configurations. They do not try to exploit any vulnerabilities they find.

> **Penetration testing**—This type of simulated attack begins with a vulnerability scan and then attempts to exploit identified vulnerabilities. A penetration test might be something as simple as a network admin clicking through the network to see what vulnerabilities surface, such as discovering that the default credentials for a networked

HVAC system were never changed, logging into these systems using the default credentials, and determining how deeply the HVAC system is interlinked with other network resources. Or it might consist of a much more robust process, relying on a professional pen testing organization to conduct a thorough examination of the company's network and resulting in a lengthy report recommending important, critical, and urgent changes to make to the network.

Risk assessment is one area where cloud platforms can offer significant assistance in identifying and preventing potential problems. Cloud security is organized according to the shared responsibility model. As illustrated in Figure 8-4, the cloud provider is partially responsible for your cloud's security, and you're responsible for the rest of it. Further, the portion of your responsibility shifts according to the type of cloud deployment.

Given this partnership in the interest of cloud security, cloud providers offer several tools to help you identify and monitor your cloud networks. For example, you can enable AWS's GuardDuty or Azure's Sentinel to analyze multiple data streams and identify behavior within your cloud account that might indicate an attack.

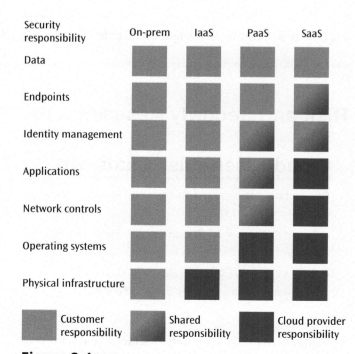

Figure 8-4 The customer's responsibility for security shifts with different cloud deployment structures

Risk Response

As risks are identified and evaluated, these findings will be tracked in a risk register, which provides documentation of risks and might be required for compliance with certain regulations. The risk register will also document measures taken to reduce or eliminate these risks.

Four layers of risk response strategies offer options according to your findings for each risk:

> **Avoidance**—In many cases, a risk can be avoided completely. For example, you can avoid the risk of vulnerabilities in legacy software by replacing that software with newer, more secure options.

> **Mitigation**—Risk mitigation reduces the risk in some way. For example, creating effective backup strategies can mitigate the risks involved in a potential ransomware attack, but a ransomware attack might still occur, and it might still cause damage that you couldn't prevent.

> **Transfer**—You might choose to have someone else to take on the risk for you. This is the essence of how insurance works, where you pay the insurance company to shoulder the risk. Another option is to write contracts in a way that the other party takes on some of the inherent risk. Note that transferring a risk doesn't eliminate the risk; it simply reduces your liability in relation to the risk.

> **Acceptance**—In some cases, it's reasonable to accept a risk as-is if the risk's probability is low or if the likely impact is sustainable.

Security Policies

A security policy for network users identifies your security goals, risks, levels of authority, designated security coordinator and team members, responsibilities for each team member, and responsibilities for each employee. In addition, it specifies how to address security breaches. It should not state exactly which hardware, software, architecture, or protocols will be used to ensure security, nor how hardware or software will be installed and configured. These details change and should only be shared with authorized network administrators or managers. The policy is written with the intent of keeping people safe; protecting sensitive data; ensuring network availability and integrity; and collecting data to determine what went wrong, who is responsible, and what actions should be taken in the future to prevent similar damage.

Incident Response

A sound security policy includes clear plans for response to incidents that affect a network's security or availability. An incident response plan specifically defines the characteristics of an event that qualifies as a formal incident and the steps that should be followed as a result. Qualifying incidents take into account the full spectrum of possible events, which might include a break-in, fire, weather-related emergency, hacking attack, discovery of illegal content or activity on an employee's computer, malware outbreak, or a full-scale, environmental disaster that shuts down businesses throughout the city or state.

An incident response is a six-stage process, which actually begins *before* the incident occurs:

Stage 1—Preparation: The response team brainstorms possible incidents and procedures for handling them. This includes installing backup systems and compiling all the information required to restore the network, such as passwords, configurations, vendor lists and their SLAs (service level agreements), locations of backup data storage, emergency contact information, and relevant privacy laws.

Stage 2—Detection and identification: All staff are educated about what qualifies as an incident and what to do if they notice a potential problem. Any system or staff alerts are routed to assigned personnel to determine whether the event requires escalation—that is, if it should be recognized as something other than a normal problem faced by IT technicians. Each company will have its own criteria for which incidents require escalation, as well as its own chain of command for notification purposes.

Stage 3—Containment: The team works to limit the damage. Affected systems or areas are isolated, and response staff are called in as required by the situation.

Stage 4—Remediation: The team finds what caused the problem and begins to resolve it so no further damage occurs.

Stage 5—Recovery: Operations return to normal as affected systems are repaired.

Stage 6—Review: The team determines what can be learned from the incident and uses this information to make adjustments in preparation for and perhaps prevention of future threats.

Now that you understand several of the more common system attacks, let's investigate what you can do to protect yourself and your company from these risks. You will begin by examining ways you can physically protect your equipment and your data.

Remember this...

> As a result of the large number of attacks on computers and networks in recent years, experts monitor threats used to exploit loopholes and vulnerabilities in networks and other systems. An attacker's goal is to somehow gain access to a system and then steal or damage data. Attackers might use one or more of many available attack vectors, including compromising users, compromising software, compromising network or system availability, or compromising accounts.

> A risk assessment is an inventory that identifies all assets that must be protected from identified threats. These assets will be classified according to sensitivity to risk factors, value to the organization, and ownership of each asset.

> Risks will be tracked in a risk register as they are identified and evaluated. This provides documentation that might be required for compliance with certain regulations.

> A security policy for network users identifies security goals, risks, levels of authority, designated security coordinator and team members, responsibilities for each team member, and responsibilities for each employee. An incident response plan

specifically defines the characteristics of an event that qualifies as a formal incident and the steps that should be followed as a result.

Self-check

1. What type of attack is most likely to result in the victim paying money to the attacker?
   a. DDoS
   b. Ransomware
   c. Rootkit
   d. Phishing
2. Which technique relies on exploitation of vulnerabilities?
   a. Penetration testing
   b. Vulnerability scanning
   c. Risk assessment
   d. Application scanning
3. Which of the following events would NOT qualify as an incident?
   a. Building break-in
   b. Tax audit
   c. Hurricane
   d. Ransomware attack

Check your answers at the end of this chapter.

Section 8-2: Network Security Technologies

Understanding the threats to your network is half the battle—the other half is protecting your network from these threats. Critical components of a comprehensive security strategy include anti-malware software, firewall devices, secure authentication techniques, and encryption technologies.

The **defense in depth** approach combines multiple layers of security to cover gaps and increase the network's overall resistance to harm. Figure 8-5 illustrates how these security layers build on each other. Weaknesses in one layer are compensated for by other layers. Each security technique discussed in this chapter, and many others, work together to provide better security than any single layer could perform on its own.

To provide adequate layers of network security, you'll need to start with limiting physical access to your devices, as described next.

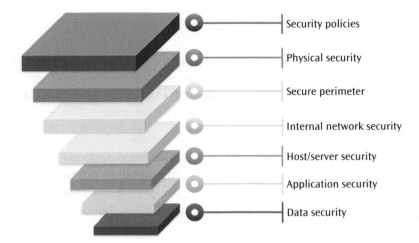

Figure 8-5 Layers of defense in depth security

Physical Security

A network's physical security refers to controlling physical access to network resources (such as server rooms or network devices) as well as managing environmental factors that affect the performance and longevity of network devices. Physical security strategies for a network can be broadly categorized as prevention methods and detection methods.

Prevention Methods

The physical protection of a computer system or network includes protecting the equipment from physical damage caused by fire, floods, earthquakes, power surges, vandalism, and similar threats. For example, to prevent electrical damage to computing equipment, high-quality surge protectors should be used on all devices that require an electrical current. The electrical circuits that provide power to devices should be large enough to adequately support them without placing a strain on the electrical system. In addition, computer devices should not run on the same circuits as electrical devices that can cause power fluctuations, such as large motors. Finally, devices that are susceptible to damage from static electricity discharges, such as memory cards and printed circuit boards, should be properly grounded.

In many cases, the techniques to prevent damage are simple steps. For example, rooms containing computer equipment should always be locked, and unauthorized persons should not be allowed to enter them. Where possible, cabling and the devices that cables plug into should not be left exposed.

Additional prevention techniques protect networks and computer systems from unauthorized access. Consider the following access control technologies:

> **Keypad**—Requires the entry of a code to open the door, which can reduce the inherent risk of lost keys. Some keypads can be used to log who comes and goes, enable or disable unescorted entry, schedule open access times, and even respond to access made under duress (with a special hostage code that trips an alarm when entered).

> **Access badge**—Identifies the person by name and perhaps includes a photo, title, and other information. These badges can be programmed to allow their owner access to some, but not all, rooms in a building.

> **Locking rack or locking cabinet**—Provides a final layer of physical defense should an attacker gain access to a data room or some other controlled space. Locking racks restrict physical access to servers, routers, switches, and firewalls installed on the rack to prevent an intruder from making configuration changes to these devices. Locking cabinets might be used to store hardware not in use, such as spare devices, radio equipment, or tools.

Detection Methods

Some equipment, obviously, must be placed in the open for public access. In this case, the equipment should be locked down. There are many kinds of antitheft devices for locking cabinets, locking cables to cabinets, and locking down keyboards and other peripheral devices. However, in many cases, the threat of discovery is more

> **Note**
>
> A door might not be the only way to enter a room containing sensitive equipment. Drop ceilings, also called suspended ceilings, can provide easy access to someone determined to get around a locked door. Secured rooms should be surrounded by impenetrable walls, ceilings, and floors. If a data room does have a drop ceiling, make sure the walls extend all the way up to the true ceiling beyond the drop ceiling grid.

of a deterrent than a secure lock. For example, Figure 8-6 shows a plastic seal on an electric meter.

While a small device like this might serve as a deterrent to some people, it wouldn't prevent someone from breaking in if the person is determined to do so. Therefore, this device offers tamper detection more than prevention.

No security system is perfect, and network breaches happen. It's important to detect these problems quickly and respond appropriately. The following list explores some methods of detecting physical intrusions and other kinds of events:

> **Motion detection**—Triggers a response, such as an alarm or video capture, when movement is detected. To reduce false alarms, AI-powered motion detectors can discern between different types of movement, such as small animals passing by, plants or trees blowing in the wind, or humans approaching a door.

> **Video camera**—Feeds a captured video stream to a CCTV (closed-circuit TV) monitoring system. Some cameras will capture video continuously while others are activated by motion detectors. Although many employees feel surveillance is an intrusion into their privacy, many network administrators consider it a good deterrent of computer vandalism and theft.

Figure 8-6 A single-use, plastic security seal

iStock.com/Maudib

> **Tamper detection**—Identifies physical penetration, temperature extremes, input voltage variations, input frequency variations, or certain kinds of radiation. Tamper detection sensors might trigger defensive measures such as an alarm or shutdown, or it might activate a video camera or other security system.

Anti-Malware

One of the most common forms of invasion delivered over communications channels is malware such as a virus, a worm, or ransomware. Anti-malware software might use any of the following techniques to detect malware and protect the system against malware attacks:

> **Scanning**—Anti-malware regularly scans all files stored in a system, and also checks any incoming files, such as web pages, files, and emails. These scans are searching for patterns of commands or instructions known to be common for malware, a process called heuristic analysis.

> **Behavior monitoring**—Rather than looking for a specific pattern of bits in a file, anti-malware today also continues to watch for activities typical of malware, such as unusual file changes or directory activity. This is another form of heuristic analysis.

> **Sandboxing**—Logically isolating a program from the rest of the system can create space to investigate potential threats before they can cause damage. Anti-malware can test run a file in this sandboxed environment to determine whether the file will perform actions indicative of malware.

> **Removal**—Identified threats are wiped from the system, hopefully before damaged has occurred.

Proxy Server

A **proxy server** is software that serves as an intermediary between internal resources and external users, much like how a librarian controls access to a library's rare books room. To ensure protection and proper handling techniques, the public are not allowed into the room and must fill out a request to see copies of the material instead.

Similarly, a transaction making a request of a company's proxy server firewall never directly connects with the company's network. Any external transactions that request something from the corporate network must first approach the proxy server, which retrieves the requested information. Because all external transactions must go through the proxy server, it provides an opportunity to create an audit log.

Access Control Lists (ACLs)

Cloud Essentials+ Exam Tip

This section discusses hardening, which is required by

- Part of Objective 4.4: Explain security concerns, measures, or concepts of cloud operations.

Configuring network devices with security in mind is called device hardening, and it's a critical component of any network security strategy. One way to harden network devices such as routers and switches is to configure ACLs (access control lists) that determine which traffic is allowed to cross the device and which traffic is, instead, dropped. An ACL acts like a filter to instruct the device to allow or deny traffic according to the protocol used, the source or destination IP address, or the TCP or UDP port number.

To do this, the device's ACL consists of a list of rules, or statements, that specify allow or deny flags based on certain criteria. When a device receives a message, it inspects each statement in its ACL, starting at the top of the list, until it finds a statement that matches the message's characteristics. The device allows or denies the message according to the matching statement. If no matching statement is found, the message is discarded by default. This last decision is called the implicit deny rule, which ensures that any traffic the ACL does not explicitly allow is denied by default.

Devices such as switches and routers don't contain configured ACLs by default and so allow all traffic through until programmed otherwise. A network admin must add an ACL to each interface. Naturally, the more statements a device must scan, or the longer the ACL, the more time it will take the device to process network

traffic and, therefore, the slower overall network performance. Increased security often results in lower network performance. Centralizing these traffic rules into a few, specialized devices can help increase performance of other network devices while still providing high security. This is the role of firewalls, which you'll read about next.

Firewalls

Cloud Essentials+ Exam Tip

This section discusses firewalls, which is required by

- Part of Objective 1.2: Identify cloud networking concepts.

A firewall is a system or combination of systems that supports an access control policy between two networks or between two segments of a network. Most commonly, the two networks are an internal corporate network and an external network, such as the Internet. A firewall can limit users on the Internet from accessing certain portions of a corporate network and can limit internal users from accessing various portions of the internal network or the Internet. Figure 8-7 demonstrates how a firewall blocks both internal and external requests.

Firewall Effectiveness

A firewall system can prevent remote logins, filter inbound or outbound emails and file transfers, and limit inbound or outbound web page requests. Most firewalls function primarily by monitoring the TCP or UDP ports of traffic crossing the firewall. These ports indicate which application is targeted by the traffic. When a message destined for a specific application enters a system, the appropriate port is included as part of the message's transport layer header. Some ports typically allowed through firewalls include:

> Web browsing, which uses HTTP on port 80 and HTTPS on port 443

> URL resolution using DNS on port 53

> Remote login using SSH (SecureShell) on port 22 or RDP (Remote Desktop Protocol) on port 3389

> Email using insecure ports 25 (SMTP), 110 (POP3), and 143 (IMAP4) or secure ports 587 (SMTP over TLS), 995 (POP3 over TLS), and 993 (IMAP4 over TLS)

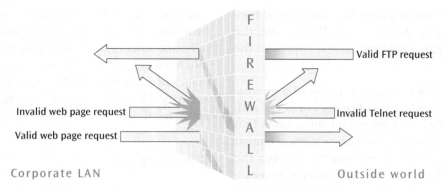

Figure 8-7 A firewall as it stops certain internal and external transactions

Note that most firewalls also allow you to identify which IP addresses can access each of these ports. Most often, you'll allow all IP addresses to send HTTP messages on ports 80 and 443 to communicate with a web server. However, if you allow remote login traffic on port 22 or port 3389, you'll want to specify the network admin's home or remote IP address so other people can't send traffic across those ports.

Firewall Functionality in the Cloud

While you won't need to install an actual firewall on the cloud-based portions of your network, you still need firewall functions to protect cloud resources. Most of the time, the cloud provider builds these tools into the relevant cloud resources. For example, suppose you are creating a web server in AWS's EC2. As you configure the server instance, you must choose which security group to assign to the EC2 instance, as shown in Figure 8-8. In AWS, a security group provides the ability to add ACL statements specifying which traffic will be allowed or denied access to the instance.

It's important to note that security groups apply to EC2 instances in AWS, not to the entire VPC (Virtual Private Cloud) or subnet. In other words, the rules in a

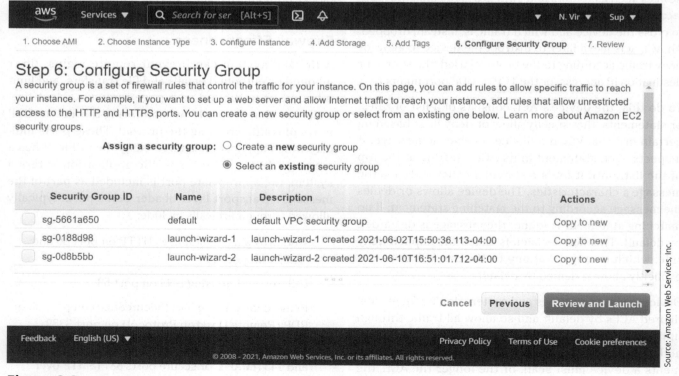

Figure 8-8 Choose a security group for an EC2 instance in AWS

security group apply only to each instance the security group is assigned to. An alternative resource is a NACL (network ACL, pronounced *nackle*). A NACL functions at the VPC level, meaning the rules in a NACL will filter traffic to and from any resource contained within that VPC.

Security groups, NACLs, and similar resources in other cloud platforms allow you to control what traffic can reach specific resources within your cloud-based network. There are variations in these tools' characteristics, however. For example, Table 8-1 shows a comparison of security groups and NACLs in AWS. Security groups deny all traffic by default. To allow traffic, you must create allow rules, and no deny rules are needed. In contrast, you can create both allow and deny rules in NACLs.

Similar services and resources are available in other cloud platforms. When deploying these resources, it's important to understand the specific characteristics and limitations of each within that environment.

Firewall Limitations

Firewalls cannot protect a network from all possible forms of attack. Because malware can hide within a document, for example, it will probably not be detected by a firewall if its host document is allowed into the system. Application layer firewalls perform deeper packet inspection and can detect problems within the message's payload, such as malware contained in a document attached to an email. This added benefit of examining the payload increases the processing time of an application layer firewall.

If an internal network user has attached a rogue access point, such as a Wi-Fi router or a hotspot on a computer, someone can bypass the firewall and gain illegal access. For a firewall system to work, a comprehensive security policy must be created, installed, and enforced. This security policy must cover the management of all possible entrances to and exits from the corporate environment.

Intrusion Detection and Prevention Systems

Many companies use an IDS (intrusion detection system) or an IPS (intrusion prevention system) to monitor data flow and system requests into, out of, and throughout their networks. If unusual activity is noticed, protective action can be taken immediately. The response to detected issues, however, differs according to the type of system used:

> An **IDS (intrusion detection system)** is a stand-alone device, an application, or a built-in feature running on a workstation, server, switch, router, or firewall. It monitors network traffic, generating alerts about suspicious activity (see the right side of Figure 8-9). Two subtypes of IDS vary according to where they're installed and what they're designed to protect:

>> If installed on the device it's monitoring, it's called an HIDS (host-based IDS). For example, an HIDS might detect an attempt to exploit an insecure application running on a server or repeated attempts to log on to the server.

>> An NIDS (network-based intrusion detection system) protects a network or portion of a network and is usually situated at the edge of the network or in a network's protective perimeter, known as a screened subnet (formerly called a DMZ, or demilitarized zone). Here, it can detect many types of suspicious traffic patterns, such as those typical of DoS attacks.

Table 8-1 Security groups vs. NACLs in AWS

Security Group	NACL
Security groups deny all traffic by default. You can only create allow rules in a security group.	NACLs allow all traffic by default and are considered a backup security measure if you decide to use them. You can create both allow and deny rules in a NACL.
A security group evaluates all its rules before allowing traffic through.	A NACL evaluates rules in order and allows or denies traffic when the first matching rule is identified.
Security groups are stateful, which means the security group matches incoming and outgoing traffic in a conversation. For example, if incoming messages from a device are allowed, corresponding outgoing messages in reply to that device are also allowed.	NACLs are stateless, which means the NACL does not match incoming and outgoing traffic. You must anticipate which outbound rules will be needed to support conversation allowed by inbound rules.

> An IPS (intrusion prevention system) stands inline between the attacker and the targeted network or host where it can prevent traffic from reaching that network or host (see the left side of Figure 8-9). IPSs were originally designed as a more comprehensive traffic analysis and protection tool than firewalls. However, firewalls have evolved, and as a result, the differences between a firewall and an IPS have diminished. Similar to IDS, IPS comes in two varieties:

> > An HIPS (host-based intrusion prevention system) protects a specific host.

> > An NIPS (network-based intrusion prevention system) can protect entire networks or sections of a network.

> Using NIPS and HIPS together increases the network's security. For example, an HIPS running on a file server might accept a hacker's attempt to log on if the hacker is posing as a legitimate client. With

the proper NIPS, however, such a request would likely never get to the server.

Remember this...

> Physical security strategies for a network can be broadly categorized as prevention methods and detection methods. The physical protection of a computer system or network includes protecting the equipment from physical damage caused by fire, floods, earthquakes, power surges, vandalism, and similar threats. Additional prevention techniques protect networks and computer systems from unauthorized access. However, no security system is perfect, and network breaches happen. It's important to detect these problems quickly and respond appropriately.

> Anti-malware software might use any of the following techniques to detect malware and protect the system against malware attacks: scanning, behavior monitoring, sandboxing, and removal.

> A proxy server is software that serves as an intermediary between internal resources and external users.

> ACLs (access control lists) determine which traffic is allowed to cross the device and which traffic is dropped. An ACL acts like a filter to instruct the device to allow or deny traffic according to the protocol used, the source or destination IP address, or the TCP or UDP port number.

Note

An IDS solution might also include **FIM (file integrity monitoring)**, which alerts the system of any changes made to files that shouldn't change, such as operating system files. FIM works by generating a baseline checksum of the monitored files and then recalculating the checksum at regular intervals to determine if anything has changed.

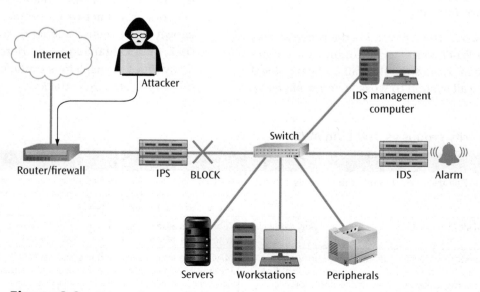

Figure 8-9 An IDS detects traffic patterns, while an IPS can intercept traffic that might threaten a corporate network

❭ A firewall is a system or combination of systems that supports an access control policy between two networks or between two segments of a network.

❭ While you won't need to install an actual firewall on the cloud-based portions of your network, you still need firewall functions to protect cloud resources. Most of the time, the cloud provider builds these tools into the relevant cloud resources.

❭ Many companies use an IDS (intrusion detection system) or an IPS (intrusion prevention system) to monitor data flow and system requests into, out of, and throughout their networks. If unusual activity is noticed, protective action can be taken immediately.

Self-check

4. What kind of physical security is offered by a video camera?
   a. Prevention
   b. Proxy
   c. Detection
   d. Hardening
5. Which device will alert network technicians to an intrusion but will not prevent an attack?
   a. IPS
   b. IDS
   c. ACL
   d. TLS
6. Which port should be opened to allow email traffic to enter your network?
   a. 22
   b. 443
   c. 80
   d. 587

Check your answers at the end of this chapter.

Section 8-3: Data Security Technologies

Data security and preventing intruders from accessing private information is significantly more complicated than it may appear. Protecting access to data is only one aspect of data security. To understand the intricacies of what various data security techniques offer, you first need to understand what these techniques are trying to accomplish as defined by the CIA triad.

CIA Triad

Cloud Essentials+ Exam Tip

This section discusses confidentiality, integrity, and availability, which are required by

- Part of Objective 4.4: Explain security concerns, measures, or concepts of cloud operations.

Security experts have long relied on a three-pronged security model to guide their efforts in securing sensitive data, a model called the **CIA (confidentiality, integrity, and availability) triad**, and it consists of the following components:

❭ **Confidentiality**—Data can only be viewed by its intended recipient or at its intended destination. Two significant technologies used to achieve confidentiality include:

 ❭ **Encryption**—Scrambles data bits to appear as gibberish unless you have the key to decrypt the data.

 ❭ **Sanitization**—Destroys unneeded data in a way that ensures no one can recover the data.

❭ **Integrity**—Data that is received is the same as the data that was sent. Integrity can be maintained by:

 ❭ **Error checking tools**—Confirm data wasn't changed in transit. Examples include checksums and hashes.

 ❭ **Data validation processes**—Ensure data communicates the information intended and limit the types of changes that could happen to that data, such as requiring ten digits in a phone number field or offering a selection of years in a birthdate field.

❭ **Availability**—Data is accessible to the intended recipient when needed, meaning the sender is accountable for successful delivery of the data. Availability can be increased with adequate backups of the data. Be sure to test recovery processes to ensure backups are working as expected and can be restored quickly when needed.

What precautions can you take to ensure that data is not corrupted or intercepted by the wrong people? Let's begin with a discussion of data security standards and regulations. You'll then examine several techniques that can be used to better secure data, including encryption, digital signatures, and blockchain.

Data Security Regulations and Compliance

Cloud Essentials+ Exam Tip

This section discusses compliance and data security categories, which are required by

- Part of Objective 4.3: Identify the importance and impacts of compliance in the cloud.

- Part of Objective 4.4: Explain security concerns, measures, or concepts of cloud operations.

The security of a company's data is not just an internal concern. Other parties, such as customers or business partners, have a vested interest in how securely their data within the company's network is protected. Governments and industry-based regulatory agencies maintain enforceable oversight of businesses' security policies and procedures.

These regulatory concerns affect many types of data, especially financial data, medical information, PHI (protected health information), and PII (personally identifiable information), such as a person's name, birthdate, and Social Security number.

A company's data can be categorized in the following ways:

> **Public**—Some data maintained by a company is considered public information, either for members of the company or for the public, and so is not restricted and does not typically require special protection to prevent access to it. For example, your school's course descriptions are likely posted to your school's website. Students also have access to names and contact information for faculty and many staff members. All school employees might have access to HR forms, standard salary information, or news about internal structural changes being made.

> **Private**—This data is confidential to some level and requires reasonable levels of protection. For example, student contact information and enrollment status constitute private data that only certain school employees can access.

> **Sensitive**—Some data is protected by government or industry regulations. These standards define minimum levels and types of protections that are more stringent than what most companies require for their private data. For example, a student's records for assessments and accommodations related to a disability contain highly protected information that only a small subset of school employees can access. Even then, that access is often time-limited. If sensitive data is compromised in a data breach where access results in the exposure, theft, or unauthorized use of data, the organization will likely face severe fines and penalties—perhaps even jail time for responsible persons—in addition to potentially irreparable damage to the organization's reputation.

These regulatory concerns deserve serious consideration by every employee who has access to protected data. As mentioned, governments have passed legislation dictating some of these requirements in the interest of protecting their citizens' privacy and rights to determine what happens with their information. Many industry-based requirements also exist to guide companies in their data security efforts, and auditing processes help ensure that companies abide by these regulations.

The most wide-reaching standards include the following:

> **GDPR (General Data Protection Regulation)**—Deployed by the EU (European Union) in 2018, this regulation applies to any company doing business with a European citizen, which encompasses nearly every sizable business in the world. Therefore, a high percentage of companies worldwide have worked to comply with these standards for all their customers, not just those in Europe. Restrictions emphasize obtaining consent, minimizing stored data, and protecting customers' rights regarding information about them.

> **CCPA (California Consumer Privacy Act)**—Similar in purpose to the GDPR, this California law applies only to medium and large businesses but enforces some standards that exceed those set by the GDPR. In some ways, this law more deeply impacts U.S. business processes, especially due to its broader

definition of what information qualifies as private data.

> **HIPAA (Health Insurance Portability and Accountability Act)**—These regulations, enforced by the OCR (Office for Civil Rights), define security and confidentiality standards for healthcare and medical data in the United States. HIPAA only applies to covered entities (most health care providers, health plan providers, health care clearinghouses, and related business associates), which means your health information with other companies (such as your employer) might not be protected by HIPAA.

> **FERPA (Family Educational Rights and Privacy Act)**—This law from the 1970s protects the privacy and access rights of parents and adults for their or their children's educational records. Some of the data not covered by HIPAA might be covered by FERPA for certain organizations.

> **PCI DSS (Payment Card Industry Data Security Standard)**—These regulations are defined and enforced by credit card companies themselves, not by any government agency. Still, the major credit card companies that oversee these regulations impose heavy fines and potential termination of services for noncompliance.

> **SOX (Sarbanes-Oxley Act)**—While more directly relevant to financial reporting, a company's IT network must still accommodate the requirements of this act by supporting the required automatic reporting, alerts, and backups.

When a company completes a transaction such as a sale, data is collected. The country where that data is collected, processed, or stored imposes its own privacy and security laws, which is called **data sovereignty**. In this way, countries can establish regulations and standards to protect their citizens' data. In some cases, countries also restrict data residency, which refers to the location data can be stored. These policies give countries greater control over what happens to that data and prevents other countries from accessing or otherwise controlling data from citizens other than their own. How do you, as a customer, know what happens to your data? For that matter, how can your company know which business associates adequately protect their systems so you don't get mixed up in a data breach caused by their laxity? Companies involved with the types of data mentioned in this section often must or optionally choose to pursue compliance certifications with the organizations that enforce these regulatory standards. For example, AWS maintains compliance certifications for PCI-DSS, HIPAA, GDPR, and others. Therefore, many companies that would otherwise struggle to meet the stringent requirements of these standards can more easily reach these benchmarks when they host some or all of their datacenter resources in AWS's cloud. You can read more about AWS's compliance offerings at *aws.amazon.com/compliance*. Other cloud providers offer similar support.

Encryption

In a network, some systems store and manipulate data, while other systems transfer data. At times, data is also accessed by users and processes. To help organize security efforts, data can therefore be classified according to its state:

> Data at rest

> Data in transit

> Data in use

Each of these states requires different strategies and tools to keep the data safe according to the CIA triad. For example, consider the security of data in transit over a fiber-optic cable. Fiber-optic cable represented a major improvement in the ability of transmission media to secure sensitive data in transit. As you might recall from Chapter 2, metal media such as twisted pair and coaxial cable conduct electrical signals and are therefore relatively easy to tap, but fiber-optic cable is much more difficult to tap because it carries pulses of light. To tap a fiber-optic system, you must either physically break the fiber-optic cable—an intrusion that would likely be noticed immediately—or you must gain access to the fiber-optic junction box, which is usually in a locked location. As you can see, using fiber-optic cable

All Things Considered

Thought Experiment

For many years, experts believed it was impossible to tap a fiber-optic cable without being detected immediately from the briefly broken signal. Network professionals have since proven this belief false. Research online to find a video showing the process a hacker could use to tap a fiber-optic cable illegally. What surprises you about this process?

in areas where the cable might be susceptible to tampering can improve the security of data in transit.

Considering these risks, sensitive data requires additional security measures. One such additional measure is to encrypt the data before it is transmitted, send the encrypted data over secure media, and then decrypt the received data to obtain the original information. **Cryptography** is the study and practice of creating and using encryption and decryption techniques. Delving into the topic of cryptography requires you to understand a few basic terms:

> **Plaintext** is data before any encryption has been performed (see Figure 8-10).

> An **encryption algorithm** is the computer code that converts plaintext into an enciphered form.

> The **key** is a unique piece of information used to alter plaintext to obscure its original form. Depending on the type of key used, the same key or a mathematically related key can then decrypt the ciphertext back into plaintext.

> **Ciphertext** is the data after the encryption algorithm has been applied. After the ciphertext is created, it is transmitted to the receiver, where the ciphertext data is decrypted.

Early cryptography algorithms used the same key for both encryption and decryption. The use of a single key greatly concerned many experts. To allow local and remote locations to send and receive encrypted data, the same key had to be provided to both local and remote parties. If this key were intercepted and fell into the wrong hands, not only could encrypted data be decrypted, but false data could be encrypted and sent to either party. Newer techniques solve this problem by allowing the use of two different but mathematically related keys. One key can encrypt the data, and the second key can decrypt the data. Single key encryption is still used in some cases today because it's faster, but usually this is only in the context of technologies that begin with encryption that relies on two keys first. Let's explore encryption techniques and then take a closer look at key-based cryptography.

Monoalphabetic Substitution-Based Ciphers

Encryption techniques include three different ciphers: monoalphabetic substitution-based ciphers, polyalphabetic substitution-based ciphers, and transposition-based ciphers. Despite its daunting name, the monoalphabetic substitution-based cipher is a simple, not secure encryption technique. A **monoalphabetic substitution-based cipher** replaces a character or group of characters with a different character or group of characters. Consider the simple example in Figure 8-11. Each letter in the plaintext row maps to the letter below it in the ciphertext row.

This ciphertext simply corresponds to the letters on a keyboard, scanning left to right, top to bottom. To send a message using this encoding scheme, each plaintext letter of the message is replaced with the ciphertext character directly below it. Thus, the message

how about lunch at noon

would encode to

IGVQW GXZSX FEIQZ FGGF

A space has been placed after every five ciphertext characters to help disguise obvious patterns. This example is monoalphabetic because one alphabetic string was used to encode the plaintext. It is a substitution-based cipher because one character of ciphertext was substituted for one character of plaintext.

Polyalphabetic Substitution-Based Ciphers

The **polyalphabetic substitution-based cipher** uses multiple alphabetic strings to encode the plaintext rather than one. Possibly the earliest example of a polyalphabetic cipher is the Vigenère cipher, devised by Blaise de

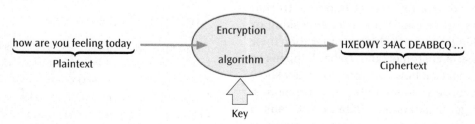

Figure 8-10 Basic encryption and decryption procedure

Plaintext:	a	b	c	d	e	f	g	h	i	j	k	l	m	n	o	p	q	r	s	t	u	v	w	x	y	z
Ciphertext:	Q	W	E	R	T	Y	U	I	O	P	A	S	D	F	G	H	J	K	L	Z	X	C	V	B	N	M

Figure 8-11   A simple example of a monoalphabetic substitution-based cipher

Vigenère in 1586. For the Vigenère cipher, a 26 × 26 matrix of characters is created, as shown in Figure 8-12.

To perform this cipher, you choose a key, such as COMPUTER SCIENCE, which you repeatedly place over the plaintext message, as shown in Figure 8-13.

To encode the message, you look at the first letter of the plaintext, *d*, and the corresponding key character immediately above it, *C*. The *C* tells you to use row C of the 26 × 26 matrix to perform the alphabetic substitution for the plaintext character *d*. You then go to column d in row C and find the ciphertext character F. This process is repeated for every character of the plaintext. The key, COMPUTER SCIENCE, must be kept secret between the encoder and decoder.

To make matters more difficult for an intruder, the standard 26 × 26 matrix with row A, row B, row C, and so on does not have to be used. Instead, the encoding and decoding can be done using a unique matrix. In this case, both the matrix and the key must remain a secret.

Transposition-Based Ciphers

A transposition-based cipher differs from a substitution-based cipher because the plaintext is not preserved. Rearranging the order of the plaintext characters makes common patterns unclear and the code much more difficult to break.

Let's consider a simple example of a transposition cipher. Choose a keyword that contains no duplicate letters, such as COMPUTER. Over each letter in the keyword, write the number that corresponds to the order in which that letter appears in the alphabet when compared to the other letters in the keyword, as shown in Figure 8-14. If you were to take the letters of the keyword COMPUTER and place them in alphabetical order, C appears first, E is second, M is third, O is fourth, and so on. Next, take a plaintext message such as "this is the best class i have ever taken" and write it under the keyword in consecutive rows going from left to right.

To encode the message, read down each column starting with the column numbered 1 and proceeding through to the column numbered 8. Reading column 1 gives TESV, and column 2 gives TLEE. Encoding all eight columns gives the following message:

TESV TLEE IEIR HBSE SSHT HAEN SCVK ITAA

The choice of the keyword is once again very important and must never be shared with unauthorized individuals. For added security, make the encryption more difficult by performing an additional substitution-based cipher on the result of the transposition cipher. To create a very difficult code, repeat various patterns of substitution- and transposition-based ciphers, one after another.

Key character	Plaintext letters																									
	a	b	c	d	e	f	g	h	i	j	k	l	m	n	o	p	q	r	s	t	u	v	w	x	y	z
A	A	B	C	D	E	F	G	H	I	J	K	L	M	N	O	P	Q	R	S	T	U	V	W	X	Y	Z
B	B	C	D	E	F	G	H	I	J	K	L	M	N	O	P	Q	R	S	T	U	V	W	X	Y	Z	A
C	C	D	E	F	G	H	I	J	K	L	M	N	O	P	Q	R	S	T	U	V	W	X	Y	Z	A	B
---	---																									
Z	Z	A	B	C	D	E	F	G	H	I	J	K	L	M	N	O	P	Q	R	S	T	U	V	W	X	Y

Figure 8-12   An example of a Vigenère 26 × 26 ciphertext character matrix

Key:	C	O	M	P	U	T	E	R	S	C	I	E	N	C	E	C	O	M	P	U	T	E	R	S	C	I
Plaintext:	d	a	t	a	c	o	m	m	i	s	t	h	e	b	e	s	t	c	l	a	s	s	e	v	e	r

Figure 8-13   Use a key to encrypt a message with the character matrix

C	O	M	P	U	T	E	R
1	4	3	5	8	7	2	6
t	h	i	s	i	s	t	h
e	b	e	s	t	c	l	a
s	s	i	h	a	v	e	e
v	e	r	t	a	k	e	n

Figure 8-14 Number each letter for the order in which these letters appear in the alphabet, then write the message in consecutive rows underneath

DES (Data Encryption Standard) and AES (Advanced Encryption Standard)

DES (Data Encryption Standard) is an older encryption method that was used by businesses to send and receive secure transactions. The basic algorithm behind the standard is shown in Figure 8-15. The DES algorithm works with 64-bit blocks of data and subjects each block to sixteen levels, or rounds, of encryption. The encryption techniques are based upon substitution- and transposition-based ciphers. Each of the sixteen levels of encryption can perform a different operation based on the contents of a 56-bit key. The 56-bit key is applied to the DES algorithm, the 64-bit block of data is encrypted in a unique way, and the encrypted data is transmitted to the intended receiver. It is the responsibility of the parties involved to keep this 56-bit key secret.

After DES's weak, 56-bit key design was cracked in 1998, attempts to design a stronger encryption technique led to the creation of triple-DES. With **3DES (triple-DES)**, the data is encrypted using DES three times—first with key A, then with key B, and finally with key A again. While this technique creates an encryption system that is virtually unbreakable, it is CPU-intensive, meaning it requires a large amount of processing time. A CPU-intensive

process is not desirable on small devices such as smartphones.

AES (Advanced Encryption Standard) is an encryption technique that is as powerful as triple-DES but also fast and compact. AES was selected by the U.S. government to replace DES. More precisely, NIST (National Institute of Standards and Technology) selected the algorithm Rijndael (pronounced *rain-doll*) in October 2000 as the basis for AES. The Rijndael algorithm involves elegant mathematical

---

Note

Encryption protocols such as DES, 3DES, and AES perform encryption on blocks of data. For example, DES encrypts blocks of 64 bits at one time while AES encrypts data in blocks of 128 bits. This works well when the volume of data to be transmitted is known, such as when sending a file across the network. In contrast, stream ciphers encrypt data one byte (or one bit) at a time.

Stream ciphers are less secure but faster and more efficient when the volume of data is unknown, such as when transmitting data during a video call or streaming audio, and thus were often used in older wireless security techniques. RC4 (Rivest Cipher 4, also called ARC4) is an example of a popular stream cipher that was part of an older, insecure wireless security technique called WEP (Wired Equivalent Privacy), which is no longer used on today's wireless networks.

---

formulas, requires only one pass instead of three, computes very quickly, is virtually unbreakable, and operates on even the smallest computing devices. With AES, one can select a key size of 128, 192, or 256 bits.

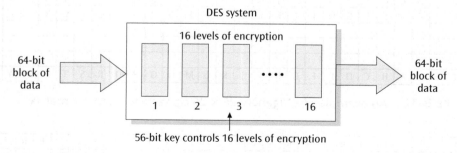

Figure 8-15 The basic operations of DES

Public Key Cryptography

All the encoding and decoding techniques shown thus far depend on protecting the key and keeping it from falling into the hands of an intruder. One of the inherent problems with a single key is that only the one key is needed to both encode and decode the message, a technique called symmetric encryption. The more people who have possession of the key, the more chances there are for someone to get sloppy and expose the key. But what if two keys are involved—one public and one private? Data encrypted with the public key can be decoded only with the private key, and data encrypted with the private key can be decoded only with the public key. This concept of two keys, public and private, is called public key cryptography. It is also called asymmetric encryption. When one key encrypts the plaintext and another key decrypts the ciphertext, it is nearly impossible to deduce the second key from the first key even if you have access to one of the keys. The encrypted data is also extremely difficult to decode without the other key, even for the experts.

How does public key cryptography work? Consider a situation in which a person browsing the web wishes to send secure information (such as a credit card number) to a web server. . Figure 8-16 illustrates the following steps:

Step 1—The user clicks a secured web page on their computer and sends the appropriate request to the server.

Step 2—The server returns a "certificate," which includes the server's public key and a list of several preferred cryptographic algorithms.

Step 3—The user's workstation selects one of the algorithms, generates a pair of public and

private keys, keeps the private key, and sends the public key back to the server.

Now both sides have their own private keys, and they both have each other's public key. Data can now be sent between the two endpoints in a secure fashion. Even if other parties intercept the transmission of the public keys, nothing will be gained because it is not possible to deduce a private key from a public key. Likewise, interception of the encrypted data will lead to nothing because the data can be decoded only with the respective private keys.

This technique can be used by most web browsers and servers when it is necessary to transmit secure data, and it relies on TLS to secure HTTP and FTP traffic, as you may recall from Chapter 7. TLS (Transport Layer Security) is the modern and improved version of the older SSL (Secure Sockets Layer) protocol—confusingly, the two protocol names are often used interchangeably and even referred to together, such as SSL/TLS. However, SSL has been deprecated for many years, and TLS is the current version. TLS works in conjunction with application layer protocols to create an encrypted session between client and server. For example, HTTPS (Hypertext Transfer Protocol Secure) is very popular and remains one of the major security techniques for transmitting secure web pages.

Public Key Infrastructure (PKI)

Suppose a company wants to open its internal LAN to the Internet, so as to allow its employees access to corporate computing resources—such as email and corporate databases—from remote locations; to allow corporate customers or suppliers access to company records; or to allow retail customers to place orders or

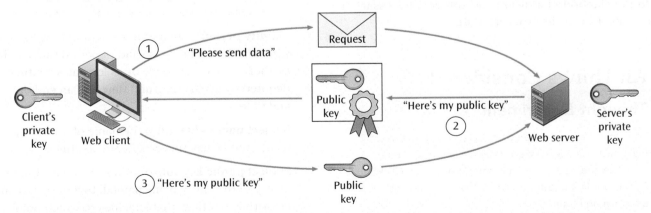

Figure 8-16 Only someone with the private key can decrypt information encrypted with their public key

inquire about previous orders. In each of these transactions, the company wants to be sure that the person conducting the transaction is a legitimate employee or customer, not a hacker trying to compromise its system. A technology that helps a company achieve this goal is public key infrastructure.

PKI (public key infrastructure) is the combination of encryption techniques, software, and services that involves all the necessary pieces to support digital certificates, certificate authorities, and public key generation, storage, and management. A company that adheres to the principles of PKI issues digital certificates to legitimate users and network servers, supplies enrollment software to end users, and provides network servers with the tools necessary to manage, renew, and revoke certificates. Average users also rely on PKI features managed by common browsers such as Chrome and Safari.

A digital certificate, or simply a **certificate**, is an electronic document similar to a passport that establishes your credentials when you are performing transactions on the web. It can contain your name, a serial number, expiration dates, a copy of your public key, and the digital signature of the certificate-issuing authority (to allow you to verify that the certificate is legitimate). Certificates are usually kept in a registry so that other users may look up a user's public key information.

Many certificates conform to the X.509 standard created and supported by the ITU-T. All certificates are issued by a **CA (certificate authority)**, which is either specialized software on a network or a trusted third-party organization that issues and manages certificates. One such third-party business is VeriSign, which is a fully integrated PKI service provider designed to provide certificates to a company that wants to incorporate PKI but does not want to deal with the elaborate hardware and software necessary to create and manage its own certificates.

Source: Google LLC

Figure 8-17 Click Certificate to see the certificate information

what information can go into a certificate. All X.509 certificates contain the following pieces of information:

> **Version**—Identifies the version of the X.509 standard that applies to this certificate.

> **Serial number**—Identifies a certificate; when a certificate is revoked, its serial number is placed in a CRL (certificate revocation list).

> **Signature algorithm identifier**—Identifies the algorithm used by the certificate authority to sign the certificate.

> **Issuer name**—Lists the name of the entity, normally a certificate authority, that signed the certificate (in some instances, the issuer signs their own name).

> **Validity period**—Limits the amount of time for which each certificate is valid (a period that can be as short as a few seconds or as long as a century), denoted by a start date and time and an end date and time.

> **Subject name**—Identifies the name of the entity whose public key this certificate identifies.

> **Subject public key information**—Provides the public key of the entity being named, together with an algorithm identifier that specifies to which public key encryption system this key belongs.

> **Digital signature**—Includes the signature of the certificate authority that verifies a legitimate certificate.

All Things Considered

Thought Experiment

You can view a website's certificate in your browser. Navigate to a secure website, such as *google.com*, and click the padlock icon in the address bar. Click the Certificate link at the bottom of the pop-up window, as shown in Figure 8-17.

When accessing a secure website's certificate in your browser, the Details tab shows the various parts of the certificate (see Figure 8-18). The X.509 standard defines

Source: Google LLC

Figure 8-18 Certificate information for a secured website

Every time you visit a secure website that uses HTTPS, your browser accesses the web server's digital certificate that was issued by a certificate authority such as VeriSign. This certificate confirms that the web server is who they say they are. The digital certificate contains the web server's public key, which the browser uses to encrypt messages sent to the web server. The web server can then use its private key to decrypt these messages. The first few messages between the browser and the web server establish secret session keys that then use symmetric encryption throughout the remainder of the session to encrypt messages in both directions. The process of establishing these session keys and secure communication is called a TLS handshake. Typically, all of this happens without the user's knowledge.

What if a certificate has been compromised in some way? A CRL (certificate revocation list) is a list of certificates that have been revoked before their originally scheduled expiration date. A certificate will be revoked if the key specified in the certificate has been compromised and is no longer valid, or if the user specified in the certificate no longer has the authority to use the key. For example, if an employee has been assigned a certificate by a company and then later quits or is fired, the CA will revoke the certificate and place the certificate ID on the CRL. The employee will no longer be able to send secure documents using this certificate. Actually, this will be true only if the software takes the time to *check* each certificate against the CRL. The decision as to whether taking the time to perform this check is worth the effort might depend on the importance of the signed document.

Companies that need to conduct secure transactions will often invest in their own PKI systems. Because PKI systems are specialized and relatively involved, they are typically very expensive. Before purchasing a PKI system, a company needs to consider whether the transactions that need to be secure will stay on their internal network, or whether they need to traverse external networks. External transactions, such as ecommerce transactions, require a system that can interoperate with the systems of other companies. The company must also consider the size of the application requiring secure transactions. If you have a small number of employees (roughly, fewer than 100), it might be more economical to purchase a PKI system that is embedded within an application. If the number of employees is larger (more than 100), then a PKI system that supports a complete system of key and certificate storage and management might be more useful.

As good as PKI sounds, it does have its problems. For one thing, it's expensive. Typical PKI systems cost tens of thousands of dollars for medium-sized businesses. Moreover, many PKI systems are proprietary and do not interact well with other PKI systems. On the positive side, the price of PKI technology, like that of most technologies, is constantly dropping. In addition, the IETF continues to work on standards to which future PKI systems can adhere. It is hoped that these new standards will increase the possibility that PKI systems will interoperate.

Technologies That Use Encryption

Basic encryption and decryption techniques have come a long way since their inception. While today's techniques often employ state-of-the-art encryption and decryption methods, many of these methods are founded on the earlier techniques. Let's examine some additional advances in cryptography, beginning with digital signatures.

Digital Signatures

When participating in financial or legal transactions, you often prove your identity through a handwritten signature or by entering a PIN (personal identification number). But how can you prove your identity when signing an electronic document so that later, you and others can know it is the document you signed, that you are the one who signed it, and that it has not been altered since you signed it?

To authenticate electronic documents as yours, you need to create a digital signature. A **digital signature** is a security procedure that uses public key cryptography and assigns a code to a document for which you alone have the key. The process involves the following steps:

1. The document is hashed using a hashing algorithm such as SHA-3. If either the document or the hash is altered, they will not match, and others will know the document is not yours.

2. The hash is encrypted using your private key. The encrypted hash becomes the digital signature and is either stored with the document or transmitted with the document.

3. Later, when someone needs to verify this is the document you signed, a new hash is created from the document. The original hash, which was encrypted with your private key, is decrypted with your public key, and the two hashes are compared. If the two hashes agree, the data was not tampered with, and the user's digital signature is valid.

One drawback to this system is that if someone discovers your private key, a digital signature could be forged. Another challenge involves the complexity of creating and managing key pairs. What if someone doesn't have a public key and private key pair, or doesn't have the resources to post the public key as needed? While the digital signature technique requires a key pair, an e-signature does not. An e-signature can be a digital version of a handwritten signature or, alternatively, it might consist of any electronic sound, symbol, or process intended by the user to approve or accept the terms of an agreement and typically is associated with other identifying information, such as the user's device IP address.

In 2000, the U.S. government approved the ESIGN (Electronic Signatures in Global and National Commerce) Act, and similar legislation has long been in place for many other countries as well. This legislation grants digital signatures and e-signatures in electronic documents the same legal standing as that of handwritten signatures on pieces of paper. It is important to note, however, there are restrictions and exceptions. For example, although home loans and mortgages may be digitally signed, documents such as divorce agreements, wills, and adoption contracts still need old-fashioned, pen-and-paper signatures.

Tunneling Protocols

One of the more serious problems with the Internet is its lack of security. Whenever data is transmitted, it is susceptible to interception. Retailers have solved part of the problem by using encryption techniques to secure many communications on their websites. Businesses that want their employees to access the corporate or cloud network from a remote site have found a similar solution: virtual private networks.

A **VPN (virtual private network)** is a data network connection that makes use of the public Internet but maintains privacy using a tunneling protocol and security procedures. A **tunneling protocol**, such as L2TP (Layer 2 Tunneling Protocol), packages data for transport between the two endpoints of the connection so the packaged messages are treated as local transmissions on both ends of the tunnel. When combined with IPsec (Internet Protocol Security) for encryption, the L2TP/IPsec configuration provides secure communications for a VPN. **IPsec (IP Security)** is a set of protocols developed by the IETF (Internet Engineering Task Force) to support the secure exchange of data packets at the network layer. For IPsec to work, both sender and receiver must exchange public encryption keys. You'll learn more about VPNs in Chapter 10.

Remember this...

> The CIA triad consists of confidentiality, which ensures data can only be viewed by its intended recipient or at its intended destination; integrity, which ensures the data that is received is the same as the data that was sent; and availability, which ensures data is accessible to the intended recipient when needed.

> Data can be classified according to its sensitivity into public, private, or sensitive categories.

> Many industry-based requirements exist to guide companies in their data security efforts, and auditing processes help ensure that companies abide by these regulations.

> Cryptography is the study and practice of creating and using encryption and decryption techniques. Early cryptography algorithms used the same key for both encryption and decryption, a technique called symmetric encryption. Newer techniques, called public key cryptography or asymmetric encryption, allow the use of two different but mathematically related keys where one key can encrypt the data, and the second key can decrypt the data.

> PKI (public key infrastructure) is the combination of encryption techniques, software, and services that involves all the necessary pieces to support digital certificates, certificate authorities, and public key generation, storage, and management.

> A digital certificate, or simply a certificate, is an electronic document similar to a passport that establishes your credentials when you are performing transactions on the web.

> Modern technologies that use encryption include digital signatures and tunneling protocols.

Self-check

7. What security concept should you most likely consider when traveling with sensitive customer data saved on your laptop?
   a. Data integrity
   b. Data in transit
   c. Data sovereignty
   d. Data availability

8. Which of the following is a stream cipher?
   a. 3DES
   b. RC4
   c. AES
   d. DES

9. If data is encrypted with a company's public key, what information is needed to decrypt that data?
   a. The company's certificate
   b. The company's digital signature
   c. The company's public key
   d. The company's private key

Check your answers at the end of this chapter.

Section 8-4: IAM (Identity and Access Management)

Controlling access to a computer network involves deciding and then limiting who can use the system, when they can access it, and how the system can be used. Consider a large corporation with many levels of employees. Those who do not need to interact with sensitive data, such as payroll information, should not have access to that level of data. Likewise, accounting employees do not need access to corporate research programs meant for top-level executives, and managers do not need access across departments. Many companies wisely limit the information access capabilities of even top-level management.

How are these access privileges managed? This is the purpose of IAM. **IAM (identity and access management)** tools can provide secure and controlled access to local and distributed resources, requiring sophisticated verification processes and granular access control. For example, a company running a hybrid cloud environment can use IAM to provide remote workers with needed access to cloud and on-prem resources while supporting activity monitoring and on-demand control to make privilege changes. Let's explore how IAM is used to manage access rights on a network.

Access Rights

IAM works by creating an identity for each object (users, servers, and other resources) that it manages. Multiple layers of controls are implemented to manage access to data and other network resources. Most of these tools are categorized according to their primary task in managing a user's access, authorizing a user's privileges, or tracking a user's activities.

IAM systems provide flexibility in the assignment of access rights to individuals or groups. **Access rights** define the network resources that a user or group of users can interact with and what they can do with those resources. Protected resources might include data, applications, or configuration rights on infrastructure devices.

In a practice called **principle of least privilege**, a company's computer network specialists and top levels of

management often work together to decide how the company should be organized into information access groups. Then they resolve each group's access rights and determine who should be included in each group, which are specified and formally documented in an access control policy. As you may recall from Chapter 6, network operating systems such as Windows Server can be very useful in the task of creating such workgroups and assigning access rights. Management and administrators should ensure that no one is given more access rights that what is required to do their job.

Access rights are managed through a framework of controls that are collectively referred to as **AAA (authentication, authorization, and accounting)** (pronounced *triple-A*). The three components of AAA are:

> **Authentication**—Authentication is the process of verifying a user's credentials (typically a username and password) to grant the user access to secured resources on a system or network. In other words, authentication asks the question, "Who are you?"

> **Authorization**—Once a user has access to the network, authorization processes determine what the user can or cannot do with network resources. In other words, authorization asks the question, "What are you allowed to do?"

> **Accounting**—The network's accounting system logs users' access and activities on the network. In other words, accounting asks, "What did you do?" The records that are kept in these logs are later audited, either internally or by an outside entity, to ensure compliance with existing organizational rules or external laws and regulations.

Authentication

Almost every system that stores sensitive or confidential data requires an authorized user to enter a password,

PIN, or other authentication factor to gain access to the system. Common authentication factors include:

> **Something you know**—Password, PIN, or biographical data

> **Something you have**—ATM card, ID badge, or key

> **Something you are**—Fingerprint, facial pattern, or iris pattern

> **Somewhere you are**—Location in a specific geographical location, building, or a secured closet

> **Something you do**—The specific way you type, speak, or walk

Note

An authentication factor that relies on "something you are" uses biometrics. **Biometrics** is a technology that performs biorecognition access in which a device scans an individual's unique physical characteristics, such as iris color patterns or hand geometry, to verify the person's identity.

For greater security, some systems require **MFA (multifactor authentication)**, where users must supply two or more authentication factors to verify their identity. Providing duplicates of a single authentication factor—a password and PIN from the "something you know category"—is not sufficient. Instead, MFA requires at least two authentication factors from different categories. A common scenario is where a user must provide something and know something. They might have to provide a one-time code from an authenticator app on their smartphone (something they have) as well as enter the correct password (something they know).

Although providing a password is the most common form of authentication, it is also one of the weakest as passwords are easily compromised. Passwords can be stored in insecure locations, but more often the password is too simple and someone can guess it to gain access. You can increase your password security by using and educating network users on the following guidelines:

> Never use the default password and change your password immediately if you suspect one has been compromised.

> Use a different password for every account. Though inconvenient, this strategy will provide you with greater protection should one of your accounts become compromised.

> Do not use personal information in your password, such as your name or the names of partner, children, and pets, or other information that can be easily guessed or publicly found.

> Misspell words or substitute some letters for numbers and symbols. Avoid obvious substitutions like @ for a and $ for s.

> Combine uppercase and lowercase letters with numbers and symbols in preferably a random pattern.

> Make sure the password is longer than ten to twelve characters—the longer the better. Statistically speaking, a shorter password is more vulnerable than a longer password, even if the longer password is less complex.

> Do not share your password with others under any circumstances; doing so invites trouble and misuse. If someone else needs access to a system, they should have their own credentials.

> Store your passwords in a safe place. Never store passwords in an unencrypted spreadsheet or document, or in a web browser. Many browsers store passwords in plaintext and can be easily hacked. Instead, consider using a password manager such as LastPass (*lastpass.com*), KeePass (*keepass.info*), or 1Password (*1password.com*). Figure 8-19 shows the LastPass vault.

Network administrators can enforce password rules for network users in the NOS or in their cloud's IAM service, as shown in Figure 8-20. Here, the network administrator can require a user to create a password, give the user the ability to change their own password, and require the user to select a password of a particular length and complexity.

Hashing

Too commonly, login credentials such as passwords are stored in plaintext in a database, spreadsheet, or other file making them vulnerable to intrusion. To increase password security, systems store passwords in a coded form called a hash that isn't designed to be decrypted. **Hashing** means to transform data through an algorithm that converts the data into a fixed-digit code and is mostly used to ensure data integrity—or verify the data, such as a downloaded file, exactly matches what is expected. Changing even a single character in the original data results in an entirely different hash that is completely unrelated to the first hash. Therefore, hashing is particularly sensitive to even minor alterations in the source data.

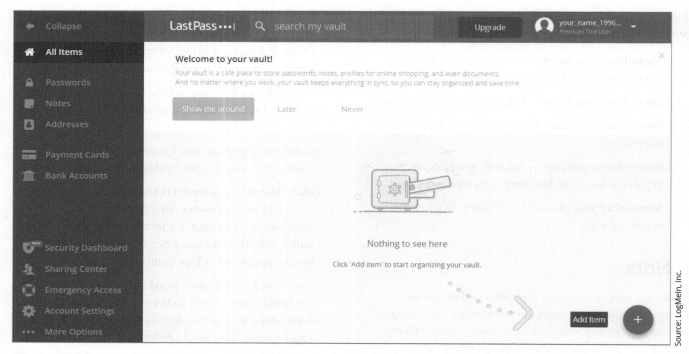

Figure 8-19   Store passwords, notes, and form information securely in the LastPass vault

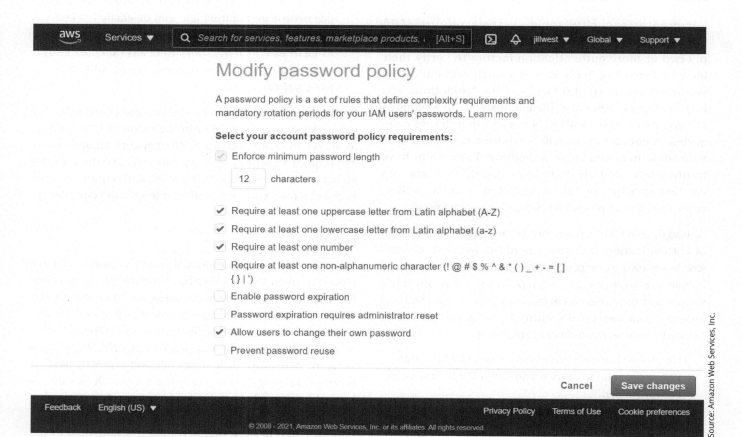

Figure 8-20   Controlling a user password with a typical network operating system

All Things Considered

Thought Experiment

Several hashing tools are available free online. One website, *onlinemd5.com*, lets you choose between three hashing algorithms: MD5 (an older, outdated hashing algorithm), SHA-1, and SHA-256. Complete the following steps:

1. In your browser, go to **onlinemd5.com**. The first tool shown on this page can hash an entire file, but you'll practice with smaller portions of text. Scroll down to the *MD5 & SHA1 Hash Generator For Text box* (see Figure 8-21).

2. **MD5** should be selected by default. Type a string of text into the box and watch the hash output calculate automatically as you type. What do you notice about the length of the string hash as you enter each additional letter?

3. Copy the final string hash into a text document for later comparison. Windows Notepad works well for this purpose.

4. Select **SHA1** and copy the new string hash into your text document for comparison.

5. Select **SHA-256** and copy the new string hash into your text document for comparison. Which string hash is longer? Why do you think that is?

6. Change exactly one character in your original text. What happens to the string hash?

7. Just a single character change results in a completely different hash. What if your original text is much longer than what you have now? Type a lot more text into the hash generator. What happens to the string hash?

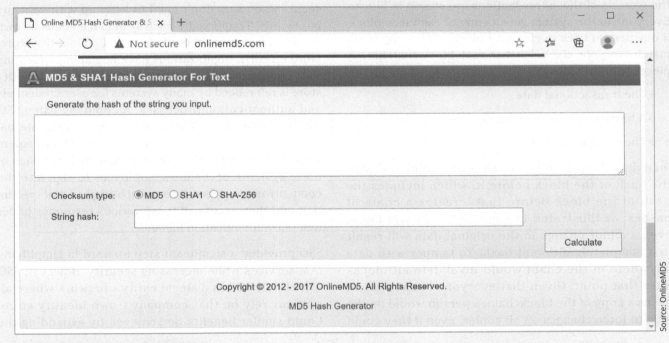

Figure 8-21   Input text to hash

If a secure hashing algorithm is used, such as SHA-2 or SHA-3 (Secure Hashing Algorithm), hashing is believed to be impossible to reverse. Anyone who gets access to this hashed password file will discover only unreadable text. This hashing technique is the reason that, when you forget your password, a technician cannot simply read a file and tell you what the forgotten password is. The password must be reset to something new.

How then does the system know when you have entered the correct password? When a user enters their login ID and password, the password is hashed and compared with the entry in the hashed password file. If the two hashes match, the login is allowed.

Blockchain

Blockchain is a key part of what makes cryptocurrencies work. Blockchain can also be used to store other kinds of transactions and data, such as property ownership or business contracts.

How does blockchain use hashing, and what makes it such a breakthrough in security technologies? Traditionally, businesses have relied on centralized record keeping where one organization (such as a government or an authorized agency) oversees management of data and keeping it safe. Blockchain takes the opposite approach and relies on decentralized, or distributed, data to ensure that data can't be changed without everyone knowing about it. As transactions, such as sales, occur, the records of those transactions are stored in blocks. Everyone in the system gets a copy of each new block. If one person tries to change a block, their copy won't match everyone else's. Further, each block contains key pieces of information:

> The transactional data

> A hash of the previous block

> The block's own hash

Including the previous block's hash, which includes the hash of the block before it, which includes the hash of the block before that, creates a chain of hashes, as illustrated in Figure 8-22. As you know, even a minor change in the original data will result in a completely different hash. To tamper with data anywhere in the chain would invalidate all blocks after that point. Given that everyone in the system keeps a copy of the blockchain, a person would not be able to force changes on all copies, even if they could

recalculate all blocks to apparently show a valid hash through the rest of the chain.

Single Sign-On (SSO) and Federated Identity Management (FIM)

As people have become more reliant on Internet-based services that require a different username and password for every account, many people have become lax in the way they manage passwords. Security researchers have found that people commonly duplicate their passwords across multiple accounts. When a hacked database of user credentials is posted on the dark web, hackers know that a high percentage of these credentials will work on other sensitive websites, such as bank accounts and employer networks. The compromised site might have informed its users to change their passwords, but other sites where users implemented the same passwords are also vulnerable.

Part of the solution to this problem lies in simplifying authentication requirements without compromising security so users don't need to keep up with so many passwords. Traditionally, each system maintains its own repository of user credentials called an identity store. More recently, organizations have begun implementing SSO (single sign-on) systems where a single identity store is referenced by many systems for user credentials and authentication processes. A company using SSO that maintains various systems for HR, payroll, internal communications, and shift scheduling would not require employees to maintain separate credentials for each of these systems. SSO allows employees to sign into the company network one time using a single set of credentials and then access all these various resources under that one authentication instance.

SSO provided a significant step forward in simplifying IAM services while increasing security. However, SSO works only within a single entity's network where all systems rely on that company's own identity store. Could similar benefits be achieved by expanding the

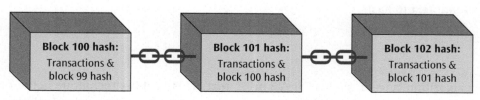

Figure 8-22 Each block contains the previous block's hash

same concept outside the organization and borrowing someone else's identity store? That's where FIM (federated identity management), also known as federated SSO or federation, comes in.

FIM (federated identity management) allows many companies to run their authentication processes against a single identity store. For example, you might use your social media account, such as Instagram or LinkedIn, to access resources on a different website, such as a streaming music service or a gaming app. In this case, the secondary site provides authentication to its services using the social media site's identity store. The term "federation" refers to a trusted relationship between entities. When applied to IAM, there is a trust relationship established between the social media provider's authentication system and the secondary site's credentialing system.

Note

When a social media site provides an identity store for FIM, the process is sometimes called social sign-on. Social media sites aren't the only providers of FIM identity stores. Email providers, such as Microsoft and Gmail, are another commonly used source for FIM.

Authorization

Modern computer systems and computer networks allow multiple users to access resources such as files, applications, printers, and other peripheral devices. Many times, however, the various resources of an organization are not supposed to be shared, or they should be shared only by a select group. If resource sharing is to be restricted, then a user or network administrator should set the appropriate access rights for a particular resource, which is managed by the authorization

component of the AAA framework. Most access rights have two basic parameters, *who* and *how*:

> The *who* parameter lists who or what is authorized to access the resource, typically the owner, a select group of users, and the entire user population. When managing access to cloud resources, nonhuman users include servers, applications, or network services.

> The *how* parameter can specify what a user can do when accessing the resource, and rights are listed as RWX for read, write, and execute, as follows:

> R includes read and print privileges.

> W includes write, edit, append, and delete abilities.

> X stands for execute, which means to run code, and should only be given for files that are applications. However, when used with a directory (also called a folder), execute permission can allow a user to enter the directory and access files in it.

When a user creates a file, the usual system defaults may grant the user full read, write, and execute access (or ALL) to modify or delete the file at any time. This user, or owner, may allow other users to access the file, but can limit them to having read access rights only or read and write access rights only. Figure 8-23 shows an example of how an OS assigns access rights to a resource.

As shown in the figure, a network administrator can use this feature to assign read, execute, modify, and other access control rights to a particular user.

Accounting

An important concept in accounting is **SoD (separation of duties)**, which refers to a division of labor that ensures no one person can singlehandedly compromise the security of data, finances, or other resources. To accomplish

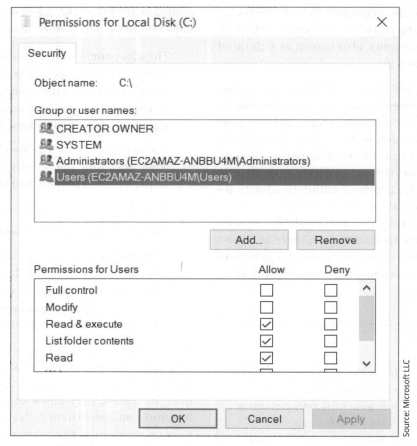

Figure 8-23 Object rights in an OS

this goal, sensitive privileges and responsibilities are distributed to multiple people. Essentially, SoD ensures that no single person is given sufficient power in a system to commit fraud or otherwise deeply compromise the system's integrity. In the context of AAA's accounting and auditing components, SoD requires that no one is responsible for monitoring and reporting on themselves, which would create a conflict of interest for that person. Accounting and auditing activities should be sufficiently spread across multiple job roles to reduce the company's vulnerability to fraud (intentional damage) or mistakes (unintentional damage).

Auditing is a core feature of the accounting component of AAA. Auditing a computer system is often a good way to deter crime and can also be useful in detecting and apprehending a person during or after the commission of a crime. As each activity, called a transaction, occurs, it is recorded into an electronic log along with the date, time, and "owner" of the transaction. If a transaction is suspected of being inappropriate, the log is scanned and this information is retrieved and reported.

Windows records events in its Event Viewer utility. In Figure 8-24, you can see an Audit Failure event related to an account that failed to log on. As you can see in the figure, Audit events appear in the Windows Logs, Security group of Event Viewer. Also, before these logon events are logged, you must use Group Policy to turn on the feature. Typical recorded events include the failure of a driver or other system components to load during system startup, possible breaches in security, and any program that might record an error while trying to perform a file operation.

Remember this...

> IAM (identity and access management) tools can provide secure and controlled access to local

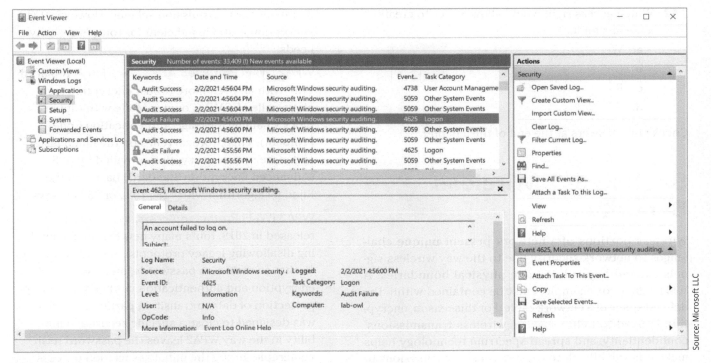

Figure 8-24   Windows Event Viewer displays a security audit event

and distributed resources, requiring sophisticated verification processes and granular access control.

> Access rights define the network resources that a user or group of users can interact with and what they can do with those resources. Access rights are managed through a framework of controls that are collectively referred to as AAA (authentication, authorization, and accounting).

> Common authentication factors include something you know, something you have, something you are, and something you do.

> If resource sharing is to be restricted, then a user or network administrator should set the appropriate access rights for a particular resource, which is managed by the authorization component of the AAA framework. Most access rights have two basic parameters, *who* and *how*.

> Auditing is a core feature of the accounting component of AAA. Auditing a computer system is often a good way to deter crime and can also be useful in detecting and apprehending a criminal during or after the commission of a crime. As each activity, called a transaction, occurs, it is recorded into an electronic log along with the date, time, and "owner" of the transaction.

Self-check

10. Which AAA concept ensures network activity can be traced back in time to retroactively confirm compliance with standards and regulations?
    a. Access rights
    b. Authorization
    c. Accounting
    d. Authentication

11. Which of the following security principles is provided by hashing?
    a. Accessibility
    b. Simplicity
    c. Confidentiality
    d. Integrity

12. Which access right would allow a user to create a file in a folder?

    a. W

    b. C

    c. R

    d. X

Check your answers at the end of this chapter.

Section 8-5: Wireless Security

Wireless portions of a network present unique challenges to network security due to the way wireless signals expand beyond defined, physical boundaries. A Wi-Fi signal, for example, can't be contained within the defined space of a network cable. For this reason, encryption is used to help preserve wireless transmissions' confidentiality, and spread spectrum technology helps make it more difficult to capture those transmissions to begin with.

Securing Wireless LANs

Wi-Fi security is provided by the following technologies:

> Security on a wireless LAN was originally provided by WEP (Wired Equivalent Privacy). Although WEP was based on relatively modern encryption techniques for the time, it suffered two serious drawbacks. First, it used weak encryption keys that were only 40 bits in length. Second, the keys were static, not dynamic. Many users felt that because of WEP's weaknesses, there was no sense in even using it, thus opening their wireless LAN transmissions to anyone within reach. Many would argue this is a poor strategy. You might still find WEP as an option on modern home routers or access points, but it should never be used.

> In order to improve upon WEP, a temporary security standard dubbed WPA (Wi-Fi Protected Access) was created. Among WPA's offerings was TKIP (Temporal Key Integrity Program). TKIP uses a 128-bit key on each packet, and it changes the key with each packet transmitted, making it difficult for an unauthorized user with a wireless device to connect to a WPA-protected signal and eventually

figure out the transmission scheme. However, TKIP encryption is still insufficient for today's security needs.

> WPA2 (Wi-Fi Protected Access, version 2) replaced TKIP with an even more robust encryption technique called CCMP (Counter Mode with Cipher Block Chaining Message Authentication Code Protocol). This protocol relies on the much faster and more secure encryption provided by AES (Advanced Encryption Standard) based on the Rijndael algorithm with 128-, 192-, or 256-bit keys.

> WPA3 (Wi-Fi Protected Access, version 3), first released in 2018, touts many new features, including disallowing legacy protocols, the ability of users to choose their own passwords, more advanced encryption and authentication methods, and better protection of data in transit. In particular, WPA3 was designed to close a specific security vulnerability in the way WPA2 leaves the password hash vulnerable during the initial association process. However, researchers are already identifying flaws in the design and security of WPA3 and believe that another round of security enhancements will be necessary.

Spread Spectrum Technology

Spread spectrum technology essentially takes the data to be transmitted and, rather than transmitting it in a fixed bandwidth, spreads it over a wider bandwidth. By spreading the data, a level of security is incorporated, thus making the eventual signal more resistant to eavesdropping or wire-tapping. One of the more common applications of spread spectrum technology is wireless communications, such as those found in Wi-Fi and Bluetooth connections. Because Bluetooth transmissions are constantly hopping channels, interference and collisions are less likely to cause significant problems with nearby Wi-Fi networks.

Frequency Hopping Spread Spectrum

Two basic spread spectrum techniques are commonly used in the communications industry today: frequency hopping spread spectrum and direct sequence spread spectrum. The idea behind FHSS (frequency hopping spread spectrum) transmission is to bounce the signal around on seemingly random frequencies rather than transmit it on one fixed frequency. Anyone trying to eavesdrop will not be able to listen because the transmission frequencies are constantly changing.

How does the intended receiver follow this random bouncing around of frequencies? The transmitter actually follows a *pseudorandom* sequence of frequencies, and the intended receiver possesses the hardware and software knowledge to follow this pseudorandom sequence.

Figure 8-25 demonstrates the basic operation of an FHSS receiver and transmitter system.

The input data enters a channel encoder, which is a device that produces an analog signal with a narrow bandwidth centered on a specific frequency. This analog signal is then modulated onto a seemingly random pattern of frequencies, using a pseudorandom number sequence as the guide. The pseudorandomly modulated signal is then transmitted to a friendly receiver. The first operation the friendly receiver performs is to "unscramble" the modulated signal, using the same pseudorandom sequence that the transmitter used to encode the signal. The unmodulated signal is then sent to the channel decoder, which performs the opposite operation of the channel encoder. The result is the original data.

Interestingly, FHSS can also be used to increase a signal's resistance to interference due to obstacles in its path. By transmitting a signal on multiple channels,

parts of the signal are more likely to get through the interference than a signal along a single channel could. Commercial wireless security systems, for example, can use FHSS to help overcome interference in commercial environments.

Direct Sequence Spread Spectrum

FHSS relies on "security by obscurity" where you attempt to protect the data by making it difficult to find. The second technique for creating a spread spectrum signal to secure communications is direct sequence spread spectrum, which includes a coding method to further secure data in transit. DSSS (direct sequence spread spectrum) spreads the transmission of a signal over a range of frequencies after coding the data using mathematical values. To understand how this works for a basic type of DSSS, you first need to understand the logical function called XOR. XOR (exclusive-OR) is a logical operation that combines two bits and produces a single bit as the result. When the two bits match, you get 0, and when they differ, you get 1. More precisely, the following combinations are possible:

> 0 XOR 0 equals 0

> 0 XOR 1 equals 1

> 1 XOR 0 equals 1

> 1 XOR 1 equals 0

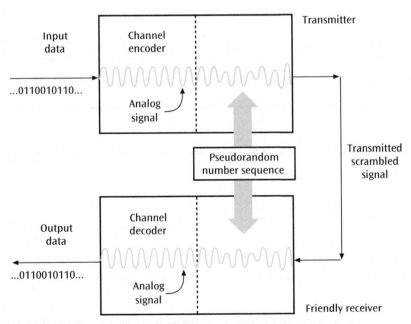

Figure 8-25 Basic operation of a frequency hopping spread spectrum receiver and transmitter system

Figure 8-26 shows that, as the original data is input into a direct sequence modulator, it is XORed with a pseudorandom bit stream called a chipping code. Thus, the output of the direct sequence modulator is the result of the XOR between the input data and the chipping code. When the data arrives at the intended receiver, the spread spectrum signal is again XORed with the same chipping code that was used during the transmission of the signal. The result of this XOR at the receiving end is the original data. Zigbee, a wireless technology used by many IoT devices, relies on DSSS.

While obscurity by itself is not considered a reliable security technique for critical data, spread spectrum technologies continue to be incorporated into wireless security strategies to help protect data in transit.

(Advanced Encryption Standard) based on the Rijndael algorithm with 128-, 192-, or 256-bit keys. WPA3 was designed to close a specific security vulnerability in the way WPA2 leaves the password hash vulnerable during the initial association process.

> Spread spectrum technology essentially takes the data to be transmitted and, rather than transmitting it in a fixed bandwidth, spreads it over a wider bandwidth. By spreading the data, a level of security is incorporated, thus making the eventual signal more resistant to eavesdropping or wire-tapping. Two basic spread spectrum techniques are commonly used in the communications industry today: frequency hopping spread spectrum and direct sequence spread spectrum.

Remember this...

> WPA2 (Wi-Fi Protected Access, version 2) replaced TKIP with an even more robust encryption technique called CCMP (Counter Mode with Cipher Block Chaining Message Authentication Code Protocol) and relies on the much faster and more secure encryption provided by AES

Self-check

13. Which Wi-Fi security technique uses TKIP?

    a. WEP

    b. WPA3

    c. WPA

    d. WPA2

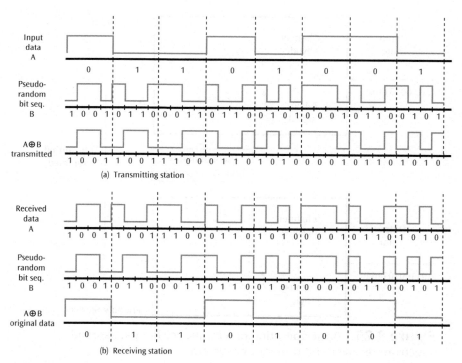

Figure 8-26 Example of binary data as it is converted into a direct sequence spread spectrum and back

14. What element does DSSS use to make it more
secure than FHSS?

    a. Signal bouncing

    b. Narrow bandwidth

    c. Random frequencies

    d. Coding method

Check your answers at the end of this chapter.

Summary

Section 8-1: Network Security Risks

> As a result of substantial attacks on computers and networks in recent years, experts monitor threats used to exploit loopholes and vulnerabilities in networks and other systems. An attacker's goal is to somehow gain access to a system and then steal or damage data. Attackers might use one or more of many available attack vectors, including compromising users, compromising software, compromising network or system availability, or compromising accounts.

> A risk assessment is an inventory that identifies all assets that must be protected from identified threats. These assets will be classified according to sensitivity to risk factors, value to the organization, and ownership of each asset.

> Risks will be tracked in a risk register as they are identified and evaluated. This provides documentation that might be required for compliance with certain regulations.

> A security policy for network users identifies security goals, risks, levels of authority, designated security coordinator and team members, responsibilities for each team member, and responsibilities for each employee. An incident response plan specifically defines the characteristics of an event that qualifies as a formal incident and the steps that should be followed as a result.

Section 8-2: Network Security Technologies

> Physical security strategies for a network can be broadly categorized as prevention methods and detection methods. The physical protection of a computer system or network includes protecting the equipment from physical damage caused by fire, floods, earthquakes, power surges, vandalism, and similar threats. Additional prevention techniques protect networks and computer systems from unauthorized access. However, no security system is perfect, and network breaches happen. It's important to detect these problems quickly and respond appropriately.

> Anti-malware software might use any of the following techniques to detect malware and protect the system against malware attacks: scanning, behavior monitoring, sandboxing, and removal.

> A proxy server is software that serves as an intermediary between internal resources and external users.

> ACLs (access control lists) determine which traffic is allowed to cross the device and which traffic is dropped. An ACL acts like a filter to instruct the device to allow or deny traffic according to the protocol used, the source or destination IP address, or the TCP or UDP port number.

> A firewall is a system or combination of systems that supports an access control policy between two networks or between two segments of a network.

> While you won't need to install an actual firewall on the cloud-based portions of your network, you still need firewall functions to protect cloud resources.

Most of the time, the cloud provider builds these tools into the relevant cloud resources.

> Many companies use an IDS (intrusion detection system) or an IPS (intrusion prevention system) to monitor data flow and system requests into, out of, and throughout their networks. If unusual activity is noticed, protective action can be taken immediately.

Section 8-3: Data Security Technologies

> The CIA triad consists of confidentiality, which ensures data can only be viewed by its intended recipient or at its intended destination; integrity, which ensures the data that is received is the same as the data that was sent; and availability, which ensures data is accessible to the intended recipient when needed.

> Data can be classified according to its sensitivity into public, private, or sensitive categories.

> Many industry-based requirements exist to guide companies in their data security efforts, and auditing processes help ensure that companies abide by these regulations.

> Cryptography is the study and practice of creating and using encryption and decryption techniques. Early cryptography algorithms used the same key for both encryption and decryption, a technique called symmetric encryption. Newer techniques, called public key cryptography or asymmetric encryption, allow the use of two different but mathematically related keys where one key can encrypt the data, and the second key can decrypt the data.

> PKI (public key infrastructure) is the combination of encryption techniques, software, and services that involves all the necessary pieces to support digital certificates, certificate authorities, and public key generation, storage, and management.

> A digital certificate, or simply a certificate, is an electronic document similar to a passport that establishes your credentials when you are performing transactions on the web.

> Modern technologies that use encryption include digital signatures and tunneling protocols.

Section 8-4: IAM (Identity and Access Management)

> IAM (identity and access management) tools can provide secure and controlled access to local and distributed resources, requiring sophisticated verification processes and granular access control.

> Access rights define the network resources that a user or group of users can interact with and what they can do with those resources. Access rights are managed through a framework of controls that are collectively referred to as AAA (authentication, authorization, and accounting).

> Common authentication factors include something you know, something you have, something you are, and something you do.

> If resource sharing is to be restricted, then a user or network administrator should set the appropriate access rights for a particular resource, which is managed by the authorization component of the AAA framework. Most access rights have two basic parameters, who and how.

> Auditing is a core feature of the accounting component of AAA. Auditing a computer system is often a good way to deter crime and can also be useful in detecting and apprehending a criminal during or after the commission of a crime. As each activity, called a transaction, occurs, it is recorded into an electronic log along with the date, time, and "owner" of the transaction.

Section 8-5: Wireless Security

❯ WPA2 (Wi-Fi Protected Access, version 2) replaced TKIP with an even more robust encryption technique called CCMP (Counter Mode with Cipher Block Chaining Message Authentication Code Protocol) and relies on the much faster and more secure encryption provided by AES (Advanced Encryption Standard) based on the Rijndael algorithm with 128-, 192-, or 256-bit keys. WPA3 was designed to close a specific security vulnerability in the way WPA2 leaves the password hash vulnerable during the initial association process.

❯ Spread spectrum technology essentially takes the data to be transmitted and, rather than transmitting it in a fixed bandwidth, spreads it over a wider bandwidth. By spreading the data, a level of security is incorporated, thus making the eventual signal more resistant to eavesdropping or wire-tapping. Two basic spread spectrum techniques are commonly used in the communications industry today: frequency hopping spread spectrum and direct sequence spread spectrum.

Key Terms

For definitions of key terms, see the Glossary near the end of the book.

3DES (triple-DES)

AAA (authentication, authorization, and accounting)

access rights

accounting

ACL (access control list)

AES (Advanced Encryption Standard)

application layer firewall

asymmetric encryption

authentication

authorization

biometrics

blockchain

breach

CA (certificate authority)

certificate

CIA (confidentiality, integrity, and availability) triad

ciphertext

cryptography

data sovereignty

DDoS (distributed denial-of-service) attack

defense in depth

DES (Data Encryption Standard)

device hardening

digital signature

DoS (denial-of-service) attack

DSSS (direct sequence spread spectrum)

encryption algorithm

FHSS (frequency hopping spread spectrum)

FIM (federated identity management)

FIM (file integrity monitoring)

hashing

IAM (identity and access management)

IDS (intrusion detection system)

incident response plan

IPS (intrusion prevention system)

IPsec (IP Security)

key

malware

MFA (multifactor authentication)

monoalphabetic substitution-based cipher

phishing

PKI (public key infrastructure)

plaintext

polyalphabetic substitution-based cipher

principle of least privilege

proxy server

public key cryptography

ransomware

risk register

security policy

shared responsibility model

social engineering attack

SoD (separation of duties)

spread spectrum technology

SSO (single sign-on)

symmetric encryption

threat

TKIP (Temporal Key Integrity Program)

TLS (Transport Layer Security)

transposition-based cipher

tunneling protocol

VPN (virtual private network)

vulnerability

WEP (Wired Equivalent Privacy)

WPA (Wi-Fi Protected Access)

WPA2 (Wi-Fi Protected Access, version 2)

WPA3 (Wi-Fi Protected Access, version 3)

Review Questions

1. What kind of attack targets a server's OS?

   a. Keylogger

   b. Phishing

   c. Social engineering

   d. Rootkit

2. In a DDoS attack, the flood of messages to the target website come from _____ servers.

   a. infected

   b. uninfected

   c. spoofed

   d. the hacker's

3. Which of the following does NOT provide physical security?

   a. Access badge

   b. Firewall

   c. Video camera

   d. Tamper detection

4. Which of these devices does NOT prevent access to a protected area?

   a. IPS

   b. Firewall

   c. Keypad

   d. IDS

5. Which of the following is the most secure password?

   a. p@$$w0rd

   b. $t@rw@r$

   c. 07041776

   d. yellowMonthMagneficant

6. Which of these encryption techniques does NOT rely on a key?

   a. Polyalphabetic substitution-based cipher

   b. Data Encryption Standard

   c. Monoalphabetic substitution-based cipher

   d. Transposition-based cipher

7. Which principle, if adequately followed, ensures a person cannot write their own employee evaluation report?

   a. Shared responsibility model

   b. Separation of duties

   c. Defense in depth

   d. Principle of least privilege

8. A digital signature supports which component of the CIA triad?

   a. Accountability

   b. Availability

   c. Confidentiality

   d. Integrity

9. After a digital signature is created, what information is needed to access the hash stored in the digital signature?

   a. The signer's private key

   b. The signer's public key

   c. The document's hash

   d. The lawyer's private key

10. Which protocol is used to secure HTTP?

   a. TLS

   b. SSH

   c. RDP

   d. IPsec

11. You have forgotten your password, so you call the help desk and ask the representative to retrieve your password. After a few moments, the help desk representative tells you your forgotten password. What do you now know about the company's password storage method?

    a. Passwords are encrypted.

    b. Passwords aren't hashed.

    c. Passwords are hashed.

    d. Passwords aren't encrypted.

12. Which of the following characteristics can a firewall NOT use to filter network traffic?

    a. Port number

    b. IP address

    c. Protocol

    d. Username

13. Which of the following is NOT an acceptable risk response strategy?

    a. Avoid   c. Accept

    b. Evaluate   d. Transfer

14. Which AWS resource filters traffic to an EC2 instance?

    a. Firewall   c. NACL

    b. Security group   d. Proxy server

15. What data classification should be applied to your company's bank statements?

    a. Sensitive

    b. Public

    c. Protected

    d. Private

16. You receive an email from a business associate that has been encrypted with your public key. What information is needed to decrypt the message?

    a. Your associate's public key

    b. Your associate's private key

    c. Your private key

    d. Your public key

17. You receive a document from a business associate that has been encrypted with their private key. Where will your browser look to retrieve the required key to decrypt the message?

    a. The browser's digital certificate

    b. A CA

    c. The DNS server

    d. A CRL

18. What security is provided by FHSS?

    a. Obscurity   c. Confidentiality

    b. Encryption   d. Hashing

19. Which authentication technique allows a student to use their Microsoft account to access their LMS (learning management system) for schoolwork?

    a. MFA   c. RWX

    b. SSO   d. FIM

20. What component stored in a block ensures the integrity of data recorded in the blockchain?

    a. The transactional data

    b. The previous block's hash

    c. The next block's hash

    d. The block's owner

Hands-On Project 8

Configure Cloud Security in AWS

Estimated time: 30 minutes

Resources:

> Windows computer with administrative privileges or with PuTTY already installed

> AWS account (created in Chapter 1)

> Internet access

›Context:

In Chapter 1, you created an AWS account and performed some tasks in the cloud. In Chapter 7, you created an EC2 instance and remoted into that instance using PuTTY and SSH. In this project, you will configure security resources in the cloud, including security groups and NACLs (network ACLs). Use the same AWS account you created in Chapter 1.

Note

Depending on the status of your account and the selections you make during this project, an EC2 instance and its supporting resources (such as storage) can deplete your credits or accrue charges. Make sure to follow these steps carefully and delete all created resources at the end of this project.

Complete the following steps to create your EC2 instance for this project:

1. Sign into your AWS management console. If you're using an AWS Academy classroom, you'll need to access your AWS management console through your AWS Academy classroom. If you're using a standard AWS account, sign in directly at **aws.amazon.com**.

2. Go to the EC2 dashboard and click the orange **Launch instance** button, and then click **Launch instance** from the list.

3. Select the free tier eligible **Amazon Linux 2 AMI**. Click through the following screens:

   a. Keep the default selection of the free tier eligible t2.micro instance type and click **Next: Configuration Instance Details**.

   b. Keep all instance details default settings and click **Next: Add Storage**.

   c. Keep storage default settings and click **Next: Add Tags**.

   d. Don't add any tags. Click **Next: Configure Security Group**.

Security groups provide a secure perimeter around each EC2 instance. Each instance can be assigned up to five security groups. A security group blocks all traffic and will only allow traffic that is explicitly allowed. As you can see, EC2 assumes you will want to SSH into your Linux EC2 instance, and it automatically suggests a rule that will allow SSH from any IP address (0.0.0.0/0) into your EC2 instance through port 22. To explore some of your options here, complete the following steps:

4. Without changing the rule type, what are three other protocols you could choose for rules in your security group?

5. What happens when you change the source to **My IP**?

6. Change the Source back to **Anywhere** and launch your instance. Be sure to use a key pair you have access to or create a new key pair—you'll need to connect with your instance shortly. If you still have it, you can use the same key you used for Hands-On Project 7. Otherwise, you can refer back to the steps in that project for guidance on how to create a new one.

Now you're ready to connect with your instance:

7. Once it's running, select your instance and click **Connect**. Click **SSH client** for detailed information about your instance. Under Example, select and copy the portion of the text from the username (ec2-user) through the URL (amazonaws.com), as shown in Figure 8-27. What is the information you copied?

8. Open PuTTY (which you used in Hands-On Project 7). Paste the information you copied from your AWS console into the Host Name field. Make sure the Port field lists **22** and make sure **SSH** is selected for the Connection type, as shown in Figure 8-28.

9. In the left pane, click **SSH** and then click **Auth**. On the right side, click **Browse** and find the private key file you chose earlier in Step 6. Click **Open**. In the security alert dialog box, click **Yes** to add your private key to PuTTY's cache.

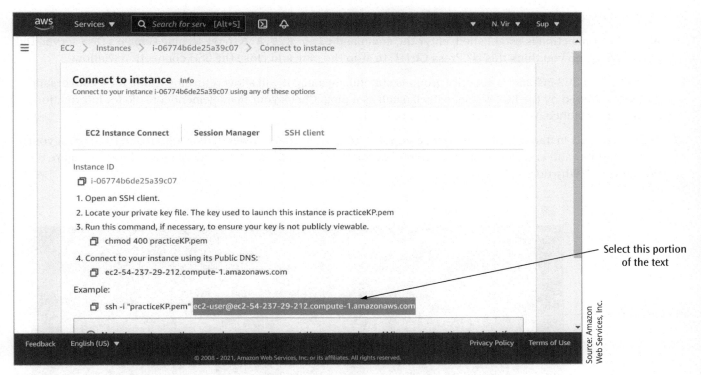

Select this portion of the text

Figure 8-27   Select the sign-in information from the username through the URL

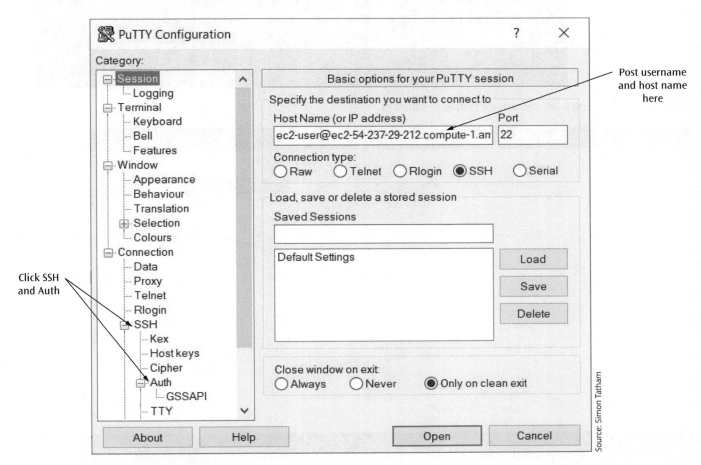

Post username and host name here

Click SSH and Auth

Figure 8-28   Paste the username and host name information from AWS in the Host Name field

Now that you're connected with your instance, let's see how well the instance's security group works:

10. When the connection is established, enter the command **ping 8.8.8.8** to try to ping Google's DNS server. Did it work? Why do you think this is? Press **Ctrl+C** to stop the ping and close the SSH connection window.

11. Recall that an EC2 instance's security group is stateful, meaning it will allow returning traffic for a conversation that was initiated by the EC2 instance itself, such as a ping. Check your management console for information about your instance. What is this instance's public IP address?

12. Try pinging this instance from your local computer. To do this, open PowerShell or Command Prompt on your local computer and enter the command **ping <instance's public IP address>**, as shown in Figure 8-29. Does it work? Why do you think this is?

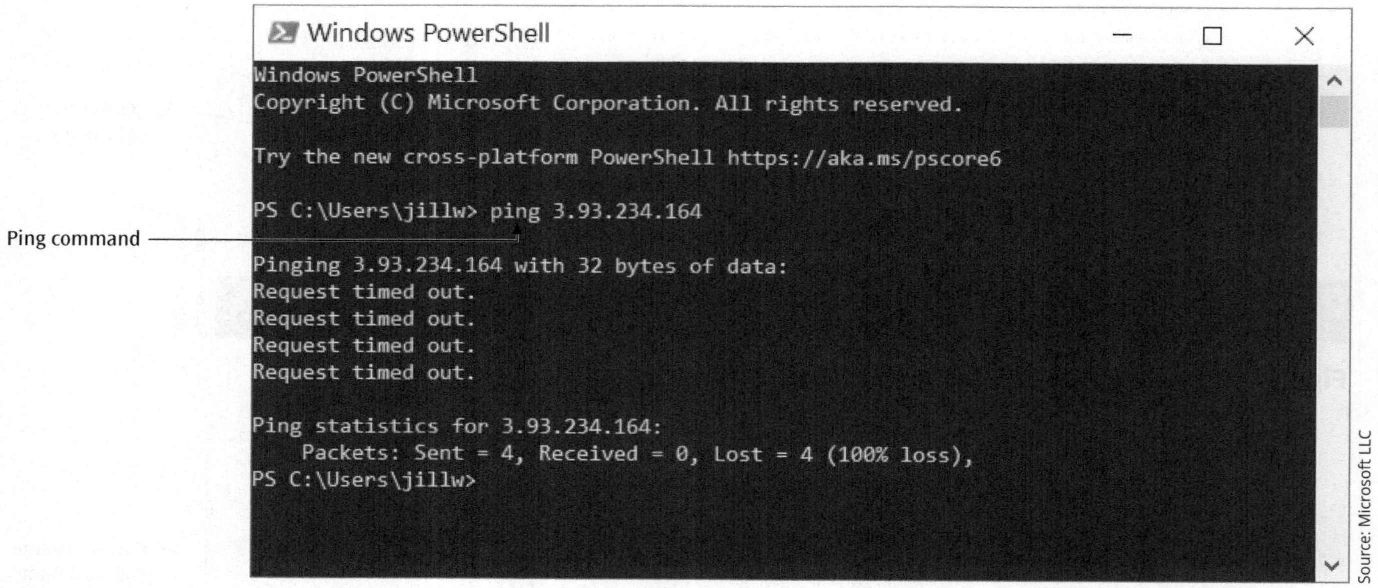

Figure 8-29 Ping your instance's public IP address

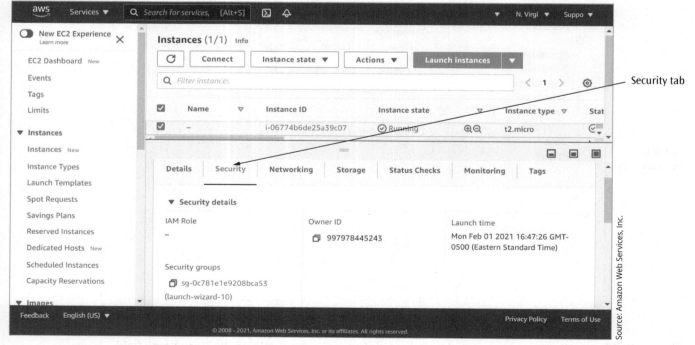

Figure 8-30 Security groups are listed on the Security tab

Let's change this. To add a new rule to your instance's security group, complete the following steps:

13. In your instance's information pane, click the **Security** tab, as shown in Figure 8-30. Scroll down to the list of Security groups and click the security group link.

14. How many inbound rules are currently listed? What traffic is currently allowed to enter the security group?

15. How many outbound rules are currently listed? What traffic is currently allowed to exit the security group?

16. On the Inbound rules tab, click **Edit inbound rules**. Add a new rule that allows **All ICMP – IPv4** traffic from any IPv4 address. (Note that the Google Chrome browser might experience a problem with this step. If so, try Mozilla Firefox.). Save the rules.

17. Try again to ping your EC2 instance from your local computer. Does it work? Why do you think this is?

By default, your VPC's (Virtual Private Cloud) NACL (network ACL) allows all traffic. You can add allow or deny rules to further control traffic into and out of each subnet. Recall that NACL rules are stateless, meaning a protocol's traffic must be allowed in both directions for a conversation such as ping to succeed. Complete the following steps:

18. Return to your instance's information pane and click the **Networking** tab. Locate and click the instance's VPC ID. This takes you to the VPC in the VPC dashboard.

19. Select the VPC listed here (there should just be one). In the VPC's information pane, click the link for the **Main network ACL**. This takes you to the NACL list.

20. Select the NACL listed here (there should just be one). In the NACL's information pane, click the **Inbound rules** tab. What inbound rules are listed here?

Notice that these rules seem contradictory—why would one rule allow all traffic and the next rule deny all traffic? Each rule is assigned a priority. The NACL checks each rule in succession from highest priority to lowest priority. As soon as a rule is found that matches the traffic, that rule is applied. To block ICMP traffic (which is currently allowed by both the NACL and the security group), complete the following steps:

21. Click **Edit inbound rules** and then click **Add new rule**. The new rule will need to be a higher priority than the existing "allow all traffic" rule that is rated at 100. Choose a number below 100 for your new rule. Continue configuring the rule so it will block ICMP – IPv4 traffic from all sources. Be sure to save your changes. **Take a screenshot** of your new NACL inbound rule; submit this visual with your answers to this project's questions.

22. If your goal is only to block outside computers from pinging your EC2 instance, is this NACL inbound rule sufficient to accomplish your goal, or do you also need a corresponding outbound rule?

23. Try again to ping your EC2 instance from your local computer. Does it work? Why do you think this is?

24. Return to your list of instances in EC2. Recall that turning the instance off does not delete any resources in your AWS cloud. In some cases, you continue to be charged for resources even if they're turned off. To delete your instance, select the instance, click **Instance state**, and click **Terminate instance**. Click **Terminate**. What is the instance state now?

Note

Depending on the status of your account and the selections you made during the AWS projects, your EC2 instance and its supporting resources (such as storage) can deplete your credits or accrue charges. Double-check to make sure you've terminated all resources you created in the AWS projects.

Reflection Discussion 8

Many people are cautious of using cloud services due to security concerns, especially considering some highly publicized cloud-based data breaches in recent years. Conduct some research online to find discussions and articles posted by cloud security professionals discussing current cloud security developments, concerns, and solutions. Then answer the following questions:

> What do you think are the biggest concerns relative to security in the cloud?

> How does cloud increase a network's security risks?

> How do cloud providers help mitigate security risks for customers' data and resources hosted in the cloud?

Go to the discussion forum in your school's LMS (learning management system). Write a post of at least 100 words discussing your thoughts about cloud security. Then respond to two of your classmates' threads with posts of at least 50 words discussing their comments and ideas. Use complete sentences, and check your grammar and spelling. Try to ask open-ended questions that encourage discussion, and remember to respond to people who post on your thread. Use the rubric in Table 8-2 to help you understand what is expected of your work for this assignment.

Table 8-2 Grading rubric for Reflection Discussion 8

Task	Novice	Competent	Proficient	Earned
Initial post	Generalized statements addressing cloud security **30 points**	Some specific statements with supporting evidence about cloud security strengths and weaknesses **40 points**	Self-reflective discussion with specific and thoughtful statements and supporting evidence about the ways cloud use both increases and decreases various network security risks **50 points**	
Initial post: Mechanics	• Length < 100 words • Several grammar and spelling errors **5 points**	• Length = 100 words • Occasional grammar and spelling errors **7 points**	• Length > 100 words • Appropriate grammar and spelling **10 points**	
Response 1	Brief response showing little engagement or critical thinking **5 points**	Detailed response with specific contributions to the discussion **10 points**	Thoughtful response with specific examples or details and open-ended questions that invite deeper discussion of the topic **15 points**	
Response 2	Brief response showing little engagement or critical thinking **5 points**	Detailed response with specific contributions to the discussion **10 points**	Thoughtful response with specific examples or details and open-ended questions that invite deeper discussion of the topic **15 points**	
Both responses: Mechanics	• Length < 50 words each • Several grammar and spelling errors **5 points**	• Length = 50 words each • Occasional grammar and spelling errors **7 points**	• Length > 50 words each • Appropriate grammar and spelling **10 points**	
			Total	

Solutions to Self-Check Questions

Section 8-1: Network Security Risks

1. What type of attack is most likely to result in the victim paying money to the attacker?

Answer: b. Ransomware

Explanation: Malware that holds a computer hostage unless the user pays a ransom to remove the malware is then called ransomware.

2. Which technique relies on exploitation of vulnerabilities?

Answer: a. Penetration testing

Explanation: A penetration test is a simulated attack that begins with a vulnerability scan and then attempts to exploit identified vulnerabilities.

3. Which of the following events would NOT qualify as an incident?

Answer: b. Tax audit

Explanation: A tax audit is a normal business process and would not qualify as an incident.

Section 8-2: Network Security Technologies

4. What kind of physical security is offered by a video camera?

Answer: c. Detection

Explanation: A video camera feeds a captured video stream to a CCTV (closed-circuit TV) monitoring system, which provides detection of potential problems and can alert security personnel to respond.

5. Which device will alert network technicians to an intrusion but will not prevent an attack?

Answer: b. IDS

Explanation: An IDS (intrusion detection system) is a stand-alone device, an application, or a built-in feature running on a workstation, server, switch, router, or firewall that monitors network traffic, generating alerts about suspicious activity but not preventing an attack.

6. Which port should be opened to allow email traffic to enter your network?

Answer: d. 587

Explanation: SMTP (Simple Mail Transfer Protocol) over TLS uses port 587.

Section 8-3: Data Security Technologies

7. What security concept should you most likely consider when traveling with sensitive customer data saved on your laptop?

Answer: c. Data sovereignty

Explanation: The country where data is collected, processed, or stored can impose its own privacy and security laws, which is called data sovereignty. Traveling with sensitive data is risky if you'll be visiting a country that insists on having access to any data entering its borders.

8. Which of the following is a stream cipher?

Answer: b. RC4

Explanation: Encryption protocols such as DES, 3DES, and AES perform encryption on blocks of data. RC4 (Rivest Cipher 4) is an example of an older but popular stream cipher.

9. If data is encrypted with a company's public key, what information is needed to decrypt that data?

Answer: d. The company's private key

Explanation: Data encrypted with a public key can be decoded only with the corresponding private key.

Section 8-4: IAM (Identity and Access Management)

10. Which AAA concept ensures network activity can be traced back in time to retroactively confirm compliance with standards and regulations?

Answer: c. Accounting

Explanation: Accounting asks, "What did you do?" The records that are kept in these logs are later audited, either internally or by an outside entity, to ensure compliance with existing organizational rules or external laws and regulations.

11. Which of the following security principles is provided by hashing?

Answer: d. Integrity

Explanation: Hashing is mostly used to ensure data integrity—that is, to verify the data exactly matches what is expected.

12. Which access right would allow a user to create a file in a folder?

Answer: a. W

Explanation: Write (W) rights include the ability to write, or create, a file.

Section 8-5: Wireless Security

13. Which Wi-Fi security technique uses TKIP?

Answer: c. WPA

Explanation: One of WPA's improvements over WEP was to use TKIP (Temporal Key Integrity Program).

14. What element does DSSS use to make it more secure than FHSS?

Answer: d. Coding method

Explanation: DSSS (direct sequence spread spectrum) includes a coding method to further secure data in transit.

Chapter 9

Wide Area Networks

Objectives

After reading this chapter, you should be able to:

- Compare CANs, MANs, and WANs

- Describe how the most common routing protocols route messages across WANs

- Describe common forms of multiplexing

- Compare lossless and lossy compression techniques

Introduction

A WAN (wide area network) is a collection of devices and computer-related equipment interconnected to perform given functions, typically using local and long-distance communications systems. The communications lines can be as simple as a standard telephone line or as advanced as a satellite system. WAN connections are typically used to transfer bulk data between two distant endpoints and provide users with web-based services such as email, remote access database systems, and access to the Internet. WANs can also assist with specialized operations in many fields, such as manufacturing, medicine, navigation, education, entertainment, and telecommunications. Consider the following cases where a WAN is needed:

> Connect branch offices owned by the same corporation, such as a bank's home office and its branch offices

> Share information between organizations in the same industry, such as sharing medical data between a medical research facility and other healthcare providers

> Support communication between businesses, such as allowing companies to place orders with vendors or manufacturers

> Provide remote access to individuals traveling or working from home, such as employees traveling to meet with customers or students taking classes from home

You might notice here that WANs are used to connect LANs. Recall from Chapter 1 that CANs (campus area networks) and MANs (metropolitan area networks) also connect LANs. The reason to make these distinctions between WANs, MANs, CANs, and LANs is because different technologies and protocols have been developed to best serve each of these markets. Networking technology that works well for a long-haul connection across hundreds of miles to support the Internet backbone isn't well suited for network connections between two buildings situated next door to each other, even though both these networks might connect multiple LANs.

To further understand the capabilities of WANs, let's review the different types of WANs, examine routing technologies used to transfer data, and discuss ways WAN technologies can optimize traffic performance.

Section 9-1: Networks That Connect LANs

A local area network, as you may recall, is a network typically confined to a single building or set of buildings that are in close proximity (as in a campus). What happens when a network expands into a metropolitan area, across a state, or across the country? To do this, you need some kind of WAN.

WANs share a few characteristics with LANs: They interconnect networks, use some form of medium for the interconnection, and support network applications. But there are many differences. For example, LANs don't need routes. LANs use switches to forward frames to local destinations, while WANs use routers to route packets from one LAN or WAN to another. WANs can interconnect huge numbers of devices on LANs and other network types so that any one device can transfer data to any other device. As the name implies, WANs can cover large geographic distances, including the entire Earth. In fact, there are even plans under way to network the planet Mars as more technology is shipped to the planet and the need for returning signals to Earth becomes greater. Thus, WANs can theoretically cover the entire solar system!

Campus Area Networks (CANs)

Typically, a CAN is a collection of LANs within a single property or nearby properties, such as buildings belonging to a school where all the buildings and most or all the network media spanning those connections are confined within land owned by the school. With a CAN, it's likely that a single organization (or group of organizations) owns all the connected LANs and most or all the networking media connecting those LANs.

To connect these LANs, the network requires routers or specialized switches and high-speed media between the LANs. Typically, high-bandwidth fiber cables are buried in the ground between buildings. Occasionally, a wireless connection might be used to connect a building that is difficult to reach with a physical cable. For example, Figure 9-1 shows a special antenna used to provide a fixed, wireless link across a nearby football field.

Metropolitan Area Networks (MANs)

Similar to a CAN, a MAN is a collection of LANs within a limited geographical area, such as a downtown area

Figure 9-1 An outdoor antenna that connects LANs across a nearby football field

or even a city, county, or province. With MANs, many customers might own one or more of the connected LANs, and a single, third-party provider leases use of the networking media connecting these LANs. These connections often must be made across property not owned by either the MAN provider or the MAN customers. MAN connections might be made available to the general public (such as when a city makes high-speed Internet access available to all downtown area residents), or it might be restricted to a single customer (such as when a hospital is connected to its satellite medical offices). The following list gives examples where MANs can be useful:

> Connecting a city's police stations

> Connecting a hospital with its regional medical centers

> Connecting a home office with its branch offices and a warehouse location

Many of the same technologies and communications protocols found in LANs and CANs are used to create MANs. Yet MANs are often unique with respect to topology and operating characteristics. MANs can be used to support high-speed disaster recovery systems and real-time transaction backup systems. They can also provide interconnections between corporate data centers and Internet service providers, and support high-speed connections among government, business, medical, and educational facilities. MANs are almost exclusively fiber-optic networks or high-speed wireless networks and so are capable of supporting data rates into the hundreds of millions of bits per second, with some technologies offering 100 Gbps transmission speeds. For the same reason, they are advertised as networks with very low error rates and extremely high throughput.

Most MANs can recover very quickly from a link, switch, or router failure. MANs are designed to have highly redundant circuits so that, in the event of a component failure, the network can quickly reroute traffic away from the failed component. This ability to reroute in the event of a failure is called **failover**, and the speed at which a failover is performed is called the failover time. Although not all MANs have low failover times, achieving them is certainly the goal of any company that offers a MAN service.

WAN Topology

More complex than CANs and MANs, WANs require specialized technology designed to manage traffic across a wide variety of devices and connection types. As you may recall, a LAN works as a star-based network in that clusters of devices, such as computers, smartphones, and IoT devices, are connected to a central switch through which these devices can transmit messages to one another. Because there are so many devices in a WAN and they are spread over large (possibly very large) distances, using a LAN-type connection is not feasible. Likewise, a network in which each device is connected to every other network device is also impractical, as there

would be so many connections into each device that the technology would be completely unmanageable. Instead, a WAN connects its devices with a mesh design and requires routing to transfer data across the network. A mesh network is one where neighbors are connected only to other neighbors (Figure 9-2). Thus, to be transmitted across a mesh network, data must be passed along a route from device to device.

A WAN's infrastructure consists of a collection of nodes and interconnecting telecommunications links. In most cases, a node is a router that accepts an incoming message, examines the message's destination address, and forward the message onto a particular communications line. The connecting media can be fiber or copper cabling or wireless connections. All these components work in concert to create the network. A user sitting at a workstation and running a network application passes their data to the local network, which passes the data to the WAN infrastructure. The WAN is responsible for getting the data to the proper destination node, which then delivers it to the appropriate destination device. Because the exact nature of the WAN infrastructure is constantly changing and adapting, it's sometimes referred to as the network cloud, as shown in Figure 9-3. Clearly, a network would not exist without a network cloud, but it should not matter to the network what the inside of the network cloud looks like. The network cloud is simply the vehicle for getting the data from sender to destination.

To understand how a WAN manages to direct traffic across nodes from source to destination, let's explore how routing works and the role routing protocols play.

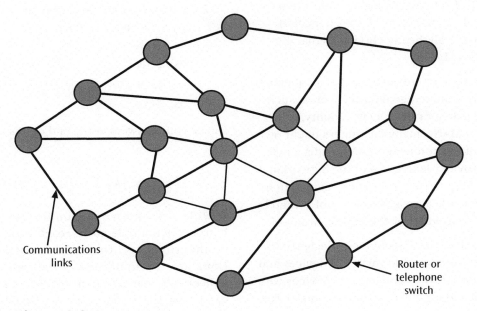

Figure 9-2 A simple mesh network

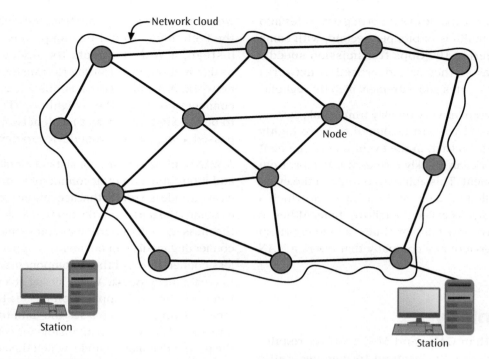

Figure 9-3   Network cloud, routers, and connected workstations

Remember this...

> A WAN (wide area network) is a collection of compute devices and computer-related equipment interconnected to perform given functions, typically using local and long-distance communications systems.

> A CAN (campus area network) is a collection of LANs within a single property or nearby properties. With a CAN, it's likely that a single organization (or group of organizations) owns all the connected LANs and most or all the networking media connecting those LANs.

> A MAN (metropolitan area network) is a collection of LANs within a limited geographical area, such as a downtown area or even a city, county, or province. With MANs, many customers might own one or more of the connected LANs, and a single, third-party provider leases use of the networking media connecting these LANs. These connections often must be made across property not owned by either the MAN provider or the MAN customers.

> WANs require specialized technology designed to manage traffic across a wide variety of devices and connection types. A WAN connects its devices with a mesh design and requires routing to transfer data across the network.

Self-check

1. Two nearby cities each have their own MAN. What network type can connect these two MANs?
   a. MAN
   b. WAN
   c. LAN
   d. CAN
2. What network type is best suited to support a city-wide smart traffic system?
   a. WAN
   b. CAN
   c. LAN
   d. MAN

Check your answers at the end of this chapter.

Section 9-2: Routing

A wide area network's underlying infrastructure consists of multiple nodes, each with multiple possible connections to other nodes within the network. Consider the hundreds of millions of routers that, collectively, manage all the traffic of the Internet. As you can guess, there can be many possible routes between a message's source and its destination. Figure 9-4

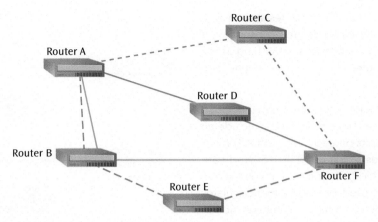

Figure 9-4   A six-node network showing multiple routes between nodes

shows a simple example with several possible routes between Node A and Node F: A-B-F, A-D-F, A-B-E-F, and A-C-F, to list a few.

How is routing through a WAN accomplished? Consider the Internet, which is a massive collection of networks, routers, and communications lines. When a data packet enters a router, the router examines the destination IP address encapsulated in the network layer of the packet and determines where the packet should go next. When there are multiple routes through a network, how is any one particular route selected? That's the job of routing protocols. When studying the routing protocols and techniques covered in this section, keep in mind that a WAN does not have to use only one form of routing. The routing protocols used across the Internet and other WANs combine several types of routing techniques.

Best Paths

There are many methods for selecting a route through a network. Often, routing protocols strive for an optimal route through a network, called a **best path**, but there are different ways to define "optimal." Consider the following possible priorities:

> Fewest hops

> Most available bandwidth

> Smallest queue lengths at the nodes along the path

> Least cost in terms of available bandwidth and expected delays

Some protocols use criteria other than optimality, such as:

> Balance the network load over many possible paths.

> Favor one type of traffic over another—for example, prioritizing delay-sensitive, real-time traffic over other traffic that can more easily tolerate delays.

> Adapt quickly, responding to changing network demands as nodes and communications links fail or become congested.

> Remain static and not switch between possible paths.

You can read about one of the underlying algorithms routing protocols use to calculate best paths for messages in the Details box titled, "Dijkstra's Least-Cost Algorithm." Clearly, routing is a complicated topic. To better understand routing in WANs, let's compare the two basic categories of routing configurations and examine some of the most common routing protocols. Most WANs use a combination of these routing techniques to achieve routing that is fair, efficient, and robust, but at the same time stable.

Details | Dijkstra's Least-Cost Algorithm

One possible method for selecting a route through a network is to choose a route that minimizes the sum of the costs of all the communications paths along that route.

A classic algorithm that calculates a least-cost path through a network is **Dijkstra's least-cost algorithm**. This algorithm is executed by each node, and the results are stored at the node and sometimes shared with other nodes. Because this calculation is time-consuming, it is done only on a periodic basis or when something in the network changes—for example, when there is a connection or node failure.

The example in Figure 9-5 depicts the same network cloud shown in Figure 9-4, but it has been modified to include an arbitrary set of associated costs on each link. Path A-B-F has a cost of 9 (2 + 7), A-D-F has a cost of 10 (5 + 5), and path A-B-E-F has a cost of 8 (2 + 4 + 2). To ensure that you find the least-cost route, you need to use a procedure that calculates the cost of every possible route, starting from a given node.

Although the human eye can quickly pick out a path through a network graph when you can see the whole network at once, there are drawbacks to "eyeballing" the data to find a solution:

> You can easily miss one or more paths.

> You may not find the least-cost path.

> WANs are never as simple as the network in Figure 9-5; thus, eyeballing the data could never be sustained as a reliable, long-term procedure.

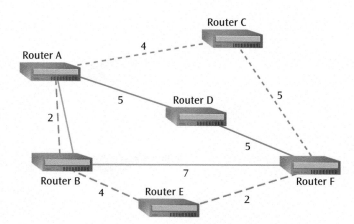

Figure 9-5   Network with costs associated with each link

Most WANs use some form of Dijkstra's algorithm to determine a least-cost route through a network, whether that cost is a measure of time or number of hops. Other algorithms include the Bellman-Ford algorithm, the Floyd-Warshall algorithm, and Johnson's algorithm.

Dynamic Versus Static Routing

When networks change, routing information needs to change too. Each router maintains a list of routes to various networks and hosts in its routing table and best paths for forwarding messages between them. When routing tables adapt to network changes, the routing system is called dynamic. Dynamic routing is an adaptive routing technique in which routing tables react to network fluctuations, such as congestion and node/link failure, and routers frequently communicate with each other to monitor network conditions. When a problem occurs in a network with dynamic routing, the appropriate information is transmitted to the routing tables, and new routes that avoid the problem areas are created. Dynamic routing raises some questions and issues: How often should information be shared, and how often should routing tables be updated? How much additional traffic is generated by messages transmitting routing information?

Unfortunately, dynamic routing can add to network congestion. Each time the network experiences a change in congestion, information about this change is transmitted to one or more nodes. The transmission of this information adds to the congestion, possibly making it worse. In addition, if the network reacts too quickly to a congestion problem and reroutes all traffic

onto a different path, it can create congestion problems in a different area. The network might then detect the congestion in this different area and possibly reroute all traffic back toward the first problem area. This back-and-forth rerouting produces a yo-yo effect, affecting network stability and decreasing efficiency. Thus, routing protocols are developed to use algorithms that minimize dynamic routing problems while maximizing the benefits.

The opposite of dynamic routing is static routing. With static routing, one or more fixed routes are added to the routing table, often when the network is installed, and are only updated when a network admin makes changes manually. Although this method is simple and eliminates the need for routers to talk to one another (thus avoiding additional traffic), it can also result in networks working with out-of-date information and thus causing inefficient or slow routing. Typically, dynamic and static routing are used together.

The majority of the network is configured for dynamic routing using one or more routing protocols, and a few connections are configured with static routing for routes that shouldn't change. Let's explore some of these routing protocols that adjust dynamically to changing network conditions while finding the most desirable route for each message.

Routing Protocols

Routing protocols can be loosely divided into categories according to how much each router knows about the surrounding network and how they communicate that information with other routers. Most routing protocols fall into one of the following categories:

> Distance vector protocols—Using a distance vector protocol, a router monitors each link and the number of hops from that link to network destinations. Some distance-vector routing protocols factor only the number of hops to the destination, whereas others consider route latency and other network traffic characteristics. Distance-vector routing protocols periodically exchange their entire routing tables with neighboring routers even if there's not been a change to a route, which requires the transfer of large amounts of data simply to keep routing tables updated. Also, routers relying on this type of routing protocol must accept the data they receive from their neighbors and cannot independently assess network conditions two or more hops away. This limitation is sometimes called "routing by rumor," and it results in slow convergence and higher likelihood of persistent errors when network conditions change.

> Link state protocols—To determine best paths, routers using link state routing protocols focus less on the number of hops between networks and more on the state of each of its connections. These protocols collect information about all their connected links and send that information to other routers on the network. Other routers, then, can use this information about links throughout the network to build their own routing tables, independently mapping the network and determining the best path between itself and a message's destination node. These protocols tend to adapt more quickly to changes in the network, but they can also be more complex to configure and troubleshoot. They also require more processing power to incorporate information from throughout the network to build each device's routing table. Part of this resource demand is offset by the fact link-state routing protocols only send information when something changes.

> Hybrid routing protocols—These protocols exhibit characteristics of both distance-vector and link-state routing protocols. For example, Cisco's EIGRP functions primarily as a distance-vector routing protocol but incorporates elements of link-state routing by syncing link information across the network only when something changes.

Most large WANs employ multiple routing protocols, which means routers must be able to choose which routes they'll save in their routing tables as this information comes from various types of routing protocols. A network administrator assigns each routing protocol an AD (administrative distance), which determines how routers will prioritize that protocol's data. Lower values are given higher priority. The following criteria are used to rate these protocols, depending on the networking environment:

> **Convergence time**—When something on the network changes, such as a failure or a configuration change, routers must identify the change and adjust their routes. The time it takes for this to happen is called convergence time. Some routing protocols are more efficient at this process than others.

> **Overhead**—The different approaches routing protocols use to collect information about the network and then to communicate that information results in varying levels of bandwidth load placed on the network and processing power required at each router. Collectively, these demands generate a burden on the network, referred to as overhead.

The following are common routing protocols, starting with the oldest: RIP (Routing Information Protocol).

Routing Information Protocol (RIP)

The first routing algorithm used on the Internet (when it was still called ARPANET) was a distance vector routing protocol called RIP (Routing Information Protocol). Every 30 seconds, each node exchanged its routing table information with its neighbors. When all its neighbors' route data came in, a node would update its own routing table with the least-cost values of all the neighbors. This protocol had some significant limitations:

> Good news, or routing information that indicated a shorter path, moved relatively slowly through the network, one router at a time. In other words, RIP suffers from a high convergence time.

> Similarly, bad news—such as a router or link failure—very often moved even more slowly through the network.

> Sharing each router's entire routing table every 30 seconds generated excessive overhead traffic on the network.

> RIP shared information only within 15 hops between routers, which means it's not suitable for larger networks where a message might need to travel through dozens of routers before reaching its destination.

A newer version, RIPv2 (Routing Information Protocol version 2), is also a distance vector protocol and is also limited to 15 hops. It generates less broadcast traffic than RIPv1 and was intended to provide greater security. By today's standards, however, RIPv2 is slow and insecure. Although insecure, it's simple to configure and so is still found on some modern networks. The Details box "How RIP Works" explains the basics of this protocol's process

for choosing a route. Although RIP is an older routing protocol, understanding how it works can help you better understand the significance of benefits offered by other routing protocols and the problems these newer protocols are designed to solve. In the project at the end of this chapter, you'll configure RIP on routers in Packet Tracer so you can study how routing protocols are configured and how they function on a network.

Details | How RIP Works

Examine the following example of how RIP works. Suppose that Router A is aware of four networks (123, 234, 345, and 789) and has routing table entries similar to the simplified version shown in Table 9-1.

Table 9-1 Representation of Router A's current routing table

Network	Hop Count	Next Router
123	8	B
234	5	C
345	6	C
789	10	D

Now suppose Router D sends out the following routing information shown in Table 9-2 (note that Router D did not send Next Router information because each router will determine that information for itself).

Table 9-2 Routing information sent by Router D

Network	Hop Count
123	4
345	5
567	7
789	10

Router A will look at each entry in Router D's table and make the following decisions:

> Router D says Network 123 is 4 hops away from Router D. Because Router D is 1 hop away from Router A, Network 123 is actually 5 hops away from Router A. That is better than the current entry of 8 hops in Router A's table, so Router A will update the entry for Network 123.

> Router D says Network 345 is 6 hops away (5 hops from Router D plus the 1 hop between Router

A and Router D). That is currently the same hop count as shown in Router A's table for Network 345, so Router A will not update its table.

> Router D says Network 567 is 8 hops away (7 hops from Router D plus the 1 hop between Router A and Router D). Because Router A has no information about Network 567, Router A will add this entry to its table. And because the information is coming from Router D, Router A's Next Router entry for network 567 is set to D.

> Router D says Network 789 is 11 hops away (10 hops from Router D plus the 1 hop between Router A and Router D), which is worse than the value in Router A's table. Normally the router would ignore information for a longer route; but since the current information in Router A's table for Network 789 came from Router D, and Router D is the one giving the new information, Router A must use this information and update its routing table accordingly.

Router A's updated routing table will thus contain information similar to that shown in Table 9-3.

Table 9-3 Updated routing table for Router A

Network	Hop Count	Next Router
123	5	D
234	5	C
345	6	C
567	8	D
789	11	D

Router A now has an updated routing table based upon the information sent from Router D. It has found a shorter path to Network 123 through Router D and has learned that Network 567 is 8 hops away from itself.

Open Shortest Path First (OSPF)

OSPF (Open Shortest Path First) protocol is a link state algorithm and is still used today by many Internet routers. Unlike RIP, OSPF has no hop limits and calculates more efficient best paths than RIP. For example, OSPF can consider network traffic conditions in choosing a best path, not just the number of hops. If OSPF learns of the failure of a given link, the router can rapidly compute an alternate path. OSPF demands more memory and CPU power for calculations, but it keeps network bandwidth use to a minimum with a very fast convergence time. Also, each router floods other routers in its area with its information only when something in the network changes. Thus, compared to RIP, which transmits every 30 seconds, OSPF transmits fewer packets of routing information.

OSPF routers communicate their routing data through link state advertisements. More precisely, the routing information is a snapshot of the current state of all the router links (to other networks) that are connected to that router. According to OSPF, there are four types of router links:

> **Point-to-point link**—Connects exactly two routers.

> **Transient link**—Connects multiple routers within the network.

> **Stub link**—Has only one router on the network.

> **Virtual link**—Created by an administrator when a link between two routers fails. More than likely, the virtual link passes through multiple routers.

OSPF's link state routing involves four steps:

> *Step 1*—Measure the delay or cost to each neighboring router. For example, each router can send out a special echo packet that gets bounced back almost immediately. By placing a timestamp on the packet as it leaves and again as it returns, the router knows the transfer time to and from a neighboring router.

> *Step 2*—Construct a link state packet containing all this timing information.

> *Step 3*—Flood the link state packets to its neighboring routers.

> *Step 4*—Compute new routes based on the updated information. Once a router collects a full set of link state packets from its neighbors, it creates or updates its routing table, usually using Dijkstra's least-cost algorithm.

Intermediate System to Intermediate System (IS-IS)

Another link state routing protocol is IS-IS (Intermediate System to Intermediate System), which uses a best-path algorithm similar to OSPF's. It was originally codified by ISO, which referred to routers as "intermediate systems," thus the protocol's name. Unlike OSPF, however, IS-IS can adapt to IPv6. Service providers generally prefer to use IS-IS in their own networks because it's more scalable than OSPF, but OSPF is still more common.

Enhanced Interior Gateway Routing Protocol (EIGRP)

EIGRP (Enhanced Interior Gateway Routing Protocol) is an advanced distance vector protocol that combines some of the features of a link state protocol and so is sometimes referred to as a hybrid protocol. With the fastest convergence time of the protocols covered here and low network overhead, it's easier to configure and less CPU-intensive than OSPF. EIGRP also offers the benefits of supporting multiple protocols and limiting unnecessary network traffic between routers.

Originally, EIGRP was proprietary to Cisco routers. In 2013, parts of the EIGRP standard were released to the public so that networks running routers from other vendors can now use EIGRP. It accommodates very large and heterogeneous networks, but it is still optimized for Cisco routers and not many manufacturers have made the transition. On LANs that use Cisco routers exclusively, EIGRP is generally preferred over OSPF.

Border Gateway Protocol (BGP)

All the routing protocols you've read about so far are used only within or on the edge of an AS (autonomous system), which is a group of networks, often on the same domain, that are operated by the same organization. For example, Cengage might have several LANs that all fall under its domain with each LAN connected to the others by core routers. An AS is sometimes referred to as a trusted network because the entire domain is under the organization's control.

BGP (Border Gateway Protocol) is the only routing protocol used across the open Internet and can span multiple autonomous systems. The following are special characteristics of BGP:

> **Path-vector routing protocol**—Communicates via BGP-specific messages that travel between routers over TCP sessions.

> **Efficient**—Determines best paths based on many factors.

> **Customizable**—Can be configured to follow policies that might, for example, avoid a certain router, or instruct a group of routers to prefer one route over other available routes.

BGP is the most complex of the routing protocols covered in this chapter. If you're responsible for an ISP's networks, you will need to understand BGP in depth.

Remember this...

> Routing protocols strive for an optimal route through a network, called a best path, but there are different ways to define "optimal." Most WANs use a combination of routing techniques to achieve routing that is fair, efficient, and robust, but stable at the same time.

> Each router maintains a list of routes to various networks in its routing table. Dynamic routing is an adaptive routing technique in which routing tables react to network fluctuations, such as congestion and node/link failure. In contrast, static routes are created once, typically when the network is installed, and then never updated again.

> Routing protocols can be loosely divided into categories according to how much each router knows about the surrounding network and how they communicate that information with other routers. Using a distance vector protocol, a router monitors each link and the number of hops from that link to network destinations. To determine best paths, routers using link state routing protocols focus less on the number of hops between networks and more on the state of each of its connections. Hybrid routing protocols exhibit characteristics of both distance vector and link state routing protocols.

Self-check

3. Which of the following is NOT a factor a routing protocol might use to determine a message's best path?

   a. Available bandwidth

   b. Traffic type

   c. Router brand

   d. Number of hops

4. You need a predictable route between your home office's network and a branch office's network. What kind of routing can you use to ensure the same route is always used for messages crossing this connection?

   a. Link state routing

   b. Static routing

   c. Distance vector routing

   d. Dynamic routing

5. Which routing protocol directs messages across the Internet?

   a. BGP

   b. EIGRP

   c. RIP

   d. OSPF

Check your answers at the end of this chapter.

Section 9-3: Multiplexing

Transferring data across a WAN often requires a lot of time, hardware resources, and network bandwidth. WAN functionality is a high priority for network admins especially with businesses increasingly relying on cloud connectivity for core business functions. What can be done to decrease the demand on limited resources and increase the effective speed of data transmissions?

Several techniques are available for WANs, and collectively, these techniques are called **WAN optimization**, or WAN acceleration. Some techniques commonly used for WAN optimization include:

> Caching, which you read about in Chapter 6 in the context of CDNs (content delivery networks) and is the process of storing copies of data in locations closer to where the data is used.

> Data compression and deduplication, which were covered in Chapter 6 in the context of storage optimization and are used to reduce the amount of data that must be stored or transmitted.

> Multiplexing, which was first introduced in Chapter 1 and is a technique of transmitting multiple signals over a single medium.

In most cases, you won't have to manage each of these processes separately—a WAN optimizer tool, such as the SolarWinds NPM (Network Performance Monitor), incorporates many technologies and can track changes and performance over time. Still, to use these tools to their full effect, it's beneficial to understand the separate processes. Multiplexing and compression, especially, play key roles in WAN optimization efforts. This section will explain types of multiplexing used to optimize WAN traffic. The next section will dig deeper into ways that compression technologies increase WAN performance for audio and video streaming.

Under the simplest conditions, a medium can carry only one signal at any point in time. For example, the twisted pair cable that connects a keyboard to a computer carries a single digital signal. Likewise, the Category 6 twisted pair wire that connects a computer to a LAN carries only one digital signal at a time on each wire. Often, however, you want a medium to carry multiple signals at the same time. When talking on the phone, for example, you want to be able to hear the other person even while you're talking. Similarly, when many people are in the same area talking on their smartphones at the same time, there is simultaneous transmission of multiple cell phone signals over the same wireless medium.

The ability to multiplex is especially relevant to WANs where many users transmit information on the same medium at any given time. ISPs must be able to manage many Internet connections from customers in the same area using the same infrastructure. The Internet itself must be able to manage nearly unimaginable volumes of traffic over the same routers and fiber-optic cables.

For multiple signals to share one medium, the medium must be "divided" somehow to give each signal a portion of the total bandwidth, similar to lanes on a large highway. Presently, a medium can be divided using one of four basic methods:

> A division of time

> A division of frequencies

> A division of wavelengths

> A division of transmission codes

Regardless of which kind of division is performed, multiplexing can make a communications link, or connection, more efficient by combining the signals from multiple sources. Let's explore further the ways a medium can be divided using various multiplexing techniques.

Time Division Multiplexing (TDM)

TDM (time division multiplexing) allows only one user at a time to transmit, and the sharing of the medium is accomplished by dividing available transmission *time* among users. Here, a user uses the entire bandwidth of the channel, but only briefly.

How does time division multiplexing work? Suppose an instructor in a classroom poses a controversial question to students. In response, several hands shoot up, and the instructor calls on each student, one at a time. It is the instructor's responsibility to make sure that only one student talks at any given moment so that each individual's response is heard. At a conceptual level, the instructor is a time division multiplexor, giving each user (student) a moment in time to transmit data (express an opinion to the rest of the class). In a similar fashion, a time division multiplexor calls on one input device after another, giving each device a turn at transmitting its data over a high-speed line. Suppose two users, A and B, wish to transmit data over a shared medium to a distant computer. A simple TDM scheme allows user A to transmit during the first second, then user B during the following second, followed again by user A during the third second, and so on. Since TDM was introduced in the 1960s, it has split into two roughly parallel but separate technologies: *synchronous* TDM and *statistical* TDM.

Synchronous Time Division Multiplexing

Sync TDM (synchronous time division multiplexing) gives each incoming source signal a turn to be transmitted, proceeding through the sources in round-robin fashion. Given *n* inputs, a synchronous time division multiplexor, or mux, accepts one piece of data, such as a byte, from the first device, transmits it over a high-speed link, accepts one byte from the second device, transmits it over the high-speed link, and continues this process until a byte is accepted from the *n*th device. After the *n*th device's first byte is transmitted, the multiplexor returns to the first device and continues to cycle through each device. Alternatively, rather than accepting a byte at a time from each source, the multiplexor may accept single bits as the unit input from each device. Figure 9-6 shows an output stream produced by a synchronous time division multiplexor.

Note that the second multiplexor, called a demultiplexor or demux, on the receiving end of the high-speed link must disassemble the incoming byte stream and deliver each byte to the appropriate destination. Because the high-speed output data stream generated by the mux does not contain addressing information for individual bytes, a precise order must be maintained. This will allow the demux to disassemble and deliver the bytes to the respective owners in the same sequence as the bytes were input.

What happens if a device has nothing to transmit? In this case, the mux must still allocate a slot for that device in

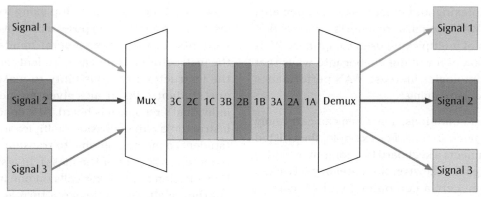

Figure 9-6 Synchronous TDM

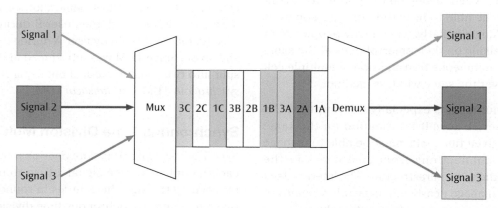

Figure 9-7 Multiplexor transmission stream with some input devices not transmitting data

the high-speed output stream; but that time slot will, in essence, be empty. Because each time slot is statically fixed in sync TDM, the mux cannot take advantage of the empty slot and reassign busy devices to it. If, for example, only a few devices are transmitting, the mux must still sample each input device (see Figure 9-7). In addition, the high-speed link that connects the two muxes must always be capable of carrying the total of all possible incoming signals, even when none of the input sources is transmitting data.

Statistical Time Division Multiplexing

As you can guess, synchronous TDM wastes a lot of unused transmission space. One solution to this problem is statistical TDM. Sometimes called asynchronous TDM, stat TDM (statistical time division multiplexing) transmits data only from active users and does not transmit empty time slots. To transmit data only from active users, the multiplexor creates a more complex frame that contains data only from those input sources that have something to send, as illustrated in Figure 9-8. Note that at any moment, the number of stations transmitting can

change. If that happens, the statistical multiplexor must create a new frame containing data from the currently transmitting stations.

How does the demux on the receiving end recognize the correct recipients of the data? Some type of address must be included with each byte of data to identify who sent that byte and for whom it is intended. The address can be as simple as a binary number that uniquely identifies the station that is transmitting. If the multiplexor transmits more than one byte of data at a time from each source, then it must also include a length field defining the length of the data block included along with the address and data. Finally, the sequence of *address/length/data/address/length/data...* is packaged into a larger unit by the statistical multiplexor, as shown in Figure 9-9, and includes the following fields:

> The flags at the beginning and end delimit the beginning and end of the frame.

> The control field provides information that is used by the sending and receiving multiplexors to control the flow of data between them.

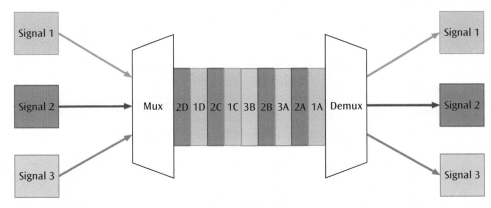

Figure 9-8   Intermittent transmissions via a statistical multiplexor

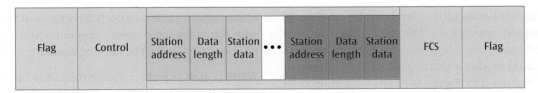

Figure 9-9   Frame layout for the information packet transferred between statistical multiplexors

> The FCS (frame check sequence) provides information that the receiving multiplexor can use to detect transmission errors within the frame.

All Things Considered

Thought Experiment

When data is transmitted using a statistical multiplexor, the individual units of data must have some form of address that tells the receiver the identity of the intended recipient of each piece of data. Instead of assigning absolute addresses to each piece of data, however, it's possible to incorporate relative addressing. What benefits do you think this would provide?

Frequency Division Multiplexing (FDM)

Frequency division multiplexing is the oldest multiplexing technique and is used in many fields of communication, including broadcast television and radio, cable television, and cell phones. It is also one of the simplest multiplexing techniques. FDM (frequency division multiplexing) is the assignment of non-overlapping frequency ranges to each user of a medium. A user might be a television station that transmits its television channel through the airwaves (the medium) into homes and businesses. A user might also be a smartphone transmitting signals over a cellular connection. To allow multiple users to share a single medium, FDM assigns each user a separate channel. A channel is a designated set of frequencies used to transmit a signal.

Many examples of FDM can be found in business and everyday life. Cable television is still one of the more commonly found applications of FDM. Another common example of FDM is cell phone systems. The telephone connection of one user is assigned one set of frequencies for transmission, while the telephone connection of a second user is assigned a different set of frequencies. Cell phone systems differ from other broadcast systems, such as radio and television, because they are dynamically assigned channels. When a user makes a call, the cellular network assigns this connection a range of frequencies based on current network availability. As you might expect, the dynamic assignment of frequencies can be less wasteful than the static assignment of frequencies.

In all FDM systems, the mux accepts input from users, converts the data streams to analog signals using either fixed or dynamically assigned frequencies, and transmits the combined analog signals over a medium that

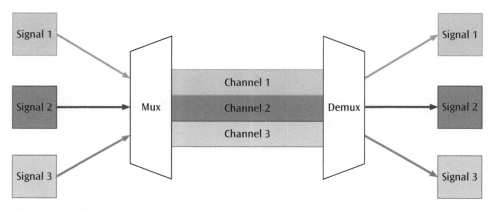

Figure 9-10   Simplified example of frequency division multiplexing

has a wide enough bandwidth to support the total range of all the assigned frequencies. The demux then accepts the combined analog signals, separates out one or more of the individual analog signals, and delivers these to the appropriate user(s). Figure 9-10 shows a simplified diagram of FDM.

To keep one signal from interfering with another signal, a set of unused frequencies called a guard band is usually inserted between the two signals to provide a form of insulation, preventing one signal from interfering with a neighboring frequency. These guard bands take up frequencies that might be used for other data channels, thus introducing a certain level of wastefulness.

Wavelength Division Multiplexing (WDM)

WDM (wavelength division multiplexing) multiplexes multiple data streams onto a single fiber-optic line. It is, in essence, a frequency division multiplexing technique that assigns input sources to separate sets of light frequencies. Wave division multiplexing uses different wavelength (frequency) lasers to transmit multiple signals at the same time over a single medium. The wavelength of each differently colored laser is called the lambda. Thus, WDM supports multiple lambdas.

The technique assigns a uniquely colored laser to each input source and combines the multiple optical signals of the input sources so they can be amplified as a group and transported over a single fiber. It is interesting to note that, because of the properties of the signals and glass fiber, plus the nature of light itself, each signal carried on the fiber can be transmitted at a different rate from the other signals. This means that a single fiber-optic line can support simultaneous transmission speeds. It can

also support signals in both directions at the same time, which enables full-duplex communication across a single fiber-optic line with the right equipment.

WDM is also scalable. As the demands on a system and its applications grow, it's possible to add additional wavelengths, or lambdas, onto the fiber, thus further multiplying the overall capacity of the original fiber-optic system. When WDM can support a large number of lambdas, it is often called DWDM (dense wavelength division multiplexing). This additional power comes with a high price tag, however. DWDM is an expensive way to transmit signals from multiple devices due to the high number of differently colored lasers required in one unit. One less expensive variation on WDM is CWDM (coarse wavelength division multiplexing), which is a less expensive technology because it is designed for short-distance connections and has only a few lambdas with a greater space between lambdas. Because the wavelengths are farther apart and not packed as closely together as they are in DWDM, the lasers used for CWDM can be less expensive and do not require extensive cooling.

Wi-Fi Multiplexing

With this understanding of the basic forms of multiplexing in hand, let's explore how multiplexing is used to improve performance of wireless networks, including Wi-Fi and cellular phones. Recall MIMO (multiple input multiple output) and MU-MIMO (multi-user MIMO) from Chapter 2. In the context of multiplexing, MIMO is sometimes used to send the same signal across multiple antennae, as illustrated in Figure 9-11. Rather than multiplexing, this is a form of diversity, providing redundancy and thereby improving a signal's reliability and resistance to noise.

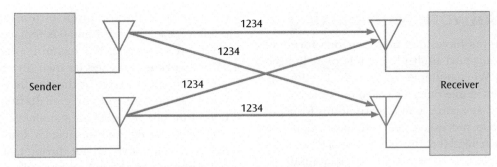

Figure 9-11   MIMO transmission for increased reliability

Alternatively, MIMO can offer a form of multiplexing called **SM (spatial multiplexing)**, or SDM (space division multiplexing), as illustrated in Figure 9-12. Two or more signals carrying different data are transmitted and received at the same time using multiple antennae, which separates the multiple signals by some distance in space. This results in slightly different signal strengths, allowing each antenna to differentiate between source antennae. Each antenna processes some of the data and, collectively, two or more antennas can work together to transmit and receive higher volumes of data at one time.

MU-MIMO, then, takes advantage of spatial multiplexing to support data exchange with multiple users at the same time. Figure 9-13 shows how the sender (such as a wireless router) can carry on multiple, simultaneous conversations due to the multiplexing allowed by the spatial distance between each wireless client. As you might suspect, MU-MIMO is most effective when wireless clients are widely spread across a geographical space, such as a warehouse floor or perhaps a home network where client devices are widely spaced apart. Also, at this time, MU-MIMO processes are supported only on network devices such as wireless routers and access points, not on end devices such as smartphones and laptops.

MIMO and MU-MIMO aren't the only technologies helping to support simultaneous signals on today's Wi-Fi networks. Wi-Fi and cellular networks both also use a form of FDM. Let's cover some basic historical background to provide context for the development of modern FDM technologies in Wi-Fi and cellular systems.

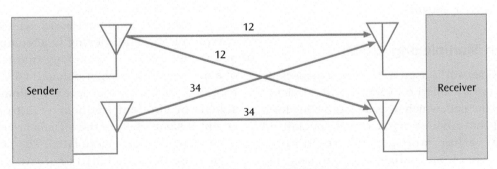

Figure 9-12   MIMO transmission for increased throughput

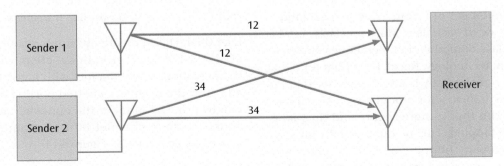

Figure 9-13   MU-MIMO transmission for supporting an increased number of devices simultaneously

Cellular Network Multiplexing

Cell phone systems have long used various forms of multiplexing to support multiple signals over limited frequency bands. When multiplexing is applied in the support of many users at one time, it's called multiple access. In the following discussion, you'll learn about forms of multiplexing used in successive generations of cell phone technology. Keep in mind that the *application* of these technologies is multiple access, which provides adaptations to the underlying multiplexing technology. For example, CDM (code division multiplexing), when used by 3G phone networks, is CDMA (code division multiple access). While they have different names, they're essentially the same technology, possibly with a few, minor adaptations.

Global System for Mobile Communications (GSM)

GSM (Global System for Mobile Communications) was first developed for 2G (2nd generation) cellular networks and later adopted for 3G (3rd generation) cellular. It uses a combination of TDM and FDM by first dividing the available bandwidth into channels, and then allocating use of each channel by time slots. GSM was widely adopted worldwide for cellular networks. Initially, it only supported voice communications but later added data services as well. GSM phones must have a SIM (Subscriber Identity Module) card to communicate with the cellular network.

Code Division Multiplexing (CDM)

Not all 2G and 3G networks used GSM—many (especially in the United States) relied on CDMA (code division multiple access) instead, which uses an interesting form of multiplexing that divides signals by a specialized code. Whereas other multiplexing techniques differentiate one user from another by either assigning frequency ranges or interleaving bit sequences in time, CDM (code division multiplexing) allows multiple users to share a common set of frequencies by assigning a unique digital code to each user. More precisely, CDM is based upon a class of modulation techniques known as spread spectrum technology. Recall from Chapter 8 that spread spectrum technology is a technique used in the communications industry for modulating a signal over a wider bandwidth that is more secure and thus more resistant to wiretapping. This technology falls into two categories: frequency hopping and direct sequence. CDM uses direct sequence spread spectrum technology to spread the transmission of a signal over a wide range of frequencies using mathematical values.

As the original data is input into a direct sequence modulator, each binary 1 and 0 is replaced with a larger, unique bit sequence. For example, each device in a CDM network is assigned its own bit sequence. When the bit sequences arrive at the destination station, the code division multiplexor can distinguish between different mobile devices' bit sequences. In reality, CDM is only used during the transmission from the cell phone office to mobile devices, not during transmission from mobile devices to the cell phone office. This is due to synchronization problems inherent in CDM.

> **Note**
>
> Sprint extensively used 3G CDMA networks to support its customers, while T-Mobile used GSM for 3G devices. After T-Mobile acquired Sprint in 2018, plans were developed to shift all customers off the older CDMA networks and onto 4G and 5G devices. At the time of this writing, Sprint's CDMA network is scheduled to be disabled by the end of 2021.

Orthogonal Frequency Division Multiplexing (OFDM)

4G (4th generation) and 5G (5th generation) cellular networks are characterized by an all-IP network for both data and voice transmissions. Beginning with LTE (Long-Term Evolution) networks, which were an early version of 4G, multiplexing is accomplished using a newer multiplexing technology that takes advantage of a mathematical sleight-of-hand. OFDM (orthogonal frequency division multiplexing) combines multiple signals of different frequencies into a single, more complex signal. Before the signals are combined, each is individually phase-modulated. The phase-modulated signals are then combined to create a compact, high-speed data stream. OFDM is widely used in modern applications, including Wi-Fi, digital television, digital radio, and home AC power-line transmissions.

Like GSM, OFDM creatively combines techniques from FDM and TDM. Earlier in this section, you learned that FDM cushions each channel with a guard band before and after the channel's allotted portion of the available bandwidth. OFDM takes the opposite tact and instead squeezes each channel into overlapping frequency spaces, as illustrated in Figure 9-14.

What keeps each channel from interfering with surrounding channels if they're using overlapping frequencies? This is where the magic of mathematics

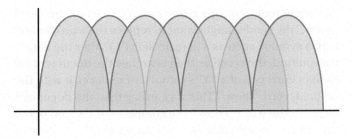

Figure 9-14 OFDM's overlapping frequencies

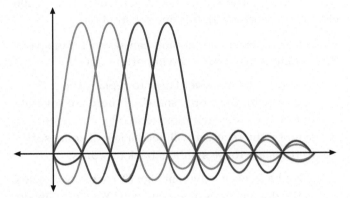

Figure 9-15 Orthogonal wave spacing

allows OFDM to manage complex signals transmitted at nearly the same time. Figure 9-15 shows how each signal occurs at a slightly different point on the timeline than any other signal. The specific spacing of these timings are orthogonal, which means the high point of one signal's wave occurs at a time when other waves are at their zero point.

All Things Considered

Thought Experiment

Which of these multiplexing techniques can be used on both conducted media and wireless media, which on only conducted media, and which on only wireless media?

Remember this...

> The technique of transmitting multiple signals over a single medium is multiplexing. For multiple signals to share one medium, the medium must be "divided," which is typically achieved using one of four basic methods: a division of time, a division of frequencies, a division of wavelengths, or a division of transmission codes.

> TDM (time division multiplexing) allows only one user at a time to transmit, and the sharing of the medium is accomplished by dividing available transmission time among users.

> Sync TDM (synchronous time division multiplexing) gives each incoming source signal a turn to be transmitted, proceeding through the sources in round-robin fashion. Sometimes called asynchronous TDM, stat TDM (statistical time division multiplexing) transmits data only from active users and does not transmit empty time slots.

> FDM (frequency division multiplexing) is the assignment of non-overlapping frequency ranges to each user of a medium. To allow multiple users to share a single medium, FDM assigns each user a separate channel. A channel is a designated set of frequencies used to transmit a signal.

> WDM (wavelength division multiplexing) multiplexes multiple data streams onto a single fiber-optic line. The wavelength of each differently colored laser is called the lambda.

> Sometimes, MIMO is used to send the same signal across multiple antennae. Rather than multiplexing, this is a form of diversity, providing redundancy and thereby improving a signal's reliability and resistance to noise. Alternatively, MIMO can offer a form of multiplexing called SM (spatial multiplexing). MU-MIMO takes advantage of spatial multiplexing to support multiplexed data exchange with multiple users at the same time.

> When multiplexing is applied in the support of many users at one time, it's called multiple access.

> OFDM (Orthogonal Frequency Division Multiplexing) combines multiple signals of different frequencies into a single, more complex signal. Before the signals are combined, each is individually phase-modulated. The phase-modulated signals are then combined to create a compact, high-speed data stream.

Self-check

6. Which form of multiplexing wastes resources by allocating transmission slots even when they're not needed?
   a. WDM
   b. Sync TDM
   c. FDM
   d. Stat TDM

7. Which technology relies on spatial multiplexing to carry on simultaneous conversations with multiple devices at one time?

    a. MIMO

    b. CWDM

    c. CDMA

    d. MU-MIMO

8. Which form of multiplexing uses overlapping frequency ranges?

    a. CDM

    b. FDM

    c. OFDM

    d. GSM

Check your answers at the end of this chapter.

Section 9-4: Compression

With multiplexing, you read how multiple data streams can be variously combined to maximize the amount of data that can be transmitted through different types of media, thus yielding a more efficient connection. Another way to make a connection more efficient is to compress the data that is transferred over the connection so there's less data to transmit to begin with. While ISPs themselves don't apply data compression within their networks as they handle customer data, ISPs do sometimes apply data caps that require customers to apply their own data compression in order to make the most of the available bandwidth. This is especially important when transferring large amounts of data, such as with multimedia streaming.

Recall from Chapter 1 that compression is the process of taking data and packing more of it into the same space whether this is in the form of a storage device, such as a hard drive or smartphone, or a medium such as a fiber-optic line. When data is compressed for transmission, it transfers more quickly because there is actually less of it, and this can result in a more efficient connection. Correspondingly, in terms of storage capacity, compression also allows for more data to be stored in the same amount of memory or disk space.

There are several compression techniques currently used in communication (and entertainment) systems, and some of these compression techniques can return an exact copy of the original data, while others cannot. The basic way to perform compression is to look for some common pattern in the data and replace each data pattern with a symbol or symbols that will consume less space during transmission or storage. For example,

if a document contains many occurrences of the word "snow," the sender might want to replace the word "snow" with a symbol, such as a percent sign (%). After the data is transmitted, the receiver then searches the document for each occurrence of a "%" symbol and replaces it with the original word "snow." This way, every time the document includes the word "snow," the compressed version of the document contains three fewer characters ("%" instead of "snow"). This space savings can add up if the document contains, for example, five hundred occurrences of the word "snow"—the compressed version will be 1,500 characters shorter with this one substitution!

While this replacement method can save a lot of space, the technique also raises two important questions:

> How does the receiver know to replace the "%" symbol with the word "snow"? If there are several different words each represented by a different symbol, the receiver will need a key of some sort to translate these symbols back to words.

> What happens if a percent sign (%) actually appears in the document as a percent sign? You certainly do not want the receiver replacing valid percent signs with the word "snow."

This example is oversimplified and is not the way compression actually works. In this section, you'll learn about real compression techniques, including their advantages and disadvantages. As you examine these examples of compression, you will discover how these and other issues are addressed.

Before you learn about compression techniques, let's divide the compression process into two categories—each compression technique discussed in this section falls into one of these two categories:

> **Lossless compression**—If a compression technique compresses data and then decompresses it back into the original data, no data is lost due to compression.

> **Lossy compression**—Some compression techniques allow for the loss of some data in a way that does not seriously compromise the user's experience of the data in exchange for the efficiency provided by compression.

Lossless Compression

As an example of lossless compression, consider a bank that wishes to compress all its customer accounts to increase its computer system's data storage space. Given the disaster that would ensue if customer accounts were to lose data due to compression, the bank would obviously want to use a lossless compression technique to perform this task. Lossless compression techniques ensure that every translation of data bits into a compressed form can be accurately reversed with no loss of bits. This can be a tedious process and often requires more processing power than lossy compression and is not as efficient. Still, these techniques are useful in cases where compression can increase network or storage efficiency without compromising data integrity.

Run-Length Encoding

One of the more common and simpler examples of lossless compression is run-length encoding. This technique replaces any repetitions of the same bit or byte that occur in a sequence of data with a single occurrence of the bit/byte and a run count, or simply with a run count. For example, this technique works at the binary level by counting either long strings (or runs) of binary 0s or long strings of binary 1s. Consider the following data string, which is composed predominantly of binary 0s:

00000100000000011000000000000000010000110000000000 00000000001000000

A compression technique based on run-length encoding would compress the 0s by first counting the "runs" of 0s—that is, it would start by counting the 0s until a binary 1 is encountered. If there are no 0s between a pair of 1s, then that pair would be considered a run that contains zero 0s. Performing this process on your data string, you find the following runs:

5 9 0 15 4 0 20 6

Thus, in the first run, you encountered five 0s, while the second run had nine 0s. The third run had zero 0s because a 1 immediately followed a 1. In the next run, you encountered fifteen 0s, followed by a run of four 0s, zero 0s, twenty 0s, and finally six 0s.

The next step in this compression technique would be to convert each of the decimal values (5, 9, 0, 15, etc.) into 4-bit binary values, or nibbles, according to the following rules:

> Because the largest decimal number that a 4-bit binary nibble can represent is 15 (which corresponds to four binary 1s—1111), you must convert a run that has a decimal value that is greater than 15 into multiple 4-bit nibbles. For example, a run of 20 would be converted into 1111 0101, in which the first nibble is the value 15, and the second nibble is the value 5.

> A caveat to this rule is that if you are converting the value of 15 itself, then you would also create two nibbles: 1111 followed by 0000. The reason for this is simply to be consistent—so that whenever a binary nibble of 1111 (or 15) is encountered, the following nibble (0000, which corresponds to a decimal value of 0) is added to that nibble.

Thus, converting the above runs of 5, 9, 0, 15, 4, 0, 20, and 6 would produce the following nibbles:

0101 1001 0000 1111 0000 0100 0000 1111 0101 0110

In this example, note that the original bit string, which consisted of 68 bits, is compressed to 40 bits—a reduction of 42 percent—and that no data has been lost (hence, the name lossless).

This technique is only worthwhile if the original data consists predominantly of one particular symbol, in this case binary 0s. As you'll see a little later in this chapter, run-length encoding is a component of compression used for video images (due to the presence of many zero values), as well as compressing other documents that have repeated characters.

Lempel-Ziv Technique

The Lempel-Ziv technique is another lossless compression technique, one which creates a dictionary of character strings and associated codes. It was published in 1977 and is often referred to as LZ77. This technique forms the basis of many modern algorithms, such as LZW (Lempel-Ziv-Welch) and LZSS (Lempel-Ziv-Storer-Szymanski). LZ77 is the underlying technology behind applications such as GIF, PKZIP, WinZip, gzip, UNIX's compress utility, and Microsoft's compressed folders. Although the actual algorithm is fairly complex, it is possible to get a basic understanding of how the algorithm works. As the string to be transmitted is processed, the sender of the data creates a "dictionary" of character strings and associated codes. This set of codes is transmitted and the receiver then re-creates the dictionary and the original data string as the data codes are received.

The Lempel-Ziv algorithm can be fairly effective in compressing data. Studies have shown that application files can be reduced to 44 percent of the original size, text files can be reduced to 64 percent of the original size, and image files can be reduced to 88 percent of the original size.

It is also possible to compress music and audio files and not lose any of the audio content. Although most portable music players use a lossy compression scheme (such as MP3), many users are turning toward lossless compression to preserve a more exact copy of their analog recordings. Likewise, most commercial users who digitize and compress analog recordings do not want to lose any of the original music. To this end, a number of lossless audio compression schemes are available. These include FLAC (Free Lossless Audio Codec), TTA (The True Audio), WavPack, ALAC (Apple Lossless Audio Codec), and Monkey's Audio. Although some of these schemes are proprietary, FLAC, TTA, and WavPack are free and/or open source. And most, if not all, can compress audio sources by at least 50 percent.

All the compression techniques described thus far have been examples of lossless compression. Lossless compression is necessary when it's important that no data be lost during the compression and decompression stages. Like application, text, and image files, video images and higher-quality audio files can also be compressed using lossless compression, but the percentage of reduction is usually not as significant. This is due to the nature of the data in video and audio files: There is not one symbol or set of symbols that occur frequently enough to produce a reasonable level of compression. For example, if you take some video and digitize it, you will produce a long stream of binary 1s and 0s. To compress this stream, you can choose to perform a lossless run-length encoding on either the 1s or the 0s. Unfortunately, however, because this type of data is dynamic, there will probably not be enough repeating runs of either bit to produce a reasonable compression. Thus, you might want to consider some other compression techniques that allow for losing data bits that you don't really need. Music and video have certain properties that can be exploited to perform an effective compression, as you'll learn about next.

Lossy Compression

Suppose you wanted to copy a song from a website to your smartphone. To do this, you would first need to compress the song. During the compression process, if some of the data got lost, you might not even notice the loss, especially if the compression algorithm were designed to intentionally "lose" only those sounds that most human ears are not likely to detect. Because certain ranges of audio and video data cannot be detected easily, lossy compression algorithms are often used to compress music, image, and video files, and thus are commonly incorporated into technological devices such as smartphones and tablets. Three of the possible file types that result from this compression are MP3 for audio, JPEG for images, and MPEG for video, as described next.

MP3 (MPEG [Moving Picture Experts Group] Audio Layer-3)

When one is listening to music, if two sounds play at the same time, the ear hears the louder one and usually ignores the softer one. Also, the human ear can hear sounds only within a certain range, which for an average person is 20 Hz to 20 kHz (20,000 Hz). There are sounds, usually occurring at the extremes of the normal hearing range, that the human ear cannot hear well or even at all. Similarly, complex audio data often includes quieter sounds that can't normally be detected when played alongside louder sounds. Audio engineers remove portions of these extreme frequency ranges and the quieter sounds to compress music through techniques called perceptual encoding, or perceptual noise shaping. Perceptual encoding processes remove those portions of the audio data that are not required in order to reproduce an equivalent listening experience by human ears. If the perceptual encoding is performed well, the compressed version of an audio stream sounds fairly close to the uncompressed version (i.e., almost CD-quality) even though some of the original data has been removed.

MP3 (MPEG [Moving Picture Experts Group] Audio Layer-3) is a common form of audio compression. In fact, the Moving Picture Experts Group has also developed compression standards for HDTV broadcasts, digital satellite systems, and DVD movies. After employing perceptual encoding tricks, the MP3 encoder produces a data stream that has a much slower data rate than that of conventional CD-quality music. A CD player is designed to reproduce music that has been encoded with 44,100 samples per second, which converts to a bitrate of 1,411 kbps (44,100 samples per second times 16 bits per sample times 2 channels) and is considered the so-called Red Book standard. An MP3 encoder typically reproduces a data stream of 128 kbps to 192 kbps with a maximum of 320 kbps, and data streaming services typically offer 128 kbps (although some drop to 64 kbps). Thus, the compression process reduces both the amount of data as well as the data transfer rate of the music.

JPEG (Joint Photographic Experts Group)

Image files can also be compressed by removing small details from the image that, in this case, the average human eye will not notice are missing. JPEG (Joint Photographic Experts Group) is a technique that is very commonly used to compress photos and other images.

Note

The JPEG file format is shortened to three letters, JPG, when these files are stored on Windows devices. Thus, you'll see a photo's file extension in Windows written as .jpg.

The process of converting an image to JPEG format involves three phases:

> **Discrete cosine transformation**—Calculates pixel value changes.

> **Quantization**—Increases the number of zeroes in each block.

> **Run-length encoding**—Counts consecutive zeroes.

To perform the discrete cosine transformation, the image is broken into multiple 8 by 8 blocks of pixels, where each pixel represents either a single dot of color in a color image or a single shade of black and white in a black and white image. Each 8 by 8 block (corresponding to 64 pixels) is then subjected to a common mathematical routine called the discrete cosine transformation. Essentially, what this transformation does is produce a new 8 by 8 block of values. These values, however, are now called spatial frequencies, which are cosine calculations of how much each pixel value changes as a function of its position in the block.

Rather than deal with the mathematics of this process, let's examine two simple examples. If you have an image with fairly uniform color changes over the area of the image—in other words, not a lot of fine details—then one of its 8 by 8 blocks of pixels might look something like the block in Figure 9-16, where each decimal value represents a particular level of color.

After applying the discrete cosine transformation to these pixels, you might then have a set of spatial frequencies as shown in Figure 9-17.

Note the many zero entries and that the nonzero entries are clustered toward the upper-left corner of the block. This is because of the discrete cosine calculations, which in essence depict the difference between one pixel's color relative to that of a neighbor's pixel rather than the absolute value of a particular pixel's color. The other reason for the clustering is that this image, as noted earlier, is one with fairly uniform color—that is, not a lot of color variation—and thus there is little change as you move away from the upper-left corner.

15	18	21	24	28	32	36	40
19	22	25	28	32	36	40	44
22	25	28	32	36	40	44	48
26	29	32	35	39	43	47	51
30	34	38	42	46	51	56	61
34	38	42	46	51	56	61	66
38	42	46	51	56	61	66	72
43	48	53	58	63	68	74	80

Figure 9-16   Original block of pixels

628	−123	12	−8	0	−2	0	−1
−185	23	−5	0	0	0	0	0
10	0	0	0	0	0	0	0
0	0	0	0	0	0	0	0
3	0	0	0	0	0	0	0
−1	0	0	0	0	0	0	0
0	0	0	0	0	0	0	0
0	0	0	0	0	0	0	0

Figure 9-17   Pixel values after discrete cosine transformation

Suppose, however, that you have an image with lots of fine detail. It will have an 8 by 8 block of pixels with widely different values and might look like Figure 9-18.

After applying the discrete cosine transformation to the pixels of this image, you might then have a set of spatial frequencies as shown in Figure 9-19.

Notice there are few zero entries in this block of spatial frequencies.

The second phase in the conversion of an image to a JPEG file is the quantization phase. The object of this phase is to try to generate more zero entries in the 8 by 8 block. To do this, divide each value in the block by some predetermined number and disregard the remainders. For example, if the pixel block contains a spatial

120	80	110	65	90	142	56	100
40	136	93	188	90	210	220	56
95	89	134	74	170	180	45	100
9	110	145	93	221	194	83	110
65	202	90	18	164	90	155	43
93	111	39	221	33	37	40	129
55	122	52	166	93	54	13	100
29	92	153	197	84	197	84	83

Figure 9-18 Original block of pixels for detailed picture

1	4	7	10	13	16	19	22
4	7	10	13	16	19	22	25
7	10	13	16	19	22	25	28
10	13	16	19	22	25	28	31
13	16	19	22	25	28	31	33
16	19	22	25	28	31	33	36
19	22	25	28	31	34	37	40
22	25	28	31	34	37	40	43

Figure 9-20 Quantization values

652	32	−40	54	−18	129	−33	84
111	−33	53	9	122	−43	65	100
−22	101	94	−32	23	104	76	101
88	33	211	2	−32	143	43	14
132	−32	43	0	122	−48	54	110
54	11	133	27	56	154	13	−94
−54	−69	10	109	65	0	27	−33
199	−18	99	98	22	−43	8	32

Figure 9-19 Detailed picture's pixel values after discrete cosine transformation

652	8	−5	5	−1	8	0	3
27	−4	5	0	7	−2	2	4
−3	10	7	2	1	4	3	3
8	2	13	0	−1	5	1	0
10	−2	2	0	4	−1	1	3
3	0	6	1	2	4	0	−2
−2	−3	0	3	2	0	0	0
9	0	3	3	0	−1	0	0

Figure 9-21 Detailed picture's pixels in quantization phase

frequency with the value 9, divide this by 10 to get the result of 0. But you don't want to divide all 64 spatial frequencies by the same value because the values in the upper-left corner of the block have more importance (due to the discrete cosine transformation operation). So, let's divide the block of spatial frequencies with a block of values in which the upper-left corner of values are closer to 1—and thus will serve to reproduce the original number in a division. An example of such a block is shown in Figure 9-20.

Now when you divide the block of spatial frequencies with this block of weighted values, you produce a new block of values with more zero entries, as shown in Figure 9-21.

But if you perform 64 divisions and toss out the remainders, won't you lose something from the original image? Yes, you will, but by selecting an optimal set of values you won't lose too much of the original image. In other words, in striving to maximize the number of zeros in each block (which will be important in the final phase), you allow the data (i.e., the image) to change a little bit—but hopefully not so much that the human eye might detect gross differences between the original file and the one that has been compressed and decompressed.

Finally, the third phase of the JPEG compression technique is to take the matrix of quantized values and perform run-length encoding on the zeros. But the trick here is that you do not run-length encode

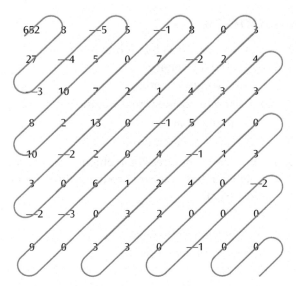

Figure 9-22   Run-length encoding of a JPEG image

the zeros by simply going up and down the rows of the 8 by 8 block. Instead, you take advantage of the fact that you can achieve longer runs of zeros if you encode on a diagonal, as is shown in Figure 9-22.

MPEG (Moving Picture Experts Group)

Similar to image files, video files can also be compressed because a video is actually just a series of images. When these images, or frames, are shown in rapid succession, it appears as if the objects in the images are moving. To make it seem as though the movement (of characters, objects, scenery) in a movie is fluid, these frames are displayed at a rate of approximately 30 frames per second. And interestingly, most of the time each frame looks very similar to the next unless there is a complete scene change.

If successive images are very similar, why transfer the full image of each frame? Why not just transfer the *difference* between the two frames? This sort of transfer is an example of differential encoding. MPEG-1 and MPEG-2—or simply **MPEG (Moving Picture Experts Group)**—are common examples of this form of compression.

To save space, not all of those 30 frames per second are complete images. MPEG creates a complete frame of information, followed by several partial, or difference,

frames, followed by a complete frame. More precisely, the frames shown in Figure 9-23 are created, as follows:

> The I-frame is a complete frame.

> The P-frame is the difference from the previous I-frame (and is created using motion-compensated prediction).

> The B-frames are the difference frames, which contain the smaller differences between the I-frame and the P-frame and are inserted between I and P frames to smooth out the motion.

Because MPEG is computationally complex, today's processor chips have been designed specifically for the compression and decompression of MPEG images.

Remember this...

> When data is compressed, it transfers more quickly because there is actually less of it, and this can result in a more efficient connection. The basic way to perform compression is to look for some common pattern in the data and replace each data pattern with a symbol or symbols that will consume less space during transmission or storage.

> Lossless compression compresses data and then decompresses it back into the original data.

> Lossy compression allows for the loss of some data in a way that does not seriously compromise the user's experience of the data in exchange for the efficiency provided by compression.

> One of the more common and simpler examples of lossless compression is run-length encoding. This technique replaces any repetitions of the same bit or byte that occur in a sequence of data with a single occurrence of the bit/byte and a run count, or simply with a run count.

> The Lempel-Ziv technique is another lossless compression technique, one which creates a dictionary of character strings and associated codes and is often referred to as LZ77. This technique forms the basis of many modern algorithms, such as LZW (Lempel-Ziv-Welch) and LZSS (Lempel-Ziv-Storer-Szymanski).

Figure 9-23   Frames in a digital MPEG video file

> MP3 (MPEG [Moving Picture Experts Group] Audio Layer-3) is a common form of audio compression. After employing perceptual encoding tricks, the MP3 encoder produces a data stream that has a much slower data rate than that of conventional CD-quality music.

> JPEG (Joint Photographic Experts Group) is a technique that is very commonly used to compress photos and other images. The process of converting an image to JPEG format involves three phases: discrete cosine transformation, quantization, and run-length encoding.

> MPEG (Moving Picture Experts Group) is used to compress motion picture images or moving video, which is a series of images. To save space, MPEG creates a complete frame of information, followed by several partial, or difference, frames, followed by a complete frame.

Self-check

9. Which compression technique relies on a self-created dictionary?
   a. Run-length encoding
   b. Discrete cosine transformation
   c. Quantization
   d. Lempel-Ziv technique

10. What lossless compression technique compresses the high number of zeroes produced during JPEG compression?
    a. LZW
    b. Run-length encoding
    c. Perceptual encoding
    d. LZ77

Check your answers at the end of this chapter.

Summary

Section 9-1: Networks That Connect LANs

> A WAN (wide area network) is a collection of compute devices and computer-related equipment interconnected to perform given functions, typically using local and long-distance communications systems.

> A CAN (campus area network) is a collection of LANs within a single property or nearby properties. With a CAN, it's likely that a single organization (or group of organizations) owns all the connected LANs and most or all the networking media connecting those LANs.

> A MAN (metropolitan area network) is a collection of LANs within a limited geographical area, such as a downtown area or even a city, county, or province. With MANs, many customers might own one or more of the connected LANs, and a single, third-party provider leases use of the networking media connecting these LANs. These connections often must be made across property not owned by either the MAN provider or the MAN customers.

> WANs require specialized technology designed to manage traffic across a wide variety of devices and connection types. A WAN connects its devices with a mesh design and requires routing to transfer data across the network.

Section 9-2: Routing

> Routing protocols strive for an optimal route through a network, called a best path, but there are different ways to define "optimal." Most WANs use a combination of routing techniques to achieve routing that is fair, efficient, and robust, but stable at the same time.

> Each router maintains a list of routes to various networks in its routing table. Dynamic routing is an adaptive routing technique in which routing tables react to network fluctuations, such as congestion and node/link failure. In contrast, static routes are created once, typically when the network is installed, and then never updated again.

> Routing protocols can be loosely divided into categories according to how much each router knows about the surrounding network and how they communicate that information with other routers. Using a distance vector protocol, a router monitors each link and the number of hops from that link to network

destinations. To determine best paths, routers using link state routing protocols focus less on the number of hops between networks and more on the state of each of its connections. Hybrid routing protocols exhibit characteristics of both distance-vector and link-state routing protocols.

Section 9-3: Multiplexing

> The technique of transmitting multiple signals over a single medium is multiplexing. For multiple signals to share one medium, the medium must be "divided," which is typically achieved using one of four basic methods: a division of time, a division of frequencies, a division of wavelengths, or a division of transmission codes.

> TDM (time division multiplexing) allows only one user at a time to transmit, and the sharing of the medium is accomplished by dividing available transmission time among users.

> Sync TDM (synchronous time division multiplexing) gives each incoming source signal a turn to be transmitted, proceeding through the sources in round-robin fashion. Sometimes called asynchronous TDM, stat TDM (statistical time division multiplexing) transmits data only from active users and does not transmit empty time slots.

> FDM (frequency division multiplexing) is the assignment of non-overlapping frequency ranges to each user of a medium. To allow multiple users to share a single medium, FDM assigns each user a separate

channel. A channel is a designated set of frequencies used to transmit a signal.

> WDM (wavelength division multiplexing) multiplexes multiple data streams onto a single fiber-optic line. The wavelength of each differently colored laser is called the lambda.

> Sometimes, MIMO is used to send the same signal across multiple antennae. Rather than multiplexing, this is a form of diversity, providing redundancy and thereby improving a signal's reliability and resistance to noise. Alternatively, MIMO can offer a form of multiplexing called SM (spatial multiplexing). MU-MIMO takes advantage of spatial multiplexing to support multiplexed data exchange with multiple users at the same time.

> When multiplexing is applied in the support of many users at one time, it's called multiple access.

> OFDM (Orthogonal Frequency Division Multiplexing) combines multiple signals of different frequencies into a single, more complex signal. Before the signals are combined, each is individually phase-modulated. The phase-modulated signals are then combined to create a compact, high-speed data stream.

Section 9-4: Compression

> When data is compressed, it transfers more quickly because there is actually less of it, and this can result in a more efficient connection. The basic way to perform compression is to look for some common pattern in the data and replace each data pattern with a symbol or symbols that will consume less space during transmission or storage.

> Lossless compression compresses data and then decompresses it back into the original data.

> Lossy compression allows for the loss of some data in a way that does not seriously compromise the user's experience of the data in exchange for the efficiency provided by compression.

> One of the more common and simpler examples of lossless compression is run-length encoding. This technique replaces any repetitions of the same bit or byte that occur in a sequence of data with a single occurrence of the bit/byte and a run count, or simply with a run count.

> The Lempel-Ziv technique is another lossless compression technique, one which creates a dictionary of character strings and associated codes and is often referred to as LZ77. This technique forms the basis of many modern algorithms, such as LZW (Lempel-Ziv-Welch) and LZSS (Lempel-Ziv-Storer-Szymanski).

› MP3 (MPEG [Moving Picture Experts Group] Audio Layer-3) is a common form of audio compression. After employing perceptual encoding tricks, the MP3 encoder produces a data stream that has a much slower data rate than that of conventional CD-quality music.

› JPEG (Joint Photographic Experts Group) is a technique that is very commonly used to compress photos and other images. The process of converting an image to JPEG format involves three phases: discrete cosine transformation, quantization, and run-length encoding.

› MPEG (Moving Picture Experts Group) is used to compress motion picture images or moving video, which is a series of images. To save space, MPEG creates a complete frame of information, followed by several partial, or difference, frames, followed by a complete frame.

Key Terms

For definitions of key terms, see the Glossary near the end of the book.

2G (2nd generation)

3G (3rd generation)

4G (4th generation)

5G (5th generation)

AD (administrative distance)

best path

BGP (Border Gateway Protocol)

CDM (code division multiplexing)

channel

CWDM (coarse wavelength division multiplexing)

demultiplexor

Dijkstra's least-cost algorithm

distance vector protocol

DWDM (dense wavelength division multiplexing)

dynamic routing

EIGRP (Enhanced Interior Gateway Routing Protocol)

failover

FDM (frequency division multiplexing)

GSM (Global System for Mobile Communications)

guard band

hybrid routing protocol

IS-IS (Intermediate System to Intermediate System)

JPEG (Joint Photographic Experts Group)

Lempel-Ziv technique

link state protocol

lossless compression

lossy compression

LTE (Long-Term Evolution)

MP3 (MPEG [Moving Picture Experts Group] Audio Layer-3)

MPEG (Moving Picture Experts Group)

multiple access

multiplexor

OFDM (orthogonal frequency division multiplexing)

OSPF (Open Shortest Path First) protocol

RIP (Routing Information Protocol)

routing table

run-length encoding

SM (spatial multiplexing)

stat TDM (statistical time division multiplexing)

static routing

sync TDM (synchronous time division multiplexing)

TDM (time division multiplexing)

WAN optimization

WDM (wavelength division multiplexing)

Review Questions

1. When a router receives multiple possible routes for the same network connection from three different routing protocols, what information will the router use to choose the route it adds to its routing table?

    a. Autonomous system
    b. Convergence time
    c. Overhead
    d. Administrative distance

2. With which network type does a single organization most likely own all the equipment?

    a. WAN
    b. SD-WAN
    c. CAN
    d. MAN

3. What technique will ensure a message arrives at its destination even if a router along the path loses power?

    a. Backup
    b. Best path
    c. Failover
    d. Multiplexing

4. Which of the following is NOT an optimal application of a MAN?

    a. Long-haul connection across states
    b. High-speed disaster recovery site
    c. Interconnection between corporate data center and ISP
    d. Real-time transaction backup

5. Which device determines the best path for a message traversing the Internet?

    a. Switch
    b. Fiber cable
    c. Router
    d. Multiplexor

6. Which algorithm is often used to help calculate the least-cost path on a network?

    a. Lempel-Ziv
    b. DWDM
    c. Dijkstra
    d. MU-MIMO

7. Which routing protocol requires that routers transmit their routing tables every 30 seconds?

    a. EIGRP
    b. OSPF
    c. IS-IS
    d. RIP

8. Which routing protocol has the fastest convergence time?

    a. EIGRP
    b. OSPF
    c. RIPv2
    d. IS-IS

9. How does OSPF advertise its routing information?

    a. It listens for update requests from each of its neighbors.
    b. It floods other routers with link state packets when something changes.
    c. It measures the delay or cost to each neighboring router.
    d. It floods other routers with its entire routing table every 30 seconds.

10. As you're designing your network across multiple, private WAN connections, you realize you need to choose a secure routing protocol for your AS. Which of the following would NOT be a reasonable choice to consider?

    a. BGP
    b. IS-IS
    c. EIGRP
    d. RIPv2

11. What type of protocol is BGP?

    a. Distance vector
    b. Hybrid
    c. Link state
    d. Path vector

12. Which routing protocol is limited to 15 hops?

    a. RIPv2
    b. EIGRP
    c. OSPF
    d. BGP

13. Which of the following is NOT an example of some variation of FDM?

    a. 5G
    b. MIMO
    c. CWDM
    d. Cable television

14. Which multiplexing technique uses a round-robin pattern?

    a. SM
    b. CWDM
    c. Stat TDM
    d. Sync TDM

15. Which multiplexing technique requires addressing to identify each data stream?

    a. CDM
    b. Stat TDM
    c. Sync TDM
    d. FDM

16. What type of medium is required to support WDM?

    a. Wi-Fi
    b. Cable TV
    c. Fiber
    d. Cellular

17. If data has a large number of one type of symbol, which type of compression would be the most effective?

    a. Lempel-Ziv technique
    b. MP3
    c. Quantization
    d. Run-length encoding

18. Which of the following is NOT a phase of JPEG compression?

    a. Run-length encoding
    b. Lempel-Ziv technique
    c. Quantization
    d. Discrete cosine transformation

19. Given the following bit string, what run-length encoding would result?
    0000 0001 0000 0110 0000 0000 00

    a. 0111 0101 0000 1011
    b. 7 5 0 11
    c. 4 3 4 1 1 4 4 2
    d. 0 1 0 6 0 0 0

20. MP3, JPEG, and MPEG all rely on what characteristic in the data in order to perform compression?

    a. The original data consists predominately of one symbol.
    b. The percentage of reduction is not significant.
    c. Most users have limited available bandwidth.
    d. Some loss of data will not be noticed by the end user.

Hands-On Project 9

Configure RIP on Routers in Packet Tracer

Estimated time: 45 minutes

Resources:

❯ Computer with Cisco Packet Tracer installed

❯ **Context:**

Devices can't communicate outside their own LAN unless the router at the edge of the LAN is configured to communicate with other routers. A routing protocol will enable connections across multiple LANs. In this project, you'll create two LANs with three routers in between. You'll then configure RIP on the routers so they can learn of each other's networks and enable communication between the networks. Complete the following steps:

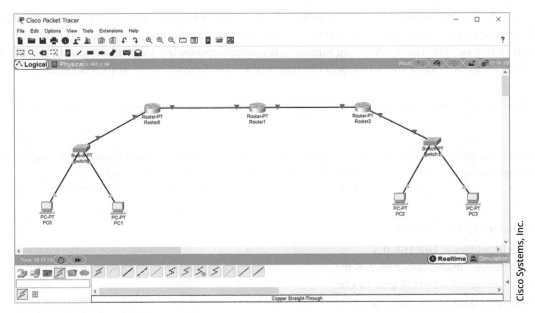

Figure 9-24 Create your network

1. Open Packet Tracer and add the following devices to your workspace, as shown in Figure 9-24:

    a. Four **PCs**

    b. Two **PT-Switches**

    c. Three **PT-Routers**

2. Use Copper Straight-Through cables to connect all PCs to their respective switches and to connect each switch to its closest router. Connect the routers to each other using Fiber cables. Your router connections will not come up automatically, but your switch connections to the PCs will.

3. In Chapter 5, you configured PCs with IP addresses and subnet masks. Refer back to that information for a refresher if you need it. Configure the PCs with the following information, and be sure to add notes to your workspace to document these configurations:

    a. PC0:

    > IP address: **192.168.0.2**
    > Subnet mask: **255.255.255.0**
    > Default gateway: **192.168.0.1**

    b. PC1

    > IP address: **192.168.0.3**
    > Subnet mask: **255.255.255.0**
    > Default gateway: **192.168.0.1**

    c. PC2

    > IP address: **192.168.10.2**
    > Subnet mask: **255.255.255.0**
    > Default gateway: **192.168.10.1**

    d. PC3

    > IP address: **192.168.10.3**
    > Subnet mask: **255.255.255.0**
    > Default gateway: **192.168.10.1**

4. Configure each router's interfaces as listed below. To do this, click each router and click the **Config** tab. The network interfaces are listed in the menu on the left of the Config window. The LAN-facing interface is the link connected to the switch. The WAN-facing interface is the link connected to another router. Be sure to make adjustments for your specific network, and document your configurations in your workspace.

Note

If at any point you need to check which interface a particular connection is using on a device, in the workspace, float your cursor over the connection. Packet Tracer will show the interface in use on each end.

---

    a. Router0's LAN-facing interface:
- IP address: **192.168.0.1**
- Subnet mask: **255.255.255.0**
- Change the Port Status to **On**.

    b. Router0's WAN-facing interface:
- IP address: **172.168.0.1**
- Subnet mask: **255.255.255.0**
- Change the Port Status to **On**.

    c. Router1's interface to Router0:
- IP address: **172.168.0.2**
- Subnet mask: **255.255.255.0**
- Change the Port Status to **On**.

    d. Router1's interface to Router2:
- IP address: **172.168.10.2**
- Subnet mask: **255.255.255.0**
- Change the Port Status to **On**.

    e. Router2's LAN-facing interface:
- IP address: **192.168.10.1**
- Subnet mask: **255.255.255.0**
- Change the Port Status to **On**.

    f. Router2's WAN-facing interface:
- IP address: **172.168.10.1**
- Subnet mask: **255.255.255.0**
- Change the Port Status to **On**.

5. Determine which PCs can talk to each other. Test the following pings:

    a. From PC0, ping PC1. Does it work?

    b. From PC0, ping any of Router1's interfaces. Does it work?

    c. From PC0, ping any of Router2's interfaces. Does it work?

    d. From PC0, ping PC3. Does it work?

6. **Take a screenshot** of your Packet Tracer network and mark all the devices PC0 can successfully ping; submit this visual with your answers to this project's questions.

7. Click **Router0**. In Router0's CLI, choose the commands you need from Table 9-4 to reach global configuration mode.

Table 9-4   Navigate CLI modes

If Your Prompt Says...	Enter This Command	Purpose
`Router>`	`enable`	Enters privileged EXEC mode
`Router#`	`configure terminal`	Enters global configuration mode
`Router (config-if)#`	`exit`	Returns to global configuration mode
`Router (config)#`	[No change needed]	Indicates global configuration mode

8. In Router0's CLI, enter the commands listed in Table 9-5.

Table 9-5   Configure RIPv2 on each router

Command	Purpose
`router rip`	Enables RIP
`version 2`	Specifies RIPv2, which is required to support classless routing
`no auto-summary`	Disables classful networking
`network 192.168.0.0`	Specifies connected network to advertise—all networks directly connected to the router must be listed to be included in RIPv2 routing tables
`network 172.168.0.0`	Specifies connected network to advertise
end and press **Enter**	Returns to privileged EXEC mode
`show ip route rip`	Displays routing table entries learned through RIP—the routing table will be empty at first for the first router, and later routers should start to add entries within a minute or two
`copy run start` and press **Enter**	Saves the current settings

9. Repeat the commands listed in Table 9-4 and Table 9-5 for each of the routers, substituting the network addresses directly connected to each router:

   a. For Router1, you'll list the network addresses 172.168.0.0 and 172.168.10.0.

   b. For Router2, you'll list the network addresses 172.168.10.0 and 192.168.10.0.

10. As RIP is enabled on each router, the router learns of the routes connected to it. To see the routes learned by Router1, enter the command **show ip route rip**. How many routes has Router1 learned through RIP, as indicated by an R in front of the route in the routing table?

11. Determine which PCs can talk to each other. Test the following pings:

   a. From PC0, ping PC1. Does it work?

   b. From PC0, ping any of Router0's interfaces. Does it work?

   c. From PC0, ping any of Router2's interfaces. Does it work?

   d. From PC0, ping PC3. Does it work?

12. **Take a screenshot** of your Packet Tracer network and mark all the devices PC0 can successfully ping; submit this visual with your answers to this project's questions.

13. When you're finished, you can close Packet Tracer. You do not need to save this network.

Reflection Discussion 9

In this chapter, you learned that routers use routing protocols to detect network configurations and conditions as they choose best paths for messages traversing the network. In all the examples given, each router manages its own routing table, collects its own information, and makes its own decisions. This is called distributed routing. In contrast, SDN (software defined networking), which you learned about in Chapter 6, centralizes most of the routing decision-making processes on a network. As you compare these two approaches, answer the following questions:

> What advantages do you think distributed routing provides a network?

> What advantages do you think SDN's centralized routing management provides a network?

> In comparing distributed routing and SDN's centralized routing management, which do you think is the most efficient in getting network traffic where it needs to go?

Go to the discussion forum in your school's LMS (learning management system). Write a post of at least 100 words discussing your thoughts about distributed routing compared to SDN's centralized routing management. Then respond to two of your classmates' threads with posts of at least 50 words discussing their comments and ideas. Use complete sentences, and check your grammar and spelling. Try to ask open-ended questions that encourage discussion, and remember to respond to people who post on your thread. Use the rubric in Table 9-6 to help you understand what is expected of your work for this assignment.

Table 9-6 Grading rubric for Reflection Discussion 9

Task	Novice	Competent	Proficient	Earned
Initial post	Generalized statements comparing distributed and centralized routing **30 points**	Some specific statements with supporting evidence comparing the advantages of distributed routing and SDN's centralized routing management **40 points**	Self-reflective discussion with specific and thoughtful statements and supporting evidence comparing the advantages and efficiency of distributed routing versus SDN's centralized routing management **50 points**	
Initial post: Mechanics	• Length < 100 words • Several grammar and spelling errors 5 points	• Length = 100 words • Occasional grammar and spelling errors 7 points	• Length > 100 words • Appropriate grammar and spelling 10 points	
Response 1	Brief response showing little engagement or critical thinking 5 points	Detailed response with specific contributions to the discussion 10 points	Thoughtful response with specific examples or details and open-ended questions that invite deeper discussion of the topic 15 points	
Response 2	Brief response showing little engagement or critical thinking 5 points	Detailed response with specific contributions to the discussion 10 points	Thoughtful response with specific examples or details and open-ended questions that invite deeper discussion of the topic 15 points	
Both responses: Mechanics	• Length < 50 words each • Several grammar and spelling errors 5 points	• Length = 50 words each • Occasional grammar and spelling errors 7 points	• Length > 50 words each • Appropriate grammar and spelling 10 points	
			Total	

Solutions to Self-Check Questions

Section 9-1: Networks That Connect LANs

1. Two nearby cities each have their own MAN. What network type can connect these two MANs?

Answer: b. WAN

Explanation: WANs interconnect LANs and other network types across large geographical areas, such as when connecting two cities.

2. What network type is best suited to support a city-wide smart traffic system?

Answer: d. MAN

Explanation: A MAN is a collection of LANs within a limited geographical area, such as a city. Because a city-wide smart traffic system will cross property not owned by the city, a MAN is a better choice than a CAN. Because the covered geographical area is contained within the city, and the network needs to be highly fault-tolerant, a MAN is a better choice than a WAN.

Section 9-2: Routing

3. Which of the following is NOT a factor a routing protocol might use to determine a message's best path?

Answer: c. Router brand

Explanation: While a router's brand might determine which routing protocol it can use, that information would not be used in determining a message's best path to its destination across a WAN.

4. You need a predictable route between your home office's network and a branch office's network. What kind of routing can you use to ensure the same route is always used for messages crossing this connection?

Answer: b. Static routing

Explanation: With static routing, a fixed route can be added to the routing table and never updated again.

5. Which routing protocol directs messages across the Internet?

Answer: a. BGP

Explanation: BGP (Border Gateway Protocol) is the only routing protocol used across the open Internet and can span multiple autonomous systems.

Section 9-3: Multiplexing

6. Which form of multiplexing wastes resources by allocating transmission slots even when they're not needed?

Answer: b. Sync TDM

Explanation: With sync TDM (time division multiplexing), if a device has nothing to transmit, the mux must still allocate a slot for that device in the high-speed output stream; but that time slot will, in essence, be empty.

7. Which technology relies on spatial multiplexing to carry on simultaneous conversations with multiple devices at one time?

Answer: d. MU-MIMO

Explanation: MU-MIMO takes advantage of spatial multiplexing to support data exchange with multiple users at the same time.

8. Which form of multiplexing uses overlapping frequency ranges?

Answer: c. OFDM

Explanation: OFDM (Orthogonal Frequency Division Multiplexing) squeezes each channel into overlapping frequency spaces to maximize bandwidth usage and use phase-modulated signals to prevent interference.

Section 9-4: Compression

9. Which compression technique relies on a self-created dictionary?

Answer: d. Lempel-Ziv technique

Explanation: When using the Lempel-Ziv technique, the sender of the data creates a "dictionary" of character strings and associated codes. This set of codes is transmitted and the receiver then re-creates the dictionary and the original data string as the data codes are received.

10. What lossless compression technique compresses the high number of zeroes produced during JPEG compression?

Answer: b. Run-length encoding

Explanation: The third phase of the JPEG compression technique is to take the matrix of quantized values and perform run-length encoding on the zeros.

Chapter 10

Connecting Networks and Resources

Objectives

After reading this chapter, you should be able to:

- Explain WAN service options for small businesses and residential consumers

- Explain WAN service options for enterprises

- Explain WAN virtualization technologies

- Describe popular cloud-supported technologies

Introduction

According to the comics, when Superman needed to change costumes, he would duck into a nearby phone booth. This was not a problem in the 1930s when Superman debuted. Today, however, the Man of Steel would need to find a utility closet or an alleyway, as phone booths have mostly disappeared from the American landscape. In fact, according to the CDC (Centers for Disease Control), most U.S. households no longer even have landline telephones and depend solely on smartphones. The shift away from the telephone system is not limited to phone calls—Internet connectivity has also moved to more modern network infrastructures.

The telephone system as originally envisioned by Alexander Graham Bell in the 1870s was designed to transfer voice signals, not data traffic. As the demand for data connectivity increased, technologies evolved that made use of the existing telephone infrastructure for data transmission across local and long distances alongside voice signals. Other network types can also deliver both data and voice traffic over local and wide areas. Unlike the telephone network, however, these networks were originally designed for data traffic.

Today, consumers and businesses have many options for connecting their own networks to the Internet. WAN connectivity technologies can also create private connections to remote sites, such as branch offices, traveling employees, or cloud networks. In this chapter, you'll learn about WAN connectivity options for consumers and small businesses, and then you'll explore more reliable—and expensive—options for larger enterprises. You'll then read about newer technologies that take advantage of virtualization and SDN (software-defined networking) to blend the best of both consumer-grade and enterprise-grade WAN connectivity options. This chapter concludes with a discussion of cloud-based services that require WAN connectivity from your on-prem network to the cloud.

Section 10-1: Small Business and Consumer-Grade WAN Services

Internet service providers offer an array of service options to connect customers to the Internet and to other remote locations. Homes and small businesses can get Internet access for relatively low prices because the technologies used to support those connections tend to be less reliable with less constant available bandwidth. However, this doesn't mean that consumer-grade Internet services aren't reliable or aren't fast. They're just not at the levels needed by larger companies. Still, you can sometimes find home Internet service that provides speeds up to 1 Gbps, which is called gigabit Internet, or gig Internet for short.

Another cost-saving factor is the fact that many of these Internet connectivity options take advantage of existing network infrastructure, such as telephone lines or cable TV connections. While these systems weren't designed with Internet connectivity in mind, they can provide decent service that satisfies the needs of most homeowners and small businesses. Additionally, the infrastructure supporting these Internet connections is shared to some degree with other customers, a technology called broadband Internet.

This section begins with a discussion of Internet provided over the existing telephone and cable lines and then explores other options made available through more dedicated technologies.

All Things Considered

Thought Experiment

Before reading about the different types of Internet connection technologies for home and small business customers, do some research on what kind of Internet connection your home network uses to connect to your ISP. If you don't have a home network, research Internet connection options available in your area.

Digital Subscriber Line (DSL)

The basic telephone system, or POTS (plain old telephone service), has been in existence since the early 1900s. During most of those years, POTS was an analog system capable of supporting voice conversations. It was not until the 1970s that POTS began carrying computer data signals as well as voice signals. The amount of data transmitted on POTS eventually grew so large that near the end of the twentieth century, the system carried more data than voice.

DSL (digital subscriber line) allows *existing* twisted pair telephone lines to transmit multimedia materials and high-speed data. To do this, DSL had to be capable of functioning within the limitations of the existing telephone system. As you saw in Chapter 3, the average human voice has a frequency range of roughly 300 to 3400 Hz (a bandwidth of 3100 Hz). Thus, the telephone network was engineered to transmit signals of approximately 3100 Hz. In practice, the telephone system actually allocates 4000 Hz to a channel and uses filters to remove frequencies that fall above and below each 4000-Hz channel. The channels and their frequencies are depicted in Figure 10-1.

All this talk about frequencies and voice transmission leads to two important points:

> The more information you wish to send over a medium, the higher the frequency of the signal you need to represent that information. (See Chapter 3 for a detailed discussion of this point.)

> If you want to send data over a telephone line, it must be able to travel in one or more 4000-Hz channels.

When you put these two statements together, a painful fact about using voice communication lines for data transmission emerges: any data transmission that is performed over a standard telephone line must fit within one or more fairly narrow bands of 4000 Hz, which means the data transmission rate will also be limited. Recall Shannon's formula from Chapter 3, which shows that the frequency, noise level, and power level of an analog signal determine the maximum rate of data transmission. With advanced modulation techniques such as discrete multitone (used in DSL) and orthogonal frequency division multiplexing (used in digital television), it is possible to create hundreds of channels on two twisted pairs. Let's examine more closely how DSL works.

DSL Basics

Most, if not all, telephone companies offer various levels of DSL service. As with any technology that can deliver multimedia data, transmission speed is an important issue. DSL transfer speeds can range from hundreds of thousands of bits per second up to several million

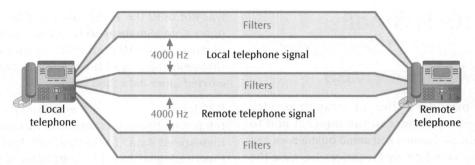

Figure 10-1 The two telephone channels and their assigned frequencies

bits per second. The transfer speed of a particular line depends on one or more of the following factors:

> The carrier providing the service determines the particular form of DSL technology and the supporting transmission formats. The form of DSL and its underlying technology determine the theoretical maximum speeds of the service.

> The distance of your house or business from the phone company's CO (central office) directly impacts the speed of the signal you experience: the closer your house or business is to the CO, the faster the possible transmission speed. This dependency on distance is due to the fact that copper-based twisted pair is susceptible to noise, which can significantly affect a DSL transmission signal. The farther the wire goes without a repeater, the more noise on the line and the slower the transmission speed. The maximum distance a house or business can be from the CO without a repeater is approximately 5.5 km (3 miles).

> The type of connection, either symmetric or asymmetric, directly affects transfer speed. A **symmetric connection** is one in which upload and download transfer speeds are equal. An **asymmetric connection** has a faster downstream transmission speed than its upstream speed. For example, an asymmetric DSL service typically provides download speeds around 5-35 Mbps, while upload speeds may be less than 10 Mbps. An asymmetric service is useful for an Internet connection in which the bulk of the traffic (in the form of web pages or streaming media) comes down from the Internet to the user's devices. Often the only data that goes up to the Internet is a request for another web page, some relatively small email messages, or a request to stream a different multimedia file. Most residential DSL services are asymmetric.

Another distinguishing characteristic of DSL is that it is an "always-on" connection. Users do not have to dial in to make a connection. Furthermore, the connection is charged at a flat, usually monthly, rate. The user does not pay a fee based on the distance of the connection or how long the connection is established, although some DSL providers may charge by the amount of data downloaded per month.

Note

Recall from Chapter 7 how any connection that is created using DHCP, which is common with DSL, may lose its connection after a period of inactivity, thus requiring DHCP to renegotiate a connection. So technically speaking, the connection is not always on. But for the typical user, it appears that way.

What does a business or home user need in order to establish a DSL connection? Currently, four components are required, as illustrated in Figure 10-2:

> The LEC (local exchange carrier) installs a special router called a DSLAM (DSL Access Multiplexer) within the telephone company's CO. This device bypasses the CO switching equipment, and it creates and decodes the DSL signals that transfer on the telephone local loop.

> The DSLAM router at the telephone company's CO must be connected to an ISP via a high-speed line because this high-speed line will support the Internet service requests from multiple users.

> The local telephone company may also install a DSL splitter on its premises, which combines or splits the DSL circuits (the upstream and downstream channels) with the standard telephone circuit of POTS. Some DSL systems transmit over the same

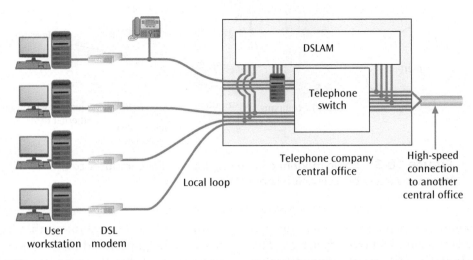

Figure 10-2 The four necessary components of a DSL connection

telephone line that runs from a CO to a home or business. Because it is the same telephone line, DSL must share the line with a POTS signal. If the DSL is of a particular form, then the DSL line does not carry a standard telephone circuit. Thus, there is no need to split the DSL signal from the telephone signal at either the sending or receiving end.

> On the user end, a DSL modem is required to convert the DSL signals into a form that the user workstation or network can understand. If the DSL circuit is also carrying a POTS telephone circuit, the user will also need a splitter to separate the regular telephone line from the DSL data line.

DSL Formats

DSL comes in a variety of formats. A number of these formats will, no doubt, fall by the wayside over time, but there is no way of knowing how long that will take. For now, an informed business network user should be aware of the various formats. Collectively referred to as xDSL, three DSL formats commonly in use today include:

> **ADSL (asymmetric digital subscriber line)**—A popular format that transmits the downstream data at a faster rate than the upstream rate. Typical downstream data rates start around 7 Mbps, while upstream data rates might reach 1-2 Mbps.

> **VDSL (very high data rate DSL)**—A very fast format (up to 100 Mbps downstream and upstream) over very short distances (less than 300 meters).

> **R-ADSL (rate-adaptive DSL)**—A format in which the transfer rate can vary depending on noise levels within the telephone line's local loop.

DSL is not the only way that a home or small business user can contract a data delivery service to connect their private network to the Internet. Let's examine a second very popular technology: the cable modem.

Cable Modems

Cable modem Internet is a communications service that allows high-speed access to WANs such as the Internet via a cable television connection. A cable modem is a physical device that separates the computer data from the cable television video signal, but many people refer to the entire system (fiber-optic cables, neighborhood distribution nodes, coaxial cables, cable modem splitter, and interface card) as a cable modem service. This connection of components is shown in Figure 10-3. Notice that much of the cabling is fiber, not coaxial. At this point, much of the cable television network has been converted to fiber and so is called an HFC (hybrid fiber coaxial) network. In an HFC network, fiber optic cabling connects the cable company's distribution center to distribution hubs and then to optical nodes near the customer. Either fiber optic or coaxial cable then connects a node to each customer's business or residence.

Most cable modems connect to a private network through a common Ethernet NIC, which is either provided by the cable company or purchased at most

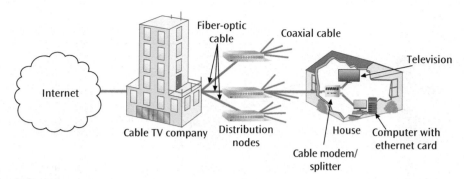

Figure 10-3 Cable modem connecting a personal computer to the Internet via a cable television connection

stores that sell computer equipment. As such, the connection is capable of transmission rates ranging as high as 10 Gbps, and, similar to DSL, these connections are typically asymmetric. Note that experienced speeds are partially determined by the DOCSIS version of the modem on the customer's end. A DOCSIS 3.0 modem maxes out around 1 Gbps while a DOCSIS 3.1 modem might be capable of supporting speeds nearing 10 Gbps. The Details box, "Cable Modem Standards," discusses the importance of DOCSIS. Despite the capabilities of cable modem technologies, experienced speeds in most cases tend to be much lower.

Cable modems provide high-speed connections to the Internet and the demand for them now is consistently high. Like the telephone system, the cable system features a kind of local loop—that is, a cable that runs from the neighborhood distribution node into a home or business. A disadvantage of cable modems is that, as traffic to and from each customer's location increases, there is a decrease in available bandwidth for each network connection. Thus, as more customers within a neighborhood use their cable modem service, throughput suffers. If you have cable Internet, you might have noticed your network performance degrading in the evenings when other cable customers in your area start streaming music or videos after work. The reason for this reduced throughput is because cable connections are quickly merged onto the same physical media and do not run on a dedicated connection to the provider for as far as a DSL connection does.

Details | Cable Modem Standards

Cable companies that offer a cable modem service use a standard called DOCSIS (Data Over Cable Service Interface Specification). Currently modems built to DOCSIS 3.1 are available with most cable companies requiring at least DOCSIS 3.0. DOCSIS 4.0 is already on the horizon with the new specs released in March of 2020. DOCSIS was designed to include all the operational elements used in delivering a data service over a cable television system, including service provisioning, security, data interfaces, and radio frequency interfaces. The basic architecture of a cable modem system is shown in Figure 10-4.

The system consists of six major components:

1. The CMTS (Cable Modem Termination System) is located at the main facility of the cable operator

and translates the incoming data packets into radio frequencies. Downstream channels cover bandwidths between 24 and 192 MHz while upstream channels vary from 6.4 to 96 MHz.

2. The combiner combines the frequencies of the data packets with the frequencies of common cable television channels.

3. These signals are then sent over a fiber-optic line.

4. The signals are received by a fiber distribution node, which resides in a user's neighborhood and can distribute the signals to 500–2000 homes.

5. From the fiber distribution node, coaxial cables carry the signals into homes where a splitter separates the data packet frequencies from the cable

channel frequencies. The cable channel frequencies go to the television set, and the data packet frequencies that have been split off go to a cable modem.

6. The cable modem converts the radio signals back to digital data packets for delivery to your computer.

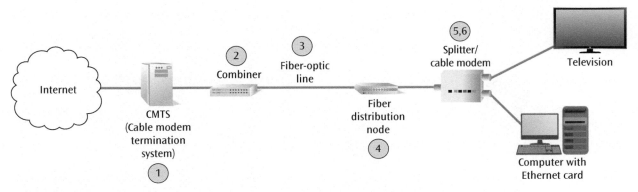

Figure 10-4   Basic architecture and components of a cable modem system

Fiber Internet

Currently, the fastest Internet service connection available to consumers and small businesses is broadband fiber Internet. Fiber Internet relies on fiber-optic cable run close to or all the way to the customer's location. Because fiber cable is not readily available from older telecommunications systems, this service option is typically more expensive, and its availability is limited.

The proximity of the fiber cable termination to its point of use partially determines the cost of fiber Internet. Most of the Internet backbone already runs on fiber. Even if you connect your new home office to the Internet via an obsolete dial-up connection, most of the distance your data travels on the Internet will run over fiber cables. It's that last mile to your location that really slows your data down. The growing trend in ISP offerings is to provide fiber closer and closer to the customer's location. In these scenarios, the ISP runs a fiber connection to one of a few nearby locations, as illustrated in Figure 10-5 and described next:

> **FTTN (fiber-to-the-node** or **fiber-to-the-neighborhood)** —A nearby service junction that serves a few hundred customers

> **FTTC (fiber-to-the-curb)**—A nearby pole or equipment cabinet that serves a few customers

> **FTTB (fiber-to-the-building)** or **FTTH (fiber-to-the-home)**—The junction box at the entry point to your building

As you can see, each progressive scenario brings the fiber closer to your own network. The closest options cost more but also reduce the distance over which your data must traverse copper cabling to reach your private network. While this option has limited availability in many market areas, those who can choose fiber often do. Fiber's higher speeds, with symmetric speeds often reaching as high as 1–2 Gbps for home or small business fiber services, offset the increased cost. Additionally, so long as the ISP can provide you with a fiber connection, your distance from their offices won't negatively affect your experienced speeds.

Fiber technology and availability to business customers —and even to residential customers—continues to improve. Rising market demand for last-mile fiber service is causing increased investments by ISPs into their access-level fiber infrastructure. Traditionally, fiber investment focused on long-haul connections across hundreds and thousands of miles. In contrast, MONs (metropolitan optical networks) bring fiber to the customer. This dense, localized grid of junctions and fiber cables attempts to make direct fiber connections available to as many customers as possible while balancing the significant expense of replacing existing telephone and coaxial cable infrastructure with fiber equipment and fiber-optimized technologies.

Recall from Chapter 9 some of the multiplexing technologies that handle multiple signals on each fiber connection, such as DWDM (dense wavelength division

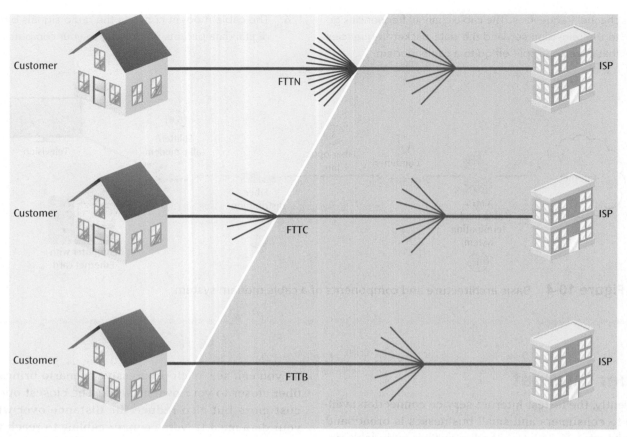

Figure 10-5   Getting fiber closer to your own network increases your Internet speeds

multiplexing). However, DWDM does not easily lend itself to handling the high numbers of communications channels and the wide variety of network protocols needed within a metro network environment. This mismatch between what pre-existing fiber technology was designed to do and what is needed in the metro market is sometimes referred to as the "metro gap." In response to these emerging needs, newer technology has been developed or adapted to support MONs and the expectations of customers in these markets. With 100 Gbps speeds already available on long-haul connections, the industry is now aiming for similar speeds for MONs on the ISP's end of broadband fiber connections.

Satellite

A limited number of companies offer satellite Internet services. Satellite Internet is typically the slowest of all Internet options, but also the most readily available in rural areas where wired connections are limited. It requires a dish-shaped antenna installed at the customer's location, and the dish is set to communicate with a geostationary satellite in orbit.

Signals via satellite travel from a ground station on Earth to a satellite in orbit around the Earth and back to another ground station on Earth, thus traversing great distances across the globe, farther than Earth-bound line-of-sight transmissions. In fact, a satellite located at the farthest possible communication point from the Earth—36,000 kilometers or 22,300 miles—can receive and send signals approximately one-third the distance around the Earth. Satellite systems can also transmit signals all the way around the Earth by bouncing them from one satellite to another.

One way of categorizing satellite systems is by how far the satellite is from the Earth. The closer a satellite is to the Earth, the shorter the times required to send data to the satellite—to uplink—and receive data from the satellite—to downlink. This transmission time from ground station to satellite and back to ground station is called propagation delay. The disadvantage to being closer to Earth is that the satellite must continuously circle the Earth to remain in orbit. Thus, these satellites are constantly moving and eventually pass beyond the horizon, ruining the line-of-sight transmission. They can only be used with applications requiring shorter periods of data transfer, such as mobile telephone systems. Satellites that are farther away can always stay over the same point on Earth and can be used for longer periods of high-speed data transfers. As Figure 10-6 shows, satellites orbit the Earth from four possible ranges:

> LEO (low Earth orbit) satellites are closest to the Earth. They maintain an altitude of 99 to 1,200 miles, which is much higher than commercial jets at 6-7 miles altitude. While jets fly at about 500 mph, LEO satellites fly at nearly 18,000 mph, and this allows a complete orbit about every 90-120 minutes. The number of LEO satellites is growing rapidly. At the end of the twentieth century, there were approximately 300 LEO satellites. By 2019, nearly 1,500 LEO satellites were in orbit, including the International Space Station and the Hubble Space Telescope. LEO satellites are used primarily for satellite imaging, weather observation, and communication constellations (several satellites working together), and are expected to play an increasingly key role in IoT (Internet of Things) networks.

> MEO (middle Earth orbit) satellites are typically found roughly 3,000 to 15,000 miles from the Earth. At the end of the twentieth century, approximately 65 MEO satellites were orbiting the Earth. Although MEO

satellite systems are not growing at the same phenomenal rate as LEO systems, industry experts estimated that the number of MEO satellites as of 2019 was over 130. These satellites are visible for longer periods, completing an orbit every 2-24 hours, and work well for many types of navigation technologies, such as the American GPS (Global Positioning System), Europe's Galileo, and Russia's GLONASS (Globalnaya Navigazionnaya Sputnikovaya Sistema). GPS (global positioning system) is a system of 29 operational satellites that were launched by the U.S. Department of Defense and are used for identifying locations on Earth. By triangulating signals from at least four GPS satellites (each of which provides the directional coordinates X, Y, Z, and time), a receiving unit can pinpoint its own current location to within a few yards or meters anywhere on Earth.

> GEO (geosynchronous Earth orbit) satellites (also known as high earth orbit) are found exactly 22,236 miles (35,786 kilometers) from the Earth and are always positioned over the same longitude at a point near the Earth's equator. Two ground stations can maintain a continuous connection with each other, conducting continuous transmissions from Earth to the satellite and back to Earth, because

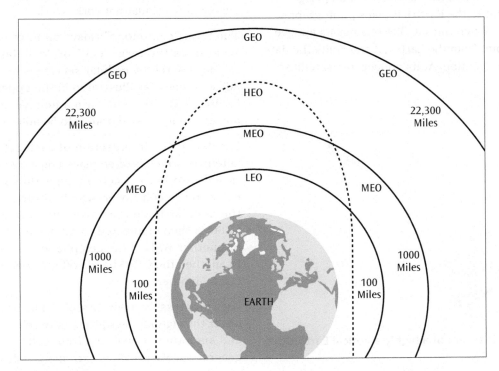

Figure 10-6   Earth and the four Earth orbits: LEO, MEO, GEO, and HEO

the satellite mostly appears "stationary" from the ground. The satellite's orbit corresponds exactly with the Earth's rotation, taking 23 hours 56 minutes and 4 seconds to complete. GEO satellites are most commonly used for signal relays for radio and television; meteorology; search and rescue beacons; monitoring solar activity; Internet connection services; and communications between other, non-GEO satellites. The primary advantage of GEO satellites is their capacity for delivering consistently available transmissions that can cover up to one-third of Earth's surface. However, due to the location of these orbits over or near the Equator, higher latitude geographies cannot rely on connectivity with these satellites. Companies that operate GEO satellites can commit all their transmission resources to one client or share the satellite time with multiple clients. The use of a GEO satellite system by a single client is expensive and usually involves the transfer of great amounts of data. Over 560 GEO satellites were in orbit by the end of 2019.

> A fourth satellite system that has unique properties is the HEO (highly elliptical orbit) satellite, which is used by governments for satellite photography, by scientific agencies for observing celestial bodies, and by non-global communications networks. An HEO satellite follows an elliptical pattern, as shown in Figure 10-7. When the satellite is at its perigee (closest point to the Earth), it takes photographs of the Earth. When the satellite reaches its apogee (farthest point from the Earth), it transmits the data to the ground station. At its apogee, the satellite

Figure 10-7 Diagram of a highly elliptical Earth orbit satellite

can also photograph objects in space. Some countries use HEO satellites to provide more consistent communications coverage to their geographical area, as an elliptical orbit can place a satellite over a specific continent for longer periods of time through the course of the orbit. For example, a satellite in the Molniya orbit, developed by Russian scientists, can spend about two-thirds of its 12-hour orbit over the northern hemisphere.

Satellite Internet works well when low-speed, asymmetrical service is sufficient for the customer's purposes. Typical speeds are 1 to 2 Mbps for the downlink and 300 Kbps for uplink. However, throughput is not reliable, and the entire satellite connection can be lost during bad weather when the line-of-sight connection is obscured by clouds and precipitation.

Cellular Networks

If you have a cell phone with access to the Internet, then you may use a cellular connection to the Internet. Most smartphones rely on two network types to access the Internet: Wi-Fi, which is a short-range connection to a nearby access point and on to a LAN, or cellular, which is a long-range connection to a cellular antenna and on to a WAN. You can review Wi-Fi in Chapters 2 and 5. Recall from Chapter 9 the generations of cellular networks in the context of multiplexing. This section discusses how cellular networks work.

The term "cell phone" raises an interesting question: What does the term "cell" or "cellular" mean? Each region covered by cellular service is broken down into adjacent cells (as illustrated in the upper-left corner of Figure 10-8). The cells form a honeycomb-like pattern and can range in size from ½ to 50 miles in radius.

Located at the intersection of each cell is an array of antennas, which is often placed on a free-standing tower (see Figure 10-9). A cell phone within a cell communicates to the cell tower, which in turn is connected to the cellular telephone switching office (CTSO). The CTSO is then connected to the local telephone system or another WAN. If the cell phone moves from one cell to another, the CTSO hands off the connection from one cell to another.

Each progressive generation of cellular technology offers faster throughput, less jitter, more reliable connections, and smoother transitions from cell to cell. The latest generation, 5G, provides extremely high-speed, wireless

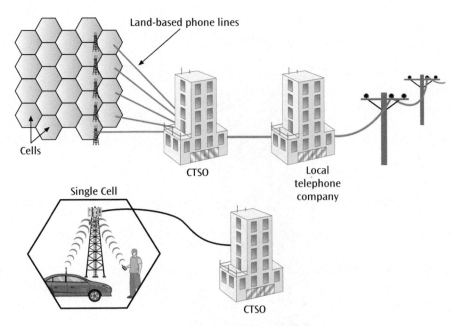

Figure 10-8 One cell phone market divided into cells

Note

In earlier generation cell phone systems, a cell phone company could tell only the cell in which you were located. It could not determine exactly where in the cell you were. Shortly after 2000, the FCC asked the cell phone companies to devise a system in which the exact location of a cell phone could be determined. One of the ideas behind this feature was that it would enable emergency services to locate a cell phone user should the user request a 911 service. Today, nearly all cell phones are enabled with a GPS chip so that in emergency situations, the cell phone company can locate the cell phone and user within 100 feet. It is also possible to locate a cell phone by triangulating on the cell phone's signal.

connectivity. You might think of cellular technology, like LTE and 4G, as mostly relevant just for smartphones. Maybe you have a cellular adapter for your laptop, or maybe your car has cellular service. But 5G will make cellular networking relevant to all kinds of connections, not just for checking your email or streaming a YouTube video on your phone.

Consider the possibilities as 5G becomes more widely available: traffic management systems, expansive AI connectivity, smart homes and smart cities, supply chain automation and increased efficiency, drone networks, robotics and automation, telemedicine breakthroughs, and as yet unimagined possibilities with virtual reality. Your home network and possibly entire business networks can connect with the Internet through 5G connections, and you wouldn't need cable or DSL or, in many cases, fiber. In fact, you won't even be limited by your own home network—you can have all your devices (such as your car, laptop, IoT, watch, and many others) connect directly to the Internet through 5G, no matter where you are or where your devices are.

The convenience and reliability of 5G will also provide more flexibility to distribute computing activities across the connection between cloud resources and mobile and IoT devices. You can have cheaper endpoint devices that are less capable but perform better because they maintain a solid connection to cloud resources that are doing the actual computing work. Many experts predict that 5G will do for cloud what interstates and highways

All Things Considered

Thought Experiment

If you have a smartphone, does your cell phone provider offer 5G service? If so, have you upgraded your phone to 5G yet? Have you noticed any differences in performance, connectivity, or reliability?

Mike West

Figure 10-9 A cell phone tower

did for travel in making distant networks and devices more connected with faster throughput and lower costs.

Remember this...

> Homes and small businesses can get Internet access for relatively low prices because the technologies used to support those connections tend to be less reliable with less constant available bandwidth. Many of these Internet connectivity options take advantage of existing network infrastructure, such as telephone lines or cable TV connections.

> DSL (digital subscriber line) allows existing twisted pair telephone lines to transmit multimedia materials and high-speed data. The type of connection, either symmetric or asymmetric, directly affects transfer speed. A symmetric connection is one in which upload and download transfer speeds are equal. An asymmetric connection has a faster downstream transmission speed than its upstream speed.

> Cable modem Internet is a communications service that allows high-speed access to WANs such as the Internet via a cable television connection. A

cable modem is a physical device that separates the computer data from the cable television video signal, but many people refer to the entire system (fiber-optic cables, neighborhood distribution nodes, coaxial cables, cable modem splitter, and interface card) as a cable modem service. Much of the cable television network has been converted to fiber and so is called an HFC (hybrid fiber coaxial) network.

❭ Currently, the fastest Internet service connection available to consumers and small businesses is broadband fiber Internet. Fiber Internet relies on fiber-optic cable run close to or all the way to the customer's location. Because fiber cable is not readily available from older telecommunications systems, this service option is typically more expensive, and its availability is limited.

❭ A limited number of companies offer satellite Internet services. Satellite Internet is typically the slowest of all Internet options, but also the most readily available in rural areas where wired connections are limited. It requires a dish-shaped antenna installed at the customer's location, and the dish is set to communicate with a stationary satellite in orbit.

❭ Most smartphones rely on two network types to access the Internet: Wi-Fi, which is a short-range connection to a nearby access point and on to a LAN, or cellular, which is a long-range connection to a cellular antenna and on to a WAN. Each region covered by cellular service is broken down into adjacent cells, which form a honeycomb-like pattern. Located at the intersection of each cell is an array of antennas, which is often placed on a free-standing tower.

Self-check

1. How fast is gigabit Internet?
   a. 1 Mbps
   b. 10 Mbps
   c. 100 Mbps
   d. 1000 Mbps

2. Which Internet service's throughput is determined by a DOCSIS version?
   a. Satellite
   b. Cable
   c. DSL
   d. Cellular

3. If your cell phone says it has a 5G connection, what kind of Internet-connection technology is it using to connect to your cell provider's network?
   a. Satellite
   b. Wi-Fi
   c. Cellular
   d. Fiber

Check your answers at the end of this chapter.

Section 10-2: Enterprise-Grade WAN Services

All the Internet connection services you've studied so far provide a connection from a device or LAN to the open Internet. Many businesses, however, need WAN connections between specific locations, such as between a corporate office and a branch office. In some cases, these connections can be made over the open Internet, sometimes called the "wild area network." In other cases, sensitive data necessitates a private connection over dedicated infrastructure where the signal cannot be easily intercepted.

Predictably, private or dedicated connections are more expensive because the costs of the underlying infrastructure are not shared among many customers. While costs have decreased over time for these types of private connections, more significant cost savings has been achieved by increasing the security and controllability of open Internet connections. Let's examine how this evolution of technology has developed.

Legacy WAN Technologies

Some older WAN technologies are still around, and you're likely to encounter them at some point. These technologies are usually still in place to service legacy networks or legacy services. Even if you don't work for a company that uses them, having a foundational understanding of what each of these is will help you better understand the improvements offered by current WAN technologies. Legacy WAN connectivity services still in use include:

❭ **T-1 line**—A leased telephone line (or group of lines) that maintains a constant, all-digital data connection between two locations and can transfer either voice or data at speeds up to 1.544 Mbps. Smaller portions of a T-1 are cheaper with lower data throughput, while combinations of multiple T-1s transmit data up to 45 Mbps.

> **Frame relay**—A permanent or temporary (called switched) data circuit provided over a telephone network or a dedicated network infrastructure that can connect locations locally or long-distance. Data transfer speeds can be faster than a T-1 at lower costs with some services reaching up to 45 Mbps. With permanent connections, the channel is always available. Switched connections, on the other hand, provide a dynamic ability to allocate bandwidth on demand. The error rate of frame relay networks is so low that the network does not have any form of error control. If an error occurs, the frame relay network simply discards the frame. It is the responsibility of the application, and not the frame relay network, to perform error control. Frame relay is a layer 2 protocol, meaning it functions at the data link layer and relies on some other technology at the physical layer (typically fiber-optic).

> **ATM (Asynchronous Transfer Mode)**—Like frame relay, a high-speed data communication service with transfer rates as fast as 622 Mbps, and even faster speeds possible in some locations. In ATM, all data is sent in small, 53-byte packages called cells. The cell size is kept small so that when a cell reaches a node (a switch point) in an ATM network, the cell will quickly pass through the node and continue on its way to its destination. This fast-switching capability gives ATM its high transfer rates. Furthermore, ATM is a fully switched network. As the cells hop from node to node through the network, each one is processed and forwarded by high-speed switches. ATM can handle a wide range of applications, including live video, music, and interactive voice. At the physical layer, ATM requires specialized cabling and hardware and so is considered to be both a layer 1 and layer 2 technology. Finally, ATM can support different classes of traffic to provide various QoS (quality of service) levels. ATM is often more expensive than other options because of the high cost and complexity of ATM equipment.

MPLS

Recall from Chapter 7 how MPLS (Multiprotocol Label Switching) can be used to create a faster and well-defined path across the Internet. MPLS achieves this goal by adding a label to each message, similar in concept to a VLAN's tag. The labeled packet traverses a predefined route across one or more ISP's networks, allowing for high-speed data transfer over very long distances for lower prices than what some of the older WAN technologies could offer. Due to this labeling, MPLS can provide reliable, high-speed connections over the public Internet infrastructure, resulting in lower costs.

As its name implies, MPLS enables multiple types of layer 3 protocols to travel over any one of several layer 2 protocols. Essentially, MPLS allows you to use any connectivity option that makes sense for each site while centrally managing bandwidth between each site. For example, in Figure 10-10, you might have your warehouse connected to the ISP using DSL while your storefronts use fiber broadband and your central office has a leased line.

Despite the various service levels of each location's connection to the ISP, you can manage segmentation and QoS (quality of service) for different types of traffic across your entire network, even if your locations are spread hundreds or thousands of miles apart. Recall from Chapter 5 that QoS refers to a group of techniques for adjusting the priority assigned to various types of traffic. For example, you might want to prioritize VoIP traffic over email traffic. Additionally, you can set routes for traffic between sites so the ISP's routers don't have to stop and think with each packet where that packet should go next. Essentially, MPLS lets routers function more like switches, working with information in layer 2 headers instead of having to dig to layer 3 and process routing information. This saves time and reduces latency.

With MPLS, the first ISP router (the provider's edge router, also called the MPLS ingress router) receives a message in a data stream and adds one or more labels to the layer 3 packet. These MPLS labels together are sometimes called a shim because of their placement between layer 3 and layer 2 headers. For this reason, MPLS is sometimes said to belong to "layer 2.5." Next, the network's layer 2 protocol header is added, as illustrated in Figure 10-11.

These MPLS labels include information about where the router should forward the message next and, sometimes, prioritization information. Each router in the data stream's path (see Figure 10-12) revises the label to indicate the packet's next hop. In this manner, routers on a network can take into consideration network congestion, QoS indicators assigned to the messages, plus other criteria; however, these transit routers, called

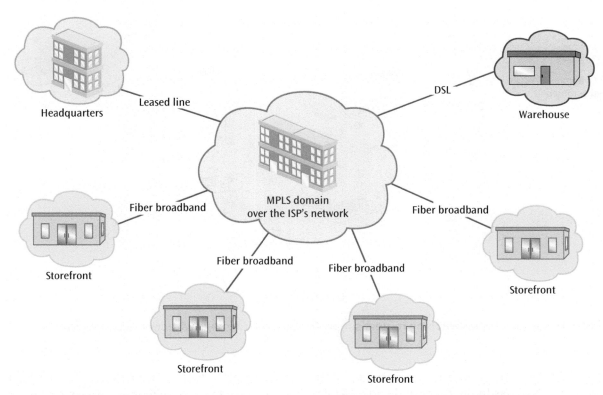

Figure 10-10   MPLS provides cohesive WAN management for multiple connection types

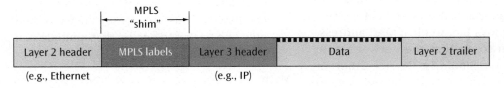

Figure 10-11   MPLS shim within a frame

LSRs (label switching routers), don't have to take time to map a path for the messages. Network engineers maintain significant control in setting these paths. Consequently, MPLS offers potentially faster transmission than traditionally routed networks.

While MPLS does offer decreased latency, this benefit is not quite as noticeable today as it was when MPLS first became available. The primary benefits of MPLS today include the following:

> MPLS connections are highly scalable for businesses, which means a business can add more and longer connections for less cost than similarly scaled leased lines.

> Customers can prioritize their own traffic across the WAN according to QoS attributes, such as giving VoIP traffic higher priority over email traffic.

> The ability to label traffic offers more reliability, predictability, and security (when properly implemented) than when using cheaper connections over the open Internet.

Ethernet

As you know, Ethernet was originally developed as a LAN technology that delivers messages from one device to the next, using information in its layer 2 header. Due to its simplicity, Ethernet has also become an attractive option for WAN and MAN connections. However, because Ethernet was not originally designed with this purpose in mind, certain adaptions were needed to make Ethernet capable of traversing WANs and MANs. The standard that emerged, as defined by the MEF (Metro Ethernet Forum), was **CE (Carrier Ethernet)**.

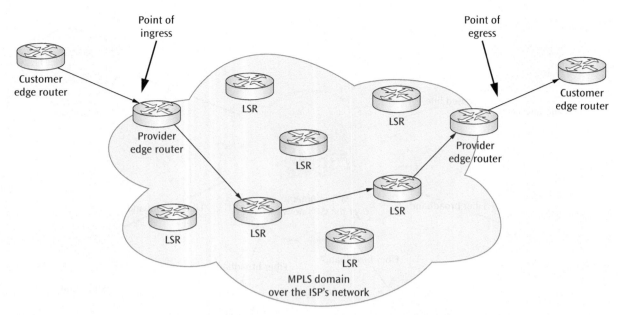

Figure 10-12 Label switching routers simply forward the message without calculating routes

Recall that Ethernet directs messages according to the destination MAC address in the Ethernet header. While MAC addresses should be unique, this is not always the case. Therefore, Carrier Ethernet needed a different method for tracking the destination of each message. The solution was IEEE 802.1ah, also called MAC-in-MAC. This addressing scheme employs hierarchical MAC addressing with encapsulation to protect the network from duplicate MAC addresses. Similarly, Carrier Ethernet uses double VLAN tagging, called QinQ (in reference to the VLAN standard, 802.1q) to provide separate inner and outer VLAN tags.

Ethernet is less expensive than other systems, is well understood, easily scalable at convenient through-put tiers (such as 10 Mbps, 100 Mbps, 1000 Mbps, or 10 Gbps), and works well to carry IP traffic over the Internet. Ethernet MANs have given rise to a service whose popularity continues to grow: Metro Ethernet. **Metro Ethernet** is a data transfer service that can connect one business to another business (or businesses) using a standard Ethernet connection:

> A direct connection between companies can use a point-to-point connection, or, for example, to two other companies using two point-to-point connections, as shown in Figure 10-13. This is similar to having a private connection between two points. A common example of this type of Metro Ethernet connection is found when a company is connected to an ISP. All the traffic on this connection is between only two locations.

> Alternatively, one company can connect to multiple companies as though they were all part of a large LAN, as shown in Figure 10-14. This is an example of a multipoint-to-multipoint connection. Here, any company can talk to one or more (or all) connected companies. Thus, a company needs to send out only one packet to ensure that multiple companies receive this data.

Metro Ethernet users can seamlessly connect their company Ethernet LANs to the larger network. Because all the involved networks are Ethernet, there is no need for time-consuming and sometimes clumsy conversions from one format to another. Thus, a corporate LAN running at 1 Gbps can smoothly connect to a Metro Ethernet service also running at 1 Gbps.

A company that has a Metro Ethernet connection can also create a bandwidth profile for that connection. This bandwidth profile describes various characteristics about the connection, such as basic data transfer rates, basic burst rates (a burst is a large surge of data that is transmitted for a short period of time), excess data transfer rates, and excess burst rates. Recall from Chapter 5 that LAN Ethernet does not allow users to set their own data transfer rates—they must simply accept the one rate corresponding to the particular brand of Ethernet (such as 100-Mbps Ethernet) they have chosen. This profile feature of Metro Ethernet is an interesting and powerful option for companies that want to tailor a connection to a particular application. For example, if a company is launching a new web

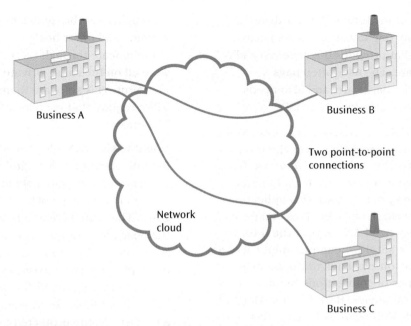

Figure 10-13   Two point-to-point connections

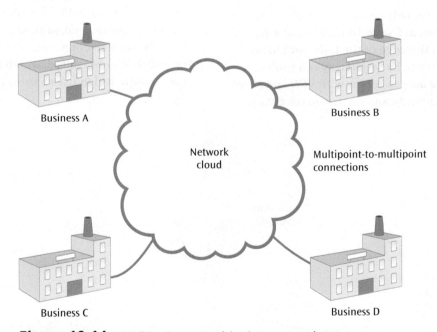

Figure 10-14   Multipoint-to-multipoint connections

application and expects a varying level of user response, the company's network personnel can set a basic data transfer rate for the average response anticipated, and then set an excess burst rate for peak periods.

Virtual Private Network (VPN)

Recall from Chapter 9 the tunneling protocols that allow a VPN (virtual private network) to create a secure tunnel across the Internet through which a business can confidently send private data. There are basically two ways a business can create a tunnel through the Internet:

> **Software**—A user installs the necessary software at each end of the tunnel and contracts an ISP to create and maintain the tunnel. This typically incurs a monthly charge from the ISP.

> **Hardware and software**—The user purchases software and physical or virtual hardware that is

placed at each end of the tunnel. The hardware is essentially a gateway (an advanced router) called the **VPN headend** that provides the necessary VPN and security software. The user often pays a one-time price for the hardware, and also needs a standard Internet connection via an ISP.

Businesses rely on VPNs for many purposes. Most often, remote workers will use a VPN over the Internet to securely connect to the company network. This connection might provide access to internal company resources, such as a file system, database, applications, or internal website. Alternatively, a business might use a robust VPN to connect two LANs across the Internet. For example, a school's satellite campus might use a VPN to connect all its resources back to the home campus. These different types of connections require different underlying VPN technologies. Based on the kinds of endpoints they connect, VPNs can be loosely classified according to three models:

> **Site-to-site VPN**—Tunnels connect multiple sites on a WAN, as shown in Figure 10-15. At each site, a VPN gateway on the edge of the LAN establishes the secure connection. Each gateway is a router, firewall, or remote access server with VPN software installed, and it encrypts and encapsulates data to

exchange over the tunnel. Meanwhile, clients, servers, and other hosts on the protected LANs communicate through the VPN gateways as if they were all on the same, private network without needing to run VPN software themselves. Site-to-site VPNs require that each location have a static public IP address.

> **Client-to-site VPN**, also called host-to-site VPN— Remote clients, servers, and other hosts establish tunnels with a private network through the VPN headend at the edge of the LAN, as shown in Figure 10-16. The tunnel created between the client and the headend encrypts and encapsulates data. This is the type of VPN typically associated with the concept of remote access. To establish a client-to-site VPN, only the VPN headend needs a static public IP address. As with site-to-site VPNs, clients and hosts on the protected LAN communicate with remote clients by way of the VPN headend and are not required to run VPN software. However, each remote client on a client-to-site VPN must either run VPN software to connect to the VPN headend or establish a more limited, web-based, clientless VPN connection, which uses a browser and is secured by TLS.

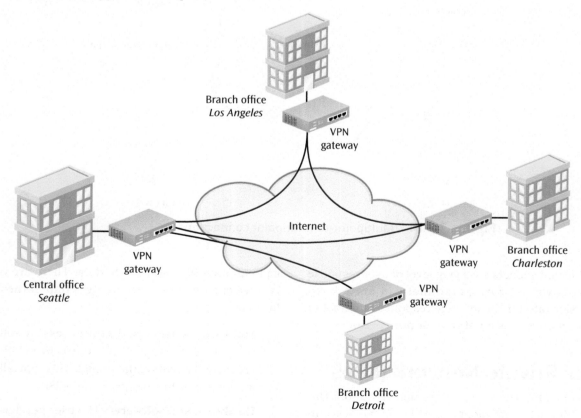

Figure 10-15 A VPN gateway connects each site to one or more other sites

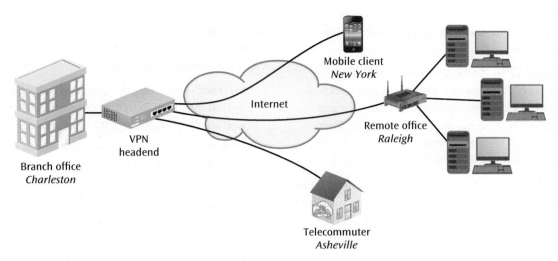

Figure 10-16   Remote clients connect to the LAN through the VPN headend

> **Host-to-host VPN**—Two computers create a VPN tunnel directly between them. Both computers must have the appropriate software installed, and they don't serve as a gateway to other hosts or resources on their respective networks. In a host-to-host VPN, usually the site that receives the VPN connection (such as a home network) needs a static public IP address. Another option, however, is to subscribe to a service such as Dynamic DNS by Oracle (**dyn.com/dns**), which automatically tracks dynamic IP address information for subscriber locations.

When a remote site or a remote worker uses a VPN to connect to the company's main network, that connection might also handle the remote site's or employee's connection to the Internet. In that case, the VPN must be capable of supporting higher bandwidths, as today's employees use many tools accessed through the Internet. Two common approaches to VPN tunneling either require all network traffic to traverse the VPN tunnel or only some of that traffic. Consider the following comparison, as illustrated in Figure 10-17:

> **Full tunnel VPN**—Captures all network traffic, whether destined for the Internet or for the

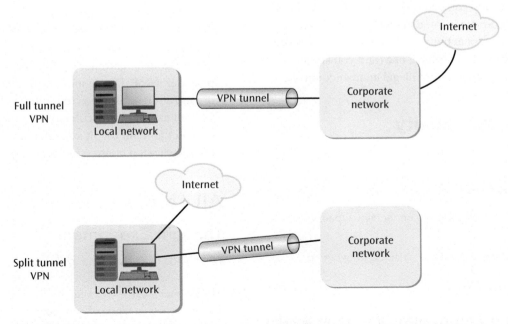

Figure 10-17   A full tunnel VPN protects all traffic, while a split tunnel VPN only captures traffic destined for the corporate network

corporate network. The client has no access to its local network and is assigned an IP address from the remote network.

> **Split tunnel VPN**—Only captures traffic destined for the corporate network. The client can communicate with local network resources directly and with Internet resources, such as Google or Zoom, through a local Internet connection. The client is assigned an IP address from the local network.

While security must be handled differently with a split tunnel VPN where the computer can still communicate with local resources, the primary benefit is that a split tunnel VPN reduces the amount of traffic routed through the corporate network, thereby increasing the user's privacy and decreasing latency. This is especially helpful if the remote user needs access to the Internet for personal reasons, such as streaming music or video, making online purchases, or performing online banking.

Software-based VPNs are also used by consumers for various purposes:

> Remotely connect to a network, such as connecting to your home computer from a laptop while traveling.

> Increase privacy and security when using an insecure Wi-Fi network, such as when using an open Wi-Fi connection at a café or coffee shop.

> Appear to connect to a website from some location other than where you are located. For example, if you're located in a region where viewing of a live event is restricted, you can use a VPN to reach the website from an IP address located in some other region. While this type of activity might be restricted according to the website's terms of use (and you should always check this), it's not illegal in most countries.

Cloud Connectivity

Considering the many resources a company is likely running in the cloud, the connection from the company's

on-prem datacenter to its cloud services directly affects the usability and reliability of those services. Most cloud platforms offer an array of options for connecting back to the customer's datacenter:

> **Internet**—Provides the simplest and cheapest option, but with high and unpredictable latency as well as significant security concerns.

> **VPN (virtual private network)**—Relies on the same VPN technologies used to connect on-premises networks with branch offices and remote workers.

> **Remote access connections**—Uses tunneling or terminal emulation technologies to increase security, including SSH and RDP.

> **Leased line**—Relies on private WAN options to reserve a dedicated amount of bandwidth between the cloud provider and the customer's premises. Depending on the respective locations of provider and customer, this might require the cooperation of multiple ISPs to reach the cloud provider's servers. Hybrid pay-per-use models are available where the customer reserves a portion of anticipated bandwidth needs, and then is invoiced for additional bandwidth used during the pay period. Works in conjunction with a private or dedicated direct connection.

> **Private or dedicated direct connection**—Maximizes predictability and minimizes latency, and of course comes with a high price tag. Some of the larger cloud service providers maintain multiple PoPs (Points of Presence) around the world. This means the provider rents space at a datacenter facility, called a colocation facility, that is shared by a variety of providers. In many cases, ISPs can offer dedicated access from a customer's premises to a cloud provider's PoP. This is more cost effective when an organization subscribes to multiple cloud providers who all use the same colocation. Amazon's Direct Connect and Microsoft's Azure ExpressRoute both offer dedicated connection services.

Remember this...

> Many businesses need WAN connections between specific locations, such as between a corporate office and a branch office. In some cases, these connections can be made over the open Internet, sometimes called the "wild area network." In other cases, sensitive data necessitates a private connection over dedicated infrastructure where the signal cannot be easily intercepted.

> Some older WAN technologies are still in place to service legacy networks or legacy services. Legacy WAN connectivity services still in use include T-1 line, frame relay, and ATM (Asynchronous Transfer Mode).

> MPLS (Multiprotocol Label Switching) allows a customer to use any connectivity option that makes sense for each site while centrally managing bandwidth between each site. Despite the various service levels of each location's connection to the ISP, the customer can manage segmentation and QoS for different types of traffic across the entire network, even if connected locations are spread hundreds or thousands of miles apart.

> Due to its simplicity, Ethernet has also become an attractive option for WAN and MAN connections. However, because Ethernet was not originally designed with this purpose in mind, certain adaptions were needed to make Ethernet capable of traversing WANs and MANs. The standard that emerged, as defined by the MEF (Metro Ethernet Forum), was CE (Carrier Ethernet).

> Based on the kinds of endpoints they connect, VPNs can be loosely classified according to three models: site-to-site VPN, client-to-site VPN, and host-to-host VPN. Two common approaches to VPN tunneling either require all network traffic to traverse the VPN tunnel (called a full tunnel VPN) or only some of that traffic (called a split tunnel VPN).

> Most cloud platforms offer an array of options for connecting back to the customer's datacenter: Internet, VPN, remote access connections, or leased lines in conjunction with a private or dedicated direct connection. Some of the larger cloud service providers maintain multiple PoPs (Points of Presence) around the world. This means the provider rents space at a datacenter facility, called a colocation facility, that is shared by a variety of providers. In many cases, ISPs can offer dedicated access from a customer's premises to a cloud provider's PoP.

Self-check

4. Which WAN connectivity technology includes QoS management capabilities?
   - a. T-1
   - b. DSL
   - c. Frame relay
   - d. MPLS
5. Which type of VPN requires both ends of the connection to have a static public IP address?
   - a. Host-to-host VPN
   - b. Site-to-site VPN
   - c. Client-to-site VPN
   - d. Host-to-site VPN
6. Which cloud connectivity option provides the fastest throughput?
   - a. Direct connection
   - b. Internet connection
   - c. RDP connection
   - d. VPN connection

Check your answers at the end of this chapter.

Section 10-3: WAN Virtualization

Gigabit broadband, which you read about earlier in this chapter, represents a new era for WAN technologies where high-speed Internet access has become available for home users and small businesses at reasonable costs. But what about larger companies? Why wouldn't these companies be able to take advantage of the same technologies?

With the advent of SDN (software-defined networking), which you may recall from Chapter 6, they can. As an application of SDN, SD-WAN (software-defined WAN) combines the advantages offered by consumer-grade WAN connections with the flexibility and scalability of software-based network management to provide businesses with adaptable, reliable, and secure worldwide network access. However, SD-WAN is merely one step along the evolutionary path. Let's examine how SD-WAN creates new options for businesses, and then explore even newer, emerging technologies.

Software-Defined WAN (SD-WAN)

Similar to its SDN cousin, **SD-WAN (software-defined WAN)** relies on abstracted, centralized control of networking devices to manage network functions across a diverse infrastructure, including managing network connections across a variety of WANs. SD-WAN offers the following benefits:

> **Transport agnostic**—As shown in Figure 10-18, an SD-WAN controller can manage network configurations at multiple locations throughout the world, regardless of the type of connection each segment uses to reach the SD-WAN (such as broadband, leased line, MPLS, cellular, and others).

> **Active-active load balancing and automatic failover**—An SD-WAN managed network offers active-active load balancing where it can choose the best physical WAN connection for different types of traffic according to traffic prioritization and current network conditions. For example, suppose a branch office has three Internet connections as shown in Figure 10-19: an MPLS connection, a broadband connection, and a 5G wireless connection. SD-WAN can route traffic over each of these connections according to each data stream's configured priority. If one WAN connection goes down, the SD-WAN controller can switch traffic to another WAN connection.

> **Intent-based management**—A network admin can indicate in the controller's GUI their intent for traffic, such as limiting bandwidth for a specific application, and the SD-WAN controller institutes all configuration changes needed on all affected network devices.

> **Zero-touch provisioning**—An SD-WAN edge device can be shipped to a branch location where a non-technical person can plug in the device without any configuration needed on-site. The device then finds and checks in with the remote SD-WAN controller for further instructions. Trained technicians at the home office can remotely finish deploying the SD-WAN configurations at the branch office without additional assistance from on-site personnel.

> **Reduced cost**—Because SD-WAN solutions can be deployed over any kind of underlying WAN connection (such as cable, DSL, fiber broadband, or 5G), expensive MPLS connections can be abandoned in favor of SD-WAN management for many of a company's connections. While the company might not replace all their MPLS connections, SD-WAN can be used to optimally manage all available WAN connections regardless of underlying technology and minimize the need for more expensive WAN services.

The advantages offered by SD-WAN are causing an industry shift away from older, more traditional WAN connectivity options. Still, improvements to SD-WAN technologies are needed surrounding security when traffic traverses the Internet, costs for underlying WAN connections (such as MPLS), and flexibility for cloud and mobile users. Let's review some emerging technologies that are designed to better address these issues.

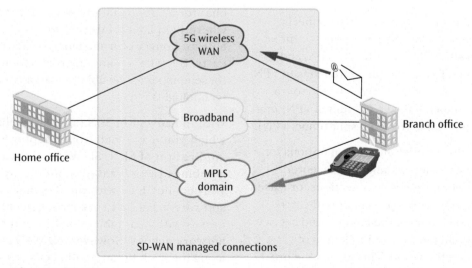

Figure 10-18 SD-WAN supports many underlying WAN connectivity technologies

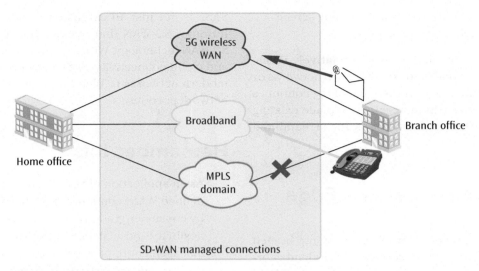

Figure 10-19 The SD-WAN controller can direct traffic through the optimal path for that traffic at a given time

Software-Defined Branch (SD-Branch)

SD-WAN provides visibility and management access for WAN connections between an organization's networks. Suppose you manage several branch networks—consider the benefits of being able to apply the same software-defined accessibility to your branch LANs as to your WAN connections leading to your branches, as shown in Figure 10-20. That's the role of SD-branch (software-defined branch) solutions, which provide centralized control of virtual network devices at remote network locations. SD-branch extends SD-WAN technology into an organization's remote LANs, thus increasing the

visibility, optimization, and security coverage of those remote locations.

SD-branch capabilities include the following examples:

> An SD-branch solution can evaluate the remote LAN's traffic as it makes decisions about which traffic should be transmitted on which WAN connection.

> SD-branch implements network segmentation similar in concept to VLANs but with simpler management that can be handled from the home office.

> When using the same vendor, SD-branch can serve as a seamless extension of SD-WAN, allowing both

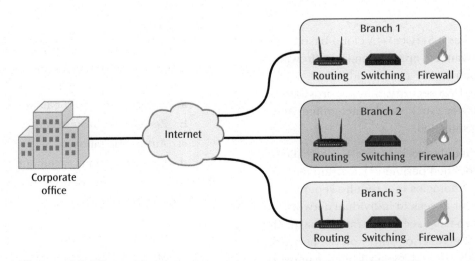

Figure 10-20 SD-branch allows remote management of a branch's networking configuration

solutions to be controlled from the same screen (a feature called "single pane of glass").

Because SD-branch technology is still relatively immature, it's primarily a good fit for small branch networks or even temporary branches. As the technology continues to evolve, companies will increasingly replace existing hardware with SD-branch solutions for streamlined management.

Secure Access Service Edge (SASE)

Where SD-branch extends SD-WAN coverage into branch offices, SASE (secure access service edge) blends corporate and branch networks with the company's cloud infrastructure. Consider a company with one home office, a warehouse location, and a dozen store locations. Each of these networks needs to communicate with each other, and they also need extensive connections with multiple cloud platforms for POS (point of sale) transactions, SaaS applications, and various other cloud-based services. Rather than managing each network's cloud connections separately, SASE (secure access service edge, and pronounced "sassy") provides cloud-based management of WAN, LAN, and cloud connections. It incorporates the following elements, which provide an increased emphasis on network security:

> CASB (cloud access security broker and pronounced "cas-b")—A security appliance, either physical or virtual and hosted on-prem or in the cloud, that is designed to detect applications and other resources running within a domain and monitor those resources according to policies set by the organization.

> FWaaS (Firewall as a Service)—A cloud-based firewall with advanced, application-layer firewall capabilities, such as ATP (advanced threat protection) and DNS security, that are provided at the point of service (such as a branch office) and can be scaled as needed.

> ZTNA (Zero Trust Network Access)—Also called SDP (software-defined perimeter), a group of policies and technologies that require separate authentication for access to individual network resources. A zero-trust security strategy makes the assumption that no user or object on the network can be inherently trusted, even within the network perimeter.

SASE is not just an extension to SD-WAN, it's an evolution of SD-WAN that is expected to replace current SD-WAN technology. With a greater emphasis on security and cloud connectivity, SASE better serves the needs of modern networks to blend on-prem, remote, and cloud network portions.

Remember this...

> As an application of SDN, SD-WAN (software-defined WAN) combines the advantages offered by consumer-grade WAN connections with the flexibility and scalability of software-based network management to provide businesses with adaptable, reliable, and secure worldwide network access. Similar to its SDN cousin, SD-WAN (software-defined wide area network) relies on abstracted, centralized control of networking devices to manage network functions across a diverse infrastructure.

> SD-branch (software-defined branch) solutions, which provide centralized control of virtual network devices at remote network locations. SD-branch extends SD-WAN technology into an organization's remote LANs, thus increasing the visibility, optimization, and security coverage of those remote locations.

> Rather than managing each network's cloud connections separately, SASE provides cloud-based management of WAN, LAN, and cloud connections. SASE incorporates the following elements: CASB (cloud access security broker), FWaaS (Firewall as a Service), and ZTNA (Zero Trust Network Access).

Self-check

7. Which characteristic of SD-WAN means that trained technicians can remotely deploy devices at a new branch location?
   a. Active-active load balancing
   b. Zero-touch provisioning
   c. Automatic failover
   d. Intent-based management

8. What kind of network does SD-branch technology manage?
   a. WAN
   b. PAN
   c. MAN
   d. LAN

9. Which SASE element requires a user to authenticate separately to each network resource?

   a. ZTNA

   b. FWaaS

   c. CASB

   d. SD-branch

Check your answers at the end of this chapter.

Section 10-4: Cloud-Supported Technologies

As you learn about new ways to connect your company's network to the cloud, you also need to understand the kinds of services and technologies your company is likely to be using in the cloud that will require these connections. Cloud computing enables many business functions that weren't possible or as streamlined without cloud. Furthermore, cloud makes available to smaller, less well-funded companies many technologies, resources, and services they couldn't afford to purchase or manage in their own datacenters.

Digital Marketing

Cloud Essentials+ Exam Tip

This section discusses digital marketing, which is required by

- Part of Objective 2.4: Identify the benefits or solutions of utilizing cloud services.

Marketing teams have always engaged creatively with available technology to attract attention and traffic from potential customers. Cloud computing offers new and expanded tools for marketing strategies that enable companies to more accurately target interested customers and provide more personalized information to these markets. Digital marketing, also called online marketing, is the use of electronic devices or the Internet to reach current and potential customers. Today's marketing strategies must account for the ways people interact with technology, their priorities when considering a purchase, and the methods they prefer for making purchases or creating subscriptions. For example, consider that a high portion of customers uses a search engine such as Google to find and research a company when there's something the person would like to purchase. SEO (search engine optimization) is the process of creating and improving a website's design to maximize its potential of appearing in appropriate search engine results. Digital marketing encompasses this process and includes other marketing strategies as well.

Today's digital marketing techniques often rely heavily on cloud technologies to provide improved performance, more accurate marketing efforts, and lower expenses. Consider the following ways that digital marketing can rely on cloud computing:

> **Email campaigns**—Salesforce, a cloud-based SaaS, is one of the most popular CRM (customer relationship management) tools for handling email campaigns. Salesforce and similar cloud-based, CRM tools can be used to manage sophisticated email campaigns that more accurately segment and target relevant consumers while supporting a wide market and geographic reach.

> **Social media**—Cloud-based CRM tools can also provide a centralized interface for managing social media communications throughout multiple platforms. For example, the Oracle social cloud tool allows companies to manage social media campaigns and communications on all popular social media sites, optimize consistent branding, monitor questions and reviews from customers, and integrate this information with their full CRM application.

> **Blogs**—Blogs serve a key purpose in a complete digital marketing approach by providing curated information for consumers, often leading to initial customer contacts and ongoing sales. A well-designed blog will help with SEO by addressing the questions and concerns that bring consumers to a search engine in the first place. Cloud-based blogging tools enable the collection of granular traffic data, including site visits, traffic patterns (where site visitors come from, what they click on the site, and where they go next), shares, and even searches that resulted in your blog appearing on the person's search results. This information can generate ideas for further blog topics, product development, and marketing strategies.

> **Tutorials**—Video tutorials and downloadable manuals, self-published e-books, or survey results provide potential customers with information they need, which helps develop a positive impression of a company. Cloud-based tools, such as YouTube,

Twitch, Vimeo, and LinkedIn, provide platforms for posting tutorials that can easily be shared in a variety of marketing scenarios.

Remote Workers

Today's employees, contractors, and consultants often work remotely, communicating and collaborating through cloud-based tools that make files, data, and tools available across the Internet. To support these remote workers and their teams, companies need cloud-based tools such as the following:

> **Data collaboration**—Cloud-based collaboration allows for multiple people to interact with and edit a file or other data concurrently over the Internet. Typically, the file or other data is stored in the cloud, such as when using Box, Dropbox, Drive, or OneDrive. Access is often provided through a SaaS, such as Office 365 and Google's Docs, Sheets, and similar apps. Cloud-based file

and data collaboration ensures that all users have access to the most recent version of the data. It also reduces the overall storage space required, as everyone accesses the same file rather than keeping multiple copies on their own devices.

> **Resource management**—In many cases, remote workers use their own devices for their work, a policy called **BYOD (bring your own device)**. However, this inconsistency in hardware often results in employees not having access to software resources they need for work, such as an expensive CAD (computer-aided design) application or an application that only works in Windows. **VDI (virtual desktop interface)** is a remote desktop implementation that offers VM instances for remote access clients. For example, Figure 10-21 shows a MacBook connected to a VDI-based Windows desktop through the Safari web browser. With VDI, you can provide a consistent desktop experience that includes installed applications your users commonly need. VDI provides flexibility with options to access VMs running many different OSs or many different configurations of installed applications. VDI can also provide either persistent or non-persistent instances. With a persistent instance, when the user remotes back into the desktop, any changes they made will still be there, including files they saved. With a non-persistent instance, the desktop is reset each time someone signs in.

Local computer's macOS desktop

Remote virtual Windows desktop

Source: Apple, Inc.

Figure 10-21 VDI connection to a Windows desktop from a MacBook

> **Project management**—Email is not a sufficient means of communicating team goals, task deadlines, and project phases because information can be so easily lost or misunderstood. Cloud-based project management tools clarify this information for the entire team and organize the information in ways that make it readily accessible and relevant to daily work. Popular tools include Trello, ProofHub, Monday, and Instagantt.

> **Time management**—When working together in an office, it's easy to see who is present and engaged at any given time. The freedom and flexibility of remote work necessitates a different means of tracking how a person uses their time and how well they're progressing toward project goals. While many companies don't believe an employee's time should be micro-managed, some accountability can help keep people on track and focused. Cloud-based tools such as Todoist, Kickidler, and Teamwork can detail deadlines and target dates, track productivity, organize task lists, and allow for invoicing tracked time or expenses.

> **Casual communication**—Not all work communication is formal and purpose driven. One of the benefits of working in an office is the casual chitchat that occurs around the proverbial water cooler, where employees get to know each other, build relationships, co-create ideas, and generate a company culture. Having employees work from home can be detrimental to this type of communication. Cloud-based apps such as Slack, Microsoft Teams, and Yammer can encourage casual communication that supports the evolution of a company culture founded on teamwork, cooperation, and encouragement. Figure 10-22 shows an example of team communications in Slack.

All Things Considered

Thought Experiment

Have you used any remote productivity tools? Perhaps you've connected remotely with VMs at your school, or you've participated in video calls online, or you've shared documents in a cloud storage service to work collaboratively with classmates or coworkers. List the tools you've used, and discuss the strengths and weaknesses you noticed about each one.

Edge Computing

Cloud Essentials+ Exam Tip

This section discusses autonomous environments, which is required by

- Part of Objective 2.4: Identify the benefits or solutions of utilizing cloud services.

One of the biggest benefits with cloud for technologies like IoT and AI is the fact that cloud computing can be fast. Cloud providers position their datacenters all over the world so customers can run their clouds in the regions closest to where they will be used. For example, if your company is located in the United States and doing a lot of business in India or Thailand, you can create many of your cloud resources in one or more of AWS's Pacific zones. That way, the data doesn't have to travel so far around the world to go into or come out of the cloud in relation to where your users are located.

Edge computing takes this concept a few steps further and brings computing power and connectivity even

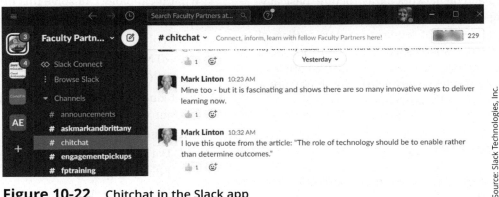

Figure 10-22   Chitchat in the Slack app

Source: Slack Technologies, Inc.

closer to where these resources are used. AWS itself provides edge locations, which are datacenters that aren't full regions but do offer the ability to store copies of data closer to customers. For example, you might cache a copy of your website at an AWS edge location in Bogota, Colombia, and then a customer in northern South America requesting the web page will get it faster than if your website was only stored in North Virginia or Ohio or anywhere else in the United States.

But edge computing is much more than this, too. Think about if you're crossing the street and an autonomous car is headed your way. The car's system is integrated with cloud resources, but you don't want the car waiting to hear back from a cloud service on whether to veer to the right or to the left—you want that car capable of making an intelligent decision on the spot. Having some of the car's computing capability in its onboard system for these split-second kinds of decisions, while still relying on cloud connectivity for things like routing and traffic reporting, is an example of edge computing.

For an even more complex example, what if edge computing devices were placed at each intersection? Then all autonomous cars approaching the intersection could communicate with each of these devices. A traffic management device at each intersection could coordinate with all approaching vehicles to manage traffic more efficiently.

Edge computing can enable autonomous environments of all kinds, not just smart cars. The same principles could apply to autonomous manufacturing processes where the IIoT (Industrial Internet of Things) consists of sensors, robotics, engines, autonomous vehicles, wireless networks, and other systems used in manufacturing, transportation, retail, utilities, and other industries. Edge computing is an extension of cloud computing and reduces the geographical gap between powerful cloud computing technologies and the endpoint user. This is critical for real-time performance issues. But it also addresses security concerns, privacy issues, data sovereignty restrictions, as well as reducing the demand on network infrastructure. Basically, edge computing distributes computing back to its point of use, but not in a way that requires massive outlays of centralized hardware resources like datacenters. It's more of a pinpoint technology that can reach into all areas of technology, from smart homes to smart cars, smart cities, smart traffic systems, and smart industry systems.

Remember this...

> Digital marketing, also called online marketing, is the use of electronic devices or the Internet to reach current and potential customers. Digital

marketing uses cloud computing for SEO (search engine optimization), email campaigns, social media, blogs, tutorials, and other methods to connect with more targeted customer segments.

> Companies need cloud-based tools to support remote workers, including tools for data collaboration, resource management, project management, time management, and casual communication.

> Edge computing brings computing power and connectivity closer to where these resources are used. Edge computing can enable autonomous environments using IoT and IIoT (Industrial Internet of Things) systems, which consists of sensors, robotics, engines, autonomous vehicles, wireless networks, and other systems used in manufacturing, transportation, retail, utilities, and other industries. Edge computing is an extension of cloud computing and cuts down the geographical gap between powerful cloud computing technologies and the endpoint user. This is critical for real-time performance issues, security concerns, privacy issues, data sovereignty restrictions, and reducing the demand on network infrastructure.

Self-check

10. How can you increase the chances potential customers will find your flooring store's website when they're searching for information about home renovations?
    a. CRM
    b. BYOD
    c. SEO
    d. VDI

11. Many of your students only have Chromebooks. However, you need to assign a project that requires software on a Windows computer. What technology can solve this problem?
    a. IIoT
    b. VDI
    c. ZTNA
    d. BYOD

12. What kind of cloud service can reduce latency for your website visitors?
    a. Autonomous car
    b. Data collaboration
    c. Edge computing
    d. Digital marketing

Check your answers at the end of this chapter.

Summary

Section 10-1: Small Business and Consumer-Grade WAN Services

› Homes and small businesses can get Internet access for relatively low prices because the technologies used to support those connections tend to be less reliable with less constant available bandwidth. Many of these Internet connectivity options take advantage of existing network infrastructure, such as telephone lines or cable TV connections.

› DSL (digital subscriber line) allows existing twisted pair telephone lines to transmit multimedia materials and high-speed data. The type of connection, either symmetric or asymmetric, directly affects transfer speed. A symmetric connection is one in which upload and download transfer speeds are equal. An asymmetric connection has a faster downstream transmission speed than its upstream speed.

› Cable modem Internet is a communications service that allows high-speed access to WANs such as the Internet via a cable television connection. A cable modem is a physical device that separates the computer data from the cable television video signal, but many people refer to the entire system (fiber-optic cables, neighborhood distribution nodes, coaxial cables, cable modem splitter, and interface card) as a cable modem service. Much of the cable television network has been converted to fiber and so is called an HFC (hybrid fiber coaxial) network.

› Currently, the fastest Internet service connection available to consumers and small businesses is broadband fiber Internet. Fiber Internet relies on fiber-optic cable run close to or all the way to the customer's location. Because fiber cable is not readily available from older telecommunications systems, this service option is typically more expensive, and its availability is limited.

› A limited number of companies offer satellite Internet services. Satellite Internet is typically the slowest of all Internet options, but also the most readily available in rural areas where wired connections are limited. It requires a dish-shaped antenna installed at the customer's location, and the dish is set to communicate with a stationary satellite in orbit.

› Most smartphones rely on two network types to access the Internet: Wi-Fi, which is a short-range connection to a nearby access point and on to a LAN, or cellular, which is a long-range connection to a cellular antenna and on to a WAN. Each region covered by cellular service is broken down into adjacent cells, which form a honeycomb-like pattern. Located at the intersection of each cell is an array of antennas, which is often placed on a free-standing tower.

Section 10-2: Enterprise-Grade WAN Services

› Many businesses need WAN connections between specific locations, such as between a corporate office and a branch office. In some cases, these connections can be made over the open Internet, sometimes called the "wild area network." In other cases, sensitive data necessitates a private connection over dedicated infrastructure where the signal cannot be easily intercepted.

› Some older WAN technologies are still in place to service legacy networks or legacy services. Legacy

WAN connectivity services still in use include: T-1 line, frame relay, and ATM (Asynchronous Transfer Mode).

› MPLS (Multiprotocol Label Switching) allows a customer to use any connectivity option that makes sense for each site while centrally managing bandwidth between each site. Despite the various service levels of each location's connection to the ISP, the customer can manage segmentation and QoS for different types of traffic across the entire network, even if connected locations are spread hundreds or thousands of miles apart.

> Due to its simplicity, Ethernet has also become an attractive option for WAN and MAN connections. However, because Ethernet was not originally designed with this purpose in mind, certain adaptions were needed to make Ethernet capable of traversing WANs and MANs. The standard that emerged, as defined by the MEF (Metro Ethernet Forum), was CE (Carrier Ethernet).

> Based on the kinds of endpoints they connect, VPNs can be loosely classified according to three models: site-to-site VPN, client-to-site VPN, and host-to-host VPN. Two common approaches to VPN tunneling either require all network traffic to traverse the VPN tunnel (called a full tunnel VPN) or only some of that traffic (called a split tunnel VPN).

> Most cloud platforms offer an array of options for connecting back to the customer's datacenter: Internet, VPN, remote access connections, or leased lines in conjunction with a private or dedicated direct connection. Some of the larger cloud service providers maintain multiple PoPs (Points of Presence) around the world. This means the provider rents space at a datacenter facility, called a colocation facility, that is shared by a variety of providers. In many cases, ISPs can offer dedicated access from a customer's premises to a cloud provider's PoP.

Section 10-3: WAN Virtualization

> As an application of SDN, SD-WAN (software-defined WAN) combines the advantages offered by consumer-grade WAN connections with the flexibility and scalability of software-based network management to provide businesses with adaptable, reliable, and secure worldwide network access. Similar to its SDN cousin, SD-WAN (software-defined wide area network) relies on abstracted, centralized control of networking devices to manage network functions across a diverse infrastructure.

> SD-branch (software-defined branch) solutions, which provide centralized control of virtual network devices at remote network locations. SD-branch extends SD-WAN technology into an organization's remote LANs, thus increasing the visibility, optimization, and security coverage of those remote locations.

> Rather than managing each network's cloud connections separately, SASE (secure access service edge, and pronounced "sassy") provides cloud-based management of WAN, LAN, and cloud connections. SASE incorporates the following elements: CASB (cloud access security broker), FWaaS (Firewall as a Service), and ZTNA (Zero Trust Network Access).

Section 10-4: Cloud-Supported Technologies

> Digital marketing, also called online marketing, is the use of electronic devices or the Internet to reach current and potential customers. Digital marketing uses cloud computing for SEO (search engine optimization), email campaigns, social media, blogs, tutorials, and other methods to connect with more targeted customer segments.

> Companies need cloud-based tools to support remote workers, including tools for data collaboration, resource management, project management, time management, and casual communication.

> Edge computing brings computing power and connectivity closer to where these resources are used.

Edge computing can enable autonomous environments using IoT and IIoT (Industrial Internet of Things) systems, which consists of sensors, robotics, engines, autonomous vehicles, wireless networks, and other systems used in manufacturing, transportation, retail, utilities, and other industries. Edge computing is an extension of cloud computing and cuts down the geographical gap between powerful cloud computing technologies and the endpoint user. This is critical for real-time performance issues, security concerns, privacy issues, data sovereignty restrictions, and reducing the demand on network infrastructure.

Key Terms

For definitions of key terms, see the Glossary near the end of the book.

asymmetric connection

broadband Internet

BYOD (bring your own device)

cable modem

CASB (cloud access security broker)

CE (Carrier Ethernet)

colocation facility

digital marketing

DSL (digital subscriber line)

edge computing

fiber Internet

FWaaS (Firewall as a Service)

gigabit Internet

GPS (global positioning system)

HFC (hybrid fiber coaxial)

Metro Ethernet

MON (metropolitan optical network)

propagation delay

SASE (secure access service edge)

SD-branch (software-defined branch)

SD-WAN (software-defined WAN)

SEO (search engine optimization)

symmetric connection

VDI (virtual desktop interface)

VPN headend

ZTNA (Zero Trust Network Access)

Review Questions

1. Which of these standards could provide the fastest throughput for a homeowner?

    a. ADSL

    b. DOCSIS 3.0 cable

    c. VDSL

    d. GEO satellite

2. Which fiber infrastructure minimizes the copper cable distance your data must travel on its way to the Internet?

    a. FTTC

    b. FTTN

    c. FTTD

    d. FTTB

3. What device does a smartphone communicate with directly when using 5G?

    a. Cellular antenna

    b. Satellite dish

    c. Wi-Fi antenna

    d. Cable modem

4. Which device on a customer's network allows telephone and data transmissions to share the same network media?

    a. DSLAM

    b. LEC

    c. Splitter

    d. Modem

5. Which orbit type ensures a satellite appears to remain stationary?

    a. MEO

    b. HEO

    c. LEO

    d. GEO

6. Which of these technologies would you most likely choose for a company's WAN connections today?

    a. Frame relay

    b. Metro Ethernet

    c. T-1 line

    d. ATM

7. Which technology relies on labels for routing traffic across WANs?

    a. VPN

    b. SD-WAN

    c. SASE

    d. MPLS

8. How does CE track the destination of each message?

    a. MAC-in-MAC

    b. VLAN tag

    c. QinQ

    d. QoS

9. When establishing a VPN connection with your company's network from home, which device does your computer communicate with on the company network's end?

   a. VPN colocation

   b. VPN headend

   c. VPN host

   d. VPN tunnel

10. Which of these connection types would provide the highest throughput between your on-prem network and your cloud resources?

    a. SSH

    b. VPN

    c. Cable modem

    d. Direct connect

11. You are the go-to tech person for an interstate trucking company. You need to maintain constant contact with your fleet of trucks. Which technology will enable you to do this?

    a. Cellular

    b. SD-branch

    c. Fiber

    d. Carrier Ethernet

12. A company wants to connect two offices located in Memphis, Tennessee, and Laramie, Wyoming. Which is the least expensive solution?

    a. T-1 line

    b. VPN

    c. Metro Ethernet

    d. Frame relay

13. Which technologies allow you to create and manage WAN connections to remote networks? *Choose TWO.*

    a. SD-branch

    b. SD-WAN

    c. SASE

    d. Edge computing

14. As you build a cloud-based web app, what tool can you use to protect this app from a DDoS attack?

    a. FWaaS

    b. ZTNA

    c. CASB

    d. SD-branch

15. Which of these technologies could best provide network security at a branch location?

    a. SASE

    b. MPLS

    c. SD-WAN

    d. VPN

16. SEO is an integral part of _____.

    a. data collaboration

    b. edge computing

    c. time management

    d. digital marketing

17. What resource could best provide information from customers to help generate ideas for product development and marketing strategies?

    a. Video tutorials

    b. Website traffic analysis

    c. Email campaigns

    d. Search engine optimization

18. Which tool could provide remote workers with multiple OSs on the same device?

    a. BYOD

    b. CRM

    c. VDI

    d. IIoT

19. Which of these cloud-based tools would most help employees prevent confusion from file version issues?

    a. Trello

    b. Todoist

    c. Yammer

    d. Dropbox

20. Where does edge computing perform compute processes?

    a. In the cloud provider's largest datacenter

    b. In a device near where the service is used

    c. In a regional datacenter where the customer is located

    d. In the customer's datacenter

Hands-On Project 10

Create WAN Links in Packet Tracer

Estimated time: 30 minutes

Resources:

❯ Computer with Cisco Packet Tracer installed

❯ **Context:**

You can create several kinds of WAN connections in Packet Tracer. In this project, you'll keep the topology simple so you can see the process instead of getting mired in the details. You'll create DSL connections between two networks and a web server, which will host your own web page. Complete the following steps:

1. Open Packet Tracer and add the following devices to your workspace, as shown in Figure 10-23:

   a. Two **PCs**

   b. One **Server**

   c. Two **PT-Switches**

   d. Two **DSL Modems** (from the Network Devices > WAN Emulation group)

   e. One **PT-Cloud** (from the Network Devices > WAN Emulation group)

2. Configure the Server with the following information:

   a. Static IP address: **192.168.2.10/24**

   b. Default Gateway: **192.168.2.1**

   c. DNS server: **192.168.2.10**

3. Configure the services you need on the Server. On the **Services** tab, click **DHCP**. Add the following information:

   a. DNS server: **192.168.2.10**

   b. Start IP address: **192.168.2.100**

   c. Subnet mask: **255.255.255.0**

   d. Maximum Number of Users: **50**

4. Click **Save** and then turn the DHCP service **On**.

5. Click **DNS**, configure the following information, click **Add** to create the new A record (which is a type of address record in a DNS database), and then turn **On** the DNS service:

   a. Name: **www.cengage.com**

   b. Address: **192.168.2.10**

6. Click **HTTP**. Next to the index.html file, click **(edit)**. As shown in Figure 10-24, delete the line that says *Welcome to Cisco Packet Tracer. Opening doors to new opportunities. Mind Wide Open.* Replace that text with your own message, such as **Welcome to Jill West's web page!!** (using your own name, of course). Click **Save** and then click **Yes**. Close the Server's configuration window.

7. Add and configure interfaces on the cloud. Click the **Cloud**. Turn off the physical device (scroll to the right to view the Power button if necessary). Drag one **PT-CLOUD-NM-1CFE** module to an available slot. Turn the physical device back on.

8. Click the **Config** tab and click **DSL**. At the top under DSL, make sure **Modem4** and **FastEthernet8** are selected for the ports and click **Add**. Then select **Modem5** and **FastEthernet8** and click **Add** again. Close the Cloud's configuration window.

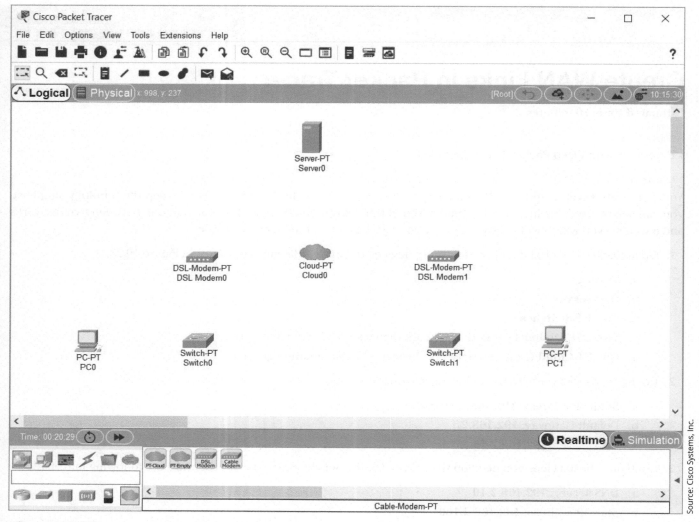

Figure 10-23 Add these devices to your network

9. Configure each PC to use **DHCP**.

10. Connect each PC to its Switch using a **Copper Straight-Through** cable.

11. Connect each Switch to its DSL Modem using a **Copper Cross-Over** cable. Use **FastEthernet** ports on the Switches, and **Port 1** on each Modem.

12. Connect each Modem to the Cloud using a **Phone** cable. On the Cloud, connect to the **Modem** ports.

13. Connect the Cloud to the Server using a **Copper Straight-Through** cable and a **FastEthernet** connection on both ends.

14. Once all ports are up, wait a couple of minutes and then confirm that each PC received an IP address. If the PCs show APIPA addresses (i.e., IP addresses beginning with 169.254) after several minutes, you can switch each PC to static addressing, and then reactivate their DHCP configurations. What IP address did PC0 get? What about PC1?

15. On each PC, ping the Server. What command did you use? Does it work? If not, troubleshoot the problem.

16. On one PC, ping **www.cengage.com**. What command did you use? Does it work? If not, troubleshoot the problem.

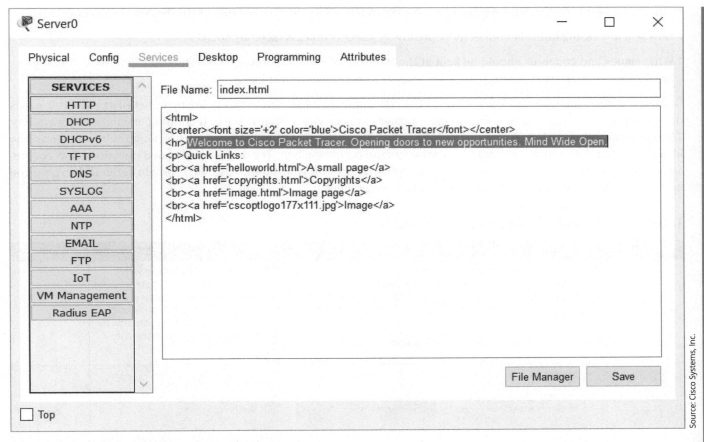

Source: Cisco Systems, Inc.

Figure 10-24 Replace the selected text with your own

17. On one PC, open a web browser and navigate to **www.cengage.com**.

18. **Take a screenshot** of the web page showing your custom text; submit this visual with your answers to this project's questions.

19. When you're finished, you can close Packet Tracer. You do not need to save this network.

Reflection Discussion 10

This chapter covered ways that cloud computing and Internet connectivity are enabling technological developments such as smart homes, smart cars, smart cities, and smart traffic systems. Many people see these developments as positive and productive. In some ways, metro Ethernet, edge computing, and related technologies could help narrow the so-called digital divide between those who have access to sophisticated technology and those who typically don't by making technology and Internet connectivity more accessible to all people. At the same time, many people are concerned about the security issues of IoT, edge computing, and autonomous systems. There are also concerns around privacy, safety, dependency on technology, and increasing complexity.

Do some research online regarding the advantages and disadvantages of increasingly incorporating Internet-based technology into daily routines and lifestyle patterns. As technology becomes more available to all layers of society, and as every part of daily life becomes more connected to the Internet, do you think of these developments as overall positive or negative? As you research, answer the following questions:

> In what ways do you think increasing Internet connectivity will affect your daily life in the next few years?

> How will increasing Internet connectivity positively affect problems faced by society?

> What issues and concerns should be kept at the forefront of conversation and consideration as these technologies are developed to prevent making problems worse or creating new problems?

Go to the discussion forum in your school's LMS (learning management system). Write a post of at least 100 words discussing your thoughts about increasing Internet connectivity and how these technologies might affect society. Then respond to two of your classmates' threads with posts of at least 50 words discussing their comments and ideas. Use complete sentences, and check your grammar and spelling. Try to ask open-ended questions that encourage discussion, and remember to respond to people who post on your thread. Use the rubric in Table 10-1 to help you understand what is expected of your work for this assignment.

Table 10-1 Grading rubric for Reflection Discussion 10

Task	Novice	Competent	Proficient	Earned
Initial post	Generalized statements discussing increasing Internet connectivity **30 points**	Some specific statements with supporting evidence comparing the advantages and disadvantages of increasing Internet connectivity **40 points**	Self-reflective discussion with specific and thoughtful statements and supporting evidence discussing the potential benefits to society and potential problems of increasing Internet connectivity **50 points**	
Initial post: Mechanics	• Length < 100 words • Several grammar and spelling errors 5 points	• Length = 100 words • Occasional grammar and spelling errors 7 points	• Length > 100 words • Appropriate grammar and spelling 10 points	
Response 1	Brief response showing little engagement or critical thinking 5 points	Detailed response with specific contributions to the discussion 10 points	Thoughtful response with specific examples or details and open-ended questions that invite deeper discussion of the topic 15 points	
Response 2	Brief response showing little engagement or critical thinking 5 points	Detailed response with specific contributions to the discussion 10 points	Thoughtful response with specific examples or details and open-ended questions that invite deeper discussion of the topic 15 points	
Both responses: Mechanics	• Length < 50 words each • Several grammar and spelling errors 5 points	• Length = 50 words each • Occasional grammar and spelling errors 7 points	• Length > 50 words each • Appropriate grammar and spelling 10 points	
			Total	

Solutions to Self-Check Questions

Section 10-1: Small Business and Consumer-Grade WAN Services

1. How fast is gigabit Internet?

Answer: d. 1000 Mbps

Explanation: Gigabit Internet is 1000 Mbps, or 1 Gbps.

2. Which Internet service's throughput is determined by a DOCSIS version?

Answer: b. Cable

Explanation: Cable Internet's experienced throughput is partially determined by the DOCSIS version of the modem on the customer's end.

3. If your cell phone says it has a 5G connection, what kind of Internet-connection technology is it using to connect to your cell provider's network?

Answer: c. Cellular

Explanation: 5G is the latest generation of high-speed cellular technology that provides a long-range connection to a cellular antenna and on to a WAN.

Section 10-2: Enterprise-Grade WAN Services

4. Which WAN connectivity technology includes QoS management capabilities?

Answer: d. MPLS

Explanation: Despite the various service levels of each location's connection to the ISP, you can manage segmentation and QoS for different types of traffic across your MPLS network, even if your locations are spread hundreds or thousands of miles apart.

5. Which type of VPN requires both ends of the connection to have a static public IP address?

Answer: b. Site-to-site VPN

Explanation: Site-to-site VPNs require that each location have a static public IP address.

6. Which cloud connectivity option provides the fastest throughput?

Answer: a. Direct connection

Explanation: A dedicated direct connection maximizes predictability and minimizes latency.

Section 10-3: WAN Virtualization

7. Which characteristic of SD-WAN means that trained technicians can remotely deploy devices at a new branch location?

Answer: b. Zero-touch provisioning

Explanation: With zero-touch provisioning, an SD-WAN edge device can be shipped to a branch location, and trained technicians at the home office can remotely finish deploying the SD-WAN configurations at the branch office without additional assistance from on-site personnel.

8. What kind of network does SD-branch technology manage?

Answer: d. LAN

Explanation: An SD-branch solution can evaluate a remote LAN's traffic as it makes decisions about which traffic should be transmitted on which WAN connection.

9. Which SASE element requires a user to authenticate separately to each network resource?

Answer: a. ZTNA

Explanation: ZTNA (Zero Trust Network Access) is a group of policies and technologies that require separate authentication for access to individual network resources.

Section 10-4: Cloud-Supported Technologies

10. How can you increase the chances potential customers will find your flooring store's website when they're searching for information about home renovations?

Answer: c. SEO

Explanation: SEO (search engine optimization) is the process of creating and improving a website's design to maximize its potential of appearing in appropriate search engine results.

11. Many of your students only have Chromebooks. However, you need to assign a project that requires software on a Windows computer. What technology can solve this problem?

Answer: b. VDI

Explanation: VDI (virtual desktop interface) is a remote desktop implementation that offers VM instances for remote access clients. With VDI, you can provide a consistent desktop experience that includes installed applications your users commonly need.

12. What kind of cloud service can reduce latency for your website visitors?

Answer: c. Edge computing

Explanation: Edge computing is an extension of cloud computing and cuts down the geographical gap between powerful cloud computing technologies and the endpoint user.

Chapter 11

Network Design and Management

Objectives

After reading this chapter, you should be able to:

- Explain how project management, application lifecycle management, and change management help with planning for changes on a network

- Identify methods to analyze a proposed design or change

- Describe tools and methods used to monitor and manage a network

- Describe tools and methods used to deploy and manage cloud resources

Introduction

For a computer network to be successful, it must be able to support current and future amounts of traffic, pay for itself within an acceptable period of time, and provide the services necessary to support users of the system. All these goals are very difficult to achieve. Why? First, computer networks are constantly increasing in complexity. In many business environments, it is extremely difficult for one person to completely understand every component, protocol, and network application. Thus, network management is becoming increasingly challenging.

A second reason these goals are difficult to achieve is related to how difficult it is for an individual or a business to properly define the future of computing within a company. Each company has its own expectations about what computing services it should provide. In addition to this, each user within the company has their own idea of the computing services that should be available. It is extremely difficult, therefore, to determine a single service or set of services that could serve the needs of an entire company.

Finally, computer network technology changes at breakneck speed. In some areas, you can expect major developments about every six months, and in other areas, new technologies are emerging almost daily. Keeping abreast of new hardware, software, and network applications is a full-time job in itself. Incorporating the new technology into existing technology, while trying to predict the needs of users, is exhausting. This ever-changing environment is one of the main reasons that designing new systems and updating current systems are areas filled with dangerous pitfalls. With one wrong decision, much time and money can be wasted.

Why is it important to understand the foundational concepts used to develop computer systems? These concepts are important because, if you pursue a career that involves computer networks, there is a good chance that sometime in the future you will either be designing or updating a network system, or assisting one or more persons who are designing or updating a network system. If you will be performing this task yourself, you will need to know how to approach the problem logically and set up a proper progression of steps. If you will be working with a team of network professionals, you will need to be cognizant of the steps involved and how you might participate in them.

Section 11-1: Planning for Changes

Every company, whether it is a for-profit or nonprofit organization, usually has several major goals, some of which might include:

> Increasing the company's customer base

> Keeping customers happy by providing the company's services as effectively as possible

> Increasing the company's profit level, or, in a non-profit organization, acquiring the funds necessary to meet the organization's goals and objectives

> Conducting business more efficiently and effectively

From these major goals, systems planners and management personnel within a company try to generate a set of questions that, when satisfactorily answered, will assist their organization in achieving its goals and move the organization forward. For example, someone in management might ask: Is there a way to streamline the order system to allow the company to conduct business more efficiently and effectively? Can we automate the customer renewal system to better serve customers and keep them happy? Is there a more efficient way to offer new products to help the company increase the customer base? Is there a better way to manage our warehouse system to increase company profits? Several disciplines contribute to discovering the answers to these questions and implementing the solutions.

Project Management

To be able to properly understand a problem, analyze all possible solutions, select the best solution, and implement and maintain the solution, you need to follow a well-defined plan. The oversight of this plan and its execution are often handled by project management

professionals or other professionals with project management training. A **project** is an effort that has a clearly defined beginning and ending. It involves many processes that are generally grouped into five categories: initiating, planning, executing, monitoring and controlling, and closing, as illustrated in Figure 11-1.

Project management is the application of specific skills, tools, and techniques to manage processes in such a way that the desired outcome is achieved. Nearly any undertaking in IT benefits from project management skills:

> **Communication**—When asked which skill a potential employer most wants in a new hire, the ability to communicate well often rises to the top of the list. When managing a project, good communication is even more critical, as many people are often involved in various levels and phases of the project. Consistent and thorough communication also involves making good decisions in specific scenarios about communication channels used, such as emails, social media channels, face-to-face meetings, and online conferencing. For example, consider the need for training an organization's users about new tools being deployed from the cloud. Knowing when to employ written communication versus arranging for face-to-face communication or a video tutorial can make a significant impact on how easily users adjust to any changes affecting their work.

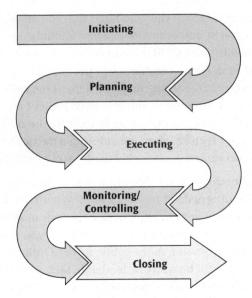

Figure 11-1 The five project management process groups

> **Negotiation**—Negotiating with vendors creates the opportunity to expand the reach of a limited budget. Knowing how to write an RFP (request for proposal), which is a document requesting that vendors submit a proposal for a product or service that the customer wants to purchase, and knowing how to negotiate favorable contractual terms will help protect the organization when something goes wrong during a project.

> **Task and time management**—Time management is the art of learning how to set realistic deadlines that ensure the project will be completed on time while not overly stressing the team. Project management training teaches how to schedule phases of a project as well as smaller, more incremental steps so the work is well paced and everyone knows what they should be doing next.

> **Cost and quality management**—In many cases, budgets place non-negotiable limits on a project. A team that regularly exceeds its budget will not be allowed to continue operations for long. What's more, a budget isn't a number that can be set at the beginning of a project and not look at it again until near the end. Ongoing expenses and projected costs must be continuously and closely monitored and revised. Like steering an airplane onto a runway, it takes a lot of planning, skill, and practice to learn how to manage costs and budgets for large projects while maintaining high quality standards.

> **Risk management**—Accepting some risks in a project will increase the likelihood that the endeavor is relevant and innovative, while minimizing unhealthy risks will prevent detrimental surprises that undermine confidence in the project's goals. Effective risk management, to a great degree, requires experience and maturity. Project management training teaches how to identify the most relevant factors when considering a particular risk and promotes greater skill in choosing risks wisely.

> **Leadership**—The value of the ability to inspire and guide others can't be overstated. Whether you're the type of person who loves being out in front of the crowd and energizing people or you prefer to offer a quieter, more subtle form of influence, you can still be a strong leader. In fact, you don't even have to be the boss to be a leader. Anyone on the team can set the pace for focus, creativity, resourcefulness, and productivity. Project

management training explains how to balance the details of a project with the big picture, and how to organize communications and activities to help everyone maximize the potential of what they have to offer the team.

All Things Considered

Thought Experiment

What certifications exist for project managers? Choose one that you think would be a good fit for your planned career path. How would this certification help you professionally? What would you need to do to prepare for passing this certification's exam?

Application Lifecycle Management (ALM)

Cloud Essentials+ Exam Tip

This section discusses continuous integration/continuous delivery, which is required by

- Part of Objective 3.2: Explain DevOps in cloud environments.

A specific use of project management is in ALM (application lifecycle management). The application lifecycle follows the progression of an application from its conception through its retirement. The various phases an application might experience are shown in Figure 11-2.

The most active portion of the ALM is the software development phase, which is also referred to as the SDLC (software development life cycle). In the past, organizations took a linear path to SDLC called the waterfall method. As shown in Figure 11-3, software development begins with an evaluation of the requirements, followed by work on the design, coding the application, testing functionality, and deploying the software. The waterfall method has a clearly defined beginning and ending, which can occur several months or even years apart.

With the increasing speed of technology advancement, organizations are finding the waterfall method can no longer keep up with demand. The need for more efficiency and faster response times has resulted in a continuous or cyclical software development approach

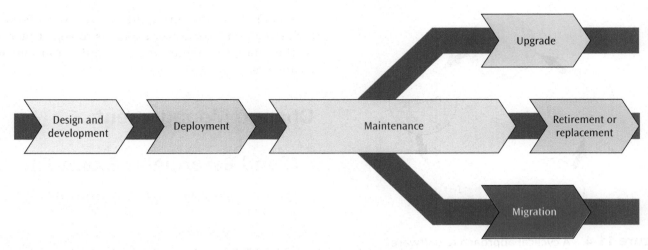

Figure 11-2   An application progresses from one end to the other

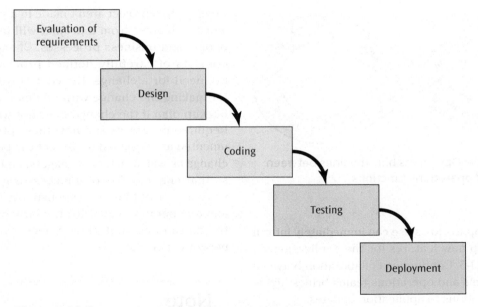

Figure 11-3   A linear progression of software development

that offers increased agility, which is the ability to adapt quickly to market demands according to increased or decreased feature use within an application. Figure 11-4 shows the software development cycle more commonly in use today. With this approach, software is constantly being updated. As soon as changes are deployed, new changes are already underway. Organizations accomplish this feat by making smaller changes much more frequently, sometimes as quickly as every 24 hours.

The idea of *phases* is critical to modern ALM. The intent of ALM is for phases not to be disjointed steps in a big plan but overlapping layers of activity. It is quite common for two and three phases of a single project to be going on at the same time. For example, the design of one component of a system can be in progress while the implementation of another component is being performed.

A second critical concept is that of the *cycle*. After a system has been maintained for a period of time, it is relatively common to restart the planning phase—hence, another cycle—in an attempt to seek a better solution to the problem. Thus, the ALM is a never-ending process.

The streamlining and built-in repetition of the application lifecycle, along with the increased collaboration between the teams working on each app, has come to be known as DevOps (development and operations). Once an application is deployed, the data gathered from

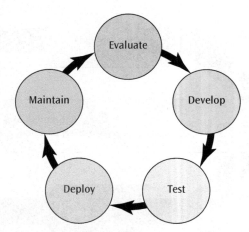

Figure 11-4 A cyclical approach to software development

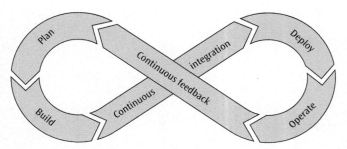

Figure 11-5 DevOps teams blur the lines between development and operations functions

monitoring the application's use can immediately inform efforts to develop new features for the application, as shown in Figure 11-5. Continuous collaboration between development teams and operations teams brings highly responsive adaptations to application updates.

Many IT professionals apply this same DevOps environment or culture to the entire network, especially cloud-based portions. The emphasis on agility results in a focused effort toward collaboration among teams, automation of processes, and faster turnover of changes:

> Changes are released more often through **continuous integration**, the practice of continuously merging all code changes from all developers working on a project.

> **Continuous delivery** deploys changes in small increments on a short time schedule, such as every 24 hours, rather than being delayed for larger, less frequent updates.

These two practices together are often referred to together as CI/CD (continuous integration/continuous

delivery). The inherent agility of software-defined technologies allows network admins to adjust quickly to the changing needs of an organization and its customers.

Change Management

Changes to a project aren't made in a vacuum—in other words, changes from a project will likely affect many people and business processes. **Change management** consists of carefully defined processes to evaluate the need for a change, the cost of the change, a plan for making the change with minimal disruption, and a backup plan if the change does not work as expected. Required processes and how these processes are documented are designed to protect the person making the change as well as users, managers, and the organization so that changes do not unnecessarily disrupt normal workflow or put undue responsibility for a problem on any one person. Generally, the larger an organization, the more documentation is necessary when making network changes.

> **Note**
>
> Minor changes, such as applying a security patch to an application that involves only a few users, are sometimes made without going through an official change request process, but are usually documented in some way, such as a technician making entries in the change management database before and after the change is made.

Here is a list of typical required steps:

Step 1: **Submit a change request document**—Find out who in the organization is responsible for submitting such a document. For example, the lead accountant might be considered the owner of an accounting application and is, therefore, the only one allowed to request an upgrade to the

Table 11-1   Parts of a change request document

Information	Example
Person submitting the change request and person who must authorize the change	The network administrator is submitting the request, and the director of IT must approve it.
Type of change	Software patch
Reason for change	To fix a bug
Configuration procedures	An upgraded application might require new data file templates be built, settings defined for an entire department of users, or existing data be converted to a new format.
Potential impact	Ten users in the Accounting Department will need three hours of training.
Grounds for rollback	The new application doesn't work as expected, and the Accounting Department head decides it's best to go back to the old way of doing things.
Notification process	Management and users will be informed of the change through email.
Timeline for the change	Anticipated downtime is two hours.

application. Still, IT personnel might be able to request a security patch be applied to the same application. In this case, the change request document might include items listed in Table 11-1.

Step 2: **Understand and follow the approval process—** The manager of a department might be able to approve a minor change to an application, hardware device, or OS, whereas major changes might need to go through a review board process. You might be expected to provide additional documentation during this review process. The complexity of the approval process is usually determined by the cost and time involved in making the change, the number of users affected, the potential risk to their work productivity, and the difficulty of rolling back the change. Sometimes a change request is entered into a change management database where many people can access the request, enter supporting documentation and questions, and weigh in with their opinions regarding the change.

Step 3: **Follow project management procedures—**After a major change is approved, a change coordinator is usually assigned to the project. This coordinator is a trained project manager responsible for overseeing all aspects of the change including user training; coordinating between departments involved in the change; documenting how and when notification of the change will happen; negotiating with users, management, and the IT Department regarding the authorized downtime for the change to happen; communicating with management regarding any unforeseen problems that arise during the change; and managing the

budget for the change. Technicians and the network administrator work closely with the change coordinator during the change process.

Step 4: **Provide additional documentation—**Depending on the organization, other required documentation might include testing documentation (for example, test data, testing scenarios, and software and hardware used for the testing), step-by-step procedures for applying the change, vendor documentation and vendor contact information, and locations of configuration backups and of backups that will be used in the event of a rollback, which is a return to the previous state if something goes wrong. Network administrators should pay particular attention to updating their own documentation regarding the network, including updating any network maps. These network documentation updates might include edits to the information shown in Table 11-2.

Step 5: **Close the change—**After the change is implemented and tested and users have settled into the change without problems, the change is officially closed. Sometimes the change coordinator will call a debriefing session where all involved can evaluate how well the change went and what can be done to improve future changes.

Project management and change management work together to oversee changes and ensure the process goes smoothly. At the same time, ALM and DevOps, in some ways, work in opposition to the restrictions of project management and change management. Instead, these models encourage smaller, more frequent changes with less resistance to change and, therefore, more

Table 11-2   Documentation edits

Documentation	Example Edits
Network configuration	The network was segmented with three new VLANs and subnets added.
IP address utilization	IP address ranges were assigned to the three new subnets.
Additions to the network	New routers and switches were installed to accommodate new VLANs to handle additional network traffic.
Physical location changes	Twenty workstations, a switch, and two printers were moved to a different building on the corporate campus.

responsiveness to the shifting needs of users. In balance, the push for innovation and the pull of caution can guide a company towards optimization of its available resources and potential.

Remember this...

> Project management is the application of specific skills, tools, and techniques to manage processes in such a way that the desired outcome is achieved. A project is an effort that has a clearly defined beginning and ending. It involves many processes that are generally grouped into five categories: initiating, planning, executing, monitoring and controlling, and closing.

> A specific use of project management is in ALM (application lifecycle management). The application lifecycle follows the progression of an application from its conception through its retirement.

> The streamlining and built-in repetition of the application lifecycle, along with the increased collaboration between the teams working on each app, has come to be known as DevOps (development and operations). Once an application is deployed, the data gathered from monitoring the application's use can immediately inform efforts to develop new features for the application.

> Change management consists of carefully defined processes to evaluate the need for a change, the cost of the change, a plan for making the change with minimal disruption, and a backup plan if the change doesn't work as expected.

Self-check

1. Which of the following is *NOT* an advantage offered by professional project management?
   a. Balanced risk taking
   b. Effective negotiation with vendors
   c. Realistic deadlines
   d. Increased physical security

2. Which application development practice ensures small but frequent incremental changes?
   a. Agility
   b. Continuous delivery
   c. Waterfall method
   d. Continuous integration

3. Which change management step initiates a change to be made in a system?
   a. Complete the approval process.
   b. Implement project management procedures.
   c. Submit a change request document.
   d. Close the change.

Check your answers at the end of this chapter.

Section 11-2: Analyzing Design

When considering changes to make to a network or its various resources, you'll need to consider both current and future requirements. To do this well, you must first know what you're starting with, and then identify what changes are needed. Network modeling helps with the first task by identifying connected systems at the WAN, MAN, and LAN levels. Gap analysis provides insights into what needs to change and for what purpose. Feasibility studies and capacity planning assist in identifying the changes that will best solve targeted problems. You also need to understand various approaches to testing to ensure the planned design will meet needs as expected. In this section, you'll explore each of these components of a sound design.

Network Modeling

Cloud Essentials+ Exam Tip

This section discusses documentation and diagrams, which are required by

- Part of Objective 2.1: Given a scenario, use appropriate cloud assessments.

When a systems analyst or architect is asked to design or update an IT system, they will typically create a set of models for both the existing system (if there is one) and the proposed system. These models are usually designed to show the flow of data through the system and the flow of procedures within the system, thus helping the analyst and other professionals visualize the current and proposed systems. The models created for a network design can either depict the current state of the network or illustrate the desired network.

Network model diagrams don't have to be elaborate creations. Oftentimes, a diagram is only a hand-drawn model that depicts the proposed design of the network. One technique used to model a corporation's network environment is to create connectivity maps. More precisely, three different modeling techniques can be used, depending on what type of network you are modeling: wide area connectivity maps, metropolitan area connectivity maps, and local area connectivity maps. Not all analysis and design projects require all three map types. For example, your company might not use a MAN to connect its LAN to the outside world, and thus will not need to create a metropolitan area connectivity map. Nonetheless, all three maps will be described here, as each type has slightly different but important characteristics. Let's begin with the big-picture perspective of the wide area connectivity map and work down to the smaller details shown in the local area connectivity map.

Wide Area Connectivity Map

To create a wide area connectivity map, the modeler begins by identifying each site or location in which the company has an office. In the example shown in Figure 11-6, each fixed site is denoted by a circle; mobile or wireless sites are indicated by circles containing the letter M; and external sites, such as suppliers or external agents, are denoted by circles containing the letter E. A solid line between two sites indicates a desired path for data transmission. The example in Figure 11-6 shows three fixed sites (Chicago, Seattle, and Los Angeles), an external site in San Antonio (which is actually a government office), and wireless users in the Chicago office (shown all together with a single circled M).

To identify the connections between sites, link characteristics can be applied to each connection, such as the following (in any order):

> d = Distance of the connection (usually shown in either miles or kilometers)

> s = Security level (high, medium, low, or none)

> dr = Data rate desired (in bps)

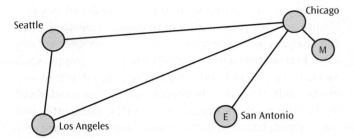

Figure 11-6 Example of a wide area connectivity map for sites in Chicago, Seattle, Los Angeles, and San Antonio

> de = Delivery rate (sometimes called throughput percentage)

> l = Latency, or acceptable delay time across the network (usually in milliseconds, or ms)

Metropolitan Area Connectivity Map

If a company desires a MAN connection between one of its offices and another of its locations or another business, such as an ISP, it can use a metropolitan area connectivity map to outline this connection and define the desired network characteristics. A metropolitan area connectivity map shares some of the characteristics of wide area maps and some of the characteristics of local area maps. Data rate and security are still important parameters at the metropolitan layer, but distance is probably not as important as it was in the wide area map. A new parameter that might have an impact on metropolitan area design is the failover time. Recall from Chapter 9 that failover time is the amount of time necessary for the MAN to reconfigure itself or reroute a packet should a given link fail. An example of a metropolitan area connectivity map is shown in Figure 11-7.

Local Area Connectivity Map

To examine the nodes in a wide area or metropolitan area connectivity map in more detail, an analyst can expand each individual site into a local area connectivity map. The LAN design can then be evaluated in one or

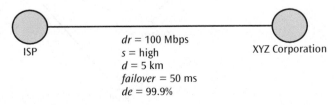

Figure 11-7 Two nodes and the connecting link in a metropolitan area connectivity map

two stages, depending upon the level of detail desired. If only an overview of a local network is desired, then the analyst can create a local area overview connectivity map. In this stage, entire logical or physical groups, such as clusters of users and workstations, are denoted as a single node. The links between such nodes are defined by factors such as distance, security, data rate, and throughput. Latency, delivery rate, and failover are usually not significant enough factors to be included at the local area level. Figure 11-8 shows an example of a local area overview connectivity map. Note that the overview map does not include any connection points, such as switches or routers.

If more detail is desired, the analyst can create a local area detailed connectivity map. A detailed map can show how individual workstations or groups of workstations are clustered with switches, routers, and server farms. For example, the local area detailed connectivity map in Figure 11-9 has zoomed in on the Marketing node from the overview map in Figure 11-8 to show this node's workstations and their interconnections with the node's switches. The level of detail shown in a local area detailed connectivity map depends on the needs of a given

project. Some projects require that all interconnections among the components be shown, while others can work from a map that shows only the major interconnections. As you can imagine, local area detailed connectivity maps generally capture a lot of information.

Collecting the information for any of these maps can be tedious. For this reason, network administrators typically use tools to discover and identify all connected nodes in a network. Even with these tools, network admins rely on familiarity with the network and frequent investigation of portions of the network to create and maintain updated documentation.

All Things Considered

Thought Experiment

Create a series of connectivity maps for either your place of work or your school. Try to include as many different external locations as possible. For one of these external locations, create one wide area connectivity map and one or more local area connectivity maps.

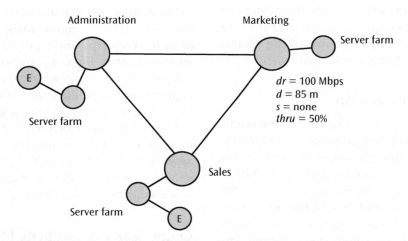

Figure 11-8   Example of a local area overview connectivity map

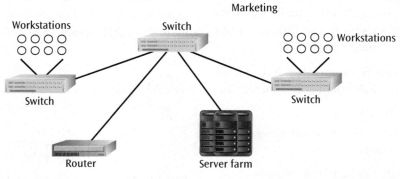

Figure 11-9   Local area detailed connectivity map for Marketing

Gap Analysis

A **gap analysis** is a study used to compare current conditions with desired conditions and identifying how to close that gap. Current conditions might include business objectives—such as number of customers, sales revenue, or rate of growth—or (as more directly relevant to the computer network) technical objectives like IT costs, number of trouble tickets, user satisfaction rates, or data throughput. Each of these factors might be one of the business's long-term **KPIs (key performance indicators)**, which is measured to indicate the efficiency and functioning of a system, or they might be newly identified measures or characteristics of the system. As each factor is quantified, you can then set goals for what you would like those numbers to be instead.

Setting a realistic goal for any of these KPIs requires consideration of available resources, current market conditions, the amount of support from higher-level decision makers, and many other factors. When identifying your goals, you'll set both a desired number for the KPI and a timeframe to reach that goal. This is called your desired state or future target. You can then chart your current state's trajectory and your desired state's trajectory to see the identified gap, as shown in Figure 11-10.

Next, the team will need to determine why the gap exists. Is there a problem that needs to be solved? Can a system's efficiency be increased? Do you need to upgrade some equipment or policies? Are you short-staffed?

Once you identify the root cause of the gap, you can strategize actions that will close the gap. Determine what changes are needed, what those changes will cost, and how long those changes will take to implement.

Feasibility Studies

As results from the gap analysis generate proposed changes, the team needs a way to determine which suggestions for change are reasonable. A **feasibility study** will consider all relevant factors to determine the practicality of proposed changes identified in the gap analysis. This includes an assessment of the company's resources and ability to accomplish the proposed changes as well as an evaluation of the added value the proposed changes could provide.

The term "feasible" has several meanings when it is applied to technology-based projects:

> The **technical feasibility** of a system is the extent to which the system can be created and

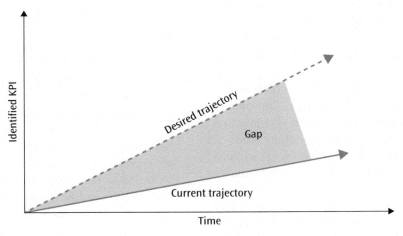

Figure 11-10 The difference between the current state's trajectory and the desired state is the gap

implemented using currently existing technology. Potential questions to answer would be: Does the technology specified in the system proposal exist, and can it be incorporated into a working solution? If technology from two or more vendors is suggested, will the differing technologies work together? Does your company have the technical expertise to build, install, or maintain the proposed system?

> A system's financial feasibility is the extent to which the system can be created, given the company's current finances. Potential questions to answer would be: Can the proposed system both solve the company's current problem and stay within budget? Will the proposed system return a profit? If so, how long will it take for this to happen?

> When a system demonstrates operational feasibility, it operates as designed and implemented. Thus, the company must ask: Will the proposed system produce the expected results? Will users be able to use the proposed system, or is there a chance that it will be so difficult or inconvenient to use that users will not adopt it?

> A system's time feasibility is the extent to which the system can be installed in a timely fashion that meets organizational needs. Potential questions to answer would be: Can the proposed system be designed, built, tested, and installed in an amount of time that all parties find reasonable and to which they can agree?

Technical, operational, financial, and time feasibility are best determined when the studies are based on a sound knowledge of the existing network, an understanding of the state of the current market and its products, and experience. Individuals involved in designing and installing a new or upgraded network system will perform better if they also understand analysis and design techniques, project and time management techniques, and financial analysis techniques. These techniques are an integral part of feasibility studies. The people involved in designing the new or updated system must also communicate effectively with key stakeholders, which include decision makers for the project (such as whether and how much funding will be made available for the project), those who will rely most heavily on or be most affected by the new or upgraded system, and those who will be responsible for helping to implement any changes within their departments.

Capacity Planning

Cloud Essentials+ Exam Tip

This section discusses benchmarking, which is required by

- Part of Objective 2.1: Given a scenario, use appropriate cloud assessments.

Capacity planning involves trying to determine the amount of network bandwidth necessary to support an application or a set of applications. Computer networks are mission-critical systems, and designing a new network or increasing the capacity of a current system requires careful planning. If a network is not capable of supporting the traffic generated within the company, response times will be sluggish, and users may not be able to complete their work on time, leading to missed deadlines, projects backing up or even failing, and low employee morale. For an online company, sluggish response times will also lead to dissatisfied customers who will quickly turn elsewhere.

At the other end of the spectrum, an overdesigned system is unnecessarily expensive and may never reach its capacity. It is probably best to err in the direction of overdesigning, especially because it is difficult to predict the growth rate of new users and applications. But the reality is that a large percentage of systems designed during the last 10 years are probably too small and will not be able to—or already cannot—support the demands placed on them. A smaller percentage of network systems are overdesigned and remain relatively idle.

Note

The problem of over- or under-designing a network is somewhat mitigated when using cloud's pay-as-you-go approach. You can design the system to scale up or down automatically—that is, it will increase or decrease the resources available to your network depending on the moment-by-moment demand on your systems. Many companies, when first migrating to the cloud, don't know to do this or don't do it well. This is one area where cloud optimization and cloud-native technologies offer extensive cost savings potential to customers.

Capacity planning is a difficult and time-consuming operation. But if capacity planning is not done well, it can be disastrously easy to plan poorly and thus design a system that will not support the intended applications. Several techniques exist for performing capacity planning, as described next:

> **Linear projection** involves predicting one or more network capacities based on the current network parameters and multiplying those capacities by some constant. If a network system of 10 nodes has a response time of x, then using a linear projection, a network system of 20 nodes will have a response time of $2x$. Not all systems follow a linear projection; applying a linear projection to these systems may produce inaccurate predictions. In these cases, an alternate strategy is required.

> A **computer simulation** involves modeling an existing system or a proposed system using a computer-based simulation tool and subjecting the model to varying degrees of user demand (called load). A computer simulation can mimic conditions that would be impossible or destructive to create on a real network, but accurate simulations are difficult to create. Any mistakes in the modeling process can be difficult to discover and can produce misleading results. Thus, extreme care must be taken when designing a simulation.

> **Benchmarking** involves generating system statistics under a controlled environment and then comparing those statistics against known measurements. Many network benchmark testing tools exist that can be used to evaluate the performance of a network or its components. Benchmarking is a relatively straightforward technique and can provide useful information when it is used to analyze a network. But setting up a benchmark test can be time consuming and, like creating computer simulations, this process can suffer from possible errors. In addition, if all the variables in the test environment are not the same as all the variables in the benchmark environment, inaccurate comparisons will result.

> **Analytical modeling** involves the creation of mathematical equations to calculate various network values. For example, to calculate the utilization of a single communications line within a network (the percentage of time that the line is being used), you can use the following equation:

$$U = t_{frame}/(2t_{prop} + t_{frame})$$

in which t_{frame} is the time to transmit a frame of data, and t_{prop} is the propagation time, the time it takes for a signal to be transferred down a wire or over the airwaves. Many experts feel analytical modeling is a good way to determine network capacity. As in the computer simulation technique, you can create analytical models representing network systems that are difficult to create in the real world. Unfortunately, it is easy to create inaccurate analytical models and thus generate results that are invalid.

Because most networks support multiple applications, a person who performs capacity planning for a network must calculate the capacity of each application on the network. Once the capacity of each application has been determined, it should be possible to determine the capacity for the entire network. You can calculate the individual capacities using analytical methods and then estimate the total network capacity using a linear projection.

Clearly, capacity planning is a difficult and nontrivial matter. Once capacity planning is properly done, however, a network administrator can determine if the company's LAN and WAN connections can support the intended applications.

Testing Environments

Cloud Essentials+ Exam Tip

This section discusses testing in QA environments, which is required by

- Part of Objective 3.2: Explain DevOps in cloud environments.

Planned changes should never be deployed directly in the active **production environment** that is currently supporting users and work processes without extensive testing first. During an app's development phase—or later, as changes are made—developers need an environment that is as nearly identical to the app's final production environment as possible. Typical environment types used through various phases of product development include:

> **Development**—This is a controlled environment where an app can be developed or changed to implement new features and improvements or to eliminate bugs.

> **Staging**—Usually a different team deploys the app in a staging environment for QA (quality assurance) testing, where testers attempt to identify bugs or security loopholes and run performance tests.

> **Production**—This is the live environment where users interact with the active version of the app.

> **Duplicate production**—It's not uncommon for an organization to run a duplicate production environment, at least temporarily, for an application or other services. One environment is active while the other environment receives updates, allows for further testing, or serves as a backup. This is called a **blue-green deployment** (see Figure 11-11), where one environment is active while the other waits on standby or receives updates. A router, load balancer, or other networking configuration (such as DNS) sends traffic only to the currently active environment and then changes traffic to the other environment after updates or other changes are successfully applied.

Various techniques offer the opportunity for QA testing before deploying changes into production:

> **Sandboxing**—A sandbox is an isolated environment where you can experiment with changes or potentially dangerous software without exposing sensitive resources to risk of damage.

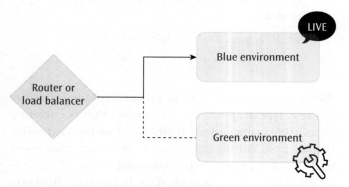

Figure 11-11 All traffic is directed to the live blue environment while the green environment receives updates

> **Load testing**—Load testing places the full force of anticipated demand on a system to determine if it can handle the load.

> **Regression testing**—This testing process confirms that changes to one system haven't negatively impacted other systems or functionality.

Remember this...

> One technique used to model a corporation's network environment is to create connectivity maps, depending on what type of network you are modeling: wide area connectivity maps, metropolitan area connectivity maps, and local area connectivity maps.

> A gap analysis is a study used to compare current conditions with desired conditions and identifying how to close that gap. When identifying your goals, you'll set both a desired number for the KPI and a timeframe to reach that goal. This is called your desired state or future target. You can then chart your current state's trajectory and your desired state's trajectory to see the identified gap.

> A feasibility study will consider all relevant factors to determine the practicality of proposed changes identified in the gap analysis. The technical feasibility of a system is the extent to which the system can be created and implemented using currently existing technology. A system's financial feasibility is the extent to which the system can be created, given the company's current finances. When a system demonstrates operational feasibility, it operates as designed and implemented. A system's time feasibility is the extent to which the system can be installed in a timely fashion that meets organizational needs.

> Capacity planning involves trying to determine the amount of network bandwidth necessary to support an application or a set of applications. Several techniques exist for performing capacity planning, including linear projection, computer simulation, benchmarking, and analytical modeling.

> Typical network environments for application development include the development environment for exploring possible changes, the staging environment for testing proposed changes, the production environment for active users, and a duplicate

production environment used as a backup or for additional testing. QA (quality assurance) testing techniques include sandboxing, load testing, and regression testing.

Self-check

4. When identifying a target number for a KPI, what other information is used to define the desired state?
   a. Current state
   b. Timeframe
   c. Gap
   d. Trajectory

5. Which type of feasibility study will ensure the new system will be convenient enough for users to use it consistently?
   a. Operational feasibility
   b. Time feasibility
   c. Technical feasibility
   d. Financial feasibility

6. Which environment do typical users interact with?
   a. Staging
   b. Production
   c. Development
   d. Duplicate production

Check your answers at the end of this chapter.

Section 11-3: Network Monitoring and Management

As changes are planned and executed, the network requires ongoing monitoring and maintenance to ensure its continued performance and reliability. This task is not as easy at it might first appear. Gaining access to the relevant information can be challenging, and sorting through all that information can be equally difficult. Further, a network admin must seek an appropriate balance between gathering all needed information and filtering information to just the important parts so staff aren't inundated with irrelevant data. To understand these processes, you'll first need an introduction to commonly used network monitoring tools. You'll then learn how some of these tools are used to create a baseline that can help IT staff identify problems quickly.

Network Monitoring Tools

Cloud Essentials+ Exam Tip

This section discusses alerts and logging, which are required by

- Part of Objective 3.1: Explain aspects of operating within the cloud.

To support a computer network and all its workstations, nodes, wiring, applications, and protocols, network administrators and their support staff need an arsenal of monitoring and diagnostic tools that provide visibility into how a network is performing and what problems it might be experiencing. These tools can be grouped into two categories: tools that test and debug the network hardware, and tools that analyze the data transmitted over the network.

Monitoring Network Hardware

Tools that test and debug network hardware range from very simple devices to more elaborate, complex devices. Three common testing devices are electrical testers (the simplest), cable testers, and network testers (the most elaborate):

> Electrical testers measure AC and DC volts, resistance, and continuity. An electrical tester will show if there is voltage on a line, and if so, how much voltage. If two bare wires are touching each other, they will create a short, and the electrical tester will show zero resistance. A continuity tester like the one shown in Figure 11-12 is a handy device that shows whether a signal is traversing a cable from one end to the other. Electrical and continuity testers are used to determine if the wires themselves are experiencing simple electrical problems.

> Cable testers are slightly more elaborate devices. They can verify connectivity and test for line faults, such as open circuits, short circuits, reversed circuits, and crossed circuits. Certain kinds of handheld cable testers can also test fiber-optic lines, such as the one shown in Figure 11-13. For example, if a connector hidden in some wiring closet contains two wires that are switched, a cable tester will detect the problem and point to the source of the problem.

Figure 11-12   A continuity tester can determine if a cable is good

One of the most elaborate devices is the network tester like the one shown in Figure 11-14. Some network testers have a display that graphically shows a network segment and all the devices attached to it. When plugged into an available network jack, these testers can troubleshoot the network and suggest possible corrections. A common problem solved by these devices is the identification and location of a NIC (network interface card) that is transmitting continuously but not sending valid data—this is called a jabber. The tester will pinpoint the precise NIC by indicating the 48-bit MAC address. A network administrator can then simply look up the particular MAC address in the system documentation and map it to a specific machine in a specific office.

Monitoring Network Traffic

The second category of diagnostic tools covers tools that analyze data transmitted over the network by examining message headers to determine many characteristics of network traffic. The most common of these are network monitors and protocol analyzers:

- A network monitor is a tool that continually monitors network traffic and might receive data from monitored devices that are configured to report their statistics.

- A similar tool, a protocol analyzer, can monitor traffic at a specific interface between a server or client and the network.

Figure 11-13   This optical power meter measures light power transmitted on a fiber-optic line

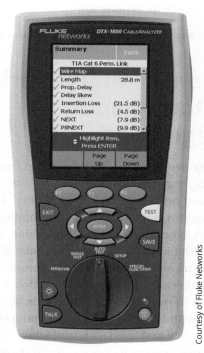

Courtesy of Fluke Networks

Figure 11-14   DTX-1800 device by Fluke Networks

In practice, these two terms—network monitor and protocol analyzer—are often used interchangeably. However, they differ significantly when it comes to the kinds of data each tool generates. Think about the difference between monitoring the traffic that a single device encounters on its connection to the network, versus monitoring devices and traffic patterns throughout the network. For example, Spiceworks is a type of network monitoring software because it can be configured to monitor multiple devices on a network at one time. Wireshark, which you used in the Chapter 4 project, is a type of protocol analyzer because it monitors traffic on the interface between a single device and the network.

Wireshark or other monitoring applications running on a single computer connected to a switch don't see all the traffic on a network—they only see the traffic the switch sends to them, which includes broadcast traffic and traffic specifically addressed to the one computer. To track more of the network traffic, a switch can be configured to use port mirroring. In port mirroring, also called SPAN (switched port analyzer), one port on a switch is configured to send a copy of the switch's traffic to the device connected to that port. The device runs a monitoring program, which can now see most of the traffic the switch receives. This configuration is managed using the `monitoring session` command on Cisco switches and consists of identifying the source interface (the port to be monitored) and the destination interface (the port where copied messages are sent). In the project at the end of this chapter, you'll configure SPAN on a switch in Packet Tracer. Then you'll monitor traffic through a device connected to the monitored port.

As traffic is monitored, each packet's protocol headers are analyzed, and statistics are generated that show which devices are talking to each other and which applications are being used. This information can then be used to update the network so that it operates more effectively. For example, if a network monitor indicates that a particular application is being used a great deal and is placing a strain on network resources, a network administrator can consider alternatives such as replacing the application with a more efficient one or redistributing the application to the locations where it is used the most.

Alerts and Logs

Some traffic monitoring tools provide real-time analysis of data, while other tools are designed to store data for retroactive analysis only as needed. Each approach results in different outcomes:

> **Alert message**—Monitoring live data allows detection of faults and other defined conditions, which can trigger alerts. An alert is a message that indicates some threshold has been met or exceeded, and it might generate notifications to IT personnel. Depending on the software used, these notifications might be transmitted either by email or text message, also called SMS (Short Message Service), or they can automatically prompt support ticket generation.

> **Log entry**—Virtually every condition recognized by an operating system or network monitor can be recorded. Records of such activities are kept in a log. Many devices, such as routers, switches, servers, and workstations, include embedded event logging tools of various types and will store logs within their own systems. Other tools collect log entries from devices across the network. These logs can be centrally collected via the syslog utility and analyzed retroactively to determine the cause of a problem or to track the effects of a problem.

Syslog

Syslog is a standard for generating, storing, and processing messages about events on many networked systems. It describes methods for detecting and reporting events and specifies the format and contents of messages. To limit the types of messages generated, transmitted, and stored, syslog assigns a severity level to each event. For example, "0" indicates an emergency situation, whereas "7" points to specific information that might help in debugging a problem, as shown in Figure 11-15.

Regulatory compliance requirements often dictate the minimum requirements for filters and other syslog configurations you implement on each device. In some cases, you must be able to track every movement of every user. By referring to information stored

Level	State indicated
0	Emergency! System unusable
1	Alert–Immediate action needed
2	Critical–Critical condition
3	Error–Error condition
4	Warning–Warning condition
5	Notification–Normal but significant condition
6	Informational–Informational message only
7	Debugging–Helpful for debugging

Figure 11-15 Syslog severity levels

in your logs, you should be able to answer the question, "Who did what activity when and in what way?" When tracking this level of information, the collective data is called an audit log, or audit trail. The data in these logs is consistent and thorough enough to retroactively prove compliance and also to defensibly prove user actions. This data is often used in forensics investigations to determine how a particular problem occurred, especially if criminal investigations are involved. Make sure you know exactly what types of actions and other events you must log on your network to meet or exceed relevant compliance standards.

Using the information collected in event logs and system logs for security and fault management requires thoughtful data filtering and sorting. Not all information in the logs points to a problem, even if it is marked with a warning. A user might have typed their password incorrectly while trying to log on to their computer, thus generating a log entry. At other times, seemingly innocuous information turns out to be exactly the data needed to diagnose a problem.

Because the syslog utility only keeps a history of messages issued by the system but doesn't send out alerts, someone must monitor the system log for issues, review the logs regularly for missed problems, or filter log data to monitor packet flow when troubleshooting a problem or checking for patterns that might indicate developing problems. Most UNIX and Linux desktop operating systems provide a GUI application for easily reviewing and filtering the information in system logs. Other

applications are available for sifting through syslog data and generating alerts.

Simple Network Management Protocol (SNMP)

Organizations often use enterprise-wide network management systems to perform real-time monitoring functions across an entire network. These systems consist of the following components, as illustrated in Figure 11-16:

> Each network device—such as routers, switches, and wireless access points—can be classified as either managed or unmanaged. A managed device has management software, called an **agent**, running on it and is more elaborate and expensive than an unmanaged element. Each managed device may contain several managed objects. This can be any characteristic of the device that is monitored, including components such as a processor, memory, hard disk, or NIC, or intangibles such as performance or utilization. Each managed object is assigned an OID (object identifier), which is standardized across all network management systems.

> Agents communicate information about managed devices via any one of several application-layer protocols. On modern networks, most agents use SNMP (Simple Network Management Protocol), which is the simplest to operate, easiest to implement, and most widely used. Recall from Chapter 1

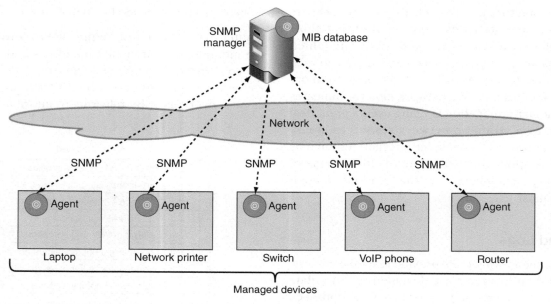

Figure 11-16 Network management architecture

that SNMP allows the numerous elements within a computer network to be managed from a single point and is an industry standard created by the IETF. One characteristic that sets SNMP apart from syslog is that SNMP can be used to reconfigure managed devices while syslog does not offer that kind of remote management control. Additionally, SNMP is used more for real-time network monitoring rather than retroactive analysis.

> **SNMP manager** software controls the operations of a managed element and maintains a database of information about all managed elements. An SNMP manager can query each agent and receive management data, which it then stores in the database. An agent can send unsolicited information to the manager in the form of an alarm. Finally, an SNMP manager itself can also act as an agent if a higher-level SNMP manager calls upon the manager to provide information for a higher-level database. All this management and passing of information can be done either locally or remotely, for example, from across the country in cases where the information is transmitted over the Internet.

> The database that holds the information about all managed devices is called the **MIB (Management Information Base)**. The information stored in the MIB can be used to repair or manage the network, or simply to observe the operation of the network. A manager can query a managed element (agent), asking for the particular details of that element's operation at that moment in time. This information is then sent from the managed element to the MIB for storage. For example, a manager might ask a router how many packets have entered the router, how many packets have exited the router, and how many packets were discarded due to insufficient buffer space. This information can later be used by a management program, which might, after looking at the information in the MIB, conclude that this particular element is not performing properly.

SNMP can also perform an autodiscovery type of operation. This operation is used to discover new elements that have been added to the network. When SNMP discovers a newly added element, the information about the element is added to the MIB. Thus, SNMP is a dynamic protocol that can automatically adapt to a changing network. This adaptation does not require human intervention (except for the intervention involved in connecting the new element to the network).

Managed elements are monitored and controlled using three basic SNMP commands:

> The read command is issued by a manager to retrieve information from the agent in a managed element.

> The write command is also issued by a manager, but it's used to control the agent in a managed element. By using the write command, a manager can change the settings in an agent, thus making the managed element perform differently.

> The trap command is used by a managed element to send reports to the manager. When certain types of events, such as a buffer overflow, occur, a managed element can send a trap to report the event.

Most, but not all, network management applications support multiple versions of SNMP. SNMP version 3 is the most secure version of the protocol. For example, a weakness of the first two versions of SNMP was the lack of security in the write command. Anyone posing as an SNMP manager could send bogus write commands to managed elements and thereby cause potential damage to the network. SNMPv3 addresses the issue of security, so that bogus managers cannot send malicious write commands.

However, some administrators have hesitated to upgrade to SNMPv3 because it requires more complex configuration. Therefore, SNMPv2 is still widely used, despite the many SNMP vulnerabilities listed in the CVE (Common Vulnerabilities and Exposures) database, one of which is displayed in Figure 11-17. When using older versions of SNMP, it's important to incorporate additional security measures, such as the following:

> Disable SNMP on devices where it's not needed.

> Limit approved sources of SNMP messages.

> Require read-only mode so devices can't be reconfigured using SNMP messages.

> Configure strong passwords, called community strings, on SNMP managed devices.

> Use different community strings on different types of devices so, for example, a compromised power backup system (which incorporates less secure protections) doesn't result in a compromised router using the same community string.

NetFlow

SNMP provides real-time monitoring of network activities and device states with an emphasis on device

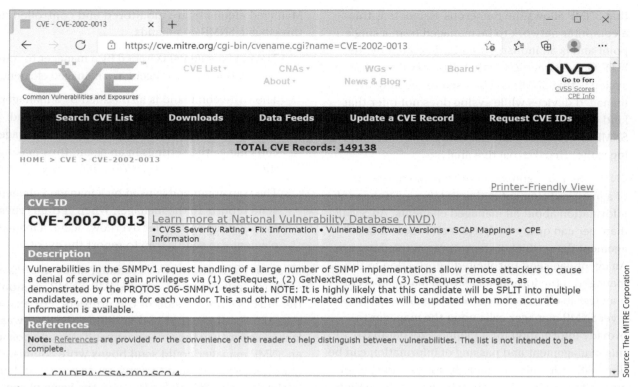

Figure 11-17 One of many SNMP vulnerabilities listed in the CVE

health, performance, and configuration. But what if a comprehensive view of network traffic across all devices is needed instead? NetFlow is a proprietary traffic monitoring protocol from Cisco that tracks all IP traffic crossing any interface where NetFlow is enabled. From that information, NetFlow creates flow records that show relationships among various traffic types. While SNMP focuses on individual devices, NetFlow focuses on the way network bandwidth is being utilized by identifying how communications from all devices are related to each other.

When NetFlow is enabled on a network device, each unique conversation is collected in a NetFlow cache as a flow record. Additional messages in the same conversation are aggregated into that one flow record. When complete, the flow record is then sent, or exported, to a centralized NetFlow analyzer. The NetFlow analyzer collates flow records from throughout the network to provide insights into traffic patterns, such as why congestion is happening, what changes are occurring, and how those changes are affecting other traffic. A NetFlow analyzer can be hardware-based or software-based, which is more common.

A significant challenge with NetFlow is determining the optimal balance between tracking all traffic and tracking enough traffic to sufficiently observe network behavior. While NetFlow can provide in-depth access to traffic

information, all the data must be transferred from the NetFlow exporter (the router, switch, or other device monitoring its traffic) to the NetFlow analyzer. NetFlow is capable of tracking nearly 100 percent of messages crossing an interface. However, transferring this volume of flow records to the analyzer will, on its own, negatively impact network performance. The trick is to sample enough traffic to get an accurate picture and catch problems early while not transferring any more flow records than necessary across the network for analysis. Still, NetFlow requires shallower examination of messages on the network and, therefore, fewer resources than other options that capture entire packets. This allows NetFlow to analyze very high volumes of traffic that would overwhelm more traditional approaches.

Creating a Baseline

Cloud Essentials+ Exam Tip

This section discusses baselines and resource management, which are required by

- Part of Objective 2.1: Given a scenario, use appropriate cloud assessments.

- Part of Objective 4.2: Explain policies or procedures.

Effective network resource management involves monitoring the demand placed on network devices and available bandwidth to ensure that network traffic flows smoothly and safely. To identify changes in network performance, the network administrator must first establish a baseline, which is a record of how a network or resource operates under normal conditions and includes performance statistics, utilization rates, and so on. Creating a baseline for an existing computer network involves measuring and recording a network's state of operation over a given period of time. This process requires capturing many network measurements over all segments of a network, including numerous measurements on workstations, user applications, routers, and switches. Once a baseline is created, the results can be used to identify network weaknesses and strengths, which can then be used to intelligently upgrade the network.

Very often, network administrators feel pressure from users and network owners to increase the bandwidth of a network. Without a thorough understanding of whether network problems actually exist—or, if they do, *where* they exist—a network administrator trying to improve network operation may inadvertently "fix" the wrong problem. Improving a network's operation may involve increasing network bandwidth, but it could just as easily involve something less expensive, such as upgrading some older equipment or segmenting a network with a new switch. By conducting a baseline study (preferably one that is *continuing*), a network administrator can gain a better understanding of the network and can improve its overall quality more effectively.

Baseline studies can be started at any time, but they're most effective when they are initiated during a time when the network is not experiencing severe problems, such as a node failure or a jabber. Therefore, before beginning a baseline study, all immediate problems should be addressed so the network is operating normally. Because a baseline generates a large number of statistics, a good database or spreadsheet application is needed to keep the data organized, or a tool designed to baseline a network can be especially useful.

The next question is: on what items will baseline information be collected? For example, information on items such as system users, system nodes, operational protocols, network applications, and network utilization levels might prove useful. Information on system users might include the maximum number of users, the average number of users, and the peak number of users.

Information included in baseline documentation must be detailed. Baseline information on system nodes should include a list of the number and types of system nodes in the network. These may include computer workstations, printers, routers, switches, and servers. It is a good practice to have up-to-date drawings of the locations of all nodes, along with their model numbers, serial numbers, and any address information such as Ethernet and IP addresses. This information should also include the name and telephone number(s) of each product's vendor, in case technical assistance is ever needed.

Collecting baseline information on operational protocols involves listing the types of operational protocols used throughout the system. Most networks support multiple protocols, such as TCP, IP, and more. If a baseline study discovers an older protocol that can be replaced, it could contribute to improving network efficiency.

The baseline study should also generate a list of all network applications found on the network, including the number, type, and utilization level of each application. Having a comprehensive list of the applications on the network will help to identify old applications that can be removed and the number of copies of each application to avoid violating software licenses. When creating a comprehensive list of network applications, don't forget to include the applications stored on both individual user workstations and network servers.

Assembling information on network utilization levels requires an extensive list of statistics. These statistics might include many of the following values:

> Average network utilization (%)

> Peak network utilization (%)

> Average frame size

> Peak frame size

> Average frames per second

> Peak frames per second

> Total network collisions

> Network collisions per second

> Total runts, which you learned about in Chapter 5

> Total jabbers

> Total CRC errors

> Node(s) with the highest percentage of utilization and corresponding amount of traffic

Once network utilization data is collected and analyzed, several important observations can be made. First, a network may be reaching saturation. Typically, a network reaches saturation when its network utilization is at or near100 percent, which means 100 percent of the usable transmission space on the network is consumed by valid data. However, a network should never need to function at 100 percent to meet demand, as its efficiency falls quickly when its available bandwidth is used up.

A second observation is when peak periods of network use occur. Making observations about peak periods of network use is easiest with a graph of network activity data. Consider the hypothetical example shown in Figure 11-18. Peak periods occur at approximately 8:30 a.m., 11:30 a.m., 1:00 p.m., and 4:00 p.m. The most likely reason for these peaks would be users logging in and checking email at 8:30 a.m. and 1:00 p.m., and users finishing work before going to lunch (11:30 a.m.) or going home (4:00 p.m.). Once regular peak periods and their underlying causes are identified, a peak period at an unusual time can prompt further investigation. Plus, knowing when peak periods occur and why they occur allows the network administrator to rearrange network resources to help lessen the load during these periods.

Examining the amount of traffic on each node also yields valuable information about network performance. Typically, a small percentage of network nodes generates a large percentage of network traffic. It is not unusual to encounter a node, such as a router or server, that is at the center of a great deal of traffic. A user workstation that generates a high amount of traffic, however, is suspect and should be examined more closely. A common example today is that of a user downloading music or video files over the corporate or school network. Music and video downloads consume a great deal of bandwidth and tie up network resources, causing delays for employees and students with legitimate network requests. Network administrators can and should detect these downloads, which are often unauthorized, and ask the user to discontinue performing them on network workstations.

Once the baseline study has been performed, the network will need ongoing observation. For a baseline study to be really effective, it must be maintained. An ongoing baseline study gives a network administrator an effective tool for identifying network problems, repairing the network, responding to complaints, improving the weak spots, and requesting additional funding.

Remember this...

> Three common hardware testing devices are electrical testers (the simplest), cable testers, and network testers (the most elaborate).

> Network monitors and protocol analyzers examine message headers to determine many characteristics of network traffic. A network monitor is a tool that continually monitors network traffic and might receive data from monitored devices that are configured to report their statistics. A protocol analyzer can monitor traffic at a specific interface between a server or client and the network.

> An alert is a message that indicates some threshold has been met or exceeded, and it might generate notifications to IT personnel. In contrast, static records of activities on an OS or a network are kept in a log.

> Syslog is a standard for generating, storing, and processing messages about events on many networked systems. It describes methods for detecting and reporting events and specifies the format and contents of messages.

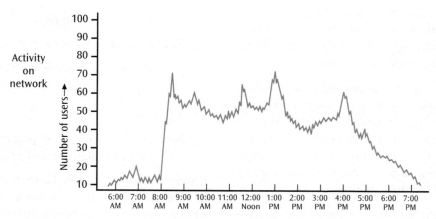

Figure 11-18   Peak periods of network activity in a typical day

> SNMP (Simple Network Management Protocol) allows the numerous elements within a computer network to be managed from a single point and supports real-time network monitoring.

> NetFlow is a proprietary traffic monitoring protocol from Cisco that tracks all IP traffic crossing any interface where NetFlow is enabled. From that information, NetFlow creates flow records that show relationships among various traffic types. While SNMP focuses on individual devices, NetFlow focuses on the way network bandwidth is being utilized by identifying how communications from all devices are related to each other.

> To identify changes in network performance, the network administrator must first establish a baseline, which is a record of how a network or resource operates under normal conditions and includes performance statistics, utilization rates, and so on. Creating a baseline for an existing computer network involves measuring and recording a network's state of operation over a given period of time. This process requires capturing many network measurements over all segments of a network, including numerous measurements on workstations, user applications, routers, and switches. Once a baseline is created, the results can be used to identify network weaknesses and strengths, which can then be used to intelligently upgrade the network.

Self-check

7. Which network tool is best for monitoring traffic on a single network interface?
   a. Network monitor
   b. Network tester
   c. Cable tester
   d. Protocol analyzer
8. Which standard yields the best big-picture view of traffic patterns on a network?
   a. SNMP
   b. NetFlow
   c. CVE
   d. Syslog
9. When is the best time to collect data to establish a network baseline?
   a. In the middle of the night
   b. During a network crisis

   c. Throughout a typical business day
   d. Over the weekend

Check your answers at the end of this chapter.

Section 11-4: Cloud Deployment and Management

Many times, changes to a company's network infrastructure includes a shift to the cloud. Expanding an on-prem network into the cloud typically includes a time of transition where resources are migrated to the cloud, followed by the deployment, monitoring, and optimization of cloud-based resources. Unlike with an on-prem network, a public cloud customer does not have access to the underlying hardware hosting cloud resources, and most of the time, traffic between these resources cannot be directly observed. This presents a challenge for network administrators who are familiar with tools used for on-prem network monitoring and management. In this section, you'll learn about different methods designed specifically to help cloud customers optimize their cloud's performance.

Cloud Migration

Cloud Essentials+ Exam Tip

This section discusses cloud migration techniques, which are required by

- Part of Objective 2.5: Compare and contrast cloud migration approaches.

For most companies, their initial migration to the cloud is performed in layers, beginning with a simple application and continuing with more complex projects. Further, a company might find that one cloud provider no longer meets their needs at some point, and they decide to migrate to another cloud provider. They might choose to extend the scope of their deployment to include additional providers and services. The accelerating growth of cloud technologies, fluctuating prices for services, and constant demand for quality improvement impel organizations to continually evolve their cloud deployments. For these and other reasons, a company will likely revisit each phase of cloud migration repeatedly throughout their engagement with the cloud.

Migration Phases

When moving an organization's IT resources to the cloud, whether a single application, a few servers, a database, or the entire network, the project consists of five major phases: assess, plan, migrate, validate, and manage. Figure 11-19 shows these phases in a cycle because the process of cloud migration is never fully complete or static.

Probably the most challenging phase of a migration to the cloud is the planning stage. However, a well-laid plan will help to ensure the migration proceeds smoothly and the outcome meets the organization's goals. The plan should consider the type of migration, whether the company is moving data, databases, applications, or network functions. An effective plan contains thorough information on the following topics:

> **Business continuity**—Consider the effects of any anticipated downtime and how to minimize or avoid it. Also consider user training that can be performed before the migration occurs. Will the migration affect how users interact with the network or applications? Will they notice any significant changes in their work processes? Do they need training on any new applications? Service desk staff hours might need to be temporarily increased immediately following the transition to support users throughout the process. Keeping users informed and helping them understand the benefits that will be achieved once the migration is complete will more effectively manage expectations.

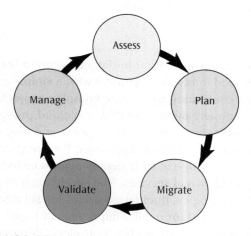

Figure 11-19 The five phases of cloud migration

> **Legal restrictions**—Countries and states have different laws for data protection. For this reason, some types of data cannot be stored at datacenters located inside countries with laws against certain kinds of data security. Some types of regulated data are required to be stored only within the geographical borders of an organization's own country. This poses a challenge for cloud-based data storage, and companies need to be aware of these issues before signing a contract. In other cases, there are limitations on what software can run on machines hosted in particular countries. An organization should have formal processes for evaluating contracts before signing them and ensure that both legal and IT experts weigh in on the terms of the agreement.

> **Baselines**—Collect extensive baselines before beginning any transition, which will indicate current functioning and configuration of the systems in the network. This includes collecting information on KPIs such as CPU and RAM usage, page load time and error rates, storage and network usage, and patch and application versions.

> **Existing systems**—Thoroughly understand and document existing systems that will be affected by the cloud migration. Recognize that systems and resources are highly interrelated—systems slated for migration interact with many components and services such as databases, network services, or applications. Sometimes these dependencies can also be moved to the cloud. Other times, the other systems relying on these same resources require that the entire web of interdependencies stay on-prem, such as when several applications—both modern and legacy—pull from a single, monolithic database. A dependency diagram shows which components rely on what other components. This diagram will help in deciding which components should be migrated and in what order. Be sure to investigate how the transition will affect the systems left behind. Also include a discovery process to identify so-called shadow IT components, which refers to resources or services running outside the knowledge or oversight of the IT department. These rogue components might have been instituted by users outside of the appropriate approval processes. However, changing systems that these shadow components rely on can interrupt work activities for the people who use them. By discovering who is using

what, frustrated complaints from co-workers can more likely be bypassed.

> **Target hosts**—Initially, resources start on the source host, which is whatever system—physical, virtual, or cloud based—that currently supports the resource. Any resource being moved is headed toward a target host. Configure this target host carefully to match the needs and anticipated growth of the transitioned resources.

> **Cloud architecture**—A cloud deployment is made up of many components, not just VMs. These cloud elements (also called target objects) include applications, databases, servers, processes, virtual appliances (such as a firewall), logs, and storage blocks or volumes. In addition, the overall cloud architecture includes the interfaces between these elements, the networking architecture that manages these interfaces, and the connections to the on-prem datacenter or users. In developing a migration plan, consider all of these aspects to the degree they'll be incorporated into the cloud deployment. Provide the appropriate structure in the target cloud for the resources and workloads it will support.

> **Order of operations**—Consider in what order elements should be moved to the cloud. Most often, a company will start with an easy application, something simple and well defined without a lot of interdependencies on other systems. Ideally, this first migration will also involve a low-priority resource so that if something goes wrong, the organization doesn't lose significant amounts of revenue or productivity while troubleshooting the problem. As they tackle more complex systems, they'll need to carefully consider which parts of each system should be moved first so that the timing of data synchronization and DNS record transitions will flow smoothly.

While hashing out the migration plan, the migration team will continue to fine-tune it even as the migration proceeds. Also, they should revisit the plan after migration is complete, evaluating the effect of this migration and considering other resources that might benefit from a shift to cloud. Migration is not a one-time event.

Migration Strategies

Each organization will take its own unique approach to its cloud migration, depending on the scope of elements being migrated and the company's intent in making the transition. Intentions can range from wanting to save money to overhauling their entire IT infrastructure, and anything in between. Throughout the industry, some general categories have emerged for cloud migration strategies that reveal a spectrum of organizational investment in the cloud. These categories have been defined by the research company Gartner (*gartner.com*), AWS, and others along the following lines:

> **Rehost**—Also called *lift and shift* or *forklift*, this migration strategy refers to moving the application or data into the cloud as it is. The process is often automated for high efficiency. One disadvantage is that weaknesses in resource design are retained. However, the speed of making this transition is appealing and can save money quickly, and then the resource can be further adapted or eventually replaced.

> **Revise or replatform**—Also called *lift tinker and shift*, this approach makes some relatively minor changes to the application or data before moving it to the cloud, such as adding a management layer or incorporating auto-scaling features.

> **Refactor, rearchitect, or rebuild**—In this approach, the changes are more significant, such as rewriting huge portions of an application's code.

> **Repurchase**—Also called *rip and replace*, this strategy refers to replacing the product with an existing or custom-designed cloud-native product. This can be a quick, easy, and inexpensive solution, especially considering the increasing variety of options in the cloud marketplace.

> **Retain**—Also called the *do-nothing* option, this is also a low-complexity strategy that means the organization keeps using an application or data as it is, without any changes. The company might revisit the resource later as circumstances continue to evolve.

> **Retire**—This is a low-complexity strategy that basically means the organization stops using the application or data.

Figure 11-20 shows how the migration process varies between the different strategy options. Study this diagram carefully, as many cloud providers and related vendors use similar diagrams to help customers consider their options.

Most companies are choosing to adopt a hybrid cloud strategy where some resources stay on-prem and others

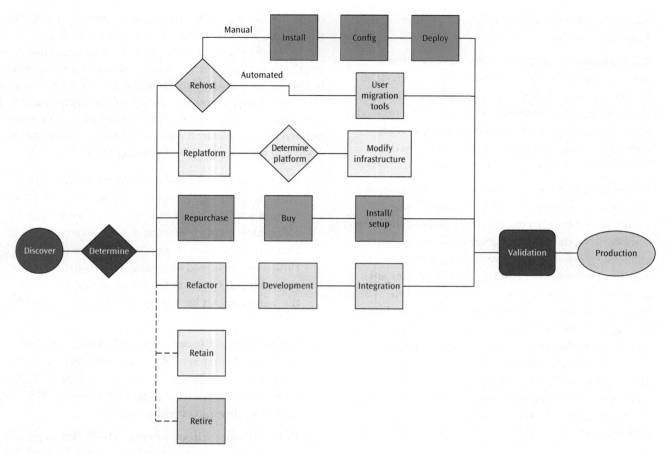

Figure 11-20   Cloud migration strategies

are moved to the cloud. In choosing which approach to take for a specific resource, consider both a practical perspective and a technical perspective. Will users have constant Internet access when using this app? Is the relevant data covered by compliance requirements? Is the app compatible with a cloud environment? Can it easily be adapted to the cloud, or is it too old or have dependencies too complex to be moved? Where the app can't reasonably be adapted, it might need to stay where it is or be replaced entirely. In many cases, some app components (such as a database) might stay on-prem while other components (such as a web server) are moved to the cloud.

Cloud Provisioning and Configuration Management

In the Chapter 7 project, you deployed an EC2 instance in AWS. To do this, you used AWS's management console, which is a GUI (graphical user interface) for interacting with your cloud resources. When companies deploy extensive cloud infrastructure—especially in a production environment—they use automated processes that can be tracked, audited, and consistently repeated.

Automation

Automation refers to the use of software-based solutions to perform a process or procedure with minimal human intervention. In the physical world, this might look like cars that can park themselves, digital assistants like Siri or Alexa that can start your coffee pot in the morning, or drones that can deliver packages (see Figure 11-21). In the cloud, this might look like an automated process for creating, cloning, or shutting down a VM instance or a server cluster, upgrading or patching a VM, configuring a virtual network, or deploying an extensive and complex

iStock.com

Figure 11-21   Companies like Amazon (amazon.com) and UPS (ups.com) are experimenting with automated drone delivery of packages

cloud environment. The idea with cloud automation is to reduce the demand on human staff's time while increasing accuracy and repeatability of common tasks.

Think about the steps you take to configure a new VM. You need to choose the boot source, size, network connections, security configurations, and storage allocations. The first time you do this, you have to think through the options and implications of your decisions. However, the next time you need a VM with the same configuration, you don't have to invest nearly so much thought. If this is a configuration you use often, you eventually reach a point where configuring a new VM consists of a series of mind-numbing clicks to implement the same decisions made the first time. And the more boring or repetitive the task, the more likely you'll make a mistake. The thing is, humans tend to be particularly bad at doing the same thing exactly the same way over and over. Computers, however, are very good at doing exactly what you tell them to do and doing it exactly the same way every time. When you find yourself doing the same thing repeatedly, this is often an ideal candidate for automation.

Automation in the cloud accomplishes several important goals, such as the following:

> **Faster deployment, adjustments, and corrections—** Monitoring tools can be programmed to respond automatically to problems. Automated tools can also deploy, replicate, or resize resources quickly to

efficiently meet increasing or decreasing demand, which, as you might recall, is called auto-scaling.

> **Better control—**Standardized processes are easier to define, monitor, and replicate. When you know a task is performed the same way every single time, you can better predict the effects of those changes and fine-tune the process as needed.

> **Lower costs—**With fewer errors and less demand on staff's time, the team can focus on higher-level, strategic activities that provide added value to the organization while paying less for cloud management and resources.

> **More secure—**It might seem counterintuitive to think of security increasing when administrators hand off some of the control to the computer. However, a well-orchestrated system is much less likely to suffer from vulnerabilities due to misconfigurations and other human errors.

Modern automation tools designed for the cloud offer flexible, robust features that can help an organization take full advantage of the cost-saving and performance benefits the cloud has to offer. Some of the maintenance and security tasks that can be performed by these tools include the following:

> Create backups.

> Clone, resize, or remove resources.

> Apply patches, updates, and upgrades.

> Restart or shut down VM instances.

> Enable or disable alerts.

> Detect signs of an attack.

> Quarantine compromised resources.

> Manage security rules.

Infrastructure as Code (IaC)

How does all of this work? How can you set up a cloud system to make good decisions reliably and perform complex tasks without human intervention?

To understand the basic principles of automation, it helps to first understand the concept of a runbook. A **runbook** is a collection of physical or digital documents that outline the precise steps to complete procedures or operations in a specific IT environment. For example, an admin might document the steps to provision a new server, update a running VM instance, or recover from a database backup. A good runbook provides sufficient detail so other people could follow the steps and obtain the exact same results each time.

A runbook is typically designed to be read and followed by humans. However, consider what could be done with a runbook that is written in a computer-readable language, such as a programming language or scripting language. With sufficient detail, runbooks could tell a computer how to spin up a VM with a specific configuration, create or replicate a database, or configure a virtual network with multiple servers. This application of the runbook concept in an automated environment is called **IaC (infrastructure as code)**, where the steps needed to configure or change a cloud environment are written in code and are deployed all at once rather than requiring a human admin to complete one step of the deployment at a time.

Several runbooks can be designed to work together to spin up multiple nodes and all the related security, networking, and OS configurations. In cooperation, these runbooks could create a large and complex testing environment complete with network services, security groups, VMs running various OSs, and predictable access keys and passwords as desired. Collections of many automated processes like this in a carefully choreographed manner is the essence of **orchestration**. Where automation accomplishes a single task (such as create a VM), orchestration designs a series of tasks in a workflow (such as creating an entire testing

environment). AWS's CloudFormation service, for example, can be used to design a separate template for each resource (such as a VM) to be created automatically, and then multiple templates are collected in a configuration file to deploy many resources in parallel.

Documenting and designing infrastructure as code presents many benefits. For example, IaC and the related automation and orchestration tools enable a more consistent environment throughout the process of developing, testing, deploying, and patching an application or service. IaC can ensure that all these environments are properly synced and updated. Applications are quickly changed and updated in a DevOps-based organization; new releases might occur every day, even multiple times a day. By maintaining consistency between the various environments representing different stages of an app's development, IaC helps minimize problems as the app is transitioned from one environment to the next.

IaC also assists in troubleshooting efforts or security investigations. What was the state of a cloud environment when a particular network connection went down or when a problematic intrusion occurred? In a large, active organization—or even in a small company—it could be nearly impossible to remember who made what changes if everything is done manually, where a staff person gives direct reconfiguration commands to the cloud deployment.

By first defining a cloud environment in a text file, changes to that environment can be tracked by examining historical versions of the file. Each time a change is executed in an environment, the previous state of the environment is still documented in the earlier version of the file. This is especially useful when the new configuration has problems and must be rolled back to a previous configuration, which can be accomplished by deploying the previous environment's configuration file.

Because IaC provides documentation of each automated environmental configuration along the way, troubleshooting or security teams can investigate historical changes made in the cloud environment to determine when a problem occurred and why. In essence, IaC provides a digital "paper trail." This same IaC documentation also helps in meeting regulatory standards to prove historical compliance, which is essential during audits or court-ordered investigations. And IaC processes increase consistency across an organization's staff members and their work, especially when the organization experiences staff turnover.

Automation and Orchestration Tools

Automation and orchestration tools might be built into the cloud platform or provided by third-party vendor applications that interact with the cloud platform through API (application programming interface) messages. Many cloud automation tools are primarily managed through a CLI (command-line interface) and rely on a variety of programming languages, such as Python, and file formats, such as JSON (JavaScript Object Notation and pronounced *j-son*) and YAML (YAML Ain't Markup Language and rhymes with *camel*). Some of these tools offer a web GUI or cloud portal, especially when using the paid version of the application. Most of these tools work from templates of some kind for managing deployments. However, by understanding the underlying file format and programming languages, scripts or custom programming can be written to design automated processes unique to a particular environment.

No single tool can meet all of an organization's automation needs. Some automation tasks address infrastructure provisioning or server configurations while other automation workflows target management of applications or IAM accounts. A tool that attempts to address all these areas typically doesn't handle any of them well. As a result, you need to know about the wide range of tools available to make good decisions for which combination of tools will best serve your situation.

As you read about the following tools, notice that each tool is optimized either for resource provisioning or for configuration management. While many automation tools can do some of both of these processes, most tools are specialized for one or the other:

> **Provisioning**—Provisioning tools deploy new cloud resources. Many kinds of automated processes can be part of IaC provisioning such as auto-scaling, which is a type of provisioning task.

> **CM (configuration management)**—CM tools configure existing resources to match a particular configuration template. Automation might also include the need to reconfigure instances after creation so they meet a certain standard of settings, software installations, and security configurations. This process is part of CM (configuration management).

Each major cloud platform includes its own automation tool, such as AWS's CloudFormation, Azure's Resource Manager, and GCP's Deployment Manager. Templates are typically configured using YAML or JSON,

both of which are machine readable while also being human-reader friendly. A third-party provisioning tool is Terraform. Terraform was developed by HashiCorp (*hashicorp.com*) and provides cloud-agnostic infrastructure provisioning. The open-source version is free to the public while the enterprise version offers additional features, such as GUI, collaboration, and governance capabilities that work well in an enterprise environment where many teams rely on the same tools. Terraform works with AWS, Azure, GCP, and more than 150 other service providers.

In contrast, the following is a list of popular, third-party tools used primarily for configuration management:

> **Ansible**—Another open-source (but not free) automation tool, Ansible (*ansible.com*) is sponsored by Red Hat and relies on YAML. Ansible requires no agent installation on managed nodes and, instead, connects to these nodes via SSH (Secure Shell) by default. For this reason, Ansible is generally considered easier to set up than other third-party options.

> **Chef**—Chef (*chef.io*) is an open-source configuration management tool that can be used to configure and manage large numbers of nodes such as servers and network devices both on-prem and in the cloud. Built on Ruby, a programming language that is easy for beginners to learn, configurations are stored in recipes that are grouped in cookbooks.

> **Puppet**—Puppet (*puppet.com*) is another configuration management tool similar to Chef but has been around longer. The Puppet DSL (Domain Specific Language) is based on Ruby. Open-source Puppet is free to use while the enterprise version is free only for up to 10 nodes. Puppet and Chef both rely on an agent installed on each managed node, which then reports to the master server for configuration management.

> **SaltStack**—SaltStack (*saltstack.com*) is an open-source CM tool that provides event-driven automation to detect problems and enforce the desired state of managed resources. SaltStack requires the installation of an agent, called a minion, on managed devices. A pillar file stores configuration details in YAML, JSON, or other formats. Like Terraform and others, open-source Salt is free to the public, while enterprise SaltStack offers additional features, such as a GUI.

Details | Choosing an Automation Tool

Initially, these lists of tools might look like a hodge-podge of options providing no clear sense of direction on how to choose one tool over another. Let's look at some of the ways to differentiate each of these tools from the others. Differentiating factors include the following:

> **Push model vs. pull model**—In a push model, the server pushes out configuration changes to managed resources, as shown in Figure 11-22. In a pull model, managed resources check in with the server to retrieve configuration details. The push model works well when the managed resources are easily identified and located, and they're consistently reachable through established network connections. For more transient resources, such as auto-scaled VMs, the pull model is typically more effective. Puppet and Chef use the pull model, while SaltStack and Ansible use more of a push configuration (although SaltStack actually uses some of both models).

> **Immutable vs. idempotent**—This characteristic determines whether a resource can be changed once created:

o Immutable environments or resources aren't changed after they're deployed. They're deployed in the state they're intended to be used. If changes are needed, the old resources

are destroyed and replaced with new resources that meet the desired configurations, such as when needing to update a server's OS. This helps prevent configuration drift where undocumented changes might cause problems that are difficult to identify. Terraform, CloudFormation, and AWS's auto-scaling groups take an immutable approach to resources.

o Idempotent means that, when running the configuration, it will make needed changes to the environment without destroying existing resources. This ability allows the idempotent system to conform configurations to their intended state by reconfiguring them rather than destroying and replacing them. For example, an OS update can be applied to existing VM servers rather than replacing servers with updated versions. Ansible and Chef rely on idempotent techniques.

> **Imperative vs. declarative**—Imperative tools require the exact steps needed to complete a task. Declarative tools, however, require less direction from the administrator. Instead, the admin tells the tool the end result they want, and the tool figures out how to accomplish that goal. Chef and Ansible take an imperative approach while Terraform, SaltStack, Puppet, and CloudFormation all offer a declarative style.

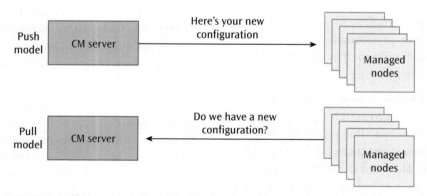

Figure 11-22 Some CM tools push configurations to managed nodes at the time the changes need to be made; other tools require that nodes check in with the server to determine if changes need to be made

Cloud Monitoring and Optimization

Cloud Essentials+ Exam Tip

This section discusses cloud reporting, right-sizing, and API integration, which are required by

- Part of Objective 2.1: Given a scenario, use appropriate cloud assessments.
- Part of Objective 3.1: Explain aspects of operating within the cloud.
- Part of Objective 3.2: Explain DevOps in cloud environments.

Many variables contribute to the fluctuation of cloud performance. For example, a VM server will perform best if its CPU utilization remains below 80 percent. However, if CPU utilization falls below 10 percent for an extended period of time, this might indicate the VM instance is no longer needed and should be deallocated. Therefore, managing the capacity of cloud resources can help to optimize cloud performance and costs. The challenge, however, is getting sufficient access to these resources to determine what's happening.

Traditional network monitoring tools often rely on having access to physical network hardware or having deep access to all network traffic, but both of these are restricted in the cloud. How can a network administrator monitor their cloud for problems? How can they make sure that users have an optimal experience interacting with the organization's cloud resources?

Cloud services generate API messages that report on various metrics for those resources. Monitoring tools, whether native to the cloud provider's platform or installed from a third-party monitoring service, capture information from those APIs and organize the data to report on the health, activities, and expenses of the monitored resources. Specific metrics are covered by these APIs. For example, consider a running VM instance in the cloud. A key metric for the VM might be CPU utilization so the number of vCPUs for a VM can be increased when needed (called vertical scaling) or, instead, additional VMs can be started in the server cluster (called horizontal scaling) if existing VMs show signs of strain. This adjustment process to efficiently meet demand as it changes while minimizing costs is called **right sizing**.

Figure 11-23 shows some metrics monitored by default in AWS for three running VM instances in EC2. Notice

> **Note**
>
> API integration is a key tenant of cloud-native computing where applications are designed in ways that best take advantage of what cloud computing has to offer. Other significant characteristics of cloud that enable cloud-native computing are serverless compute, containers, DevOps, automation, and IaC.

the lines of different color for each instance and the various metrics being monitored—such as CPU utilization, disk reads and writes, and network traffic. This figure also shows an alarm that's been triggered. A cloud admin would need to dig into the alarm's information to determine what went wrong and whether the related resources need additional attention.

Data collected on these metrics can be monitored on the service's own page, such as the page for a specific VM instance, or data from many services can be collected in a central location to give a bigger picture of a cloud's overall health. For example, AWS provides the CloudWatch service, which allows cloud technicians to monitor metrics across AWS services by collating data in one or more dashboards, tracking events, or generating alerts for compute, network, storage, security, and other types of services. Figure 11-24 shows the Cross service dashboard in CloudWatch. Azure Monitor and GCP's Stackdriver service perform similar functions in their respective platforms.

Dashboards provide a passive viewpoint for cloud admins to monitor cloud resources. This information might prompt further research or immediate human intervention. Automated responses to certain types of conditions can also be configured to relieve technicians of some of the time commitment required for cloud monitoring.

> **Note**
>
> How do you choose which data should be included on your dashboard? In the past, IT professionals have been primarily concerned with technical KPIs and thresholds that indicate how well the technology is performing in comparison to what it might be capable of. In today's cloud-run businesses, you've got to learn to think about the bigger picture. How do your cloud services fit into the business strategy of your organization? More specifically, how are users experiencing the services provided by your cloud resources? As many experts are now saying, "Slow is the new down." Outages might not be common in the cloud, but these days, slow services will lose business almost as quickly as outages will.

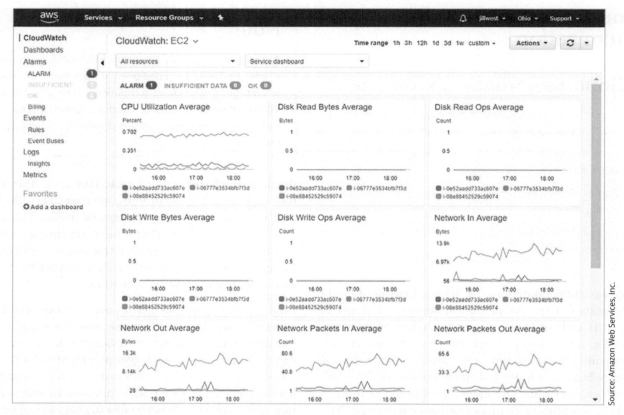

Figure 11-23 By default, AWS monitors EC2 KPIs such as CPU utilization, failed status checks, and disk read operations

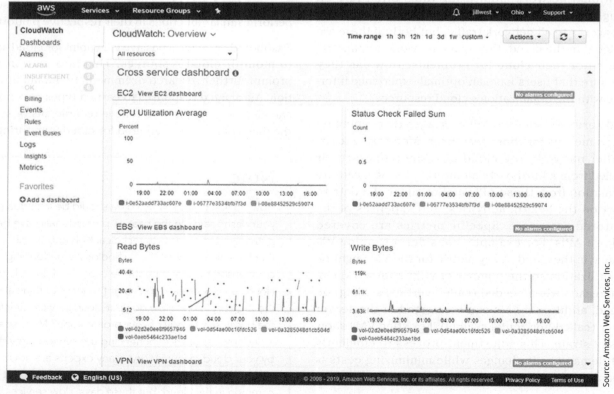

Figure 11-24 The Cross service dashboard includes data on EC2 and EBS

Remember this...

> Cloud migration consists of five major phases: assess, plan, migrate, validate, and manage.

> General categories for cloud migration strategies include rehost (also called lift and shift), revise (also called lift tinker and shift), repurchase (also called rip and replace), refactor, retain (also called do-nothing), and retire. In reality, most companies are choosing to adopt a hybrid cloud strategy where some resources stay on-prem and others are moved to the cloud.

> Automation refers to the use of software-based solutions to perform a process or procedure with minimal human intervention. Automated tools can deploy, replicate, or resize resources quickly to efficiently meet increasing or decreasing demand, which is called auto-scaling. Collections of many automated processes in a carefully choreographed manner is the essence of orchestration. Where automation accomplishes a single task (such as create a VM), orchestration designs a series of tasks in a workflow (such as creating an entire testing environment).

> The application of the runbook concept in an automated environment is called IaC (infrastructure as code), where the steps needed to configure or change a cloud environment are written in code and are deployed all at once rather than requiring a human admin to complete one step of the deployment at a time.

> Automation and orchestration tools might be built into the cloud platform or provided by third-party vendor applications that interact with the cloud platform through API messages. Many cloud automation tools are primarily managed through a CLI and rely on a variety of programming languages, such as Python, and file formats, such as JSON and YAML. Some of these tools offer a web GUI or cloud portal, especially if you're using the paid version of the application. Most of these tools work from templates of some kind for managing deployments.

> Provisioning tools deploy new cloud resources. CM (configuration management) tools configure existing resources to match a particular configuration template.

> Cloud services generate API messages that report on various metrics for those resources. Monitoring tools, whether native to the cloud provider's platform or installed from a third-party monitoring service, capture information from those APIs and organize the data to report on the health, activities, and expenses of the monitored resources. Specific metrics are covered by these APIs. This adjustment process to efficiently meet demand as it changes while minimizing costs is called right sizing.

Self-check

10. Which of these migration strategies would cause the least amount of change for the user?
    a. Refactor
    b. Rip and replace
    c. Lift and shift
    d. Lift tinker and shift

11. Which tool is primarily used for provisioning cloud resources?
    a. Ansible
    b. Puppet
    c. Chef
    d. Terraform

12. What resource can best provide a cloud monitoring tool with information about a running VM in the cloud?
    a. IaC
    b. API
    c. Alerts
    d. Dashboard

Check your answers at the end of this chapter.

Summary

Section 11-1: Planning for Changes

> Project management is the application of specific skills, tools, and techniques to manage processes in such a way that the desired outcome is achieved. A project is an effort that has a clearly defined beginning and ending. It involves many processes that are generally grouped into five categories: initiating, planning, executing, monitoring and controlling, and closing.

> A specific use of project management is in ALM (application lifecycle management). The application lifecycle follows the progression of an application from its conception through its retirement.

> The streamlining and built-in repetition of the application lifecycle, along with the increased collaboration between the teams working on each app, has come to be known as DevOps (development and operations). Once an application is deployed, the data gathered from monitoring the application's use can immediately inform efforts to develop new features for the application.

> Change management consists of carefully defined processes to evaluate the need for a change, the cost of the change, a plan for making the change with minimal disruption, and a backup plan if the change doesn't work as expected.

Section 11-2: Analyzing Design

> One technique used to model a corporation's network environment is to create connectivity maps, depending on what type of network you are modeling: wide area connectivity maps, metropolitan area connectivity maps, and local area connectivity maps.

> A gap analysis is a study used to compare current conditions with desired conditions and identifying how to close that gap. When identifying your goals, you'll set both a desired number for the KPI and a timeframe to reach that goal. This is called your desired state or future target. You can then chart your current state's trajectory and your desired state's trajectory to see the identified gap.

> A feasibility study will consider all relevant factors to determine the practicality of proposed changes identified in the gap analysis. The technical feasibility of a system is the extent to which the system can be created and implemented using currently existing technology. A system's financial feasibility is the extent to which the system can be created, given the

company's current finances. When a system demonstrates operational feasibility, it operates as designed and implemented. A system's time feasibility is the extent to which the system can be installed in a timely fashion that meets organizational needs.

> Capacity planning involves trying to determine the amount of network bandwidth necessary to support an application or a set of applications. Several techniques exist for performing capacity planning, including linear projection, computer simulation, benchmarking, and analytical modeling.

> Typical network environments for application development include the development environment for exploring possible changes, the staging environment for testing proposed changes, the production environment for active users, and a duplicate production environment used as a backup or for additional testing. QA (quality assurance) testing techniques include sandboxing, load testing, and regression testing.

Section 11-3: Network Monitoring and Management

> Three common hardware testing devices are electrical testers (the simplest), cable testers, and network testers (the most elaborate).

> Network monitors and protocol analyzers examine message headers to determine many characteristics of network traffic. A network monitor is a tool that

continually monitors network traffic and might receive data from monitored devices that are configured to report their statistics. A protocol analyzer can monitor traffic at a specific interface between a server or client and the network.

> An alert is a message that indicates some threshold has been met or exceeded, and it might generate notifications to IT personnel. In contrast, static records of activities on an OS or a network are kept in a log.

> Syslog is a standard for generating, storing, and processing messages about events on many networked systems. It describes methods for detecting and reporting events and specifies the format and contents of messages.

> SNMP (Simple Network Management Protocol) allows the numerous elements within a computer network to be managed from a single point and supports real-time network monitoring.

> NetFlow is a proprietary traffic monitoring protocol from Cisco that tracks all IP traffic crossing any interface where NetFlow is enabled. From that information, NetFlow creates flow records that show relationships among various traffic types. While SNMP focuses on individual devices, NetFlow focuses on the way network bandwidth is being utilized by identifying how communications from all devices are related to each other.

> To identify changes in network performance, the network administrator must first establish a baseline, which is a record of how a network or resource operates under normal conditions and includes performance statistics, utilization rates, and so on. Creating a baseline for an existing computer network involves measuring and recording a network's state of operation over a given period of time. This process requires capturing many network measurements over all segments of a network, including numerous measurements on workstations, user applications, routers, and switches. Once a baseline is created, the results can be used to identify network weaknesses and strengths, which can then be used to intelligently upgrade the network.

Section 11-4: Cloud Deployment and Management

> Cloud migration consists of five major phases: assess, plan, migrate, validate, and manage.

> General categories for cloud migration strategies include rehost (also called lift and shift), revise (also called lift tinker and shift), repurchase (also called rip and replace), refactor, retain (also called do-nothing), and retire. In reality, most companies are choosing to adopt a hybrid cloud strategy where some resources stay on-prem and others are moved to the cloud.

> Automation refers to the use of software-based solutions to perform a process or procedure with minimal human intervention. Automated tools can deploy, replicate, or resize resources quickly to efficiently meet increasing or decreasing demand, which is called auto-scaling. Collections of many automated processes in a carefully choreographed manner is the essence of orchestration. Where automation accomplishes a single task (such as create a VM), orchestration designs a series of tasks in a workflow (such as creating an entire testing environment).

> The application of the runbook concept in an automated environment is called IaC (infrastructure as code), where the steps needed to configure or change a cloud environment are written in code and are deployed all at once rather than requiring a human admin to complete one step of the deployment at a time.

> Automation and orchestration tools might be built into the cloud platform or provided by third-party vendor applications that interact with the cloud platform through API messages. Many cloud automation tools are primarily managed through a CLI and rely on a variety of programming languages, such as Python, and file formats, such as JSON and YAML. Some of these tools offer a web GUI or cloud portal, especially if you're using the paid version of the application. Most of these tools work from templates of some kind for managing deployments.

> Provisioning tools deploy new cloud resources. CM (configuration management) tools configure existing resources to match a particular configuration template.

> Cloud services generate API messages that report on various metrics for those resources. Monitoring tools, whether native to the cloud provider's platform or installed from a third-party monitoring service, capture information from those APIs and organize the data to report on the health, activities, and expenses of the monitored resources. Specific metrics are covered by these APIs. This adjustment process to efficiently meet demand as it changes while minimizing costs is called right sizing.

Key Terms

For definitions of key terms, see the Glossary near the end of the book.

agent

agility

alert

ALM (application lifecycle management)

analytical modeling

automation

baseline

benchmarking

blue-green deployment

capacity planning

change management

computer simulation

connectivity map

continuous delivery

continuous integration

DevOps (development and operations)

feasibility study

financial feasibility

gap analysis

IaC (infrastructure as code)

jabber

key stakeholder

KPI (key performance indicator)

linear projection

load testing

local area detailed connectivity map

local area overview connectivity map

log

metropolitan area connectivity map

MIB (Management Information Base)

NetFlow

network monitor

operational feasibility

orchestration

port mirroring

production environment

project

project management

protocol analyzer

regression testing

RFP (request for proposal)

right sizing

runbook

sandboxing

shadow IT

SNMP manager

syslog

technical feasibility

time feasibility

waterfall method

wide area connectivity map

Review Questions

1. Which ALM phase is the most active?

   a. Development

   b. Upgrade

   c. Maintenance

   d. Deployment

2. With which connectivity map is distance most relevant as a connection characteristic?

   a. Local area overview connectivity map

   b. Wide area connectivity map

   c. Local area detailed connectivity map

   d. Metropolitan area connectivity map

3. Which feasibility study will most likely discover any discrepancies between vendor claims and actual functionality?

   a. Financial feasibility

   b. Time feasibility

   c. Operational feasibility

   d. Technical feasibility

4. Which capacity planning approach will compare a network's actual performance with expected statistics?

   a. Analytical modeling

   b. Computer simulation

   c. Benchmarking

   d. Linear projection

5. When you arrive at work one morning, you find several new trouble tickets complaining of slow network performance. You take a few moments to capture some network traffic using Wireshark. What information will help you identify variances between this network capture and previous network traffic?

   a. Connectivity map   c. Sandbox

   b. Baseline   d. Syslog

6. What kind of professional training can help a manager develop better time management skills for their team?

    a. Change management

    b. Network modeling

    c. Capacity planning

    d. Project management

7. What software allows a managed device to communicate information about itself via SNMP?

    a. Agent

    b. Manager

    c. MIB

    d. CVE

8. Which SNMP message type is issued by a managed element?

    a. Write

    b. Save

    c. Read

    d. Trap

9. During which change management phase are users retrained?

    a. Understand and follow the approval process.

    b. Follow project management procedures.

    c. Submit a change request document.

    d. Provide additional documentation.

10. You are performing a baseline study for your company, which is located on the East Coast with many remote workers on the West Coast. You note that a peak network utilization occurs at approximately noon, when most of your East Coast employees are on lunch break. What could be causing this peak activity?

    a. Security breach

    b. Employees working during lunch

    c. Time zone differences

    d. Malfunctioning workstations

11. Which network tool would be the easiest to use to determine if a cable has been severed by rodents?

    a. Continuity tester

    b. Network tester

    c. Cable tester

    d. Network monitor

12. Which standard creates static records used for retroactive analysis?

    a. NetFlow

    b. Syslog

    c. SNMP

    d. Sandbox

13. As you migrate your application's resources to the cloud, you want to create a cloud-based environment that mimics your on-prem datacenter as closely as possible so you can run the application in the cloud alongside its counterpart on-prem. What kind of deployment is this?

    a. Production

    b. Sandbox

    c. Benchmark

    d. Blue-green

14. Ansible can be used to create _____ cloud resources that can be reconfigured after deployment.

    a. imperative

    b. idempotent

    c. declarative

    d. immutable

15. What kind of file is needed to deploy a cloud-based network using IaC?

    a. Snapshot

    b. Multimedia

    c. Text

    d. Image

16. Your web server needs to increase resources to handle increased traffic after a successful email campaign. Your server is configured to clone itself to create a larger cluster of servers. What kind of scaling is your auto-scaling group using?

    a. Directional

    b. Diagonal

    c. Vertical

    d. Horizontal

17. Which of the following is *NOT* an advantage of automation?

    a. Better control

    b. More secure

    c. Slower deployment

    d. Lower costs

18. Which cloud migration strategy aims to best take advantage of cloud technologies?

    a. Repurchase

    b. Rehost

    c. Retain

    d. Replatform

19. Which development model follows a linear path?

    a. Agile

    b. Waterfall

    c. DevOps

    d. CI/CD

20. You've just deployed an update to an HR application that is widely used throughout your company. Which type of testing should you conduct to ensure your scheduling and shift planning software has not been adversely affected by the HR application update?

    a. Load testing

    b. Progressive testing

    c. Benchmark testing

    d. Regression testing

Hands-On Project 11

Configure SPAN and Syslog in Packet Tracer

Estimated time: 1 hour

Resources:

> Computer with Cisco Packet Tracer installed

> **Context:**

In this module, you read about various ways to capture network traffic for analysis and monitoring. In this project, you'll experiment with two of these technologies: SPAN on switches and a syslog server. Complete the following steps:

1. In your Packet Tracer workspace, add a 2960 switch and three PCs.

2. Configure static IP addresses on all three PCs within the same subnet:

    a. PC0: IP 192.168.10.10, subnet mask 255.255.255.0

    b. PC1: IP 192.168.10.20, subnet mask 255.255.255.0

    c. PC2: IP 192.168.10.30, subnet mask 255.255.255.0

3. Connect the PCs to the first three switch ports (FastEthernet 0/1 – 0/3). Wait for all connections to come up.

4. In the bottom right corner, click **Simulation**. This opens the Simulation Panel.

5. By default, the simulation will display all messages from all protocols on the network once you start the simulation—you can see a list of applicable filters in the *Event List Filters – Visible Events* section. For this project, you only want to see ICMP messages. At the bottom of the Simulation Panel, click **Show All/None**, which clears all visible event types. Click **Edit Filters**. In the PacketTracer7 filters window, check the box on the IPv4 tab for **ICMP**. Close the PacketTracer7 filters window. Confirm ICMP is the only visible event type listed in the Simulation Panel.

6. When you start the simulation in the next step, you will run pings between PCs on your network, and the results will display in the PDU List Window in the bottom right corner of your Packet Tracer interface. If you don't see this pane, click the left arrow at the far right border of your Packet Tracer window, directly under the Simulation button. See Figure 11-25.

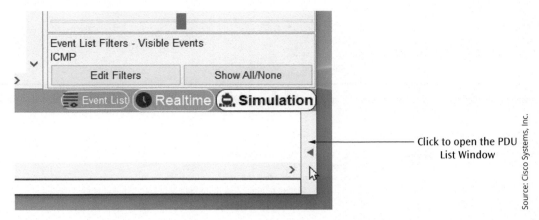

Figure 11-25   Click the left arrow to open the PDU List Window

7. For a more convenient arrangement, in the bottom middle pane, click **Toggle PDU List Window** to move this pane to a larger space in your Packet Tracer interface. If desired, you can also grab the top bar of the Simulation Panel to move this module around on your screen in a separate window.

8. On the common tools bar, click the **Add Simple PDU (P)** button, which looks like a closed envelope. This will create a ping-based conversation between two devices. Click **PC0** as the source device and click **PC1** as the destination device.

9. In the Simulation Panel, click the **Play (Alt + P)** button. As the simulation begins, a PDU leaves PC0 and arrives at the switch. Watch the traffic carefully. To which device does the switch send the first PDU? Why do you think this is?

10. At the bottom of the interface, click the **Delete** button to stop the simulation for this scenario. Click **Realtime** to return to Realtime mode.

Now you're ready to add a sniffer to the network that will monitor all traffic on the switch. Complete the following step:

11. From the End Devices group, add a **Sniffer** to the workspace. Connect the sniffer's Ethernet0 port to the switch's FastEthernet 0/24 port. The sniffer does not need an IP address to do its job.

With these devices connected to your network, you're ready to configure a SPAN monitoring session on the switch. Complete the following steps:

12. On the switch's CLI tab, enter the commands in Table 11-3. You might first have to press **Enter** to access the prompt.

Table 11-3   Configure a SPAN monitoring session on a switch

Command	Purpose
`enable`	Enables privileged EXEC mode
`configure terminal`	Enters global configuration mode
`monitor session 1 source int fa0/1 - 3`	Configures source interfaces for the monitoring session
`monitor session 1 destination int fa0/24`	Configures the destination interface for the monitoring session (there can be only one)
`do show monitor`	Displays the monitoring session configuration; confirm your configuration matches that shown in Figure 11-26

13. To test your monitoring session, enter Simulation Mode and send a simple PDU from PC0 to PC1 again. Watch the traffic carefully. To which device(s) does the switch send the PDU this time? Why do you think this is?

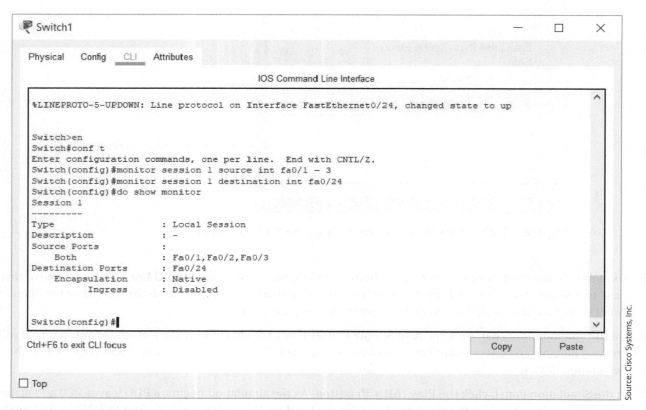

Figure 11-26 SPAN monitoring session from three interfaces to FastEthernet 0/24

14. To see the captured traffic, click the Sniffer and click its **GUI** tab. Apply the same filter here as the one you used for Simulation Mode in Step 5. Clear the buffer and run the ping again. Click any of the captured ICMP messages. What are the source and destination IP addresses of the message you chose? Stop the simulation and return to **Realtime** mode.

Syslog is another way to capture network traffic; however, syslog functions differently by capturing messages processed on a monitored device. To compare SPAN and syslog functionality, complete the following steps:

15. Add a 2901 router and a server to the workspace. Connect both to the switch.

16. On the server's Services tab, confirm the Syslog service is turned on. Configure the server with the static IP address 192.168.10.50, subnet mask 255.255.255.0.

17. Configure the router with the static IP address 192.168.10.1, subnet mask 255.255.255.0, and turn on the interface connected to the switch.

Syslog logging is enabled by default on the router, but additional information is needed to send the required logs to the server. Complete the following steps:

18. To configure syslog logging on the router's CLI, enter the commands listed in Table 11-4, starting in global configuration mode (most likely, you need to enter **exit** to access global configuration mode, depending on how quickly you moved to this step from the previous step).

19. Check the logging configuration on your router. Where are the router's logs being sent? What port are these messages using?

20. To test your syslog configuration, ping one of your PCs from your router (it might take a couple of tries to get a successful ping). Return to your syslog server to examine captured traffic. **Take a screenshot** of the Syslog Service window showing logged traffic; submit this visual with your answers to this project's questions. How many ICMP messages are logged?

Table 11-4   Configure syslog on a router

Command	Purpose
`logging 192.168.10.50`	Tells the router where to send syslog messages
`logging trap debugging`	Requires all messages from the debugging level (level 7, which is the lowest severity level) and above to be logged with the server; note that Packet Tracer only supports logging at level 7 (debugging), which includes all severity levels
`exit` press **Enter** again	Returns to privileged EXEC mode
`debug ip icmp`	Enables debugging for ICMP messages
`show debugging`	Displays debugging configuration; confirm ICMP packet debugging is on
`show logging`	Displays syslog configuration

21. Syslog captured the ICMP messages for a ping between the router and a PC. Now ping between two PCs. Return to your syslog server to examine captured traffic. How many ICMP messages are logged now? Why do you think this is?

22. When you're finished, you can close Packet Tracer. You do not need to save this network.

Reflection Discussion 11

Cloud-native computing refers to infrastructure design that is built to best take advantage of the technologies offered by the cloud. In this chapter, you learned that cloud-native computing relies on API integration, serverless compute, containers, DevOps, automation, and IaC. In 2002, Jeff Bezos, the founder of Amazon, issued what has since been called the Bezos API Mandate. One portion of the mandate essentially states that any functionality built by Amazon must be exposed through an API.

Search online to read the entire Bezos Mandate on APIs, and do some research on the impact this mandate has had on software development and cloud native thinking since then. Next, answer the following questions:

> How has the API mandate shifted business strategies as cloud has evolved?

> How does the API mandate affect software innovation?

Go to the discussion forum in your school's LMS (learning management system). Write a post of at least 100 words discussing your thoughts about how APIs and cloud have shifted business and software development. Then respond to two of your classmates' threads with posts of at least 50 words discussing their comments and ideas. Use complete sentences, and check your grammar and spelling. Try to ask open-ended questions that encourage discussion, and remember to respond to people who post on your thread. Use the rubric in Table 11-5 to help you understand what is expected of your work for this assignment.

Table 11-5   Grading rubric for Reflection Discussion 11

Task	Novice	Competent	Proficient	Earned
Initial post	Generalized statements discussing the API Mandate **30 points**	Some specific statements with supporting evidence discussing the effects of the API Mandate on business and software innovation **40 points**	Self-reflective discussion with specific and thoughtful statements and supporting evidence discussing ways the API Mandate has shifted business strategies and reorganized priorities for software innovation **50 points**	

Initial post: Mechanics	• Length < 100 words • Several grammar and spelling errors **5 points**	• Length = 100 words • Occasional grammar and spelling errors **7 points**	• Length > 100 words • Appropriate grammar and spelling **10 points**	
Response 1	Brief response showing little engagement or critical thinking **5 points**	Detailed response with specific contributions to the discussion **10 points**	Thoughtful response with specific examples or details and open-ended questions that invite deeper discussion of the topic **15 points**	
Response 2	Brief response showing little engagement or critical thinking **5 points**	Detailed response with specific contributions to the discussion **10 points**	Thoughtful response with specific examples or details and open-ended questions that invite deeper discussion of the topic **15 points**	
Both responses: Mechanics	• Length < 50 words each • Several grammar and spelling errors **5 points**	• Length = 50 words each • Occasional grammar and spelling errors **7 points**	• Length > 50 words each • Appropriate grammar and spelling **10 points**	
			Total	

Solutions to Self-Check Questions

Section 11-1: Planning for Changes

1. Which of the following is *NOT* an advantage offered by professional project management?

Answer: d. Increased physical security

Explanation: Physical security is the responsibility of security teams, IT teams, and all employees in general. Typically, project management professionals are not specifically focused on physical security.

2. Which application development practice ensures small but frequent incremental changes?

Answer: b. Continuous delivery

Explanation: Continuous delivery is the practice of deploying changes in small increments on a short time schedule, such as every 24 hours, rather than being delayed for larger, less frequent updates.

3. Which change management step initiates a change to be made in a system?

Answer: c. Submit a change request document.

Explanation: The person responsible for a particular application can initiate a change to the application by submitting a change request document. IT personnel might also be able to submit a change request related to security or required updates.

Section 11-2: Analyzing Design

4. When identifying a target number for a KPI, what other information is used to define the desired state?

Answer: b. Timeframe

Explanation: When identifying your goals, you'll set both a desired number for the KPI and a timeframe to reach that goal. This is called your desired state or future target.

5. Which type of feasibility study will ensure the new system will be convenient enough for users to use it consistently?

Answer: a. Operational feasibility

Explanation: When assessing operational feasibility, a company must ask if users will be able to use the proposed system or if it will be too difficult or inconvenient for users to commit to using it.

6. Which environment do typical users interact with?

Answer: b. Production

Explanation: The production environment is the live environment where users interact with the active version of an application.

Section 11-3: Network Monitoring and Management

7. Which network tool is best for monitoring traffic on a single network interface?

Answer: d. Protocol analyzer

Explanation: A protocol analyzer monitors traffic at a specific interface between a server or client and the network.

8. Which standard yields the best big-picture view of traffic patterns on a network?

Answer: b. NetFlow

Explanation: NetFlow tracks all IP traffic crossing any interface where NetFlow is enabled. From that information, NetFlow creates flow records that show relationships among various traffic types. While SNMP focuses on individual devices, NetFlow focuses on the way network bandwidth is being utilized by identifying how communications from all devices are related to each other.

9. When is the best time to collect data to establish a network baseline?

Answer: c. Throughout a typical business day

Explanation: Baseline studies are most effective when they are initiated during a time when the network is not experiencing severe problems and when the network is experiencing fairly normal operation, such as throughout a typical business day.

Section 11-4: Cloud Deployment and Management

10. Which of these migration strategies would cause the least amount of change for the user?

Answer: c. Lift and shift

Explanation: Lift and shift, also called rehost, refers to moving the application or data into the cloud as it is.

11. Which tool is primarily used for provisioning cloud resources?

Answer: d. Terraform

Explanation: A third-party provisioning tool is Terraform, which provides cloud-agnostic infrastructure provisioning.

12. What resource can best provide a cloud monitoring tool with information about a running VM in the cloud?

Answer: b. API

Explanation: Cloud services generate API messages that report on various metrics for those resources. Monitoring tools, whether native to the cloud provider's platform or installed from a third-party monitoring service, capture information from those APIs and organize the data to report on the health, activities, and expenses of the monitored resources.

Chapter 12

Business Principles in IT

Objectives

After reading this chapter, you should be able to:

- Describe ways to manage people resources related to computer networking

- Explain methods and documentation in handling vendor relationships for new projects

- Evaluate financial aspects of deploying resources to the cloud

- Compare components of business continuity and disaster recovery preparations

Introduction

Businesses today rely heavily on their IT infrastructure, whether those resources reside on-premises or in the cloud. Nearly every decision regarding a company's network must be made in the context of its effect on the business. At the same time, business processes, principles, and priorities have become deeply integrated into the way companies handle technology. IT is a service-oriented industry that supports employees and their companies in a myriad of ways.

This chapter takes a step back from the technical side of networking and examines technology through the lens of a business professional. It addresses the following questions:

> What skills do people need and how can companies support their employees as technology changes?

> How are B2B (business-to-business) relationships handled in the service of the company's network and cloud infrastructures?

> How can cloud technologies save companies money while improving their progress toward business goals?

> What measures should companies take to protect themselves when something goes wrong with their technology resources?

If you're preparing for the CompTIA Cloud Essentials+ exam, this chapter covers a large portion of the exam's objectives with a focus on the non-technical concepts. This chapter will help you apply the technical concepts you've learned to the practicalities of how the business world works.

Section 12-1: People Resources

A network administrator is responsible for keeping a network infrastructure and cloud deployment running. This work involves making repairs on failed components, installing new applications and updating the existing ones, keeping the system's existing users up-to-date, and looking for new ways to improve the overall system and service level. It is not an easy job. With the complexity of today's networks and businesses' dependence on their applications, network administrators are highly valuable, often visible, and always engaged with the network and the people using it. This section covers a network admin's responsibilities as well as ways someone in this or a related position might need to support technical and nontechnical staff through training and policy development.

> ## Note
>
> Some companies are starting to call this position a network architect, although network architects tend to perform more network design while network administrators may perform more network upkeep. Regardless, these terms are somewhat interchangeable.

Network Administrator Skills and Certifications

Because many network administrators are dealing with both computers and people, they need the skills necessary to work with both. To make effective use of limited resources, a network admin should also possess several common management skills:

> **Technical skills**—These skills include, but are not limited to, knowledge of LANs, WANs, cloud computing, voice and data transmission systems, multimedia transmission, basic hardware concepts, and basic software skills.

> **Interpersonal skills**—These skills help network admins to be better managers. Managing people requires the ability to talk with users to service problems and explore new applications.

> **Training skills**—These skills are required for providing education related to the network. A network admin will likely need to train users or other network support personnel.

> **Budget management skills**—These skills include knowing how to prepare a budget to justify continuing funds or to request additional funds.

> **Basic statistical skills**—These skills include collecting and using system statistics to justify the performance of existing systems or to validate the addition of new ones.

> **Time management skills**—These skills apply to daily routines as well as special projects. A network admin will be expected to manage not only their own time, but also that of projects and any IT workers who may be working with the admin.

> **Project management skills**—These skills center on the ability to keep a project on schedule and to use project-estimating tools, project-scheduling tools, and other methods for continuous project assessment.

> **Policy creation and enforcement skills**—These skills include creating policies concerning the use of computer systems, access to facilities, password protection, access to applications, access to databases, distribution of hardware and software, replacement of hardware and software, and the handling of service requests.

To learn new skills and demonstrate proficiency within a particular area, a network admin can consistently work toward obtaining additional industry certifications or renewing their existing certifications. They might become certified on a particular type of network operating system such as Windows Server, on a particular brand of network equipment such as Cisco routers, or in a particular cloud platform such as AWS. Many of these certifications require continuing education or a retake of the test every two to three years to keep the certification active, which requires certified professionals to continue learning new concepts and skills, which, in turn, helps these professionals keep up with changing technology. The following is a list of some of the more popular certifications in networking:

> **CompTIA Network+**—This vendor-neutral certification verifies a network professional's understanding and ability to apply a wide variety of foundational network concepts and skills in a range of networking environments, including LANs, WANs, and the cloud.

> **Cisco CCNA (Certified Network Associate)**—This certification covers the topics of installing, configuring, operating, and troubleshooting enterprise-level routers and switched networks.

> **CWNA (Certified Wireless Network Administrator) by CWNP (Certified Wireless Network Professionals)**—This certification addresses basic wireless LAN concepts and lays a foundation for more advanced enterprise Wi-Fi expertise.

> **VMware VCP (VMware Certified Professional)**—This certification validates a candidate's ability to install, configure, and administer virtual networking in a VMware environment.

> **AWS Cloud Practitioner**—This certification addresses basic concepts and services in the AWS cloud and serves as a gateway to many, highly respected AWS certifications.

> **CompTIA Cloud Essentials+**—This vendor-neutral certification bridges the gap between the technical and business interests in cloud computing to provide a common language for professionals from both areas of expertise.

All Things Considered

Thought Experiment

Scan local job listings online. What percentage of advertisements seeking network support personnel require an industry certification?

Professional Development

Cloud Essentials+ Exam Tip

This section discusses professional development, which is required by

- Part of Objective 2.2: Summarize the financial aspects of engaging a cloud provider.

Network administration is a demanding, challenging, and always changing position that requires the network admin to keep up with rapidly evolving technology and constantly learn new skills. This same principle applies to everyone in the IT department. Companies that are willing to invest in their human capital—their employees—will prioritize professional development for all staff involved in managing, improving, securing, and optimizing the company's network resources. Professional development enables employees to improve and update their skills in ways that contribute to the company's well-being.

It's expensive to compensate for high employee turnover with lengthy hiring processes and train new employees on company policies and procedures. Many employers have realized that training, or upskilling, existing employees leads to improved employee performance and satisfaction as well as financial savings for the companies themselves. Companies that invest in their employees are more frequently able to promote from within, which streamlines business processes as employees are cross-trained in various job roles.

Whether your employer is providing professional development or you're pursuing this work on your own time and at your own expense, many programs are available to develop your skills, help you keep track of changes, and progress within your industry. Consider the following possibilities:

> **Continuing education**—These programs provide short-term or part-time training and is often required to maintain certain certifications or licenses.

> **On-the-job training**—To increase vertical movement within a company, employers can provide on-the-job training to pre-qualify their existing employees for positions the company needs filled. This kind of training might include job shadowing where a person follows someone else as they perform typical duties.

> **Conferences**—Industry conferences offer professionals the opportunity to network with others in their field, learn from experts during sessions that address current trends and concerns, and identify emerging technologies that can benefit the company. Many industry conferences are free, especially for students, and many are offered online for convenience, such as the one listed in Figure 12-1.

> **Workshops**—Half-day or full-day training workshops cover a focused skillset with a specific purpose. For example, a network technician might take a one-day workshop to learn about a new virtualization platform.

> **Mentoring**—Many experts in their field enjoy guiding less-experienced coworkers at their own company or colleagues at other companies. This kind of informal guidance can be invaluable as you make difficult decisions about job opportunities or as you face challenges in your existing position. Some companies institute formal, short-term mentoring programs to acclimate new hires to the company culture.

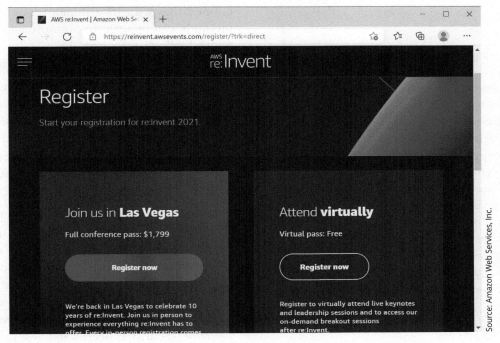

Figure 12-1 Virtual registration is often free, even for expensive conferences

› **Certifications**—The pursuit of higher-level certifications ensures you will continually challenge your current abilities and will help you keep up with changes and new technologies. Adding certifications that aren't necessarily in your direct line of expertise (such as a network admin obtaining a project management certification) will expand your understanding of your job's business context as well as open perhaps unexpected avenues for advancing your career. Vendor-neutral certifications, such as CompTIA's Cloud Essentials+, can help lay a solid foundation with core concepts while vendor-specific certifications, such as AWS's Cloud Practitioner (see Figure 12-2), can help build skills in a particular platform.

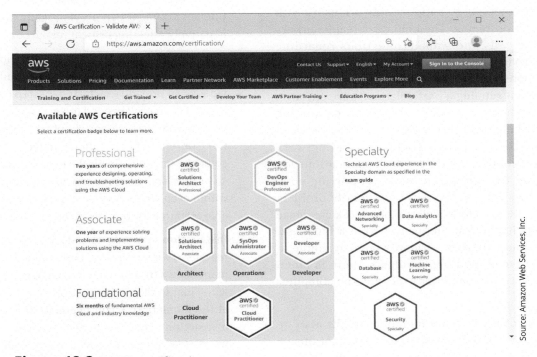

Figure 12-2 AWS certifications

Note

Consider attending a few conferences within your industry while you're still completing coursework so you can network with other professionals. You can learn from their conversations about their concerns, endeavors, and interests. One or more of these contacts might even provide you with a job opportunity when you're ready. Also, consider taking a few certification exams, especially if you take courses (such as this one) that are built around the learning objectives covered by one or more certifications. Many employers require or request these certifications to verify your practical skills beyond your academic learning, and some employers won't consider job applicants who have no industry certifications even if they have a degree.

Training Users

Cloud Essentials+ Exam Tip

This section discusses training, which is required by

- Part of Objective 2.2: Summarize the financial aspects of engaging a cloud provider.

Network administrators and IT staff often have a help desk in their company to support network users with questions and problems. The help desk team answers all telephone calls and walk-in questions regarding computer services within the company. Whether they are called upon to address hardware problems, answer questions about running a particular software package, or introduce the company's users to new computing services, the help desk serves as the gateway between the user and the company's computing and network services. Fortunately, good help desk applications are available that the operations staff supporting computing services can use to track and identify problem areas within the system. A well-run help desk can make an enormous impact on the users within a business. When users know there is a friendly team available to help them solve computing problems, there is much less friction between computer users and the computer system.

Help desk or other IT team members might also be responsible for training users on new applications or other resources. User training might also be done in

cooperation with HR (human resources) staff. Many methods can be used to promote new user skills and understanding:

- **Instructor-led training**—This traditional approach requires dedicated time from the instructor and the learners. While coordinating schedules for a company or team to gather at the same time in the same place can be challenging, instructor-led training can provide the most adaptable and personable training, especially for users who lack confidence in their ability to learn new IT skills.

- **eLearning**—Digital learning products can provide flexible learning opportunities at a time and place that works for the individual. Many vendors provide eLearning for their own products that can be distributed to users. Other eLearning programs can be purchased for targeted training, such as the one shown in Figure 12-3 that helps refresh users on cybersecurity concerns and best practices.

- **Hands-on training**—Direct experience with a new platform, tool, or application can give users confidence in their new skills as well as provide an opportunity for experimentation and exploration.

- **Simulations**—Some virtual learning environments can provide simulated hands-on experience with the flexibility of eLearning. For example, giving a user a sandbox environment to practice new skills before needing to apply those skills in the production environment can prevent many mistakes from negatively affecting critical resources.

- **Videos**—Instructional videos can give how-to demonstrations of specific tasks. For non-technical users, videos can provide exact, step-by-step demonstrations of each click needed to accomplish a specific goal. Instructional videos should be short (less than three or four minutes), should move slowly enough so someone unfamiliar with the material can follow the steps, and should cover specific and limited topics within each video. A video library can be an invaluable resource for both users and technical staff.

- **Instruction manuals**—Used as a reference resource, well-organized and concise instruction manuals written in plain language can provide users with "just in time" information about specific tasks at the moment the user needs it. Non-technical instruction manuals can also give users confidence to try new things or provide a convenient reference to help fill in gaps left by earlier training.

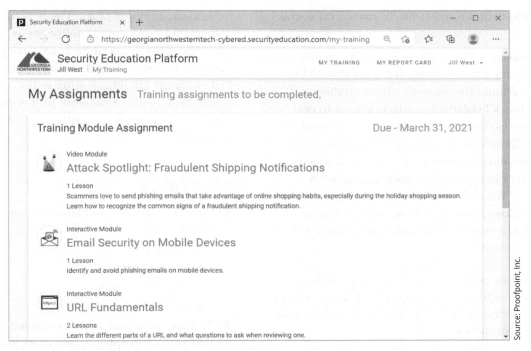

Source: Proofpoint, Inc.

Figure 12-3 Security awareness training

Policies and Procedures

A company training new and experienced users needs to aim for some level of consistency in how all users perform each type of task. Many corporations establish standards to ensure consistency as different employees perform the same complex tasks. These **SOPs (standard operating procedures)** define steps for a specific process to maintain consistency and avoid errors. For example, the process of adding a new user to the network should consist of a specific series of steps performed in a specific order to ensure all components of the user account are properly and securely configured.

Some policies might apply companywide while others are specific to certain departments. For example, some network security policies will apply only to network technicians given elevated access to network resources. In contrast, many security policies will apply to all network users. Most network security

breaches begin or continue due to human error. A network security policy will address issues such as acceptable use of network resources, ways the network may be accessed, and how to protect against email phishing attacks.

Some company policies will address expectations for what and how information should be communicated inside and outside the organization. Because IT systems are an integral part of company communication paths, these policies directly affect network professionals and, in many cases, might be written or enforced by the IT staff. For example:

> **Passwords**—How long must passwords be? How often must they be changed? What kinds of complexity will be enforced for passwords to various types of resources?

> **Device usage**—If employees are provided with laptops or cell phones, what can they use these devices for? What security restrictions are needed to protect these devices in the event of loss or theft? What data is not allowed to be stored on these mobile devices?

> **Social media**—How is social media used by employees? Can they access social media during work hours or using company computers? Are there restrictions on how employees interact with the public through social media? What

information should never be discussed on social media?

> **Internet usage**—For which job tasks do employees need Internet access? Which websites should be avoided? Should the network admin establish a website block list (which restricts access to certain websites) or a website allow list (which allows access only to websites listed)? What kind of information should employees not be allowed to access during work hours or using company network resources? What are the repercussions if someone is caught downloading obscene or illegal material, invading someone's privacy, or using pirated software or content?

These and other policies will need to be developed, enforced, and updated so employees know what's required of them and how they can help protect company network resources.

Remember this...

> To make effective use of limited resources, a network admin should also possess several common management skills, including technical skills, interpersonal skills, training skills, budget management skills, basic statistical skills, time management skills, project management skills, and policy creation and enforcement skills.

> Companies that are willing to invest in their human capital—their employees—will prioritize professional development for all staff involved in managing, improving, securing, and optimizing the company's network resources. Professional development enables employees to improve and update their skills in ways that contribute to the company's well-being. Professional development options include continuing education, on-the-job training, conferences, workshops, mentoring, and certifications.

> The help desk or other IT staff might be responsible for training users on new applications or other resources. Training methods include instructor-led training, eLearning, hands-on training, simulations, videos, and instruction manuals.

> Many corporations establish standards to ensure consistency as different employees perform

the same complex tasks. These SOPs (standard operating procedures) define steps for a specific process to maintain consistency and avoid errors. Because IT systems are an integral part of company communication paths, these policies directly affect network professionals and, in many cases, might be written or enforced by the IT staff.

Self-check

1. CompTIA Cloud Essentials+ is what kind of certification?
   a. Hands-on
   b. Vendor-neutral
   c. Vendor-specific
   d. Highly technical

2. To apply for a promotion, you need to validate that you are keeping up with new industry trends. Which of these professional development options will best help you accomplish this goal?
   a. Conference
   b. Workshop
   c. Certification
   d. Continuing education class

3. Which technique can ensure a new workstation on the network is properly connected, segmented, and secured?
   a. SOP
   b. SLA
   c. SaaS
   d. SSH

Check your answers at the end of this chapter.

Section 12-2: Vendor Relations

Network professionals must communicate regularly with more people than just company employees. Many vendors require a close working relationship to ensure a company's network functions reliably and benefits from their products and services. Managing vendor relationships involves business acumen and an in-depth understanding of expectations for B2B interactions.

Vendor Services

When choosing a vendor for a network, cloud platform, or third-party service within the cloud, several factors affect the decision-making process. One of the first questions to ask is, what skills does the internal team currently offer that might make one vendor easier for the company to use than another? For example, a network admin that has worked with AWS in the past might prefer to start with the AWS cloud as they begin migrating resources from the on-prem datacenter to the cloud. In contrast, if the team already relies heavily on Active Directory in Windows, migrating to Microsoft Azure might offer a more natural transition. And similarly, if the datacenter runs on VMware's virtualization products, the admin might prefer to take advantage of a VMware deployment in the cloud, such as VMware in AWS.

However, current skill availability does not have to restrict available options. Many vendors offer extensive training for customers, and often, this training is completely free to the customer. In fact, AWS, Azure, Google, and other large providers offer free training to anyone, customer or not, who wants to learn more about their products and perhaps even earn a few vendor certifications.

In addition to training, large service providers offer other support services to ease a customer's migration onto their platform. Professional services to look for and other factors to consider when comparing vendors include the following items.

Support Plans

What kinds of technical and customer support does the vendor offer, and how much does the customer have to pay for it? For example, as shown in Figure 12-4, AWS offers three tiers of paid support plans:

> **Developer**—The lowest tier is affordable even for individual developers, startups, or small businesses and provides general guidance within 24 hours or assistance with an impaired system within 12 hours.

> **Business**—The middle tier is designed for slightly larger businesses that need support for a failed production system within an hour.

> **Enterprise**—The most expensive support plan is priced for very large enterprises that require a response time of less than 15 minutes if a business-critical system is down.

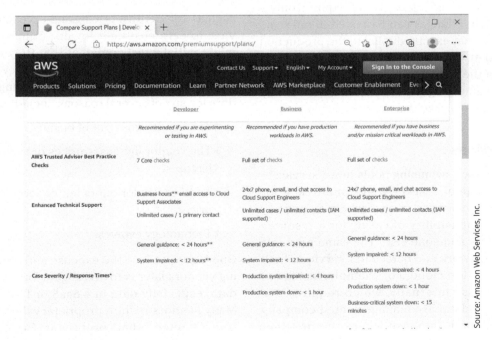

Source: Amazon Web Services, Inc.

Figure 12-4 AWS support tiers

Many vendors offer similar support tiers, and sometimes minimal support is included for free. Perhaps a customer anticipates only needing support during the initial migration, or maybe they expect to need support indefinitely. Either way, this expense should be factored into vendor comparisons.

> **Note**
>
> The differences between support tiers are commonly covered in vendor cloud certification exams, such as AWS's Cloud Practitioner exam.

Time to Market

Existing team skills are not the only compatibility factor when considering how long it will take to migrate services from on-prem to the cloud. How compatible are existing applications and workflows with cloud-native design? What kinds of refactoring or replacements should be incorporated into the migration timeline? How much user retraining will the migration require?

The initial transition is not the only important timeline to consider. Migrating to the cloud can significantly decrease a company's time to market with business innovations, website or application updates, and overall network and application performance optimizations. Because most of the cloud infrastructure is managed through IaC (infrastructure as code), changes can be tracked in detail and made quickly while a rollback to a previous state if something goes wrong requires only a few clicks. Similarly, changes can be tested in full-scale test environments that exactly duplicate the production environment rather than being limited to a small-scale representation of the production network. The ability to adapt quickly to emerging trends and new technology decreases the time to market for future changes.

Managed Services

Many people who own swimming pools hire a service to regularly clean the pool, test the water, and treat it for problems. This is a managed service where a company takes over the responsibility of caring for a resource owned and used by someone else. The same principle applies to many network and datacenter services, both on-premises and in the cloud. For example, instead of managing a database internally, which requires one or more experts in database management, a company might use a managed database where the provider ensures availability of the database, oversees any

relevant licensing, applies updates, and scales storage space as needed. An MSP (managed service provider) might handle the network's VoIP system, cybersecurity, data storage or backup, help desk, specific applications, or even provide virtual CIO (Chief Information Officer) services to help with analyzing, planning, and strategizing the business's technology infrastructure needs and changes.

Managed services can help fill the gap between the talent existing team members offer and the company's needs. When considering vendors and their platforms along with the team's skill availability and budget, what managed services from the cloud vendor or from another platform vendor can help fill the gap? Are these services cost effective, and does the vendor have a good reputation for reliability and adaptability? Which is a better fit for the company: a local provider who knows the market and can offer a long-term, individualized relationship? Or a national or international provider with a global footprint and extensive experience?

Vendor Lock-In

Once a vendor is selected, it can be difficult and expensive to shift to a different vendor later. This phenomenon is called vendor lock-in and specifically refers to the ominous expense of changing vendors that often prevents customers from considering any competitors' products later. Knowing this is often a concern, many vendors are increasingly offering portability options to attract customers. They instead rely on other factors, such as competitive pricing and excellent customer service, to earn customer loyalty. Still, while a company might initially feel confident that they've made a good selection of vendors and services from what is currently available, they should anticipate needing to change vendors for any of several reasons, including the following:

› The vendor goes out of business.

› The vendor increases prices or reduces needed features.

› Another vendor offers better services for better prices.

› Technology evolves.

One way to reduce the expense and difficulty of changing vendors later is to investigate formatting options for data, especially data in a SaaS or PaaS cloud service. Many vendors require proprietary data formats. Recall from Chapter 2 that "proprietary" refers to a technology developed by a company for its own use and is restricted from use or may be licensed for use by other companies. This is in contrast to open-source technologies that are available for anyone to use and change. While open-source standards encourage freedom of movement between platforms, proprietary standards prevent data portability, which is the ability to export data from one service and import it to a different vendor's service. Similarly, the ability to move applications from one cloud platform to another without requiring significant refactoring is called application portability.

> ## Note
>
> A similar concept that might also affect vendor selection is **interoperability**, or the ability of a cloud system to successfully interact with other systems. Interoperability requires the use of open-source technologies and industry standards, such as APIs or certain data formats. When choosing vendors, a customer should confirm that all relevant services from each vendor meet interoperability requirements for all relevant systems.

Vendor Documentation

> ## Cloud Essentials+ Exam Tip
>
> This section discusses vendor documentation, which is required by
>
> - Part of Objective 2.1: Given a scenario, use appropriate cloud assessments.
> - Part of Objective 2.2: Summarize the financial aspects of engaging a cloud provider.
> - Part of Objective 2.3: Identify the important business aspects of vendor relations in cloud adoptions.

The process of investigating and then building relationships with vendors relies on a variety of documents that are somewhat standardized in their purposes and application. The following discussion covers documents you should be familiar with and the role they serve in the vendor relationship.

Request for Information (RFI)

To thoroughly consider vendor options for a new cloud service or platform and make the best selection for the company's needs, a significant amount of information must be collected. One place to start this research process is with an RFI (Request for Information), which asks vendors to submit information about their products and services that will address many of the customer's initial questions. An RFI is non-binding, meaning that the customer is simply asking for general information and they're not yet committing themselves to any vendor.

A well-written RFI will indicate the customer's goals, some general company background, what they're looking for, and a date when they need to receive the vendor's response. These responses to the RFI will help the customer create comparable vendor profiles across a range of possible vendors and will help determine next steps in the information gathering process. This information can also be saved for future reference as other projects arise. The process of collecting this information will also establish a primary POC (point of contact) with the vendor—this is a single person who will become familiar with the customer and their needs to facilitate more efficient communication in the future.

As questions about vendors become more targeted and detailed, the customer will move to other documents, such as:

> RFP (Request for Proposal)—Asks for more detailed responses from the vendor that are specific to the project.
>
> RFQ (Request for Quotation)—Asks for detailed pricing information specific to the project.

Statement of Work (SOW)

Once a vendor is selected, the project can begin with an SOW. An SOW (Statement of Work) documents in detail the work that must be completed for a particular project, and includes specifics such as tasks, deliverables, standards, payment schedule, and work timeline. An SOW is legally binding, meaning it can be enforced in a court of law. Many times, an SOW is used to define the terms of each new project as an addendum to an existing MSA. An MSA (Master Service Agreement) is a contract that defines the terms of future contracts between parties, such as payment terms or arbitration arrangements.

Service-Level Agreement (SLA)

Another document to establish at the beginning of a project is an SLA. Recall from Chapter 1 that an SLA (Service-Level Agreement) is a legally binding contract or part of a contract that defines, in plain language and in measurable terms, the aspects of a service provided to a customer, such as the service provided by an ISP. Details specified might include contract duration (minimum or maximum), guaranteed uptime, options for compensation if outages exceed defined thresholds, problem management, performance benchmarks, and termination options.

Project Evaluations

When exploring the possibilities of a new project or acquisition with vendors, the customer will also need to gather and organize information about the project itself in addition to the nature of the agreement between their company and the vendor. Documents that help to guide the work on this process include:

> **PoC (Proof of Concept)**—The PoC answers the question: Will a solution effectively address the problem they're trying to solve? The PoC might not be particularly detailed and is often one of the first documents to be produced when exploring a new product or service. The PoC takes more of a qualitative approach in describing the ideas, concepts, and "what if…" scenarios that led to the company's interest in the solution.

> **PoV (Proof of Value)**—The PoV builds on evidence from the PoC and answers the question: What value will the solution bring to the company in terms of financial savings, workflow efficiency, or satisfaction improvements? The PoV quantifies anticipated costs, savings, workflow changes, and effects on employee or customer satisfaction.

Both the PoC and PoV might consist solely of documentation based on research and educated guesses. In contrast, they might also involve generating a small test version of the proposed project, such as when developing a new application, to validate the projected effects of the proposal. This small-scale test might require only a few days' work and is not intended to fully represent the entire proposed system. Figure 12-5 shows the PoC's position in a diagram showing the progression of time and scope of a software development project.

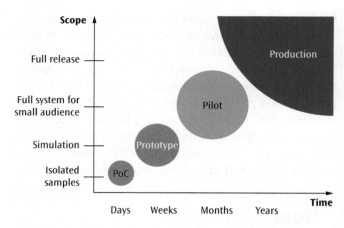

Figure 12-5 Progression from PoC to production

In the context of software development projects, larger-scale tests gradually increase in both scope and time investment:

> **Prototype**—This draft-scale product allows for initial user testing without needing to incorporate real data or compatibility with other systems. The prototype lays out some general designs for user interfaces with clickable links. These drafts help users start to visualize the design and provide feedback to be incorporated in the next iteration.

> **Pilot**—This larger scale product expands the earlier test versions and likely reflects some widespread changes to the overall design based on early user feedback. The pilot provides core functionality to allow for adequate testing and accurate user feedback on more detailed features. While minor issues, such as spelling errors or static graphics, are acceptable for a pilot, the primary features of the product should be reliably functional and ready for extensive user testing, including using actual data.

> **MVP (minimum viable product)**—The pilot phase is sometimes referred to as the MVP (minimum viable product), or the MVP might be a transitional phase between the pilot and production. The MVP is a stable, functioning product that incorporates the core functionality of the product and is built with the intention of expanding functionality before releasing to full production.

> **Production**—The final stage is to release the product to its full, intended audience. While future iterations might be required to address problems or to expand functionality, these later iterations are usually considered versions of the product rather than initial developmental phases. Still, development

phases such as PoC or prototyping might be required again later if the product needs to undergo extensive renovation for future expansion.

How does a company determine, at any point along this path, if the proposal warrants further development? During each phase, they will evaluate the proposal in terms of predefined success criteria. In general, these success criteria revolve around three major measurements:

> **Cost (or budget)**—Can the product be developed within budget? Will the product bring a greater return than it costs?

> **Time (or schedule)**—Can the product be developed within the required timeframe? Which people will need to contribute time to this project, and how will those work hours affect the overall cost of the project?

> **Scope**—Will the product adequately address the problems originally identified? Will any additional functionality increase user satisfaction and efficiency? Is the complexity of the project expanding beyond the company's ability to complete this project within the allocated time and budget?

Note

In project management, the combination of cost, time, and scope as success criteria for a project are sometimes referred to as the "iron triangle" or the "triple constraint." Various stakeholders in a project will prioritize each of these criteria differently. The project manager must balance tradeoffs between these three factors to achieve desired quality. Too great an emphasis on any one point of this triangle will result in compromises to the budget, the schedule, or functionality. See Figure 12-6.

Figure 12-6   The iron triangle of project management

At every step along the path toward product development, everyone on the team should be on guard against potential scope creep, which is the tendency to add more functionality than is really needed, thereby increasing cost, time to production, and scope of the project.

Remember this...

> Vendors might offer professional services and other features to increase their appeal to customers. For example, many vendors offer support tiers, such as AWS's Developer, Business, and Enterprise tiers. Compatibility with the customer's existing applications, workflows, and user skills will affect the migration timeline available from one vendor compared to another. Migrating to a cloud platform that supports thorough testing and quick rollback can significantly decrease a company's time to market with business innovations, website or application updates, and overall network and application performance optimizations. A vendor's managed services offerings can help fill the gap between the talent existing team members offer and the company's needs. Finally, many vendors are increasingly offering portability options to attract customers.

> The process of investigating and then building relationships with vendors relies on a variety of documents that are somewhat standardized in their purposes and application: RFI (Request for Information), SOW (Statement of Work), and SLA (Service-Level Agreement).

> Documents that help to guide project development include a PoC (Proof of Concept) and PoV (Proof of Value). Either of these might include generating a test version of the proposed project. Larger-scale tests that gradually increase in both scope and time investment include a prototype, pilot, and MVP (minimum viable product).

Self-check

4. If your company is concerned about vendor lock-in, which of these factors is most relevant to that concern?
   a. SLA requirements
   b. Skill availability
   c. Time to market
   d. Migration costs

5. The development of which document will first establish a POC?

    a. SOW

    b. MSA

    c. SLA

    d. RFI

6. Which test stage is most likely to use real data?

    a. Prototype

    b. Pilot

    c. PoV

    d. PoC

Check your answers at the end of this chapter.

Section 12-3: Financial Aspects of Cloud

Companies like Flexera and Global Knowledge conduct regular surveys of IT professionals to determine what their concerns and challenges are in using the cloud. Recently, one of the biggest issues that has consistently appeared at the top of these lists is cost optimization in the cloud. Of course, cost optimization is always a concern with nearly any business endeavor. Why is cost optimization such a high priority with the cloud? A big part of the answer to this question involves the variability of cloud expenses, the challenges in tracking these expenses, and the options for reducing cloud costs. This section will explore what expenses you're likely to see detailed in your cloud expense report and ways to optimize your cloud resource configurations to keep those numbers within budget.

CapEx vs. OpEx

Cloud Essentials+ Exam Tip

This section discusses CapEx and OpEx, which are required by

- Part of Objective 2.2: Summarize the financial aspects of engaging a cloud provider.

- Part of Objective 3.3: Given a scenario, review and report on the financial expenditures related to cloud resources.

Not only does cloud represent a shift in the way companies do IT, it also brings a shift in the way companies pay for IT resources. With traditional networks, companies invest large amounts of money at a time into purchasing expensive hardware and software. These are CapEx (capital expenditures) where the benefits are experienced over a long time (more than one year) after the investment is made. Using the pay-as-you-go model, however, most cloud resources are paid for in smaller amounts every month or quarter. These are OpEx (operational expenditures) where benefits are experienced in about the same period as when the expenses are paid for those benefits. This shift requires a different mindset when managing cloud expenses. Rather than researching and making large purchases every several months or years, cloud professionals must consider how to manage monthly costs to ensure their company is getting their IT needs met with minimal ongoing expenses.

Consider the cost of purchasing a new server for a company's on-prem datacenter. This server will need robust CPU and RAM resources as well as high-bandwidth network connectivity. In most cases, the server must contain duplicates of some of its hardware, such as duplicate power systems. While some companies might rent a server like this, many companies choose to purchase the server. On average, a typical, small-business server will cost two or three thousand dollars. For larger corporations running dozens or hundreds of servers, they might spend even more for some of the servers, perhaps upwards of $10,000 or more. In contrast, consider the costs associated with an EC2 instance in AWS. A moderately sized instance might cost around $.12 per hour. With 8,760 hours per year, this server will cost just over a $1,000 each year even if the server is run all the time. The company could realize additional savings if they run the server only when it's needed.

While it's tempting to try to compare dollar-for-dollar the cost of purchasing a server with the cost of running a server instance on AWS, the reality is not this simple. Additional costs for each include the following:

> On-prem server:

    ○ Utilities

    ○ HVAC system

    ○ Racks with wiring and UPS (uninterruptible power supply) systems

    ○ Insurance on physical infrastructure

    ○ Building insurance and rent or taxes

    ○ Time and costs for maintenance and repair to the physical infrastructure

> Cloud instance:

    ○ Storage space

    ○ Networking features (such as public IP address and outbound traffic)

- ○ Maintenance and upgrades to IaaS cloud resources
- ○ Optional cloud customer support plan

Most cloud providers offer cost calculators so customers can experiment with cost comparisons before committing to a cloud migration or new deployment. In the project at the end of this chapter, you'll practice estimating expenses for cloud resources using some of these calculators.

The primary benefit of OpEx over CapEx is that expenditures fluctuate with demand, which is usually closely related to company income. In other words, instead of making large investments in hardware to meet anticipated future need, a company can make small investments in virtualized resources as needs occur. Figure 12-7 shows how expenditures can track closely with demand and prevent over- or under-investments in hardware. Notice the gap near the center of the figure where CapEx investments would not fully meet the actual need. Fluctuating OpEx resources in the cloud can ensure that resources always exceed the actual need by a small margin.

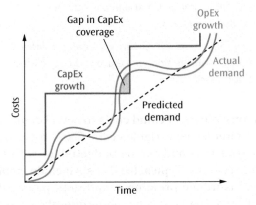

Figure 12-7   CapEx vs. OpEx

Tracking Cloud Expenses

Cloud Essentials+ Exam Tip

This section discusses cloud expenses, which is required by

- Part of Objective 2.2: Summarize the financial aspects of engaging a cloud provider.
- Part of Objective 3.3: Given a scenario, review and report on the financial expenditures related to cloud resources.

To effectively manage cloud costs, you first need to know what you're getting charged for. Each cloud provider requires fees for different types of services and resources. Common patterns you'll see among many cloud providers include the following:

- ❯ Some cloud resources are available for free all the time, such as a small VM instance.
- ❯ In addition to the cost of the VM instance itself, you must budget for any storage volumes attached to that instance or other storage space used by the instance, even if the instance itself is free.
- ❯ Some cloud providers offer a public IP address for each instance for free while others charge for this service.
- ❯ In most cases, data inbound to your cloud resources can be transferred for free, while data outbound from your cloud resources will incur charges.

Cloud services are often categorized according to the type of process being performed. The three primary, high-level categories are compute, network, and storage:

- ❯ **Compute**—These services perform some kind of computing process that receives input and produces output. For example, running a virtual server in the cloud is mostly a compute service (although it also relies on other types of services). A simpler example is serverless compute, such as AWS's Lambda, where you input code directly into the cloud service, and the service outputs some kind of data or action. The service is active perhaps only for milliseconds, and you might pay a fraction of a cent for the compute process. These kinds of serverless processes can be run hundreds or even millions of times an hour for a relatively low cost and require very little maintenance from the customer's side.
- ❯ **Network**—A cloud resource that assists with moving data from one resource, application, or storage space to another is typically identified as a networking service. Examples include public IP addresses, virtual network spaces (such as subnets), and WAN network connections between cloud resources or from the cloud to the on-prem datacenter. Sometimes these costs are included with other services. For example, AWS includes one public IP address per EC2 instance with no

additional charge, and an AWS virtual network (called a VPC, or virtual private cloud) is free to configure and use. Other services incur additional fees, such as a reserved public IP address that you can assign repeatedly to any instance or a direct connection from AWS's infrastructure to your on-prem datacenter.

> **Storage**—Data saved within the cloud, whether as files, objects, databases, or volumes, takes up space. This space is collectively referred to as storage and usually represents a separate expense from other types of services. For example, if you create a virtual server in AWS, you also need to attach a storage volume to the instance so you can install the server's OS. Unless you're using free tier options, this storage volume will appear as a separate cost on your cloud bill.

Note

When you delete a virtual machine in the cloud, always be sure to also delete the attached storage volume. In some cloud platforms, the storage resource is not automatically deleted with the instance, and it can continue to incur charges even though the VM no longer exists.

Sometimes these broad categories are broken down into more specific groupings. Some examples from AWS include Machine Learning (a collection of mostly compute services), Database (a form of storage), and Migration & Transfer (mostly network services).

To effectively track these expenses, most cloud providers incorporate some kind of resource tagging option when configuring cloud services. A **tag** is a key-value pair that attaches a customized label to cloud resources. These tags can be used to categorize resources according to their purpose, owner, or environment. For example, you might assign the tag "Department" with the value "Accounting" so you can identify all cloud resources that serve your accounting department. These tags enable **chargebacks**, which are cost allocations of individual cloud expenses to specific internal accounts or business units. In this manner, the overall cloud bill can be distributed to various departments, projects, or activities within your company rather than collecting all cloud expenses within the IT department's budget.

Note

A similar approach to the chargeback model is the showback model, which tracks usage of cloud resources without attributing specific costs to that usage. This serves the purpose of increasing cost awareness without introducing the complexity of mixing responsibility for the funding of cloud services. Either way, cloud cost monitoring provides an opportunity to granularly monitor cloud consumption per user, customer, team, project, or department and make adjustments where needed.

Cloud Cost Optimization

Cloud Essentials+ Exam Tip

This section discusses variable and fixed costs, which are required by

- Part of Objective 2.2: Summarize the financial aspects of engaging a cloud provider.
- Part of Objective 3.1: Explain aspects of operating within the cloud.
- Part of Objective 3.3: Given a scenario, review and report on the financial expenditures related to cloud resources.

The responsiveness of cloud costs to actual demand creates a counter issue: variable costs. **Fixed costs** are predictable over time and can be budgeted for with a high degree of accuracy. Typical fixed costs include employee salaries, insurance premiums, and debt payments. In contrast, **variable costs** change frequently and unpredictably, possibly with a large range of possible values. Typical variable costs include some utility expenses, such as electricity bills that fluctuate significantly with the weather. A large, fixed expense can be easier to budget for than a smaller but variable expense. Cloud's variable expenses that increase or decrease along with the demand placed on cloud resources require a different approach to budgeting that allows for the higher end of potential costs but, in most months, will fall below the budgeted amount and save the customer money.

Similarly, the way costs are calculated in the cloud can fluctuate as new, money-saving features and services are released. Cloud admins continually look for and research possible ways to further reduce cloud expenses, and some of these options can significantly reduce a company's cloud expenses. Some of these available cost-saving options include converting variable cloud costs to fixed costs where the customer commits to using a resource for a longer term. For example, suppose a company has a web server that maintains a relatively consistent amount of traffic and rarely needs to scale up or out in response to traffic fluctuations. They can save money by agreeing to use that VM for several months, a year, or even multiple years.

Instance Pricing Options

Instance pricing options vary slightly from cloud platform to platform. The following list explains instance pricing options from AWS as an example:

> **On-demand instance**—This is the arrangement you've already seen in your AWS project. The customer pays a premium to create the instance when they choose, terminate the instance when they choose, and run it only when they choose. This pricing option also offers the most freedom to respond to fluctuating demand on cloud resources.

> **Reserved instance**—A reserved instance offers lower prices in exchange for a commitment to use the instance over a longer period of time. For example, if a customer reserves the instance for a year, they'll get about a 40 percent discount compared to an on-demand instance run for that same period of time. If they fully pay for the year up front (i.e., pay

for the year all at once when they contract for the instance), they can get an even bigger discount.

> **Spot instance**—Sometimes, customers reserve more instances than they end up needing, or they need to shift to a different instance configuration than what they reserved. Many cloud platforms allow customers to then sell their reserved instance in the cloud provider's marketplace for a market-enabled rate. The prices for these resold instances fluctuate often. Buyers can purchase spot instances very inexpensively—Figure 12-8 shows this option in the EC2 instance configuration process. When the market rate for the desired instance type falls within a set range, buyers are given access time to the number of spot instances they've requested at that rate. Once the market rate rises above a certain threshold, those spot instances are returned to the pool available for other buyers who are willing to pay more. The benefit with a spot instance is that customers can get compute time for much lower prices than what they would pay to the cloud provider for an on-demand or a reserved instance. The challenge is that they can only run processes on those instances if those processes can be started and stopped at unpredictable times. The customer receives a brief warning, such as an hour, that the instance rate has risen above their threshold. They must terminate their processes on the instance during that time so they don't lose data once the

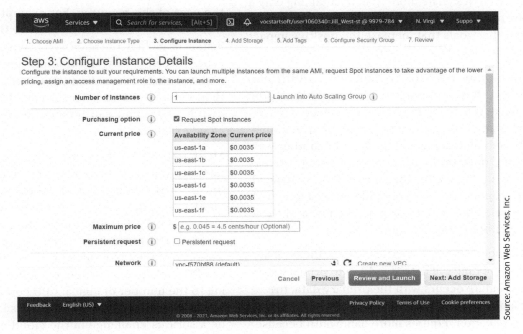

Figure 12-8   Request a spot instance in EC2

spot instance is pulled from their account. Note that all of these processes of starting and stopping processes on spot instances can be handled automatically through the use of scripts.

All Things Considered

Thought Experiment

Search the AWS website and find the current price for an a1.large on-demand EC2 instance. Then find the current price for an a1.large spot instance. What is the percent discount for using a spot instance instead of an on-demand instance?

Data Replication Cost vs. Benefit

In optimizing cloud costs, clearly the goal isn't always to reduce costs. Other priorities include increasing performance, availability, and security. For example, a company might decide the cost of storing a copy of their customer database is warranted because they can't afford to lose that data should something happen to their original database.

Strategies used to protect and optimize data are collectively called **data management**. Part of data management is **data replication**, or keeping multiple copies of data, to decrease latency and increase data resiliency and application performance. While copying data and storing these copies costs more than maintaining only a single copy of data, the added expense also helps a company meet other goals that increase the positive impact a business can make in its market.

Once a company decides to invest in additional functionality, they still must decide to what degree they will make this investment. It's a nuanced decision that offers many possibilities for saving a little money in one way and increasing functionality in another way. For example, data replication is an ongoing process that must be updated after the source data is changed. Updates to replicated data are made either along with changes to the source data or periodically, and these options affect both price and functionality:

› Synchronous replication writes data to the replica at the same time the data is written to primary storage. If a failure occurs with the primary data, the replica provides an exact, updated copy. Synchronous replication requires more bandwidth because

data is written to two locations at the same time and is the more expensive option while providing the most accurate copy of the source data.

› Asynchronous replication writes data to primary storage first and then periodically copies this data to the replica. Asynchronous replication requires less bandwidth and so is cheaper, but it can also result in some data loss due to the delay in writing to the replica.

Licensing in the Cloud

Cloud Essentials+ Exam Tip

This section discusses licensing, which is required by

- Part of Objective 3.3: Given a scenario, review and report on the financial expenditures related to cloud resources.

Separate from the virtual resource itself (such as a virtual server), a cloud customer must also manage licenses, such as OS or other software licenses. For example, a Windows Server VM in AWS requires a legitimate Windows license. Similarly, many cloud database services require a license for the database software running in the database instance.

In some cases, the cost of the license is included in the cost of the resource. For example, some of AWS's EC2 instances and RDS (Relational Database Service) instances include the Microsoft license with the instance type. Alternatively, a customer might already have high-volume licenses that they would like to import to their cloud resources. This is called BYOL (bring your own license) and can be an effective way to reduce cloud expenses.

Most people are familiar with obtaining software licenses per user or per device. The technical term for this arrangement is CAL (client access license). In many cases, however, high-volume software licensing costs are calculated not according to the number of users or the number of machines on which the software is installed but, instead, according to the number of CPU sockets in a system or (more recently) according to the number of logical CPU cores used to execute that software. For this reason, license management can be a serious challenge in the cloud when the number of vCPUs can change if an instance is configured to scale up (i.e., to increase the number of its vCPUs in response to increasing demand on the server). Any kind of auto-scaling configured on instances that rely on licenses should take into account the limitations imposed by those licenses.

Many types of licenses, such as subscription licenses for Office 365 or pay-as-you-go licenses for AWS services, require ongoing payments to maintain the license. If the bill doesn't get paid, the licenses expire. This might seem like a minor thing, and yet it can cause major problems. SLM (software license management) can help minimize license expenses by eliminating unneeded licenses and renewing licenses before expiration, thereby avoiding fees or legal fines. If you're responsible for these processes, be sure to keep license documents and receipts in a central repository (not your email inbox), and set reminders or appointments in your calendar or schedule email reminders to yourself to renew or update licenses periodically.

Remember this...

> With traditional networks, companies invest large amounts of money at a time into purchasing expensive hardware and software. These are CapEx (capital expenditures) where the benefits are experienced over a long time (more than one year) after the investment is made. Using the pay-as-you-go model, however, most cloud resources are paid for in smaller amounts every month or quarter. These are OpEx (operational expenditures) where benefits are experienced in about the same period as when the expenses are paid for those benefits.

> Cloud services are often categorized according to the type of process being performed. Compute services perform some kind of computing process that receives input and produces output. A cloud resource that assists with moving data from one resource, application, or storage space to another is typically identified as a networking service. Data saved within the cloud, whether as files, objects, databases, or volumes, takes up space. This space is collectively referred to as storage and usually represents a separate expense from other types of services.

> To effectively track cloud expenses, most cloud providers incorporate some kind of resource tagging option when configuring cloud services. A tag is a key-value pair that attaches a customized label to cloud resources. These tags enable chargebacks, which are cost allocations of individual cloud expenses to specific internal accounts or business units.

> Fixed costs are predictable over time and can be budgeted for with a high degree of accuracy. In contrast, variable costs change frequently and unpredictably, possibly with a large range of possible values.

> With an on-demand instance, the customer pays a premium to create the instance when they choose, terminate the instance when they choose, and run it only when they choose. This pricing option offers the most freedom to respond to fluctuating demand on cloud resources. A reserved instance offers lower prices in exchange for a commitment to use the instance over a longer period of time. Buyers can purchase spot instances when the market rate for the desired instance type falls within a set range. The benefit with a spot instance is that customers can get compute time for much lower prices than what they would pay to the cloud provider for an on-demand or a reserved instance. The challenge is that they can only run processes on those instances if those processes can be started and stopped at unpredictable times.

> Strategies used to protect and optimize data are collectively called data management. Part of data management is data replication, or keeping multiple copies of data, to decrease latency and increase data resiliency and application performance.

> An arrangement to obtain a software license per user or per device is called a CAL (client access license). In many cases, high-volume software licensing costs are calculated instead according to the number of CPU sockets in a system or (more recently) according to the number of logical CPU cores used to execute that software. SLM (software license management) can help minimize license expenses by eliminating unneeded licenses and renewing licenses before expiration, thereby avoiding fees or legal fines.

Self-check

7. What kind of expense is a subscription for a customer support plan?
   a. OpEx
   b. Storage
   c. CapEx
   d. Network

8. What resource allows you to identify a server that belongs to the Marketing department?
   a. IP address
   b. Storage volume
   c. Tag
   d. VPC

9. Which instance type would be best suited to an email server that must be available 24 hours a day, seven days a week?
   a. Spot instance
   b. Public instance
   c. On-demand instance
   d. Reserved instance

Check your answers at the end of this chapter.

Section 12-4: Continuity and Recovery

Computer networks are in a constant state of change. New users and applications are added, while former users and unwanted applications are deleted. Hardware is upgraded, replaced, virtualized, or migrated to the cloud. Because the technology changes so quickly and networks are constantly being called upon to support new and computationally intensive applications, a network administrator is constantly working on improving data transfer speed and throughput of network applications, optimizing cloud services, and preparing for problems.

Problems a network might face could be something relatively minor, such as a misconfiguration that slows data throughput, or it could be something major or even devastating, such as a long-term service outage, theft, or fire. Preparation for these problems begins long before the problem itself occurs. With all preparations, the priorities are safety and the ability of the business to continue operations throughout a failure or disaster. This section discusses the types of preparations that need to be made.

Business Continuity

BC (business continuity) refers to a company's ability to weather a failure, crisis, or disaster of some kind while maintaining continuity of operations, especially for critical services to customers and income-generating activities. Part of the business continuity planning process is developing a BIA (business impact analysis) that evaluates how different departments and components of an organization's business would, if lost, affect the company's bottom line. Corporate guidelines will help in the decision-making process to determine what services should be prioritized for business continuity protection and how much money should be invested in protecting those resources.

Business continuity strategies hinge on redundancy, which is the duplication of key resources so one can take over if the other fails. As you read about in Chapter 1, redundancy seeks to eliminate all SPOFs (single points of failure) so that any critical component or system is duplicated. Examples include duplicate or triplicate connectivity to the Internet and other offsite resources, or backup services for loss of communications or power.

Some forms of redundancy include alternate sites. Outsourcing to third-party services or sites is also an option. Backup locations host backup hardware, data, and services in preparation for use during an emergency, according to the following categories (also shown in Figure 12-9):

> **Cold site**—Computers, devices, and connectivity necessary to rebuild a network exist, but they are not appropriately configured, updated, or connected. Therefore, restoring functionality from a cold site could take a long time.

> **Warm site**—Computers, devices, and connectivity necessary to rebuild a network exist, with some pieces appropriately configured, updated, or connected. Recovery using a warm site can take hours or days, compared with the weeks a cold site might require. Maintaining a warm site costs more than

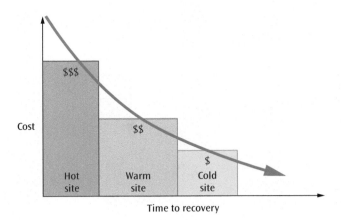

Figure 12-9 The most expensive option also provides the fastest recovery

maintaining a cold site, but not as much as maintaining a hot site.

> **Hot site**—Computers, devices, and connectivity necessary to rebuild a network exist, and all are appropriately configured, updated, and connected to match your network's current state. For example, you might use server mirroring to maintain identical copies of your servers at two locations. In a hot site contingency plan, both locations would also contain identical connectivity devices and configurations and thus would be able to stand in for the other at a moment's notice. As you can imagine, hot sites are expensive and potentially time-consuming to maintain. For organizations that cannot tolerate downtime, however, hot sites provide the best disaster recovery option.

Cloud providers build in available redundancy options for their cloud services and for the customer's cloud resources. Large cloud providers, like Amazon and Microsoft, host many datacenters throughout the world. Each datacenter contains built-in redundancies for power sources, WAN connections, connections between network segments, and many other critical infrastructure components. In the case of AWS, each collection of datacenters is called an **AZ (Availability Zone)**. A group of AZs is called a region. At the time of this writing, AWS has 81 AZs in 25 regions worldwide. This distribution of redundant components in various regions is called **geo-redundancy**. It ensures that, if one regional area is struck by a widespread disaster (such as a hurricane or earthquake), other AZs or regions can take over responsibility for certain cloud services. Depending on the service, it is often the cloud customer's responsibility to ensure their resources in the cloud are adequately spread across multiple AZs or regions to provide their required level of geo-redundancy.

Disaster Recovery

Ensuring business continuity during a disaster covers only part of the process. A company must also ensure their network can recover quickly after the disaster and return to full functionality. **DR (disaster recovery)** refers to the strategies and tools that facilitate an organization's recovery from an adverse event. "Business continuity" and "disaster recovery" are two related but distinct terms. While business continuity refers to an organization's ability to continue doing business *during* a crisis, disaster recovery refers to the process of getting back to normal *after* the crisis is over. Typically, DR planning is considered a subset of BC planning.

MTBF and MTTR

The following statistics, as illustrated in Figure 12-10, are useful in quantifying DR preparedness:

> **MTBF (mean time between failures)** is the average time a device or system will operate before it fails. This value is sometimes generated by the manufacturer of the equipment and passed along to the purchaser. But often this value is not available, and the owner of the equipment must generate an MTBF value from the equipment's past performance. Although every device is different, the longer the MTBF, the better.

> **MTTR (mean time to repair)** is the average time necessary to repair a failure within the network. This time includes the time necessary to isolate the failure. It also includes the time required to either swap the defective component with a working component or repair a component—either on-site or by removing the component and sending it to a repair center. Finally, MTTR includes the time needed to bring the system back up to normal operation. The value of MTTR depends on each installation and, within an installation, on each type of component.

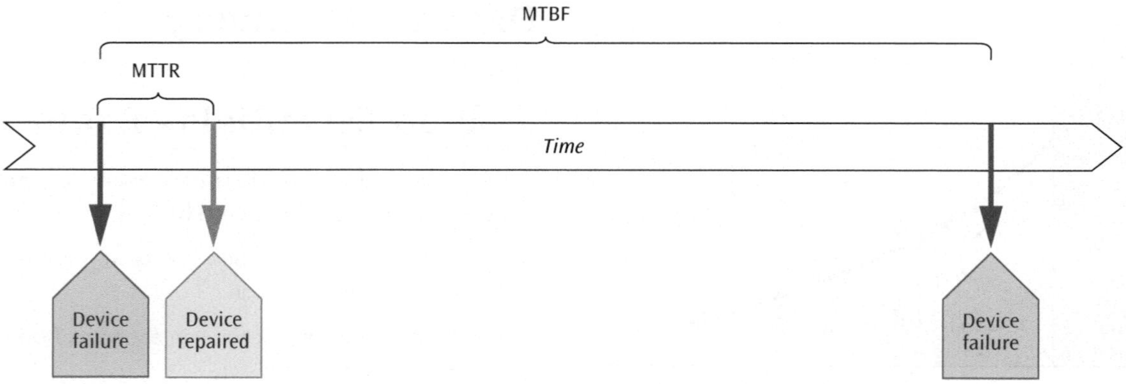

Figure 12-10   MTBF and MTTR

For example, a network server with hot-swappable devices should have a shorter MTTR than a device that has to be shut off, opened, repaired, and then rebooted. In contrast, a virtual server in the cloud will have a very low MTTR because typically, virtual servers can be deleted and replaced within minutes.

Details | Calculating Availability and Reliability

When you know a system's MTTR and MTBF, you can then calculate the system's availability and reliability. Recall from Chapter 1 that availability is the probability that a particular component or system will be available during a fixed time period. A component or network with a high availability (near 1.0) is almost always operational. Software that generates statistics often calculates the value for availability based on MTTR and MTBF values. Components with a small MTTR and a large MTBF will produce availability values very near to 1.0. For simplicity, however, you can calculate availability by simply subtracting the downtime from the total available time and then dividing by the total available time:

Availability% = (Total available time − Downtime)
/Total available time

Suppose you want to calculate the availability of a printer for one month (24 hours per day for 30 days, or 720 hours), knowing that the printer will be down (inoperable) for 2 hours during that period.

Availability% = (720 − 2) / 720 = 0.997

Because the availability is near 1.0, there is a very high probability that the printer will be available during that one-month period.

To calculate the availability of a system of components, you should calculate the availability of each component and find the product of all availabilities. For example, if a network has three devices with availabilities of 0.992, 0.894, and 0.999, the availability of the network is the product of 0.992 × 0.894 × 0.999, or 0.886. Companies typically like to see availability values expressed as "nines," as you read in Chapter 1, with the more nines the better. For example, 0.9999 ("four nines") is better than 0.999 ("three nines").

Recall that reliability calculates the probability that a component or system will be operational for the duration of a transaction of time t. Reliability is defined by the equation

$$R(t) = e^{-bt}$$

in which

$$b = 1/\text{MTBF}$$
t = the time interval of the transaction

What is the reliability of a router if the MTBF is 3000 hours and a transaction takes 20 minutes, or ⅓ of an hour (0.333 hour)?

$$R(0.333 \text{ hour}) = e^{-(1/3000)(0.333)} = e^{-0.000111} = 0.99989$$

What if the reliability of a second device was calculated and found to be 0.995? Although this value also appears to be near 1.0, there is a difference between the two reliabilities of 0.00489. What this difference basically means is that, in 1000 repetitions of a trial, a particular failure may occur five more times in the second device. On a network, many events occur or repeat thousands of times, so you would not want to experience five additional device failures for every one thousand events, especially during the transmission of data. Therefore, many network administrators strive to maintain system availability and reliability values of 0.9999 (four nines) to 0.99999 (five nines).

All Things Considered

Thought Experiment

A component has been operating continuously for three months. During that time, it has failed twice, resulting in 4.5 hours of downtime. Calculate the availability of the component during this three-month period.

Backups

Some cloud resources are disposable resources, meaning they can be replaced with another resource if something goes wrong. For example, if your web server becomes corrupted, you can delete it and replace it with a new one faster and cheaper than trying to fix the broken one. Other resources in the cloud, however, can't be so easily replaced. For example, a customer database contains valuable data that, if destroyed, might be difficult or impossible to reassemble. Data and similar resources must be backed up so they can be recovered if something happens to the first copy.

A significant portion of DR planning is determining the type of backup a company will maintain and how often these backups will be made. Different backup types affect the point in time represented by the backup. The challenge is to maximize the use of available storage space and minimize the cost of storing backups while meeting company goals for what their backups can do if those files are needed. Consider the following backup types:

> **Full backup**—Backs up everything every time a backup is performed.

> **Incremental backup**—Backs up only data that has changed since the last backup of any kind.

> **Differential backup**—Backs up data that has changed since the last *full* backup.

Figure 12-11 illustrates the conceptual differences between these backup types.

It might help to imagine the different file sizes if you were to look at a full backup file, incremental backup file, and differential backup file side by side. The full backup would be the largest because it copies all the original data, even old data that hasn't changed in a long time. The time to recover data from a full backup would be relatively short because all the backed-up data exists in one place. However, full backups take up a lot of space and require a lot of time to create.

The incremental backup would be the smallest file. It only includes data that has changed since the last backup of any kind. For example, if you perform a full backup on Sunday, then an incremental backup would copy whatever changed on Monday, the next incremental backup would copy whatever changed on Tuesday, and so on. You have one full backup from early in the week, with several smaller files containing changes for each day. To recover this data, you would need to start with the full backup, then apply changes from Monday, then changes from Tuesday, and so on. This creates a series of dependencies between backup files. Incremental backups don't take up much space and don't require much time to create. However, you must make these backups frequently and allow more time to recover when using incremental backups.

The size of a differential backup (also called a delta backup or delta differential backup) falls between the other two. It includes all data changed since the last full backup (this changed data is called the delta) regardless of any other smaller backups performed since then. To recover this

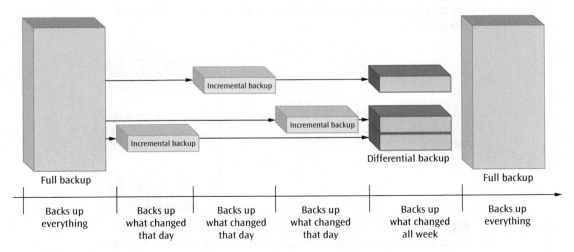

Figure 12-11 Incremental and differential backups require fewer resources

data, you would need to start with the full backup and then apply only the latest differential backup, which would contain all changes since the latest full backup was performed.

Backup professionals suggest, at the minimum, following the 3-2-1 Rule for backups. This rule states, as shown in Figure 12-12, that a company should keep at least three copies of their data (that's one production copy and two backup copies), stored on at least two different kinds of media (such as disk and tape), with one copy stored in a location geographically separate from the original data. For an on-prem network, this means storing one backup copy locally is okay while the other backup should be stored in a remote location, preferably in a different geographic area where a natural disaster that affects the local network would not endanger the remote backup. For more sophisticated backup strategies that rely more natively on the cloud, consider following variations of this rule, such as 3-1-2 (Figure 12-13) or 4-2-3 (Figure 12-14).

> **Note**
>
> It's important to understand the difference between archived data and backup data. Archived data is cold data that is no longer used and rarely accessed. It might be an earlier version of the data that is in use, or it might be the master copy of old data that is no longer accessed (such as medical records for former patients). Typically, archived data is stored in cold storage that is less expensive but not easily accessible. It's not synced to any active systems. While backup data is not regularly accessed, it must be frequently updated to match active data, and it should be quickly accessible should something bad happen to the data in use. Backups might include versioning, which keeps different versions of a file that has been changed multiple times.

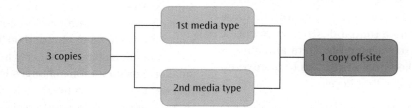

Figure 12-12 Three copies of data, stored on two different kinds of media, with one copy stored off-site

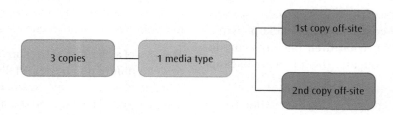

Figure 12-13 Three copies of data, stored on one kind of media (such as SSD), at two geographically isolated locations in the cloud

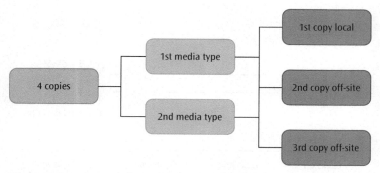

Figure 12-14 Four copies of data, stored on two different kinds of media, with one backup stored locally and two in geographically isolated locations in the cloud

RTO and RPO

The various backup types point to another pair of statistics commonly used to measure disaster recovery effectiveness: RPO (recovery point objective) and RTO (recovery time objective). Consider the diagram in Figure 12-15.

The RPO shows at what point in the past data was most recently backed up, and so this is the point before which data will be recovered. Data that was created or changed since that point will be lost because data backups do not generally copy data in real time. For example, relying on a full backup that's created only once a week will result in multiple days' worth of lost data if the disaster happens later in the week. However, if incremental or differential backups are made each day, the RPO would lose less than a day's worth of data.

In contrast, the RTO shows at what point in the future full functionality will be restored (less any lost data). If a full backup is created each month and differential backups each day, the full backup and one differential backup together contain all backed up data. If, however, an incremental backup is created each day, then the backed-up data is spread across the full backup and all incremental backups since the last full backup, which is more files and will take more time to restore. While incremental backups take up less space and take less time to create, they require more time to recover and therefore result in more recovery time needed after a loss.

RPOs and RTOs in the cloud have the potential to reach near-zero numbers. Cloud DR options open many new avenues of preparedness with much lower costs due to the pay-as-you-go nature of public cloud services. DRaaS (Disaster Recovery as a Service) can greatly reduce RTO because it doesn't take nearly as long to create new VMs from existing images as it does to reinstall OS images on physical servers (called bare metal restore). RPO also benefits from cloud due to inexpensive data replication and storage options. DRaaS is available natively in most major cloud platforms and is also widely available from third-party providers.

> ### Note
>
> When planning for a cloud RTO, also consider bandwidth or ISP limitations and costs for transferring files from backup locations back into the main datacenter or cloud location.

Figure 12-16 shows the spectrum of recovery tiers available in AWS to illustrate the relationship between RPO, RTO, and cost. These tiers are described as follows:

> ❯ Cold backup services are relatively inexpensive, such as storing regular snapshots of VMs and databases but none of these resources are running in duplicate. This means you'll need hours to recover from a loss.

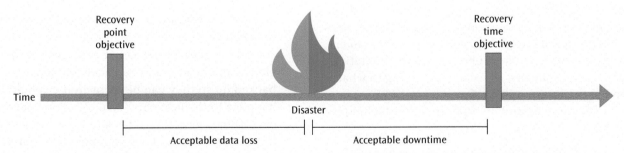

Figure 12-15 RPO defines how much data loss is acceptable while RTO defines how much downtime is acceptable

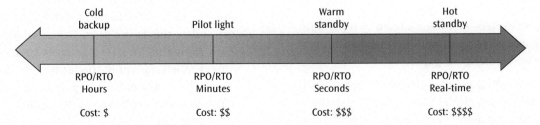

Figure 12-16 Various tiers of recovery services offer faster and more expensive recovery times

› AWS developed a new DR approach called pilot light that allows a customer to design the backup resources they need and leave them in a stopped state—this is less expensive than paying for running services. Perhaps the database is kept running so it's regularly updated, and the server images should be periodically updated but they're not left running indefinitely. Recovery requires the amount of time needed to start these replacement services from a stopped state.

› Warm standby means copies are designed and created, and a scaled-down version of the environment is left running for immediate failover. This arrangement might buy enough time to start the remaining resources for full backup services if needed.

› Hot standby provides real-time failover with no significant data loss. For example, site mirroring copies the current version of a website to a duplicate web server cluster. A load balancer or DNS server can transfer traffic over to the mirrored site instantly if the original web service becomes overloaded or fails completely. Ideally, an active-active, multi-site configuration keeps both sites working and productive at all times to balance the load and provide faster response times. However, each site is large enough to handle the entire workload if the other site fails.

Existing SLAs for disaster recovery scenarios define expectations for service during a crisis, and these requirements partially determine which of the DR tiers is most appropriate for any specific cloud deployment. It's important to help users understand the limitations of any DR arrangements, especially according to what is defined in the relevant SLAs. Consider the CSP's guidelines for DR planning and incorporate other techniques as needed.

Whatever BC plan or DR plan an organization develops, it should be thoroughly tested two or three times a year, or more often if required by relevant compliance regulations. These tests might look like any of the following scenarios:

› **Tabletop exercise**—Involves a team of representatives from each department reviewing the plan together and looking for gaps.

› **Structured walk-through**—Requires each department to walk through the plan in detail, usually with a specific disaster scenario in mind.

› **Disaster simulation testing**—More involved and requires the presence and participation of all personnel, including business partners and vendors.

Remember this...

› BC (business continuity) refers to a company's ability to weather a failure, crisis, or disaster of some kind while maintaining continuity of operations, especially for critical services to customers and income-generating activities. Business continuity strategies hinge on redundancy, which is the duplication of key resources so one can take over if the other fails. Some forms of redundancy include alternate sites according to the following categories: cold site, warm site, hot site.

› DR (disaster recovery) refers to the strategies and tools that facilitate an organization's recovery from an adverse event. Typically, DR planning is considered a subset of BC planning.

› MTBF (mean time between failures) is the average time a device or system will operate before it fails. MTTR (mean time to repair) is the average time necessary to repair a failure within the network. This time includes the time necessary to isolate the failure, repair or replace the defective component, and bring the system back up to normal operation.

› Some cloud resources are disposable, meaning they can be replaced with another resource if something goes wrong. Other resources in the cloud can't be so easily replaced and must be backed up so they can be recovered if something happens to the first copy. A full backup backs up everything every time a backup is performed. An incremental backup backs up only data that has changed since the last backup of any kind. A differential backup backs up data that has changed since the last full backup.

› The RPO (recovery point objective) shows at what point in the past data was most recently backed up, and so this is the point before which data will be recovered. The RTO (recovery time objective) shows at what point in the future full functionality will be restored (less any lost data). RPOs and RTOs in the cloud have the potential to reach near-zero numbers.

Self-check

10. Only one person having access to core network passwords is an example of _____.

   a. AZ

   b. SPOF

   c. BC

   d. BIA

11. A web server that fails often has a low _____.

   a. RTO

   b. MTTR

   c. MTBF

   d. RPO

12. Which backup type generates the largest file?

   a. Differential

   b. Incremental

   c. Cold

   d. Full

Check your answers at the end of this chapter.

Summary

Section 12-1: People Resources

> To make effective use of limited resources, a network admin should also possess several common management skills, including technical skills, interpersonal skills, training skills, budget management skills, basic statistical skills, time management skills, project management skills, and policy creation and enforcement skills.

> Companies that are willing to invest in their human capital—their employees—will prioritize professional development for all staff involved in managing, improving, securing, and optimizing the company's network resources. Professional development enables employees to improve and update their skills in ways that contribute to the company's well-being. Professional development options include continuing education, on-the-job training, conferences, workshops, mentoring, and certifications.

> The help desk or other IT staff might be responsible for training users on new applications or other resources. Training methods include instructor-led training, eLearning, hands-on training, simulations, videos, and instruction manuals.

> Many corporations establish standards to ensure consistency as different employees perform the same complex tasks. These SOPs (standard operating procedures) define steps for a specific process to maintain consistency and avoid errors. Because IT systems are an integral part of company communication paths, these policies directly affect network professionals and, in many cases, might be written or enforced by the IT staff.

Section 12-2: Vendor Relations

> Vendors might offer professional services and other features to increase their appeal to customers. For example, many vendors offer support tiers, such as AWS's Developer, Business, and Enterprise tiers. Compatibility with the customer's existing applications, workflows, and user skills will affect the migration timeline available from one vendor compared to another. Migrating to a cloud platform that supports thorough testing and quick rollback can significantly decrease a company's time to market with business innovations, website or application updates, and overall network and application performance optimizations. A vendor's managed services offerings can help fill the gap between the talent existing team members offer and the company's needs. Finally, many vendors are increasingly offering portability options to attract customers.

> The process of investigating and then building relationships with vendors relies on a variety of documents that are somewhat standardized in their purposes and application: RFI (Request for Information), SOW (Statement of Work), and SLA (Service Level Agreement).

> Documents that help to guide project development include a PoC (Proof of Concept) and PoV (Proof of Value). Either of these might include generating a test version of the proposed project. Larger-scale tests that gradually increase in both scope and time investment include a prototype, pilot, and MVP (minimum viable product).

Section 12-3: Financial Aspects of Cloud

> With traditional networks, companies invest large amounts of money at a time into purchasing expensive hardware and software. These are CapEx (capital expenditures) where the benefits are experienced over a long time (more than one year) after the investment is made. Using the pay-as-you-go model, however, most cloud resources are paid for in smaller amounts every month or quarter. These are OpEx (operational expenditures) where benefits are experienced in about the same period as when the expenses are paid for those benefits.

> Cloud services are often categorized according to the type of process being performed. Compute services perform some kind of computing process that receives input and produces output. A cloud resource that assists with moving data from one resource, application, or storage space to another is typically identified as a networking service. Data saved within the cloud, whether as files, objects, databases, or volumes, takes up space. This space is collectively referred to as storage and usually represents a separate expense from other types of services.

> To effectively track cloud expenses, most cloud providers incorporate some kind of resource tagging option when configuring cloud services. A tag is a key-value pair that attaches a customized label to cloud resources. These tags enable chargebacks, which are cost allocations of individual cloud expenses to specific internal accounts or business units.

> Fixed costs are predictable over time and can be budgeted for with a high degree of accuracy. In contrast, variable costs change frequently and unpredictably, possibly with a large range of possible values.

> With an on-demand instance, the customer pays a premium to create the instance when they choose, terminate the instance when they choose, and run it only when they choose. This pricing option offers the most freedom to respond to fluctuating demand on cloud resources. A reserved instance offers lower prices in exchange for a commitment to use the instance over a longer period of time. Buyers can purchase spot instances when the market rate for the desired instance type falls within a set range. The benefit with a spot instance is that customers can get compute time for much lower prices than what they would pay to the cloud provider for an on-demand or a reserved instance. The challenge is that they can only run processes on those instances if those processes can be started and stopped at unpredictable times.

> Strategies used to protect and optimize data are collectively called data management. Part of data management is data replication, or keeping multiple copies of data, to decrease latency and increase data resiliency and application performance.

> An arrangement to obtain a software license per user or per device is called a CAL (client access license). In many cases, high-volume software licensing costs are calculated instead according to the number of CPU sockets in a system or (more recently) according to the number of logical CPU cores used to execute that software. SLM (software license management) can help minimize license expenses by eliminating unneeded licenses and renewing licenses before expiration, thereby avoiding fees or legal fines.

Section 12-4: Continuity and Recovery

> BC (business continuity) refers to a company's ability to weather a failure, crisis, or disaster of some kind while maintaining continuity of operations, especially for critical services to customers and income-generating activities. Business continuity strategies hinge on redundancy, which is the duplication of key resources so one can take over if the other fails. Some forms of redundancy include alternate sites according to the following categories: cold site, warm site, hot site.

> DR (disaster recovery) refers to the strategies and tools that facilitate an organization's recovery from an adverse event. Typically, DR planning is considered a subset of BC planning.

> MTBF (mean time between failures) is the average time a device or system will operate before it fails. MTTR (mean time to repair) is the average time necessary to repair a failure within the network. This time includes the time necessary to isolate the failure, repair or replace the defective component, and bring the system back up to normal operation.

> Some cloud resources are disposable, meaning they can be replaced with another resource if something goes wrong. Other resources in the cloud can't be so easily replaced and must be backed up so they can be recovered if something happens to the first copy. A full backup backs up everything every time a backup is performed. An incremental backup backs up only data that has changed since the last backup of any kind. A differential backup backs up data that has changed since the last full backup.

> The RPO (recovery point objective) shows at what point in the past data was most recently backed up, and so this is the point before which data will be recovered. The RTO (recovery time objective) shows at what point in the future full functionality will be restored (less any lost data). RPOs and RTOs in the cloud have the potential to reach near-zero numbers.

Key Terms

For definitions of key terms, see the Glossary near the end of the book.

application portability	interoperability	prototype
AZ (Availability Zone)	managed service	reserved instance
BC (business continuity)	MSP (managed service provider)	RFI (Request for Information)
CapEx (capital expenditures)	MTBF (mean time between failures)	scope creep
chargeback	MTTR (mean time to repair)	SOP (standard operating procedure)
data management	MVP (minimum viable product)	
data portability	on-demand instance	SOW (Statement of Work)
data replication	OpEx (operational expenditures)	spot instance
disposable resource	pilot	tag
DR (disaster recovery)	POC (point of contact)	variable cost
fixed cost	PoC (Proof of Concept)	vendor lock-in
geo-redundancy	PoV (Proof of Value)	
human capital	professional development	

Review Questions

1. You've requested reports from your network admin that will help your team determine whether to invest more heavily in security improvements or hardware upgrades. Which skillset will most assist the network admin in assembling the requested information?

   a. Project management skills

   b. Basic statistical skills

   c. Interpersonal skills

   d. Training skills

2. Your company has noted a high turnover rate with new hires due to unusual company policies that work well long-term but require a lengthy adjustment period. Which professional development technique would most likely support new employees by helping them adapt more quickly?

   a. Workshop

   b. Conference

   c. Continuing education

   d. Mentoring

3. Which user training technique is most likely offered by a manufacturer at no additional cost to the customer?

   a. Instruction manuals

   b. Hands-on training

   c. Simulations

   d. Instructor-led training

4. Which cloud platform offers native integration with Active Directory?

   a. AWS

   b. Azure

   c. Google

   d. Alibaba

5. Which support plan feature decreases along with the plan's tier?

   a. Covered cloud resources

   b. Monthly cost of the plan

   c. Available methods to contact the support team

   d. Support response time

6. What cloud feature decreases time to market for new innovations?

   a. Custom user training

   b. Redundant resources distributed in different regions

   c. IaC deployment of test environments

   d. SLA-backed data durability

7. Which of the following is NOT directly benefited by open-source standards?

   a. Skill availability

   b. Data portability

   c. Platform interoperability

   d. Application portability

8. Which document directly addresses questions about ROI?

   a. RFQ

   b. SOW

   c. RFP

   d. SLA

9. Which of the following produces the smallest scale application?

   a. Pilot

   b. Prototype

   c. MVP

   d. PoC

10. Which of the following is NOT a component of the iron triangle?

    a. Schedule

    b. Budget

    c. Scope

    d. Service

11. What kind of expense is a monthly mortgage payment?

    a. OpEx

    b. RPO

    c. CapEx

    d. RTO

12. What kind of cloud service is a network file system?

    a. Storage
    b. Security
    c. Compute
    d. Network

13. How can a company distribute cloud costs to multiple departments?

    a. Machine learning
    b. Chargebacks
    c. IP addresses
    d. Showbacks

14. Which instance type is best suited to a workload that increases and decreases at unpredictable times?

    a. Spot instance
    b. Reserved instance
    c. On-demand instance
    d. Cold instance

15. Which replication method ensures the lowest possible RPO?

    a. Asynchronous
    b. Fixed
    c. Variable
    d. Synchronous

16. Which document will identify the full cost to the company caused by a ransomware infection?

    a. RFQ
    b. PoV
    c. BIA
    d. SLA

17. Which site type would provide the fastest recovery?

    a. Cold
    b. Hot
    c. Warm
    d. Ambient

18. Which takes up the most geographical space?

    a. AZ
    b. Hot site
    c. Datacenter
    d. Region

19. Which of these statistics would ideally be zero?

    a. MTBF
    b. RTO
    c. Availability
    d. Reliability

20. Which recovery technique relies on a configured but stopped cloud resource?

    a. Hot
    b. Pilot
    c. Cold
    d. Warm

Hands-On Project 12

Calculating Cloud Costs

Estimated time: 30 minutes

Resources:

> Internet access

> **Context:**

This chapter discussed a few popular ways to optimize cloud expenses, such as purchasing reserved instances in EC2 or efficiently managing data replication options. You also learned that cloud providers offer pricing calculators to help customers estimate and plan for the costs of a cloud deployment. In this project, you'll practice using AWS's Pricing Calculator to determine the monthly and yearly costs of a theoretical cloud infrastructure design. Complete the following steps:

1. In your browser, go to the website **https://calculator.aws/#/** as shown in Figure 12-17. Read through the information on AWS's Pricing Calculator. What are the ways you can share your estimate once it's complete?

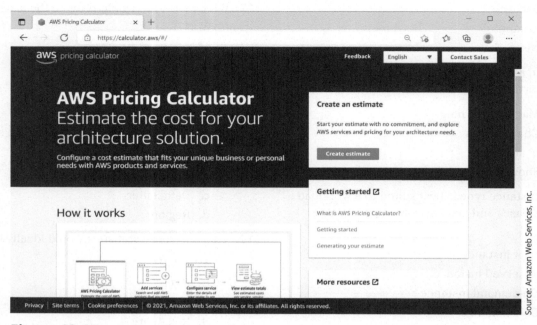

Figure 12-17 AWS Pricing Calculator

2. Suppose you need to determine the monthly costs of a basic web server running in an EC2 instance. To begin designing this estimate, click **Create estimate**.

3. In the search box, enter **EC2**. When the **Amazon EC2** tile appears in the search results, click **Configure** in that tile as shown in Figure 12-18.

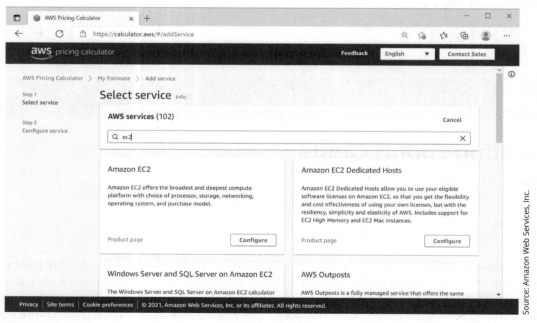

Figure 12-18 Configure each service individually

4. On the next page, you can choose configuration options for your EC2 instance that will host your web server. Give the instance a description, and then make the following selections:

   a. Region: **US East (Ohio)**

   b. **Quick estimate**

   c. Operating system: **Linux**

   d. Instance type: Search for the lowest cost instance type that offers **4** vCPUs and **16** GiB of memory. Which instance type did you choose?

   e. Quantity: **1**

   f. Utilization: **100**

   g. Pricing model: **On-Demand Instances**

   h. Keep the default selections for the Amazon EBS section.

5. What is your monthly price for your web server and its block storage? How much of this cost covers the instance itself (and not the storage)? How much would this server cost you if you pay this rate for three years?

6. Experiment with available pricing strategy options. What is the lowest cost you can find for this instance over a period of three years? What pricing strategy did you use to find this rate?

7. Add this instance to your overall estimate.

8. Most businesses need a lot more resources than a single web server instance. Add the following services to your estimate using default settings except where indicated:

   a. **Amazon RDS for MySQL**: db.m5.xlarge reserved instance for three years paid upfront

   b. **Elastic Load Balancing**: Network Load Balancer processing 20 GB per hour for TCP

   c. **Amazon Virtual Private Cloud (VPC)**: Data Transfer of 1 TB per month both Inbound from Internet and Outbound to Internet

9. What is the total cost of your deployment now?

10. Add a **Business** support plan, as shown in Figure 12-19. What is the total cost of your deployment now?

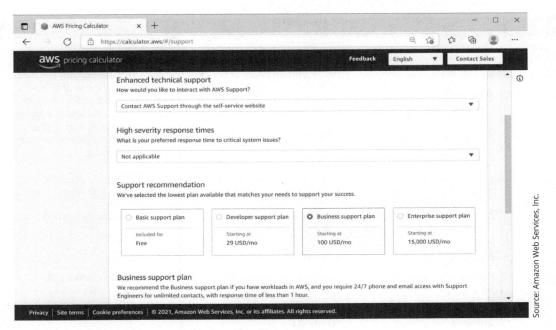

Figure 12-19   Choose the Business support plan

11. Create a shareable link for your estimate. **Take a screenshot** of the link in the Save estimate window; submit this visual with your answers to this project's questions.

12. What is the link to your estimate? Leave your estimate intact (in other words, don't change or clear your estimate) so your instructor can check your configuration if needed.

Reflection Discussion 12

Throughout this course, you've learned how the cloud is now deeply integrated into the way business does IT. While cloud computing offers many benefits and opportunities, there are also legitimate concerns that should be kept in mind as a company designs their cloud infrastructure, whether that's cost optimization, security, connectivity, geo-redundancy, or cloud-native design. Imagine that, in the near future, you're given the task of deciding if and how your company might migrate some of its core infrastructure to the cloud, and then answer the following questions:

> What is a lingering concern you have about the cloud that might affect your decision?

> Find three or four resources that address this issue: one that agrees with your concerns, one that counters your concerns, and one or two additional resources that discuss both sides. Make sure these resources are produced by professionals in the industry. What resources did you find?

> After reading these resources, what do you now know about this issue that you didn't before you started this discussion assignment?

Go to the discussion forum in your school's LMS (learning management system). Write a post of at least 100 words discussing your concerns about cloud computing, what you've learned on this issue, and what you still need to know. Then, respond to two of your classmates' threads with posts of at least 50 words discussing their comments and ideas. Use complete sentences, and check your grammar and spelling. Try to ask open-ended questions that encourage discussion, and remember to respond to people who post on your thread. Use the rubric in Table 12-1 to help you understand what is expected of your work for this assignment.

Table 12-1   Grading rubric for Reflection Discussion 12

Task	Novice	Competent	Proficient	Earned
Initial post	Generalized statements discussing a cloud computing issue **30 points**	Some specific statements with supporting evidence discussing an issue of concern with cloud computing along with some resources addressing this issue **40 points**	Self-reflective discussion with specific and thoughtful statements and supporting evidence discussing an issue of concern with cloud computing, listing three or four resources addressing this concern, and critically discussing valid points on both sides of the issue **50 points**	
Initial post: Mechanics	• Length < 100 words • Several grammar and spelling errors **5 points**	• Length = 100 words • Occasional grammar and spelling errors **7 points**	• Length > 100 words • Appropriate grammar and spelling **10 points**	
Response 1	Brief response showing little engagement or critical thinking **5 points**	Detailed response with specific contributions to the discussion **10 points**	Thoughtful response with specific examples or details and open-ended questions that invite deeper discussion of the topic **15 points**	

Response 2	Brief response showing little engagement or critical thinking **5 points**	Detailed response with specific contributions to the discussion **10 points**	Thoughtful response with specific examples or details and open-ended questions that invite deeper discussion of the topic **15 points**	
Both responses: Mechanics	• Length < 50 words each • Several grammar and spelling errors **5 points**	• Length = 50 words each • Occasional grammar and spelling errors **7 points**	• Length > 50 words each • Appropriate grammar and spelling **10 points**	
			Total	

Solutions to Self-Check Questions

Section 12-1: People Resources

1. CompTIA Cloud Essentials+ is what kind of certification?

Answer: b. Vendor-neutral

Explanation: CompTIA Cloud Essentials+ is a vendor-neutral certification that bridges the gap between technical and business interests in cloud computing.

2. To apply for a promotion, you need to validate that you are keeping up with new industry trends. Which of these professional development options will best help you accomplish this goal?

Answer: c. Certification

Explanation: The pursuit of higher-level certifications ensures you will continually challenge your current abilities and will help you keep up with changes and new technologies.

3. Which technique can ensure a new workstation on the network is properly connected, segmented, and secured?

Answer: a. SOP

Explanation: SOPs (standard operating procedures) define steps for a specific process to maintain consistency and avoid errors.

Section 12-2: Vendor Relations

4. If your company is concerned about vendor lock-in, which of these factors is most relevant to that concern?

Answer: d. Migration costs

Explanation: Vendor lock-in specifically refers to the ominous expense of migrating to a different vendor that often prevents customers from considering any competitors' products later.

5. The development of which document will first establish a POC?

Answer: d. RFI

Explanation: The process of collecting information through an RFI (Request for Information) will first establish a primary POC (point of contact) with the vendor.

6. Which test stage is most likely to use real data?

Answer: b. Pilot

Explanation: While minor issues, such as spelling errors or static graphics, are acceptable for a pilot, the primary features of the product should be reliably functional and ready for extensive user testing, including using actual data.

Section 12-3: Financial Aspects of Cloud

7. What kind of expense is a subscription for a customer support plan?

Answer: a. OpEx

Explanation: OpEx provides benefits that are experienced in about the same period as when the expenses are paid for those benefits, such as a subscription for a service.

8. What resource allows you to identify a server that belongs to the Marketing department?

Answer: c. Tag

Explanation: A tag is a key-value pair that attaches a customized label to cloud resources. These tags can be used to categorize resources according to their purpose, owner, or environment.

9. Which instance type would be best suited to an email server that must be available 24 hours a day, seven days a week?

Answer: d. Reserved instance

Explanation: A reserved instance offers lower prices in exchange for a commitment to use the instance over a longer period of time. An email server is likely to be needed for the long-term and can't tolerate being shut down and restarted.

Section 12-4: Continuity and Recovery

10. Only one person having access to core network passwords is an example of _____.

Answer: b. SPOF

Explanation: Only one person having access to network passwords is an example of an SPOF (single point of failure). Redundancy seeks to eliminate all SPOFs, including the ability to perform certain tasks and access critical network information.

11. A web server that fails often has a low _____.

Answer: c. MTBF

Explanation: MTBF (mean time between failures) is the average time a device or system will operate before it fails. A web server that fails often has a low MTBF.

12. Which backup type generates the largest file?

Answer: d. Full

Explanation: A full backup file would be the largest because it copies all the original data, even old data that hasn't changed in a long time.

CompTIA Cloud Essentials+ CLO-002 Certification Exam Objectives

This text covers material related to all the exam objectives for the CompTIA Cloud Essentials+ exam CLO-002 that CompTIA (the Computing Technology Industry Association) released in 2019. The official list of objectives is available at CompTIA's website, *comptia.org*. For your reference, the following tables list each exam objective and the modules of this course that explain the objective, plus the amount of the exam that will cover each certification domain. Each objective belongs to one of four domains (or main categories) of cloud computing expertise. For example, the task of comparing and contrasting cloud migration approaches belongs to Objective 2.5 in the "Business Principles of Cloud Environments" domain, which altogether accounts for 28 percent of the exam's content.

Domain	Percentage of examination
1.0 Cloud Concepts	24%
2.0 Business Principles of Cloud Environments	28%
3.0 Management and Technical Operations	26%
4.0 Governance, Risk, Compliance, and Security for the Cloud	22%
Total	**100%**

As you read through the exam objectives, pay close attention to the verbs used in each objective, as these words indicate how deeply you should know the content listed. For example, an objective that begins, "Explain the purposes" or "Compare and contrast" expects you to understand the concepts listed, be able to identify those concepts in a scenario, and answer questions about the concepts. However, an objective that begins, "Given a scenario, use" or "Given a scenario, implement" expects you to be able to put those concepts to work.

Domain 1.0 Cloud Concepts—24% of Exam

Cloud Essentials+ Exam Objectives	Section	Bloom's Taxonomy
1.1 Explain cloud principles.	1-3: Common Network Examples	Understand
• Service models	1-5: Cloud Computing	
○ SaaS		
○ IaaS		
○ PaaS		
• Deployment models		
○ Public		
○ Private		
○ Hybrid		
• Characteristics		
○ Elastic		
○ Self-service		
○ Scalability		
○ Broad network access		
○ Pay-as-you-go		
○ Availability		
• Shared responsibility model		
1.2 Identify cloud networking concepts.	6-4: Virtualization	Remember
• Connectivity types	7-2: Locating a Resource on the Internet	
○ Direct connect	7-4: Internet Services	
○ VPN	8-2: Network Security Technologies	
• Common access types	10-2: Enterprise-Grade WAN Services	
○ RDP		
○ SSH		
○ HTTPS		
• Software-defined networking (SDN)		
• Load balancing		
• DNS		
• Firewall		
1.3 Identify cloud storage technologies.	6-1: Network Servers and Software	Remember
• Storage features	6-4: Virtualization	
○ Compression	6-5: Cloud Computing	
○ Deduplication		
○ Capacity on demand		
• Storage characteristics		
○ Performance		
○ Hot vs. cold		

Cloud Essentials+ Exam Objectives	Section	Bloom's Taxonomy

• Storage types
  ○ Object storage
  ○ File storage
  ○ Block storage
• Software-defined storage
• Content delivery network		

1.4 Summarize important aspects of cloud design.
• Redundancy
• High availability
• Disaster recovery
• Recovery objectives
  ○ RPO
  ○ RTO
	1-5: Cloud Computing
	12-4: Continuity and Recovery
		Remember

Domain 2.0 Business Principles of Cloud Environments—28% of Exam

Cloud Essentials+ Exam Objectives	Section	Bloom's Taxonomy

2.1 Given a scenario, use appropriate cloud assessments.
• Current and future requirements
• Baseline
• Feasibility study
• Gap analysis
  ○ Business
  ○ Technical
• Reporting
  ○ Compute
  ○ Network
  ○ Storage
• Benchmarks
• Documentation and diagrams
• Key stakeholders
• Point of contact
	11-2: Analyzing Design
	11-3: Network Monitoring and Management
	11-4: Cloud Deployment and Management
	12-2: Vendor Relations
		Apply

(Continued)

Cloud Essentials+ Exam Objectives	Section	Bloom's Taxonomy

2.2 Summarize the financial aspects of engaging a cloud provider.
 	
• Capital expenditures
• Operating expenditures
• Variable vs. fixed cost
• Licensing model
  ○ BYOL
  ○ Subscription
• Contracts
• Billing
• Request for information
• Human capital
  ○ Training
  ○ Professional development
	6-1: Network Servers and Software
	6-5: Cloud Computing
	12-1: People Resources
	12-2: Vendor Relations
	12-3: Financial Aspects of Cloud
		Remember

2.3 Identify the important business aspects of vendor relations in cloud adoptions.
 	
• Professional services
  ○ Time to market
  ○ Skill availability
  ○ Support
  ○ Managed services
• Statement of work (SOW)
• Service level agreement (SLA)
• Training
• Evaluations
  ○ Pilot
  ○ Proof of value
  ○ Proof of concept
  ○ Success criteria
• Open-source vs. proprietary
	12-2: Vendor Relations	Remember

2.4 Identify the benefits or solutions of utilizing cloud services.
 	
• Identity access management
  ○ Single sign-on
  ○ Multifactor authentication
  ○ Federation
• Cloud-native applications
  ○ Microservices
  ○ Containerization
	1-5: Cloud Computing
	6-5: Cloud Computing
	7-4: Internet Services
	8-4: IAM (Identity and Access Management)
	10-4: Cloud-Supported Technologies
		Remember

Cloud Essentials+ Exam Objectives	Section	Bloom's Taxonomy
• Data analytics		
○ Machine learning		
○ Artificial intelligence		
○ Big Data		
• Digital marketing		
○ Email campaigns		
○ Social media		
• Autonomous environments		
• IoT		
• Blockchain		
• Subscription services		
• Collaboration		
• VDI		
• Self-service		
2.5 Compare and contrast cloud migration approaches.	11-4: Cloud Deployment and Management	Understand
• Rip and replace		
• Lift and shift		
• Hybrid		
• Phased		

Domain 3.0 Management and Technical Operations— 26% of Exam

Cloud Essentials+ Exam Objectives	Section	Bloom's Taxonomy
3.1 Explain aspects of operating within the cloud.	11-3: Network Monitoring and Management	Understand
• Data management	11-4: Cloud Deployment and Management	
○ Replication	12-3: Financial Aspects of Cloud	
○ Locality	12-4: Continuity and Recovery	
○ Backup		
• Availability		
○ Zones		
○ Geo-redundancy		
• Disposable resources		
• Monitoring and visibility		
○ Alerts		
○ Logging		
• Optimization		
○ Auto-scaling		
○ Right-sizing		

(Continued)

Cloud Essentials+ Exam Objectives	Section	Bloom's Taxonomy

3.2 Explain DevOps in cloud environments.
 	
• Provisioning
  ○ Infrastructure as code
  ○ Templates
• Continuous integration/continuous delivery
• Testing in QA environments
  ○ Sandboxing
  ○ Load testing
  ○ Regression testing
• Configuration management
  ○ Orchestration
  ○ Automation
  ○ Upgrades and patching
• API integration
	11-1: Planning for Changes
	11-2: Analyzing Design
	11-4: Cloud Deployment and Management
		Understand

3.3 Given a scenario, review and report on the financial expenditures related to cloud resources.
 	
• Storage
• Network
• Compute
• Chargebacks
  ○ Resource tagging
• Maintenance
• Instances
  ○ Reserved
  ○ Spot
• Licensing type
• Licensing quantity
	12-3: Financial Aspects of Cloud	Apply

Domain 4.0 Governance, Risk, Compliance, and Security for the Cloud—22% of Exam

Cloud Essentials+ exam objectives	Section	Bloom's taxonomy

4.1 Recognize risk management concepts related to cloud services.
 	
• Risk assessment
  ○ Asset inventory
  ○ Classification
  ○ Ownership
	8-1: Network Security Risks
	12-2: Vendor Relations
		Remember

Cloud Essentials+ exam objectives	Section	Bloom's taxonomy

• Risk response
 	
  ○ Mitigation
 	
  ○ Acceptance
 	
  ○ Avoidance
 	
  ○ Transfer
 	
• Documentation
 	
  ○ Findings
 	
  ○ Risk register
 	
• Vendor lock-in
 	
• Data portability		

4.2 Explain policies or procedures. • Standard operating procedures • Change management • Resource management • Security policies ○ Incident response • Access and control policies • Department specific policies • Communication policies	8-1: Network Security Risks 8-4: (IAM) Identity and Access Management 11-1: Planning for Changes 11-3: Network Monitoring and Management 12-1: People Resources	Understand
4.3 Identify the importance and impacts of compliance in the cloud. • Data sovereignty • Regulatory concerns • Industry-based requirements • International standards • Certifications	8-3: Data Security Technologies	Remember

4.4 Explain security concerns, measures, or concepts of cloud operations.
 	
• Threat
 	
• Vulnerability
 	
• Security assessments
 	
  ○ Penetration testing
 	
  ○ Vulnerability scanning
 	
  ○ Application scanning
 	
• Data security
 	
  ○ Categories
 	
    ■ Public
 	
    ■ Private
 	
    ■ Sensitive
	8-1: Network Security Risks
	
	8-2: Network Security Technologies
	
	8-3: Data Security Technologies
	
	8-4: IAM (Identity and Access Management)
		Understand

(Continued)

Cloud Essentials+ exam objectives	Section	Bloom's taxonomy
○ Confidentiality		
• Encryption		
• Sanitization		
○ Integrity		
• Validation		
○ Availability		
• Backup		
• Recovery		
○ Breach		
• Application and infrastructure security		
○ Audit		
○ Access		
○ Authorization		
○ Hardening		

Glossary

1000Base-LX An 802.3 standard, created by IEEE for Ethernet (or CSMA/CD LANs), that incorporates 1000-Mbps baseband (digital) signaling for transmitting data over single-mode or multimode fiber-optic cable that is being used to support longer-distance cabling within a single building.

1000Base-SX An 802.3 standard, created by IEEE for Ethernet (or CSMA/CD LANs), that incorporates 1000-Mbps baseband (digital) signaling for transmitting data over multimode fiber-optic cable that is being used to support relatively close clusters of workstations and other devices.

1000Base-T An 802.3 standard, created by IEEE for Ethernet (or CSMA/CD LANs), that incorporates 1000-Mbps baseband (digital) signaling for transmitting data over Cat 5e or higher twisted pair cable for a maximum segment length of 100 meters.

100Base-FX An 802.3 standard, created by IEEE for Ethernet (or CSMA/CD LANs), that incorporates 100-Mbps baseband (digital) signaling for transmitting data over fiber-optic cable.

100Base-TX An 802.3 standard, created by IEEE for Ethernet (or CSMA/CD LANs), that incorporates 100-Mbps baseband (digital) signaling for transmitting data over two pairs of Cat 5 or higher twisted pair for a maximum segment length of 100 meters.

10Base-T An 802.3 standard, created by IEEE for Ethernet (or CSMA/CD LANs), that incorporates 10-Mbps baseband (digital) signaling for transmitting data over twisted pair for a maximum segment length of 100 meters.

10GBase-T An 802.3 standard, created by IEEE for Ethernet (or CSMA/CD LANs), that incorporates 10-Gbps baseband (digital) signaling for transmitting data over twisted pair.

10-Gbps Ethernet A general term to represent 10-Gbps Ethernet LANs.

2G (2nd generation) Early cellular phone networks.

3DES (triple-DES) A temporary solution for the shortcomings of DES security (which has now been replaced with AES) in which data is encrypted using DES three times; in many cases, the first time by the first key, the second time by a second key, and the third time by the first key again.

3G (3rd generation) Third generation mobile phone service released in the early 2000s that supported up to 384 Kbps.

4B/5B A digital encoding scheme that takes 4 bits of data, converts the 4 bits into a unique 5-bit sequence, and encodes the 5 bits using NRZI.

4G (4th generation) Fourth generation mobile phone service that is characterized by an all-IP network for both data and voice transmission and throughput of 100 Mbps up to 1 Gbps.

5G (5th generation) Fifth generation mobile phone standard requiring minimal throughput of 1 Gbps and maxing out at 20 Gbps download and 10 Gbps upload. Actual speeds vary greatly depending on the bands, cell density, channels, and client volume.

802.11a The IEEE standard for a wireless networking technique that uses multiple frequency bands in the 5-GHz frequency range and provides a theoretical maximum throughput of 54 Mbps.

802.11ac The IEEE standard for a wireless networking technique that exceeds benchmarks set by earlier standards by increasing its useful bandwidth and amplitude. 802.11ac is the first Wi-Fi standard to approach Gigabit Ethernet capabilities.

802.11ax The IEEE standard for a wireless networking technique that operates in both the 2.4-GHz and 5-GHz bands and relies on newer modulation techniques to offer theoretical maximum data rates nearing 10 Gbps with an emphasis on supporting more clients (hundreds or thousands) at shorter distances.

802.11b The IEEE standard for a wireless networking technique that uses DSSS (direct-sequence spread spectrum) signaling in the 2.4-GHz frequency range and provides a theoretical maximum throughput of 11 Mbps.

802.11g The IEEE standard for a wireless networking technique designed to be compatible with 802.11b in the 2.4-GHz frequency range while using different data modulation techniques that allow it to reach a theoretical maximum capacity of 54 Mbps.

802.11n The IEEE standard for a wireless networking technique that may issue signals in the 2.4-GHz or 5-GHz band and can achieve actual data throughput between 65 Mbps and 600 Mbps.

802.1Q The IEEE standard that specifies how VLAN and trunking information appears in frames and how switches and bridges interpret that information.

A

AAA (authentication, authorization, and accounting) A category of protocols that establish a client's identity, authorize a user for certain privileges on a system or network, and keep an account of the client's system or network usage.

access point The interconnecting bridge between a wireless local area network workstation and the wired local area network.

access rights Permissions assigned to a network resource such as a file or device; determine how a user or group of users may access the resource.

accounting In the context of network security, the process of logging users' access and activities on a network.

ACL (access control list) A list of statements used by a router or other device to permit or deny the forwarding of traffic on a network based on one or more criteria.

AD (Active Directory) A hierarchical structure in Windows Server that stores information about all the objects and resources in a network and makes this information available to users, network administrators, and applications.

AD (administrative distance) A number indicating a protocol's reliability, with lower values being given higher priority. This assignment can be changed by a network administrator.

AES (Advanced Encryption Standard) An encryption technique selected by the U.S. government to replace the aging DES (Data Encryption Standard). AES is based on the Rijndael algorithm and uses 128-, 192-, and 256-bit keys.

agent The software that runs in a network element; an element that has an agent is considered a managed element and can react to SNMP commands and requests.

agility The ability to adapt quickly to market demands according to increased or decreased feature use within a system or application.

AI (artificial intelligence) The ability of computers to adapt to changing circumstances.

alert A message generated when a pre-defined event occurs, which is then logged by the system.

ALM (application lifecycle management) The oversight of an application through its development, maintenance, and retirement.

amplification The gain of the signal strength (power) of an analog signal.

amplitude The height of the wave above or below a given reference point.

analog data Data that is represented by continuous waveforms, which can be at an infinite number of points between some given minimum and maximum.

analog signal Signal that is represented by continuous waveforms, which can be at an infinite number of points between some given minimum and maximum.

analytical modeling The creation of mathematical equations to calculate various network values during network analysis.

API (application programming interface) An access point into a software's available processes through which a specific type of request generates a particular kind of response.

application layer The topmost layer in the OSI model and TCP/IP protocol suite, which provides direct support to applications.

application layer firewall A firewall that accepts or denies access to a network based upon data contained within the application layer of messages.

application portability The ability to move applications from one cloud platform to another without requiring significant refactoring to do so.

arithmetic checksum An error-detection technique in which the ASCII values of the characters to be transmitted are summed and included at the end of the message.

ARP (Address Resolution Protocol) A core protocol in the TCP/IP suite that functions in the data link layer of the OSI model. ARP works in conjunction with IPv4 to discover the MAC address of a node on the local network and to maintain a database that maps local IP addresses to MAC addresses.

ASCII (American Standard Code for Information Interchange) A 7-bit code that is used to represent all the printable characters on a keyboard plus many non-printable control characters.

ASK (amplitude shift keying) A modulation technique for encoding digital data using various amplitude levels of an analog signal.

asymmetric connection A connection in which data flows in one direction at a faster transmission rate than the data flowing in the opposite direction. For example, there are numerous systems that have a faster downstream connection (such as from the Internet) and a slower upstream connection.

asymmetric encryption An encryption technique in which two keys are used: one to encrypt and one to decrypt; often known as public key cryptography.

attenuation The continuous loss of strength (power) that a signal experiences as it travels through a medium.

authentication The process of comparing and matching a client's credentials with the credentials in a client database to enable the client to log on to the network.

authorization The process that determines what a user can and cannot do with network resources.

automation The use of technology to perform a process or procedure with minimal human intervention.

auto-scaling The ability of a virtual resource to automatically increase or decrease in capacity as demand on the resource changes.

availability A measure of how consistently and reliably a file, device, connection, or other resource can be accessed by authorized personnel.

AZ (Availability Zone) A collection of physical datacenters within a region.

B

backbone The central conduit of a network that connects network segments and significant shared devices (such as routers, switches, and servers) and is sometimes referred to as a "network of networks."

backplane The main hardware of a device (such as a LAN switch) into which all supporting printed circuit boards connect.

bandwidth The absolute value of the difference between the lowest and highest frequencies.

baseline A record of how a network or resource operates under normal conditions.

baud rate The number of signal element or signal level changes per second.

BC (business continuity) A company's ability to weather a failure, crisis, or disaster of some kind while maintaining continuity of operations, especially for critical services to customers and income-generating activities.

benchmarking The generation of system statistics under a controlled environment and then comparing those statistics against known measurements.

best path The most efficient route from one network to another, as calculated by a router.

BGP (Border Gateway Protocol) Dubbed the "routing protocol of the Internet," this path vector routing protocol is currently the only routing protocol used on the open Internet. It's capable of considering many factors in its routing metrics.

big data Large-volume data sets.

biometrics Security techniques that use parts of the body, such as fingerprints or iris prints, for verification.

block storage Consistently sized storage spaces within a SAN that each hold up to a certain amount of data; a block's location in the SAN is referenced by a LUN (logical unit number).

blockchain A distributed ledger technology where each new block of transactional data incorporates a hash of the previous block so that earlier blocks can't be changed without breaking the chain of blocks.

blue-green deployment A pair of environments where one environment is active while the other waits on standby or receives updates.

Bluetooth A low-power wireless technology that provides close-range communication between devices such as computers, smartphones, tablets, and peripheral devices.

bps (bits per second) The number of bits that are transmitted across a medium in a given second.

breach Unauthorized access or use of sensitive data.

broad network access The ability to connect to cloud-hosted resources from anywhere on the Internet using a variety of device types.

broadband Internet A WAN technology where the network media and available bandwidth are shared between multiple customers.

broadcast domain Logically grouped network nodes that can communicate directly via broadcast transmissions. By default, switches and repeating devices, such as hubs, extend broadcast domains.

BSS (Basic Service Set) The transmission area surrounding a single access point in a wireless local area network; it resembles a cell in a cellular network.

bus topology A topology in which a single cable connects all nodes on a network without intervening connectivity devices.

BYOD (bring your own device) The practice of allowing people to bring their personally owned smartphones, laptops, or other technology into a facility for the purpose of performing work or school responsibilities.

BYOL (bring your own license) A policy that allows cloud customers to implement their existing software licenses on cloud resources.

C

CA (certificate authority) An organization or software on a network that issues and maintains digital certificates as part of the PKI (public-key infrastructure).

cable modem A communication device that allows high-speed access to WANs, such as the Internet, via a cable television connection.

caching The process of storing copies of data in locations closer to where the data is used.

CAN (campus area network) A network that spans the area of a campus, such as one or more adjacent buildings on an academic campus or a business campus.

capacity planning A time-consuming operation in the process of computer network development that involves trying to determine the amount of network bandwidth necessary to support an application or a set of applications.

CapEx (capital expenditures) Costs whose benefits are experienced over a long period of time after the investment is made.

CASB (cloud access security broker) A security appliance, either physical or virtual and hosted on-prem or in the cloud, that is designed to detect applications and other resources running within a domain and monitor those resources according to policies set by the organization.

Cat 5 (Category 5) A form of UTP that contains four wire pairs and supports up to 100-Mbps

throughput and a 100-MHz signal rate. Required minimum standard for Fast Ethernet.

Cat 5e (Enhanced Category 5) A higher-grade version of Cat-5 wiring that supports a signaling rate of up to 350 MHz and a maximum throughput of 1 Gbps, making it the required minimum standard for Gigabit Ethernet.

Cat 6 (Category 6) A twisted-pair cable that contains four wire pairs, each wrapped in foil insulation. Additional foil insulation can cover the bundle of wire pairs, and a fire-resistant plastic sheath might cover the second foil layer. The foil insulation provides excellent resistance to crosstalk and enables Cat 6 to support a signaling rate of 250 MHz and throughput up to 10 Gbps.

Cat 6a (Augmented Category 6) A higher-grade version of Cat 6 wiring that further reduces attenuation and crosstalk, and allows for potentially exceeding traditional network segment length limits.

Cat 7 (Category 7) A twisted-pair cable that contains multiple wire pairs, each separately shielded then surrounded by another layer of shielding within the jacket.

Cat 7a (Augmented Category 7) A higher-grade version of Cat 7 wiring with a 1 GHz bandwidth.

Cat 8 (Category 8) A twisted-pair cable that includes heavy shielding, high bandwidth, and increased throughput that rivals fiber-optic cable at short distances while providing the option to use backwards-compatible connectors.

CDM (code division multiplexing) A multiplexing technique in which binary 1s and 0s are replaced with larger, unique binary sequences to allow multiple users to share a common set of frequencies. Based on spread spectrum technology.

CDN (content delivery network) A distributed storage structure that allows customers to store files in locations closer to where their users are located.

CE (Carrier Ethernet) An adaptation to the Ethernet standard that makes Ethernet capable of traversing WAN and MAN connections.

certificate An electronic document, similar to a passport, that establishes a resource's credentials for the purpose of performing transactions online.

change management Carefully defined processes to evaluate the need for a change, the cost of the change, a plan for making the change with minimal disruption, and a backup plan if the change doesn't work as expected.

channel A path or connection typically supporting one user.

character set A list of all textual characters or symbols and their corresponding binary patterns for a particular character encoding scheme, such as ASCII or Unicode.

chargeback A cost allocation of an individual cloud expense to a specific internal account or business unit.

CIA (confidentiality, integrity, and availability) triad A three-tenet, standard security model describing the primary ways that encryption protects data. Confidentiality ensures that data can only be viewed by its intended recipient or at its intended destination. Integrity ensures that data was not modified after the sender transmitted it and before the receiver picked it up. Availability ensures that data is available to and accessible by the intended recipient when needed.

CIDR (Classless Interdomain Routing) notation A shorthand method for identifying network and host bits in an IP address.

ciphertext Data after an encryption algorithm has been applied.

client/server system A distributed computing system consisting of a server and one or more clients that request information from the server.

cloud The network substructure of nodes (routers and switches) and high-speed links.

cloud computing The flexible provision of virtualized data storage, applications, or services to clients across a network from a software-defined environment.

coaxial cable A type of cable that consists of a central metal conducting core, surrounded by an insulator, shielding, and an outer cover. Today coaxial cable, called "coax" for short, is used to connect cable Internet and cable TV systems.

codec A device that accepts analog data and converts it into digital signals. This process is known as digitization.

collision The result of signals from two or more devices colliding on a network medium.

collision domain The portion of an Ethernet network in which collisions could occur if two nodes transmit data at the same time. Today, switches and routers separate collision domains.

colocation facility A datacenter facility that is shared by a variety of providers. Also called a carrier hotel.

compression The process of manipulating data such that it fits into a more compact physical space in storage or along a connection.

computer network An interconnection of computers and computing equipment that uses either wires or radio waves over small or large geographic areas.

computer simulation A software program used to simulate an often-complex operation, such as simulating a nuclear explosion, or the addition of an additional runway at an airport.

computer terminal A relatively non intelligent device that allows a user to input data into a system or displays data from the system.

connectivity map A series of figures used for modeling computer networks; types include wide area connectivity maps, metropolitan area connectivity maps, and local area overview and detailed connectivity maps.

container A lightweight, self-contained environment that provides the services needed to run an application in nearly any OS environment.

containerization The application development process that breaks an application into microservices to run in separate containers.

contention-based protocol A first-come, first-served protocol—the first device to recognize that no one is transmitting data is the first device to transmit.

continuous delivery The practice of deploying changes in small increments on a short time schedule, such as every 24 hours, rather than being delayed for larger, less frequent updates.

continuous integration The practice of continuously merging all code changes from all developers working on a project.

control plane The process of decision making, such as routing, blocking, and forwarding, that is performed by protocols.

corporate license An agreement that allows an application to be installed anywhere within a corporation, even if the installation involves multiple sites.

CRC (cyclic redundancy check) An error detection technique that typically adds between 8 and 32 check bits to potentially large data packets and approaches 100 percent error detection.

crosstalk A type of interference caused by signals traveling on nearby wire pairs infringing on another pair's signal.

cryptography The study of creating and using encryption and decryption techniques.

CSMA/CA (carrier sense multiple access with collision avoidance) A contention-based medium access control protocol for wireless networks in which wireless workstations can only transmit at designated times, in an attempt to avoid collisions.

CSMA/CD (carrier sense multiple access with collision detection) A contention-based medium access control protocol for bus and star-wired bus LANs in which a workstation wanting to transmit can only do so if the medium is idle; otherwise, it must wait. Signal collisions are detected by transmitting workstations, which then back off and retransmit.

CSP (cloud service provider) A business that offers one or more cloud services to other businesses or individuals.

CWDM (coarse wavelength division multiplexing) A less expensive form of wavelength division multiplexing that involves the transfer of a small number of streams of data over a single optical fiber using multiple lasers emitting light of differing wavelengths.

D

daisy-chaining The technique of plugging one peripheral into another, rather than running a separate line from each peripheral to the computer.

DAS (direct attached storage) Storage that is directly attached to the computer or server that uses it.

data Entities that convey meaning within a computer or computer system.

data analytics The study of raw data to detect patterns, anomalies, and insights.

data communication The transfer of digital or analog data using digital or analog signals.

data link layer The second lowest layer of the OSI model and of the TCP/IP protocol suite in a 5-layer model or the lowest layer in a 4-layer model; it defines the frame that incorporates flow and error control and, when combined with the physical layer to make the lowest layer, also defines the physical medium that transmits the signal. In the TCP/IP suite, it's also called network access layer or link layer.

data management Strategies used to protect and optimize data.

data plane An SDN (software-defined networking) construct made up of physical or virtual devices that receive and send network messages. Also called infrastructure plane.

data portability The ability to export data from one service and import it to a different vendor's service.

data rate The speed at which data is transmitted between two devices; often referred to in bits per second (bps).

data replication The technique of keeping multiple copies of data to decrease latency and increase data resiliency and application performance.

data sovereignty The right of a country to impose privacy and security laws on data collected, processed, or stored within its borders.

dB (decibel) A relative measure of signal loss or gain that is used to measure the strength of a signal.

DDoS (distributed denial-of-service) attack An attack in which multiple hosts simultaneously flood a target host with traffic, rendering the target unable to function.

de facto standard A standard that has not been approved by a standards-making organization, but has become a standard through widespread use.

deduplication A process that eliminates multiple copies of data in a storage system.

defense in depth Layers of security implemented to protect a network from multiple attack vectors.

delta modulation A method of converting analog data to a digital signal in which the incoming analog signal is tracked and a binary 1 or 0 is transmitted, respectively, when the analog signal rises or falls.

demultiplexor A multiplexor that un-multiplexes the data stream and delivers the individual streams to the appropriate devices. Also called a demux.

DES (Data Encryption Standard) An older, now insecure encryption method that subjects each 64-bit block of data to 16 levels, or rounds, of encryption.

device hardening Preventive measures that can be taken to secure a device from network- or software-supported attacks.

DevOps (development and operations) A cultural shift toward continuous collaboration between development teams and operations teams that brings highly responsive application updates.

DHCP (Dynamic Host Configuration Protocol) A network protocol that dynamically assigns IP addresses to devices as they request a connection to the network.

differential Manchester code A digital encoding scheme that transmits a binary 0 when there is a voltage change at the beginning of the bit frame, and transmits a binary 1 when there is no voltage change at the beginning of the bit frame. This technique ensures that there is always a voltage transition in the middle of the bit frame.

digital data Entity that is represented by discrete waveforms, rather than continuous waveforms. Between a minimum value X and a maximum value Y, the discrete waveform takes on only a finite number of values.

digital marketing The use of electronic devices or the Internet to reach current and potential customers. Also called online marketing.

digital signal The electric or electromagnetic encoding of data that is represented by discrete waveforms rather than continuous waveforms. Between a minimum value X and a maximum value Y, the discrete waveform takes on only a finite number of values.

digital signature A technology that uses public key cryptography to assign to a document a code for which only the creator of the document has the key.

digitization The process of converting an analog signal or data into digital data.

Dijkstra's least-cost algorithm A procedure that determines the least-cost path from one node in a network to all other network nodes.

disk mirroring A RAID technique in which multiple copies of data are stored on two or more drives simultaneously to provide data redundancy.

disposable resource A cloud resource that can be replaced with another, duplicate resource if something goes wrong rather than needing to repair the resource.

distance vector protocol The simplest type of routing protocols; used to determine the best route for data based on the distance to a destination.

DNS (Domain Name System) A large, distributed database of Internet addresses and domain names.

domain name The second part of a URL, such as www.mycompany.com. Usually, a domain name is associated with the company's name and its type of organization, such as a school or nonprofit organization.

DoS (denial-of-service) attack An attack in which a legitimate user is unable to access normal network resources because of an attacker's intervention.

DR (disaster recovery) Strategies and tools designed to facilitate an organization's recovery from an adverse incident.

DSL (digital subscriber line) A technology that allows existing twisted pair telephone lines to transmit multimedia materials and high-speed data.

DSSS (direct sequence spread spectrum) A modulation technique that, like other spread-spectrum technologies, distributes lower-level signals over several frequencies simultaneously.

durability A resource's ongoing existence.

DWDM (dense wavelength division multiplexing) An expensive form of wavelength division multiplexing that involves the transfer of a large number of data streams over a single optical fiber using multiple lasers emitting light of differing wavelengths.

dynamic routing An adaptive routing technique in which routing tables react to network fluctuations when calculating the best path between networks.

E

echo The reflective feedback of a transmitted signal as the signal moves through a medium.

edge computing The placement of computing devices at or near the location of their use.

effective bandwidth The bandwidth of a signal after noise and other factors such as environmental conditions have been applied.

EIGRP (Enhanced Interior Gateway Routing Protocol) An advanced distance vector routing protocol developed by Cisco that combines some of the features of a link state routing protocol and so is sometimes referred to as a hybrid protocol.

elasticity A cloud resource's ability to scale up or down automatically without requiring human intervention.

electrical component One of the four components of an interface's design; deals with voltages, line capacitance, and other electrical characteristics.

EMI (electromagnetic interference) A type of interference that can be caused by motors, power lines, televisions, copiers, fluorescent lights, or other sources of electrical activity.

encapsulation The process by which control information is added to a data packet as it moves through the layers of the communications architecture.

encryption algorithm A computer program that converts plaintext into an enciphered form.

enterprise network One or more local area networks managed by an organization such as a school or business.

error control The process of detecting an error and then taking some type of corrective action. The three options for response include: drop the message (do nothing), return a message, and correct the error.

ESS (Extended Service Set) In a wireless LAN topology, the collection of all the Basic Service Sets attached to the local area network through its access points.

Ethernet The first commercially available LAN system (and currently the most popular). Almost identical in operation to CSMA/CD.

extranet An intranet extended outside the corporate walls and made available to suppliers, customers, or other external agents.

F

failover The process of a network reconfiguring itself if a network failure is detected.

Fast Ethernet The group of 100-Mbps Ethernet standards designated by the IEEE 802.3u protocol.

FDM (frequency division multiplexing) The oldest and one of the simplest multiplexing techniques, FDM involves assigning non-overlapping frequency ranges to different signals or to each user of a medium.

feasibility study An analysis of all relevant factors to determine the practicality of proposed changes.

FEC (forward error correction) The process that enables a receiver, upon detecting an error in the arriving data, to correct the error without further information from the transmitter.

FHSS (frequency hopping spread spectrum) A wireless signaling technique in which a signal jumps between several frequencies within a band in a synchronization pattern known to the channel's receiver and transmitter.

fiber Internet A connection to the Internet that relies on fiber cable close to or all the way to the customer's location.

fiber-optic cable A form of cable that contains one or more glass or plastic fibers in its core. Data is transmitted via a pulsing light sent from a laser or LED (light-emitting diode) through the central fiber or fibers.

file system A hierarchical structure to organize files into folders, which can also be nested inside other folders.

FIM (federated identity management) The use of a single identity store by multiple companies for their various authentication processes.

FIM (file integrity monitoring) A security technique that alerts the system of any changes made to files that shouldn't change, such as operating system files.

financial feasibility The characteristic of a project that it can be completed as set forth within the budgetary constraints set by the company.

firewall A device (either a router, a dedicated device, or a computer running special software) that selectively filters or blocks traffic between networks.

fixed cost An expense that is predictable over time and can be budgeted for with a degree of accuracy.

frame A cohesive unit of raw data. The frame is the package of data created at the data link layer of the OSI model or the network access layer of the TCP/IP protocol suite.

frequency The number of times a signal makes a complete cycle within a given time frame.

FSK (frequency shift keying) A modulation technique for encoding digital data using various frequencies of an analog signal.

FTP (File Transfer Protocol) One of the first services offered on the Internet, FTP's primary functions are to allow a user to download a file from a remote site to a local computer, and to upload a file from a local computer to a remote site.

full-duplex connection A connection between two devices in which data can be transmitted in both directions at the same time.

functional component One of the four components of an interface's design; defines the function of each pin or circuit that is used in a particular interface.

FWaaS (Firewall as a Service) A cloud-based firewall with advanced, application-layer firewall capabilities that are provided at the point of service and can be scaled as needed.

G

gap analysis A study used to compare current conditions with desired conditions and identify how to close that gap.

Gaussian noise A relatively constant type of noise, much like the static when a radio is tuned between two stations. Also called white noise.

generator polynomial An industry-approved bit string that is used to create the CRC remainder.

geo-redundancy The distribution of redundant components in various geographical regions.

Gigabit Ethernet An Ethernet specification for transmitting data at 1 billion bits per second.

gigabit Internet An Internet connection that supports up to 1 Gbps throughput.

GPL (General Public License) A software license that allows the creator to distribute the software for free; recipients may alter the software as they wish, but must still give the altered software away for free.

GPS (global positioning system) A system of satellites that can locate a user's position on Earth to within several meters.

GSM (Global System for Mobile Communications) A second-generation mobile telephone technology that is based on a form of time division multiplexing.

guard band A set of unused frequencies between two channels on a frequency division multiplexed system.

H

H.323 An older VoIP standard that is complex and time-consuming to set up and manage, and is slowly being replaced by SIP (Session Initiation Protocol).

HA (high availability) The precise percentage of time during which a system, resource, or network functions reliably.

half-duplex connection A connection between two devices in which data can be transmitted in only one direction at a time.

Hamming code A code that incorporates redundant bits so if an error occurs during transmission, then the receiver may be able to correct the error.

Hamming distance The smallest number of bits by which character codes (in a character set such as ASCII) differ.

hashing The transformation of data through an algorithm that is mathematically irreversible and generally reduces the amount of space needed for the data. Hashing is mostly used to ensure data integrity—that is, to verify the data has not been altered.

header The bits at the beginning of a packet where protocols add control information.

HFC (hybrid fiber coaxial) A physical infrastructure where fiber-optic cabling connects the cable company's distribution center to distribution hubs and then to optical nodes near customers; either fiber-optic or coaxial cable then connects a node to each customer's business or residence.

host ID The portion of an IP address that identifies the host on a network.

hot pluggable A component that can be installed or removed without disrupting operations. Also called hot swappable.

hot swappable The ability to remove a component from a device without turning off the power to the device.

HTML (Hypertext Markup Language) A set of codes inserted into a document (web page) that is used by a web browser to determine how the document is displayed.

HTTP (Hypertext Transfer Protocol) An Internet protocol that allows web browsers and servers to send and receive web pages.

HTTPS (Hypertext Transfer Protocol Secure) An extension to HTTP that requires data be exchanged between client and server using SSL or TLS encryption.

hub An outdated connectivity device that connects two or more workstations in a star-wired bus topology and broadcasts incoming data onto all outgoing connections.

human capital Employees that are considered to be resources for the company.

hybrid cloud A deployment model in which both private and public clouds or both cloud-based and on-prem services are used simultaneously.

hybrid routing protocol A routing protocol that exhibits characteristics of both distance vector and link state routing protocols.

hypervisor The element of virtualization software that manages multiple guest machines and their connections to the host (and by association, to a physical network).

I

IaaS (Infrastructure-as-a-Service) A cloud service that allows consumers to deploy a cloud-based network with services such as operating systems, applications, storage, and virtual devices.

IaC (infrastructure as code) The provisioning and management of IT infrastructure through computer-readable configuration files that can be automated rather than interactive tools that require manual configuration.

IAM (identity and access management) A framework of techniques and tools for managing the identities of people and applications that allow for access to cloud resources.

ICMP (Internet Control Message Protocol) A core protocol in the TCP/IP suite that notifies the sender when something has gone wrong in the transmission process and packets were not delivered.

IDS (intrusion detection system) A stand-alone device, an application, or a built-in feature running on a workstation, server, switch, router, or firewall. It monitors network traffic, generating alerts about suspicious activity.

IEEE (Institute of Electrical and Electronics Engineers) An organization that creates protocols and standards for computer systems—in particular, local area networks.

IFS (interframe space) The time in which a workstation waits before transmitting on a wireless LAN. There are typically three different IFSs, depending upon the function to be performed.

IMAP4 (Internet Message Access Protocol version 4) A mail retrieval protocol that allows users to store messages on the mail server while reading, responding to, and organizing the messages. The most current version of IMAP is version 4 (IMAP4).

impulse noise A nonconstant noise that is one of the most difficult errors to detect because it can occur randomly.

incident response plan A document specifically defining the characteristics of an event that qualifies as a formal incident and the steps that should be followed as a result.

insertion loss A measure of attenuation, or loss of the signal strength between two points before and after an inserted connector or other passive network component on a fiber-optic cable connection.

interactive user license An agreement in which the number of concurrent active users of a particular software package is strictly controlled.

interfacing The process of creating an interconnection between a peripheral device and a computer, between a computer and a network, or between two network devices such as routers or switches.

interoperability The ability of a cloud system to successfully interact with other systems.

intranet A TCP/IP network inside a company that allows employees to access the company's information resources through an Internet-like interface.

IoT (Internet of Things) Devices connected to the Internet that normally wouldn't be expected to do so along with networking devices that allow for remote or voice activated control.

IP (Internet Protocol) The software that prepares a packet of data so that it can move from one network to another on the Internet or within a set of networks in a corporation.

IPS (intrusion prevention system) A stand-alone device, an application, or a built-in feature running on a workstation, server, switch, router, or firewall that stands in-line between an attacker and the targeted network or host and can prevent traffic from reaching that network or host.

IPsec (IP Security) A layer 3 protocol that defines encryption, authentication, and key management for TCP/IP transmissions.

IPv6 (Internet Protocol version 6) A standard for IP addressing that is gradually replacing the current IPv4. Most notably, IPv6 uses a newer, more efficient header in its packets and allows for 128-bit source and destination IP addresses, which are usually written as eight blocks of hexadecimal numbers, such as 2001:0DB8:0B80:00 00:0000:00D3:9C5A:00CC.

IR (infrared) A wireless technology that uses a bandwidth just below the spectrum that is visible to the human eye, with longer wavelengths than red light.

IS-IS (Intermediate System to Intermediate System) A link state routing protocol that uses a best-path algorithm. IS-IS was originally codified by ISO, which referred to routers as "intermediate systems," thus the protocol's name.

ISO (International Organization for Standardization) An organization that creates protocols and standards for a wide variety of systems and functions.

J

jabber   A NIC (network interface card) that is transmitting continuously but not sending valid data.

jitter   A kind of noise that can result from small timing irregularities during the transmission of digital signals and can become magnified as the signals are passed from one device to another.

JPEG (Joint Photographic Experts Group)   A technique commonly used to compress images.

K

key   The unique piece of information that is used to create ciphertext and then decrypt the ciphertext back into plaintext.

key stakeholder   A person who holds decision making power for a project, whose work will be significantly affected by the changes implemented by the project, or who will be responsible for helping to implement changes for the project.

KPI (key performance indicator)   A specific performance factor measured to indicate the efficiency and functioning of a system.

L

LAN (local area network)   A communication network that interconnects a variety of data communicating devices within a small geographic area and broadcasts data at high data transfer rates with very low error rates.

latency   The delay between the transmission of a signal and its receipt.

Lempel-Ziv technique   A compression technique that offers lossless compression by creating a dictionary of character strings and associated codes. Also called LZ77, this technique forms the basis of many modern compression algorithms.

licensing agreement   A legal contract that describes a number of conditions that must be upheld for proper use of a software package.

licensing model   The legal structure of a software license that defines certain aspects of the agreement, including where the software can be installed, who can use it, and when payments are made.

Lightning   An interface standard (power and data) that uses an 8-pin, reversible connector on some Apple devices.

linear projection   A capacity planning technique that involves predicting one or more network capacities based on the current network parameters and multiplying by some constant.

link aggregation   The ability to combine multiple connections between two devices within a LAN to increase data transfer rates.

link state protocol   A type of routing protocol that enables routers to share performance and status information about their connected links with routers throughout the network, after which each router can independently map the network and determine the best path between itself and a message's destination node.

LLC (logical link control) sublayer   A sublayer of the data link layer of the OSI model that identifies the message type and might provide error control and flow control information.

load balancer   A device that distributes traffic intelligently among multiple devices or connections.

load testing   A testing process that places the full force of anticipated demand on a system to determine if it can handle the load.

local area detailed connectivity map   A simple drawing which outlines the workstation, server, router, and cable placement for a local area network. Used during the network design phase.

local area overview connectivity map   A simple drawing which outlines the locations and/or departments included in a local area network. Used during the network design phase.

log   A record of activities or state changes on a device or in an operating system.

logical connection   A nonphysical connection between sender and receiver that allows an exchange of commands and responses.

logical topology   A map showing how data moves around a network from device to device, including how access to the network is controlled and how specific resources are shared on the network. A network's logical topology may differ from its physical topology.

longitudinal parity   This type of parity check tries to solve the main weakness of simple parity, in which all even numbers of errors are not detected; sometimes called longitudinal redundancy check, horizontal parity, or two-dimensional parity.

lossless compression   A compression technique in which data is compressed and then decompressed such that the original data is returned—that is, no data is lost due to compression.

lossy compression   A compression technique in which data is compressed and then decompressed, but this process does not return the original data—that is, some data is lost due to compression.

LTE (Long-Term Evolution)   A transitional cellular network technology between 3G and 4G that takes advantage of some improved 4G technologies to exceed 3G speeds, but it does not reach 4G throughput requirements.

M

MAC (medium access control) address   A 48- or 64-bit network interface identifier that includes two parts: the OUI, assigned by IEEE to the manufacturer, and the extension identifier, a unique number assigned to each NIC by the manufacturer.

MAC (medium access control) sublayer   A sublayer of the data link layer of the OSI model that identifies the destination and source MAC addresses as well as the checksum in the frame's trailer.

MAC address table   A table of MAC addresses that shows which device is connected to each of a switch's ports.

malware   A program or piece of code designed to intrude upon or harm a system or its resources.

MAN (metropolitan area network)   A network that serves an area of 3 to 30 miles—approximately the area of a typical city.

managed service   The outsourcing of the responsibility of caring for a resource.

managed switch   A switch that can be configured via a command-line interface or a web-based management GUI, and sometimes can be configured in groups.

Manchester code   A digital encoding scheme that ensures each bit has a signal change in the middle of the bit and thus solves the synchronization problem.

mechanical component   One of the four components of an interface's design; deals with items such as the connector or plug description.

medium access control protocol   A protocol that allows a device (such as a workstation) to gain access to the medium (the transmission system) of a LAN.

Metro Ethernet   A data transfer service that can interconnect two businesses at any distance using standard Ethernet protocols.

metropolitan area connectivity map   A simple drawing which outlines the locations and/or departments included in a metropolitan area network. Used during the network design phase.

MFA (multifactor authentication)   An authentication process that requires information from two or more categories of authentication factors.

MIB (Management Information Base)   The database that holds the information about each managed device in a network that supports SNMP.

microservice   A component of an application that can be run in a separate cloud resource than other application components.

MIME (Multipurpose Internet Mail Extensions)   The protocol used to attach a document, such as a word processor file or spreadsheet, to an email message or to send non-ASCII characters in an email.

MIMO (multiple input multiple output)   A technology used in wireless LANs in which sending and receiving devices have multiple antennas and transmit data over multiple streams in an effort to send data faster with fewer errors.

ML (machine learning)   The ability of computers to learn from data analysis rather than from explicit programming.

modulation   The process of converting digital data into an analog signal.

MON (metropolitan optical network)   A dense, localized grid of junctions and fiber cables designed to make direct fiber connections available to as many customers as possible.

monoalphabetic substitution-based cipher   A fairly simple encryption technique that replaces a character or group of characters with a different character or group of characters.

MP3 (MPEG [Moving Picture Experts Group] Audio Layer-3)   A compression/encoding technique that allows a high-quality audio sample to be reduced to a much smaller sized file.

MPEG (Moving Pictures Expert Group)   A technique used to compress motion picture images or moving video; MPEG is often an abbreviation for versions such as MPEG-1 and MPEG-2.

MPLS (Multiprotocol Label Switching)   A technique that enables a router to switch data from one path onto another path.

MSP (managed service provider)   A company that takes over the responsibility of caring for a resource owned and used by someone else.

MTBF (mean time between failures) The average time a device or system will operate before it fails.

MTTR (mean time to repair) The average time necessary to repair a failure within a network.

multimode transmission A fiber-optic transmission technique that sends a broadly focused stream of light through thick (62.5/125) fiber-optic cable.

multiple access The application of multiplexing in the support of many users at one time.

multiplexing Technology that allows transmitting multiple signals on one medium at essentially the same time.

multiplexor The device that combines (multiplexes) multiple input signals for transmission over a single medium and then demultiplexes the composite signal back into multiple signals. Also called a mux.

MU-MIMO (multi-user MIMO) An improvement to older MIMO (multiple-input, multiple-output) technology that allows access points to issue multiple signals to different stations at the same time, thereby reducing congestion and contributing to faster data transmission.

MVP (minimum viable product) A stable, functioning product that incorporates core functionality and is built with the intention of expanding functionality before releasing to full production.

N

NAS (network attached storage) A specialized storage device or group of storage devices that provides centralized, fault-tolerant file system storage and relies on network infrastructure to provide file access.

NAT (Network Address Translation) A network protocol that allows all clients on a LAN to assume the identity of one public IP address.

NetFlow A proprietary traffic monitoring protocol from Cisco that tracks all IP traffic crossing any interface where NetFlow is enabled.

network architecture A template that outlines the layers of hardware and software operations for a computer network and its applications.

network ID The portion of an IP address common to all nodes on the same network or subnet.

network layer A layer in the OSI model and TCP/IP protocol suite that is responsible for creating, maintaining, and ending network connections. Often referred to as "layer 3."

network management The design, installation, and support of a network and its hardware and software.

network monitor A tool that continually monitors network traffic and might receive data from monitored devices that are configured to report their statistics.

NFC (near-field communication) A short-range wireless technology that transfers data (often automatically) between near or touching devices.

NFV (network functions virtualization) A network architecture that merges physical and virtual network devices.

NIC (network interface card) An electronic device, typically in the form of a computer circuit board, that performs the necessary signal conversions and protocol operations so that a workstation or other networked device can send and receive data on a network.

node Any computer or other device on a network that can be addressed on the network.

noise Unwanted electrical or electromagnetic energy that degrades the quality of signals and data.

NOS (network operating system) A large, complex program that can manage all the resources that are commonly found on most LANs, in addition to performing the standard functions of an OS.

NRZI (nonreturn to zero inverted) A digital encoding scheme that assigns a binary 1 or a binary 0 by the voltage change or lack of voltage change, respectively, at the beginning of the bit.

NRZ-L (nonreturn to zero-level) A digital encoding scheme that assigns a binary 1 or a binary 0 to a low or high voltage level, respectively.

Nyquist's theorem A theorem that states that the data transfer rate of a signal is a function of the frequency of the signal and the number of signal levels.

O

object storage A cloud-native storage infrastructure that packages stored data along with metadata about the stored objects in a flat namespace.

OFDM (orthogonal frequency division multiplexing) A modern multiplexing technology that combines FDM and TDM techniques and takes advantage of mathematical manipulation of wavelengths to compress multiple signals within a smaller bandwidth.

on-demand instance A cloud VM that can be created, run, and terminated whenever the customer chooses.

on-demand pricing model A payment arrangement where the customer pays for a resource as capacity is needed. Also called a pay-as-you-go model.

open source Software whose code is publicly available for use and modification.

operational feasibility The characteristic of a project that it will operate as designed and implemented.

OpEx (operational expenditures) Costs whose benefits are experienced in about the same period as when the expenses are paid for those benefits.

orchestration The provisioning and management of IT infrastructure through computer-readable configuration files that can be automated rather than interactive tools that require manual configuration.

OS (operating system) The software that is loaded into computer memory when the computer is turned on; it manages all the other applications and resources (such as disk drives, memory, and peripheral devices) in a computer.

OSI (Open Systems Interconnection) model A template that consists of seven layers and defines a model for understanding, developing, and troubleshooting computer-to-computer communications.

OSPF (Open Shortest Path First) protocol A link state routing protocol that improves on some of the limitations of RIP (Routing Information Protocol) and can coexist with RIP on a network.

P

PaaS (Platform-as-a-Service) An intermediate level of cloud capability which allows consumers to deploy applications on various platforms without having to manage lower-layer infrastructure.

packet The entire network layer message, which includes the segment (TCP) or datagram (UDP) from the transport layer, plus the network layer header.

PAN (personal area network) A network that involves wireless transmissions over a short distance, such as a few meters. Often used between devices such as laptop computers, smartphones, personal printers, and wireless peripheral devices.

parity bit The bit added to a character of data to perform simple parity checking.

pay-as-you-go The ability for a customer to pay only for the resources being used, which reduces waste.

pay-as-you-go model A payment arrangement where the customer pays for a resource as capacity is needed. Also called an on-demand pricing model.

payload Data that is passed between applications or utility programs and the operating system and includes control information.

PCM (pulse code modulation) An encoding technique that converts analog data to a digital signal. Also known as digitization.

period The length, or time interval, of one cycle.

perpetual license An agreement that requires a single payment upfront for the right to use an application.

phase The position of the waveform relative to a given moment in time or relative to time zero.

phishing A practice in which a person attempts to glean access or authentication information by posing as someone who needs that information.

physical connection The actual connection between sender and receiver at the physical layer where the digital content of a message (actual 1s and 0s) is transmitted.

physical layer The lowest layer of the OSI model or TCP/IP protocol suite; it handles the transmission of bits over a communications channel. Often referred to as "layer 1."

physical topology The physical layout of media, nodes, and devices on a network. A network's physical topology may differ from its logical topology.

piggybacking The concept of combining two or more fields of information into a single message, such as sending a message that both acknowledges data received and includes additional data.

pilot A larger scale draft product that reflects widespread changes to the overall design based on earlier user feedback.

PKI (public key infrastructure) The use of certificate authorities to associate public keys with certain users.

plaintext Data before any encryption has been performed.

plenum The area above the ceiling tile or below the subfloor in a building.

POC (point of contact) The single person at a vendor's company who will become familiar with the customer and their needs to facilitate more efficient communication.

PoC (Proof of Concept) A document that answers the question: Will a solution effectively address the problem a customer is trying to solve?

PoE (Power over Ethernet) A form of Ethernet LAN in which the electrical power to operate the device is transmitted over the data cabling such that a separate connection to an electrical outlet is not necessary.

polyalphabetic substitution-based cipher Uses multiple alphabetic strings to encode the plaintext rather than one alphabetic string.

POP3 (Post Office Protocol version 3) An application layer protocol used to retrieve messages from a mail server. When a client retrieves mail via POP, messages previously stored on the mail server are downloaded to the client's workstation, and then deleted from the mail server. The most commonly used form of POP is POP3.

port A number in the transport layer header that identifies a process, such as an application or service, running on a computer.

port mirroring A monitoring technique in which one port on a switch is configured to send a copy of all the switch's traffic to the device connected to that port. Also called SPAN (switched port analyzer).

PoV (Proof of Value) A document that answers the question: What value will the solution bring to the customer in terms of financial savings, workflow efficiency, or satisfaction improvements?

presentation layer A layer of the OSI model that performs a series of miscellaneous functions that need to be carried out in order to present the data package properly to the sender or receiver.

principle of least privilege A security measure that ensures employees and contractors are only given enough access and privileges to do their jobs, and these privileges are terminated as soon as the person no longer needs them.

private cloud A deployment model in which flexible data storage, applications, or services are managed centrally by an organization or service provider on hardware dedicated to that one organization.

private IP address IP addresses that can be used on a private network but not on the Internet. IEEE recommends the following IP address ranges for private use: 10.0.0.0 through 10.255.255.255; 172.16.0.0 through 172.31.255.255; and 192.168.0.0 through 192.168.255.255.

private VoIP A VoIP system that is found within the confines of a company's system of networks and does not extend to the Internet.

procedural component One of the four components of an interface's design; describes how the particular circuits are used to perform an operation.

production environment An active computing environment that is currently supporting users and work processes.

professional development Resources that help employees to improve and update their skills.

project An effort that has a clearly defined beginning and ending.

project management The application of specific skills, tools, and techniques to manage processes in such a way that the desired outcome is achieved.

propagation delay The time it takes for a signal to travel through a medium from transmitter to receiver.

proprietary A technology developed by a company for its own use and is restricted from use or may be licensed for use by other companies.

protocol analyzer A software package or hardware-based tool that can capture and analyze data on a network.

protocol A set of hardware and/or software procedures that allows communications to take place within a computer or through a computer network.

prototype A draft product that allows for initial user testing without needing to incorporate real data or compatibility with other systems.

proxy server A computer running proxy server software that acts as an intermediary between the external and internal networks, screening all incoming and outgoing traffic.

PSK (phase shift keying) A modulation technique for encoding digital data using various phases of an analog signal.

public cloud A deployment model in which shared and flexible data storage, applications, or services are managed centrally by service providers.

public IP address An IP address that is valid for use on public networks, such as the Internet.

public key cryptography A two-key system in which one key encrypts the plaintext and another key decrypts the ciphertext.

Q

QAM (quadrature amplitude modulation) A modulation technique that incorporates multiple phase angles with multiple amplitude levels to produce numerous combinations, creating a bps that is greater than the baud rate.

QoS (quality of service) A group of techniques for adjusting the priority a network assigns to various types of transmissions.

QPSK (quadrature phase shift keying) A modulation technique that incorporates four different phase angles, each of which represents 2 bits: a 45-degree phase shift represents a data value of 11; a 135-degree phase shift represents 10; a 225-degree phase shift represents 01; and a 315-degree phase shift represents 00.

R

RAID (Redundant Array of Independent Disks) A distribution of data copies stored on multiple disk drives; provides a level of data security, performance improvement, or both.

ransomware A program that locks a user's data or computer system until a ransom is paid.

RDP (Remote Desktop Protocol) An application layer protocol that uses TCP/IP to transmit graphics and text quickly over a remote client-host connection. RDP also carries session, licensing, and encryption information.

redundancy The use of more than one identical component, device, connection, or other resource to ensure that high availability benchmarks are achieved.

reflectance The amount of loss caused by a light signal reaching the end of a fiber-optic cable where some of the light is reflected back into the cable toward its source.

reflection In the context of wireless signaling, the phenomenon that occurs when an electromagnetic wave encounters an obstacle and bounces back toward its source.

refraction In the context of wireless signaling, the way in which a wave alters its direction, speed, and wavelength when it travels through different transmission mediums.

regression testing A testing process that tests pre-existing functionality after a change to confirm that changes haven't negatively impacted other systems.

reliability A measurement of how well a resource functions without errors.

repeater A device used to regenerate a digital signal in its original form. Repeaters operate at the physical layer of the OSI model.

reserved instance A cloud VM that is discounted according to the customer's commitment to use the instance over a certain period of time, such as a year.

resiliency The measurement of a resource's ability to recover from errors, such as when it becomes unavailable during an outage.

RFI (Request for Information) A document that requests information from a vendor about their products or services that will address many of the customer's initial questions.

RFP (request for proposal) A document requesting that vendors submit a proposal for a product or service that a company wants to purchase.

right sizing The adjustment process to efficiently meet demand as it changes while minimizing costs.

right-of-way Permission to install a medium across public or private property.

RIP (Routing Information Protocol) The oldest routing protocol that is still widely used. RIP and RIPv2 are distance-vector protocols that use hop count as their routing metric and only allow up to 15 hops.

risk register A document used to track risks of a system or project and might be required for compliance with certain regulations.

RJ45 connector The standard connector used for twisted pair cables and compatible devices.

router A layer 3 device that uses logical addressing information to direct data between two or more networks and can help find the best path for traffic to travel from one network to another.

routing table A database stored in a router's memory that maintains information about the location of hosts and networks and the best paths for forwarding messages between them.

RTP (Real-Time Protocol) An application layer protocol used to deliver streaming audio and video data to a user's browser.

RTSP (Real-Time Streaming Protocol) An application layer protocol used to deliver streaming audio and video data to a user's browser.

runbook A collection of physical or digital documents that outline the precise steps to complete procedures or operations in a specific IT environment.

run-length encoding A compression technique in which a commonly occurring symbol (or symbols) in a data set is replaced with a simpler character and a count of how many times that symbol occurs.

runt A frame on a LAN that is shorter than 64 bytes.

S

SaaS (Software-as-a-Service) The provision of application services through the cloud where those applications can be accessed from many different types of devices without having to manage any of the underlying infrastructure.

SAN (storage area network) A distinct network of storage devices and the infrastructure that supports them in providing centralized, fault-tolerant block storage.

sandboxing A testing process that creates an isolated environment for experimenting with changes to a system or with potentially dangerous software without exposing sensitive resources to risk of damage.

SASE (secure access service edge) A network management product that provides cloud-based management of WAN, LAN, and cloud connections.

scalability The ability to adjust the size (vertical scaling) or the number (horizontal scaling) of resources over time in response to changing needs.

scope creep The tendency to add more functionality than is really needed, thereby increasing cost, time to production, and scope of the project.

SD-branch (software-defined branch) Abstracted, centralized control of virtual network devices at remote network locations.

SDN (software-defined networking) A centralized approach to networking that removes most of the decision-making power from network devices and instead handles that responsibility at a software level.

SDS (software-defined storage) A centralized approach to storage management that removes most of the organizational and read/write decision-making from storage devices and instead handles that responsibility at a software level.

SD-WAN (software-defined WAN) Abstracted, centralized control of networking devices that manage network functions across a diverse infrastructure.

security policy A document or plan that identifies an organization's security goals, risks, levels of authority, designated security coordinator and team members, responsibilities for each team member, and responsibilities for each employee. In addition, it specifies how to address security breaches.

segmentation The process of separating network traffic for increased security or efficiency.

self-clocking A characteristic of a signal in which the signal changes at a regular pattern, which allows the receiver to stay synchronized with the signal's incoming bit stream.

self-service The ability for a customer to make configuration changes to cloud resources without assistance or involvement from the cloud service provider.

SEO (search engine optimization) The process of creating and improving a website's design to maximize its potential of appearing in appropriate search engine results.

server A computer or application that provides a service, such as data or other resources, to other devices or applications.

server license A license which applies to the installation and use of an application on a particular server and is priced according to the number of CPU cores or sockets the server has.

server OS An OS optimized for use on a server that hosts network services for client devices.

serverless computing A cloud-native, streamlined technology for hosting cloud-based applications where use of a server runs for short bursts only when needed by an application or service.

session layer A layer of the OSI model that is responsible for establishing sessions between users and for handling the service of token management.

shadow IT IT resources or systems in an organization that were not submitted to formal approval processes and likely exist outside the knowledge or oversight of the IT department.

Shannon's theorem A theorem that demonstrates that the data rate of a signal is proportional to the frequency of the signal and its power level, and inversely proportional to the signal's noise level.

shared responsibility model The division of labor between a cloud service provider and a cloud customer for the management, configuration, and security of a cloud service.

signal The electric or electromagnetic encoding of data. Signals are used to transmit data.

simple parity A simple error detection technique in which a single bit is added to a character in order to preserve an even number of 1s (even parity) or an odd number of 1s (odd parity).

single-mode transmission A fiber-optic transmission technique that sends a tightly focused stream of light through thin (8.3/125) fiber-optic cable.

single-user-multiple-station license An agreement that allows a user to install a copy of an application on multiple computers—for example, on a desktop computer and also on a laptop.

single-user-single-station license An agreement that allows a user to install a single copy of an application on only one computer.

SIP (Session Initiation Protocol) A signaling protocol that is used to make an initial connection between hosts but that does not participate in data transfer during the session. SIP is a common application layer protocol used by voice gateways to initiate and maintain connections.

site license An agreement that allows a company to install copies of an application on all the machines at a single site.

SLA (Service-Level Agreement) A legally binding contract or part of a contract that defines, in plain language and in measurable terms, the aspects of a service provided to a customer. Specific details might include contract duration, guaranteed uptime, problem management, performance benchmarks, and termination options.

sliding window protocol A protocol that allows a station to transmit a number of data packets at one time before receiving an acknowledgment.

SM (spatial multiplexing) A form of multiplexing that relies on multiple antennae transmitting and receiving in different locations so that signals are separated by some distance in space. Also called SDM (space division multiplexing).

smart speaker A voice controlled IoT device that provides an embedded personal assistant app used to access information and control other IoT devices.

SMTP (Simple Mail Transfer Protocol) An application layer protocol responsible for moving messages from one email server to another.

sniffer Software or hardware device that can monitor a network to determine if there are invalid messages being transmitted, report network problems such as malfunctioning NICs, and detect traffic congestion problems.

SNMP (Simple Network Management Protocol) An industry standard created by the Internet Engineering Task Force; it was originally designed to manage Internet components, but is now also used to manage wide area network and telecommunications systems.

SNMP manager Software that controls the operations of a managed element and maintains a database of information about all the managed elements in a given network.

social engineering attack An attack that tries to trick a user into giving up confidential information or otherwise allowing unauthorized access to a computer or network, such as clicking a link that results in dangerous software being downloaded to the user's computer.

socket A combination of IP address and TCP port number that is used to recognize an application on a server.

SoD (separation of duties) A division of labor that ensures no one person can singlehandedly compromise the security of data, finances, or other resources.

SOP (standard operating procedure) Defined steps for a specific process to maintain consistency and avoid errors.

SOW (Statement of Work) A document that details the work that must be completed for a particular project and includes specific tasks, deliverables, standards, payment schedule, and work timeline.

spectrum The range of frequencies that a signal spans from minimum to maximum.

spot instance A cloud VM that is deeply discounted according to shifting supply and demand and might be terminated on short notice if the price increases beyond the customer's threshold rate.

spread spectrum technology A high-security transmission technique that, instead of transmitting a signal on one fixed frequency, bounces the signal around on a seemingly random set of frequencies.

spyware Software that a user unknowingly downloads from the Internet and, when executed on the user's machine, begins spying on the user's activities.

SSH (Secure Shell) A terminal emulation program for TCP/IP networks, such as the Internet, that allows users to securely log in to a remote computer.

SSO (single sign-on) The use of a single identity store by multiple authentication systems.

star topology   A topology where every node on the network is connected through a central device.

star-wired bus topology   A topology where a hub (or similar device) is the connection point for multiple workstations and may be connected to other hubs.

stat TDM (statistical time division multiplexing)   A form of time division multiplexing in which the multiplexor creates a data packet of only those devices that have something to transmit.

static routing   The use of one or more fixed routes manually added to the routing table, often when the network is installed.

stop-and-wait error control   An error control technique usually associated with a class of protocols, also called stop-and-wait, in which a single message is sent, and then the sender waits for an acknowledgment before sending the next message.

STP (shielded twisted pair)   A type of copper-based cable containing twisted-pair wires that are not only individually insulated, but are also surrounded by a shielding made of a metallic substance such as foil.

STP (Spanning Tree Protocol)   An algorithm used by LAN switches that evaluates all available paths within a network and creates a tree structure that includes only unique paths between any two points. Switches use STP to avoid sending data across redundant paths (loops) within a network. Replaced by RSTP (Rapid Spanning Tree Protocol).

striping   A RAID technique in which data is broken into pieces, which are then stored on different disk drives to provide increased storage performance.

subnetting   The process of segmenting a network into smaller networks that requires calculations of IP address ranges within a larger IP address range.

subnetwork   The underlying physical system of nodes and communications links that support a network.

subscription license   An agreement that relies on a monthly or annual payment schedule to continue using an application.

subscription service   A payment arrangement where the customer commits to paying for a resource over a period of time in exchange for a lower price.

switch   A device that interconnects multiple workstations and can filter out frames, thereby providing a segmentation of the network.

symmetric connection   A type of connection in which the transfer speeds in both directions are equivalent.

symmetric encryption   A form of encryption in which the same key is used to encode and decode the data; often called private key encryption.

sync TDM (synchronous time division multiplexing)   A multiplexing technique that gives each incoming source a turn to transmit, proceeding through the sources in round-robin fashion.

syslog   A standard for generating, storing, and processing messages about events on a system.

T

tag   A key-value pair that attaches a customized label to cloud resources.

TCP (Transmission Control Protocol)   A core protocol of the TCP/IP suite that makes a connection with the end host, checks whether data is received, and resends it if it is not.

TCP/IP protocol suite   A suite of networking protocols that includes TCP, IP, UDP, and many others. TCP/IP provides the foundation for data exchange across the Internet.

TDM (time division multiplexing)   A multiplexing technique in which the sharing of a signal is accomplished by dividing the available transmission time on a medium among the medium's users.

technical feasibility   The characteristic of a project that it can be created and implemented using currently existing technology.

Telnet   A terminal emulation protocol used to log on to remote hosts using the TCP/IP protocol.

threat   An attack vector used to take advantage of loopholes or vulnerabilities in systems.

throughput   The amount of data that a medium transmits, either theoretically or practically, during a given period of time.

Thunderbolt   A high-speed interface standard developed by Intel that now uses a USB-C connector.

time feasibility   The characteristic of a project that it can be installed in a timely fashion that meets organizational needs.

timeout   An action that occurs when a transmitting or receiving workstation has not received data or a response in a specified period of time.

TKIP (Temporal Key Integrity Program)   An encryption key generation and management scheme used by WPA (Wi-Fi Protected Access).

TLS (Transport Layer Security) An update to SSL (Secure Sockets Layer) standardized by the IETF (Internet Engineering Task Force). TLS uses slightly different encryption algorithms than SSL and is more secure, but otherwise is very similar to the most recent version of SSL.

topology How the parts of a whole work together.

trailer Control information attached to the end of a packet by a data link layer protocol.

transport layer The layer of software in the TCP/IP protocol suite and OSI model that provides a reliable end-to-end network connection. Often referred to as "layer 4."

transposition-based cipher An encryption technique in which the order of the plaintext is not preserved, as it is in substitution-based ciphers.

tunneling protocol A protocol that encapsulates one type of protocol inside another.

twisted-pair cable A type of cable similar to telephone wiring that consists of color-coded pairs of insulated copper wires. Every two wires are twisted around each other to form pairs, and all the pairs are encased in a plastic sheath.

type 1 hypervisor A hypervisor that installs on a computer before any OS and is sometimes erroneously called a bare-metal hypervisor.

type 2 hypervisor A hypervisor that installs in a host OS as an application and is called a hosted hypervisor.

U

UDP (User Datagram Protocol) A core protocol in the TCP/IP suite that does not guarantee delivery because it does not first make the connection before sending data or check to confirm that data is received.

Unicode A character encoding standard that can represent symbols from all the languages on the planet.

unmanaged switch A switch that provides plug-and-play simplicity with minimal configuration options and has no IP address assigned to it.

URL (Uniform Resource Locator) An addressing technique that identifies files, web pages, images, or any other type of electronic document that resides on the Internet.

USB (Universal Serial Bus) A modern standard for interconnecting peripheral devices to computing devices. Also used as power connectors for mobile and peripheral devices.

utility A type of network software that often operates in the background and supports one or more functions to keep the network or computer running at optimal performance.

UTP (unshielded twisted pair) A type of copper-based cable that consists of one or more insulated twisted-pair wires encased in a plastic sheath, which does not contain additional shielding for the twisted pairs.

UWB (ultra-wideband) A wireless transmission technique that sends data over a wide range of frequencies at low power so as to not interfere with other signals.

V

variable cost An expense that changes frequently and unpredictably, possibly with a large range of possible values.

VDI (virtual desktop interface) A remote desktop implementation that offers VM instances for remote access clients.

vendor lock-in The ominous expense of changing vendors that often prevents customers from considering competitors' products.

virtualization Technology that uses software to emulate the functions of hardware.

VLAN (virtual LAN) A network within a network that is logically defined by grouping ports on a switch so that some of the local traffic on the switch is forced to go through a router, thereby limiting the traffic to a smaller broadcast domain.

VM (virtual machine) A logical computer running an operating system that borrows hardware resources from its physical host computer and otherwise functions as a completely independent system.

VNC (Virtual Network Computing) Software that uses the cross-platform protocol RFB (remote frame buffer) to remotely control a workstation or server.

VoIP (Voice over IP) The provision of telephone service over a packet-switched network running the TCP/IP protocol suite.

VoIP gateway The device that converts an analog telephone call (voice and signals) into data packets (and vice versa) for traversal over an IP-based network.

VPN (virtual private network) A data network connection that makes use of the public network infrastructure, but maintains privacy through the use of a tunneling protocol and security procedures.

VPN headend   A VPN gateway that manages multiple tunnels from individual VPN clients.

vulnerability   A weakness of a system, process, or architecture that could lead to compromised information or unauthorized access to a network.

W

WAN (wide area network)   An interconnection of computers and computer-related equipment that performs a given function or functions, typically uses local and long-distance telecommunications systems, and can encompass parts of states, multiple states, countries, and even the world.

WAN optimization   Techniques used to decrease the demand on limited WAN resources and increase the effective speed of data transmissions over WAN connections. Also called WAN acceleration.

waterfall method   A linear path of software development with a clearly defined beginning and ending, and a distinct progression of phases in between.

WDM (wavelength division multiplexing)   The multiplexing of multiple data streams onto a single fiber-optic cable through the use of lasers emitting lights of varying wavelength.

web app   An application accessed through a user's browser.

WEP (Wired Equivalent Privacy)   A key encryption technique for wireless networks that uses keys both to authenticate network clients and to encrypt data in transit.

wide area connectivity map   A simple drawing which outlines the locations and/or departments included in a wide area network. Used during the network design phase.

Wi-Fi (wireless fidelity)   A set of protocols supporting the IEEE 802.11 family of wireless local area network technologies.

Wi-Fi 5   A new name for 802.11ac Wi-Fi.

Wi-Fi 6   A new name for 802.11ax Wi-Fi.

Wi-Fi 6E   An expanded version of 802.11ax (also called Wi-Fi 6) that will use the unlicensed 6-GHz frequency range.

wireless   A shorthand term often used to denote the transmission of radiated signals without the use of wires.

wireless LAN   A network configuration that uses radio waves for intercommunication.

workstation   A personal computer or microcomputer where users perform computing work.

WPA (Wi-Fi Protected Access)   A wireless security method that dynamically assigns every transmission its own key.

WPA2 (Wi-Fi Protected Access, version 2)   A wireless security method that improves upon WPA by using a stronger encryption protocol called AES (Advanced Encryption Standard).

WPA3 (Wi-Fi Protected Access, version 3)   An improvement to WPA2 intended to close security vulnerabilities and increase usability features.

X

XaaS (Anything as a Service)   The provision of a service (such as computing, networking, or storage) across the Internet rather than requiring a local provision of resources.

Y

Z

Zigbee   A wireless transmission technology for the transfer of data between smaller, often embedded devices that don't require high data transfer rates and can operate with low power consumption.

ZTNA (Zero Trust Network Access)   A group of policies and technologies that require separate authentication for access to individual network resources. Also called SDP (software-defined perimeter).

Index

Note: Boldface entries include definitions